REA's Test Prep Books Are The Best!

(a sample of the <u>hundreds of letters</u> REA receives each year)

" I did well because of your wonderful prep books... I just wanted to thank you for helping me prepare for these tests. "

Student, San Diego, CA

" My students report your chapters of review as the most valuable single resource they used for review and preparation. "

Teacher, American Fork, UT

" Your book was such a better value and was so much more complete than anything your competition has produced—and I have them all! "

Teacher, Virginia Beach, VA

" Compared to the other books that my fellow students had, your book was the most useful in helping me get a great score. "

Student, North Hollywood, CA

" Your book was responsible for my success on the exam, which helped me get into the college of my choice... I will look for REA the next time I need help. "

Student, Chesterfield, MO

" Just a short note to say thanks for the great support your book gave me in helping me pass the test... I'm on my way to a B.S. degree because of you! "

Student, Orlando, FL

(more on next page)

(continued from front page)

" I just wanted to thank you for helping me get a great score on the AP U.S. History exam... Thank you for making great test preps! "

Student, Los Angeles, CA

" Your *Fundamentals of Engineering Exam* book was the absolute best preparation I could have had for the exam, and it is one of the major reasons I did so well and passed the FE on my first try. "

Student, Sweetwater, TN

" I used your book to prepare for the test and found that the advice and the sample tests were highly relevant... Without using any other material, I earned very high scores and will be going to the graduate school of my choice. "

Student, New Orleans, LA

" What I found in your book was a wealth of information sufficient to shore up my basic skills in math and verbal... The section on analytical ability was excellent. The practice tests were challenging and the answer explanations most helpful. It certainly is the *Best Test Prep for the GRE*! "

Student, Pullman, WA

" I really appreciate the help from your excellent book. Please keep up the great work. "

Student, Albuquerque, NM

" I am writing to thank you for your test preparation... your book helped me immeasurably and I have nothing but praise for your *GRE* preparation. "

Student, Benton Harbor, MI

(more on back page)

REA: THE TEST PREP AP TEACHERS RECOMMEND

AP LATIN: VERGIL

2nd Edition

TestWare® Edition

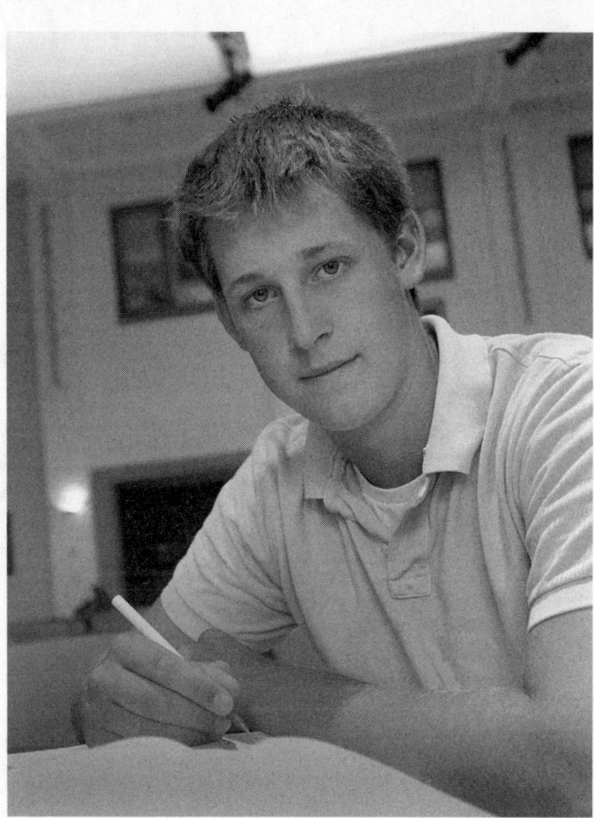

Ronald B. Palma, M.A.
Holland Hall School
Tulsa, Oklahoma

Research & Education Association
Visit our website at: www.rea.com

Planet Friendly Publishing
✔ Made in the United States
✔ Printed on Recycled Paper
Text: 10% Cover: 10%
Learn more: www.greenedition.org

At REA we're committed to producing books in an Earth-friendly manner and to helping our customers make greener choices.

Manufacturing books in the United States ensures compliance with strict environmental laws and eliminates the need for international freight shipping, a major contributor to global air pollution.

And printing on recycled paper helps minimize our consumption of trees, water and fossil fuels. This book was printed on paper made with **10% post-consumer waste.** According to Environmental Defense's Paper Calculator, by using this innovative paper instead of conventional papers, we achieved the following environmental benefits:

Trees Saved: 7 • Air Emissions Eliminated: 1,505 pounds
Water Saved: 1,323 gallons • Solid Waste Eliminated: 444 pounds

For more information on our environmental practices, please visit us online at **www.rea.com/green**

Research & Education Association
61 Ethel Road West
Piscataway, New Jersey 08854
E-mail: info@rea.com

AP LATIN: VERGIL EXAM

Printed in the United States of America

Library of Congress Control Number 2010920460

ISBN-13: 978-0-7386-0706-1
ISBN-10: 0-7386-0706-1

B10-0101

CONTENTS

About Our Author

Ronald B. Palma has been teaching Latin and other classics courses at Holland Hall School in Tulsa, Oklahoma, for the past 36 years. He holds an A.B. in Classics from Cornell University and an M.A. in Classics from the University of Cincinnati, where he did doctoral work funded by a Louise Taft Semple Fellowship. He has co-authored *Ecce Romani: A Latin Reading Program* (Prentice-Hall, 2008), now in its fourth edition, and is also the author of REA's *Best Test Preparation for the SAT Subject Test: Latin*. Palma has received numerous fellowships and awards for both teaching and scholarship, including Rockefeller and Fulbright grants, the Summer Fellowship of the Classical Society of the American Academy in Rome, a Presidential Scholar Award from the U.S. Department of Education, a Special Recognition Award from the College Board, and the Excellence in Pre-Collegiate Teaching Award from the American Philological Association.

Author Acknowledgments

I would like to acknowledge several individuals for their invaluable personal and professional support in the production of this book. A thousand thanks to Diane Goldschmidt, Senior Editor, Research & Education Association, for her guidance and patience; to Professor Tom Benedicktson, Dean of the College of Arts and Sciences, University of Tulsa, for his expert proofreading of the first edition of this book and Andrew Holm, AP Latin teacher at Hillsdale Academy in Hillsdale, Mich., for proofreading the second edition of this book.

Most importantly, I extend my thanks and appreciation to Fay, my wife of 42 years, whose continual support throughout my career has given me both the opportunity and the confidence to share with others my love of the past. I would also like to thank those readers who have corrected my Latin in the first edition of this book and those who have offered suggestions and advice on how to improve it.

Proviso

The author assumes all responsibility for the content of this study guide, as the College Board does not sanction or recommend any such publications. Although the author has relied upon much information provided by the College Board itself, he has endeavored to use discretion in revising or supplementing the wording of such information, while giving close attention to producing original AP-style questions in the chapter discussions and Practice Exams.

Dedication

This book is dedicated to my high school Latin teacher (1960–64), Marion Harvey, of Bernards High School in Bernardsville, New Jersey, where she taught Latin for thirty-four years. I still share with my own students her daily mantra, "Latin is a language of endings!"

Ronald B. Palma
Holland Hall School
Tulsa, Oklahoma

About Research & Education Association

Founded in 1959, Research & Education Association is dedicated to publishing the finest and most effective educational materials—including software, study guides, and test preps—for students in elementary school, middle school, high school, college, graduate school, and beyond. Today, REA's wide-ranging catalog is a leading resource for teachers, students, and professionals. We invite you to visit us at *www.rea.com* to find out how "REA is making the world smarter."

Staff Acknowledgments

In addition to our author, we would like to thank Larry B. Kling, Vice President, Editorial, for his overall direction; Pam Weston, Vice President, Publishing, for setting the quality standards for production integrity and managing the publication to completion; John Cording, Vice President, Technology, for coordinating the design and development of REA's TestWare®; Diane Goldschmidt, Senior Editor, for project management; Alice Leonard, Senior Editor, for editorial contributions; Heena Patel, Technology Project Manager, for design contributions and software testing efforts; Weymouth Design for designing our cover; and Kathy Caratozzolo of Caragraphics for typesetting this edition.

A Note from Our Author

Congratulations on reaching the pinnacle of your high school Latin career! You are preparing to join the elite fraternity of those who will take the Advanced Placement Latin Exam, among whom are counted the nation's best Latin students. Because of an increase in interest in the study of Latin and because of the growing availability of the opportunity to take college classes in high school, the number of students taking the AP Latin Exam has been rising in recent years. This book is designed to assist you in reaching your goal of doing your best on what may be either the end of your study of Latin or the beginning of a new phase of that study in college.

This study guide provides you with an abundance of practice questions and answers that are aligned with the AP Latin: Vergil Exam in both subject matter and level of difficulty. There are two complete Practice Tests available at the end of this book. There are also materials for a brief but comprehensive review of Latin grammar and syntax and plenty of tips on how you might strengthen not only your test readiness, but your overall skills in Latin. A new chapter, on questions and answers, has been added to this section. Also, many of these grammar review chapters now include activities that refer directly to the Latin text of the *Aeneid*. The content and organization of this guide are products of the author's leadership of and participation in conferences, in-service presentations, and workshops on AP Latin, experience as an Exam Reader (grader), and service on the Advisory Committee for the National Latin Exam. Additionally, the author's preparation for writing this book also includes a formal analysis of the AP Latin Exam, as well as 30 years of experience in teaching AP Latin to eleventh and twelfth grade students. It is the author's hope that it will also be useful to other teachers, both those who are beginning an AP Latin program in their schools and those veterans who may be seeking approaches that are new or who hope to reinforce those long held.

You should know that in the spring of 2008 the College Board announced the elimination of the AP Latin Literature option for the AP Latin Exam. Accordingly, this study guide has been revised to assist you as you prepare to take the AP Latin Exam on Vergil's *Aeneid*. The latter Exam will be the only option for the years 2009–2010, 2010–2011, and 2011–2012. In the academic year 2012–2013, a single AP Latin Exam will test the Aeneid plus a prose author, probably Caesar, both of which will be covered in a single, year-long course.* This book has been updated to reflect the current change in the AP Latin program and therefore focuses entirely on the *Aeneid*. Features of this revised edition include new chapters on vocabulary and on reviewing the Aeneid in its entirety, plus a completely revised chapter on translation, the latter in response

---

* This information was provided in an e-mail of September 24, 2009, from Prof. Mary Pendergraft of Wake Forest University, current Chief Reader of the AP Latin Exam.

to requests from readers for more assistance with preparing for the literal translation currently required on the Exam.

Some notes on changes in the format of this book. Endnotes referred to in the chapters are located at the end of each chapter. Updated and annotated recommendations for print and online resources are now included in a separate chapter-by-chapter appendix found at the end of the book. Note that all websites listed in this book are active as of summer, 2009. References to the Latin text of the *Aeneid* will be given as Book and line number(s) in Arabic numerals, e.g., 1.1–11 means Book 1, lines 1 through 11. The word "Exam" refers to the AP Latin: Vergil Exam.

Ronald B. Palma
Holland Hall School

5 Weeks to a 5

AP Latin

Week	Activities
1	At the beginning of this first week, plan your review schedule and organize or join a study group. Read Chapters 1, 2, and 3 of this book, which will give you a general overview of the content and format of the Exam. Begin reading your published translation of the *Aeneid* to get a sense of the entire work, and visit the appendices of this book to discover and explore those resources that might help you review most effectively. See especially the Appendix for Chapter 10, the AP Vergil Metasites created by Latin teacher Tim Abney and Jerard White, and the activities and games on Vergil and the *Aeneid* at the *Quia.com* website for Latin.
2 and 3	During these next two weeks, continue reading the *Aeneid* in translation. Supplement this activity by using the overview provided in this book and by referring to any websites that appeal to you. Read Chapter 5 on translation and then begin to review the required Latin of Books 1, 2, 4, and 6. Open your textbook at random and practice translating five- to ten-line passages, or consult in Chapter 5 the list of passages recommended for practice. During these two weeks, it would also be useful to revisit the AP Latin: Vergil website to obtain passages for translation practice. Be sure to check your versions against the sample translation provided in the Scoring Guidelines to ensure that your translations are sufficiently literal.
4	Week Four should be devoted both to continuing your reading of the *Aeneid* in translation and to final preparations for the analytical essay questions. By now, you should have mastered the techniques of poetic analysis, but it wouldn't hurt to revisit Chapters 8 and 9. The development of skills for writing effective analytical essays takes time, however, you might find it both helpful and reassuring to return to Chapter 6 (long and short essays), Chapter 8 (using figures of speech), and the AP Latin: Vergil website to practice with AP-style and actual AP questions, respectively. By practice, we don't mean endless hours of writing (which you wouldn't do, anyway), but we do mean reminding yourself about expectations, such as how to cite Latin support correctly. Read the author's sample essays in the chapters mentoned above to remind yourself about the significance of the acronym SODA—support, organize, develop, and analyze—in writing an effective essay.

Continued →

(Continued from previous page)

Week	Activities
5	This final week before the actual AP Latin Exam should be devoted to completing your reading of the *Aeneid* in English. This will refresh your memory of the latter Books, which we have put aside. Your other goal should be to simulate as closely as possible, the actual experience of taking the AP Latin Exam. Use the AP-style Practice Exams provided at the end of this book. Spend the time to assess your own performance by consulting the answers. Again, the author's sample answers to essay questions are necessarily subjective, but you will receive additional reminders about some of the issues we addressed in Week Four. Discussions with a classmate or classmates will provide "feedback" and help build confidence. The final step is to take an actual AP Latin Exam under simulated conditions. Go online to the AP Latin: Vergil website, pick an Exam year at random, print out the free-response section for that year, and spend time taking the Exam and then using the Scoring Guidelines provided to help you to assess your performance.

PART I

The AP Latin Course and Exam

Chapter 1

Content and Format of the AP Latin Exam

Content of the AP Latin Exam

For the past decade, the number of students taking the AP Latin Exam has slowly but steadily increased.[1] Whether or not this indicates that more students are studying Latin, it does indicate that more students are studying Latin at the college level while in high school. The AP Latin Exam tests the proficiency of high school Latin students when compared to college students who have taken a fourth- through a sixth-semester Latin course.[2] The focus of this book is to help you prepare for the AP Latin Exam, that is, to help you expand and assess your skills of comprehending, translating, analyzing, and interpreting the meaning of the Latin you read. The specific content, format, and scoring of the AP Latin Exam, also referred to in this book as "the Exam," is described in greater detail in succeeding chapters.

AP Latin Syllabus

The Latin reading content for the Vergil Exam consists of the following lines of the *Aeneid*. The remainder of the *Aeneid* is to be prepared in English.[3]

Book #	Number of Lines	Total Lines	Running Total
Book 1:	lines 1–519	519 lines	519
Book 2:	lines 1–56, 199–297, 469–566, and 735–804	323 lines	842
Book 4:	lines 1–449, 642–705	513 lines	1355
Book 6:	lines 1–211, 450–76, and 847–901	293 lines	1648
Book 10:	lines 420–509	90 lines	1738
Book 12:	lines 791–842, 887–952	118 lines	1856

In 1999, selections in Latin from Books 10 and 12 were added to the syllabus because there was concern among college teachers that AP Vergil students were not acquainting themselves with the entire work of the *Aeneid*. Keep this in mind as you prepare for the AP Latin Exam. Your preparation of the Latin of the *Aeneid* is evaluated in the syllabus-based question on the multiple-choice section and in four of the five questions on the free-response section. Your familiarity with the characters and situations of the epic as a whole in English is tested on the second of the 20-minute short essay questions found in the free-response section.

General Format of the AP Latin Exam

The AP Latin Exam, the format of which was changed in 1999, now consists of two parts: a multiple-choice section (40 percent) and a free-response section (60 percent).[4] You must read in English those portions of the *Aeneid* that you have not prepared in Latin. The total time for the AP Latin Exam is three hours, plus about one-half hour of administrative and break time.

The Multiple-Choice Section

The multiple-choice section of the Vergil exam consists of 50 multiple-choice questions over three sight readings/passages of poetry and prose, plus one syllabus-based passage covering the lines of the *Aeneid* required in Latin. You have 60 minutes in which to answer all questions. For the specific skills tested and for additional information on the multiple-choice section, see the next chapter.

The Free-Response Section

The free-response section of the Vergil exam consists of five questions, for which you have 1 hour and 45 minutes, plus a 15-minute "reading period" for preparation. These questions, which consist of translations, long and short essays, and a question on the poem as a whole, evaluate your preparation of the assigned syllabus. For the specific skills tested and for more information on the free-response section, see Chapter 3.

Terms Used in AP Latin

- **Acorn book:** see **syllabus**.
- **background question:** sometimes called the global essay, this is the final question on the free-response section. This question tests knowledge of those portions of the *Aeneid* read in English, requires 20 minutes, and counts for 15 percent of your score on the free-response section.
- **chunk:** see **segment**.
- **free-response:** the larger part of the AP Latin Exam in time (1 hour, 45 minutes) and weight (60 percent), the free-response consists of five questions that call for you to translate, compose essays in English, and demonstrate your knowledge of the *Aeneid* in its entirety.
- **global essay:** see **background question**.
- **gloss:** annotations at the foot of a Latin text, in either the multiple-choice or free-response sections. Glosses occur rarely, but when they do, they

provide assistance with a particularly difficult or uncommon word or form. Glosses no longer include variations in the spelling of the Latin.

- **item:** College Board terminology for an AP Exam question. The word "question" will be used in this book.
- **"literal":** the rendering of Latin in English with attention to the precise and accurate expression of all vocabulary and forms.
- **long essay:** a written analytical discussion of a given passage or passages of Latin on the free-response section. The suggested time for the long essay for Vergil, which is worth 35 percent of your score on the free-response section, is 45 minutes. See also **short essay**.
- **multiple-choice:** the smaller part of the AP Latin Exam in time (one hour) and weight (40 percent). There are 50 questions on three sight passages, each 10–15 lines long, from Latin poets and at least one prose author. One additional passage comes from the prepared syllabus of Vergil. Each multiple-choice question consists of four answers, one of which is correct.
- **prompt:** a term used mostly by those who produce or grade the exam. It refers to the essential question being asked within the wording of an essay question on the free-response section.
- **Reader:** a volunteer high school or college teacher who grades the AP Latin Exam in mid-June. Readers are organized into groups, each of which is guided by a Table Leader, or more experienced grader. Readers spend their grading time evaluating one specific question on the Exam. Questions are frequently re-graded at random to ensure consistency.
- **reading period:** the 15-minute preface to writing answers in the pink answer booklet. This time is provided to encourage you to think through and organize your answers before actually writing. You may make notes anywhere on your green test sheets.
- **released exams:** every five years or so, the entire AP Latin Exam (both multiple-choice and free-response sections) is published by the College Board for use by students and teachers.
- **scoring guidelines:** these are the rubrics, or criteria, used by the Readers in scoring your exam. They are published by the Chief Reader sometime after the exams have been graded and include sample student responses, along with their scores. You might find these guidelines useful in determining how the exams are graded and therefore how you might improve your preparation. In addition to finding information about the scoring of the AP Latin Exam in this book, you may consult the College Board web pages for AP Latin or the annual report published by the Chief Reader in *The Classical Outlook* (see Appendix).
- **segment:** a small combination of syntactically related words, used in determining units of sense within a Latin sentence. Segments are used as the criteria in evaluating a literal translation. For examples other than those

provided in this book, see the scoring guidelines online or the appropriate article in *The Classical Outlook*.

- **short essay:** the short essays, which are the final two questions on the Exam, consist of a short analytical essay and a "background" question covering the entirety of the *Aeneid.* The suggested time is 20 minutes, although the point-value of these questions varies from 20 percent to 15 percent, respectively (see Chapters 6 and 7 for details). The length of your writing, i.e., the number of pages it takes you to answer the question, is of little consequence. The difference between short and long essays, in addition to the suggested time and point value, concerns the length of the passage under consideration and the corresponding expectation of increased breadth and depth in your analysis on the long essay. See also **background question** and **long essay**.
- **sight reading:** a passage that has not been previously seen, i.e., it is unfamiliar or unprepared.
- **"suggested time":** the College Board provides a "suggested time" for each free-response question, in order to help you plan your time. It is assumed that you have practiced taking timed tests during your preparation for the AP Latin Exam and that you have some idea about how you perform under the pressure of time. The simplest advice for you to remember is that you should not use substantially more or less time than that suggested. You are not penalized if you do not stay within the suggested time.
- **syllabus-based:** this phrase refers to the passage from the Latin syllabus of Vergil given in the multiple-choice section of the Exam.
- **syllabus:** refers to an outline or summary of the reading required for the AP Latin Exam. This is published semi-annually by the College Board in the *AP Latin Course Description* or so-called Acorn Book (the acorn is the logo of the College Board).
- **. . . "throughout the passage/s":** this phrase appears in the instructions for the essay questions on the free-response section of the exam. It is designed to remind you to consider the passage *as a whole* in your answer and to draw support for your discussion from the entirety of the Latin text. Failure to do this is a common shortcoming and often leads to a reduced score on the question.
- **"well-developed":** this phrase is found in the directions for the long essay. A well-developed essay is not necessarily a long essay. A well-developed essay includes organization, coherence, completeness, and sound analysis, which makes liberal use of specific and relevant references to the entire Latin text. When references are made to figures of speech, attention should be paid to how the figure affects the meaning of the Latin.

Endnotes

[1] The total number of students taking the AP Latin Exam in 2009, the most recent year for which such statistics are available, was 8388, of whom 4706 took the Vergil Exam. In 2005, the total number was 7892, of which 4362 took the Vergil Exam. Ten years earlier, in 1999, the respective numbers were 5606 for all Latin and 3398 for Vergil alone.

[2] Traditionally, one semester of college study has been approximately equivalent to one year of high school study.

[3] For those portions of the *Aeneid* not required in Latin, see Chapter 7.

[4] For recommended print and online resources on the AP Latin program and on the AP Latin Exam, see Appendix 1.

Chapter 2

The Multiple-Choice Section

Overview

The multiple-choice section is the first of two sections of the AP Latin Exam; the other is the free-response section, which will be covered in the next chapter. As indicated in the previous chapter of this book, these two sections differ in content, format, and length. The multiple-choice section consists of 50 multiple-choice questions on three sight reading passages and one syllabus-based passage, the latter of which comes from the lines of the *Aeneid* prepared in Latin. At the end of this chapter, you will find several examples of the types of passages and questions (with answers) that you will meet on this section of the Exam.

Content

The questions on this section of the Exam approximate those on the Reading Comprehension Section of the SAT Subject Test in Latin.[5] That is, they require demonstration of your ability to translate or interpret a phrase or sentence, to identify in context basic grammatical forms and syntactical uses, and to explicate references, allusions, and words understood. The remaining questions focus on the mechanics of literary analysis, e.g., figures of speech and metrics, which will be presented in later chapters of this book. The types of questions found on the multiple-choice section cover translation, comprehension, grammar, reference, figures of speech, metrics, and background.[6]

Skills Tested on the Multiple-Choice Section

35–45 percent (17–23 questions)	Translation or comprehension of the meaning of a phrase or sentence
20–30 percent (10–15 questions)	Grammar: contextual questions on grammar, syntax, and word meaning
20–30 percent (10–15 questions)	Reference: identification of the person or thing to which a pronoun or adjective refers; inference of meaning from words that are assumed or understood; recognition of references or allusions to a specific person, place, or event mentioned in the text
2–5 percent (1–3 questions)	Figures of speech

(continued)

2–5 percent (1–3 questions)	Metrics (the hexameter line)
2–5 percent (1–3 questions)	Literary and cultural background questions (syllabus based passages only)

The Format of Latin Passages on the Multiple-Choice Section

Here is a sample to illustrate the format of the Latin text in the multiple-choice section:

Brief title	**Mourning for Phaethon**
Sentences with initial caps No macrons	Naides Hesperiae trifida[1] fumantia flamma corpora dant tumulo, signant quoque carmine saxum: "Hic situs est Phaethon, currus auriga paterni;
Lines numbered every five lines	quem si non tenuit, magnis tamen excidit ausis." Nam pater obductos, luctu miserabilis aegro, condiderat vulnus: et si modo credimus, unum isse diem sine sole ferunt. Incendia lumen praebebant, aliquisque malo fuit usus in illo.
Glossing of unfamiliar words	[1] <u>trifidus</u>, -<u>a</u>, -<u>um</u>, adj.: three-forked

Notes:

1. Titles are provided for Latin passages in the multiple-choice section, but not in the free-response section.
2. Passages given in the multiple-choice section are <u>not</u> attributed, i.e., the author and work are not identified. Passages <u>are</u> identified in the free-response section.
3. Accusative plurals of third declension **i**-stems appear as **–es**, rather than **–is**, e.g., **cives** rather than **civis**; consonantal **i** is used instead of **j**, i.e., **iam** rather than **jam**.
4. Initial capitals are used.
5. The letter v appears, instead of u, which appears in the official Oxford text, e.g., **obviam,** rather than **obuiam.**
6. Note that macrons (long marks) do not appear on the AP Latin Exam.

FAQs About the Multiple-Choice Section

- **What types of questions on the multiple-choice section am I likely to find difficult?**

  Most wrong answers occur in the areas of grammatical and syntactical usage.[7] Note that the AP Latin Exam does not ask for recognition or production of <u>specific</u> descriptive terms, e.g., ablative of time, and that all questions are asked in the context of the passage of Latin provided. Here are some examples of areas that continually prove troublesome:

  - Identifying the contextual form of a noun or adjective, e.g., "The case and number of **corpora** is . . . ," or "The case of **corpora** is determined by . . . ."

- Pronoun reference, e.g., "In line 3, **se** refers to . . . ."
- Adjective–noun agreement, e.g., In line 4, **omnes** modifies . . . ."
- Identifying the subject, tense, or mood of a verb, e.g., "The subject of **sacravit** is . . . ."
- The tense and mood of **possim** are . . . ."
- Translation of an individual word in context, e.g., "In line 6, the word **cum** is translated . . . . "

- **How can I best prepare for this part of the exam?**

  Here are some general tips for the long term:[8]

  1. Read as much authentic Latin as you can!
  2. Approach your daily reading assignments as sight readings. Attempt to do as much of the decision-making as possible without recourse to references.
  3. Master the fundamentals of Latin: spend extra time during class grammar review and review regularly on your own. When you read, pay particular attention to noun/pronoun-adjective agreement, identification of the references of pronouns, and the proper rendering of verb forms, as well as to the guidewords that define phrases and clauses. Ask your teacher for suggestions on how to strengthen your weak areas. (Don't do this on the eve of the exam!)
  4. Become familiar with the types of questions asked on the multiple-choice section by practicing with the sample materials found in this book and with those provided by the College Board. Actual multiple-choice questions are available only on exams that are released every five years or so (the last one of which was in 2005).[9]

- **Should I guess on this section if I'm not sure of the answer?**

  It is best not to "random guess." There is a penalty of 1/3 pt. for each wrong answer, as opposed to 1/4 pt. on the SAT. Random guessing will likely lower your score because the Exam is penalty-graded and because it wastes time. If you can narrow your choices to two, then go for it! This constitutes an "educated guess." In making an educated guess, use all the language skills at your disposal, such as recall, analogy and deduction, and reference to English and other languages. You have 60 minutes to answer 50 questions, which means you have 15 minutes to spend on each of the four passages. This averages out to about one question per minute. You need not answer every question correctly in order to achieve a solid score on this section of the test, nor do you even need to answer every question. If you are stumped and cannot eliminate one or two answers as incorrect, move on.

- **How will my performance on the multiple-choice section influence my overall score?**

  The multiple-choice section counts for 40 percent of your total Exam score (for further information, see Part II). It is important to remember that the multiple-choice section is tested first during the Exam period and is considered by many students to be the more difficult of the two sections, so don't become discouraged.[10]

Types of Questions Asked on the Multiple-Choice Section

Remember that questions such as these are always asked in the context of a reading passage.

Translation

Romae (line 2) is best translated . . .

In line 3, **occurri** is translated . . .

In lines 6–7, **ad urbem defendendam** is best translated . . .

Which of the following is a literal translation of the sentence **Es germana . . . fluctus** (lines 7–8)?

Comprehension

From the words **Sed . . . affugerat** (lines 8–9), we learn that . . .

From the clause **cum . . . vidisset** (lines 9–10), we learn that . . .

The sentence **Occidit . . . Troia** (line 11) states that . . .

From lines 10–12 (**Si voluit . . . est resistendum**), we learn that . . .

Grammar and Syntax

The case of **gaudio** (line 1) is dependent upon . . .

The case and number of **templa** (line 2) are . . .

The case of the words **dolori, irae,** and **gaudio** (lines 2–3) is . . .

The case and number of **haec** (line 4) are . . .

In line 5, **tantas** modifies . . .

The main verb in **Cum . . . vocari** (lines 4–5) is . . .

The gender of **posita** (line 6) is determined by . . .

The subject of **spectavisse** (line 7) is . . .

The direct object of **dedit** (line 11) is . . .

What part of speech is **munere** (line 8)?

In line 9, both **vive** and **ama** are . . .

The tense of **tradiderint** (line 10) is . . .

Reference

In line 1, **eos** refers to . . .

The word **illo** (line 2) refers to the same person as . . .

In line 4, the word **quae** refers to . . .

In line 5, **se** refers to . . .

In line 6, the word **suos** in the phrase **suos viros** refers to . . .

-que (line 7) joins **optimis** to . . .

In line 8, **advocati** refers to . . .

The implied subject of **conspicit** (line 9) is . . .

Festinate (line 10) is addressed to . . .

Figures of Speech

The words **non . . . ignara** (line 1) are an example of . . .

What figure of speech occurs in **hic illius arma, hic currus fuit** (lines 16–17)?

Metrics (dactylic hexameter)

How many elisions occur in line 4?

The metrical pattern of the first four feet of line 3 is . . .

Note: Answers will be given in the form "dactyl-spondee-spondee-dactyl."

Background (asked with reference to the syllabus-based passage only)

The speaker in this passage is . . .

Another individual who gives a speech that outlines Aeneas' destiny is . . .

The Sight Reading Passages

Authors selected for sight readings are equivalent in difficulty to the following intermediate authors: for prose, Caesar, Cicero, Gellius, Livy, Nepos, Pliny the Younger, and Sallust; for poetry, Lucan, Lucretius, Martial, Ovid, Propertius, and Tibullus. Here are the authors that appeared on the past three released Exams:

1994	Martial, Pliny, Vergil, Catullus (no syllabus-based passage)
1999	Ovid, Cicero, Tibullus, Vergil (*Aeneid* 6.162–174, syllabus-based)
2005	Vergil (*Aeneid* 4.90–104, syllabus-based), Juvenal, Livy, Statius

For practice with sight reading, consult the College Board's AP Vergil Web site and the reading comprehension passages from Levels III, IV, and V of previous National Latin Exams (1999-current).[11]

How to Sight Read a Passage of Latin on the Multiple-Choice Section

Your success on this part of the AP Latin Exam will be the product of your background in reading Latin. Presumably, before reading Vergil you will have had some experience in making the transition from "made-up" to authentic Latin, that is, you will have read some Latin written by an ancient Roman. The tips given in this book are meant to supplement, rather than substitute for, daily practice in reading authentic Latin. There seems to be general agreement that the basic reason for studying Latin is learning how to read the language, preferably without resource (some define "reading" as translation, others as comprehensive understanding of the meaning). More about this in Chapter 5.

Sight Reading Passage 1 (Prose)

As you have learned, there are currently four Latin passages on the multiple-choice section: one sight passage of prose and two sight passages of poetry, plus one syllabus-based passage on the required Latin of Vergil. The following section consists of a sample passage of prose, plus AP-style questions, followed by answers and discussion. First of all, however, here are some steps to follow that will help you read sight passages with success:

Pliny misses his wife

C. Plinius Calpurniae Suae S.[1]

Incredibile est quanto desiderio tui tenear. In causa amor primum, deinde quod non consuevimus abesse. Inde est [quod magnam noctium partem in imagine tuā vigil exigo; inde quod interdiu, quibus horis te visere solebam], ad diaetam[2] tuam ipsi me (ut verissime dicitur) pedes ducunt; quod denique aeger et maestus ac similis excluso a vacuo limine recedo. Unum tempus his tormentis caret, quo in foro et amicorum litibus[3] conteror[4]. Aestima tu quae vita mea sit, cui requies in labore, in miseria curisque solacium. Vale.

1 S. = Salutem dicit: sends greetings
2 diaeta, diaeta, f.: room
3 lis, litis, f.: lawsuit, court
4 contero, contere, contrivi, contritum: wear out

Step 1

Read quickly through the entire passage in the order in which the Latin is given. The explicit instructions given for this section are "Read each of the following selections carefully for comprehension."[12] Try to follow the main ideas and the general drift of the meaning without translating. You will find it helpful to approach a multiple-choice passage by getting a sense of the meaning of the whole before venturing on to the analytical questions that accompany the passage. It is not recommended that you jump immediately into the task of answering the questions without getting a sense of their context. Do not translate the reading passage word-for-word unless instructed to do so in answer to a specific question. In the sight passage above, the greeting **C. Plinius Calpurniae Suae S(alutem dicit)** and the salutation **Vale** at the end indicate that this is a letter written by Pliny to his wife, Calpurnia. The information you pick up as you read the Latin for the first time may be subtle, but it will begin the process of comprehension.

Step 2

Pay attention to the clues given in the English title and glossed vocabulary and incorporate their hints into your understanding of the passage. The title of the passage "Pliny misses his wife" and the clause **quanto desiderio tui tenear** (line 2) suggest right away that the writer is separated from, and longs for, his wife. The early sentences of a passage usually introduce information that is important for establishing context and they also help to set the mood and tone.

Step 3

Read quickly through the passage in Latin a second time, noting more specifically the main constructions, idiomatic expressions, and transition points in the writer's thinking. Remember that Latin prefers to use subordinate clauses and participles whose meaning is equivalent to subordinate clauses. As you read, focus on groups of words that go together, paying particular attention to:

noun–adjective agreement

antecedents and references of pronouns

tense, voice, and mood of verbs

boundaries of phrases and clauses

Some students are assisted in their comprehension by use of a more graphic expression of the Latin. Feel free to mark up the text, using arrows, circles, parentheses, square brackets, and underlining to designate connections between words or word groups, and thus guide you to greater comprehension. As you read again through the passage of Pliny above, give attention to the following elements of the Latin as examples of things to notice.

Sentence 1 Remember to concentrate less on individual words than on word groups, such as the clause **quanto . . . tenear**. **Quanto** is the type of word that introduces a subordinate clause (indirect question), which is confirmed by the subjunctive verb **tenear**. Word selection can sometimes give some insight into the general direction in which the meaning of the passage is heading. For instance, the key word **desiderio**, *longing,* suggests to the reader how the writer feels, which is confirmed by the title of the passage. As you proceed, note whether there is a verb tense that appears consistently in the Latin (here, it is the present tense).

Sentence 2 In this sentence, the juxtaposed words **primum, deinde** (3) indicate that there are two ideas being expressed, in sequential order. The first clause, **In causa amor primum** (2–3), which is a bit confusing as it lacks a verb, has something to do with love (**amor,** 2). The second clause, **quod . . . abesse** (3), is likely to be causal, as there is no neuter antecedent to which **quod** might refer if it were a relative pronoun, and the position and meaning of the phrase **in causa** in the first clause is suggestive of causation. Therefore, it is logical that these clauses give reasons for something, i.e., why the writer misses his wife. The verb **consuesco** may be unfamiliar, but the meaning of **abesse** suggests that something is away or apart, most likely the writer from his wife, given the sense so far. Thus, the first reason for his longing is that he loves his wife, and the second reason (probably) has something to do with being apart from her. If you know the meaning of **(non) consuevimus**, you can confirm that they are not accustomed to being apart.

Sentence 3 This long sentence (lines 3–8) is the centerpiece of the passage. You may have noticed its length and structure during your first reading. It contains three **quod** (causal) clauses, each separated from the previous by a semi-colon. The respective repetitions of **inde** (3, 4), *from there, as a result*, and the appearance of **denique** (7), *finally,* suggest that the writer is listing reasons that indicate to his wife why he misses her so much, which is a logical inference from what has been said so far. In each clause, **quod . . . exigo** (3–4), **quod . . . ducunt** (5–6), and **quod . . . recedo** (6–8), the writer explains one of these reasons.

The first is that he spends a great part of his nights (**magnam noctium partem . . . exigo**) awake with her image (**in imagine tua vigil**), i.e., thinking of her. Pay attention to ambiguous situations, such as the proper agreement of the words in the phrase **magnam noctium partem.**

The second consequence of his wife's absence is that during the day the writer's feet, on their own, lead him to her room (**interdiu . . . ad diaetam tuam ipsi me . . . pedes ducunt**), i.e., he goes to her room. Remember to consult the glosses for words that are unfamiliar, such as **diaetam**. Determining the meaning of clauses within clauses, such as **quibus . . . solebam** (5), which is embedded in **quod . . . ducunt** (5–6), and parenthetical expressions such as **ut verissime dicitur** (6), may be temporarily postponed until you deal with any accompanying multiple-choice questions. The idea at this stage is to locate the main clause or, in this case, the primary subordinate clause (**quod . . . ipsi . . . pedes ducunt**) in order to determine how the sentence is organized.

The third and final consequence is that the writer leaves the empty room (**a vacuo limine recedo**), depressed (**aeger et maestus**) at not finding his wife there. A judgment will need to be made here as to whether **excluso** is a substantive or is to be taken with **a vacuo limine**. Knowledge that **similis** takes a dative, a requirement fulfilled by the form **excluso**, and that **excluso** is found outside of the prepositional phrase **a vacuo limine** (which is a stylistic feature found in poetry, but less so in prose) leads to the conclusion that **excluso** is better taken as a substantive with **similis** than with **a vacuo limine**, giving a meaning such as "similar to someone who has been shut out." Thus far, we have learned that Calpurnia's absence has three consequences for Pliny (3–8):

a) he stays awake a large part of the night thinking about her

b) he wanders into her room during the daytime

c) he finally leaves her room, heartsick and disconsolate

Sentence 4 The meaning of the sentence **Unum . . . conteror** (8–9) may be readily comprehended by taking the Latin in the order in which it is written. "One time from/by these torments is free from, in the forum and of (my) friends by the lawsuits I am worn out." The meaning of **caret**, if unfamiliar, may be deduced from context. (**Careo,** *to be free from, to lack,* contains the idea of separation and is followed by the ablative, here, **his tormentis**.) Use the glosses for **litibus** and **conteror** (9) to help you establish the context for the general meaning of this sentence. Note that **conteror** is present passive, *I am being worn out,* making it likely that **litibus** is an ablative of cause or means and that it is to be taken as part of a genitive phrase with **amicorum**, *by means of the lawsuits of (my) friends.*

Sentence 5 This sentence is controlled by the imperative **Aestima** (9). The succeeding subjunctive clause, **quae vita mea sit,** is further elaborated upon by two gapped and elliptical clauses – **cui requies in labore (est), (cui) in miseria curisque solacium (est)** – that seem to summarize the writer's unhappiness (**labore, miseria curisque**). Resolve the meaning of each clause before beginning the next.

And so, a more careful reading of this sight passage has led us to learn that:

1) Pliny is writing to his wife (line 1);
2) He misses his wife dearly, because he loves her and because they are unaccustomed to being apart (2–3);
3) His wife's absence has three consequences for Pliny (3–8):
    a) he stays awake a large part of the night thinking about her
    b) he wanders into her room during the daytime
    c) he finally leaves her room, heartsick and disconsolate
4) His one consolation is the distraction provided by his work in the forum and in the lawcourts (8–9);
5) He is so lonely and depressed that he finds comfort in his misery (9–10).

Step 4

Finally, work from each multiple-choice question back to the text, trying to locate the specific answer. Note that the questions are asked in the sequence of the sentences in the passage and that there is usually at least one question for each sentence. Line numbers and Latin citations are always provided in the question to assist you in locating the relevant Latin quickly. Remember, if you are stumped and cannot eliminate one or two answers as incorrect, move on.

Now, see if you can answer correctly the following typical multiple-choice questions on the Pliny passage, which is repeated below for your convenience. Look over each answer, rather than rush to judgment, because distractors, or red herrings, do appear. Each question below will be followed by the answer, with explanation. Following this sample, you will find two additional passages for practice with multiple-choice questions, one a syllabus-based passage from Vergil and the other a sight reading from the poet Catullus. Answers to these are also provided.

Questions and Answers on the Prose Sight Reading

Pliny misses his wife

C. Plinius Calpurniae Suae S.[1]

Incredibile est quanto desiderio tui tenear. In causa amor primum, deinde quod non consuevimus abesse. Inde est [quod magnam noctium partem in imagine tuā vigil exigo; inde quod interdiu, quibus horis te visere solebam], ad diaetam[2] tuam ipsi me (ut verissime dicitur) pedes ducunt; quod denique aeger et maestus ac similis excluso a vacuo limine recedo. Unum tempus his tormentis caret, quo in foro et amicorum litibus[3] conteror[4]. Aestima tu quae vita mea sit, cui requies in labore, in miseria curisque solacium. Vale.

1. S. = Salutem dicit: sends greetings
2. diaeta, diaeta, f.: room
3. lis, litis, f.: lawsuit, court
4. contero, contere, contrivi, contritum: wear out

1. In line 2, quanto . . . tenear is translated
   (A) with what longing I will hold you
   (B) how many times I will be held by your longing
   (C) with how much longing for you I am held
   (D) when I long to be held by you

(C) From your initial readings, you will have determined that **quanto . . . tenear** is a subordinate clause. More specifically, **quanto**, which means "how much" and modifies the noun **desiderio**, introduces an indirect question bounded by the present subjunctive verb **tenear.** Answer (A) mistranslates the tense and voice of **tenear**, which is present passive. Answer (B) both mistranslates **quanto** and expresses **tenear** as a future passive indicative (which would be **tenebor**). Answer (D) mistranslates **desiderio** as a verb and **tenear** as a present passive infinitive.

2. In line 3, Pliny says he misses his wife partly because
   (A) she is so far away
   (B) they are unaccustomed to being apart
   (C) traveling is dangerous
   (D) they have only recently been married

(B) Disregard answers (C) and (D), which do not include the meaning of the verb **abesse**; answers (A) and (B) are both worthy of consideration if the meaning of **consuevimus** is unknown, but (B) expresses correctly the meaning of **abesse** as an infinitive. <u>Use the wording of the questions on the passage to help you confirm your understanding of the meaning of particular words that may be unfamiliar.</u> Here, answer (B), which contains the correct meaning of **abesse**, translates **consuevimus** as "unaccustomed," which is likely to be and is, in fact, correct.

3. In lines 3–4, we learn that Pliny
   (A) stays awake thinking of his wife
   (B) sleeps the night through
   (C) has frightening nightmares
   (D) tries not to think of his wife

(A) Answer (B) misunderstands or ignores the meaning of **vigil**; answer (C) might be suggested by the distractor **in imagine tua** (4), but "has frightening nightmares" seems inappropriate to, or an exaggeration of, the emotional context of the passage. Answer (D) is incorrect because the Latin does not contain or suggest the word "tries" or a negative ("not to think").

4. The case and number of <u>noctium</u> (line 4) are
   (A) accusative singular
   (B) accusative plural
   (C) genitive plural
   (D) nominative singular

(C) The noun **nox, noctis** is a 3rd declension **i**-stem noun, making **noctium** genitive plural. The temptation, of course, is for you to take **noctium** as accusative, accompanying **magnam partem**, which also ends in **–m,** but remember that a genitive usually links two nouns. If your memory of the endings fails, the context should help you with the meaning.

5. The adjective vigil (line 4) modifies
   (A) partem (4)
   (B) imagine (4)
   (C) the subject of exigo (4)
   (D) Calpurnia, understood

(C) It should be clear that the adjective **vigil** is nominative, eliminating (A), which is accusative, and (B), which is ablative. Since Pliny is writing this letter to Calpurnia in the 1st person, the answer must be (C), rather than (D). Do not be distracted by the fact that you may not know the meaning of the verb **exigo**.

6. In line 6, ut is best translated
   (A) that
   (B) as
   (C) in order to
   (D) when

(B) You may not have worked out the meaning of **ut verissime dicitur** in your initial readings, but the punctuation and context indicate that the writer is making a parenthetical comment here, probably in response to **ipsi . . . pedes**, 6 (for which, see the answer to the next question).The verb **dicitur** is indicative, which removes the **ut** here from consideration as a subjunctive clause of purpose or result (A and D). The word **ut** does not have the meaning "when" (D).

7. From lines 4–6 (inde . . . ducunt), we can infer that Pliny
   (A) continues to visit his wife's room at the usual times
   (B) sleeps in his wife's room out of loneliness
   (C) avoids his wife's room, which reminds him of her absence
   (D) cleans his wife's room during the day

(A) Answer (A) comes closest to the meaning of **ad diaetam tuam ipsi me . . . pedes ducunt**. Pliny says literally "(my) feet on their own (**ipsi pedes**) lead me (**me**) to your room (**ad diaetam tuam**). "Continues" and "at the usual times" is expressed by the use of the imperfect tense and the meaning of **solebam** and the phrase **quibus horis** in the subordinate clause **quibus . . . solebam** (5). Answers (B), (C), and (D) are not supported by the Latin, i.e., there is no sleeping, avoiding, or cleaning here.

8. The words aeger et maestus (line 7) describe Pliny's mood as
   (A) gloomy
   (B) angry
   (C) apathetic
   (D) puzzled

(A) This question is not necessarily typical, in that it asks for a generalized interpretation. The answer will come from 1) knowledge of the vocabulary, or 2) deduction from proper inference of the mood of the writer. **Aeger, -a, -um**, "sick" and **maestus, -a, -um**, "sorrowful," are relatively common in Latin literature. There is nothing in the Latin that justifies the interpretation that Pliny is angry, apathetic, or puzzled.

9. The phrase <u>similis excluso</u> (line 7) suggests a

   (A) trusted confidante (C) condemned criminal

   (B) freed slave (D) spurned lover

(D) The word **excluso** is a past participle used here as a substantive (for discussion of the form of this word, see above, Step 4, Sentence 3). The concept of exclusion present in this word is closest in meaning to "spurned lover." The word "lover" here is inferred from the context, given the fact that Pliny was in his wife's room.

10. In line 8, <u>his tormentis</u> is ablative because it

    (A) is in a prepositional phrase

    (B) expresses time

    (C) completes the meaning of the verb <u>caret</u>

    (D) indicates location

(C) Although you might not be familiar with the meaning or the syntax required by the word **caret** here (see above, Step 4, Sentence 4), Answers (A), (B), and (D) may be eliminated because the Latin does not contain a preposition (A) and **his tormentis** expresses neither time (B) nor place (D).

11. From lines 8–9 (<u>Unum</u> . . . <u>conteror</u>), we learn that Pliny

    (A) is never at ease in his wife's absence

    (B) feels the loneliest when he has to be in public

    (C) finds sole consolation in his work in the courts

    (D) is exhausted by socializing with friends in the forum

(C) This question asks for comprehension of the Latin. The glosses help to convey some of the meaning of this sentence. Answers (A) and (B) do not do justice to the Latin, i.e., there is nothing stated or suggested about feeling "ill at ease" or "lonely when in public." In Answer (D), "exhausted" might express the meaning of **conteror** adequately, but Pliny is not "socializing with friends in the forum."

12. The pronoun <u>cui</u> (line 10) refers to

    (A) Calpurnia (C) the reader

    (B) Pliny (D) the lawcourt

(B) **Cui** is a dative of possession referring to Pliny, who is describing the sort of life he asks his wife to imagine in **Aestima tu quae vita mea sit.**

13. A figure of speech that occurs in line 10 (cui . . . solacium) is

(A) metonymy
(B) enjambment
(C) apostrophe
(D) ellipsis

(D) The missing verb from both clauses is likely to be **est**, given the sense implied by the context. Figures of speech, such as ellipsis, will be covered in a later chapter of this book.

Practice Multiple-Choice Questions

This section includes a syllabus-based passage from Vergil and a sight passage of poetry from Catullus. For your convenience, the answers to these questions are provided at the end of this chapter, along with translations of both passages.

About the Syllabus-Based Passage

- Syllabus-based passages are often selected from the less familiar portions of the required Latin reading. Be sure to prepare all required lines thoroughly!
- Glance over the passage quickly in Latin to see if you can recognize a familiar word, phrase, sentence, or proper name that will help to orient you. If you do not recognize the passage, use what knowledge you have of its general context and then apply your sight-reading skills. Remember to avoid random guessing.

The Syllabus-Based Passage

The destiny of the Romans is assured

"Et nunc cedo equidem pugnasque exosa relinquo.
Illud te, nulla fati quod lege tenetur,
pro Latio obtestor, pro maiestate tuorum:
cum iam conubiis pacem felicibus (esto)
component, cum iam leges et foedera iungent,
ne vetus indigenas nomen mutare Latinos
neu Troas fieri iubeas Teucrosque vocari
aut vocem mutare viros aut vertere vestem.
Sit Latium, sint Albani per saecula reges,
sit Romana potens Itala virtute propago:
occidit, occideritque sinas cum nomine Troia."

14. The emotion expressed by the speaker in line 1 is

(A) confusion
(B) joy
(C) resignation
(D) contemplation

15. Based upon your knowledge of this passage, who is speaking to whom?
    - (A) Juno to Aeneas
    - (B) Latinus to Aeneas
    - (C) Aeneas to Jupiter
    - (D) Juno to Jupiter

16. Illud (lines 2) refers to
    - (A) what is said in the previous line
    - (B) fate
    - (C) what is said in lines 4–8
    - (D) Latium

17. The metrical pattern of the first four feet of line 3 is
    - (A) dactyl-dactyl-spondee-spondee
    - (B) dactyl-spondee-spondee-spondee
    - (C) spondee-spondee-dactyl-spondee
    - (D) spondee-dactyl-spondee-dactyl

18. In line 4, cum is best translated
    - (A) when
    - (B) since
    - (C) with
    - (D) although

19. What figure of speech occurs in lines 4–5?
    - (A) hyperbole
    - (B) anaphora
    - (C) simile
    - (D) apostrophe

20. According to lines 4–5 (cum . . . iungent), what two things will join the Trojans and the Latins?
    - (A) peace and happiness
    - (B) pressure from others and conscience
    - (C) intermarriage and laws
    - (D) language and culture

21. The figure of speech occurring in line 6 is
    - (A) chiasmus
    - (B) asyndeton
    - (C) aposiopesis
    - (D) interlocked word order (synchysis)

22. In lines 6–7, ne . . . iubeas is translated
    (A) may you not command
    (B) you are not commanding
    (C) do not command
    (D) you will not command

23. As it appears in line 7, -que joins
    (A) iubeas and Teucros
    (B) ne (line 6) and neu
    (C) Troas fieri and Teucros vocari
    (D) Latinos (line 6) and Teucros

24. In lines 6–8, we learn that all but which of the following will remain unchanged except the
    (A) clothing
    (B) language
    (C) name
    (D) religion

25. In line 10, Itala modifies
    (A) Romana
    (B) virtute
    (C) propago
    (D) a noun that is understood

26. The technique of anaphora found in 9–10 is used to
    (A) confuse
    (B) explain
    (C) emphasize
    (D) understate

27. Sit Latium (line 9) is translated
    (A) There is Latium
    (B) Let Latium be
    (C) Latium can be
    (D) Latium was

28. In line 11, the speaker wishes that
    (A) the Roman people should adopt the identity of Trojans
    (B) Troy should avenge her destruction
    (C) anyone with the name Trojan should die
    (D) even the name Troy should disappear

Sight Reading Passage 2 (Poetry)

A holiday gift

Di magni, horribilem et sacrum libellum,
quem tu scilicet ad tuum Catullum
misti, continuo ut die periret
Saturnalibus, optimo dierum!
Non non hoc tibi, salse,[5] sic abibit:
nam, si luxerit,ad librariorum
curram scrinia,[6] Caesios, Aquinos,
Suffenum, omnia colligam venena,
ac te his suppliciis remunerabor,
vos hinc interea valete abite
illuc, unde malum pedem attulistis,
saecli incommoda, pessimi poetae.

5 salsus: scoundrel, rascal, rogue; substantive of salsus, -a, -um
6 scrinium, -i, n.: a case or box for books
Caesius, Aquinus, Suffenus: notoriously bad poets of the day

29. The words horribilem et sacrum libellum (line 1) are accusative because they
   (A) express the direct object of misti (line 3)
   (B) are the subject of an indirect statement
   (C) are an exclamation
   (D) express the object of an understood preposition

30. What do we learn from lines 1–3 (Di . . . misti)?
   (A) that the gods have given the addressee a book
   (B) that the addressee has given Catullus a book
   (C) that the gods have given Catullus a book
   (D) that Catullus has given the addressee a book

31. The form misti (line 3) is translated
   (A) to be sent
   (B) you have sent
   (C) you are sending
   (D) having been sent

32. In line 3, ut . . . periret is a
   (A) result clause
   (B) fear clause
   (C) indirect command
   (D) purpose clause

33. Si luxerit (line 6) is translated
   (A) If it is permitted
   (B) If dawn arrives
   (C) If he will have been allowed
   (D) Unless he is sorry

34. The object of the preposition ad (line 6) is
    (A) librariorum (line 6)
    (B) scrinia (line 7)
    (C) Caesios, Aquinos, Suffenum (lines 7–8)
    (D) venena (line 8)

35. The use of venena (line 8) is an example of
    (A) metaphor
    (B) transferred epithet
    (C) apostrophe
    (D) zeugma

36. As we learn in lines 7–9 (ac . . . remunerabor), Catullus intends to
    (A) look forward to another gift from the addressee
    (B) write abusive poems about the addressee
    (C) give the addressee a book of bad poems
    (D) pick out a book that the addressee will enjoy

37. Line 10 contains an example of the figure of speech
    (A) asyndeton
    (B) chiasmus
    (C) onomatopoeia
    (D) hyperbole

38. In lines 10–11 (vos . . . attulistis), Catullus suggests that those addressed here should
    (A) write in a different meter
    (B) strive to improve their writing
    (C) stop writing bad poetry
    (D) go back to where they came from

Answers

Syllabus-Based Passage	Sight Passage 2 (Poetry)
14. C	29. A
15. D	30. B
16. C	31. B
17. B	32. D
18. A	33. B
19. B	34. B
20. C	35. A
21. D	36. C
22. A	37. A
23. C	38. D
24. D	
25. B	
26. C	
27. B	
28. D	

Translations of Sight and Syllabus-Based Passages

Sight Reading Passage 1 (Prose)

Gaius Pliny sends greetings to his Calpurnia

It is unbelievable with how much longing for you I am held (prisoner). (My) love (for you) is the first reason, then the fact that we have not grown accustomed to being apart. As a result, I spend a great part of (my) nights staying awake thinking of you; and, too, throughout the day, during the hours when I was in the habit of visiting you, my feet lead me of their own accord (I say this very truly) to your room; and finally, sick and sorrowful like a spurned lover, I withdraw from (your) empty doorway. The one time that I am free from these torments is when I wear myself out in the Forum and with the lawsuits of my friends. Imagine what life there is for me, for whom there is rest in work and distraction in unhappiness and anxiety. Farewell. (Pliny, *Epistulae* 7.5)

Syllabus-Based Passage

"And now I yield, yes, and hating the fighting, I abandon it. To the following, which is held by (under the control of) no law of fate, for the sake of Latium and for the sake of the greatness of your own (descendants), I call upon you as a witness: when now they will make peace with happy bridal rites — so be it! — when now they will join in laws and agreements, may you not command the native Latins to change their ancient name nor to become Trojans and be called Teucrians, nor to change their language or alter their clothing. Let there be Latium, let Alban kings last throughout the generations, let Roman offspring be mighty in Italic valor: may you allow Troy to fall, and with it the (very) name of Troy." (Vergil, *Aeneid* 12.818–28)

Sight Reading Passage 2 (Poetry)

Great gods, a dreadful and detestable little book (it was) that you sent to your Catullus, so that he may surely perish on the day of the Saturnalia, best of days! No, no, you scoundrel, this will not end here for you: for, if the morning should come, I will run down to the bookcases of the booksellers, gather up the Caesii, the Aquini, and Suffenus, all poisonous (writers), and I will pay you back with these instruments of torture. All of you (poets), meanwhile, farewell, be gone from here to that place from which you brought your wretched feet (of the body and of verse), (you) afflictions of our age, (you) worst of poets. (Catullus 14.12–23)

Endnotes

[5] See the author's study guide *SAT Subject Test: Latin*, published by Research & Education Association, 2006.

[6] In Part I of this book, a separate chapter is devoted to each of these skills except for grammar and syntax, which are covered in Part II.

[7] Statistical analyses of student performances on the multiple-choice sections are published with the released AP Latin Exams, for which, see Chapter 1 of the Appendix.

[8] For short-term strategies on preparing for the AP Latin Exam, see Chapters 10 and 11.

[9] Sample multiple-choice questions may be found in the current Acorn book, available in print or online, and online at the AP Latin: Vergil Course Homepage. For complete multiple-choice sections of released AP Latin exams, see the resources listed under Chapter 1 of Appendix 1. For excellent teacher-produced AP-style multiple-choice questions with self-check answers, go to "Approximately AP-Style Test Items" at *http://abney.homestead.com/aeneid.html*. For a number of resources for teachers on the subject of multiple-choice questions, see "Latin Tutorial 4: Format of the Multiple-Choice Section," at *http://apcentral.collegeboard.com/apc/members/courses/teachers_corner/9614.html*.

[10] Based upon the statistics available for the multiple-choice section of the most recently released Exam (2005), the mean scores for each of the four passages were 6.8 out of 12 pts., 3.9 out 13, 4.3 out of 11, and 5.7 out of 13 pts. The total accuracy for this section was 42% correct.

[11] Go to *http://www.nle.org/exams.html#exams_previous* (answers are provided). For each of Books 1, 2, 4, 6, 10–12 of the *Aeneid,* there are sight reading passages with multiple-choice questions and answers at Tim Abney's AP Vergil site *http://abney.homestead.com/aeneid.html#anchor_80*. The format is a running Java banner that forces you to read the Latin as Latin, and is excellent for teaching or testing comprehension. For some additional online sight passages (no questions), see Jerard White's site at *http://www.frapanthers.com/teachers/white/Apl_sight_reading.html*. Also on this website, there is a handy multiple-choice template that demonstrates the format for the types of questions asked on the multiple-choice section of the AP Latin Exam.

[12] *2005 AP Latin Literature and Latin: Vergil Released Exams*, page 41. For a discussion of reading for comprehension vs. translation as it pertains to the AP Latin Exam, see Chapter 5.

Chapter 3

The Free-Response Section

The free-response section is the second of the two sections of the AP Latin Exam.[13] (Remember that you will be given a short break between the two sections.) As indicated in Chapter 1 of this book, the free-response section differs from the multiple-choice section in content, format, length, and value. The free-response section on the *Aeneid* consists of five questions. This section, which requires two hours — a 15-minute reading period and 1 hour and 45 minutes for writing — counts 60 percent of your total score.

Content of the Free-Response Section

You are called upon to demonstrate your command of the prepared Latin by answering translation and essay questions that assess your ability both to give a close reading of the Latin text and to express your understanding of that text with regard to a specific question.

As mentioned, there are five free-response questions on the Vergil Exam. The free-response section of the Vergil Exam contains two translation questions, a long essay, and two short essays. One short essay calls for you to be able to produce a comparative analysis of characters or situations in the context of those portions of the *Aeneid* that you read in English. For specific information about the various types of questions that appear on the free-response section of the AP Latin Exam, see the chapters that follow.

Abilities Tested on the Free-Response Section

The free-response section anticipates that you can:[14]

- write a literal English translation of a prepared Latin passage;[15]
- analyze excerpts from the required reading of the *Aeneid*, compare and contrast different parts of the poem, and draw generalized conclusions about keynote themes and motifs expressed in these excerpts as they relate to the entire work;
- examine and interpret the writing style of the author, including characteristic elements such as organization and structure, word choice, mood and tone, imagery and figures of speech, and the relation of sound to sense;
- demonstrate knowledge of the *Aeneid* as a whole.

The Format of the Free-Response Section

Exam questions on Vergil are designated as Question V1, Question V2, etc.

Question V1: 10-minute translation (15 percent)

Question V2: 10-minute translation (15 percent)

Question V3: 45-minute long essay (35 percent)

Question V4: 20-minute short essay (20 percent)

Question V5: 20-minute short essay (15 percent)

FAQs About the Free-Response Section

- **What is the free-response section like?**

  This section tests the specific reading syllabus that you've prepared, whether this preparation occurred in a course specifically designated as Advanced Placement, in an advanced Latin course not labeled as AP, or in a self-taught or tutorial setting. The free-response section measures your ability to read and understand the Latin that you have prepared, as well as your ability to express your understanding in organized and coherent English. You will write your answers in longhand in a booklet roughly equivalent to the blue book used in colleges (except that it's pink!)

- **What is the "15-minute reading period"?**

  Before you begin writing on the free-response section, you will be given a 15-minute "reading period" to look over the five questions on this second section of the Exam (essentially, two translations and three essays) in order to assess the time you think you will need to answer each question and to begin thinking about and planning your answers. Some refer to this as pre-reading or brainstorming. Look over every question in your free-response booklet and try to recognize the Latin passages being tested (each passage of Latin is identified). Circle or otherwise highlight the "prompt" or essential element in the English wording of each essay question. In addition, think about how you will approach each answer and circle or otherwise highlight Latin words, phrases, clauses, lines, or sentences in the texts that are relevant to your answer. You may make marginal or intratextual notes directly on your green Exam booklet, outlining the main points you wish to make during your formal discussion. Note that the green book is returned to your teacher after the Exam and will not be considered by the Readers in evaluating your performance.

- **How can I best prepare for the free-response section?**

  Your success on this section is directly proportional to the amount of the syllabus that you have prepared and to the thoroughness of that preparation.

1) Prepare your daily assignments thoroughly and consistently. Don't fall behind, which will leave gaps in your preparation and therefore in your recognition and comprehension of the Latin. Prior to the exam, it is best not to rush through uncompleted portions of the syllabus at the last minute, as this will only create confusion and anxiety. Concentrate on preparing thoroughly what you have done and use your sight-reading skills and ability as a writer to address that question or those questions on passages that you do not recognize. Not every student can answer every question!
2) When you are preparing your daily reading assignments, minimize your reliance on reference materials, such as reading or class notes, published translations, dictionaries, online resources, friends, or tutors.
3) Learn to support your interpretative analysis by providing proper Latin citations from throughout the passage.[16] Pretend that each unit test you take in class is an AP Latin Exam and adjust your test-taking style to practice coping with the challenges of thinking and writing under the pressure of time. Also, practice answering untimed and timed free-response questions from previous AP Latin Exams.
4) Leave time for review before the AP Latin Exam.

Catalogues of Passages Tested on the Free-Response Section of Recent AP Latin Exams

Remember that there are two translation passages and three essays on the free-response section. The catalogues of reading passages provided on the next page illustrate the length and degree of difficulty of the Latin passages appearing on the free-response section. From the listing of two passages for the same question, it is apparent that the long or short essay question sometimes asks you to compare and contrast two different passages from the same Book or different Books.[17] Note that it is not customary for the same passage to be tested in consecutive years and that each of the five free-response questions covers a different one of the six Books of the *Aeneid* that you prepared in Latin.

Free-Response Questions By Year of Exam[18]

2009

Translation: 1.23–28

Translation: 10.459–465

Long Essay: 4.337–350, 6.110–122

Short Essay: 12.903–918

Short Essay: desire for material possessions

2008

Translation: 4.429–434

Translation: 12.791–796

Long Essay: 2.234–253

Short Essay: 6.65–76

Short Essay: shows hospitality

2007

Translation: 4.68–73

Translation: 6.847–853

Long Essay: 1.36–52, 12.818–828

Short Essay: 2.533–545

Short Essay: sufferings of the Trojans

2006

Translation: 1.378–85

Translation: 2.560–66

Long Essay: 6.868–86

Short Essay: 10.491–96, 500–505

Short Essay: function in plot

2005

Translation: 2.201–207

Translation: 12.930–36

Long Essay: 1.92–101, 1.198–209

Short Essay: 6.83–94

Short Essay: **pietas**

2004

Translation: 2.10–16

Translation: 6.893–899

Long Essay: 1.124–141, 4.84–89

Short Essay: 10.467–475

Short Essay: reasonable vs. rash

2003

Translation: 4.160–166

Translation: 12.803–809

Long Essay: 2.768–793

Short Essay: 1.450–465

Short Essay: deception

2002

Translation: 12.908–914

Translation: 2.289–294

Long Essay: 4.20–29, 4.320–330

Short Essay: 1.291–296

Short Essay: unfair events

2001

Translation: 10.451, 453–456

Translation: 2.237–243

Long Essay: 1.37–49, 12.818–828

Short Essay: 4.675–685

Short Essy: revealing the future

Free-Response Passages by Type of Question

Translation	Long Essay	Short Essay
1.23–28 (2009)	1.36–52, 12.818–828 (2007)	1.291–296 (2002)
1.378–385 (2006)	1.37–49, 12.818–828 (2001)	1.450–465 (2003)
2.10–16 (2004)	1.92–101, 198–209 (2005)	2.533–545 (2007)
2.201–207 (2005)	1.124–141, 4.84.89 (2004)	4.675–685 (2001)
2.237–243 (2001)	1.198–209, 92–101 (2005)	6.65–76 (2008)
2.289–294 (2002)	2.234–253 (2008)	6.83–95 (2005)
2.560–566 (2006)	2.768–793 (2003)	10.467–475 (2004)
4.68–73 (2007)	4.20–29, 4.320–330 (2002)	10.491–496, 10.500–505 (2006)
4.160–166 (2003)	4.84–89, 1.124–141 (2004)	
4.429–434 (2008)	4.337–350, 6.110–122 (2009)	12.913–918 (2009)
6.847–853 (2007)	6.110–122, 4.337–350 (2009)	
6.893–899 (2004)	6.868–886 (2006)	
10.450, 453–456 (2001)	10. none	
10.459–465 (2009)	12.818–828, 1.36–52 (2007)	
12.791–796 (2008)	12.818–828, 1.37–49 (2001)	
12.803–809 (2003)		
12.908–914 (2002)		
12.930–936 (2005)		

Free-Response Passages by Book of the *Aeneid*

Book 1	Book 4	Book 10
23–28 (2009)	20–29 (2002)	450, 453–456 (2001)
36–52 (2007)	68–73 (2007)	467–475 (2004)
37–49 (2001)	84–89 (2004)	459–465 (2009)
92–101 (2005)	160–166 (2003)	491–496 (2006)
124–41 (2004)	320–330 (2002)	500–505 (2006)
198–209 (2005)	337–350 (2009)	
291–296 (2002)	429–434 (2008)	
378–385 (2006)	675–685 (2001)	
450–465 (2003)		
Book 2	**Book 6**	**Book 12**
10–16 (2004)	65–76 (2008)	791–796 (2008)
201–207 (2005)	83–94 (2005)	803–809 (2003)
234–253 (2008)	110–122 (2009)	818–828 (2001, 2007)
237–43 (2001)	847–853 (2007)	903–918 (2009)
289–294 (2002)	868–886 (2006)	908–914 (2002)
533–545 (2007)	893–899 (2004)	930–936 (2005)
560–566 (2006)		
768–793 (2003)		

Endnotes

[13] For additional information on the free-response section, see Chapter 1 of this book, the current Acorn book, and the AP Latin: Vergil Exam page.

[14] The succeeding chapters of this book will help you to prepare for the types of questions that evaluate the abilities described here.

[15] For the meaning of the term "literal" translation, see Terms Used in AP Latin, Chapter 1 and Chapter 5.

[16] Proper citation from the Latin will be covered in Chapter 6.

[17] With the exception of the years 2003 and 2008, every AP Latin Exam has contained a question with two passages.

[18] Remember that links to the entire free-response sections of the Exams, including the actual questions themselves, together with scoring guidelines and sample student answers with commentary, are provided on both the AP Latin: Vergil Homepage and the AP Latin: Vergil Exam page. See the Appendix for Chapter 1. For AP Vergil free-response questions from previous Exams, see also the websites of Timothy S. Abney, Michael B. Myer, and David Pellegrino in the Appendix for Chapter 1. Sample questions for this section are available in the Acorn book.

Chapter 4

The Vocabulary of Vergil's *Aeneid*

Many students and teachers will agree that the most difficult challenge in reading the *Aeneid* is the vocabulary. However, it is Vergil's use of language that makes his epic poem a classic. For instance, instead of using the word **mare** for *sea* each time he wants to refer to the sea, he uses **aequor, altum, fluctus, pelagus, pontus,** or **unda,** bringing variety and therefore interest to his writing.[19] Professional classicists continue to argue about which Latin words should make up a student's "working vocabulary." [20] For many years, Latin textbook publishers typically built their programs around a Caesar-based vocabulary, because Caesar was traditionally the first authentic Latin author read by students.[21] (Many parents and grandparents, when asked, can still quote "Gallia est omnis divisa in partes tres.") In recent decades, the availability of computers to conduct word-frequency studies of Latin literature has helped textbook authors and publishers, especially those of comprehension or context-based reading programs, broaden their presentation of Latin vocabulary to include more authors that are commonly read at the secondary level.[22] Retention of a Latin word comes easily to some and with considerable difficulty to others.[23] It is important to realize that you are the one responsible for learning vocabulary and that you will save much time and frustration by discovering exactly how you learn and retain vocabulary most effectively. It is not the purpose of this book to teach you a simple way to master Vergil's vocabulary: there is none! But here are several general ways to help you remember words in Latin.

1) Say the word aloud or to yourself.[24] It is important to verbalize the Latin words whose meaning you are trying to grasp. This simply gives your brain another pathway to become acquainted with the word. Vocalize and visualize.
2) Find some kind of "hook" or mnemonic device (memory trick) to help you retrieve the word or its relevant meaning.[25] Try to relate it to another word that you know. Above all, try to figure out the meaning of the word before checking the vocabulary list or notes or looking it up in the dictionary.
3) The availability of vocabulary on pages facing the text makes it easy to ignore the importance of actually acquiring the words. Say the word or write it down several times. Practice recalling the word.

As mentioned, your success in reading Latin in general and on the AP Latin Exam specifically will depend partly upon your overall ability to retain lexical informational about the Latin words that you have met.[26] (This does not mean that only those who can readily memorize translations will find success on the AP Latin Exam!) Many teachers now introduce Vergil in Latin III, or in the year before

AP Latin, to give their students extra time to adjust to the diversity of Vergil's vocabulary.

Building Vocabulary at an Advanced Level of Study[27]

By the time you read authentic Latin literature, you should be paying less attention to the meanings of individual words and more to the meanings of word groups, such as phrases and clauses.[28] That said, of importance to the development of your vocabulary at this level of study is your ability to discriminate among different meanings of the same word, i.e., that you learn to read contextually and critically. (You have probably already discovered that the same Latin word can have opposite meanings, such as **hospes**, which can mean both *guest* and *host*.) For example, with respect to the phrase **tot volvere casus** (1.9), you may have previously learned the meaning of the verb **volvere** as *turn (around), roll, revolve*. That meaning won't do here, will it? This word can refer to the passing of time (**volventibus annis**, 1.234, **volvendis mensibus**, 1.269), the unscrolling of a book (**volvens fatorum arcana movebo**, 1.262), or thread, (**sic volvere Parcas**, 1.22), the flowing of the waves of the sea (**vastos volvunt ad litora fluctus**, 1.86), the act of pondering or meditating (**Talia flammato secum dea corde volutans**, 1.50 [**volutare** is a frequentative form of **volvere**], and **per noctem plurima volvens**, 1.305), in addition to the physical act of rolling something along (**manibus subvolvere saxa**, 1.424) or rolling or tumbling off (**magister volvitur in caput**, 1.115). Vergil uses this word because he wants the reader to appreciate the fact that Aeneas has gone through a series of misfortunes (**tot . . . casus**), so that here **volvere** is more likely to mean *undergo, endure,* or *suffer.*

Another aspect of vocabulary building at an advanced level of study is the need for greater attention to how Latin words are formed, i.e., the use of prefixes, roots/stems/bases, suffixes and affixes. Word lists designed for mastery at advanced levels of study in Latin often include a preponderance of compound words, especially verbs. To enlarge and strengthen your Latin vocabulary through word building, consult your textbook or one of the many resources available on word formation to help you improve your understanding of the range of meaning that a Latin word can have.[29] As you explore the topic of word formation in Latin, appreciate how the Romans, who actually had a relatively small vocabulary, managed to use the elements of their language to full advantage. You should begin to see groups of words that are similar in form or that have the same basic root meaning as word families, e.g., adjectives ending in **-idus, -a, -um**, a suffix having the meaning *in a condition* or *state of* . . . , such as **candidus, fervidus, fluidus, frigidus, horridus, lucidus, splendidus, timidus, validus,** and **vividus.** Consider further how these adjectives relate to the verbs from which they come, e.g., **candidus** from **candeo** (*shine*), **fervidus** from **ferveo** (*boil*), **fluidus** from **fluo** (*flow*), **frigidus** from **frigeo** (*be cold*), **horridus** from **horreo** (*bristle*), **lucidus** from **luceo** (*be light*), **splendidus** from **splendeo** (*shine*), **timidus** from **timeo** (*fear*), **validus** from **valeo** (*be strong*), and **vividus** from **vivo** (*live*). Knowledge of the rules for the use of prefixes, such as assimilation, will also help you to build your vocabulary quickly in both Latin and English.[30]

Word Lists

Word lists generally consist of an alphabetized list or column of Latin vocabulary words side by side with one or two of the most common English meanings of that word. Learning vocabulary in lists creates the basic problem of tempting the user to cheat and peek at the answer, even if one of the columns is covered up.[31] Research indicates that we remember words best in the way we learned them. If we learn vocabulary in a list, it will become more difficult for us to apply the appropriate meaning to a particular word when seen in context. We also have a tendency to think that, if we know most of the words on a list, we know them all, thus neglecting the unknown words. Some texts of the *Aeneid* have become popular precisely because they are designed to help you master Vergil's vocabulary. For instance, a standard high school text of the *Aeneid,* by Clyde Pharr (revised by Barbara Weiden Boyd), contains inside the back cover a foldout mastery list of words found 12–23 times in the *Aeneid*, which is considered to be "working vocabulary" for the poem. The Pharr/Boyd text gives further assistance by printing all glossed vocabulary in Roman font in the running text, and all unglossed vocabulary, i.e., the words you should already know, in italics.

Flashcards

The use of flashcards is a tried-and-true method of learning Latin words, especially in the early stages of your study.[32] A flashcard consists of an individual Latin word written on one side of a 3 × 5 card, with the English on the reverse. Many students and teachers believe that "card learning" is a much more efficient and effective way to learn Latin vocabulary than word lists. Furthermore, flashcards are more interactive, i.e., there is physical movement involved, and the cards can be carried anywhere, shuffled, grouped by category, color-coded, and so forth.

Websites

There are a growing number of publisher- and teacher-produced websites online for Latin, many of which are useful for the acquisition and improvement of vocabulary skills. Those which are recommended for the study of Vergilian vocabulary have been provided for your convenience in the Appendix for this chapter. There are several websites which provide software that allows teachers to design and publish their own interactive learning materials for specific Latin classes, levels, textbooks, or topics for their students, or anyone else, to use online. The two that are the most valuable for (AP) Latin are *Quia* (Key-ah) and Quizlet.[33] The activities and games on both sites cover all aspects of Vergil and the *Aeneid*, especially vocabulary and content. *Quia* contains learning activities that include Java games such as *Matching*, *Word Search*, *Concentration*, *Battleship*, *Hangman*, *Flashcards*, *Rags-to-Riches*, and the like. All activities are self-administered and self-evaluated. On the Quizlet website, go to the *Aeneid* Flashcard Set where you will find many teacher-produced vocabulary flashcard and other activities, starting with tasks titled *Familiarize, Learn, and Test*, then followed by various games, such as *Scatter* and *Space Race*. This site even includes several voice recognition activities (*Voice Race*, *Voice Scatter*) and printable flashcards.

Although literal translation, which requires you to account for the meaning and form of every word in a Latin passage, is required on the AP Latin Exam, experience will teach you that you need not learn every word that Vergil wrote to enable you to read his Latin and to appreciate the beauty of his poetry. But, as Wilfred Funk has said, "The more words you know, the more clearly and powerfully you will think and the more ideas you will invite into your mind." So, work on that vocabulary!

Endnotes

[19] In the space of six lines in Book 1 (124–129), Vergil uses six different words for the sea: **pontus, vadum** (the depths), **altum, unda, aequor,** and **fluctus.**

[20] The standard word list for many years, organized by level of study, has been John K. Colby's *Latin Word Lists*, first published in booklet form by Independent School Press in 1972. For more on the general subject, see the item "Latin Vocabulary" at Latinteach Resources *http://www.latinteach.com/Site/RESOURCES/Entries/2008/7/16_Latin_Vocabulary_.html* and the listings for this chapter in the Appendix.

[21] Interestingly, as of this writing, the College Board is considering Caesar as the prose alternative to Vergil for the AP Latin Exam.

[22] For websites contributing to vocabulary development in the more commonly-used Latin textbook programs, see the list of resources for this chapter in the Appendix.

[23] Opinions differ about the importance of memorization in acquiring vocabulary. In a study guide for Vergil from 1930, one finds the statement, "The mechanical memorization of words should be avoided and the functional [sic] method followed whenever possible." (*Suggestions for Teachers of Vergil in Secondary Schools*, Service Bureau, The American Classical League, April, 1930, page 74). On the other hand, Colby says in his preface, "Time spent in memorizing the meanings of these words (i.e., the ones in his booklet) pays a student rich dividends in the task of translating from Latin to English."

[24] The classicist W.H.D. Rouse wrote, "The ear is the natural receptive organ of language, the tongue the expressive. To substitute the eye is a vital blunder. Mastery can be obtained only by training eye, ear, tongue, and memory at the same time. The sounds will become second nature, so that you no longer think about them, but think in them." ("What's the Use of Latin?" *Latin Teaching* (June, 1967), page 191.)

[25] See "Mnemonic Techniques and Specific Memory Tricks to Improve Memory, Memorization" (Intelegen, Inc.) at *http://brain.web-us.com/memory/mnemonic_techniques.htm*. See also "Latin Mnemonics," at *http://en.wikipedia.org/wiki/Latin_mnemonics* at Wikipedia. Examples of common Latin mnemonics include SID SPACE for the prepositions that require the ablative, or Let's eat caviar for the vowels of the present subjunctive, or PUFFY (PUFFV), the special deponents that take the ablative, i.e., **potior, utor, fruor, fungor,** and **vescor**.

[26] Poor command of vocabulary is continually mentioned in the annual Chief Reader's report on student performance for any particular year of the AP Latin Exam. See, for example, the following comment on Question V3 (the long essay) of the 2008 Vergil Exam: "A common problem was vocabulary; poor command of vocabulary made it difficult for students to understand what transpired in the passage, to discuss the Trojans' perceptions, and to support their arguments from the text. Students mistook, for example, *canunt* (line 6) for *currunt* and *dolos* (line 19) for *dolor* or *donum*." ("Student Performance Q & A," 2008 AP Latin Vergil Free-Response Questions, *http://apcentral.collegeboard.com/apc/public/repository/ap08_latin_vergil_qa.pdf*.)

[27] For online resources for building a basic Latin vocabulary, as well as for acquiring and strengthening your knowledge of vocabulary for reading Vergil's *Aeneid*, see the Appendix for this chapter.

[28] This is not to say, however, that individual words are not important. For instance, in the *Aeneid,* the recurring word **furor**, which means *violent madness, frenzy, passion,* has important meaning for the development of the characters to whom this word is applied, as well as for an understanding of the unstable political context in which this poem was composed.

[29] One of the best resources for learning about Latin word formation is Joseph M. Pax, *Word Mastery for Students of Latin*, Scott Foresman and Co., 1965, which, alas, is out of print. For other recommended resources in print and online, see the appropriate section for this chapter in the Appendix.

[30] Assimilation is the spelling change some verbal prefixes undergo (usually for reasons of pronunciation) when they are joined to stems that begin with certain consonants, e.g., **ad + capere = accipere.**

[31] For a defense of word lists in acquiring vocabulary in a second language, see the online article "In Defense of Learning Words in Word Pairs" (Rob Waring, Notre Dame Seishin Univ., Okayama, Japan), at *http://www.perlingua.com/LatinHome/LatVocab/LatVocab.htm*.

[32] See "How to Make Vocabulary Flashcards" at *http://www.dl.ket.org/latin1/review/*. For websites on which you can create and share your own vocabulary flashcards online, see the Appendix. For online flashcards of the Pharr/Boyd vocabulary, go to the vocabulary section of Tim Abney's website for AP Vergil and to Virginia Kehoe's *Quia* website, also in the Appendix.

[33] For the links to the nearly 3000 teacher-created activities and games for Latin, including the *Aeneid,* go to *http://www.quia.com/shared/latin*. For Quizlet, go to *http://quizlet.com/subject/aeneid/*. For additional vocabulary games for AP Latin, see Jo Green in the Appendix for this chapter.

Chapter 5

The Free-Response Section: Translation

Literal Translation

> Ipse suas sectatur oves et filius agnos
> et calidam fesso comparat uxor aquam.
>
> Tibullus, *Elegies*, I.10.41–42

> He gains his own eggs but procures a son from
> the lambs and a wife from the cold water.[34]
>
> Student's translation

Many of us who have learned to read Latin admit, albeit grudgingly, that we have produced such "translations" as the one above at some point. This translation demonstrates the pitfalls into which one who attempts to translate Latin into English must inevitably stumble.[35] When students translate Latin into English, many students create a new language, known as "translationese." This language is usually the by-product of the hunt 'n' peck or decoding method of translating, a procedure that has been called "a series of disconnected word puzzles."[36] All Latin students know that it is difficult to render one language in another, especially in poetry.[37] The fact remains that your ability to translate Latin literally is considered important by those who teach Latin at the college level, as indicated by the fact that translation now counts as 30 percent of your score on the free-response section of the Exam.[38]

Instructions on the translation questions of the AP Latin Exam ask you to "translate the passage as literally as possible." What does this mean? It means that you must account in English for every word and every form in the passage. Stated a bit differently, you should "stay as close to the Latin forms and structure as good English allows."[39] One classicist has defined literal translation as, "the process by which the exact thought of a Latin sentence is transferred to an English one, identical insofar as English idiom, word-order, emphasis, and style will permit."[40] On the translation section of the AP Latin Exam, you must demonstrate your ability to translate the Latin rather than present an English translation from memory.[41] Furthermore, it is a "literal," not a "literary," translation that is sought. A literary translation perhaps preserves more of the poetic essence or spirit of the original. In this regard, another classicist has written "A good translation must carry over the very soul and spirit, the feelings and the emotions, that are concealed between the lines but pervade the whole text."[42] Here are several recent literary translations of the following Latin passage, one in prose and one in verse:[43]

Fracti bello fatisque repulsi
ductores Danaum tot iam labentibus annis
instar[1] montis equum divina Palladis arte
aedificant, sectaque intexunt abiete costas;
votum pro reditu simulant; ea fama vagatur.

[1] instar: "likeness"

***Aeneid* 2.13–17**

"Year after year the leaders of the Greeks had been broken in war and denied by the Fates, until, with the aid of the divine skill of Pallas Athene, they built a horse the size of a mountain, cutting pine trees to weave into it for ribs. They pretended it was a votive offering for their safe return to Greece, and that was the story on men's lips."

(David West, 1991)

"The years of war had broken
The Greek kings; destiny had pushed them back.
They built a mountainous horse, with woven ribs
Of fir – Athena's genius aided them.
"An offering for a safe voyage home!" The news spread.

(Sarah Ruden, 2009)

Ruden's translation of **votum pro reditu simulant** as "An offering for a safe voyage home!" is creative, but it is by no means literal. So, how does one arrive at a literal translation that is acceptable to an Exam Reader? In the paragraphs that follow, we will go through the process of translating the Latin passage above literally, working step by step through the text. Obviously, the first and most important way to meet or surpass the standard for literal translation on the AP Latin Exam is to prepare thoroughly the assigned to be read in Latin. You will certainly feel more confident during and after the Exam if you are able to translate one or both of the passages. In addition to thorough preparation of the assigned lines, to achieve success on the translation questions you will need the following: 1) a working knowledge of Latin grammar and syntax, 2) common sense, and 3) plenty of practice translating Latin. You probably already have a generous supply of all three of these or you wouldn't be a candidate to take the AP Latin Exam! With respect to translating Latin, most would agree on two main principles:

1) that you should read and render the Latin in sense units or word-groupings, such as noun–adjective combinations, phrases, and clauses, and avoid translating words individually;
2) that you should make accuracy and precision your goal and avoid simply giving a general impression of what the Latin says.

In translating accurately, you need to pay attention to the precise expression of such specific grammatical elements as noun–adjective agreement; subject–verb agreement; the tense, voice, number, and mood of verbs; and the time relationship between the verbs in main clauses and those in subordinate elements, such as dependent clauses, participial phrases, and infinitives in indirect statement.[44] Although close paraphrasing is allowed on analytical questions of the free-response section, paraphrasing does not substitute for precision on the translation question of the AP Latin Exam. One teacher has written, "The College Board never penalizes for being too literal, but may very well penalize for not being literal enough."[45] When asked to translate literally, remember that you are better served by staying true to the Latin, regardless of the requirements of English, than by producing a "free" translation or paraphrase for the sake of better English expression. And remember, too, that your translations must make sense!

Making Use of Punctuation When Translating

The Romans, of course, did not have the advantages of punctuation (from **punctus,** *point*).[46] The official Latin text used for the AP Latin Exam is that of Sir Roger A.B. Mynors, which, although published by Oxford University Press, uses initial caps (however, the vowel *u* is retained for *v*, e.g., **obuiam,** not **obviam**).[47] Given the fact that standard English punctuation is used in Mynors' text and in the American editions of the *Aeneid* commonly used in AP Latin courses (where *u* is "corrected" to *v*, e.g., **obviam,** not **obuiam**), you should take full advantage of the use of English punctuation in helping you to determine the meaning of the Latin. We will now give examples of how punctuation can assist you in reading and comprehending Latin. The punctuation marks commonly used in Latin texts, in addition to the period, are commas, semi- and full colons, parentheses, dashes, exclamation points, quotation marks, and capital letters. Such marks, especially quotation marks and exclamation points, are particularly useful in determining the context and mood of a passage. Commas, semi-colons, and colons supplement Latin guidewords, such as **cum, quod,** and **ut,** to create boundaries for units of thought or sense.

- **Commas** ("take a breath") quite often indicate asyndeton (lack of conjunctions), which speeds the narrative along. Look carefully at the following example, which describes Aeolus releasing the raging winds from their cave (1.81–83):

  Haec ubi dicta, cavum conversa cuspide montem
  impulit in latus; ac venti, velut agmine facto,
  qua data porta, ruunt et terras turbine perflant.

  Note how the commas contribute to the speed of the narrative to suggest how the winds exit in a rush. Commas can give the sense of piling up or accumulation when used to list items, e.g., **Ipse ignotus, egens, Libyae deserta peragro, / Europae Asiae pulsus** (1.384–385). Asyndeton often accompanies alliteration or anaphora to create emphasis through repetition. Here's an example, where Aeneas scans the scenes of the murals in the temple of Juno at Carthage (1.485–487). Note the repetition of **ut:**

  Tum vero ingentem gemitum dat pectore ab imo,
  ut spolia, ut currus, utque ipsum corpus amici
  tendentemque manus Priamum conspexit inermis.

Commas are often followed by connectors, such as **et, ac, -que,** or **nec,** or by semi-colons, and so designate main or subordinate clauses or other types of sense-units.

- **Colons** and **semi-colons** are used to break up long sentences into smaller units of thought, or to create some other break in the thought.[48] Here is the beginning of Jupiter's reply to Venus in Book 1 (257–260):

  Parce metu, Cytherea, manent tuorum immota
  fata tibi; cernes urbem promissa Lavini
  moenia, sublimemque feres ad sidera caeli
  magnanimum Aenean; neque me sententia vertit.

  Through the use of semi-colons and commas, this four-line sentence is divided into five main clauses, containing separate but related thoughts:

Clause 1	Parce metu, Cytherea:
Clause 2	manent tuorum immota / fata tibi;
Clause 3	cernes urbem promissa Lavini / moenia,
Clause 4	sublimemque feres ad sidera caeli / magnanimum Aenean;
Clause 5	neque me sententia vertit.

  Here is another example, where Jupiter is describing for Venus what will become the Augustan *Pax Romana* (291–294). Note how the colons, commas, and semi-colons are used:

  Aspera tum positis mitescent saecula bellis:
  cana Fides et Vesta, Remo cum fratre Quirinus
  iura dabunt; dirae ferro et compagibus artis
  claudentur Belli portae; Furor impius intus . . .

  Colons are used to explain or to illustrate. In the **Parce metu** passage above, the colon separates Jove's request for Venus to calm down from the list of reasons that he gives for why she should do so. In the **Aspera tum** passage, Jove states that wars will end and that peace will come; the colon provides a pause which prepares the listener/reader for a list of examples of what this will mean for the Roman world. So, a colon may be used to separate a generalized statement from specific examples that illustrate that statement.

- **Parentheses** enclose asides or personal comments made by the writer. They can also enclose additional information that illustrates or clarifies what came previously in a sentence or set the mood for what comes ahead. Venus, in her speech to Jupiter, comments about the loss of Trojan ships by saying **navibus (infandum!) amissis** (1.251). Note how Vergil comments on the wondrous event of Venus enveloping Aeneas and Achates in a fog (1.429–440): **Infert se saeptus nebula (mirabile dictu) per medios.** Here is Vergil commenting on the terrifying sight of the twin serpents swimming towards the Trojan shore: **Ecce autem gemini a Tenedo tranquilla per alta / (horresco referens) immensis orbibus angues** (2.203–204).

- **Dashes** are used to interrupt or to explain, e.g., when an indignant Neptune is at a loss for words, he is so angry at the winds: **Quos ego -- sed motos praetstate componere fluctus** (1.135). When Venus questions Jove about her son's fate, she asks, **Certe hinc Romanos . . . hinc fore ductores . . . pollicitus (es) — quae te, genitor, sententia vertit?** (1.234–237)

- **Exclamation points** punctuate emphatic statements, such as apostrophes, exclamations or interjections, and imperatives. The meaning implied usually involves dramatic or sudden emotion, such as anger or amazement, e.g., **O fortunati quorum iam moenia surgunt!** (1.437), where Aeneas interjects his personal feelings into the narrative. Sometimes exclamation points serve as counterpoints to (rhetorical) questions, especially in speeches, e.g., Aeneas' opening soliloquy in the *Aeneid,* **O terque quaterque** (1.94–101), which consists of two exclamations and a question. Juno's opening soliloquy (1.37–49) consists of three questions and an exclamation, which gives evidence of high emotion. The word *O,* by its meaning, introduces an interjection or apostrophe, e.g., Aeneas to Juno, **O regina** (1.76), Aeneas to his shipmates, **O socii** (1.198), Venus to Jupiter, **O qui res hominumque deumque . . . regis** (1.229), Aeneas to Venus, **O quam te memorem, virgo?** (1.327), or Aeneas to Troy, **O patria, O divum domus Ilium** (2.241).

- **Question marks** often terminate questions that are rhetorical, that is, they do not require an answer. In Latin, these are regularly used to persuade someone of something, including the listener/reader. As we saw just above, question marks and exclamation points often punctuate soliloquies or interchanges in speeches or dialogues, especially when they are used in consecutive sentences, e.g., Venus' plaintive series of questions inquiring of Jupiter about her son's future, which ends with **Hic pietatis honos? Sic nos in sceptra reponis?** (1.253). Note how persuasive is the litany of Laocoon's impassioned questions to his fellow Trojans in Book 2 (42–44):

  O miseri, quae tanta insania, cives?
  Creditis avectos hostes? Aut ulla putatis
  dona carere dolis Danaum? Sic notus Ulixes?

  Or read or listen to Dido's angry speeches in Book 4. A question can even have the force of an exclamation, e.g., **Tantaene animis caelestibus irae?**

- **Capital letters** can indicate allegory, allusion, or personification, e.g., **Fama** (4.173), **cana Fides** and **Belli portae** (1.292 and 294). Words such as **fortuna** or **penates** are often personified.

A Method for Translating a Passage "as Literally as Possible"

Here is an AP-style translation question that will serve as the reference point for our discussion below. Depending upon your background in translating Latin, some of you will read this passage rather intuitively, others more analytically. Many Latin students consider the literal translation questions the most difficult of those on the free-response section of the Exam.[49] Some students who have used the first edition of this book have asked for a more thorough-going discussion of how to produce a literal translation, so here we go!

Question V1 (15 percent)

(Suggested time – 10 minutes)

Begin your answer to this question on a clean page.

Fracti bello fatisque repulsi
ductores Danaum tot iam labentibus annis
instar[1] montis equum divina Palladis arte
aedificant, sectaque intexunt abiete costas;
votum pro reditu simulant; ea fama vagatur.

1 instar: "likeness"

***Aeneid* 2.13–17**

Translate the passage above as literally as possible.

Step 1

Before you get underway, note the location of this particular passage in the corpus of the *Aeneid*. It is from the beginning of Book 2, which we know contains Aeneas' narrative of the fall of Troy. Also, it appears to be a descriptive or expository passage, as there are no quotation marks used.[50] These bits of information offer clues that may help us to establish the context.

As we should do when we attempt to understand the meaning of any passage of Latin, first we read the entire passage completely in Latin, that is, in the sequence in which the words are written.[51] Look at all the words of the passage in context. Particular Latin phrases or words may help us to recall the passage, or at least its context, e.g., **Fracti bello fatisque repulsi** (noticeable because of the patterned word order), **instar montis** (memorable because of its figure of speech, hyperbole), or **divina Palladis arte** or **votum pro reditu simulant** (familiar because of the storyline of the *Aeneid*). And, of course, the word **equum**!

Some or all of these clues indicate that the passage has something to do with the wooden horse. We should begin to process mentally how the words relate to one another, trying to understand the meaning as we read. We want to understand how the passage is organized, i.e., its general structure. One *caveat,* before we go any further: if you have not prepared the first translation passage on the Exam or you do not recognize it, move on to the second passage and then come back to the first and work through it as a sight reading, if you have time. We have established so far that our passage is a descriptive narrative from early in Book 2 and that it has something to do with building the wooden horse (**equum . . . aedificant,** 3–4). We might observe that the structure of the passage consists of a single sentence of five lines, which is interrupted by two semi-colons (lines 4 and 5). As we have seen, a semi-colon is a kind of super-comma used to separate related but independent thoughts that occur within a long sentence. Based upon the punctuation, the first four lines (**Fracti . . . costas,** 1–4) are probably closely connected in meaning. In fact, the part of the sentence up to the first semi-colon contains two main clauses that are connected by **-que** in line 4 (**Fracti . . . aedificant** and **sectaque . . . costas**), followed by two more main clauses, which are separated by semi-colons in lines 4 and 5 (**votum . . . simulant** and **ea . . . vagatur**). We can now say that this long sentence consists of four main clauses that contain related but independent thoughts. It is also useful to know at this stage that all the actions in a Latin sentence are narrated in the order in which they occur, which informs us that the actions of **aedificant, intexunt, simulant,** and **vagatur**, which are the verbs of these clauses, are happening in that particular sequence. Even though we are not yet ready to translate, it is also useful to realize now that it is acceptable to break up one long Latin sentence into two or more smaller English sentences while keeping the same sequence as the Latin. Use the punctuation, as here, to help you to understand how the sense of the passage unfolds. Thus, in the upcoming act of translating, we may break up the four main clauses of our Latin passage into three smaller English sentences: **Fracti . . . aedificant** and **sectaque . . . costas** (1–4), **votum . . . simulant** (5), and **ea . . . vagatur** (5). We are, of course, free to retain the use of semi-colons in our translation.

We now have a very general sense of the basic content and structure of this passage, but we are not yet ready to translate. We should keep in mind the excellent advice of B. Dexter Hoyos, who says, "If translating, translate only when you have seen exactly how the sentence works and what it means. Do not translate in order to find out what the sentence means. Understand first, *then* translate."[52]

Step 2

After we have read through the passage in Latin, we then read it through a second time in Latin. In our first reading, we attained some basic understanding of the meaning of the passage – it is Aeneas' narrative description of the building of the wooden horse by the Greeks, plus attendant information – so this time we want to read with greater attention to establishing the details of what Aeneas is describing. We must pay closer attention to the sense-units within the four main clauses that we have observed and apply what we know about the way Latin works in order to arrive at a more precise understanding of the meaning. This will eventually lead us to an accurate translation. At this stage, we must confirm what we know and, using inference and common sense, begin to deduce or guess what we do not know. In other words, we must use what Hoyos calls "logical expectation," i.e., infer what is likely to happen next, based upon what has already happened. We need to ask questions of the text and seek out their answers, e.g., with regard to **Fracti bello fatisque repulsi,** Who or what is involved here? Why are they described in this way? What is likely to happen as a result of this situation?, and so forth. We must establish the way in which the words in each sentence (in our case, the main clauses) are ordered, in the sequence in which they appear, using punctuation and guide words to help us recognize the boundaries of each unit of sense.[53] (We already began this process in Step 1 by making some general observations about how the Latin of the passage was organized.) Sense-units can consist of simple sentences, subordinate clauses, or phrases, such as a prepositional or infinitive phrase. They contain a single thought, action, or descriptive element consisting of words that are what Hoyos calls "syntactically coherent."[54] Simply put, a sense-unit consists of words that "go together," either in lexical sense or grammatical form. Sense-units may stand independently, such as the participial phrase **Fracti bello** (1) or the prepositional phrase **pro reditu** (5), or they may contain other sense-units, e.g., this passage from Venus' speech to Jupiter later in Book 1: **Certe hinc Romanos olim volventibus annis, / hinc fore ductores, revocato a sanguine Teucri, / [qui mare], [qui terras omnes dicione tenerent], pollicitus (es)** (1.234–237). Note how the indirect statement of the main clause, **Romanos . . . fore . . . pollicitus (es)** embraces the two participial phrases, **volventibus annis** and **revocato a sanguine Teucri**, and the relative clauses, **qui mare (dicione tenerent)** and **qui terra omnes dicione tenerent.**

Next, we will identify and discuss the various sense-units that appear in *Aeneid* 2.13–17, preliminary to translating, or "carrying over," these into English.

The First Main Clause (*Fracti . . . aedificant,* 1–4)

Fracti bello fatisque repulsi are two sense-units, each consisting of a past participle and a noun.[55] These two participial phrases appear to be parallel and coordinate (-**que**) in construction, which is reinforced by the chiastic A-B-B-A word order of the grammatical forms.[56] This figure of speech contributes to our understanding of what words "go together" in these sense-units. Since the Latin words here have meanings that are familiar, we can easily understand that **fracti bello** means "some people or things have been broken by means of war," and that **fatis repulsi** means "some people or things have been driven back by the fates." Moving on in our thinking, we know that participles generally modify or describe something, so we look for an upcoming noun or pronoun and one that serves as the nominative subject of our sentence, since the endings **-i** of the participles **fracti** and **repulsi** are most likely nominative plural. And, lo, we come upon a likely candidate, **ductores,** in the next line. Actually, **ductores** taken with **Danaum**, constitutes another word group, which supplies the subject of the sentence. Through our experience in reading Vergilian Latin, we know that Vergil often employs contraction, or syncope, making it likely that **Danaum** is **Danaorum**, a genitive plural form that links with and completes the meaning of **ductores** as "leaders of the Greeks." And being good students of Vergil, we also note the emphatic use of alliteration here, which also helps us to link **ductores** with **Danaum.** So far, then, we have established that the first three word groups tell us that the Greek leaders (**ductores Danaum**) are the victims of both war (**bello**) and the fates (**fatisque**). One general point here. In Latin, once a phrase or subordinate clause is begun, it must be completed syntactically before the rest of the sentence can proceed. Put another way, the words found within the boundaries of a phrase go together and do not cross the boundaries of the phrase, i.e., one of the words in the participial phrase **Fracti bello** cannot wander off into another part of the sentence, such as the succeeding participial phrase **fatisque repulsi**. Each sense-unit is self-contained and must be completed before continuing with the rest of the sentence, that is, the meaning of the sense-unit **Fracti bello** must be established before moving on to **fatisque repulsi.** As we proceed—remember, we are still reading through the Latin—the next group of words that seem to go together is **labentibus annis**. **Labentibus annis** is another participial phrase, this time containing a present participle, **labentibus,** which we recognize as a form of the deponent verb **labor,** *pass by, slip,* or *glide*. **Laboro,** *work,* is another possibility, but we reason that this verb belongs to the first conjugation, which requires an **-a-** vowel in the participle. So, "the years are passing by." We will postpone our understanding of the precise meaning of this sense-unit (which is most likely an ablative absolute), until we fit in the words **tot** and **iam,** which mean *so many* and *now, already,* respectively. The word **tot** is an (indeclinable) adjective, so it makes sense to take **tot** with the closest succeeding noun, which is **annis**. These words, when taken together, give the meaning "so many years." Having established the word-group as **tot iam labentibus annis**, we then have "while so many years are/were already passing by." (The time of the participle here, that is, whether its meaning is "are passing" or "were passing," will depend upon the tense of the main verb, which we haven't yet met.) We now understand from the Latin of the first four sense-units that the Greeks have been overcome by both war and the fates and that some time has passed. Continuing to comprehend the meaning of our first main clause, we use the lexical information from the gloss of the uncommon word **instar**, *likeness*, to determine that this word is a noun. The next word, **montis** (genitive singular), to which it can be linked using word position, then completes a sense unit, "the likeness of a mountain."[57] What has "the likeness of a mountain"? Have we met anything so far that could be described in this way? We deduced above that the subject of this main clause is probably **ductores,** so **instar,** which looks nominative but is singular in form, cannot modify **ductores,** which is plural.

Therefore, **instar** must modify something else. We know from having prepared these lines and/or from our familiarity with the storyline, that the next word, **equum,** is probably what has "the likeness of a mountain." Therefore, the word group **instar montis** logically goes with **equum,** which has the form of an accusative direct object. But the direct object of what? If we have a direct object, we need a verb, so we move along in the clause until we find **aedificant** (4), which completes the sense-unit **equum . . . aedificant,** "they build a horse," completing the core information of the first main clause. The relative placement of **ductores Danaum** and **aedificant** illustrate the fundamental principle of Latin that the words most emphasized by the writer are usually placed at the beginning and end and that all the intervening words contribute to the overall sense. Note also that, although **equum . . . aedificant** form a sense-unit, these words are found in different lines. They are a sense-unit because they are "syntactically coherent," that is, they go together. We now take the remaining words before the comma (which serves as break in the thought and the end of the first main clause) as a sense-unit: **divina Palladis arte**. We know from our knowledge of the storyline that Pallas Athena/Minerva helps the Greeks with the inspiration for the wooden horse, which confirms our understanding about her "divine skill" in this sentence. To summarize, the first and longest main clause of our passage, **Fracti . . . aedificant** (1–4), contains the following sense-units, which lead us to a good understanding of the meaning of these lines.

Sense-unit	Function in clause
Fracti bello	participial phrase
fatisque repulsi	participial phrase
ductores Danaum	subject of first main clause
tot iam labentibus annis	participial phrase
equum . . . aedificant	object and verb of first main clause
instar montis	appositional phrase

The Second Main Clause (*sectaque . . . costas,* 4)

The enclitic **-que,** the appearance of a second present indicative verb, **intexunt,** and the semi-colon after **costas** at the end of line 4, all lead us to conclude that these words inclusively form a second main clause that coordinates with the first. As we continue our second pass through the Latin, we must determine how the words **sectaque intexunt abiete costas** fit together. Remembering that **ductores Danaum** served as the subject of the first main verb, **aedificant,** we might assume that the same holds true for **intexunt,** giving the meaning "they (the leaders of the Greeks) wove together." (The derivative *textile* prompts the meaning of **intexo** and, again, as good Vergil students, we know that Athena was patron goddess of domestic crafts, which include weaving.) What did they weave together? The accusative direct object must be **costas,** giving us the meaning of the sense unit **intexunt . . . costas** as "they weave together (its) ribs," most likely referring to the infrastructure of the wooden horse, given the context. (If you know your anatomy, you know that *intercostal* muscles are those that run between the ribs.) We are left with the participial phrase **secta . . . abiete**. **Secta,** from **seco,** *cut, cleave,* as in *bisect* or *intersect*, tells us that something has been cut, probably **abiete.** The latter, meaning fir tree or its wood, is an unusual word and may be remembered because Vergil is inconsistent in identifying the wood used in the construction of the horse, a detail that may have been left unedited by the poet's untimely death. What is it that is probably being cut in the context of building the wooden horse? Wood, of course. (Those who really know their grammar will recognize this is an example of the ablative of material.) So, our two sense units **intexunt . . . costas** and **sectaque . . . abiete** in this main clause provide details about the horse's construction.

Sense-unit	Function in main clause
intexunt . . . costas	verb and object of second main clause
sectaque . . . abiete	participial phrase

The Third Main Clause (*votum . . . simulant,* 5)

We established during our first read-through that the words between the semicolons in this sentence constitute another, shorter, main clause, that is, a related but independent thought that can be rendered as a separate sentence. We have established that **ductores Danaum** serves as the subject of the main verbs met so far in this sentence (**aedificant, intexunt**). Let's assume that this is still the case. So, **ductores Danaum** is the subject of **simulant** and the leaders of the Greeks are pretending something. What is it? The answer is given in the accusative direct object **votum**, providing us with another simple verb–object sense-unit, **votum . . . simulant,** "they pretend an offering." We are assisted with this sense-unit by way of the verb–object examples, **equum aedificant** and **intexunt . . . costas**, in the previous two main clauses. Recognition of the ellipsis of **esse,** i.e., "they pretend (that it, the horse, is) an offering" is not necessary for comprehension at this point. For what was the horse an offering? **Pro reditu,** "for (their) return," an example of a prepositional phrase serving as a sense-unit. So, this third main clause gives some details about the purpose of the wooden horse.

Sense-unit	Function in main clause
votum . . . simulant	object and verb of main clause
pro reditu	prepositional phrase

The Fourth and Final Main Clause (*ea . . . vagatur,* 5)

This long sentence winds down with a three-word final main clause, which simply consists of subject (**ea fama**) and verb (**vagatur**). **Ea fama,** "That rumor," logically refers to the pretense stated in the previous clause (**simulant**), which was the pretext that the Greeks were giving for building the horse. **Vagatur,** the meaning of which may be triggered by the derivatives *vagrant* or *vagabond,* concludes this final sense unit, the last main clause, and the sentence as a whole. The meaning of this verb is best rendered as passive rather than as a true deponent, given the sense required by the context.

Sense-unit	Function in main clause
ea fama vagatur	main clause

Having completed our second read-through of the Latin, we now have a comprehensive understanding of the entire passage. (As mentioned, some of you will no doubt be able to read this passage without resorting to the direct analysis used in the discussion above. If so, congratulations!) We are nearing the end of our four-step journey. Prior to translating, then, let us summarize how the Latin of *Aeneid* 2.13–17 fits together, using the sense-units that we have established:

1. **fracti bello**
2. **fatisque repulsi**
3. **ductores Danaum**
4. **tot iam labentibus annis**
5. **equum aedificant**

6. **instar montis**
7. **divina Palladis arte**
8. **sectaque . . . arte**
9. **intexunt . . . costas**
10. **votum simulant**
11. **pro reditu**
12. **ea fama vagatur**

Step 3

It is now time to translate, i.e., "to carry over" into English, our understanding of the meaning of *Aeneid* 2.13–17, sense-unit by sense-unit.[58] You may have already begun to work out in your head the English wording as you read through the Latin.

Fracti bello (Broken in war) **fatisque repulsi** (and driven back by the fates), **ductores Danaum** (the leaders of the Greeks) **tot iam labentibus annis** (while so many years are passing by), **equum . . . aedificant** (build a horse), **instar montis** (the likeness of a mountain), **divina Palladis arte** (with the divine skill of Pallas Athena), **sectaque . . . abiete** (and with cut fir) **intexunt . . . costas** (they weave together its ribs); **votum . . . simulant** (they pretend [that it is] an offering) **pro reditu** (for [their] return); **ea fama vagatur** (that rumor is spread abroad).

Notes:

1. Past participles, may be translated as "having been . . . ," i.e., **Fracti,** "(having been) broken . . . ," or as a clause, "After they had been broken . . . ," as long as the tense and voice of the participial relative to that of the main verb is correct. In other words, "While they were breaking . . ." is incorrect because, although it is rendered as a clause, the participle is translated in the active voice, rather than in the passive.

2. As soon as we meet the main verb **aedificant,** we must consider the element of time (tense) in the sentence. The verb **aedificant** is present tense, which we can translate literally as "they are building, they build," or as historical present, i.e., past tense, "they built." If we choose the latter, the meaning of the previous sense unit **tot iam labentis annis** must be "while so many years were passing by," because the participle is now expressing an action contemporary with what is now past time. Remember that, if you use the historical present in translating, you must use it consistently throughout the passage.

3. In this passage, there are several opportunities to use scansion in order to determine the case/function of a noun in its context.[59] (Remember that macrons are not used on the AP Latin Exam.) The adjective **divina** is ablative because scansion of line 3 determines that the **-a** in the ending is long, thus confirming that **divina** modifies **arte,** a more obvious ablative form. The same holds true for **sectaque,** which modifies **abiete** in line 4.

4. The verb **vagor, vagari, vagatus sum** is deponent and means *wander, spread abroad.* Although it is incorrect to express the meaning of a deponent verb as pas-

sive, in this case there is lexical precedent for doing so. A translation of "That rumor spreads abroad" is obviously also acceptable.

Step 4

We have one more step to take on our journey toward achieving a successful literal translation. Can you guess what it is? Right! Proofreading. Read through your translation, making adjustments and corrections as needed, and, above all, making sure that your translation makes sense. West says simply, "The fundamental law (of translation) is not to write nonsense."[60] You will be given several opportunities to apply the method outlined above in the practice translation passages at the end of this chapter.

Some FAQs about the Translation Questions on the AP Latin Exam

What is the format?

As mentioned earlier, the first two questions on the free-response section ask you to "translate as literally as possible" two passages from the Latin of the *Aeneid* that you have prepared. The suggested time is 10 minutes for each passage. The passages, which are six to eight lines long, come from different Books of the *Aeneid* and are identified on the Exam page by Book and lines.

What is the best way to prepare for the translation questions?

As mentioned, the most effective way to insure your success on these questions is to complete a close reading of the lines of the *Aeneid* which were assigned in Latin. While you are preparing your daily assignments, don't just "get the gist" of what is happening, but work through the Latin carefully and critically. If a daily literal translation is not required by your teacher, you may find it helpful to produce one on your own.[61] Ask your teacher to check it. Practice meeting the twin challenges of discovering the meaning of the Latin and of articulating it in appropriate English. (This will also help your English skills!) Avoid the temptation to incorporate someone else's translation into your own.[62] Practice translating the passages given below and those from former AP Latin: Vergil Exams provided on the AP Latin: Vergil website. (See below for a list of passages appearing on recent Exams.)

How are translated passages evaluated by Exam Readers?

We have already met the terms "chunks" or "segments" as they apply to the assessment of a literal translation on the AP Latin Exam. When scored, your translations are divided into 18 segments (which we've called sense-units), each of which counts as one point, for a total of 18 points.[63] The passage we translated above has twelve segments and is thus worth twelve points. (Remember that passage is shorter than the average passage for translation on the Exam.) The scoring of the translation questions is explained here, because an understanding of how a translation is scored will hopefully give you further insight into what those who develop the AP Latin Exam mean by a "literal translation." Alternative meanings and renderings for each word or phrase in the sense-unit, within a range of acceptability, are provided to the Reader, as illustrated below. The numbers refer to the sense-units we established in the discussion above.

Acceptable meanings

1. **fracti**: *(having been) broken, broken, shattered, destroyed*; must modify **ductores**

   bello: *by war, by means of war*; must reflect ablative
2. **fatisque**: *by (the) fates*; must reflect ablative

   repulsi: *and (having been) driven back, repelled, spurned*; must modify **ductores**
3. **ductores Danaum**: *the leaders, commanders, generals of the Danaans, of the Greeks*

   [**Danaum** must be genitive plural = **Danaorum**]; must be subject of **aedificant**
4. **tot**: *so many*; must modify **annis**

   annis: *with year, time*; must indicate ablative, not acc. of extent of time

   iam: *already, now*; must modify **labentibus**

   labentibus: *(while) sliding, gliding, slipping, passing, flowing*; must take with **annis**; may be expressed literally as an ablative absolute or as a clause, using *while, when*, etc.
5. **equum**: *horse*; must be the direct object of **aedificant**

   aedificant: *they build, are building, do build, construct, fashion, craft, erect, establish*; may be translated as past tense = historical present
6. **instar**: *the likeness* or *image*; must be taken with **montis**

   montis: *of a mountain*; must be construed with **instar** and be in apposition to **equum**
7. **divina**: *by, by means of, with the divine*; must modify **arte**

   Palladis: *Pallas Athena, Pallas, Athena, Minerva*; must be construed with **arte**

   arte: *art, skill, craftsmanship, technique*; must link with **Palladis**
8. **sectaque**: *and (having been) cut, cleaved, sliced, hewn*; must modify **abiete**

   abiete: *by means of, with fir*
9. **intexunt**: *they weave together, twine together, interweave, plait, put together*; may be past tense = historical present

   costas: *rib/side*; must be direct object of **intexunt**

10. **votum**: *vow, pledge, (votive) offering, prayer*; must be direct object of **simulant**

    simulant: *they pretend, feign, imitate, simulate, give the appearance of*; may be translated as past tense = historical present

11. **pro**: *for, on behalf of, for the sake of*

    reditu: *return, homecoming, going back*; must be object of **pro**

12. **ea fama**: *this, that rumor, report, gossip, word of mouth*; must be subject of **vagatur**

    vagatur: *wander, rove, drift*; deponent verb; may have a passive meaning, i.e., *is spread abroad,* and may be translated as past tense = historical present

Here are some hypothetical sample student responses and their scores:

Student Response A:

Having been broken in war and repelled by fate, the leaders of the Greeks, as so much time is already passing, build a big-as-a-mountain horse with divine Athena's skill, and they interweave the ribs with fir wood that has been cut. They pretend that it (the horse) is a vow for their return. That rumor spreads abroad.

This student receives full credit of 12 points, as all twelve segments have been rendered correctly.

Student Response B:

In war and in fate, I drove back and broke the Greek leaders, while so many years were already passing, built a mountain-sized horse with the divine skill of Athena and wove the cut wood together into ribs. They pretended a vow to return; that gossip was passed around.

No credit for Segments 1 and 2, as the student's translation "in war and in fate" expresses abl. of time/place, rather than means, and incorrectly assumes that **fracti** and **repulsi** are forms of the first person singular of the perfect tense active. In Segment 3, **ductores** is mistranslated as an object, rather than a subject. Segment 4 receives credit for correctly expressing the ablative absolute **labentibus annis** (1 pt.) Segments 5, 6, and 7 also receive full credit, (1 pt. + 1 pt. + 1 pt.). Segment 8 receives full credit (1 pt.), as does Segment 9, although "into ribs" does not completely do justice to **costas** as a direct object (1 pt.). Segment 10, "they pretended a vow" for **votum simulant** receives credit (1 pt.), but Segment 11 does not receive credit because **pro reditu** cannot mean "to return;" Segment 12 is acceptable (1 pt.). Thus, the score is eight points out of 12.

Student Response C:

With war broken (discontinued) and the fates driven away, the leaders build a Greek horse, working for years, ___ (standing?) mountain with Pallas' divine skill they cut and weave ___. (?) They pretend to vote for the return (home). The news gets out.

This effort is intermittently a translation and a paraphrase, with words missing or misidentified. There is only a general sense of what is happening. Segments 1 and 2 don't work because **fracti** is taken as modifying **bello** and **repulsi** as modifying **fatis**. Segment 3 is unacceptable because **Danaum** does not modify **equum**, despite the common ending. The student mistranslates the verb **labor (labentibus)** as **laboro** and omits **tot** and **iam** (also **annis** cannot express extent of time). Segments 6 and 7 are acceptable (1 pt. + 1 pt.), but 8 and 9 are only partially correct ("cut and weave" is satisfactory for **sectaque intexunt**). "Vote" is not an acceptable meaning for **votum** in Segment 10. Segment 11 is acceptable (1 pt.), but Segment 12, although close, omits **ea** and gives an imprecise meaning of **vagatur**, which means that the news is not just broadcast, but it is broadcast far and wide. This student receives a score of three points out of 12.

Translation Passages from the *Aeneid* Appearing on AP Latin: Vergil Exams, 2001–2009

Book 1: 23–28 (2009), 378–385 (2006)

Book 2: 10–16 (2004), 201–207 (2005), 237–243 (2001), 289–294 (2002), 560–566 (2006)

Book 4: 68–73 (2007), 160–166 (2003), 429–434 (2008)

Book 6: 847–853 (2007), 893–899 (2004)

Book 10: 450, 453–456 (2001), 459–465 (2009)

Book 12: 791–796 (2008), 803–809 (2003), 908–914 (2002), 930–936 (2005)

Passages in the *Aeneid* Suitable for Translation Practice

Each of the following passages contains six to eight lines of continuous Latin. These have been selected for their particular relevance to the storyline.

Book 1: Lines 26–32; 50–57; 65–70; 81–87; 94–101; 113–119; 124–130; 132–139; 187–194; 198–206; 229–237; 272–279; 297–304; 327–334; 348–356; 378–385; 430–436; 459–465; and 513–519

Book 2: Lines 13–20; 25–32; 42–48; 50–56; 203–212; 220–227; 234–240; 241–249; 281–286; 289–295; 526–532; 559–566; 735–740; 745–751; and 790–795

Book 4: Lines 1–8; 45–53; 68–73; 107–114; 211–218; 296–303; 305–311; 333–339; 351–358; 365–371; 393–400; 651–658; 663–671; 685–692; and 700–705

Book 6: Lines 65–70; 125–131; 847–853; 860–66

Book 10: Lines 433–438; 445–451; and 491–497

Book 12: Lines 800–806; and 938–944

How to Use the AP Latin: Vergil Website for Translation Practice

As suggested elsewhere in this chapter, one way to practice for the translation questions on the AP Latin Exam is to simulate the experience by going to the AP Latin: Vergil homepage website, where you will find links to AP Latin: Vergil Exams from previous years. Click on a link to any Exam, find a passage for translation (Question V1 or V2), and then write out your literal translation using the method described above (or your own). Be sure to limit your time to 10 mins. per passage, although you need not time yourself until you have practiced a bit. Concentrate on accuracy first, then work on time. When you have finished your translation, check it against the sample provided in the scoring guidelines (be aware that not every Exam has sample translations) and take some time to assess your performance using as reference the list of sense-units that accompanies the translation.

Practicing Translation Skills 1

Identifying Sense-Units in a Latin Sentence

For each of the following sentences of the episode from Book 2 where Hector appears to Aeneas in a dream-vision, list the sense-units in the order of their appearance. Be aware that occasionally one sense-unit may be interrupted by another. Remember that sense-units consist of words that go together and are "syntactically coherent." Translate each sentence, paying close attention to the sense-units you have identified. The first is done for you. The author's other versions are provided at the end.

1. Nos delubra deum miseri, quibus ultimus esset / ille dies, festa velamus fronde per urbem. (2.248–249. There are six sense-units in this sentence.)

   Answer:

   Sense-units

1st	Nos . . . miseri
2nd	delubra de(or)um . . . velamus
3rd	quibus . . . esset
4th	ultimus . . . ille dies
5th	festa . . . fronde
6th	per urbem

   Translation: *We unhappy ones, for whom that was the final day, are draping the shrines of the gods with holiday garlands throughout the city.*

2. Vertitur interea caelum et ruit Oceano nox / involvens umbra magna terramque polumque / Myrmidonumque dolos; fusi per moenia Teucri / conticuere; sopor fessos complectitur artus. (2.250–253. There are 10 sense-units in this sentence.)

3. Et iam Argiva phalanx instructis navibus ibat / a Tenedo tacitae per amica silentia lunae / litora nota petens, flammas cum regia puppis, / extulerat, fatisque de(or)um defensus iniquis / inclusos utero Danaos et pinea furtim / laxat claustra Sinon. (2.254–259. There are 13 sense-units in this sentence.)
4. Illos patefactus ad auras / reddit equus laetique cavo se robore prount / Thessandrus Sthenelusque duces et dirus Ulixes, / demissum lapsi per funem, Acamasque Thoasque /Pelidesque Neoptolemus primusque Machaon / et Menelaus et ipse doli fabricator Epeos. (2.259–264. There are 11 sense-units in this sentence; the personal names may be grouped in various ways)
5. Invadunt urbem somno vinoque sepultam; / caeduntur vigiles, portisque patentibus omnes / accipiunt socios atque agmina conscia iugunt. (2.265–267. There are seven sense-units in this sentence.)

Now do the same activity, without the benefit of knowing the number of sense-units in each sentence.

6. 'Quae causa indigna serenos / foedavit vultus? Aut cur haec vulnera cerno?' (2.285–286)
7. Ille nihil, nec me quaerentem vana moratur, / sed graviter gemitus imo de pectore ducens, / 'Heu fuge, nate dea, teque his,' ait, 'eripe flammis.' (2.287–289)
8. 'Sat patriae Priamoque datum: si Pergama dextra / defendi possent, etiam hac defensa fuissent.' (2.291–292)
9. 'Sacra suosque tibi commendat Troia penates; / hos cape fatorum comites, his moenia quaere / magna, pererrato statues quae denique ponto.' (2.293–295)
10. Sic ait et manibus vittas Vestamque potentem / aeternumque adytis effert penetralibus ignem. (2.297–297)

Author's versions

2. Vertitur interea caelum

   et ruit Oceano nox

   involvens . . . terramque polumque

   umbra magna

   Myrmidonumque dolos;

   fusi . . . Teucri

   per moenia

   conticuer(unt);

   sopor . . . complectitur

   fessos . . . artus.

Translation: *Meanwhile the sky turns/is turned and night hastens from the Ocean wrapping both land and heaven in great darkness, along with the deceptions of the Myrmidons; the Trojans, scattered throughout the city walls, grew quiet; drowziness embraces (their) weary limbs.*

3. Et iam Argiva phalanx . . . ibat

   instructis navibus

   a Tenedo

   tacitae . . . lunae

   per amica silentia

   litora nota petens

   flammas cum . . . extulerat

   regia puppis

   fatisque deorum . . . iniquis

   defensus . . . Sinon

   inclusos utero Danaos

   et pinea . . . claustra

   furtim laxat.

   Translation: *And now the Argive battle-formation was moving, the ships arranged (in battle order), through the friendly silence of the quiet moon, from Tenedos, making for the familiar shore, when the royal (flag)ship had raised the fire-signal, Sinon, defended by the unfair will of the gods, furtively releases the pinewood latches and the Greeks enclosed in the belly.*

4. Illos . . . reddit

   equus patefactus

   ad auras

   laetique . . . se . . . promunt

   cavo . . . robore

   Thessandrus Sthenelusque duces et dirus Ulixes

   demissum . . . per funem

   lapsi Acamasque Thoasque Pelidesque Neoptolemus

   primusque Machaon et Menelaus

   et ipse . . . Epeos

   doli fabricator.

   Translation: *The horse, laid open, gave them back to the air, and happily they bring themselves forth from the hollow oakwood, the leaders Thessandrus and Sthenelus and fearsome Ulysses, having slipped along the let-down rope, as well as Acamas, Thoas, Neoptolemus of Peleus, noble Machaon and Menelaus, and Epeos himself, architect of the treachery.*

5. Invadunt urbem . . . sepultam

   somno vinoque;

   caeduntur vigiles

   portisque patentibus

   omnes accipiunt socios

   atque agmina conscia iungunt.

   Translation: *They attack the city, buried in sleep and wine; the guards are killed and, at the open gates, receive all (their) comrades and join together the like-minded bands (of Greeks).*

6. Quae indigna causa

   serenos...vultus

   foedavit?

   Aut cur...cerno

   haec vulnera?

   Translation: *'What unworthy circumstance has defiled (your) calm features? Or why do I look upon these wounds?'*

7. Ille nihil (dicit),

   nec . . . moratur,

   me quaerentem vana

   sed graviter gemitus . . . ducens,

   imo de pectore

   'Heu, fuge,

   nate dea,

   teque . . . eripe'

   ait

   'his . . . flammis.'

   Translation: *He (says) nothing, nor pays attention to me asking useless (questions) but deeply drawing out a groan from deep in his chest, he says, 'Alas, flee, goddess-born, rescue yourself from these flames.'*

8. 'Sat . . . datum (est a te)

   patriae Priamoque,

   si (qua) dextra

   Pergama . . . defendi possent,

   etiam hac (dextra mea)

   (Pergama) defensa fuissent.'

Translation: *'Enough has been given (by you) to homeland and to Priam: if Pergama could have been defended by (any) right hand, it would have been defended by this (right hand of mine).'*

9. 'Tibi commendat Troia

   sacra suosque . . . penates;

   hos . . . fatorum comites,

   cape . . . his . . . quaere

   moenia . . . magna,

   quae denique statues

   pererrato . . . ponto.'

   Translation: *'To you Troy entrusts (her) sacred objects and household gods; these companions of (your) destiny, take them and seek out for them great city-walls, which you will finally establish after you have wandered over the sea.'*

10. Sic ait

    manibus . . . effert

    vittas Vestamque

    aeternumque . . . ignem

    adytis . . . penetralibus.

    Translation: *So he speaks and in his hands brings forth the sacred headbands and Vesta and the everlasting fire from the innermost sanctum.*

Practicing Translation Skills 2

Here are some AP-style translation questions. Passage A includes a sample literal translation and scoring guidelines, for which, see below. Give yourself a score!

Passage A

Talia flammato secum dea corde volutans
nimborum in patriam, loca feta furentibus Austris,
Aeoliam venit. Hic vasto rex Aeolus antro
luctantes ventos tempestatesque sonoras
imperio premit ac vinclis et carcere frenat.
Illi indignantes magno cum murmure montis
circum claustra fremunt.

***Aeneid* 1. 50–57**

Passages B and C are followed by sample literal translations (see pages 64–65).

Passage B

"I, sequere Italiam ventis, pete regna per undas.
Spero equidem mediis, si quid pia numina possunt,
supplicia hausurum scopulis et nomine Dido
saepe vocaturum. Sequar atris ignibus absens
et, cum frigida mors anima seduxerit artus,
omnibus umbra locis adero. Dabis, improbe, poenas.
Audiam et haec manes veniet mihi fama sub imos."

***Aeneid* 4. 381–87**

Passage C

Nescia mens hominum fati sortisque futurae
et servare modum rebus sublata secundis!
Turno tempus erit magno cum optaverit emptum
intactum Pallanta, et cum spolia ista diemque
oderit. At socii multo gemitu lacrimisque
impositum scuto referunt Pallanta frequentes.

***Aeneid* 10.501–506**

Sample Translations and Scoring of Practice Passages

Passage A

Sample Literal Translation:

While pondering such things in her inflamed heart, the goddess came into Aeolia, the homeland of clouds, a place teeming with raging winds. Here, in an immense cave, King Aeolus controlled with his command the wrestling winds and howling storms and tamed (them) with chains and imprisonment. They, angry, with a loud rumble of (within) the mountain, roared around (their) enclosure(s).

Sense-units (Each sense-unit, numbered consecutively below, is worth 1 pt., for a total of 18 pts.)

1. Talia
2. secum . . . volutans
3. flammato corde
4. dea . . . venit
5. in Aeoliam
6. nimborum in patriam

7. loca feta
8. furentibus Austris
9. Hic . . . vasto antro
10. rex Aeolus
11. luctantes ventos
12. tempestatesque sonoras
13. imperio premit
14. ac vinclis et carcere frenat
15. Illi indignantes
16. magno cum murmure montis
17. circum claustra
18. fremunt

Acceptable meanings:

1. **Talia**: *such things* or *thoughts, things* or *thoughts of this kind*; must be object of **volutans**
2. **secum**: **se** must refer to **dea** and be taken with **volutans**

   volutans: *turning, revolving*; must modify **dea**; can be taken with **secum** to mean *pondering, considering*
3. **flammato**: *(having been) inflame, set on fire, kindled, seething*

   corde: *heart, spirit, feelings*; must include the understood preposition **in** or be expressed as an ablative absolute
4. **dea**: *the goddess, the goddess Juno, the deity*

   venit: *come, arrive, reach*; may be translated as past tense = historical present
5. **in Aeoliam**: *into Aeolia*; **Aeoliam** must be in apposition to **nimborum in patriam**; **in** must mean *into*
6. **nimborum**: *clouds*; must be linked with **patriam**

   in patriam: *into the homeland, country, fatherland*; **in** must be rendered as *into*
7. **loca**: *a place*; may be singular

   feta: *teeming with, swarming with, full of, pregnant with*; must modify **loca** and must accompany **furentibus Austris**
8. **furentibus**: *raging, raving*

   Austris: *south winds, winds*
9. **Hic**: *here, in this place*; cannot mean *this*

   vasto: *immense, vast /enormous, huge*

   antro: *cave, cavern*

10. **rex**: *king/lord/master*; must be in apposition to **Aeolus**

    Aeolus: *Aeolus*; must be the subject of both **premit** and **frenat**
11. **luctantes**: *wrestling, brawling, struggling*; must modify **ventos**

    ventos: *winds*; must be the object of both **premit** and **frenat**
12. **tempestatesque**: *storm, gale, tempest*; must be the object of both **premit** and **frenat**

    sonoras: *howling, resounding, roaring*; must modify **tempestates**
13. **imperio**: *command, authority, power, dominion, control*; must reflect ablative

    premit: *control, (re)press*; may be translated as past = historical present
14. **ac**: *and*; must join clauses **imperio premit** and **vinclis et carcere frenat**

    vinclis: *chain, bond, shackle*

    carcere: *imprisonment, prison, dungeon, enclosure*

    frenat: *tame, bridle, curb, check, restrain*; may be translated as past = historical present
15. **Illi**: *Those/They*; *These winds* is acceptable; must be subject of **fremunt**

    indignantes: *be angry, chafe*; must modify **Illi;** may be taken adverbially with **fremunt**
16. **magno**: *great*, etc., *loud*; must modify **murmure**

    murmure: *rumble, roar, crash, thunder*

    montis: *of the mountain*; must be linked with **murmure**
17. **circum**: *around*

    claustra: *enclosure, wall, barrier*; must be object of **circum**; may be taken as singular
18. **fremunt**: *roar, bluster*; may be translated as past = historical present

Practice Passages B and C are translated literally; Passage B is separated into 18 sense-units, as per exam scoring guidelines, and Passage C into 17 sense-units.

Passage B

"Go (**I**), follow Italy with the winds (**sequere Italiam ventis**) seek a kingdom over the waves (**pete regna per undas; regna** may be singular). If in any way (**Si quid**) divinities can be just (**pia numina [esse] possunt**), truly, I hope that (you) will swallow down your punishment (**spero equidem . . . supplicia ausurum [esse]**; **supplicia** may be singular) in the midst of rock-cliffs (**mediis . . . scopulis**) and (I hope that you) will repeatedly call Dido by name (**et nomine Dido saepe vocaturum [esse]**). Apart (from you) I will follow (you) (**Sequar . . . absens**) with dark firebrands (**atris ignibus**) and, when cold death will have separated (**cum frigida mors . . . seduxerit**) limb from soul (**anima . . . artus; artus** may be singular) I will be as a ghost (**anima . . . adero**) in every place (**et omnibus . . . locis**). You will pay the price, cruel one (**Dabis, improbe, poenas**;

poenas may be singular). I will listen (**Audiam**) and this story will come to me (**et haec . . . veniet mihi fama**) (among) the shades deep below (**manes . . . sub imos**)."

Passage C

The mind of man (**mens hominum**; **hominum** may be singular), ignorant of fate (**Nescia . . . fati**) and future destiny (**sortisque futurae**) and (how) to preserve moderation (**et servare modum**) (having been) lifted up (**sublata**) by favorable circumstances (**rebus . . . secundis**)! For Turnus there will be a time (**Turno tempus erit**) when, at a great (price) (**magno**), he will have wished (**cum . . . optaverit**) that Pallas (having been) uninjured (**intactum Pallanta**) had been redeemed (**emptum [esse]**) and when he (Turnus) will have hated (**cum . . . oderit**) those spoils and (that) day (**spolia ista diemque**). But (his) companions, in a crowd (**At socii . . . frequentes**), with much moaning and crying (**multo gemitu acrimisque**), bear Pallas back (**referunt Pallanta**), (having been) placed on his shield (**impositum scuto**).

Endnotes

[34] Quoted from David West, page 110 (see the Appendix). This author's translation: *He follows after (tends) his own sheep and his son the lambs and the wife makes the water hot (i.e., heats up the water) for the weary (man)*. For another gem, Horace's **vis consili expers mole ruit sua** is read *the unexpected weight of the consul fell upon the soft pig*, Classical Association Review (UK) (June, 1996), No. 14, page 20. This reads, *Force, without wisdom, collapses (rushes to ruin) by its own weight* (*Odes,* III.4.65). Other favorites: **Labor omnia vincit,** *Work will kill anybody;* **Dido et dux,** *Dido ate ducks;* **Multi nullum honorem habent in locis ubi nati sunt,** *Many have no honor in the places where they swim;* **Cave canem,** *Beware, I may sing!*

[35] One of these pitfalls is the practice of writing interlinear translations in the textbook, that is, writing the meaning of each word above the Latin. This leads to all sorts of bad habits, not the least of which is the decoding method of translation mentioned later in this paragraph. For more pitfalls of "hunt-the-verb," see Hoyos 1 in the Appendix. This method is most likely responsible for the old saw, "Latin is a language, as dead as it can be. First it killed the Romans, and now it's killing me."

[36] West, page 110. For a nice summary of the various methods of teaching Latin, see the Latinteach Resources website listed in the Appendix. There has been much discussion in recent years about the place of translation in the teaching and learning of Latin. The traditional grammar-translation approach, represented by the Jenney Latin Program (now published by Prentice-Hall), and now most commonly by B.L. Ullman's *Latin for Americans*, has gradually been supplanted in popularity by the so-called reading (or contextual) method, represented by text programs such the Cambridge Latin Course, *Ecce Romani*, and the Oxford Latin Course. (For those interested in the direct method of teaching or learning Latin, go to the Association for Latin Teaching website (UK) at *http://www.arlt.co.uk/dhtml/directmethod1.php*; for Hans Oerberg's *Lingua Latina,* see *http://www.lingua-latina.dk/*.) For more on the general subject of translation, see the articles by Hoyos,

Mayer, Perry, and Singh, cited in the Appendix. B. Dexter Hoyos, a professor at the University of Sydney (Australia), is a recent apologist for teaching the reading of Latin by building comprehension skills rather than by requiring a literal translation. In the method outlined below, the author will attempt to combine elements of both the grammar-translation and the reading approach. See Appendix 2.

[37] There's an Italian saying, *traduttore, traditore*, "translator, traitor." Robert Frost said that poetry is what is lost in translation.

[38] The current importance of translation on the AP Latin Exam is also suggested by the fact that, in 1999, the translation question in the free-response section was increased from one passage to the current two.

[39] 2005 AP *Latin Literature and AP Latin: Vergil Released Exams*, page 4.

[40] Dorrance Stinchfield White, *The Teaching of Latin*, Scott-Foresman, Chicago, IL, 1944, pp. 142–143.

[41] Note that the passage given below is slightly shorter than those found in the actual free-response section. For actual Exam questions, as well as scoring guidelines, sample literal translations (since 2005), and examples of student answers, see the AP Latin: Vergil website. Passages from the *Aeneid* used for translation questions on recent AP Latin: Vergil Exams are listed later in this chapter.

[42] Charles W. Siedler, *Guide to Cicero*, Oxford Book Co., NY, 1935, page 87. Some teachers ask their students to produce two translations, one literal and one literary. See Margaret A. Brucia, page 124.

[43] The translations used here are those of David West (Penguin Books, 1991) and Sarah Ruden (Yale Univ. Press, 2009). See Steve Donoghue's review of Sarah Ruden's well-received new translation and the first full translation of the poem ever published by a woman, at *http://openlettersmonthly.com/issue/book-review-aeneid-vergil-translated-sarah-ruden/*.

[44] See the Acorn book, in print or online, page 20. With regard to accuracy and precision, traditional renderings of verbs in the perfect tense are equally acceptable, i.e., **amavit**, *he loved* (simple past) or *he has loved* (present perfect), as long as the action expressed is both past and completed. The historical present, or use of the present tense which has the meaning of the past, is permitted on the AP Latin Exam, as long as its use is consistent within the given passage. See the two literary translations for examples of this usage. **Amabat** must be translated as *he was loving* or *he loved* (but not *he did love*), i.e., it must be rendered as an incomplete action. Plural nouns may be translated in the singular to express the meaning of poetic plural. For literal translation of figures of speech, see Chapter 8.

[45] David Perry, in a discussion about translation on The College Board Electronic Discussion Group (online) for Saturday, July 22, 2006.

[46] For information about how word order is used in poetic figures of speech, see Chapter 8.

[47] For a visual demonstration of how a Vergilian text looks without punctuation, see "*Aeneid* Book 1, lines 1–100 in Several Formats" (William Harris, Middlebury College), *http://community.middlebury.edu/%7Eharris/Classics/VergilAen1uncial.html.* The first 100 lines are given in typical modern format, then in all caps but with word separation, and finally with all caps and no word separation. The British still

grant a small concession to this lack of punctuation by avoiding the use of capitals when beginning sentences in Latin texts.

[48] The Greek root word *kolon,* whose literal meaning is member or limb, may refer to a clause of a sentence.

[49] The mean score on Question V1 of the 2008 Exam, the last Exam for which a Reader's Report was available as of this writing, was 4.4 out of a possible 18 points. The mean score on Question V2 was 7.15 out of a possible 18 points. Some of the reasons mentioned by the Chief Reader for such low averages were: difficulty with vocabulary, esp. mistaking one word for another (**manus** or **murus** for **munus**), missing the part of speech (translating **pulchro** as "beauty," instead of "beautiful"), and mistranslations of grammar and syntax, such as rendering an independent subjunctive as future tense (**det,** "he will give"). Pendergraft writes, "In many cases single mistranslations then led students to lose the context of the passage and thus mistranslate the next phrase or sentence." See Pendergraft, page 50.

[50] When speeches appear as translation passages on the AP Latin Vergil Exam, quotation marks are used. Use this as a contextual clue. Quotation marks are not used for passages from Aeneas' "speech" in Book 2.

[51] At Tim Abney's AP Vergil site *http://abney.homestead.com/aeneid.html#anchor_80*, you will find, for each of Books 1, 2, 4, 6, 10–12, sight reading passages with multiple-choice questions and answers. The format is a running banner that forces you to read the Latin as Latin, which is an excellent method for teaching or testing reading for comprehension.

[52] For this important idea, see Hoyos 2, Rule 5, page 3. See also Ginny Lindzey's advice to her AP Latin class at *http://drippingvergil.livejournal.com/*.

[53] Sense-units are called "chunks" or "segments" when referring to word-groups of a passage for translation on the AP Latin Exam. The use of sense-units (or "chunks" or "segments") in assessing the accuracy of a literal translation on the AP Latin Exam will be discussed further below. Some teachers now teach literal translation using the "chunking" method. The identification of sense-units is, of course, subjective. The author attempts to be consistent in identifying as sense-units those word-groups whose elements are what Hoyos calls "syntactically coherent."

[54] Hoyos 2, page 23.

[55] The assumption is made in the following discussion that you have a basic working knowledge of Latin grammar and can recognize, for instance, a participle as a participle.

[56] For chiasmus and other figures of speech, see Chapter 8.

[57] The meaning "big as a mountain" is perhaps sufficient, if not precisely literal.

[58] For a somewhat different way of using sense-units for both comprehension and translation, see Appendix 2.

[59] For scansion, see Chapter 9.

[60] West, page 110.

[61] Some teachers assign a "scribe" to take notes on class discussion or translation of an assigned passage, which can then be shared with the class. This allows students to concentrate on reading and interpreting the Latin, instead of desperately transcribing word-for-word everything that is read or said.

[62] Many teachers are now accustomed to asking their students to read an English translation of the *Aeneid* as part of their preparation for the AP Latin Exam, especially as summer reading. Be advised to avoid the temptation of relying too much on published translations when you are preparing your daily reading for Latin class. Not only is this unethical, it will not contribute to your improvement in reading Latin (quite the contrary). Be advised that your teacher is likely to be familiar with the more commonly-used translations.

[63] The point total for translation questions was changed in 2008 from 9 pts. (1/2 pt. per segment) to 18 pts. (1 pt. per segment.) The latter system is used in this book.

Chapter 6

The Free-Response Section: The Long and Short Essays

The Long and the Short of It

The free-response section of the AP Latin Exam requires that you produce both "long" and "short" essays in answer to questions that ask you to analyze a given passage or set of continuous lines.[64] This chapter will include specific information about the content and form of long and short essay questions and the passages that accompany them, some tips about how to write an effective essay on the AP Latin Exam, a sample short essay question for practice, guidance on how essays are assessed, and some direction on practicing with essays from previous AP Latin: Vergil Exams online. The so-called "background question," which will be covered in the next chapter, is also a short essay question. Here is a summary of the essay portions of the free-response section:

Long Essay		Short Essay		Background Question	
Minutes	Percentage	Minutes	Percentage	Minutes	Percentage
45	35	20	20	20	15

Essays on the AP Latin Exam

The word most commonly found in an AP Latin Exam essay question is "discuss." Hopefully, during your study of Latin, you have often been asked by your teacher or a classmate to answer a question and to give a reason for your answer, e.g., "In the story, how does Erroneus feel?" "Why does Erroneus feel this way?" "What Latin tells you this?" In simple form, this is the general idea of an essay question on the AP Latin Exam. In your discussion on an essay, you may be asked to analyze and interpret a single passage or to compare and contrast two passages with regard either to their content or structure or to some critical statement about the passage(s). Although you are not held accountable for using the strict format of an English essay on an essay for AP Latin, your writing is expected to be "well-developed." Well-developed means that your writing is coherent, concise, focused, organized, substantive, and copiously and properly documented from the Latin text. More on these points a bit later.

Of critical importance to your writing on Latin essay questions is the following statement, which appears in boldface in the Acorn book: "The responsibility rests with the student to convince the Reader that the student is drawing conclusions from the Latin text and not from a general recall of the passage."[65] In order to meet this responsibility, you must make specific reference to the Latin text throughout your discussion, including translated or closely paraphrased citations from the text. Failure to cite any Latin in an essay will result in a grade of no more than half-credit (3 of 6 pts.). We will say more about this at the end of the chapter.

The Long Essay

More often than not, the long essay is based on several passages that are related in theme, with each passage consisting of 10–15 lines, either from the same book of the *Aeneid* or from different books. The other option consists of a single passage of 20–25 lines. The long essay is the single most important question on the free-response section, as it requires the most working time (45 mins.) and carries the most weight (35 percent of your score on the free-response section). Its value is more than 20 percent of your total score on the Exam, which is equal to about two of the multiple-choice passages. The long essay question (Question V3) immediately follows the translation questions.

Passages of the *Aeneid* Appearing in Long Essay Questions

Vergil Exams, 2001–2009[66]

Book 1: 36–52 (with 12.818–828, 2007), 37–49 (with 12.818–828, 2001), 92–101 (with 198–209, 2005), 124–141 (with 4.84–89, 2004), 198–209 (with 92–101, 2005)

Book 2: 234–253 (2008), 768–793 (2003)

Book 4: 20–29 (with 320–330, 2002), 84–89 (with 124–141, 2004), 320–330 (with 20–29, 2002), 337–350 (with 6.110–122, 2009)

Book 6: 110–122 (with 4.337–350, 2009), 868–886 (2006)

Book 10: none

Book 12: 818–828 (with 1.36–52, 2007), 12.818–828 (with 1.37–49, 2001)

Topics on Recent Long Essay Questions

2009: The arguments Aeneas uses in justifying his departure from Carthage and his visit to his father in the Underworld (4.337–350 with 6.110–122)

2008: How the Trojans viewed the wooden horse at the time it was received and how Aeneas perceived this event afterwards (2.234–253)

2007: How Juno is characterized at the beginning and end of the *Aeneid* (1.36–52 with 12.818–828)

2006: Anchises grieves for the death of Marcellus (6.868–86)

2005: The character of Aeneas in action, via his speeches (1.92–101 with 198–209)

2004: The behavior of sovereigns in their realms (1.124–41 with 4.74–89)

2003: How the Trojan war disrupts the lives of Aeneas and Creusa (2.768–93)

2002: Dido's feelings at the beginning and end of her relationship with Aeneas (4.20–29 with 320–30)

2001: Juno's positions on the Trojan mission (1.37–49 with 12.818–28)

The Short Essay

The short essay topic is usually confined to a single passage, consisting of an average of 11 lines.[67] Note that the suggested time for the short essay is 20 minutes; the weight is 20% of your score on the free-response section. You are asked to analyze or interpret, and discuss, a specific topic relating to a character or event that appears in the prepared lines, which is the same as for the long essay. The difference between the long and the short essay is usually the length of the Latin passage under discussion. The expectations regarding producing a well-developed essay and referring specifically to the Latin throughout the passage to support your essay remain the same as for the long essay. Since the passage accompanying the short essay contains less Latin, there are fewer contextual clues to assist in identification, so the prompt may give you more guidance. On the Exam, the short essay (Question V4) immediately follows the long essay.

Passages of the *Aeneid* Appearing in Short Essay Questions

Vergil Exams, 2001–2009

Book 1: 291–296 (2002), 450–465 (2003)

Book 2: 533–545 (2007)

Book 4: 675–685 (2001)

Book 6: 65–76 (2008), 83–95 (2005)

Book 10: 467–475 (2004), 491–496 (with 500–505, 2006)

Book 12: 903–918 (2009)

Topics on Recent Short Essay Questions

2009: Turnus' desperation in failing to hit Aeneas with a boulder (12.903–918)

2008: Aeneas' request of and promise to the Sibyl (6.65–76)

2007: Priam confronts Pyrrhus (2.533–545)

2006: Turnus as hero (10.491–496 with 500–505)

2005: Sibyl's prophecy (6.83–94)

2004: Pallas fights Turnus: hope vs. reality (10.457–465)

2003: Aeneas' emotions in witnessing mural of the Trojan War (1.450–465)

2002: Jupiter characterizes Rome's future (1.291–296)

2001: The effect of Dido's suicide on Anna (4.675–685)

Points to Consider in Writing a Good Essay

The word "essay" produces anxiety in some students. As mentioned, you are not required to have a topic sentence, three or five body-paragraphs, and a concluding paragraph or sentence, however, it is a good idea be sure that your essay has a beginning, a middle, and an end.[68] The effectiveness of your essay is at least partly a product of the way you organize your thinking and writing. "How can I do my best on the essay questions in the free-response section?" You can find success on the essay questions in the same way that you can reach Carnegie Hall: practice, practice, practice! Write as often as you can, both within the context of your AP Latin course and in the context of your other courses. Ask your Latin teacher, your English teacher, your Mom and Dad, your friends, and anyone else who is willing, to read and comment on your writing. Practice thinking and writing under the pressure of time. Hopefully, your teacher will have prepared you for what you will find on the AP Latin Exam by challenging you with AP-style Latin questions throughout the year.[69] If not, practice on your own. The resources provided in this book should help you to improve your analytical writing for the AP Latin Exam, especially if you study the answers to the sample Practice Exam essays. Here are some points to consider in writing a good essay. The major points may be summarized by using the acronym SODA (Support, Organize, Develop, Analyze).

- Read the question and the accompanying passage(s) several times, i.e., during the reading period and again before writing.
- Answer the specific question asked. This continues to be a concern voiced in the Chief Reader's annual report on student performance on the AP Latin Exam and it should therefore be addressed by future candidates, such as yourself. Furthermore, if there are two parts to a question, be sure to address both parts. To help you maintain your focus when writing, consider the following:

  a. Use the 15-minute reading period productively.[70]

  b. Begin your lead or topic sentence by quoting or approximating key elements from the prompt of the question. Here is an example using a successful student response to the actual short essay question on the 2008 Exam:

  Question V4: In the passage above (6.65–76), Aeneas prays for an end to the troubles of the displaced Trojans. In a short essay, discuss the request he makes and what he promises the Sibyl.

Student's opening statement: "Having finally reached the Sibyl at Cumae, Aeneas prays and asks for his fate to be fulfilled, and to make his offer more appealing he proposes ways to worship Apollo."[71]

c. Organize your thinking. Avoid making vague generalizations and "free-writing," that is, writing everything you know about the subject as soon as it occurs to you. Conversely, do not leave out relevant or essential observations by assuming that these are obvious. Avoid making casual reference to other passages or other authors, unless specifically directed to do so, as this is distracting and rarely contributes to the topic under discussion.

d. If there is time, quickly proofread your writing. If you must delete, erase or cross out thoroughly; if you must add, consider doing this in a numbered endnote; if you must edit, do so neatly and clearly.

- Remember to use a fresh page for each new answer. It is useful to skip lines when you write your essay, to provide you with room for possible later editing.
- Avoid being descriptive or narrative in your discussion, that is, don't simply give a line-by-line paraphrase (or translation) of the passage. Be focused and critical in your writing, explaining how the evidence drawn from the Latin text supports each observation. Lack of analysis will earn a low score on an essay.
- Essays that receive full credit make frequent reference to the relevant Latin in the correct format (see below).
- Thoroughness is an important consideration, and one which has prompted very specific wording on each free-response essay question. The directions read "Be sure to refer specifically to the Latin **throughout** the passages to support your essay." This is an area where points are often lost unnecessarily. The word "throughout" means that you are to include documented reference to the entire Latin passage or passages—beginning, middle, and end—in your discussion. It is helpful to determine during the reading period how the Latin passages are organized, i.e., where the sense-breaks in the thought occur. Also, if the question involves two passages, you must address both. (Failure to consider one of the two passages will only earn half-credit.) Lastly, you will strengthen your essay if you briefly establish the context of the passage for the Reader, especially with regard to speeches, even if the question does not explicitly ask for this information.
- Avoid collecting figures of speech in order to make this collection the basis of the arguments in your essay, unless specifically requested to do so.[72]
- Be aware that the length of your answer to an essay question is of little or no consequence to its quality. How much is enough is whatever it takes to answer the question asked in a manner that is "developed" (for which, see above).

- Here are several pieces of personal advice with regard to your writing: write legibly (speed sometimes reduces even the finest calligraphy to scribble!), use proper English, and avoid slang or "bad language."

Guidelines for Citing Latin Correctly in an Essay

Just as it is true that providing no citation from the Latin in your essay will lead to a score no higher than 3 pts. (of 6 pts.), it is also to be expected that copious citation with no or limited analysis will obtain a score no higher than 4 pts.[73] You must demonstrate both your ability to read and cite the Latin accurately and your ability to form an opinion or interpretation and support it with appropriate citations from the Latin. The integration of citations within responses requires both perceptiveness and practice.

1. Select only the Latin that is relevant to your discussion. Don't write out several lines or an entire sentence of Latin text in the hope that the evidence is contained somewhere therein. This is time-consuming and will rarely be considered acceptable evidence for the point you are making. You are not expected to cite Latin from each line of the passage(s), but you are expected to make contact with each of the passage's sentences or thought-groups. Be sure to explain the connection between the Latin you are citing and the point that it is supporting in the discussion. (See below for more on this point.)
2. Translate or give a close paraphrase of the specific Latin that you have cited. Be sure to include all the Latin. When translating, use parentheses or quotation marks to distinguish the English from the Latin, e.g., for the line **agnosco veteris vestigia flammae** (*Aeneid* 4.23):

   Translation: "I recognize traces of the old flame."

   Close paraphrase: Dido says that she believes she is falling in love again.

   Avoid a loose paraphrase, such as "I feel the old fire."
3. Write out the Latin and cite line numbers. When referring to a specific word or short phrase, write out the Latin. It is a good idea to underline the Latin cited, as this is correct format in quoting a foreign language in English (italics are used, otherwise) and it also brings the Reader's attention to your support. You may use ellipsis points for longer citations, that is, quote the first word, indicate the intervening and assumed words by three ellipsis points (. . .), and then close the citation with the final relevant word. Thus, if you were using the first two lines of the *Aeneid* to support a point in your discussion, you should write Arma . . . venit (lines 1–2) or Arma . . . venit (1–2). Remember that, although ellipsis points may be used in citing longer clauses or sentences, it is a good idea to limit the length of your citations to a few relevant words. Use words or phrases, or better yet, sense-units, whenever possible and avoid giving vague citations, such as "in lines 1–10." When citing, you should integrate the Latin and its meaning into the structure of the sentence that contains the observation you are

supporting. Here are several ways to cite Latin in support of a discussion on an essay:

Example 1

Write out the relevant Latin, followed by an English translation in parentheses or quotation marks:

> "In the opening words of the *Aeneid,* Arma virumque cano, (I sing of arms and a man), Vergil alludes to his Homeric sources, the *Iliad* and the *Odyssey.*"

Example 2

Quote the English translation, followed by the relevant Latin:

> "In the opening words of the *Aeneid*, 'I sing of arms and a man' (Arma virumque cano), Vergil alludes to his Homeric sources, the *Iliad* and the *Odyssey.*"

Example 3

A third way to support directly from the Latin is to cite the Latin and give a close paraphrase of its meaning (or vice versa):

> "In the opening words of the *Aeneid,* where Vergil relates that he is singing about war and a man (Arma virumque cano), he alludes to his Homeric sources, the *Iliad* and the *Odyssey.*" Be sure to include line numbers with your citations.

Compare-and-Contrast Essay Questions

A question that asks you to compare and contrast two Latin passages from the same or different books of the *Aeneid* is a favorite on the exam.[74] Compare and contrast means that you are to identify and discuss both similarities and differences between the passages provided. You are expected to describe any similarities and differences and then evaluate them. In answering such questions, state the points of comparison and contrast as explicitly as you are able. Here are two effective ways to answer a compare-and-contrast question:

1) create two separate paragraphs, each devoted to an analysis of one of the two passages, and then summarize the similarities and differences in a concluding paragraph in which you compare the passages directly;
2) outline the main points of similarity and difference before writing, and then cover each point by interweaving your analysis of both poems together, so that you are comparing or contrasting the two passages directly and immediately as you proceed through the Latin. Discuss both passages at the same time, back and forth.

Choose the approach that best suits your writing style or the one that is most effective in communicating your understanding of the meaning of the Latin in the context of the question asked. Finally, it is helpful in writing your answer to a compare-and-contrast question to use linking phrases such as "In comparison . . . ," "In contrast . . . ," "Likewise . . . ," or "Similarly . . . ." Such phrases keep you connected to the question and the Reader connected to you. We will now present and discuss an AP-style short essay question.

A Sample Short Essay Question

Question V4 (20 percent)

(Suggested time – 20 minutes)

Begin your answer to this question on a clean page.

Dixerat, atque illam media inter talia ferro
collapsam aspiciunt comites, ensemque cruore
spumantem sparsasque manus. It clamor ad alta
atria; concussam bacchatur Fama per urbem.
Lamentis gemituque et femineo ululatu
tecta fremunt, resonat magnis plangoribus aether,
non aliter, quam si immissis ruat hostibus omnis
Karthago aut antiqua Tyros, flammaeque furentes
culmina perque hominum volvantur perque deorum.
Audiit exanimis, trepidoque exterrita cursu
unguibus ora soror foedans et pectora pugnis
per medios ruit ac morientem nomine clamat.

***Aeneid* 4.663–674**

Preceding the passage above, Queen Dido has just taken her own life. In a **well-developed** essay, discuss the ways in which the poet expresses the reaction to the news of the queen's death.

Be sure to refer specifically to the Latin **throughout** *the passage to support your essay*. Do NOT simply summarize what the passage says. (When you are asked to refer specifically to the Latin, you must write out the Latin and/or cite line numbers AND you must translate, accurately paraphrase, or make clear in your discussion that you understand the Latin.)[75]

Note: The author has perhaps been more thorough in his analysis of this passage than is necessary, however, the following essay is provided as an illustration of how a successful answer might be framed. Pay attention to the support, the organization, the development, and the analysis (SODA).

Sample Answer

Vergil uses a variety of stylistic features—sound, selection and placement of words, imagery—to create and enhance his description of the consequences of an event that would be difficult to exaggerate: a queen's self-murder. This passage may be divided into three parts, each of which is a complete sentence and each of which provides for the listener/speaker a different perspective on the same events. The first part is a graphic description of what Dido's attendants witness when they first see her, dying (lines 1–3). The second, or middle, part consist of lines 3–9, which describe the physical and emotional reaction of those who now realize what has happened, a description which is supported by an extended simile in lines 7–9 (non aliter . . . deorum). The final part of this passage, and perhaps the most poignant, describes the personal agony of Dido's sister Anna (10–12).

In the first part (1–3), Vergil "sets the stage," which contains the queen, who is pouring out her life's blood from the self-inflicted wound made by using Aeneas' sword, while the court (comites, 2) rushes in to find her collapsed (illam . . . collapsam, 1–2). The camera quickly pans from dying queen and shocked court to the sword, frothy with her blood (ensemque crurore spumantem, 2), and finally to her spattered hands (sparsasque manus, 3). The mention of the sword twice in this sentence (ferro, 1, ensem, 2), once using the metonymy of ferro (1), elicits the impression of cold steel and hot blood (crurore spumantem, 2–3) that is almost tactile. The three elisions in the first one and a half lines perhaps suggest the weakening and final collapse of the queen (atque illam and media inter, 1, and collapsam aspiciunt, 2). The dramatic effect of the words spumantem and sparsasque is further enhanced by alliteration and the visual effects of frothing and spattering (both participles). Furthermore, the insistent rhythm of the trisyllables ensemque cruore spumantem sparsasque suggests that the blood is still pumping around the wound. The scene is very "visual."

The second part of this passage (3–9) is, perhaps, even more poetically dramatic and provides a striking use of imagery in nearly every line. These lines, which describe the "collapse" of the palace household and the city at the news, emphasize sound effects: It clamor ad alta atria (3–4), ululatu (5), tecta fremunt (6), and resonat magnis plangoribus aether (6). There is additional noteworthy use of imagery, such as metaphor (bacchatur Fama, 4) and simile (7–9), that combine with the sound effects to provide a striking image in nearly every line. The resulting effect on the listener/reader is that there is confusion and the sounds of grief everywhere: clamor (3), Lamentis gemituque et femineo ululatu . . . fremunt (5–6), and plangoribus (6). The amount of wailing and lamenting is amplified by the rhythm of line 5, by the elision of gemituque et, and by the hiatus that magnifies the onomatopoeia in femineo ululatu. The outcries reach not only to the high halls (of the palace) (ad alta atria, 3–4) but to heaven itself (resonat . . . aether, 6). The metaphor, concussam bacchatur Fama per urbem (4), "Rumor runs riot through the shaken city," is reminiscent of the allegory of Rumor earlier in Book 4, after Dido and Aeneas have "married." This is most likely a deliberate (and masterful) allusion to those circumstances, which have brought about the event we are now witnessing in this passage. Fama races again through the city, which is shaken as if by some blow (note the powerful sound of concussam . . . urbem), like a Bacchant, the image reinforced by the juxtaposition of bacchatur with concussam, a word often used to describe the shaking of the Bacchic thyrsus. The whole clause suggests a lack of control, which was surely the case after the queen's death. This scene ends with a lengthy and compelling simile (non aliter quam . . . , 7), the language and imagery of which recalls the fall of Troy. The situation in Dido's city is as if the enemy were at the gates (immissis . . . hostibus, 7) and Carthage, or its mother-city Tyre, were to come crashing down, and raging flames (flammaeque furentes, 8;

note the emphatic alliteration) were to roll over the homes of both men and the gods (culmina perque hominum . . . perque deorum, 9). The repetition of perque suggests the image of wave after wave of fire sweeping over the city.

We come to the third and final part of this passage, which focuses on how Dido's death has affected a single individual – her sister Anna. She is breathless (exanimis, 10) with shock, a perception that the poet amplifies by contracting the verb audivit to audiit. Several subsequent participial phrases describe Anna's rush through the crowd (per medios ruit, 12): she is frightened and trembling (trepidoque exterrita cursu, 10; note the effectiveness of the harsh sounds and the elision here) and she claws at her face with her fingernails and pummels her breast with her fists (unguibus . . . pugnis, 11) in the age-old manner of expressing grief (cf. plangoribus in line 6, above). The poet draws attention to these actions through the percussive alliteration of pectora pugnis (11) and through the chiastic patterning and sound play of the words unguibus ora . . . pectora pugnis. The passage ends with Anna plaintively calling the name of her dying sister, perhaps an allusion to the Roman custom of conclamatio, which consisted of calling out the name of a dying person three times in an attempt to awaken them.

Queen Dido has taken her own life as a consequence of her unrequited love for Aeneas, who has sailed away to meet his destiny. In her unprecedented position as founder of a city (Carthage), she has built a community in which she was admired, respected, and honored, judging from what we learn about her in Book 4. This leads us to the logical conclusion that the queen's death, especially her suicide, will have serious repercussions among those who respect and love her. In this passage, Vergil successfully calls upon the best of his poetic skills to communicate the terrible effect that the news of the queen's death has on her community.

Some Additional Topics for Practice in Writing Essays on the *Aeneid*

These suggestions for essay topics are intended to supplement those questions that appear in this book and on previous AP Latin Exams. These questions may be worded somewhat differently from what you might expect on the Exam, but they are nonetheless intended to get you thinking and writing about the *Aeneid.*

- In Book 2 of the *Aeneid,* lines 281–295 and 776–789, a phantom appears to Aeneas. Compare and contrast the speeches given to the hero by these phantoms. Include in your discussion their respective identities and their purpose in addressing Aeneas.
- In Books 4.234–245 and 6.46–51, Dido and the Cumaean Sibyl have become possessed by forces that cause in them a dramatic change. Compare and contrast how the poet portrays each transformation.
- In Book 4, lines 305–330, of the *Aeneid,* Dido makes several addresses to Aeneas in which she takes exception to his decision to leave. In a well-developed essay, discuss the various ways in which the queen attempts to appeal to Aeneas upon his departure. What are the different arguments that she uses? Does she change her strategy during the speech? If so, how?

- Two passages in the *Aeneid* make reference to someone being "hard as flint" (Books 4.365–370 and 6.469–476). In a short essay, identify both individuals, then describe the circumstances that account for this characterization and how these circumstances relate to one another psychologically.
- Two speeches in the *Aeneid* portray different attitudes held by the same character (Books 1.65–70 and 12.818–828). Compare and contrast these two attitudes and account for the change.
- Compare and contrast the speeches of Creusa and the Cumaean Sibyl to Aeneas that reveal his destiny. (Books 2.776–789 and 8.86–97, respectively.)
- Compare and contrast the speeches of Neoptolemus (Pyrrhus) and Turnus to their murder victims. (Books 2.547–550 and 10.491–405, respectively.)

Some Thought Questions for Class Discussion or Theme Writing

As you prepare for the AP Exam over the long term, it is wise to practice literary analysis of Vergil's Latin by speaking up during class discussions, i.e., by asking and answering questions, and by writing essays, whether they are research papers, simulated AP-style essays, etc.

Here are some topics for class discussion or theme writing.

- With respect to the promise of Rome's future greatness, compare Jupiter's prophetic speech (Book 1.257–96), with that of Anchises in the "Parade of Heroes" (Book 6.756–886) and/or the Shield of Aeneas (8.626–728).
- One scholar has written about the dominant imagery of Book 2: the serpent and the flame.[76] Write an essay in which you discuss the relevance of these images to each other and to the context of Book 2.
- Explore the content of Dido's curses (Book 4.380–391 and 607–629) in the context of the historical enmity between Carthage and Rome.
- In Books 1 and 4, discuss the specific points of comparison in the orator simile (1.148–153), the bee simile (1.430–436), Dido the huntress simile (4.68–73), the ant simile (4.402–407), and the oak tree in a high wind simile (4.441–446). In Books 10 and 12, discuss these similes: the lion and the bull (10.454–456), the mountain rockfall (12.684–690), the dream-state (12.908–914), and the shot from a catapult (12.921–923).
- T.S. Eliot called Aeneas' meeting with Dido in the Underworld (Book 6.450–76) "the most civilized passage in all of Western literature." Comment on the reason(s) why you think Eliot felt this way.
- Write a character study of Turnus as the anti-hero who displays the passion that is the counterpoint to the self-control of Aeneas. Support your observations with examples from the second half of the *Aeneid.*
- Explore the conflict between **pietas** (rational judgment) and **furor** (mindless emotion) as an essential theme of the *Aeneid.*

- The word **fatum** in its various forms appears many times in the early books of the *Aeneid.* Argue from the poem the place of fate in the workings of the gods and in the lives of men.
- The noble Roman understood his duty to the gods, his homeland, his friends and followers, and most importantly, his family, through the person of the father. Explore the subject of patriarchal responsibility and filial duty as a major theme of the *Aeneid.*
- In the manner of Ovid's *Heroides,* compose imaginary conversations between Aeneas and Achates, Dido and Aeneas, Aeneas and Ascanius, or Iarbas and Dido, or perhaps a diary of Aeneas' wanderings as he perhaps would have kept it, or Dido's impressions as they developed day by day.

How to Use the AP Latin: Vergil Website for Practice Writing Essays

As suggested previously in this book, one way to practice for the essay questions on the AP Latin Exam is to simulate the experience by going to the AP Latin: Vergil Homepage website, where you will find links to AP Latin: Vergil Exams from previous years. Click on a link to any Exam, find an essay question (Question V3 is the long essay, Question V4, the short essay), and then write out your response to the question. Be sure to limit your time as suggested (45 mins. and 20 mins for the long and short essays, respectively), although you need not time yourself until you have practiced a bit. First, concentrate on following the guidelines for writing a good essay given above, then work on time. When you have finished your essay, check it against the criteria provided in the scoring guidelines and commentary. Take time to compare your response to that of students who received high scores.

How Essays are Scored

All essays on the free-response section, both long and short, are graded on a six-point scale, which provides Readers with both discretion and boundaries (remember that the assessment of writing is necessarily subjective). Scores of 6 and 5 are excellent, 4 and 3 good, and 2 and 1 minimal. A zero is assigned if the answer is random, irrelevant, or totally disconnected from the question. No score is given if there is no attempt at answering the question, or if the answer is off-task, such as doodling or a "personal anecdote." It should be mentioned that a paper does not need to be flawless to earn a score of 6 pts. Mistakes are allowed, as long as the general competence of the essay is not compromised. To provide you with some context, the average score on the long essay question for the 2008 Vergil Exam was 3.19 out of 6 pts. (53 percent of expectation) and the average score on the short essay for that year was 2.85 out of 6 pts. (48 percent). In the Practice Exams at the end of this book, you will find sample AP-style essay questions, with answers, that will help you to assess your readiness for such questions on the actual AP Latin: Vergil Exam. Be sure to compare your answers carefully with the suggested answers produced by the author. Below you will find sample scoring guidelines for essays to give you an idea of the range and scope of expectations on essay questions.

Six

A six is awarded to an effective essay that completely answers the question and is supported with relevant and copious documentation from the Latin. The writing is characterized by sound argument and discussion that is coherent and persuasive. Minor mistakes in interpretation or translation are acceptable and usually do not compromise an overall impression of competence.

Five

This essay is solid and competent, but perhaps lacking in effective development (depth), textual references, or sophistication. The student understands the question asked and is acquainted with the Latin text, but falls short of the top mark in one or more areas.

Four

The essay that earns a four is adequate or satisfactory. It may fall somewhat short of a six or five in the quality and/or quantity of its citations, in failing to address the question completely, e.g., addressing only one of two passages substantively, or in presenting a narrative or paraphrase without adequate analysis of the text.

Three

This score arises from failing to cite any of the Latin text, continually citing Latin that is immaterial, giving inadequate attention to one of the two passages, or answering the question in a manner that is superficial or inaccurate. Sometimes only a translation is given.

Two

This essay is unsatisfactory because it does not answer the question asked or completely ignores one of the two passages; presents statements that are vague, incorrect, or unsubstantiated; ignores the Latin text or includes citations that do not indicate comprehension.

One

This essay answers the question in a minimal way. It is apparent that the student recognizes the passage but is unable to respond to the question in any coherent way, either because the question is not understood or because the student's command of the text is faulty or based on memorization. There is no substantive discussion and little or no relevant support.

Endnotes

[64] The topic of what the word "essay" means in terms of the AP Latin: Vergil Exam will be discussed further below.

[65] Acorn book, page 21.

[66] Further information and tips re. essays on the AP Latin Exam may be found on the AP Latin: Vergil website, with which you should now be familiar, the most recently published released Exam (2005), the annual Reader's report, and the latest Acorn book (in-print or online). See also the articles by Crooker and by Davis listed in the Appendix for this chapter.

[67] But see the short essay question for the 2006 Exam, which contains two passages.

[68] Resources on the general topic of writing good essays are provided in the Appendix for this chapter.

[69] For each essay question on a test, one teacher gives her students a "sample template," which consists of the headings "opening statement," "discussion with Latin support (Latin quoted *and* translated or paraphrased)," and "the conclusion (*not* a reiteration of the above, but your final analysis based upon discussion)." See Crooker's article, cited in the Appendix.

[70] For the reading period, see Chapter 3.

[71] See Pendergraft, page 57, cited in the Appendix for Chapter 5. For the term "prompt," see the glossary in Chapter 1.

[72] For discussion about how to integrate figures of speech into a poetic analysis using the SWIMTAG technique, see Chapter 8 and Appendix 3.

[73] The scoring of essays will be discussed later in this chapter.

[74] On Exams of the past nine years (2001–2009), three of nine long essay questions contained compare-and-contrast questions (2002, 2003, 2007).

[75] The length of the Latin passage here is shorter than that usually found on the Exam. The format of the author's question is adopted from the most recent AP Latin: Vergil Exam 2009, for which, see the AP Latin: Vergil Website. The wording of the question is the author's. The wording of the instructions is that of the AP Latin Exam Development Committee, including the use of boldface and all caps.

[76] Bernard Knox, "The Serpent and the Flame: The Imagery of the Second Book of the *Aeneid*," *Virgil:A Collection of Critical Essays*, Steele Commager, ed., Prentice-Hall, Englewood Cliffs, NJ, 1966.

Chapter 7

The Free-Response Section: The Background Question

The fifth and final free-response question that we will discuss is known as the "background question." This question evaluates your familiarity with the *Aeneid* as a whole, especially those parts read in English.[77]

More generally, your familiarity with the life and times of Vergil and with the "literary" and mythological backgrounds of Homer, the *Iliad* and *Odyssey*, and the story of Troy are anticipated, although they are not tested directly. In addition, some familiarity with epic poetry as a genre is expected, along with a general knowledge of Roman cultural, political, and social history, especially that of the Augustan Age. This final question is designed for 15 minutes of writing time and counts as 20 percent of your score on the free-response section.

The background question is the only Exam question that is not based on a Latin passage and that does not ask you to cite or translate Latin. This question asks you to discuss one specific set of characters or events in the story to illustrate your familiarity with the *Aeneid* as an entire work of literature. The background question now consists of two sets of three characters or events, from each set of which you are to choose one item for your essay in response to a topic stated in the question. This, essentially, means you are to compose a two-part essay in which each part addresses the assigned topic. Specific details are requested. Although no citations of the Latin are required, some analysis is required to demonstrate knowledge of your chosen characters or events.[78] Here is a sample background question:

Question V5 (15 percent)

(Suggested time – 20 mins.)

Begin your answer to this question on a clean page.

Within the action of the *Aeneid*, there are various turning points that occur in which the action is redirected. Select two of the following events, **one from Group A and one from Group B,** and in a **short essay** discuss how each represents a turning point in the story. Be sure to support your essay with specific details.

Group A	Group B
Cupid substitutes for Ascanius	Sinon is captured by the Trojans
The Trojan women attempt to burn the ships in Sicily	Allecto comes to Turnus as an old woman
The ghost of Aeneas appears to Turnus	Tiberinus, god of the Tiber River, visits Aeneas in a dream

Since this question is an essay question, it is also scored on a scale of 0–6 pts.[79] The background question often produces the highest mean score of those on the Exam: for the 2008 Exam, the mean score on the background question was 3.31 out of a possible 6 pts. (55 percent).[80] For practice with actual background questions (Question V5), remember to check the AP Latin: Vergil website.

Background Questions on AP Latin: Vergil Exams, 2001–2009

Here are some characters and events in the *Aeneid* that have been selected for attention in the background question on AP Vergil Exams, 2001–2009. Characters are now given a short tag to help you begin, e.g., Latinus, king of the Latins, or Pallas, son of Evander. The characters, who are often supporting actors both mortal and divine, and events often appear in those lines and books not read in Latin. For a glossary of characters and events appearing in the *Aeneid,* see later in this chapter. In the chart below, Amata, Camilla, and Juturna are favorites; others appearing at several times are Allecto, Helenus, Lausus, and Sinon.

Year	Topic	Characters or Events (two groups per question)
2009	Desire for material possessions	Pygmalion, Polydorus, Cacus and Euryalus, Turnus, Camilla
2008	Concept of hospitality	Acestes, Evander, Sinon and Amata, Andromache, Anna
2007	Sufferings of Trojan wanderers	Strophades and Harpies, women setting fire to the ships, Ascanius and the stag and the shield of Aeneas, Turnus in the Trojan camp, the death of Pallas
2006	Minor characters performing critical functions	Helenus, Iarbas, Lausus and Allecto, Camilla, Juturna

(continued)

Year	Topic	Characters or Events (two groups per question)
2005	**Pietas**	Anchises during fall of Troy, Dares or Entellus (the boxers), Helenus, the prophet and Amata, queen of the Latins, Camilla, the warrior, Juturna, sister of Turnus
2004	Tension between reasonable and rash behavior	Aeneas' encounter with Helen during Troy's destruction, Trojan women's attempt to burn their ships in Sicily, boxing match between Dares and Entellus and Amata's behavior after Lavinia's engagement to Aeneas, story of Hercules and Cacus, nighttime expedition of Nisus and Euryalus
2003	Purpose of disguise or deception	Cupid, Sinon and Allecto, Iris, Juturna
2002	Events that are fair or unfair	Camilla, Palinurus, Lausus, one of the games in Book V, Amata
2001	Ways in which the future is revealed	

A Glossary of Proper Names Appearing in the *Aeneid*

Characters

Locations in the *Aeneid* that are indicated below reflect the greatest frequency of appearance. Those bearing an asterisk have appeared on a background question of the Vergil Exam. The entries are alphabetized within each category.

The Greeks: Achivi (Achaeans), Argives, Danai (Danaans), Grai, Pelasgae (Pelasgians).

Achaemenides: companion of Ulysses who was left behind on Sicily, land of the Cyclopes. Rescued by Aeneas, he helps the Trojans sail along the island's coast (Book 3).

Achilles: protagonist of the *Iliad* and slayer of Trojan Hector (Book 2).

The Atridae (sons of Atreus = **Agamemnon** and **Menelaus**): Agamemnon of Mycenae is leader of the Greek armies at Troy; his brother Menelaus is the husband of Helen (both are mentioned occasionally.)

Helen*: wife of Menelaus, abducted by Paris and cause of the Trojan War (Books 2 and 6)

Pyrrhus (also **Neoptolemus**): son of Achilles, and the Greek who slays Priam (Book 2).

Sinon*: Greek spy who allows himself to be captured by the Trojans in order to convince them to bring the wooden horse into Troy (beginning Book 2).

Tydides (Diomedes): son of Tydeus, one of the greatest Greek warriors at Troy; refuses to join the Latins when asked by Turnus to join him against the Trojans (Books 8 and 11).

Ulixes (also Ithacus; Odysseus, Ulysses): "many-sided" hero of the *Odyssey* who has the idea of the wooden horse (Book 2).

The Trojans: Aeneadae (men of Aeneas), Dardanidae (Dardanians), Phrygii (Phrygians), Teucri (Teucrians), Troes (Trojans).

The Trojan Royal Family

Andromache*: wife of Hector; she later marries the surviving Trojan Helenus.

Cassandra: daughter of Priam and Hecuba, cursed by Apollo with the gift of prophecy, but no one believes her. She foretells the fall of Troy (Book 2).

Hector: the son of Priam and Hecuba and husband of Andromache. The greatest of the Trojan warriors, he is slain by Achilles in a duel and his body is dragged around the walls of the city. He later appears to Aeneas in a vision with a warning to abandon Troy (Book 2).

Hecuba: wife of Priam and mother of Cassandra, Hector, and Paris (Book 2).

Polites: young son of Priam and Hecuba who is killed by Pyrrhus as Priam watches (Book 2).

Priam: noble king of Troy, husband of Hecuba, slain by Pyrrhus during the sack of Troy (Book 2).

Other Trojans playing a role

Acestes*: king of Sicily who is friendly to the Trojans and helps them during the time of indecision about the future. The Trojans who remain behind in Sicily after the torching of the ships name a city in his honor (Book 5).

Dares and **Entellus***: Trojan boxers at the funeral games for Anchises. Dares is the favorite, but Entellus wins (Book 5).

Helenus*: son of Priam, and a prophet, who becomes the second husband of Andromache. After the Trojan War, he settles in Epirus, where he helps Aeneas with directions and prophecies, including that of the white sow with thirty piglets (Book 3).

Laocoon: Trojan priest of Neptune who precipitates the bringing of the wooden horse into the city after he and his two sons are strangled by serpents in response to defiling the horse as a gift to Athena/Minerva (Book 2).

Nisus and **Euryalus***: young Trojans and best friends who help each other during a foot race at the games in Sicily (Book 5) and who later break out to summon Aeneas from Pallanteum. They pass through the Rutulian camp, killing many, but then they themselves are killed (Book 9).

Polydorus*: son of Priam, slain in Thrace by Polymnestor; he speaks to Aeneas from his burial mound and tells him to leave Thrace (Book 3).

Aeneas' Family

Aeneas (also **Anchisiades**, son of Anchises)*: son of Venus and Anchises, prince of Troy who settles in Italy. He is characterized as **pius** (*god-fearing, dutiful*) throughout the *Aeneid*.

Anchises*: Trojan father of Aeneas, who as an old man is carried on his son's shoulders from the burning city of Troy. He dies in Sicily before the Trojans are driven by a storm to Africa. He appears to Aeneas in the Underworld and narrates the "Parade of Heroes" that foretells the future of Rome (Books 2, 3, 5, and 6).

Creusa: Trojan wife of Aeneas and mother of Ascanius. She appears to Aeneas in a vision while they are escaping from the city and advises him to leave without her, as a new bride awaits him in Italy (end of Book 2).

Iulus/Ascanius*: Trojan son of Aeneas and Creusa, called Iulus after the fall of Troy (Ilion/Ilium). He assists in the action and is given military responsibilities when on Italian soil. Ascanius later founds Alba Longa (as the son of Aeneas and Lavinia?) Vergil uses the name Iulus for Ascanius in tribute to his literary patron Augustus, who belongs to the **gens Iulia (Julia)**.

Aeneadae

Achates: faithful (**fidus**) companion of Aeneas; his best appearance occurs in Book 1 when he accompanies Aeneas on a hunt and both are enveloped in a mist by Venus.

Cloanthus, Nisus and **Euryalus, Entellus** and **Dares, Eurytion**: Trojan participants in the funeral games on Sicily (Book 5).

Ilioneus: Trojan who leads the surviving Trojans after they are separated from Aeneas by the storm; he introduces the Trojans to Dido (Book 1) and he also addresses Latinus on behalf of the Trojans (Book 7).

Misenus: Trojan bugler who dies at the hands of an envious Triton. He is found dead on the shore and is buried by Aeneas after consulting the Sibyl (Book 6). The location in Italy is still known as *Capo Miseno*.

Nautes: elderly Trojan who advises that the Trojans who are unhappy should be left behind on Sicily (Book 5).

Palinurus*: skillful helmsman of Aeneas' ship who, on the journey from Sicily to Italy, drifts into sleep, falls overboard, and dies (Book 5). He meets Aeneas in the Underworld and describes what had happened (Book 6).

Carthaginians: Poeni (Phoenicians), Tyrii (people of Tyre)

Anna*: Dido's sister, who encourages Dido's love for Aeneas but is then duped into assisting in her suicide (Book 4).

Barce: the nurse whom Dido sends to summon Anna on the eve of her suicide (Book 4).

Dido (also **Elissa, Phoenissa, Sidonia**): queen and foundress of Carthage, a colony of Phoenician Tyre, husband of the deceased Sychaeus, and sister of Pygmalion. She falls in love with Aeneas and then, abandoned by him, kills herself (Book 4).

Iarbas*: an African prince from whom Dido obtains the land for Carthage and whom she later rejects as a suitor. His prayer to Jupiter leads to Mercury's warning to Aeneas that he leave Troy (Book 4).

Pygmalion*: brother of Dido; he murders her husband Sychaeus, as Dido herself describes in Book 1.

Sychaeus: husband of Dido, murdered by her greedy brother Pygmalion (Book 1).

Turnus and His Allies: the Rutuli or Rutulians; city Ardea

Camilla* (of the Volsci): heroic ally of Turnus, leader of the cavalry, and devotee of the goddess Diana; she is wounded in battle by the Etruscan Arruns and saved by Diana (Book 11).

Juturna*: sister of Turnus; she helps him when he drops his sword in battle, and rescues him from imminent death. She is also a water nymph of fountains, springs, and wells.

Lausus*: son of Mezentius, who faces Pallas in battle and eventually dies defending his father (Book 10).

Mezentius (also called Tyrrhenus = the Tuscan): renegade Etruscan king who becomes the ally of Turnus. He is slain by Aeneas after being gallantly defended by his son Lausus (Book 10).

Turnus*: leader of the Rutulians who desires marriage with Lavinia and pursues war with the newly-arrived Trojans. His sister is Juturna, the water nymph. Turnus first appears in Book 7. The *Aeneid* ends with his death at the hands of Aeneas in a duel (Book 12).

The Latins: Latini or Laurentes; city Laurentum

Amata*: queen of the Latins, wife of Latinus, and mother of Lavinia, who believes that Turnus is the appropriate and rightful husband for her daughter. She hangs herself when she hears (mistakenly) that Turnus has been killed (Books 7 and 12).

Latinus: king of the Latins, husband of Amata, and father of Lavinia. He believes that Aeneas is the "foreigner" whom Lavinia is prophesied to marry (Book 7).

Lavinia: Latin daughter of Latinus and Amata and pawn in the marriage-brokering of the latter half of the *Aeneid.* She is the "foreign bride" alluded to in the prophetic speeches of Creusa (Book 2) and the Sibyl (Book 6) and plays Helen to Aeneas' Paris. She eventually marries Aeneas, who founds Lavinium in her name.

Silvia: it was her pet deer that Allecto causes Anchises to slay and thus advance hostilities between the Latins and the Trojans (Book 7).

Aeneas' Allies: the Arcades or Arcadians; city Pallanteum

Evander*: Arcadian king of Pallanteum who sends his son Pallas with an armed force to assist Aeneas against the Latins (Books 8, 10, and 11).

Pallas*: young son of Evander, who puts him in the service of Aeneas. Pallas is killed in a pathetic duel with Turnus, who takes from him the swordbelt that eventually leads to Turnus' own death at the hands of Aeneas. (See Book 10 for Pallas).

Tarchon: an Etruscan ally of Aeneas who offers to make him chief of the Etruscans. Tarchon is instrumental in the battle at the ships and in the field (Book 10).

Places

Italy: Italia; also Ausonia, Hesperia, Lavinian shores, Oenotrian land, Saturnian land.

Alba Longa: town, southeast of Rome, founded by Ascanius.

Cumae: site of the Sibyl, oracle of Apollo, upcoast from the Bay of Naples.

Latium: the region of west-central Italy in which the Latins ruled and, ultimately, Rome was founded.

Laurent(i)um: city of Latinus and the Latins; famous later as the location of Pliny's seaside villa.

Lavinium: settlement founded by Aeneas and named after his wife, Lavinia.

Mt. Aetna: still-active volcano on the northeast coast of Sicily, thought to be the home of Vulcan and his forge.

Pallanteum: home-city of Evander and the Arcadians and future site of Rome.

Sicily (or Trinacria): the island to the southeast of the boot of Italy that figures heavily into the journey of Aeneas to Italy (Books 3 and 5).

Thybris (Tiber River): the river that runs northeast to southwest through Rome, ending at Ostia. The waterway much travelled by the Trojans and Arcadians during the hostilities.

Asia Minor

Mt. Ida: also the name of a mountain in Crete, this mountain near Troy was a refuge for the fleeing Trojans after Troy was sacked.

Phrygia: area east of Troy in the west-central or Anatolian highland of Asia Minor (Turkey).

Tenedos: the island off the northwest coast of Turkey behind which the Greek ships hid.

Troia (Greek Ilion, Latin Ilium or Pergamum, the citadel): city-state in western Anatolia, a seaport and gateway to the Black Sea in ancient times. Famous for its walls, horses, and windy location. Site of the legendary conflict between the Greeks and the Trojans during the Bronze Age (12th century B.C.), later celebrated in the *Iliad* and the *Odyssey* by Homer.

Xanthus and **Simois Rivers**: rivers near Troy that served as battle sites. Equated to the Tiber in Sibyl's speech to Aeneas in Book 6.

Greece

Argos: second-oldest city of Greece, close to Mycenae in the Peloponnesus. Greeks in the *Aeneid* were generically referred to as "Argives."

Mycenae: walled city of the "Lion Gate" in the northeast portion of the Peloponnese, which was ruled by Agamemnon, commander-in-chief of the Greek forces at Troy. This city was the dominant Greek city-state during the Late Bronze Age and produced both an entire culture (the Mycenaean = My-sin-ee-an) and the first language considered Greek. Mycenae is mentioned periodically in the *Aeneid*, but is often confused with Argos.

Strophades Islands*: small islands off the northwest coast of the Greek Peloponnese and home of the Harpies.

Africa (also known as Libya)

Carthage (Karthago, also Byrsa): north African colony of the Phoenician cities of Tyre and Sidon founded by Dido (Elissa) in the 9th century B.C. Antagonist of Rome during the historical Punic Wars.

Numidia: a Berber kingdom in present-day Algeria, governed by Iarbas, benefactor and suitor of Dido.

Phoenicia

Tyre and **Sidon**: major coastal Phoenician cities of what is now Lebanon. Often substituted for each other by Vergil.

The Underworld (also referred to as Avernus, Dis, Elysium, Erebus, or Tartarus)

Rivers: Acheron (river of lamentation), Cocytus (river of woe), Lethe (river of forgetfulness), Phlegethon (river of fire), Styx (river of unbroken divine oaths). The Acheron and Styx are interchangeable in the *Aeneid.*

Cerberus: three-headed dog who guards the portals of the Underworld (Book 6, lines 417–25).

Charon: ferryman of souls across the river Styx (or Acheron) (Book 6, lines 298–330).

Deities

Main Players

Juno (also Saturnia): wife and brother of Jupiter and queen of the gods. She is Aeneas' nemesis throughout the *Aeneid* for reasons outlined in Book 1.

Jupiter/Jove (also Saturnius): often addressed as father (**genitor**), king of the gods and husband/brother of Juno. He appears periodically in the *Aeneid*: in Book 1, he gives a long speech to Venus about the future history of the Trojans; in Book 4, he intervenes in the events at Carthage; and in Book 12, he finally brings Juno under control.

Phoebus (Apollo): with respect to the events of the *Aeneid*, Apollo is most important as god of prophecy, via the Sibyl Deiphobe. In Book 6, Aeneas' promise to build what is to become the Augustan temple of Apollo enables him to secure the cooperation of the god with regard to fulfilling his father Anchises' request to meet him in the Underworld.

Venus (also Cytherea): goddess of love and beauty, mother of Aeneas, and, with Mars, parent of Rome. Venus protects the interests of her son and the Trojans throughout the *Aeneid*, in disguise (as a huntress), through her son Cupid (who substitutes for Ascanius), and as a means to thwart Juno's attempts to destroy Aeneas.

Supporting Actors

Aeolus: ruler of the winds who, at Juno's insistence, allows them to escape in order to create the storm which causes the detour of Aeneas into Dido's kingdom in north Africa.

Allecto*: "she who does not rest" is one of the Furies (for which, see below). Juno sends Allecto to stir up trouble in a final attempt to control or influence Aeneas' destiny by instigating Turnus' anger at the prospect of losing Lavinia to him (Book 7).

Mercury (son of Maia; Cyllenius): In Book 4, Mercury serves several times as Jupiter's emissary to Aeneas, prompted first by Venus and then by Iarbas. On Jove's behalf, Mercury warns Aeneas to leave Carthage.

Neptune: god of the sea, Neptune calms the winds (see the famous orator simile in Book 1) so that Aeneas can continue his journey.

Pallas Athena (Minerva, Tritonia): Minerva's main scene in the *Aeneid* is her association with the wooden horse (she is said to have inspired Ulysses with the whole idea). Vergil indicates that Diomedes and Ulysses had stolen the Palladium, an ancient and sacred wooden image of Pallas (Athena/ Minerva), which had the city of Troy under its protection (see Sinon's speech in Book 2). More common tradition held that Aeneas rescued the statue from Troy and brought it to Italy, where it was known as the Penates.

Vulcan: the god of fire is spotlighted in Book 8, where he is asked by his wife Venus to make armor and weapons for her son Aeneas in anticipation of his confrontation with Turnus. Vulcan complies, designing a wonderful shield upon which are engraved high-points of Roman history, including Augustus' victory over Antony and Cleopatra at the Battle of Actium.

Bit Parts

Aquilo, Auster, Eurus, Zephyrus: personifications of various winds (north, south, east, west). **Notus** is another name for the south wind.

Atlas: Titan turned into a mountain by Perseus and mentioned in a wonderfully descriptive passage in Book 4 (lines 246–253) while Mercury is flying to Carthage.

Aurora: goddess of the dawn; Greek Eos.

Cacus*: fire-breathing giant and son of Vulcan. He lived in a cave on the Aventine Hill, on the future site of Rome, and consumed human flesh. He was overcome by Hercules, in whose honor a feast is given by King Evander. The story is told in Book 8 (lines 184–279) after Aeneas has arrived in Pallanteum.

Celaeno: a Harpy, encountered on the Strophades Islands. She gave Aeneas prophecies to assist him on his journey.

Cupid*: son of Venus, Cupid was asked by his mother to impersonate Ascanius with the purpose of making Dido fall in love with Aeneas (end of Book 2).

Cybele: the great Mother of the Gods (*Magna Mater*) or Earth Mother, Cybele was worshipped by Eastern cultures. In Book 2, Cybele keeps Creusa in Troy. As the first to teach men how to fortify cities, she is depicted as Rome personified, wearing a crown of turrets as she rides in a chariot pulled by lions (Book 6, lines 784–787).

Diana: the goddess of nature and sister of Apollo, Diana appears several times in the *Aeneid*. In a simile in Book 1, Dido is compared to Diana in stately array. She also appears in Book 11, when she tries to protect Camilla during the fighting.

Faunus: father of Latinus and grandson of Saturn, associated with the Greek Pan, and patron god of agriculture and livestock. He appears throughout Book 7, when Aeneas is being introduced to the legends and traditions of Latium.

The Furies (also known as the **Dirae**, "The Terrible Ones" or, in Greek, *Erinyes*, "The Angry Ones"): three goddesses of justice (or vengeance), who are Allecto, Megaera, and Tisiphone. They are mentioned generically in Books 4, 8, and 12. See also **Allecto.**

Harpies*: ugly winged bird-women who were vicious and cruel and lived on the Strophades; they stole food from Phineus in the *Odyssey* (Book 3). See also **Strophades.**

Hercules*: cult-hero of Evander's city of Pallanteum, because he slays Cacus, the flesh-eating giant (see **Cacus**). The presence of Hercules in Latium was extensive (cf. the early round temple still standing near the Tiber). In Book 10, Evander's son Pallas calls upon Hercules to assist him in his confrontation with Turnus, but the hero is "warned off" by Jupiter.

Iris*: messenger goddess, who mostly assists Juno in the *Aeneid*: she cuts a lock of Dido's hair to release her soul (Book 4) and later rouses the Trojan women to burn the ships in Sicily (Book 5) and Turnus to attempt to burn the Trojan ships in Italy (Book 9).

The Parcae (The Fates): three sisters, Clotho (who spins the thread of life), Lachesis (who measures the thread), and Atropos (who cuts the thread at the allotted end of one's life). (See Book 1, line 22.)

Tiberinus: god of the Tiber River who assists Aeneas several times, including appearing to him in a vision in which he encourages Aeneas that he is, indeed, in the promised land because the white sow and thirty piglets are close by (Book 8).

Practice Background Questions[81]

1. The concept of **fides,** trustworthiness or honesty, is essential to all personal relationships in Roman culture. Select one of the relationships from Group A and one from Group B listed below and, in a short essay, discuss whether the relationship does or does not possess this quality.

Group A	Group B
Anchises and Aeneas	Dido and Anna
Aeneas and Evander	Juturna and Turnus
Venus and Aeneas	

2. Omens, oracles, prophecies, and prodigies abound in the *Aeneid*. Among these are dream-visions, in which a mortal or an immortal appears to Aeneas with some direct or indirect information about what is to happen next. An oracle is an oral prediction by a god or a god's representative, usually in a temple or shrine. Choose one character from Group A, each of which appears to Aeneas in a dream-vision and one from Group B, each of which serves as giver of an oracle. In a short essay, discuss the effect that one dream-vision and one oracle has on Aeneas' future.

Dream-Vision	Oracle
Anchises	Apollo at Delos
Penates	Faunus
Tiberinus	Helenus

3. Because of the roles of Juno and Dido, it has been observed that women are portrayed in the *Aeneid* as subordinates and that they are continually subject to the authority of men. In a short essay, discuss whether you agree or disagree with this statement, choosing one character from Group A and one from Group B to illustrate your points.

Group A	Group B
Amata	Creusa
Camilla	Hecuba
Cassandra	Juturna

4. Strictly speaking, ecphrasis is a rhetorical device used to describe one work of art by means of another, e.g., poetry. Select two of the following examples of ecphrasis from the *Aeneid* and write a short essay in which you discuss the significance of the artwork in its context.

Mural of the temple of Juno at Carthage (Book 2)
Bronze doors of the temple of Apollo at Cumae (Book 6)
Shield of Aeneas (Book 8)

5. In the *Aeneid,* minor deities sometimes have important, if not major, roles. In a short essay, discuss the role played by each of the following, choosing one deity from Group A and one from Group B.

Group A	Group B
Allecto	Iris
Cupid	Mercury
Diana	Tiberinus, god of the Tiber river

Endnotes

[77] For the complete Vergil syllabus, see Chapter 1.

[78] Again, the format is that found on the actual Exam; the question is the author's. For topics covered in background questions on recent Exams, see the list later in this chapter.

[79] The scoring of essays is covered in the previous chapter.

[80] Here are the mean scores (averages) for each question on the 2009 and 2005 AP Latin: Vergil Exams. Remember that the point total for translation questions was changed from 9 points to 18 points in 2008.

	2008	2005
1st Translation	4.95 out of 18 (28%)	4.43 out of 9 (49%)
2nd Translation	7.15 out of 18 (40%)	3.03 out of 9 (34%)
Long Essay	3.19 out of 6 (53%)	3.34 out of 6 (56%)
Short Essay	2.85 out of 6 (48%)	3.28 out of 6 (55%)
Background Question	3.31 out of 6 (55%)	3.33 out of 6 (56%)

The first set of statistics is found in the Chief Reader's annual report for the 2008 Exam, and the second set is found in the *AP Latin Teacher's Guide*. For more on scoring, see Chapter 11.

[81] For review of the *Aeneid* as a whole, see Chapter 10.

Chapter 8

Techniques of Poetic Analysis: Figures of Speech

Figures of speech (also referred to as poetic techniques or rhetorical devices) present a way of saying something in a manner that is not obvious or ordinary. They allow writers to express their inner voices creatively. The Acorn book lists 34 figures of speech to be mastered for the AP Latin Exam. These are tested explicitly in context on the multiple-choice section, as well as implicitly in the essay questions on the free-response section that ask for analysis of Vergil's style.[82] Based upon information gathered from past AP Latin Exams, the figures of speech that are most important for mastery include asyndeton, anaphora, chiasmus, hendiadys, litotes, metaphor, and synchysis.[83] Also of considerable importance are ellipsis, irony, metonymy, and simile, all of which appear in the *Aeneid*. This information is provided not to suggest that these are the only figures of speech worth knowing, but to suggest that, for the Vergil Exam, some figures are more important than others. For instance, aposiopesis appears only once in the lines required for the Exam, and praeteritio and prosopopoeia, which are essentially Ciceronian figures, rarely, if ever.

Here is the list of figures to be mastered for the AP Latin Exam, all of which will be defined in this chapter, with examples in both English and Latin. Additional figures considered important for poetic analysis are also provided later in this chapter. It is important to re-state here that analysis of the use of figures of speech in essay questions should be a means to an end and not an end in itself (see Chapter 7). The author recalls with a chuckle the classroom scene from the film *Dead Poet's Society* in which Mr. Keating (Robin Williams) requires his students to rip out of their textbooks the introduction, which defines poetry and calculates the success of a poem using graphs and formulas. "We're not laying pipe," he remarks. Although figures of speech enhance a writer's style, they should not be considered definitive, and should be used with discretion in your responses on essay questions. We have covered this a bit in the discussion on writing essays in Chapter 6, but the discussion will continue in this chapter. Here is the list of figures required for the AP Latin Exam:[84]

allegory	enjambment	onomatopoeia	simile
alliteration	hendiadys	oxymoron	synchysis
anaphora	hyperbaton	personification	synecdoche
aposiopesis	hyperbole	pleonasm	tmesis
apostrophe	hysteron proteron	polyptoton	transferred epithet
asyndeton	irony	polysyndeton	tricolon crescens
chiasmus	litotes	praeteritio	zeugma
ecphrasis	metaphor	prolepsis	
ellipsis	metonymy	prosopopoeia	

In your review of figures of speech, pay particular attention to those figures that have similar functions or that are easily confused with another figure, such as apostrophe and personification, chiasmus and synchysis, hendiadys and zeugma, metonymy and synecdoche, and metaphor and simile. It is unlikely, however, that you will be asked to distinguish between two easily-confused figures of speech, such as metonymy and synecdoche, in the same question. Of those figures and other devices not required for the Exam but helpful to know in order to create a successful critical analysis of (poetic) style, we will also review the following: anastrophe, archaism, assonance, diminutive, euphemism, foreshadowing, gapping (condensation), golden line, Grecism (Hellenism), juxtaposition, parallelism, poetic plural, prime position, rhetorical question, and sound and word play.[85]

As over 200 figures of speech have been recognized, it is best not to take any classification of function as absolute. Many figures can perform several functions simultaneously, e.g., hyperbaton (framing) and chiasmus: **speluncam Dido dux et Troianus eandem** (Dido and Aeneas are together inside the same cave, *Aeneid* 4.124), or can achieve heightened effectiveness in conjunction with another figure, e.g., the sound effects of the simile of the sacrifice of the bull in **qualis mugitus, fugit cum saucius aram / taurus et incertam excussit cervice securim** (*Aeneid* 2.223–224), or the alliteration and onomatopoeia of the words **fit sonitus spumante salo,** describing the sound of the sea while suggesting the sound of the snakes as they slither along (*Aeneid* 2.209). The pace of the Latin may be speeded up through the use of asyndeton and ellipsis, or slowed down through the use of polysyndeton, and so forth. Vergil favors combining asyndeton and anaphora, such as in this example describing the sudden physical changes taking place in the Sibyl when permeated by the god Apollo: **Cui talia fanti / ante fores subito non vultus, non color unus, non comptae mansere comae** (*Aeneid* 6.46–48). Sometimes, the poet throws in condensation (gapping) and ellipsis for good measure: **Cui talia fanti / ante fores subito non vultus (mansit), non color unus (mansit), non comptae mansere comae**. (If you do not recognize the figures mentioned in this paragraph, you will be able to do so after reading this chapter.) There are two important things to remember about figures of speech:

1) a figure of speech is important only because of the effect that the figure has on the meaning of what is being expressed;

2) the listing and defining of figures of speech is never, by itself, an efficient or effective way to produce a style analysis of a passage of Latin. Consider only those that are obvious.

As mentioned, some students believe that searching through a Latin passage for figures of speech is like collecting Easter eggs. The more you have, the better off you'll be. Such an approach never addresses the explicit analysis called for in a free-response essay question. Recognition and citation of a few relevant figures, with explanation of their effect on the context in which they are found, is certainly useful support for your analysis, but this will never substitute for a thoughtful and well-focused essay.

Based upon inferences from comments made in the Chief Reader's reports on recent Exams, it is best to translate a figure of speech as literally as possible. For ambiguous figures of speech, such as transferred epithet, it is probably best to produce a translation that is grammatically correct. For instance, the phrase **mare velivolum** (*Aeneid* 1.224) is translated literally as *sail-flying sea*, although it is actually the ships and not the sea that are *sail-flying*. In the Chief Reader's report on the 2008 Vergil Exam, the translation of **rex omnipotentis Olympi** (*Aeneid* 12.791) as "omnipotent king of Olympus" was deemed incorrect.[86] If you are uncertain about how to handle a particular figure of speech in your essay, translate it literally and then include a brief explanatory comment in parentheses or a footnote.

All the figures of speech required for the exam, as well as the others mentioned in this introduction, are reviewed below and are then followed by practice activities and directions to resources for further practice. For additional discussion on how these devices may be used in an analysis of style on the free-response section of the exam, see the analysis of the sample short essay question in Chapter 6 and the sample passage analysis provided below. See also the answers to the Practice Exam questions at the end of this book.

Here is a sample question on figures of speech of the type that might appear on the multiple-choice section.[87]

Question:

1. The words <u>nec, quid Hymen, quid Amor, quid sint conubia, curat</u> (line 1) contain an example of
   (A) litotes
   (B) apostrophe
   (C) anaphora
   (D) litotes

Answer: (C) anaphora

Glossary of Figures Required for the AP Latin Exam

The first examples of each figure of speech are underlined, to assist you in your recognition of the figure and in your understanding of its effects. Practice identifying the figure on your own in the remaining examples. Some entries include practice activities, more of which will be provided after this section. Additional information is included to assist you in obtaining mastery, including examples from an author or authors besides Vergil and examples of those figures which are often confused with the figure under discussion. All references are to the *Aeneid,* unless noted otherwise.

- **allegory** (adj., allegorical): An extended metaphor. A narrative in which abstract ideas figure as circumstances or persons.

  Effects: adds interest, teaches a moral lesson.

  Latin: The personification of **Fama** (Rumor) in 4.173–197 and 655–656.

- **alliteration**: repetition of the same consonantal sound, usually at the beginning of two or more successive words, e.g., **magno cum murmure montis** (1.55). The term **consonance** is also used to describe alliteration. **Alliteration** is often combined with **asyndeton**. See also **assonance** and **word play**.

  Effects: emphasizes, enlivens.

  English: Peter Piper picked a peck of pickled peppers.

  Let us go forth to lead the land we love. (John F. Kennedy)

  Latin: **Veni, vidi, vici.** (Emphatic; Julius Caesar)

  Hic aliud maius miseris multoque tremendum. (Awesome, ominous; 2.19.)

  Technically, these next examples are **consonance**, i.e., repetition of internal consonants, but, in Latin, it is acceptable to characterize them as **alliteration**. By the way, the repetition of an internal -m- sound in Latin is suggestive of the solemn and serious, and it is often used in descriptions of sorrow or death. See also **word play**, in the second section of this glossary.

  Nimborumque facis tempestatumque potentem. (Aeolus is king of the winds. 1.80)

  Praesentemque viris intentant omnia mortem. (The storm brings death. 1.91)

  Taurus et incertam excussit cervice securim. (The sound of cutting or chopping during the sacrifice of a bull. 2.224.)

  Collocat . . . colla . . . mollibus. (Rhyme. Ovid, *Metamorphoses* 10.267–69; cf. 280, 285)

  Compare **assonance**: **paucis, si tibi di favent, diebus.** (Catullus, 13.2) Compare **onomatopoeia**: **namque mei nuper Lethaeo in gurgite fratris.** (A single word, suggesting the sound of gurgling water. Catullus, 65.5)

- **anaphora**: repetition of a word, usually at the beginning of successive phrases, clauses, or lines. Anaphora, which appears frequently in Vergil, is often accompanied by **asyndeton**.

  Effect: demands attention, emphasizes.

  English: Blessed are the poor in spirit . . . / Blessed are the meek . . . / Blessed are they who mourn. . . . (Beatitudes, *Gospel of Saint Matthew*)

  We shall not flag or fail. We shall go on to the end. We shall fight in France, we shall fight on the seas and oceans . . . we shall never surrender. (Winston Churchill)

Latin: **Tu mihi quodcumque hoc regni, tu sceptra Iovemque / concilias, tu das epulis accumbere divum.** (Note the asyndeton here and in the examples following; 1.78–79.)

Ut spolia, ut currus, utque ipsum corpus amici . . . conspexit. (1.486–487)

Hic Dolopum manus, hic saevus tendebat Achilles; / classibus hic locus, hic acie certare solebant. (2.29–30)

Domum, si forte pedem, si forte tulisset, me refero. (2.756)

Dein mille altera, dein secunda centum, / deinde usque altera mille, deinde centum. (Catullus, 5. 8–9)

With **asyndeton**: **nostra sunt tropaea, nostra monumenta, nostri triumphi.** (Cicero, *Pro Archia Poeta* 21)

Note: Most repeated words or phrases, while technically not anaphora, are nonetheless emphatic in Latin, e.g., **iam iamque** (2.530 and 12.940), **iterum iterumque** (2.770), and **Pallas te hoc vulnere, Pallas immolat**. (Note also the juxtaposition and condensation in this dramatic line, 12.948.)

- **aposiopesis**: an abrupt break in a sentence, wherein the speaker is seemingly overwhelmed with anger, fear, excitement, or some other excessive emotion. An unfinished thought, the implied meaning of which is usually clear. Being at a loss for words. The only example appearing in the syllabus is provided here below.

Effect: creates dramatic energy

English: He said he realized he was wro . . . I stopped mid-word, awestruck.

His behavior was . . . but I blush to mention that.

Oh, go to . . . !

Latin: **Quos ego ---! sed motos praestat componere fluctus.** (Neptune, 1.135)

Which I – but it is better to calm the troubled waters.

Compare **ellipsis**: **Sic notus (est) Ulixes?** (2.44)

- **apostrophe**: a "turning away" from one to address another; often used to address an absent personified object or a person. Apostrophe differs from **personification** in that it addresses an object directly, rather than merely describing it in human terms. Apostrophe appears frequently in Vergil.

Effects: expresses deep emotion and pathos; draws the reader into the situation

English: For Brutus, as you know, was Caesar's angel.

Judge, O you gods, how dearly Caesar loved him. (Shakespeare, *Julius Caesar*)

Alas, poor Yorick, I knew him, Horatio! (Shakespeare, *Hamlet*)

Latin: **O patria, O divum domus Ilium!** (2.241)

Troiaque nunc staret, Priamique arx alta maneres. (2.56)

Improbe Amor, quid non mortalia pectora cogis! (4.412)

Locate the apostrophe in each example below.

Ante, pudor, quam te violo aut tua iura resolvo. (4.27)

Dulces exuviae, dum fata deusque sinebat. (4.651)

Tu quoque magnam / partem opere in tanto . . . , Icare, haberes. (6.30)

Heu pietas, heu prisca fides. (6.878)

O dolor atque decus magnum rediture parenti. (10.507)

Invide, dicebant, paries, quid amantibus obstas? (Ovid, *Metamorphoses* 4.73)

Compare **personification**: **et Claros et Tenedos Patareaque regia servit.** (Apollo's cult sites "serve" him as slaves do a master. Ovid, *Metamorphoses*, 1.516.)

- **asyndeton:** the omission of connectors (**et, nec, vel,** etc.) in a closely related series. Creates a rapid statement of ideas. Common in Vergil when combined with **anaphora**. See also **tricolon crescens** and, in the second section, **gapping** and **parallelism**.

Effects: accelerates the words or actions; expresses non-stop action or violence.

English: But in a larger sense, we cannot dedicate, we cannot consecrate, we cannot hallow this ground. (Abraham Lincoln)

We shall pay any price, bear any burden, meet any hardships, support any friend, oppose any foe, to assure the survival and the success of liberty. (John F. Kennedy)

Latin: **Saevus ubi Aeacidae telo iacet Hector, ubi ingens / Sarpedon, ubi tot Simois correpta sub undis / scuta virum.** (Note the anaphora here and in the following examples. 1.99–100.)

hic Dolopum manus, hic saevus tendebat Achilles; / classibus hic locus, hic acie certare solebant. (2.29–30)

Unus natorum Priami, per tela, per hostes . . . fugit. (2.527–528)

Quotiens . . . nox operit terras, quotiens astra ignea surgunt . . . . (Note the parallel phrasing. 4.352)

I, sequere Italiam ventis, pete regna per undas. (4.381)

Per ego has lacrimas dextramque tuam te. . . , per conubia nostra, per inceptos hymenaeos . . . . (Note the anaphora and parallel phrasing. 4.314–316.)

Digna indigna pati. (Adjectives may be paired in asyndeton. 12.811; cf.12.930.)

Chartae regiae, novi libri, novi umbilici, lora rubra, membranae. (Catullus, 22.5–7)

Compare **polysyndeton**: **haec a te dictaque factaque sunt.** (Catullus, 76.8)

- **chiasmus** (Greek for "crossing," adj. chiastic): arrangement of two sets or pairs of corresponding or syntactically parallel words in opposite or reverse order.[88] Consider this line from a love poem of Horace:

  Cervicem roseam cerea / . . . laudas bracchia. (Horace, *Odes* 1.13.2–3). **Cervicem roseam** and **cerea . . . bracchia** are syntactically parallel, i.e., they are both direct objects of **laudas**. The order of the words, however, in the second noun-adjective pair is reversed from the first, that is, instead of the parallel phrasing **Cervicem roseam bracchia cerea**, we have **Cervicem roseam cerea bracchia**. The term **chiasmus** comes from the shape of the Greek letter chi (X), which applies to the criss-crossing of the words in the figure, e.g.,

  Cervicem **roseam** noun adjective
  X or X
  cerea **bracchia** adjective noun

  This figure usually consists of nouns and adjectives, in the pattern **A-a-b-B**, or **AabB**, e.g., noun – adjective – adjective – noun, often rendered as ABBA (= AB-BA, not A-BB-A). (In the first example, capital letters are used for nouns, lower case for adjectives.) In a broader sense, the word order of an example such as **vasto rex Aeolus antro** may be considered chiastic, but the pairing isn't the same, i.e., **vasto** does not go with **rex**, nor does **Aeolus** with **antro**. This is an example of **hyperbaton**, or **framing**, for which, see below. See also **synchysis** and **golden line**.

  Effects: balances, contrasts, embraces, creates a word picture.

  English: The cat jumped in, out jumped the mouse.

  Fair is foul, and foul is fair. (Shakespeare, *Macbeth*)

  Renown'd for conquest, and in council skill'd. (Joseph Addison)

  I am Sam, Sam I am. (Dr. Seuss, Theodor Geisel)

  Latin: There are several different ways to pattern the words in **chiasmus**, the most common of which is **AabB**, or noun – adj. – adj. - noun (see above). The cases or tenses of the words in chiasmus are not relevant, as long as the words in each pair correspond or are parallel as parts of speech. The endings may sometimes create their own chiasmus, as in the first example below (acc. – abl. – abl. – acc.):

  A a b B
  (Aeneas) Ilionea petit dextra laevaque Serestum. (1.611)

A a b B
Gravedo frigida et frequens tussis. (Catullus 44.13)

Fors ignara dedit, sed saeva Cupidinis ira. (Ovid, *Metamorphoses* 1.453)

An example of **aABb**, modifier – noun – noun – modifier:

a A B b
Fracti bello fatisque repulsi. (2.13)

A B a b
Compare **synchysis**: **paries domui communis utrique.** (Note how the walls of the houses of Pyramus and Thisbe interlock. Ovid, *Metamorphoses* 1.66)

a b B A
Compare **hyperbaton**: **Eque sagittifera prompsit duo tela pharetra**. (Note how the arrangement of the words places the arrows (**tela**) in the quiver. Ovid, *Metamorphoses* 1.468)

a b V A B
Compare **golden line**: **obviaque adversas vibrabant flamina vestes.** (Ovid, *Metamorphoses* 1.528–9)

- **ecphrasis:** a digression vividly describing a place, object, or event. In epic poetry, this device creates transition to a new scene.

Effect: adds vividness, interest.

Latin: See 1.159–70 for the elaborate description of the harbor into which Aeneas' fleet limps after the storm, the murals in the temple of Juno at Carthage (Book 4.456ff.), the description of the doors of the temple of Apollo at Cumae (Book 6.20–33), or the description of Aeneas' shield in Book 8.626–728.

- **ellipsis:** omission of an easily understood or assumed word in order to avoid repetition, to secure rapidity of narration, or to accommodate the requirements of meter. Ellipsis differs from **gapping** in that the understood word is often a form of **esse**, but it can also be a form of the verb **ago, dico, facio, inquit,** or **loquor**.

Effects: confusion, economy, acceleration of the narrative; creates variety of style.

English: Ellipsis points are used in questions throughout the AP Latin Exam, e.g., "In lines 3–4 (Melpomene . . . dedit) . . . ."

Latin: **Tantae animis caelestibus irae?** (= **[Suntne] tantae animis caelestibus irae?** 1.11)

Aeolus haec contra. (= **Aeolus haec contra [dixit]**, 1.76)

Hic pietatis honos? (= **Hic pietatis honos [est]?** 1.253).

Now try these.

Hic amor, haec patria est. (4.347)

Nusquam tuta fides. (4.373)

Et mi genus ab Iove summo. (6.123)

Facilis descensus Averno. (6.126)

Sic pater Anchises. (6.854)

Quis, pater, ille, virum qui sic comitatur euntem? (6.863)

Vovit . . . electissima pessimi poetae / scripta tardipedi deo daturam. (= **Vovit . . . electissima pessimi poetae / scripta tardipedi deo daturam [esse]**, Catullus, 36.6–7)

- **enjambment** (also spelled **enjambement**): in verse, the building of suspense by postponing to the next line a significant word or words related to the previous line. A run-on line. Common in Vergil.

  Effect: develops suspense and creates surprise.

  English: That honourable grief lodged here which burns
  Worse than tears drown. (Shakespeare, *The Winter's Tale*)

  All in the valley of death
  rode the six hundred. (Tennyson)

  Latin: **Litora – multum ille et terris iactatus et alto**
  <u>vi superum</u>. (1.3–4)

  Exstinctus pudor et, qua sola sidera adibam,
  fama prior. (4.322–323)

  Pasiphae mixtumque genus prolesque biformis
  Minotaurus inest. (6.25–26)

  Arcades, haec, inquit, memores mea dicta referte
  Evandro. (10.491–492)

  Venator in campis nivalis
  Haemoniae, daret ut catenis
  fatale monstrum. (Horace, *Odes* 1.37.20–21)

  Da mihi perpetua, genitor carissime, dixit,
  virginitate frui. (Ovid, *Metamorphoses* 1.486–87)

- **hendiadys**: the use of two nouns connected by a conjunction and having the meaning of a single modified noun, e.g., **<u>vulgus et multitudo</u>**, *the rabble and mob* (= the common herd) and **<u>vi et armis</u>**, *by force and by arms* (= by force of arms). Often known as "two for one." Common in Vergil.

  Effect: amplifies, adds force.

  English: He arrived despite the <u>rain and weather</u>. (= He arrived despite the <u>rainy weather</u>.)

  It is nice and cool today! (= nicely cool)

  Latin: **Hoc metuens, <u>molemque et montes</u> insuper altos** (= **molem montium**, a mass of mountains. 1.61).

Dirae <u>ferro et compagibus artis</u> / claudentur Belli portae. (Here, the gates are closed by iron and close-fitting joints, instead of close-fitting iron joints. 1.293–2944. See also **hysteron proteron** and **zeugma**.)

<u>Barbarico</u> postes <u>auro spoliisque</u> superbi. (= **spoliis barbarici auri**, the doorposts are not fancy *with foreign gold and with spoils*, but are fancy *with the spoils of foreign gold.* 2.504)

Paulum <u>lacrimis et mente</u> morata / incubuitque toro. (= **misera memoria**, in unhappy recollection. 4.649–650)

Da ... fortunam atque viam. (= **fortunatam viam**. 10.421–422)

Saevi monimenta doloris exuviasque hausit. (Aeneas does not really see two different things here, **monimenta doloris** and **exuvias**, but only the swordbelt, **exuvias**. 12.945–946)

Non belle uteris in ioco atque vino (= **in ebrioso ioco**, in drunken revelry. Catullus, 12.2)

Quod si, ut suspicor, hoc novum ac repertum (= **novissime repertum**, newly discovered. Catullus, 14a.8)

Tecum Philippos et celerem fugam / sensi. (Horace experienced with Pompey the swift rout at Philippi. Horace, *Odes* 2.7.9–10)

Mille domos adiere locum requiemque petentes. (= **locum requietis**, place of rest. Ovid, *Metamorphoses* 8.628)

In iudiciis periculisque. (= **in iudiciorum periculis**. Cicero, *Pro Archia Poeta* 3)

Compare **zeugma**: **crudeles <u>aras</u> traiectaque <u>pectora</u> ferro <u>nudavit</u>.** (*He <u>laid bare</u> the cruel <u>altars</u> and <u>his breast</u> pierced with steel,* describing Sychaeus' death. 1.355–356)

- **hyperbaton** (literally, "stepping over"): a significant departure from normal word order, sometimes referred to in English as **anastrophe** (for which, see below). **Hyperbaton** is the separation of words, most commonly an adjective from its noun, that logically belong together. The first word, the adjective, is placed in an emphatic position. One scholar calls this "verbal leapfrogging." **Hyperbaton** enables the writer to place words in a **framing** or bracketing position for emphasis or sound, rather than grammar. Words can actually surround objects, which may be said to be "embedded," e.g., **<u>vasto</u> rex Aeolus <u>antro</u>** (Aeolus, king of the winds, is inside his cave, 1.52). **Hyperbaton** is important in the formation of **chiasmus, synchysis**, or **golden line**.

Effects: emphasizes the first of the separated words; creates images and word play.

English: Glistens the dew upon the morning grass.

Why should their liberty than ours be more? (Shakespeare, *Comedy of Errors*)

Size matters not! Judge me by my size, do you? (Yoda, *The Empire Strikes Back*

Latin: **Tantae animis caelestibus irae?** (1.11)

Speluncam Dido dux et Troianus eandem. (Dido and Aeneas are together in the same cave. 4.124.)

Gelidus . . . per dura cucurrit / ossa tremor. (6.54–55)

Totum ut te faciant, Fabulle, nasum. (The size of Fabullus' would-be nose is exaggerated by the distance between **totum** and **nasum**. Note the anastrophe of **totum** and **ut**. Catullus, 13.14)

Aequam memento rebus in arduis / servare mentem. (The arduous circumstances are exaggerated by the long separation of **Aequam** from **mentem**. Horace, *Odes* 2.3.1–2)

Innumeris tumidum Pythona sagittis. (Apollo slays the Python with innumerable arrows. Ovid, *Metamophoses* 1.460)

Ad populi Romani gloriam laudemque celebrandam. (Cicero, *Pro Archia Poeta* 19)

Now you find the framing in the examples below. Think about what effect this figure has on the meaning of each.

Frigidus Arcadibus coit in praecordia sanguis (10.452)

Ille rapit calidum frustra de vulnere telum. (10.486)

Non cursu, saevis certandum est comminus armis. (12.890)

Genua labant, gelidus concrevit frigore sanguis. (12.905)

Answers:

Frigidus . . . sanguis; **calidum . . . telum**; **saevis . . . armis**; **gelidus . . . sanguis**.

- **hyperbole:** exaggeration for emphasis or rhetorical effect; overstatement. Its opposite is **litotes**, understatement.

Effect: stresses the importance or seriousness of a situation; helps the reader to experience it with those involved.

English: I must have walked a million miles this summer.

How do I love thee? Let me count the ways. I love thee to the depth and breadth and height my soul can reach. (Elizabeth Barrett Browning)

Publishing a volume of verse is like dropping a rose-petal down the Grand Canyon and waiting for the echo. (Don Marquis)

Latin: **Fluctusque ad sidera tollit.** (The wind raises the waves to the stars. 1.103)

Cumulo praeruptus aquae mons. (Referring to a wave of the sea as mountainous. 1.105)

Vix illum lecti bis sex cervice subirent. (A boulder the size of which only twelve men could lift. 12.899–900)

Puto esse ego illi milia aut decem aut plura / perscripta. (Catullus, 22.4)

Disertissime Romuli nepotum, / quot sunt quotque fuere, Marce Tulli, / quotque post aliis erunt in annis. (Cicero is the most learned of all Romans! Catullus, 49.1–3)

Stravimus innumeris tumidum Pythona sagittis. (Ovid, *Metamorphoses* 1.460)

Compare **litotes**: **Salve, nec minimo** (= **magno**) **puella naso.** (Catullus, 43.1)

- **hysteron proteron:** reversal of the normal or expected sequence of events in order to put the more important idea, which logically would come later in time, first. "Later-earlier." Hysteron proteron has also been defined as "a chiasmus of ideas," e.g., "You ask who I am and how old I am? I am thirty-nine and my name is Bob."[89] An uncommon figure. Cf. **prolepsis**.

Effect: emphasizes a particular word or idea, or stresses the result of an action.

English: Put on your shoes and socks! (Socks go on before shoes.)

I fled when I saw the monster. (Although the sense requires that the monster appears before the fear arises, in the word order, the fleeing precedes the seeing.)

Latin: **Fatisque deum defensus iniquis / inclusos utero Danaos et pinea furtim / laxat claustra Sinon.** (Sinon releases the Greeks inside the horse before releasing the bolt securing the trapdoor. 2.257–59. See also **zeugma**, below.)

Moriamus et in media arma ruamus. (Let us die and rush into battle. 2.353.)

Natat uncta carina, / frondentesque ferunt remos et robora silvis / infabricata fugae studio. (A complex example, wherein the ships are afloat, then their oars still are leafy, i.e., newly-hewn, and finally, the wood of both oars and ships is still in the forest. 4.398–400)

Ut tecum loquerer simulque ut essem. (Speaking is placed before being together. Catullus 50.13)

Misero quod omnes / eripit sensus mihi. (The poet is unhappy before he has lost his senses. Catullus 51.5–6)

Praedicari de se ac nominari volunt. (One's name must be known, **nominari,** before it can be made public**, praedicari**. Cicero, *Pro Archia Poeta* 26)

- **interlocked word order** (see **synchysis**)
- **irony:** the expression of something contrary to what is intended, i.e., the words say one thing but actually mean another. This usage is a sort of humor, ridicule, or light sarcasm that states an apparent fact with the manifest intention of expressing its opposite.

  Effect: adds humor or sarcasm.

  English: We brave men do quite enough if we merely stand there looking. (The supposition is that we are cowards and for that reason we do nothing.)

  Yet Brutus says he (Caesar) was ambitious; and Brutus is an honorable man. (Shakespeare, *Julius Caesar*)

  Latin: **Nos munera templis / quippe tuis ferimus**. (Iarbas sarcastically suggests that worshipping Jove has no payoff for mortals. 4.218)

  Iunone secunda, *with Juno's favor.* (The opposite is meant. 4.45)

  Scilicet in superis labor est, *of course this is work for the gods.* (This implies that the gods would not be concerned with such trifles. 4.379)

  Tanto pessimus omnium poeta / quanto tu (Cicero) optimus omnium patronus, as much as (I *am) the worst poet of all, so are you the best benefactor of all.* (This implies that Cicero is as good a benefactor as Catullus is a bad poet, which of course he would not admit. Catullus, 49.6–7)

- **litotes:** an understatement or double negative. Litotes usually consists of a negative word, such as **non** or **nec/neque**, and a following adjective with a negative prefix, e.g., <u>**non indecoro**</u> **pulvere sordidi**, *soiled with <u>not unbecoming</u>, i.e., glorious, dust* (Horace, *Odes* 2.1.22). This figure usually asserts something by denying its opposite. Its meaning is weaker than an expression of the positive, such as **praeclarus** for **non indecoro** in the example above. Some common words are derived from litotes, e.g., **nonnulli (non nulli)** and **nonnumquam (non numquam)**. Its counterpoint figure is **hyperbole**, overstatement.

  Effect: emphasizes.

  English: He is <u>not</u> a <u>bad</u> ballplayer. = He is a good ball player.

  I <u>kid</u> you <u>not</u>. = I am serious.

  It is <u>not</u> <u>unusual.</u> = It is normal.

  Latin: **<u>Neque</u> enim <u>ignari</u> sumus.** (1.198)

  Cum sic unanimam adloquitur <u>male sana</u> sororem. (4.8)

  <u>Nec</u> <u>non</u> Aeneas opera inter talia primus / hortatur socios. (6.183–184)

See if you can spot and translate the examples of litotes here below.

Non sane illepidum neque invenustum. (Catullus, 10.4)

Salve, nec minimo puella naso. (Catullus, 43.1)

Non sine (= cum) vano / . . . metu. (Horace, *Odes* 1.23.3–4)

Nec sumus ingrati: tibi nos debere fatemur. (Ovid, *Metamorphoses* 4.76)

Et hic Romae propter tranquillitatem rei publicae non neglegebantur. (Cicero, *Pro Archia Poeta* 5)

Compare **hyperbole: Servata centum clavibus et mero.** (Horace *Odes*, 2.14.26)

- **metaphor:** an implied comparison, made through the figurative use of words that suggest a likeness between what is actually being described and something else, e.g., **Agnosco veteris vestigia flammae** (fire for passion, 4.23). Metaphors apply the qualities of something familiar to give form and substance to something less familiar. The comparison is made in the mind of the reader and is expressed by a single word more often than not. As figurative language, **metaphor** and **simile** are more common in poetry than prose.

Effect: creates interest, or further understanding of something unfamiliar; stimulates the imagination.

English: to bite the bullet; unbridled anger; don't count your chickens before they're hatched; that's a horse of a different color; to be on an even keel; to take the bull by the horns; a wildcat strike.

All the world's a stage, / and all the men and women merely players / they have their exits and their entrances. (Shakespeare, *As You Like It*)

A bad-tempered elbow. (V.S. Pritchett)

Latin: **remigio alarum,** *the oarage of his wings* (Speaking of Mercury's wings as ship's oars. 1.301)

Invadunt urbem somno vinoque sepultam. (Note also the foreshadowing in the word "buried" here. 2.265)

Illum ardens infesto vulnere Pyrrhus insequitur. (Fire for passion. 2.529–530)

At regina gravi iamdudum saucia cura / vulnus alit venis et caeco carpitur igni. (Dido is seriously wounded by her love for Aeneas. Note the interlocking of **regina gravi . . . saucia cura,** and the mixed images of nursing a wound [**vulnus alit**] and being consumed by blind fire [**caeco carpitur igni**]. 4.1–2)

Spot the metaphor in the Latin, given the English clues.

Nec dulci declinat lumina somno. (Light for eyes. 4.195)

Et Numidae infreni cingunt (The Numidians, superior horsemen, are unbridled. 4.41.)

Saevit inops animi totamque incensa per urbem / bacchatur. (Dido has just learned of Aeneas' plans to leave. 4.300–301.)

Ignes interiorem edunt medullam. (She's feeling the passion of love-fire. Catullus, 35.15)

Aspera / nigris aequora ventis / (emirabitur insolens). (The youth wonders at Pyrrha, who is compared to a storm at sea. Horace, *Odes* 1.5.6–7)

Uritur, et sterilem sperando nutrit amorem. (Fire again is used as a metaphor for [Apollo's] passion. Ovid, *Metamorphoses*, 1.496)

Compare **simile**: **ac venti, velut agmine facto.** (The word **veluti**, *as, even as, just as,* explicitly compares the winds to a line of soldiers. 1.82)

- **metonymy:** use of one noun for another which it suggests, such as the substitution of the name of a deity for an attribute, e.g., Ceres, goddess of agriculture, for grain. It can also be used to refer to an object by means of the material of which the object is made, e.g., *he was stabbed with cold steel*. The distinction between **metonymy** and the closely-related figure **synecdoche** is subtle and confusing; many use metonymy as a term for both. **Metonymy** is a benchmark of epic style.

Effects: avoids commonplace words; conveys what is abstract in concrete terms.

English: *jock* for *athlete*, *brass* for *military officers*, *salt* for *sailor*, *Band-Aid* for *bandage*, *Coke* for *soft drink*, *Kleenex* for *tissue*, *Xerox* for *photocopy*.

He is a man of the cloth. (He wears a collar or vestment and is therefore a clergyman.)

The pen is mightier than the sword. (Discourse and diplomacy get better results than war.)

The White House (President of the United States) is too uncommunicative with the press (News media).

Think outside the bun. (Television commercial referring to food that is not hamburger.)

Latin: **Arma virumque cano.** (= **bellum**. 1.1)

Cererem corruptam undis. (= **frumentum**. 1.177)

Implentur veteris Bacchi pinguisque ferinae. (= **vini**. 1.215)

Deformare domum et luctu miscere hymenaeos. (= **nuptiae**. 12.805)

For what do the underlined examples of metonymy substitute?

Tum omnibus una omnes surripuit Veneres. (Catullus 86.6)

Funus et imperio parabat. (Horace, *Odes* 1.37.8)

In aeternum / exsilium impositura cumbae. (= Charon's skiff = the Underworld = ? Horace, *Odes* 2.3.27–28)

Frustra cruento Marte carebimus. (Horace, *Odes* 2.14.13)

Here are some examples where the substitution is the material of which an object is made:

Aut hoc inclusi ligno occultantur Achivi. (= **equo.** 2.45)

Dixerat, atque illam media inter talia ferro collapsam aspiciunt comites. (= **gladio** or **ense**. 4.663–664)

Hic Turnus ferro praefixum robur acuto . . . iacit (= **hastam**. 10.479)

Quoque erat accinctus, demisit in ilia ferrum. (Ovid, *Metamorphoses* 4.119)

Compare **synecdoche: ibis in auratis aureus ipse rotis.** (Wheels for chariot. Ovid, *Amores* 1.3.42.)

- **onomatopoeia:** "sound-sense," the poetic use of a single word whose sound suggests its meaning; often associated with alliteration. In this line from Ovid, **illa dedit turpes raucis bubonibus umbras,** note the noisy cry of the owl in **raucis** and the repetition of the "Hoo, Hoo" mimicked in **bubonibus** (*Amores* 1.12.19)

Effect: creates interest and illustrates or reinforces lexical meaning.

English: Babble, bang, bobwhite, buzz, chickadee, click, crack, cuckoo, hiss, hum, meow, moo, murmur, quack, swish, thud

Latin: **Magnum cum murmure montis.** (The wind-cave echoes. 1.55)

Qualis mugitus, fugit cum saucius aram. (Mooing by a bull being sacrificed. 1.223)

Lamentes gemituque et femineo ululatu. (Women wailing or howling. 4.667)

Ad solam dominam usque pipiabat. (Suggests the chirping of a bird. Catullus, 3.10)

Tintinant aures. (Suggests the ringing of a bell. Catullus, Poem 51.11)

Quod mare conceptum spumantibus exspuit undis. (With alliteration and consonance, the word **exspuit**, with **spumantibus . . . undis**, suggests the sound of the salt sea spray. Catullus, 64.155)

Lenesque sub noctem susurri. (The sibilation suggests gentle whispers at night. Horace, *Odes* 1.9.19)

- **oxymoron** (Greek for "deliberately foolish"): paradox, or the juxtaposition of opposite or contradictory words in the same phrase, e.g., **Festina lente**, *Make haste slowly* (Augustus, attributed by Suetonius). Oxymoron often appears as a noun and an adjective and is associated with **antithesis** and **juxtaposition**.

Effect: creates curiosity, surprise, "double-take."

English: Authentic reproduction, definite maybe, detailed summary, elevated subway, forward lateral, pretty ugly, jumbo shrimp, open secret, resident alien, silent alarm, uninvited guest, virtual reality, wireless cable

The silence was deafening.

Hurts so good. (John Cougar Mellencamp)

Latin: <u>**Plenus**</u> **sacculus est** <u>**aranearum**</u>**,** *a purse full of cobwebs.* (Here, cobwebs serve as a metaphor for emptiness, therefore the oxymoron is "full of emptiness." Catullus, 13.8)

Virenti canities. (Note the juxtaposition of the metaphors, green = youth, grey-white = old age. Horace, *Odes* 1.9.17)

Arida nutrix. (Dry wetnurse. Horace, *Odes,* 1.22.16)

Insaniens . . . sapientiae. (Horace, *Odes,* 1.34.2)

Cum tacent, clamant. (Cicero, *In Catilinam* 1.8)

Compare **antithesis** and **juxtaposition**: <u>**omnes**</u> <u>**unius**</u> **aestimemus assis.** (Catullus, 5.3)

- **personification:** the attribution of human qualities to inanimate objects, animals, or concepts, in order to stimulate the reader's imagination and thus gain vividness. Abstractions are often capitalized when personified, e.g., **Cana Fides . . . iura dabunt**. (1.292), *Grey-white (i.e., venerable) Honor will pass laws* (Jupiter, 1.292) or **ante, Pudor, quam te violo aut tua iura resolvo**, *before, O Shame, I violate you or your laws* (Dido, 4.27). See also **apostrophe** and **prosopopeia**.

Effects: stimulates the imagination and creates vividness; makes the abstract concrete.

English: Mother nature.

Justice is blind.

The bowels of the earth.

Flowers danced about the lawn.

England expects every man to do his duty. (Lord Nelson)

Latin: **Aeolus . . . /** <u>**luctantes ventos**</u> **. . . imperio premit**. (The winds are wrestling. 1.52–54)

<u>Eripiunt</u> subito <u>nubes</u> caelumque diemque / Teucrorum ex oculis. (The clouds snatch away sky and daylight. 1.88–89)

<u>Suadent</u>que cadentia <u>sidera</u> somnos. (Note how the spirants suggest the gentle, rhythmic breathing of sleep. 2.9)

<u>Phaselus</u> ille . . . <u>ait</u> fuisse navium celerrimus. (Boats can't talk; Catullus' bean-boat is personified throughout this poem. Catullus, 4.1–2)

Aut quam sidera multa, cum tacet nox, / furtivos hominum vident amores. (The stars see the lovers. Catullus, 7.7–8)

Cui Pudor et Iustitiae soror, incorrupta Fides, nudaque Veritas. (Personifications of the values of the Romans. Horace, *Odes* 1.24.6–7)

Saxis, unde loquaces / (lymphae) (Bandusia's waters are talkative. Horace, *Odes* 3.13.15)

Postero nocturnos Aurora removerat ignes. (Note also the antithetical juxtaposition of **nocturnos Aurora** and the metaphor of **nocturnos ignes** for stars. Ovid, *Metamorphoses* 4.81)

Ferrea cum vestris bella, valete, modis. (Ovid bids farewell to epic meter, i.e., epic poetry. Ovid, *Amores* 1.1.28)

Compare the direct address of apostrophe: **O dolor atque decus magnum . . . .** (10.507)

- **pleonasm:** the use of redundant, superfluous, or unnecessary words. Common in Vergil.

  Effects: clarifies, reinforces, or lends reassurance or an air of dignity.

  English: I saw him do it with my very own eyes.

  I'll meet you at 12 noon.

  It's *deja vu* all over again. (Yogi Berra)

  Latin: **Sic <u>ore effata</u>**, *and thus having spoken with her mouth.* (2.524)

  Et . . . in tenuem <u>ex oculis evanuit</u> auram. (4.278)

  Patriosque vocavi / voce deos. (4.680–681)

  Finem dedit ore loquendi. (6.76)

  Compare the opposite, **ellipsis**: **facilis (est) descensus Averno.** (6.126)

- **polyptoton:** repetition either of the same word in different forms of case or tense or of different words having a close etymological relationship.[90]

  Effect: adds interest, clarifies.

  English: Winners never quit, and quitters never win.

  With eager feeding food doth choke the feeder. (Shakespeare, *Richard II*)

The only thing we have to fear is fear itself. (Franklin D. Roosevelt)

Choosy Mothers Choose Jif (commercial slogan for Jif peanut butter)

Latin: Version 1:

Illum absens absentem auditque videtque. (4.83)

Sternitur Arcadiae proles, sternuntur Etrusci. (10.429)

Occidit, occideritque sinas cum nomine Troia. (12.828)

Vicisti et victum tendere palmas / Ausonii viderunt. (12.936–937)

Gemelle Castor et gemelle Castoris. (Catullus, 4.27)

Tam te basia multa basiare. (Catullus, 7.9)

Version 2:

Illum ego per flammas . . . eripui; . . . ille meum comitatus iter . . . . (6.110, 112)

Observans quae signa ferant, quo tendere pergant. (6.198)

Sunt geminae Somni portae, quarum altera fertur / cornea, qua veris facilis datur exitus umbris. (6.893–894)

Quicum ludere, quem in sinu tenere / cui primum digitum dare appetenti. (Catullus, 2.2–3)

- **polysyndeton:** the use of more conjunctions (**et, -que, atque, nec**) than is needed in a series of coordinate words, phrases, or clauses. The opposite is **asyndeton.**

Effect: produces a cumulative effect, a "heaping up"; drawing out or rushing.

English: He ran and laughed and jumped for joy.

(I love Rome) for its greatness, and its antiquity, and its beauty, and its populousness, and for its power, and its wealth, and its successes in war. (John Chryostom)

Latin: **Eurusque Notusque ruunt creberque . . . / Africus.** (1.85–86)

Exstinxti te meque, soror, populumque patresque Sidonios urbemque tuam. (4.682–683)

Quin tu animo offirmas atque istinc teque reducis / et . . . desinis esse miser? (Catullus, 76.11–12)

Laudat digitosque manusque bracchiaque. (Ovid, *Metamorphoses* 1.500–1)

Note that the meaning of **et . . . et**, *both . . . and*, may be intended if there are only two items that are connected. 2.251)

Involvens umbra magna terramque polumque. (2.251)

Quem non incusavi amens hominumque deorumque (2.745).

Do quod vis, et me victusque volensque remitto. (12.833)

Et me recuravi otioque et urtica. (Catullus, 44.15)

Compare **asyndeton: sed pleni omnes sunt libri, plenae sapientium voces, plena exemplorum vetustas.** (Cicero, *Pro Archia Poeta* 14)

- **praeteritio:** this Ciceronian figure of persuasion draws attention to an idea by pretending to pass over it. This figure is also known as preterition or paraleipsis/paralipsis.

  Effect: a kind of irony; draws more attention to something by pretending to ignore it.

  English: Not to mention . . . , or We need say nothing of . . . , or Far be it from me to say . . . .

  Pay no attention to the man behind the curtain. *The Wizard of Oz*

  Let's not mention my opponent's habit of lying.

  Latin: **Illa nimis antiqua praetereo**, *I pass over those (next examples) as too distant in time.*

  Obliviscor iam iniurias tuas, Clodia, depono memoriam doloris mei.

  I am forgetful of your injuries (to me), Clodia, and I am putting aside the memory of my pain. (The injuries and pain are still mentioned! Cicero, *Pro Caelio*, 50)

- **prolepsis**: speaking of something future as already completed or existing; anticipation or preconception, a "looking forward." Often a noun that receives the action of an anticipatory verb follows it. See also **hysteron proteron**.

  Effect: "flashforward"; prioritizes or puts in prime position what is considered most important.

  English: If my wife finds out, I'm a dead man!

  Precolonial United States (speaking of the U.S. before it was so designated)

  Consider the lilies of the field, how they grow.

  Latin: **Summersas obrue puppes.** (The ships are sunk before they are overwhelmed. 1.69)

  Vixi et quem dederat cursum fortuna peregi.

  I have lived and I have followed the path that fortune had given (me). (4.653)

- **prosopopoeia**: a Ciceronian prose figure, prosopopeia is the impersonation of an absent or imaginary speaker as speaking, for dramatic effect. Prosopopoeia is a special type of **personification**.

  Effect: adds drama.

  English: If Miller Huggins were alive today, he'd be turning over in his grave. (Yogi Berra)

- **simile:** an expressed comparison introduced by words such as "like" or "as" (**qualis, similis, ut, velut**, **veluti**, and others). Similes, which are characteristic of epic poetry, are often lengthy. For such extended similes, see these examples: orator, *Aeneid* 1.148–53, bees, 1.430–36, the wounded deer, 4.68–72, the bacchant, 4.300–3, ants, 4.402–7, and the oak tree, 4.441–6.

  Effect: describes or illustrates the unfamiliar by way of the familiar.

  English: As heavy as lead, as light as a feather.

  My love is as a fever, longing still / For that which longer nurseth the disease. (Shakespeare, Sonnet 147)

  Reason is to faith as the eye to a telescope. (David Hume)

  Like ancient trees, we die from the top. (Gore Vidal)

  Latin: **Ac veluti magno in populo cum saepe coorta est / seditio**, etc. (Neptune, in calming the seas, is compared to an orator calming riots in the Forum. 1.148)

  Quasi mugitus, fugit cum saucius aram / taurus (2.223–224)

  Qualem . . . aut videt aut vidisse putat per nubila lunam. (Dido in the Underworld as the moon peeking through the clouds. 6.454)

  Amorem, / qui illius culpa cecidit velut prati / ultimi flos. (The poet compares his lost love to a flower. Catullus, 11.22–23)

  Vitas inuleo me similis, Chloe. (Chloe is like a fawn. Horace, *Odes* 1.23.1)

  Atqui non ego te tigris ut aspera / . . . frangere persequor (Horace is like a tiger. Horace, *Odes* 1.23.9–10)

  Accipiter velut / molles columbas. (Octavian is a hawk to Cleopatra's doves. Note the anastrophe of **accipiter velut**. Horace, *Odes* 1.37.17–18)

  Videt igne micantes / sideribus similes oculos. (Daphne's eyes are compared to stars. Ovid, *Metamorphoses* 1.498–99)

  Exhorruit aequoris instar / quod tremit . . . ([Thisbe's face] shivers like the sea, which ripples . . . . Ovid, *Metamorphoses* 4.135–36)

See if you can identify what is being compared in these similes from Vergil. Be sure to identify the Latin word that introduces the simile.

> **Ac veluti magno in populo cum saepe coorta est / seditio saevitque animis ignobile vulgus**. (1.148–149)
>
> **Qualis apes aestate nova per florea rura / exercet sub sole labor . . . fervet opus redolentque thymo fragrantia mella**. (1.430–436)
>
> **Qualis coniecta cerva sagitta, / quam procul incautam nemora inter Cresia fixit / pastor agens telis liquitque volatile ferrum / nescius**. (4.69–72)
>
> **Ac velut annoso validam cum robore quercum / Alpini Boreae nunc hinc nunc flatibus illinc / eruere inter se certant.** (4.441–443)
>
> **Utque leo, specula cum vidit ab alta / stare procul campis meditantem in proelia taurum**. (10.454–456)

Compare **metaphor**: **raditur hic elegis ultima meta meis,** *The final turning-post is grazed by my elegies.* (Ovid, *Amores* 3.15.2)

- **synchysis** (Greek for "a pouring together"; also spelled **synchesis** and often referred to as **interlocked word order**): synchysis emphasizes specific words by varying the usual word order found in prose. Words are arranged so that one word of a pair is placed between the words of the other pair, or **abAB** pattern, e.g., adj. a, adj. b, noun A, noun B, such as **amissos longo socios sermone** (1.217). (Remember that capital letters signify nouns and lowercase, verbs.) An adjective will usually precede the noun it modifies. By the rules of agreement, the case endings of the words in each pair will be the same within the pair (see the examples below). The every-other-one pattern of **synchysis** can have several different arrangements by part of speech, e.g.,

  abAB, or adj. – adj. – noun – noun:

  > **Saevae memorem Iunonis ob iram**. (1.4)
  >
  > **Aeternum hoc sanctae foedus amicitiae**. (Catullus 109.6)

  AbaB, or noun – adj. – adj. – noun:

  > **Maecenas atavis edite regibus**. (Horace, *Odes* 1.1.1)

  aBAb, or adj. – noun – noun – adj.:

  > **Ista decent umeros gestamina nostros**. (Ovid, *Metamorphoses* 1.457)

Effect: variety, emphasizes the close association of the word pairs and gives a closely-knit expression.

a b A B

Latin: **aurea purpuream subnectit fibula vestem**. (4.139)

a b A B
His medium dictis sermonem abrumpit. (4.388)

Eliso percussis aere pennis. (Ovid, *Metamorphoses* 1.466)

Pulchra verecundo suffunditur ora rubore. (Ovid, *Metamorphoses* 1.484)

Now you try it, using the **abAB** for the first four examples and the underlining method for the second three.

Teucri . . . et litore celsas / deducunt toto naves. (4.397–398)

Cocytusque sinu labens circumvenit atro. (6.132)

Aspice, ut insignis spoliis Marcellus opimis / ingreditur. (6.855)

Aeternum hoc sanctae foedus amicitiae. (Note how these words all share themselves with each other. Catullus, 109.6)

Aspera / nigris aequora ventis. (Winds and waves are brought together, with the help of juxtaposition and transference. Horace, *Odes* 1.5.6–7)

Damna tamen celeres reparant caelestia lunae. (Note the juxtaposition of **caelestia** and **lunae**. Horace, *Odes* 4.7.13)

In rigidum parvo silicem discrimine versae. (The interlocking merges the image of the Propoetides becoming hard-hearted and their transformation into stone. Ovid, *Metamorphoses* 10.242)

Answers:

A b a B
Teucri . . . et litore celsas / deducunt toto naves. (4.397–398)

A B a b
Cocytusque sinu labens circumvenit atro. (6.132)

a B A b
Aspice, ut insignis spoliis Marcellus opimis / ingreditur. (6.855)

a b A B
Aeternum hoc sanctae foedus amicitiae.

Aspera / nigris aequora ventis.

Damna tamen celeres reparant caelestia lunae.

In rigidum parvo silicem discrimine versae.

a A B a

Compare **chiasmus**: **ut quos certus amor, quos hora novissima iunxit.** (Ovid, *Metamorphoses* 4.156)

a b V A B

Compare **golden line**: **Et scelerata fero consumite viscera morsu.** (Ovid, *Metamorphoses* 4.113)

- **synecdoche**: synecdoche is the use of the part for the whole (*pars pro toto*) for variety of expression. Vergil frequently uses **puppis** (properly the stern of a ship) in place of **navis** (the entire ship), or **tectum** (properly the roof of a house) for **domus** (the house itself). Synecdoche is often described as a type of metonymy and the two are often confused. When the distinction between metonymy and synecdoche is made, it is the following: when A is used to refer to B — it is a synecdoche if A is a part of B, and a metonym if A is commonly associated with B, but is not a part of it. Here is a convenient summary of the distinction between **metonymy**, **synecdoche**, and **metaphor**.

  Therefore, "The White House reported" would be a metonymy for the President and his staff, because the White House (A) is not a part of the President or his staff (B), it is merely closely associated with them because of physical proximity. On the other hand, asking for "All hands on deck" is a synecdoche because hands (A) are actually a part of the men (B) to whom they refer. There is an example which displays synecdoche, metaphor and metonymy in one sentence. "Fifty keels ploughed the deep", where "keels" is the synecdoche as it takes a part (of the ship) as the whole (of the ship); "ploughed" is the metaphor as it substitutes the concept of ploughing a field for moving through the ocean; and "the deep" is the metonym, as "deepness" is an attribute associated with the ocean. [91]

Effect: variety of expression.

English: "hands" referring to workers, "head" for cattle, "the law" for policemen, "mortal" for man, "sail" for ship, "shades" for sunglasses, "threads" for clothing, "wheels" for a car.

Friends, Romans, Countrymen, lend me your ears! (Antony in Shakespeare's *Julius Caesar*)

Latin: **Incute vim ventis summersasque obrue puppes.** (Literally, the sterns of the ships. 1.69)

Numquam Dardaniae tetigissent nostra carinae. (Keels for ships. 4.658)

Lamentis gemituque et femineo ululatu / tecta fremunt. (Roof for house. 4.667–668)

Labore fessi venimus Larem ad nostrum. (Lares, household gods, for home, might also be considered metonymy. Catullus, 31.9)

Caesar ab Italia volantem / remis adurgens. (Oars for ships. Horace, *Odes* 1.37.16–17)

Tutus caret obsoleti / sordibus tecti. (Roof for house. Horace, *Odes* 2.10.6–7)

Animus ex hoc forensi strepitu reficiatur et aures convicio defessae conquiescant. (Cicero's mind and ears, as suggestive of his whole person, are given a rest from the noise of public life. Cicero, *Pro Archia Poeta*, 12)

Compare **metonymy**: **<u>taedae</u> quoque iure coissent / sed vetuere patres.** (Marriage torch for marriage. Ovid, *Metamorphoses* 4.60)

- **tmesis**: the separation of parts of a compound word by one or more intervening words, e.g., **<u>circum</u> dea <u>fundit</u>**, for **circumfundit** (1.412). More common in poetry, especially Vergil, than prose.

  Effect: interrupts, stresses enclosed word(s).

  English: How heinous e'er it be (for However heinous it be.) (Shakespeare, *Richard II*)

  whatsoever (for whatever)

  any-old-how (for anyhow)

  a-whole-nother (for another)

  Latin: **Bis collo squamea <u>circum</u> / terga <u>dati</u>.** (For **circumdati**. 2.218–19)

  Ante, pudor, quam te violo aut tua iura resolvo. (For **antequam**. 4.27)

  Et quo quemque modo fugiatque feratque laborem. (For **quomodo**. 6.892)

  Non prius ex illo flagrantia declinavit / lumina, quam cuncto concrepit corpore flammam. (For **priusquam**. Catullus, 64.91–92)

  Quem Fors dierum cumque dabit lucro. (For **quemcumque**. Horace, *Odes* 1.9.14)

- **transferred epithet** (also known as hypallage): an **epithet** is the consistent use of an adjective to characterize some person or thing, such as the Homeric descriptive terms <u>swift-footed</u> Achilles, <u>rosy-fingered</u> Dawn, and <u>wine-dark</u> sea. In Latin, **pius** is an epithet in the phrase **pius Aeneas** (1.378)

  A **transferred epithet** is an adjective that agrees grammatically with one noun but is placed close to, and shares its meaning with, another noun, e.g., in **saevae memorem Iunonis ob iram** (1.4), **memorem** logically describes **Iunonis**, but grammatically describes **iram**. This use of an epithet reinforces or emphasizes by sharing the meaning of one word with two others, heightening the meaning of all.

Effect: reinforces or emphasizes.

English: The ploughman homeward plods his weary way (weary modifies way, grammatically, but more appropriately describes the ploughman.) (Thomas Gray)

Here comes Jim in his smartarse leather coat (transferred from Jim to coat).

Latin: **Despiciens mare velivolum terrasque iacentes** (Properly, **velivolum**, *sail-flying*, describes ships and not **mare**, the sea. 1.224)

Templumque vetustum desertae / Cereris. (It is the temple, and not Ceres, that is deserted, although she too, by association, is also abandoned. Therefore, **desertae** is taken grammatically with **Cereris** but has a meaning more appropriate to **templum** here. 2.713–14)

Iunonem interea rex omnipotentis Olympi (It is the king and not Olympus that is all-powerful. 12.791)

Oraclum Iovis inter aestuosi. (Both the oracle in Egypt and Jove are "steamy." Catullus, 7.5)

Tintinant aures, gemina teguntur / lumina nocte. (Scansion of this line reveals that the **-a** at the end of **gemina** is long, and that therefore **gemina** modifies **nocte** grammatically (*twin night*). In sense it can also describe **lumina** (*twin eyes*). Catullus, 51.11–12)

Ad aquae lene caput sacrae. (Note the double transfer here of **lene** to both **aquas** and **caput** and **sacrae** to both **aquae** and **caput**. Horace, *Odes* 1.1.22)

Regina dementes ruinas. (Cleopatra is insane, and not the ruins. Horace, *Odes* 1.37.7)

Plura locuturum timido Peneia cursu. (Strictly speaking, it is Daphne, and not her flight, that is frightened; note the juxtaposition of **timido** and **Peneia**. Ovid, *Metamorphoses* 1.525)

- **tricolon crescens:** the use of three closely-connected or parallel descriptive elements, increasing in size and emphasis, to modify a person or thing. Also known as tricolon crescendo or ascending tricolon, this figure is often accompanied by **anaphora** and **asyndeton.** A tricolon is simply a sentence or line of verse with three separate but equal parts.

Effect: gives the impression of a series.

Examples of a tricolon:

English: A happy life is one spent in learning, earning, and yearning. (Lillian Gish)

Of the people, by the people, and for the people (Abraham Lincoln, *Gettysburg Address*)

Latin: **Veni, vidi, vici.** (Julius Caesar)

Examples of a tricolon crescens:

Latin: **I, sequere Italiam ventis, pete regna per undas.** (Dido becomes increasingly more agitated as she rebukes Aeneas. Note the asyndeton. 4.381)

Nec te noster amor, nec te data dextera quondam / nec moritura tenet crudeli funere Dido? *Does neither our love, nor your right hand once given in pledge, nor Dido, about to die a cruel death, hold you?* (Note the anaphora. 4.307–8)

Quicum ludere, quem in sinu tenere, / cui primum digitum dare appetenti. (The sparrow plays with Lesbia. Note the asyndeton and polyptoton. Catullus, 2.2–3)

Sive per Syrtes iter aestuosas / sive facturus per inhospitalem / Caucasum vel quae loca fabulosus / lambit Hydaspes. (Wherever the poet goes, Lalage will be with him. Note the anaphora. Horace *Odes* 1.22.5–8)

Non incola montis, / non ego sum pastor, non hic armenta gregesque / horridus observo. (Apollo is not an ordinary man. Note the anaphora, asyndeton, and the gapping of **sum**. Ovid, *Metamorphoses* 1.512–14)

- **zeugma** (Greek for "yoke"): the use of one part of speech (usually a verb, but sometimes a noun) with two objects, when strictly speaking the word can be applied to only one of them. A condensed expression in which one word has two different senses simultaneously, one sense often being wrong. **Zeugma** is "one for two," i.e., one word/verb with two meanings, for instance, **Aeneas tulit dolorem et patrem Troia**, *Aeneas carried grief and his father from Troy*. This figure includes condensation and parallelism: **Aeneas tulit dolorem et (tulit) patrem Troia**. (See below for both of these latter devices.)

Effect: condenses.

English: The farmers in the valley grew potatoes, peanuts, and bored.

We serve Devonshire cream, Beaujolais Nouveau, and 71 cities in Europe. (a magazine ad)

If we don't hang together, we shall hang separately. (Benjamin Franklin)

As Vergil guided Dante through the Inferno, the Sibyl Aeneas Avernus. (Roger D. Scott)

Latin: **Fatisque deum defensus iniquis / inclusos utero Danaos et pinea furtim / laxat claustra Sinon.** (The word **laxat** properly describes the release of the bolts, **claustra**, of the trapdoor securing the Greeks inside the wooden horse, rather than the Greeks themselves. See also **hendiadys** and **hysteron proteron**, above. 2.257–59)

Oculos dextramque precantem / protendens. (**Protendens**, *extending*, is to be taken figuratively with **oculos** and literally with **dextram**. 12.930)

Studium atque aures adhibere posset. (He was able to lend his support and his ears. Cicero, *Pro Archia Poeta*, 5)

Avium citharaeque cantus. (Here, the singing comes from both the birds and the lyre. Horace, *Odes* 3.1.20)

Illa redit, iuvenemque oculis animoque requirit. (**Requirit** means "search for" with **oculis** and "long for" with **animo**. Ovid, *Metamorphoses* 4.129)

Compare **hendiadys**, which is "two for one," i.e., two words/nouns with a single meaning, such as, **<u>umbram et silvam</u> petebat**, *he sought shade and the woods,* instead of **umbrosam silvam**, *the shady woods*.

Glossary of Additional Figures and Devices Useful for Poetic Analysis

Here is a list of additional stylistic features. These are not required for the AP Latin Exam, but they will nonetheless assist you to get the most out of reading Vergil and to write a more perceptive essay. Remember that the study of advanced Latin is not only about what the Latin says, but how the Latin is written.

anastrophe	framing	poetic plural
archaism	gapping (condensation)	rhetorical question
assonance	golden line	sound play
diminutive	Grecism	word play
euphemism	juxtaposition	
foreshadowing	parallelism	

- **anastrophe** (Greek for "turning back"): a general term that describes the deliberate reversal or inversion of normal word order, often with the effect of emphasizing the word(s) placed earlier. In Latin, anastrophe is commonly found as a conjunction that is delayed or a preposition following its object, such as **Karthago**, **<u>Italiam contra</u>**, *Carthage, opposite Italy* (in both senses of the word **contra**, i.e., opposing each other both geographically and as political and economic rivals. 1.13). Here, the preposition and its object are reversed to create the juxtaposition of Carthage and Italy. The term postposition is often used to refer to the placement of any word later than expected, e.g., a clause may <u>precede</u> its antecedent in poetry. For example, **fidus <u>quae tela</u> gerebat Achates**, *<u>weapons which</u> the faithful Achates was carrying* (= **<u>tela quae</u> fidus Achates gerebat**. 1.188).

  Effects: emphasizes the word appearing first; provides variety of style.

English: Up the hill went Jack and Jill.

When he himself might his quietus make. (Shakespeare, *Hamlet*)

What care I for my reputation? (George Jacques Danton)

Latin:

With prepositions:

Errabant acti fatis maria omnia circum (= **circum maria omnia**. 1.32)

Quos inter medius venit furor. (1.348)

Te propter Libycae gentes Nomadumque tyranni. (4.320)

Oraclum Iovis inter aestuosi. (Catullus, 7.5)

With conjunctions and adverbs:

Daret ut catenis / fatale monstrum. (Horace, *Odes* 1.37.20–21)

Accipiter velut (adurget) / molles columbas (= **velut accipiter**. Horace, *Odes* 1.37.17–19)

Postposition with relative clauses. Note how the repositioning of some words from their more normal positions creates emphasis on the meaning of those words.

Sum pius Aeneas, raptos qui ex hoste penates / . . . veho (= **qui penates raptos ex hoste . . . veho.** 1.378)

Fractum qui veteris pedem grabati (= **qui fractum . . . .** Catullus, 10.22)

Sancte puer, curis hominum qui gaudia misces (= **qui curis hominum gaudia misces**. Catullus, 64.95)

Now, find the misplaced word(s) and rewrite the sentence with the words arranged as in prose. The answers are given just below (do not peek!)

Haberes / magnum adiutorem, posset qui ferre secundas (Horace *Satires* 1.9.45–46)

In vacuo quae vulnera pectore fecit (Ovid, *Metamorphoses* 1.520)

Iusta precor: quae me nuper praedata puella est (Ovid, *Amores* 1.3.1)

Quae iacerent in tenebris omnia, nisi litterarum lumen accederet. (Cicero, *Pro Archia Poeta* 14)

Answers:

qui posset . . . ; quae in vacuo . . . pectore fecit; puella quae . . . ; omnia quae.

Compare **hyperbaton**, which is also anastrophe: **misero quod omnes eripit sensus mihi.** (Catullus, 51.5–6). This example also includes the postpositioned relative pronoun **quod**, which normally introduces the clause, i.e., precedes **misero** = **quod misero mihi omnes sensus eripit**.

- **antithesis:** striking contrast of juxtaposed words or ideas, such as **Non ego cum Danais Troianam exscindere gentem** (4.425). The figure **oxymoron** is necessarily a contrast between opposites and therefore includes **antithesis**. See also **juxtaposition**, below.

Effect: contrast.

English: A time to be born, and a time to die. (*Ecclesiastes*, 3)

Not that I loved Caesar less, but that I loved Rome more. (Brutus, Shakespeare, *Julius Caesar*)

Love is an ideal thing, marriage a real thing. (Johann Wolfgang von Goethe)

Extremism in defense of liberty is no vice, moderation in the pursuit of justice is not virtue. (Barry Goldwater)

Latin: **Sequar atris ignibus absens**. (4.384)

Digna indigna pati. (Note also the asyndeton. 12.811)

Odi et amo. (Catullus, 85.1)

Find the examples of antithesis and explain how their elements contrast.

At vobis male sit, malae tenebrae / Orci, quae omnia bella devoratis: / tam bellum mihi passerem abstulistis. / O factum male! (Catullus 3.13–16)

Amant amantur. (Note the asyndeton. Catullus 45.20)

Lumina nocte. (Lumina is also a metaphor for eyes. Catullus 51.11–12)

Cogit amare magis, sed bene velle minus. (Catullus 72.8)

Cum esset . . . in Siciliam profectus et cum ex ea provincia . . . decederet. (Note the parallel clauses. Cicero, *Pro Archia Poeta*, 6)

Compare **oxymoron**: **virenti canities** (green = youth, grey-white = old age. Horace, *Odes*1.9.17)

Compare **juxtaposition**: **speluncam Dido dux et Troianus eandem.** (Note also the hyperbaton/framing. 4.124.)

- **archaism:** the use of words or expressions that are antiquated or out of fashion, e.g., the use of *Thou* in English. In Latin, this includes the use of words whose spelling suggests their Greek origins, such as **gnatus** for **natus**. Vergil makes frequent use of archaisms.

Effect: lends authority, sometimes evokes pathos.

Latin: **O gnate, ingentem luctum ne quaere tuorum**. (= **nate**, voc. of **natus**, from **nascor**. 6.868)

Troiae sub moenibus altis / tot gnati cecidere deum. (10.469–470)

Urbs antiqua fuit (Tyrii tenuere coloni). (= **tenuerunt**. 1.12)

Nec latuere doli fratrem Iunonis et irae. (= **latuerunt**. 1.130)

Quis ante ora patrum Troiae sub moenibus altis / contigit oppetere! (= **Quibus**. 1.95–96)

Olli subridens hominum sator atque deorum / vultu. (= **Illi**. 1.254)

Syncopation (contraction):

Multum ille et terris iactatus et alto / vi superum. (= **superorum; virum** for **virorum** and **deum** for **deorum** are also common. 1.4)

Vos . . . / accestis scopulos. (= **accessistis**. 1.201)

Exstinxti te meque, soror. (= **exstinxisti**. 4.682)

O virgo, nova mi facies inopinave surgit. (= **mihi**. 6.104)

The opposite is **anachronism**, which deliberately or mistakenly brings the future into the present, e.g., Vergil's description of a ship's anchor, **dente tenaci ancora** (6.3–4), as having prongs. Bronze Age ships had anchors made of boulders, a fact which it is unlikely that Vergil knew.

- **assonance:** repetition of internal sounds, usually vowels, in successive words. The effect of assonance can be "musical" or onomatopoetic. What vowel sound seems to be emphasized in the line **multa tibi ante aras nostra cadet hostia dextra** (1.334)? Right, it is the vowel -**a**-. Repetition of initial, internal, and even final sounds is common in poetry. The related term **consonance**, which is often used as a synonym for alliteration, technically refers to the repetition of internal consonants. Sometimes, vowels even play together within a line, e.g., **O fortunatam natam me consule Romam!** (Cicero, *de Consulatu*).

Effects: emphasizes or draws attention; reinforces meaning; brings pleasure.

English: Mankind can handle most problems. (assonance of a)

Fleet feet sweep by sleeping geeks. (assonance of e)

Try to light the fire. (assonance of i)

Thy kingdom come thy will be done. (assonance of o)

Latin: **Accipiunt inimicum imbrem, rimisque fatiscunt.** (1.123)

Amicos longo socios sermone. (1.217)

Cum primum Iliacas, Danai, venistis ad oras. (2.117)

Find the dominant sound in these examples by reading each aloud. Identify as alliteration, assonance, or consonance (see alliteration in the first section of this glossary).Which are light-hearted and playful? Sad or scary? Clipped and abrupt?

Interea magno misceri murmure pontum. (1.124)

Hic aliud maius miseris multoque tremendum / obicitur. (2.199)

Fit via vi. (2.494)

Vivamus, mea Lesbia, atque amemus. (Catullus, 5.1)

Sperne puer neque. (Horace, *Odes* 1.9.16)

Lalagen amabo. (Note the sing-song of **Lala-** and **ama-**. Horace, *Odes* 1.22.23)

Sideribus similes oculos; videt oscula. (Note the accompanying alliteration and the powerful assonance of the sound-alikes **oculos** and **oscula**. Ovid, *Metamorphoses* 1.499)

- **diminutive**: the suffixes **-ulus** (**-olus** after a vowel), **-(i)culus,** and **-ellus** (sometimes **-illus**) alter the meaning of a noun or adjective by diminishing its size. This often increases the level of affection, e.g., **caligula,** soldier's boot, a diminutive of **caliga,** producing Caligula, "L'il Boots."

Effect: elicits feelings of affection and endearment.

English: cigarette (-ette), duckling (-ling), kitty (-ey, -ie, -y), piglet (-let); German *-chen* or *-lein*, Italian, *-etta*, Russian *-chka* or *-ka*, Spanish *-ito*.

Latin: **Ante fugam suboles, si quis mihi <u>parvulus</u> aula / luderet Aeneas.** (Dido's imagined little boy is made younger and therefore more endearing by the use of the diminutive **parvulus** instead of **parvus**. 4.328)

Vae miselle passer! . . . / Flendo <u>turgiduli</u> rubent <u>ocelli</u>. (Catullus, 3.16, 18)

Ut Veraniolum meum et Fabullum. (Catullus, 12.17)

Multum lusimus in meis tabellis / . . . scribens versiculos uterque nostrum. (Catullus, 50.2–4)

Sideribus similes oculos; videt oscula. (Ovid, *Metamorphoses* 1.499)

Munera fert illi: conchas teretesque lapillos. (Ovid, *Metamorphoses* 10.260)

- **euphemism**: Greek for "well said" (*eupheme* is the opposite of *blaspheme*), this figure is used to express in a more subtle or agreeable manner a subject that is blunt or potentially uncomfortable. The popular term "politically correct" is used in such circumstances, e.g., it has become unacceptable to use the term *crippled*, a usage which over time has evolved into *handicapped, disabled,* and now *physically challenged.*

Effect: creates variety and interest.

English: Alternative ways of expressing the fact that someone has died: passed away, departed, kicked the bucket, bought the farm, met his Maker, gone to be with the Lord, checked out, bit the big one, bitten the dust, cashed in their chips, shuffled off this mortal coil, given up the ghost.

Latin: **Breviter Troiae supremum audire laborem** (= **ruinam** or **mortem**. 2.11)

Quibus ultimus esset ille dies. (2.248–249)

Ruit alto a culmine Troia. (2.290)

Quid moror? (i.e., **mortem meam**, says Dido. 2.325)

Infelix Dido, verus mihi nuntius ergo / venerat exstinctam (esse), ferroque extrema secutam (esse)? (6.456–457)

Et terram hostilem moriens petit ore cruento. (Another way, albeit grisly, of expressing the act of dying. 10.489)

Here are several non-euphemistic but periphrastic ways of describing someone dying or about to die.

Mox illos sua fata manent maiore sub hoste. (10.438)

Nescia mens hominum fati sortisque futurae / et servare modum rebus sublata secundis! (10.501–502)

Vitaque cum gemitu fugit indignata sub umbras. (12.952, the final line of the *Aeneid*.)

- **foreshadowing**: a clue or hint that suggests what will happen in a story. A verbal premonition. Vergil also uses verbal reminiscences, i.e., words that are suggestive of previous happenings, to great advantage in building suspense.

Effect: builds anticipation and suspense

English: The classic example of foreshadowing is (Anton) Chekhov's gun. A gun is hanging on the wall in a certain scene in his story. That the gun is loaded is mentioned in passing. Later, of course, this gun is taken off the wall and fired.

Latin: **donum exitiale** (speaking of the wooden horse before taking it into the city. 2.31)

fatalis machina (taking the horse into the city. 2.237)

monstrum infelix (placing the horse on the citadel. 2.245)

Invadunt urbem somno vinoque sepultam. (2.265)

- **framing**: see **hyperbaton**.

- **gapping** (also known as **condensation**): a form of ellipsis (for which, see above), this technique creates brevity or economy of expression. A word common to two or more parallel expressions is often expressed in the second one only. The appearance of such words as being "understood" or assumed is a characteristic feature of Latin. Gapping is common in Latin poetry and is routinely found with **parallel phrasing**, for which, see below. It is also accompanied by **asyndeton** and **anaphora**. Extremely common in Vergil.

  Effect: shortens, economizes, accelerates.

  Latin: **Hic amor, haec patria est.** (= **Hic amor [est], haec patria est**. This is ellipsis because a form of the verb **esse** is omitted or gapped. 4.347)

  Ut spolia, ut currus, utque ipsum corpus amici / . . . conspexit. (= **Ut spolia [conspexit], ut currus [conspexit], utque ipsum corpus amici . . . conspexit**. Note the anaphora and asyndeton. 1.486–487)

  Templa . . . centum . . . , / centum aras posuit. (= **Templa . . . centum . . . , [posuit], centum aras posuit**. 2.199–200)

  Domum, si forte pedem , si forte tulisset, me refero. (= **Domum, si forte pedem [tulisset], si forte (pedem) tulisset.** 2.756)

  Flammaeque furentes / culmina perque hominum volvantur perque deorum. (= **Flammaeque furentes / culmina perque hominum volvantur perque [culmina] deorum [volvantur]**). 4.670–671)

  Qui dare certa ferae, dare vulnera possumus hosti. (= **Qui dare certa [vulnera] ferae [possumus], dare [certa] vulnera possumus hosti**. Note the asyndeton, and the use of poetic plural. Ovid, *Metamorphoses* 1.458)

Rely on parallel phrasing and asyndeton to determine which word(s) is/are gapped in the following examples. Remember that the gapped word(s) are usually expressed in the second clause.

Quas gentes Italum aut quas non oraveris urbes. (6.92)

Hoc opus, hic labor est. (6.129)

Fugat hoc, facit illud amorem. (Ovid, *Metamorphoses* 1.469)

Non incola montis, / non ego sum pastor . . . . (Note the anaphora and asyndeton. Ovid, *Metamorphoses* 1.512–14)

Sic deus et virgo; est hic spe celer, illa timore. (Ovid, *Metamorphoses* 1.539)

In frondem crines, in ramos bracchia crescunt. (Ovid, *Metamorphoses* 1.550)

Vota tamen tetigere deos, tetigere parentes. (Ovid, *Metamorphoses* 4.164)

Figat tuus omnia, Phoebe, te meus arcus. (Ovid, *Metamorphoses* 1.463)

Regum timendorum in proprios greges / reges in ipsos imperium est Iovis. (Horace, *Odes* 3.1.5–6)

Answers:

Quas gentes Italum (non oraveris) aut quas non oraveris urbes,

Hoc opus (est), hic labor (est).

Fugat hoc (amorem), facit illud amorem.

Non incola montis (sum), non ego sum pastor.

Sic deus et virgo; est hic spe celere, illa (est) timore celer.

In frondem crines (crescunt), in ramos bracchia crescunt.

Vota tamen tetigere deos, (vota) tetigere parentes.

Figat tuus (arcus) omnia, Phoebe, te meus arcus (figat).

Regum timendorum in proprios greges (imperium est), reges in ipsos imperium est Iovis.

- **golden line**: a form of interlocked or chiastic word order in which a centrally-placed verb is surrounded by two modifiers, usually adjectives, on one side and two nouns on the other, with each modifier describing a noun, i.e., **abVAB**, where modifier **a** goes with noun **A** and modifier **b** with noun **B**, e.g.,

a b V A B
Aspera tum positis mitescent saecula bellis.
modifier modifier noun noun

The word order within this golden line is synchysis, i.e., **abAB**. The words in the next example, which is called a silver line, **abVBA**, are grammatically chiastic, **abBA** (acc. – abl. – abl. – acc).

a b V B A
Disiectam Aeneae toto videt aequore classem.
modifier modifier noun noun

In both examples, as with most types of word order, the poet is attempting to draw the attention of the mind's ear and eye to something significant. Only the hexameter line accommodates this figure. John Dryden described the golden line as a hexameter line "of two substantives and two adjectives with a verb betwixt to keep the peace" (preface to *Sylvae*).

Effect: draws attention.

See if you can match up the words correctly in these golden lines.

Irrita ventosae linquens promissa procellae. (Catullus, 64.59)

Omne capax movet urna nomen. (Horace, *Odes* 3.1.16)

Pulchra verecundo suffunditur ora rubore. (Ovid, *Metamorphoses* 1.484)

Answers:

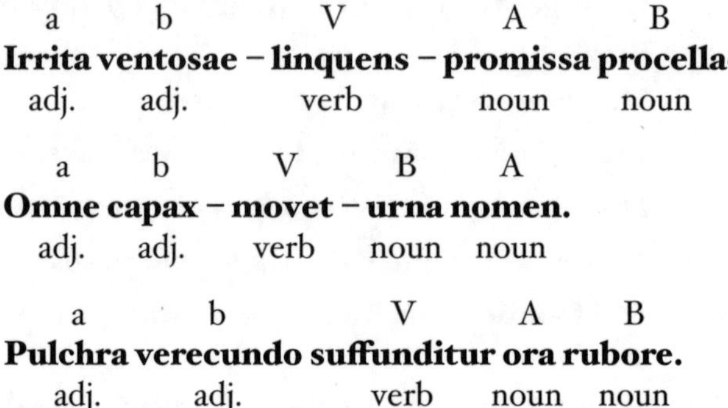

a b V A B
Irrita ventosae – linquens – promissa procellae.
adj. adj. verb noun noun
a b V B A
Omne capax – movet – urna nomen.
adj. adj. verb noun noun
a b V A B
Pulchra verecundo suffunditur ora rubore.
adj. adj. verb noun noun

- **Grecism (Hellenism)**: a patronym (adj., patronymic), which is a component of a personal name based upon the name of one's father, often contains forms of the Greek suffix **-ides** or **-idos**, e.g., **Anchisiades** = Aeneas, son of Anchises. Grecisms can give a sense of antiquity and therefore majesty, but they can also be used to demonstrate the erudition of the writer.

  Effect: lends dignity and respect; gives an air of antiquity or authority; creates variety.

  Latin: **Saevus ubi <u>Aeacidae</u> telo iacet Hector.** (Descendant of Aeacus = Achilles. 1.99)

  Defessi <u>Aeneadae</u> quae proxima litora cursu. (Descendants/followers of Aeneas. 1.157)

  Crinibus <u>Iliades</u> passis peplumque ferebant (Trojan women; note the mention of the **peplus/peplos**, a Greek female garment. 1.480).

  Caede Neoptolemum geminosque in limine <u>Atridas</u> (= Sons of Atreus = Agamemnon and Menelaus. 2.500)

  Te precor, Alcide, coeptis ingentibus adsis. (originally named Alcides = Hercules. 10.461)

  Note: Other Greek usages occur in poetry, wherein Greek endings are found on Greek names or words, especially in the case of accusatives. The Greek **-n** is the Latin **-m** and denotes the so-called Greek accusative, e.g., **Aenean** (4.74, 260, 191, et al.), **Oronten** (1.113), and **Anchisen** (2.747).

- **juxtaposition** (Latin **iuxta**, from **iungo**, means "beside, next to, side by side"): placement of words that are closely allied in meaning next to one another, in order to compare or contrast the two. This device is characterized by an absence of linking words between the words (see **asyndeton**). The parts of speech need not be the same. **Juxtaposition** is often used in other figures that use word order to draw attention to or contrast meaning. See also **antithesis** and **oxymoron**.

Effect: compares or contrasts; can create surprise.

Latin: **Ille meos, primus qui me sibi iunxit, amores** (Sychaeus and Dido. 4.28)

Quam tu urbem, soror, hanc cernes (Dido and Carthage. 4.47)

Illum ego per flammas . . . . / eripui (Anchises and Aeneas. 4.110)

Ego te, quae plurima fando / enumerare vales, numquam, regina, negabo (Aeneas and Dido. 4.333–334)

Me patris Anchisae, . . . terret imago (Aeneas and Anchises. 4.351, 353)

Now identify these examples of juxtaposition on your own.

Fata obstant placidasque viri deus obstruit aures (4.440)

Hoc illud, germana, fuit? (4.675)

Exstinxti te meque, soror. (4.682–683)

Gnatique patrisque, alma, precor, miserere. (6.116)

Interea soror alma monet succedere Lauso / Turnum (10.439–440)

Non me tua fervida terrent dicta, ferox; di me terrent et Iuppiter hostis. (There are two examples here. 12.894–895)

Pallas te hoc vulnere, Pallas immolat (12.948)

Ego te, miseranda, peremi. (Ovid, *Metamorphoses* 4.110)

Answers:

viri deus; Hoc illud; te meque; gnatique patrisque; Lauso Turnum; me tua and **di me**; **Pallas te**; **Ego te**.

- **parallelism:** the symmetrical arrangement of equal or balanced phrases or clauses. Parallel structures are commonly joined by coordinating conjunctions, such as **et** or **vel**, but they are also found frequently with **asyndeton** and **gapping**. **Parallelism** oftens appears as a **tricolon**.

Effect: creates equality and balance.

English: In a larger sense, we cannot dedicate, we cannot consecrate, we cannot hallow this ground. (Abraham Lincoln)

Government of the people, by the people, and for the people shall not perish from this earth. (Abraham Lincoln)

Latin: **Nec te teneo neque dicta refello.** (**Nec** parallels **neque**, **te** parallels **dicta** and **teneo refello**. 4.380)

Pars grandia trudunt . . . , pars agmina cogunt (pars) castigantque moras. (Note the asyndeton and condensation. 4.405–407)

Quod si tantus amor menti (est), si tanta cupido (menti) est . . . (Note the asyndeton and condensation. 6.133, 136)

Solus ego in Pallanta feror, soli mihi Pallas debetur. (Note the asyndeton. 10.442–443)

Illum . . . maiores nostri in civitatem receperunt; nos hunc . . . de nostra civitate eiciamus? (Note the asyndeton. Cicero, *Pro Archia Poeta* 22)

Now look for the parallel expressions in these examples, remembering that parallelism is frequently accompanied by asyndeton, anaphora, and gapping.

Quod facit, auratum est et cuspide fulget acuta, / quod fugat, obtusum est et habet sub harundine plumbum. (The two arrows of Cupid. Ovid, *Metamorphoses* 1.470–471)

Saepe pater dixit, "Generum mihi, filia, debes"; saepe pater dixit, "Debes mihi, nata, nepotes." (Peneus' speech to Daphne. Ovid, *Metamorphoses* 1.481–482)

Nec prosunt domino, quae prosunt omnibus, artes! (Apollo acknowledges to Daphne the ineffectiveness of his divine power. Note the anastrophe/postposition of **artes**. Ovid, *Metamorphoses* 1.524)

Lux . . . / praecipitatur aquis, et aquis nox exit ab isdem. (The sun sets and night falls. Ovid, *Metamorphoses* 4.92)

Quique a me morte revelli / heu sola poteras, poteris nec morte revelli. (Thisbe's speech to the dead Pyramus. Ovid, *Metamorphoses* 4.152–153)

Answers:

Quod facit auratum est et cuspide fulget acuta;
quod fugat, obtusum est et habet sub harundine plumbas.

Saepe pater dixit, "Generum mihi, filia, debes";
saepe pater dixit, "Debes mini, nata, nepotes."

Nec prosunt domino (artes),
quae prosunt omnibus, artes!

Lux . . . praecipitur aquis,
et aquis nox exit ab isdem.

(Tu) quique a me morte revelli heu sola poteras, poteris nec morte revelli.

- **poetic plural:** the use of the plural form of a pronoun or adjective in place of the singular, for metrical purposes or to create a more poetic expression. Equivalent in English to the so-called "royal we," e.g., "We are not amused," said the queen, speaking for her entire country. **Poetic plurals** may be translated as singular on the AP Latin Exam.

Effect: accommodates meter.

Latin: **Tantaene animis caelestibus irae?** (1.11)

Tu mihi quodcumque hoc regni, tu sceptra Iovemque / concilias. (1.78–79)

Crudeles aras traiectaque pectora ferro. (In Pygmalion's murder, there was most probably only one altar and definitely only one chest that was stabbed. 1.355)

Which words in the following lines are poetic plurals?

Illinc fas regna resurgere Troiae. (2.210)

Soles occidere et redire possunt. (Catullus 5.4; cf. 8.3)

Haec si, inquam attuleris, venuste noster. (To Cat's good friend Fabullus. Catullus 13.6)

Me doctarum hederae praemia frontium / dis miscent superis. (Horace, *Odes* 1.1.29)

Ista decent umeros gestamina nostros. (Ovid, *Metamorphoses* 1.457)

Answers:

regna for **regnum; Soles** for **Sol; noster** for **meus; hederae** for **hedera; nostros** for **meos.**

- **prime position**: an unofficial term denoting emphatic placement of a word at the beginning or end of a clause, line, or sentence. Such a word often "controls" the meaning of the unit of thought. See also **hyperbaton** and **anastrophe**.

Latin: **Femina, quae nostris errans in finibus urbem / exiguam pretio posuit**. (Iarbas, complaining to Jupiter about Dido. 4.211–212)

Te propter Libycae gentes . . . odere. (Anastrophe. Dido holds Aeneas for the hostility of neighbors. 4.320–321)

Italiam non sponte sequor. (Aeneas defends his mission to Dido. 4.361)

In each of the following examples, try to determine why the particular word is placed first or, in one case, last.

> **Ego te, quae plurima fando / enumerare vales, numquam, regina, negabo.** (Aeneas and Dido. Note the juxtaposition. 4.333–334)
>
> **Eadem me ad fata vocasses**. (Anna to Dido. 4.678)
>
> **Funeris heu tibi causa fui?** (Aeneas to Dido. 6.458)
>
> **Utque leo, specula cum vidit ab alta / stare procul campis meditantem in proelia taurum.** (A simile. What effect does the poet achieve by his relative placement of the lion and the bull? 10.454–455)
>
> **Non me tua fervida terrent dicta, ferox; di me terrent et Iuppiter hostis**. (Turnus to Aeneas. There are several examples of prime position here. 12.894–895)
>
> **Oculos ubi languida pressit nocte quies**. (Note the hyperbaton.12.908–909)
>
> **Victum quem vulnere Turnus / straverat**. (12.943–944)
>
> **Ille, oculis postquam saevi monimenta doloris / exuviasque hausit**. (12.945–946)

- **rhetorical question:** see the discussion about punctuation in Chapter 5.
- **sound play**: writers often simply like to play with the sounds of words. Sound play often accompanies or heightens the effect of another figure of speech. "The sound must seem an echo to the sense," writes Alexander Pope. See also the examples accompanying **alliteration**, **assonance**, and **onomatopoeia**.

Effects: illustrates, reinforces, heightens the sense.

Latin: **Stetit illa tremens, uteroque recusso / insonuere cavae gemitumque dedere cavernae.** (Note the trisyllables at the beginning of the line, reinforced by the repetition of **utero** and **recusso** and the **insonuere cavae . . . dedere cavernae,** all suggesting the twanging back and forth of the spear shaft after it hits the wooden horse. 2.52–3.)

> **Ardentesque oculos suffecti sanguine et igne / sibila lambebant linguis vibrantibus ora.** (The hissing of the twin serpents. 2.210–11)
>
> **Nequiquam ingeminans iterumque iterumque vocavi.** (Note the redundancy of the mournful **m/n** sounds as Aeneas searches for the lost Creusa, and the contribution of the polysyndeton and rhetorical repetition of **iterum**. 2.770)
>
> **Cui dono lepidum novum libellum.** (Rhyme. Catullus, Poem 1.1)

Qui nunc it per iter tenebricosum. (The bird hopping into Hell? Catullus, 3.11)

Loquente saepe sibilum edidit coma. (The rustling of leaves. Note the personification of **loquente . . . coma**. Catullus, 4.12)

Rumoresque senum severiorum. (The whispering of gossipy old men. Catullus, 5.2)

Litus ut longe resonante Eoa / tunditur unda. (Suggests the beating of the waves on the shore. Catullus, 11. 3–4)

Thyniam atque Bithynos. (The redundant sounds suggest the boredom of Bithynia. Note the elision. Catullus, 31.5)

Nicaeaeque ager uber aestuosae. (Catullus, 46.5)

Si quicquam mutis gratum acceptumve sepulcris (on the death of Calvus' wife; the consonance of **-m-** sounds are often used to express solemnity and sorrow, Catullus, 96.1)

Te rursus in bellum resorbens / unda fretis tulit aestuosis. (The salt sea seems to suck Pompeius back into the fray with its seething foam. Horace, *Odes* 2.7.15–16)

Fractisque rauci fluctibus Hadriae. (The harsh **c/t** sounds evoke the dangerous waters of the Adriatic. Horace, *Odes* 2.14.14; cf. *Odes* 1.1.15)

Quod fugat, auratum est et cuspide fulget acuta. (The hard **c/g** suggests the sharp cutting edge of the golden arrowhead. Ovid, *Metamorphoses* 1.417)

Obviaque adversas vibrabant flamina vestes. (The alliteration of **v** and **s** and the trisyllabic words suggest the rhythmic flapping of Daphne's clothes as she runs. Ovid, *Metamorphoses* 1.528)

Murmure blanditiae minimo transire solebant. (Note how the **m/n** alliteration suggests the gentle murmuring of the lovers. Ovid, *Metamorphoses* 4.70)

Corpus erat: saliunt temptatae pollice venae! (The jumpy sounds perhaps mimic the lively beat of the pulse. Ovid, *Metamorphoses,* 10.289)

- **word play (word picture)**: word choice or position is used by poets to suggest something beyond the literal meaning. Often a "mind picture" is created. Word play often contains more than one figure of speech. See also the examples accompanying **chiasmus, hyperbaton,** and **synchysis**.

  Effects: stimulates the imagination; reinforces sense.

Latin: **Sectaque intexunt abiete costas.** (The words are interwoven, **intexunt,** much as the ribs of the wooden horse; note the harsh **c**-sounds, perhaps the cutting of the wood? 2.16)

Uterumque armato milite complent. (The belly is filled with armed men. 2.20)

Hic Dolopum manus, hic saevus tendebat Achilles, / classibus hic locus, hic acie certare solebant. (Note how the anaphora produces the cinematic effect of a camera panning the shore, **hic . . . hic . . . hic . . . hic.** 2.29–30)

Scinditur incertum studia in contraria vulgus. (The back-and-forth adjective–noun combinations suggest the uncertainty of the crowd. 2.39)

Sopor fessos complectitur artus. (Sleep embracing the weary limbs [of the Trojans] perhaps suggests the previous strangling of and feeding on Laocoon by the serpent **in miseros morsu depascitur artus,** 2.215ff., 2.253.)

Illum absens absentem auditque videtque. (Dido is hallucinating. Note the polyptoton of **absens,** the polysyndeton, and the rhyming verbs, which all contribute to her "double vision." 4.83; cf. Turnus' "dream scene" in 12.903ff.)

Cum frigida mors anima seduxerit artus. (Death separates soul from limbs. 4.385)

Moriemur inultae, / sed moriamur. (Dido seeks her own death. 4.659–660)

Qui volucri curru medium secat agmen. (Turnus cuts through the middle of the ranks with his chariot. 10.440)

Hic Turnus ferro praefixum robur acuto. (The iron tip, **ferro . . . acuto**, is fixed to the end of the spear's shaft, **praefixum robur**. 10.479)

Passer mortuus est meae puellae. (Death comes between the sparrow and Lesbia. Catullus, 3.3)

Orci, quae omnia bella devoratis. (Hell devours all that is beautiful. Catullus, 3.14)

Paene insularum, Sirmio, insularumque. (Sirmio is a promontory sticking out in the middle of the verse. Catullus, 31.1)

Manusque collo / ambas iniciens. (The neck is embraced with both arms, **manus . . . ambas**. Catullus, 35.9–10)

Sicine subrepsti mi atque intestina perurens / . . . nostrae crudele venenum / vitae. (For his betrayal, Rufus is described in terms suggestive of a venomous snake. Note the sibilants, which suggest a hissing snake. Catullus, 77, lines 3 and 5)

Viridi membra sub arbuto. (Limbs recline beneath an evergreen. Horace, *Odes* 1.1.21)

Catulis cerva fidelis. (The doe is surrounded by the trusty hounds. Horace, *Odes* 1.1.27)

Teretes Marsus aper plagas. (The boar, **Marsus aper**, is caught in the net, **Teretes . . . plagas**. Horace, *Odes* 1.1.28)

Quae nunc oppositis debilitat pumicibus mare. (The cliffs and sea, **pumicibus mare**, oppose each other. Horace, *Odes* 1.11.5)

Saeviet circa iecur ulcerosum. (Note the harsh sounds that surround Lydia's liver, **iecur**, the seat of passion, as the poet taunts her. Horace *Odes* 1.25.15)

Fortis et asperas / tractare serpentes. (Listen to the snakiness of Cleopatra's asp. Horace *Odes* 1.37.26–27)

Post equitem sedet atra Cura. (Gloomy Anxiety sits behind the horseman. Horace, *Odes* 3.1.40)

Gelidos . . . / rubro sanguine rivos. (The dark/hot blood mingling with the clear/cold water foreshadows the death of the kid-goat. Was the goat immersed in the spring? Horace, *Odes* 3.13.6–7)

Lascivi suboles gregis. (The herd protects its offspring. Horace, *Odes* 3.13.8)

Cavis impositam ilicem / saxis. (The oak grows out of the hollow rock. Horace, *Odes* 3.13.14–15)

Eque sagittifera prompsit duo tela pharetra. (The two arrows are inside the quiver. Ovid, *Metamorphoses* 1.468)

Ut canis in vacuo leporem cum Gallicus arvo. (The hound, **canis . . . Gallicus**, has trapped the hare, **leporem**, in the field. Ovid, *Metamorphoses* 1.533)

Vidit et obscurum timido pede fugit in antrum. (Thisbe is actually enclosed in the dark cave, **obscurum . . . antrum**.) Ovid, *Metamorphoses* 4.100)

Interea niveum mira feliciter arte sculpsit ebur. (Note how the chiastic arrangement centers on **feliciter,** *successfully*; so that the "art is revealed by its art," as in **ars adeo latet arte sua.** Ovid, *Metamorphoses*, 10.247–248 and 252)

Armata vulgus inerme manu. (The unarmed mob is surrounded by those with weapons. Ovid, *Amores* 1.9.22)

Some Important Points to Remember about How Latin Poetry Works

As we discussed in Chapter 6, there are several ways to improve your success in writing a critical essay on the AP Latin Exam. One is to practice writing essays by answering free-response essay questions, using the AP Latin: Vergil website and this book. Another way is to become familiar with the fundamentals of literary analysis in Latin, which include the techniques discussed above, and meter, which will be discussed in the next chapter. Some students prefer to use one of several formulaic approaches to poetic analysis that have been developed by experienced AP Latin teachers. The most well-known is designated SWIMTAG.[92] The acronym SWIMTAG, which is actually SW^{2}IM^{2}T^{2}AG when expanded, means Sounds, Word order, Word choice, Images, Meter, Mood, Tone, Theme, Allusions, and Grammar. These categories sum up the poetic qualities worthy of consideration when you analyze and discuss a passage of Latin poetry. Use SWIMTAG to train your ear and eye to hear and see the Latin in a more critical way. Not every Latin passage will contain all of these elements, but using SWIMTAG, particularly in the early stages of learning how to critique a passage of Latin literature, will help you to understand why the *Aeneid* is classic, as well as classical, literature. Now that you have revisited some of the individual elements of poetic analysis, let us summarize. This summary will include activities on some of the more common figures and stylistic devices appearing in the *Aeneid*, which will be followed by a series of further activities for practice. The assignment of a particular figure to a particular category below is necessarily subjective, and may even seem arbitrary, but it provides a convenient way to organize the major elements used in defining how a Latin poet writes. All references immediately below are to the *Aeneid*, unless indicated otherwise.

The Selection of Words

This category of techniques consists of the particular words selected by a writer (words in parentheses are not required for the AP Latin Exam): (archaism), (Grecism), (poetic plural), and tmesis. These techniques have to do with the way a Latin word is spelled or the form that it takes in context. We learned in our discussion about Vergil's vocabulary in Chapter 5 how uniquely varied is the poet's use of words. To take the category of word selection a bit further, what about verbal echoes and reminiscences? Words that flash back or foreshadow? Why does the writer choose to use the particular words that he employs? What effect does their use have on what he is trying to communicate? One particular feature of Vergil's style worth mentioning is his use of allusion. As an example, the poet uses metaphorical language throughout the early stages of Book 2. One scholar has made a compelling argument for the fact that Vergil deliberately used figurative language in Book 2, through the iconic imagery of the serpent and the flame, to suggest that the snakes and the Greek fleet were one and the same: both come from Tenedos, both float on the sea in formation, both head for shore, and both bring blood and fire to Troy (**ardentesque oculos suffecti sanguine et igni**, 2.210).[93] A bit later in this passage, words used to describe the twin snakes are also used to describe the wooden horse, tempting the listener/reader to equate the horse with the serpents. **Insinuat pavor** (2.229), in describing the panic that ensues after Laocoon's grisly murder, suggests the sinuousness of snakes. As the horse is towed into the city, it slides or glides in threateningly, **mediaeque minans inlabitur urbi** (2.240); **inlabitur** is reminiscent of the word **lapsu**, which describes the serpents slithering beneath Minerva's shield (2.225) and which is used generically to represent the motion of a snake. (Remember that Vergil lived on a farm, where he most likely became acquainted with the habits and behavior of snakes.) Sleep embraces the weary limbs of the Trojans, **sopor fessos complectitur artus** (2.253) using language that is similar to that employed in portraying the serpents when strangling Laocoon and sons: **corpora natorum serpens amplexus uterque/implicat et miseros morsu depascitur artus** (2.214–215). **Amplexi** appears again a few lines later (2.218). Further along, after the Trojans celebrate, a foreboding silence slithers in like a snake: **quies . . . gratissima serpit** (2.268–269). Such verbal echoes create the following equation: the snakes = the Greeks = the horse = the fall of Troy. Vergil artfully sets all this up with his portrayal of Laocoon sacrificing the bull (2.201–202, and the ensuing simile of Laocoon bellowing like a wounded bull in 223–224), from which the listener/reader infers that the bull is Laocoon is Troy.

With further regard to word choice, Vergil often uses proper nouns to add variety and interest (**Mycenae** for Greece, **Aeacidae** or **Pelides** for Achilles), to validate current tradition (**Anchisiades** for Aeneas, **Iulus** for Ascanius), to give the feeling of august antiquity (**Iliades** for Trojan women, **Alcides** for Hercules, **Saturnia** for Juno), or simply to show off (**Achivi, Argivi, Danai, Grai,** and **Pelasgae**, plus **Dolopes** and **Myrmidones**, who were Achilles' men, and **Doricus** as an adjective, all denoting the Greeks).

The Positions of Words

The word order of poetry is often the same as that of prose, but "poetic license" allows poets to relocate words from their expected positions, due to considerations of meter or style. These devices can reveal or reinforce the poet's meaning. Here are some figures of speech that use the placement of a word or words in the clause, line, or sentence to communicate or emphasize meaning: (anastrophe), apostrophe, chiasmus, enjambment, (golden line), hyperbaton, hysteron proteron, (juxtaposition), oxymoron, (prime position), prolepsis, and synchysis.[94] We will now provide some review of those figures of word placement that are particularly common in Vergil: anastrophe, chiasmus, hyperbaton, and synchysis. First, a quick refresher lesson, and then an activity.

Anastrophe is a general term referring to the displacement of words from their usual or expected loctations. Remember **Karthago Italiam contra**? Or **Sum pius Aeneas, raptos qui ex hoste penates . . . veho**? Hyperbaton, which is a type of anastrophe, refers specifically to the separation of an adjective from its noun, both to emphasize the meaning of the adjective and sometimes to frame the words in between in order to create a word picture, e.g., **infelix umero cum apparuit alto / balteus** (12.941–942), where **infelix** is dislocated from its noun, **balteus**. The placement of **infelix**, which is also emphatic, allows the poet to create a word picture with the intervening words **umero cum apparuit alto**, wherein the swordbelt of Pallas appears to be literally hanging from Turnus' shoulder (note also the added effect of the enjambment of **balteus**). The patterning of words in chiasmus and synchysis is more formulaic. Like hyperbaton, Vergil uses these figures both to emphasize certain words or pairs of words or to create word pictures. In this line from Book 1, Vergil employs chiasmus (AabB) to portray Aeneas as being so overjoyed at seeing again his long-lost companions, that he seems to shake hands with both hands: **Ilionea petit dextra laevaque Serestum** (1.611; **Ilionea** is acc. sing.). In this line from the *Metamorphoses*, Ovid uses synchysis (AbaB) to describe Apollo's pursuit of Daphne, who is compared to a hare which a hound is pursuing: **ut canis in vacuo leporem cum Gallicus arvo /vidit** (1.533). Note how the interlocking of **canis – vacuo – Gallicus – arvo** allows the hare to be placed in an empty field (**vacuo leporem. . . arvo**) where he is out-flanked by the hound (**canis . . . leporem . . . Gallicus**).

The Frequency of Words

The repetition or omission of words is found frequently in Latin poetry. In this section, we will consolidate the figures of speech that relate to word frequency.

- Here are some figures that depend upon repetition or redundancy to communicate or emphasize: alliteration, anaphora, parallelism, pleonasm, polyptoton, polysyndeton, tricolon crescens.
- And here are some figures that depend upon words that are omitted by the writer and are to be assumed or understood by the listener/reader: aposiopesis, asyndeton, ellipsis, gapping, hendiadys, zeugma.[95]

Remember that anaphora repeats words at the beginning of successive, phrases, clauses, or lines and that it is frequently accompanied in Vergil's writing by asyndeton and gapping. These devices, along with parallelism and tricolon crescens, create series of words, phrases, or clauses that can build up or let down an emotion or a situation.

After reviewing these devices, complete the following activity. In each of the examples below, circle the words in anaphora and draw a connecting line or bracket between words containing asyndeton (look for the commas). Also "close the gaps" by including the words that are missing and understood. Not every example will contain all three techniques. Finally, comment on how these devices communicate and/or reinforce the meaning of the Latin.

a. **Cui talia fanti / ante fores subito non vultus, non color unus, / non comptae mansere comae**. (6.46–48)

b. **Quid Thesea, magnum quid memorem Alciden?** (6.122–123)

c. **Quod si tantus amor menti, si tanta cupido est, . . . accipe quae peragenda prius**. (6.133–136)

d. **Sternitur Arcadiae proles, sternuntur Etrusci / et vos , . . . Teucri**. (10.429–430)

e. **Sit Latium, sint Albani per saecula reges, / sit Romana potens Itala virtute propago**. (12.826–827).

Answers:

a. **Cui talia fanti / ante fores subito non vultus (mansit), non, color unus (mansit), / non comptae mansere comae**. This sentence uses anaphora, asyndeton, and gapping to create a dramatic picture of the transformation of the Sibyl as a sequence of events.

b. **Quid Thesea (memorem), magnum quid memorem Alciden?** Aeneas speaks to the Sibyl about his right, as the son of a divinity, to enter the Underworld. The figures, plus the allusions to great legendary heroes, express Aeneas' emotional state.

c. **Quod si tantus amor menti (est), si tanta cupido est, . . . accipe quae peragenda prius**. The Sibyl replies to Aeneas' insistence by telling him, with equal insistence, what he must do, divinity or not.

d. **Sternitur Arcadiae proles, sternuntur Etrusci / et vos , . . . Teucri (sternimini)**. The repetition of stated and implied forms of **sterno** and the asyndeton heighten the consequences of Lausus' battle-frenzy.

e. **Sit Latium, sint Albani per saecula reges, / sit Romana potens Itala virtute propago**. The repetition and prime position of **sit-sint-sit**, the asyndeton, and the parallel structure of the clauses in this tricolon crescens all draw attention to the solemnity of Juno's concessions.

Another figure that depends upon word frequency is hendiadys, or "two for one," which consists of two nouns joined by a conjunction instead of a single modified noun. For example, as Jupiter is outlining Rome's future history to Venus, he says **cernes urbem et promissa Lavini moenia** (1.258–259), *you will see the city and the promised walls of Lavinium*. Vergil chooses to embellish the greatness of Lavinium by using hendiadys for the expected and more prosaic **promissa moenia urbis Lavini**, *the promised walls of the city Lavinium*.

In each of the following examples, locate the hendiadys and indicate why the figure might be used.

a. **Paulum lacrimis et mente morata / incubuitque toro**. (Dido is lying on her couch, contemplating her suicide. 4.649–650)

b. **Saevi monimenta doloris exuviasque hausit**. (Aeneas has caught sight of Pallas' swordbelt on Turnus' shoulder. 12.945–946)

c. **Non sine vano / aurarum et silvae metu** (A young girl is afraid of even the breezes in the woods. Note the example of litotes, **Non sine**. Horace, *Odes* 1.23.4)

d. **Mollierant animos lectus et umbra meos**. (Ovid is relaxing under a shade-tree. Ovid, *Amores* 1.9.42)

Answers:

a. **lacrimis et mente** (= **misera memoria**, in unhappy recollection)

b. **monimenta doloris exuviasque** (Aeneas does not really see two different things here, but only the swordbelt, **exuvias**.)

c. **aurarum et silvae metu** (= **aurarum silvae**, breezes of the woods)

d. **lectus et umbra** (= **umbrosus lectus**, a shaded couch)

A quick sidebar.

Confused about the difference between hendiadys and zeugma? Let's use some examples to clarify the difference.

Hendiadys: **Lucem et solem**, *light and the sun*, i.e., **Lux solis**, *light of the sun*.

Zeugma: **Cadaver et veritatem vidit**. *He saw the dead body and the truth*, i.e., **Cadaver vidit et veritatem cognovit**. *He saw the dead body and he knew the truth*.

So, hendiadys, or "two for one," uses two combined words to create one meaning, and zeugma, or "one for two," uses one word to create two meanings.

Now, explain how you interpret the meaning of the zeugma in this example: **crudeles aras traiectaque pectora ferro nudavit** (Dido's husband Sychaeus has just been murdered by Pygmalion. 1.355–56).

Answer:

Crudeles aras traiectaque pectora ferro nudavit. *He laid bare the cruel altars and his breast, pierced with steel.* The verb **nudavit** governs two direct objects, **aras** and **pectora**, only one of which really fits the sense of the verb.

The Sounds of Words

Because Latin poetry is rarely read aloud or heard, much of its beauty as poetry is lost. To determine whether there is poetic use of sound in a line of verse, read it aloud! Poetry is, after all, verbal music. The sounds within and between words have suggestive, and sometimes prescriptive, associations with their meanings. For instance, the sounds of b, c, d, g, p, and t give an abrupt, harsh, rigid sound, such as when the bull is sacrificed in Book 2, **taurus et incertam excussit cervice securim** (2.224), or the sound of striking sparks from flint, **Ac primum scilici scintillam excudit Achates** (1.174).[96] Some scholars believe that the repetition and sound of the words **Sic, sic** in Dido's death scene (**Sic, sic iuvat ire sub umbras**, 4.660) suggest Dido's repeated stabs. Phonetic devices are often found together, such as alliteration and onomatopoeia, e.g., **Fit sonitus spumante salo** (2.209), which plays on the ear to suggest both the sibilant hissing of the twin serpents as they slide through the water and the resulting sound of the sea spray. As with many poetic devices, the repetition of sounds is often emphatic. We have met several uses of initial and internal sounds used in this way. Alliteration or consonance repeats the sound of a particular consonant, while assonance repeats that of a particular vowel.

alliteration: repetition of successive or nearby initial consonants; alliteration is a special case of consonance, wherein the repeated consonant is an initial sound.

English: She sells sea shells down by the sea shore. (Traditional)

Latin: **Musa, mihi causas memora, quo numine laeso**. (*Aeneid* 1.8)

assonance: repetition of internal vowel sounds to create internal rhyming.

English: On a proud round cloud in a white high night. (e.e. cummings, "If a Cheer Rules Elephant Angel Child Should Sit")

Latin: **Quod fugat, obtusum est et habet sub harundine plumbum**. (Ovid, *Metamorphoses* 1.471)

consonance: repetition of internal consonants in short succession.

English: All mammals named Sam are clammy. (Wikipedia, s.v. "Literary consonance")

Latin: **Ut te postremo donarem munere mortis / et mutam nequiquam adloquerer cinerem.** (Catullus, 101.3–4)

Are the sounds of the following line happy or sad? **Nequiquam ingeminans iterumque iterumque vocavi.** (Sad; Creusa has just disappeared. 2.770.) It is likely that your response to these sounds and rhythm is almost intuitive, conditioned by the steady pulse of your mother's heartbeat when you were in the womb. Don't the sounds of this next line suggest that it is raining? **Accipiunt inimicum imbrem, rimisque fatiscunt.** (This line describes the aftermath of the storm scene. 1.123.) If you were asked what sound might describe the pummeling of someone's chest with their own fists, an age-old expression of grief, what sound would you choose? Listen to the percussive sound of Anna beating her breast in grief over the death of her sister: **pectora pugnis** (4.673). Sound play, which is a non-technical but useful term, often combines several different phonetic techniques, including rhythm, which creates interest by placing in sequence

/ / / / /

words containing the same number of syllables, e.g., **Stetit illa tremens** (2.52), where the disyllables mimic the twanging back and forth of Laocoon's spear after it has struck the wooden horse. Listen to the almost-inexorable drumbeat of the

/ / /

trisyllables describing the scene at the news of Dido's death: **collapsam aspiciunt**

/ / / / / / / / / / / / / / /

comites, ensemque cruore / spumantem sparsasque manu (4.664–665; note the elision of **collapsam aspiciunt** as the queen falls). The sounds of Latin can be almost as much fun for the listener/reader as for the writer! This author believes that Vergil was being deliberately evocative by using sibilants in the line **Demissum lapsi per funem, Acamasque Thoasque** (2.262). I hear the Greeks sliding down the rope. Do you?

Words as Images

Just because Roman writers lived several millenia ago doesn't mean they could not, or did not, use their imaginations when they wrote. The fact that we can understand and even relate to most of what they wanted to say tells us something about the commonality of human experience. Vergil relates to us best through his personal experience. Life on the farm made a great impression on him and he returns to the farm, and to nature, for much of his imagery. Imagery and imagination are connected, after all. What pictures does your mind create when you read? Imagery provides the special effects of poetry, e.g., "The simile that solitary shines / In the dry desert of a thousand lines" (Alexander Pope).

Here is a list of figures that Latin poets, particularly Vergil, use to express their imaginations: allegory, antithesis, ecphrasis, hyperbole, irony, metaphor, metonymy, simile, synecdoche, oxymoron, personification, and word play. The figures allegory, irony, metonymy, metaphor, metonymy, and synecdoche are also known as tropes, which is a general term in English that refers to word-play. We will now revisit several of these figures that are important for our study of epic poetry: metaphor, metonymy, and simile. Of course, there are other images that do not have names but should, images that are nonetheless compelling, images that touch our senses, such as the description of Venus as huntress or the Cyclopes laboring in Vulcan's forge, or that affect our emotions, such as the storm, the fall of Troy, Dido's death scene, the killing of Pallas, or the duel between Aeneas and Turnus. As you have learned, metaphor and simile are defining elements of epic poetry. Both are used to apply the qualities of something familiar for the purpose of giving form and substance to something less familiar. Imagery is often associated with some kind of comparison, whether direct (simile) or implied (metaphor). Remember that metaphors depend upon the mind of the listener/reader for their meaning and usually consist of a single word, whereas similes, which are introduced by guide words such as **ac, qualis, similes, ut,** and **velut(i)**, identify the comparison and can extend for multiple lines.

Here are some similes and metaphors that appear in the *Aeneid*. Distinguish each as one or the other and indicate what is being compared.

a. **Qualis in Eurotae ripis aut per iuga Cynthi / exercet Diana choros . . . ; illa pharetram / fert umero gradiensque deas supereminet omnes**. (1.500–501)

b. **Invadunt urbem somno vinoque sepultam**. (2.265)

c. **Saevit inops animi totamque incensa per urbem / bacchatur**. (4.300–301)

d. **Ac veluti ingentem formicae farris acervum / cum populant hiemis memores tectique reponunt**. (4.402–403)

e. **Quasi mugitus, fugit cum saucius aram / taurus**. (2.223–224)

f. **His dictis impenso animum flammavit amore**. (4.54)

Answers:

a. Simile (**qualis**, etc.); Dido, when she arrives with her retinue and is seen by Aeneas for the first time, is compared to the goddess Diana.

b. Metaphor (**sepultam**); the city of Troy is "buried" in wine and sleep after celebrating the departure of the Greeks and their possession of the horse.

c. Metaphor (**incensa**); upon learning of Aeneas' plans to leave Carthage, Dido rages like a maenad and is "on fire."

d. Simile (**veluti**, etc.); the arrangements of the Trojans for departure from Troy are compared to those of ants preparing for winter.

e. Simile (**quasi**, etc.); Laocoon, who is being attacked by the serpents, bellows like a bull wounded at a sacrifice.

f. Metaphor (**flammavit**); Dido reacts to Anna's words of encouragement by feeling the fire of passion.

Metonymy is a substitution, word for word, made by a poet when he wishes to describe something in a less commonplace or less prosaic way. For example, instead of using the word **hasta** for *spear*, he chooses an associated word, such as **robur** (*oak-wood*). Contrary to metaphors and similes, which are used to describe a person or thing in terms more familiar to the reader, the poet uses metonymy to stretch the listener/reader's mind and experience. Vergil also uses metonymy to substitute the name of a god or goddess for something with which the deity is associated, e.g., Bacchus for wine, Ceres for grain, Mars for war, or Vulcan for fire. A third common Vergilian use of metonymy is the substitution of a word for an object by a word that indicates the material from which the object is made, e.g., **lignum** for (the wooden) **equus**, **ferrum** for **gladius** or **ensis**, and so forth. Such substitutions make for more interesting reading. Synecdoche, a sub-category of metonymy, is the one-word substitution of a part of something for the whole (*pars pro toto*), e.g., **puppis** or **carina** for **navis**, or **tectum** for **domus**.

Practice Questions on Figures of Speech

The following questions that test your mastery of the techniques of poetic analysis approximate, in range and scope, those appearing on the AP Latin Exam. Occasionally you will find a question on a poetic technique or usage that is not required by the College Board. For additional practice with techniques of poetic analysis, consult Levels III-IV Poetry and Level V of previous National Latin Exams and the resources listed in the Appendix.[97] Answers to all of the following questions are provided at the end of this chapter.

Matching Question 1

From the list of terms provided, match the poetic term with its English examples. Not all figures are used.

English Examples

A. anaphora	E. diminutive	I. alliteration
B. personification	F. litotes	J. apostrophe
C. transferred epithet	G. onomatopoeia	K. antithesis
D. hyperbole	H. metaphor	L. metonymy

___ 1. Hunger sat shivering in the road.

___ 2. Plop, plop, fizz, fizz, O what a relief it is! (Alka Seltzer commercial)

___ 3. Nothing like a good glass of Bacchus to go with the pasta.

___ 4. My recollection of Latin grammar is minuscule.

___ 5. The moon is a ghostly galleon.

___ 6. We shall not flag or fail. We shall go on to the end. (Churchill)

___ 7. Sighted ship sank same. (WWII sub report)

___ 8. I must have taken a million Latin tests by now.

___ 9. The ice was so cold that it felt warm to the touch.

___10. Robin Williams is not an unfunny guy.

___11. Alas, poor Yorick, I knew him, Horatio! (Shakespeare)

Matching Question 2

Match the figure from the *Aeneid* with its corresponding identification.

___ 1. Quos ego - - - !	A. ellipsis
___ 2. Molemque et montes	B. tmesis
___ 3. Finem dedit ore loquendi	C. pleonasm
___ 4. Summersas obrue puppes	D. prolepsis
___ 5. Amissos longe socios sermone	E. aposiopesis
___ 6. Velut agmine facto	F. metonymy
___ 7. Invadunt urbem somno vinoque sepultam	G. synchysis
___ 8. Bis collo squamea circum /terga dati	H. zeugma
___ 9. Fluctusque ad sidera tollit	I. alliteration
___10. Fracti fatis bello repulsi	J. metaphor
___11. Fit sonitus spumante salo	K. chiasmus
___12. Facilis descensus Averno	L. hyperbole
___13. Crudeles aras traiectaque pectore . . . nudavit	M. simile
___14. Implentur veteris Bacchi	N. hendiadys

Multiple-Choice Question 1 (Books 1–6)

Select the correct answer. Each figure of speech is underlined for your convenience. All examples are from the *Aeneid.*

1. What figure of speech occurs in hic illius arma, hic currus fuit?
   (A) simile (C) hyperbole
   (B) anaphora (D) tmesis

2. The word desertae in the phrase templumque vetustum desertae Cereris is
   (A) zeugma (C) personification
   (B) apostrophe (D) transferred epithet

3. The line iamque faces et saxa volant, furor arma ministrat contains an example of
   (A) ellipsis (C) asyndeton
   (B) tricolon crescens (D) chiasmus

4. What figure of speech occurs in involvens umbra magna terramque polumque
   (A) tmesis (C) aposiopesis
   (B) polysyndeton (D) alliteration

5. Dulces exuviae, dum fata deusque sinebat is an example of
   (A) enjambment (C) apostrophe
   (B) synchysis (D) polyptoton

6. Ac velut magno in populo cum saepe coorta est / seditio is
   (A) simile (C) zeugma
   (B) asyndeton (D) chiasmus

7. What figure of speech occurs in multum ille et terris iactatus et alto / vi superum?
   (A) synchysis (C) onomatopoeia
   (B) prolepsis (D) enjambment

8. The figure of speech in saevus ubi . . . iacet Hector, ubi ingens Sarpedon, ubi tot . . . / scuta virum galeasque et fortia corpora solvit is an example of
   (A) hendiadys (C) pleonasm
   (B) tricolon crescens (D) tmesis

9. Longum per valles armenta sequuntur agmen is an example of

   (A) hyperbaton (C) simile

   (B) aposiopesis (D) apostrophe

10. The figure of speech that appears in sic ore effata is

   (A) hyperbole (C) enjambment

   (B) personification (D) pleonasm

Multiple-Choice Question 2 (Books 10 and 12)

Select the correct answer for each figure. When there is no underlining, consider the entire sentence.

1. Quisquis honos tumuli, quidquid solamen humandi est, / largior. (Book 10.493–494)

   (A) polyptoton (C) metonymy

   (B) anaphora (D) tricolon crescens

2. O dolor atque decus magnum rediture parenti. (Book 10.507)

   (A) aposiopesis (C) enjambment

   (B) tmesis (D) apostrophe

3. Hinc Pallas instat et urget, hinc contra Lausus. (Book 10.433–434)

   (A) assonance (C) hyperbole

   (B) anaphora (D) polysyndeton

4. Per patris hospitium et mensas, quas advena adisti. (Book 10.460)

   (A) transferred epithet (C) hendiadys

   (B) hyperbaton (D) litotes

5. Infelix umero cum apparuit alto / balteus. (Book 12.941–42)

   (A) zeugma (C) hyperbaton

   (B) pleonasm (D) anaphora

6. Hic Turnus ferro praefixum robur acuto. (Book 10.479)

   (A) apostrophe (C) ellipsis

   (B) asyndeton (D) metonymy

7. Consurgunt gemitu Rutuli totusque remugit. (Book 12.928)
   (A) polyptoton (C) personification
   (B) onomatopoeia (D) transferred epithet

8. Oculos dextramque precantem / protendens. (Book 12.930–1)
   (A) transferred epithet (C) zeugma
   (B) synchysis (D) litotes

9. Volat atri turbinis instar. (Book 12.923)
   (A) asyndeton (C) oxymoron
   (B) simile (D) prolepsis

10. Tempus desistere pugnae. (Book 10.441)
   (A) ellipsis (C) hyperbole
   (B) zeugma (D) aposiopesis

Answers to Short-Answer Questions on Figures of Speech

Answers to Matching Question 1

1. B	3. L	5. H	7. L	9. K	11. J
2. G	4. E	6. A	8. D	10. F	

Answers to Matching Question 2

1. E	3. C	5. G	7. J	9. L	11. I	13. H
2. N	4. D	6. M	8. B	10. K	12. A	14. F

Answers to Multiple-Choice Question 1

1. B	3. C	5. C	7. D	9. A
2. D	4. B	6. A	8. B	10. D

Answers to Multiple-Choice Question 2

1. A	3. B	5. C	7. B	9. B
2. D	4. C	6. D	8. C	10. A

Practice Using Poetic Analysis in Writing an Essay on the AP Latin Exam

The next practice questions ask you to apply what you've learned about poetic analysis to several AP-style essay questions.[98] Remember that you are both demonstrating your ability to read Latin with comprehension and your ability to analyze it in a critical manner. Review the rubrics for correct Latin citation in Chapter 6, if necessary. Sample answers are provided after the last question.

Passage A

"Quae iam finis erit, coniunx? Quid denique restat?
Indigetem Aenean scis ipsa et scire fateris
deberi caelo fatisque ad sidera tolli.
Quid struis? Aut qua spe gelidis in nubibus haeres?
Mortalin decuit violari vulnere divum?
Aut ensem (quid enim sine te Iuturna valeret?)
ereptum reddi Turno et vim crescere victis?

***Aeneid* 12.791–799**

Identify by name or description in the nearest margin the underlined poetic techniques and usages that appear in the preceding passage (there are seven). Be sure to comment on the effect each has on Jupiter's indignant speech to his wife. Each figure is limited to the line in which it is found, except for the one that is double-underlined.

Extra credit: what word is gapped that is necessary to the meaning of the final line? (Hint: Upon what does the infinitive form **reddi** depend?)

Passage B

Talia iactanti stridens Aquilone procella
velum adversa ferit, fluctusque ad sidera tollit.
Fraguntur remi, tum prora avertiti et undis
dat latus, insequitur cumulo praeruptus aquae mons.
Hi summo in fluctu pendent; his unda dehiscens
terram inter fluctus aperit, furit aestus harenis.

***Aeneid* 1.102–107**

Identify the three examples of hyperbole that appear in this passage and discuss the poetic effect of this figure on Vergil's description of the storm.

Passage C

Talibus Aeneas ardentem et torva tuentem
lenibat dictis animum lacrimasque ciebat.
Illa solo fixos oculos aversa tenebat
nec magis incepto vultum sermone movetur
quam si dura silex aut stet Marpesia cautes.
Tandem corripuit sese atque inimica refugit
in nemus umbriferum.

***Aeneid* 6.467–473**

The passage above describes Dido is “effectively consumed by her anger” (Pharr, *Aeneid*, page 191, note for lines 467–468). In a short essay, validate this observation. Refer to the Latin **throughout** the passage to support what you say.

Write your essay using as support those portions of the text that are underlined. Double-underlining is used to distinguish a second word-group appearing in the same line, or coordinate expressions. This activity is designed to help you see what Latin is relevant to the question.

Passage D

“Dissimulare etiam sperasti, perfide, tantum
posse nefas tacitusque mea decedere terra?
Nec te noster amor nec te data dextera quondam
nec moritura tenet crudeli funere Dido?
Quin etiam hiberno moliri sidere classem
et mediis properas Aquilonibus ire per altum,
crudelis? Quid, si non arva aliena domosque
ignotas peteres, et Troia antiqua maneret,
Troia per undosum peteretur classibus aequor?
Mene fugis? Per ego has lacrimas dextramque tuam te
(quando aliud mihi iam miserae nihil ipsa reliqui),
per conubia nostra, per inceptos hymenaeos,
si bene quid de te merui, fuit aut tibi quicquam
dulce meum, miserere domus labentis et istam,
oro, si quis adhuc precibus locus, exue mentem.
Te propter Libycae gentes Nomadumque tyranni
odere, infensi Tyrii; te propter eundem
exstinctus pudor et, qua sola sidera adibam,
fama prior. Cui me moribundam deseris hospes
(hoc solum nomen quoniam de coniuge restat)?
Quid moror? An mea Pygmalion dum moenia frater
destruat aut captam ducat Gaetulus Iarbas?
Saltem si qua mihi de te suscepta fuisset
ante fugam suboles, si quis mihi parvulus aula
luderet Aeneas, qui te tamen ore referret,
non equidem omnino capta ac deserta viderer.”

***Aeneid* 4.305–330**

In this speech, Dido uses a number of different ways to persuade Aeneas to stay in Carthage. Outline these in the sequence in which they appear. Include the relevant Latin for each point, correctly cited.

Passage E

Haec ubi dicta, cavum conversa cuspide montem
impulit in latus: ac venti velut agmine facto,
qua data porta, ruunt et terras turbine perflant.
Incubuere mari totumque a sedibus imis
una Eurusque Notusque ruunt creberque procellis
Africus et vastos volvunt ad litora fluctus:
insequitur clamorque virum stridorque rudentum.
Eripiunt subito nubes caelumque diemque
Teucrorum ex oculis; ponto nox incubat atra.
Intonuere poli et crebris micat ignibus aether
praesentemque viris intentant omnia mortem.

***Aeneid* 1.81–91**

In the passage above, Aeolus releases the winds at the command of Juno. In a **well-developed** essay, discuss the ways in which the poet expresses the consequences of this act.

Be sure to refer specifically to the Latin **throughout** the passage to support your essay. Do NOT simply summarize what the passage says. (When you are asked to refer specifically to the Latin, you must write out the Latin and/or cite line number AND you must translate, accurately paraphrase, or make clear in your discussion that you understand the Latin.)

Answer to Passage for Analysis A

Line 1: **Quae . . . Quid . . .**, polyptoton.

Line 2: **Indigetem (Aenean)**, prime or emphatic position.

Line 3: **ad sidera**, hyperbole.

Lines 4, 5, 6, and 7: rhetorical questions (see Chapter 5).

Line 5: **Mortali . . . vidum**, antithesis or contrast; **violari vulnere**, alliteration.

Line 6: juxtaposition of **te** (Juno) and **Iuturna** (Juturna).

Line 7: **ereptum reddi**: antithesis.

Answer to Passage for Analysis B

1. **fluctusque ad sidera tollit**, line 2
2. **cumulo praeruptus aquae mons**, line 4
3. **unde dehiscens terras inter fluctus aperit**, lines 5–6.

Conclusion: these examples of hyperbole exaggerate the force of the storm and thus the danger to Aeneas and the Trojans.

Sample Answer to Passage for Analysis C

As Aeneas passes through the underworld, he chances upon Dido in the place where people go who have died for love. Prior to the passage here, Aeneas' expresses contrition and heartfelt pain (lenibat dictis . . . lacrimasque ciebat, 2) at confirming the rumor that Dido has killed herself. In this context, the poet describes that her mind (or heart, animum, 2) is both fiery (ardentem, 1) and fiercely attentive (? the meaning of torva tuentem . . . animum, 1–2, is problematic). The passage, going on to designate Dido impersonally as Illa (3), describes her as having turned away (aversa, 3) and as holding her eyes fixed upon the ground (solo fixos oculos . . . tenebat, 3). So far the queen's demeanor, both stated and implied, indicates that she is indeed angry with Aeneas for betraying her. She continues to ignore him by appearing to be unmoved by his words (nec . . . vultum . . . movetur, 4) and by standing there in stony silence. The two-part simile of magis . . . quam si dura silex and stet Marpesia cautes (5) is powerful in depicting the queen as hard and flinty and as a Marpesian crag (or as the hard flint of a Marpesian crag). Finally, she doesn't simply depart, but "snatches herself away" (corripuit, 6), which is an expression that suggests high emotion, and runs off (refugit, 6) into the shadow (or shade)-filled grove. The word inimica, a personal enemy, leaves both Aeneas and the listener/reader feeling that "Hell hath no fury like a woman scorned."

Sample Answer to Passage for Analysis D

1. Dido is enraged at the news, reported in the previous lines by Rumor, that Aeneas is leaving. (She hisses at him, Dissimulare . . . sperasti, 1, calls him treacherous, perfide, 1, and includes the word nefas, something impious or unspeakable, in her accusations, 2).
2. The queen then implores Aeneas, justifying her supplication by referring to their love and marriage vows (te noster amor . . . tenet and data dextera quondam, 3–4; note the juxtaposition of te noster). She also threatens him with guilt, were she to die as a result of his rejection of her (moritura . . . crudeli funere Dido, 4).
3. Angry again in lines 5–9 (Dido calls Aeneas crudelis, "heartless," 7), she chastizes him for picking the most inopportune season, winter (hiberno . . . sidere, 5, and mediis properas Aquilonibus, 6), to leave, implying that he wanted to escape from her at the earliest possible opportunity. The queen mocks him with the rhetorical question that he wouldn't be leaving for Troy (if it were still standing) in the winter, would he? Mene fugis? Is it me that you are running away from she asks. (10)
4. Dido tearfully (Per . . . has lacrimas, 10) returns to the subject of marriage, again imploring (oro, si quis adhuc precibus locus, 15) Aeneas to remember his commitment to her and his vows (per conubia nostra, per inceptos hymenaeos, 12). She introduces the guilt-trip again by suggesting that Aeneas will be responsible for the downfall of her house (miserere domus labentis, 14). She buffers these comments with pleas: all I have left for myself is this marriage (quando aliud mihi iam miserae nihil ipsa reliqui, 11), "if I have ever deserved

any kindness from you" (si bene quid de te merui, 13), and "if anything of mine has been sweet in your sight" (fuit aut tibi quicquam / dulce meum, 13–14).

5. In lines 16–19, beginning with the powerful anastrophe and anaphora of Te propter (16, 17), the blame-game now becomes a pity-party. Iarbas and the rest of her African neighbors, and even her own people, now hate her because of Aeneas (Libycae . . . Tyrii, 6–17). And she has lost her honor, exstinctus pudor et . . . fama prior, 18–19).
6. In lines 19–20, Dido flip-flops back to using words of retribution, sarcastically calling Aeneas "guest" (hospes, 19) instead of husband.
7. The queen's rhetorical question Quid moror? (21), means, essentially, I'll kill myself. What do I have to live for? I will be at the mercy of my brother Pygmalion, or Gaetulian Iarbas, (or any other man, she implies, 21–22).
8. After appealing to Aeneas as her protector, Dido plays her trump card. I could deal with all this more easily if only I had a little Aeneas playing in the hall (si quis mihi parvulus aula / luderet Aeneas, 25–26). Dido's strong character and personality as a queen, which is evident at times in this speech, finally yields to her role as a wife, mother, and woman, in which she appeals to Aeneas on the basis of love (amor, 3), marriage (data dextera, 3, conubia, 12, hymenaeos, 12, and coniuge, 20), and motherhood (suboles, 24, parvulus . . . Aeneas, 24–25).

Sample Answer to Passage for Analysis E

In Book 1, Juno uses complaints, stern words, and a bribe to pressure Aeolus, king of the winds, into creating a storm to finish off her hated Trojans. Aeolus yields to her wishes (perhaps tempted by her offer of a nymph as a bride) and, setting free the winds from their mountain cave, creates a huge tempest that all but destroys the Trojan fleet. Vergil devises a scene, as the reader might expect, that is highly visual and sonorous. This passage is full of sounds, images, and word manipulation that creates a dramatic picture of chaos and danger.

Vergil begins the scene by abruptly ending Juno's speech — using ellipsis of dicta (est) to do so—and cutting right to the chase. Note the harsh yet rhythmic alliteration of cavum conversa cuspide as Aeolus drives his scepter against the mountain, summoning the winds. He uses a simile from the military, forming a battle line (velut agmine facto, 2), that suggests the forthcoming "battle," and the winds storm out and blast across the land. Note the alliteration/ consonance of the t's in ruunt et terras turbine perflant (3), prompted by those in qua data (est) porta, whose repetition perhaps suggests how the winds are insistently pushing against each other to get out. A dramatic beginning to the storm!

The middle section of lines (4–7) describes some specifics of what is happening as the tempest grows. All the winds, thick with storms (creber procellis, 5), struggle against each other, the ensuing force upheaving the entire ocean, totum (mare) . . . ruunt (4–5), from its lowest depths and rolling vast waves to the short (vastos volvunt ad litora fluctus, 6). Note the wave-like redundancy of the alliteration and how the hyperbaton of vastos . . . fluctus seems to engulf the entire shore. The polysyndeton of -que, -que, and -que in line 5 adds to the effect of the winds piling up on top of one another. The parallel and gapped clauses (insequitur clamorque virum and [insequitur] stridorque rudentum, "there follow the cries of men and the creaking of the rigging," 7), the interlocking of men and rigging (clamorque virum stridorque rudentum), and the virtual onomatopoeia of stridor all suggest that the consequences of the storm for the Trojans are dire, indeed.

The next two lines (8–9) intensify the drama by describing how darkness suddenly (subito, 8) falls upon the land, as personified clouds snatch away both sky and daylight, Caelumque diemque, 8). The hendiadys of the latter phrase, meaning "the light of/from the sky" ("the light of day") and the polysyndeton of -que both emphasize the darkness. Vergil returns to incumbo (cf. line 4), now to describe the dark night "brooding over" the sea. The third section of this passage ends with a description of the thunder (Intonuere poli, 10) and lightning (crebris micat ignibus aether) that accompany the blasts and the darkness of the storm. The reappearance of creber, "thick, crowded" (cf. 5) and the metonymy of polus for caelum suggest that all of heaven is tempest-tossed.

The upshot of all this is that the Trojans are faced with annihilation, which is powerfully suggested by the juxtaposition of omnia mortem, the hyperbaton of praesentem . . . mortem (11), and the emphatic position of praesentem. Death is all around the Trojans. These observations all support the conclusion that Vergil intensifies the force of the gale to heighten both the tragedy the Trojans suffer and the present and subsequent difficulties that pius Aeneas must face as their leader.

Endnotes

[82] For the multiple-choice section, see Chapter 2. For the essay questions on the free-response section, see Chapters 3 and 6.

[83] Synchysis is also spelled synchesis. The former will be used in this book.

[84] Acorn book for 2010–2011, page 20.

[85] Rhetorical questions were discussed in the section on punctuation in Chapter 5. Some of these terms, such as poetic plural, prime position, and sound and word play, are traditional, if not formal.

[86] See Pendergraft, page 52, cited in the Appendix for Chapter 5.

[87] Additional examples of multiple-choice questions on figures of speech may be found in the multiple-choice section of the current Acorn book, and in the multiple-choice section of the most recently-released AP Latin Exam (2005). For collections of figures of speech and activities for mastery, see the resources cited in the Appendix for this chapter.

[88] Chiasmus is a complex and confusing figure, to the extent that it was apparently misidentified by Exam Readers on a recent AP Latin Exam. See Laura Gibbs' website *http://latinviaproverbs.pbworks.com/Chiasmus*, which contains an interesting method of learning chiamus, i.e., via proverbs, e.g., **Mors sequitur, fugit vita**. See also "Chiasmus: Correspondence and Reversal" at *http://grammatice.blogspot.com/2009/05/chiasmus-correspondence-and-reversal.html* for an extremely thoroughgoing explication of the figure, with many examples. Dr. Mardy's site for "lovers of wit and wordplay," includes a whole series of pages devoted just to chiasmus (in English): *http://www.drmardy.com/chiasmus/definition.shtml*. He explains here the ABBA designation often used by classicists.

[89] Thanks to Prof. Tom Benediktson, University of Tulsa, for this example.

[90] I have adopted the definition of polyptoton given by Jerard White on the school website *http://www.frapanthers.com/teachers/white/literary_devices.htm*. This is designated as Version 1. In the revision of Pharr's *Aeneid* (Grammatical Appendix), Boyd gives a more restrictive definition of polyptoton: "the repetition of a noun or pronoun in different cases at the beginning of successive phrases or clauses," page 78. This is designated Version 2. In English, the repeated words can be different parts of speech, e.g., a noun and a verb or two verbs. See the English examples provided.

[91] "Metonymy" at Wikipedia, *http://en.wikipedia.org/wiki/Metonymy*.

[92] For SWIMTAG, developed by Sally Davis, see Chapter 6 and Appendix 3.

[93] For development of this idea, see Bernard Knox, "The Serpent and the Flame: The Imagery of the Second Book of the *Aeneid*," *Virgil: A Collection of Critical Essays*, Steele Commager, ed., Prentice-Hall, Englewood Cliffs, NJ, 1966.

[94] Apostrophe has been included here because the person or thing addressed is usually found at the beginning of its sentence. This, however, is not a universal rule.

[95] Hendiadys and zeugma have been included in this category because of their use of parallelism and ellipsis, i.e., understood words.

[96] For other examples of sound play, refer back to the Glossary of Additional Figures earlier in this chapter.

[97] For previous National Latin Exams, go online to http://www.nle.org.

[98] For essay questions on the free-response section of the AP Latin Exam, see Chapter 6.

Chapter 9

Techniques of Poetic Analysis: Meter and Scansion

In the last chapter, we spoke about the relevance of sound to poetic meaning in Latin. We explored several figures of speech that involve the sounds of words: alliteration, assonance, consonance, and onomatopoeia, the first and last of which are required for the AP Latin Exam. In this chapter, we will concentrate more on the rhythm of the verse, specifically the way in which Vergil makes use of dactylic hexameter, the language of epic poetry. One further point, worth repeating, was made in the previous chapter: to appreciate and even enjoy poetry in any language, you must read it aloud or listen to it.[99] Some of you will have learned the correct pronunciation of Latin early in your study, others will find this area of Latin completely alien to you. Hopefully, this chapter will prove instructive, whatever your background.

Meter (the metrical structure of verse) and scansion (the analysis of the metrics of verse) are essential for the mastery of Latin poetry and they are therefore evaluated on the AP Latin Exam. This chapter presents you with a quick-study of both meter and scansion. We will begin with definitions of terms. Note that the metrical terms caesura, diaeresis, hiatus, and synizesis are not relevant for the Exam, but it is helpful to be familiar with the concepts these terms represent when you are trying to understand the art of rhythm in Latin.

The Language of Meter

- **anceps** (meaning "two headed" or ambiguous): a syllable that can be either long or short. In dactylic hexameter, the last vowel/syllable in a line is anceps and is marked with an x.
- **caesura** (sih-zoor′-ah), a pause between two words within a metrical foot, sometimes emphasizing the word before or after the pause. In the line below, the caesura falls between **animis** and **caelestibus**.

  - uu- - - u u - - - uu - x

  impulerit. Tantaene animis caelestibus irae? (1.11)
- **consonantal vowel**: the letter **i** is sometimes consonantal, as in **iam** or **Iuno**, which are spelled **jam** or **Juno** in some Latin texts. Determine whether an **i** is consonantal by thinking of a derivative from the Latin

word. If the word begins with a **j**, then the **i** is consonantal, e.g., **iocus** gives *joke*, so the **i** in **iocus** is consonantal. Sometimes the contraints of meter require a consonantal **i** where one would not be expected, e.g., the second **i** in **Lavinia**, to allow the line to be scanned. Note: the **o** in the common word **Troia**, which is followed by a consonantal **i**, is long. The vowel **u** can be used as a vowel, e.g., **equus**, or as a consonant, **uideo**, when it has the sound **v**. (Many older or British texts retain the consonantal **u.**) The consonant **h** is not usually considered a full consonant, as it is not aspirated or sounded. It will not cause a vowel to be long by position, e.g., in the phrase **premit hasta**, the syllable -**it** at the end of **premit** is not long by position, but short.

- **dactyl** ("finger"): one long syllable, followed by two short syllables: - u u.
- **diaeresis** (dye-air′-eh-sis; also spelled **dieresis**; "division between"): a pause in the middle of a line where the end of a word matches the end of a metrical foot. It is therefore similar to caesura (which comes within a foot), e.g., in

  \- u u - u u - - - - - u u - -
  Arma vir/umque ca/no Troi/ae qui / primus ab / oris
  (1.1), the diaeresis falls after **qui**.
- **diphthong** ("split-" or "double-tongue"): a double vowel with a single sound. There are six in Latin: **ae (aestas)**, **au (Plautus)**, **ei (deinde)**, **eu (eheu)**, **oe (coepit)**, and **ui (qui)**. All diphthongs are long. Double vowels that have two sounds are not diphthongs, e.g., **filia**. The common vowel combination **ue**, as in -**que**, gives a single sound, which may be either long or short, depending upon its position (see the examples below). This **u** is not considered a separately-scanned vowel.
- **elision** (verb, *to elide*): to slur an end vowel with an initial vowel, e.g., **quaeque ipse**, an end vowel with an initial **h**, e.g., **meminisse horret**, or a final -**m** with an initial vowel or with **h**, e.g., **quamquam animus** or **animam hanc**. The words are slurred together when read, e.g., **quaequipse**. When the word **est** is involved in an elision, the vowel at the end of the first word phonetically overrides the **e** in **est**, e.g., **Maro est** is pronounced **Marost**, which is a kind of reverse elision. Sometimes an elision does not occur when expected (see **hiatus**), in order to achieve a particular poetic effect. Such lines are not tested on the AP Latin Exam.
- **foot**: a metrical unit consisting of a poetic unit, such as a dactyl or spondee. There are six feet in a dactylic line, only the first four of which are tested on the AP Latin Exam. The final two feet are formulaically a dactyl then a spondee, i.e., -uu / - x. See the example **Arma virumque** above, under diaeresis, for a demonstration of where to place the foot-breaks. The designation of feet is not required on the AP Latin Exam.

- **hexameter** (*hexa*, six, + *metron*, measure): a line of verse containing six metrical units. Dactylic hexameter, known as the "heroic hexameter," is used in both Greek and Latin poetry.
- **hiatus** (hye-ay′-tus, "yawning"): where two words that would normally be elided are not, e.g., **femineo ululatu** (4.667). This technique often enhances onomatopoeia, as in the preceding example, and often appears at the end of a clause, e.g., **posthabita coluisse Samo; hic illius arma** (1.16) or **et vera incessu patuit dea. Ille ubi matrem** (1.405).
- **prosody**: the systematic study of the metrical structure of verse, i.e., meter.
- **scansion (scandere,** *to climb*; verb, *to scan*): the determination of the length of each syllable in a line of verse as long or short.
- **spondee**: two long syllables, — — within a foot.
- **syncope**: the omission of an alphabetic component within a word, e.g., **virum** for **virorum** (see the entry "archaism" in the supplementary glossary in the previous chapter). A contraction. Latin words, often verbs, can be abbreviated or shortened to accommodate the meter or to achieve some sound effect. Note the difference between syncope and elision.
- **synizesis** (sin-ih-zee′-sis, "sitting together"): where two consecutive vowel sounds are pronounced as a single sound, e.g., in

  \- \- \- u u \- u u \- \- \- uu \- x

  Eurum ad se Zephyrumque vocat, dehinc talia fatur (1.131), the word **dehinc** is pronounced as a single syllable, **dinc**, by synizesis.
- **vowel**: **a, e, i, o, u**, both long and short; occasionally **y** (the Greek *upsilon*), e.g., **adytis** (2.297).

Scansion

Each syllable of a line of Latin verse is characterized by a vowel, a diphthong, or an elision, consisting of a long or a short sound. Whether the sound is long or short reflects the amount of time the sound was held when spoken. In many Latin textbooks, long vowels are marked with a macron, e.g., **ā**. Macrons are not provided on the AP Latin Exam.[100] The combination of these long and/or short sounds is called a foot, which originally equalled the time it took, while dancing, to raise one foot and lower it to the ground. (The word **pes** can refer to a metrical foot.) Much of what we know about the use of rhythm in poetry comes from the Greeks.

The only meter now required for the AP Latin Exam is dactylic hexameter, the meter used by Vergil in the *Aeneid*. On the Exam, you are expected to be able to identify elisions and to mark the sound of a vowel as long or short. You need not concern yourself with separating a line into feet (but see below), or with the more technical aspects of scansion. Because of the ambiguity of the anceps syllable in the final foot of the hexameter, you are allowed to mark the final syllable long.

Dactylic Hexameter

Each line of hexameter verse contains six feet, or six units of rhythm. The basic metrical unit of dactylic hexameter, i.e., the "fingers and feet" meter, is the dactyl. In sound-sense, the rhythm – u u is equivalent to "dum-diddy-diddy." The following hexameter in English may help you to remember this rhythm:

/ / / / / / / / /

Down in a deep dark dell sat an old cow munching a beanstalk.

English, of course, is a stress-accented language, whereas Latin is not, but the stroke marks above, equal to long sounds in hexameter, give a sense of the rhythm in Latin, which would be:

- u u - - - u u - - - u u - -

Down in a deep dark dell sat an old cow munching a beanstalk.

In dactylic hexameter, a spondee (- -) may be substituted for a dactyl (- u u) in any of the first <u>four</u> feet in order to provide the poet with more opportunities for variety of rhythm. For the purposes of the AP Latin Exam, <u>the final two feet are formulaic, that is, they are always to be considered a dactyl and a spondee in succession</u>: - u u / - -. The detailed rules for the assignment of long and short values to syllables lie outside the scope of this book. To review these, ask your teacher, consult your Latin textbook or reader, or go online to the one of the websites suggested in the Appendix.

Long Syllables

In general, sounds are long if they are <u>long by nature</u>, i.e., have a naturally long sound when pronounced, such as the final vowels in the ablative singular form **servo**, the ablative plural form **dominis**, the accusative plural form **cives**, or the first person singular present tense form **amo**. (You may already know this simply by having learned the correct pronunciation of Latin.) When you are reading Latin poetry and you come upon an end-vowel that is ambiguous—is it **puella** or **puellā**?—you will be able to use scansion to determine the length of that syllable, and therefore its grammatical function. For instance, here is a line from the *Aeneid* without macrons: **bellaque iam fama totum vulgata per orbem** (1.457). Does the modifier **vulgata** go with **bella** or **fama**? Scansion of the line ---

- u u - - - - - - - u u - -

bellaque iam fama totum vulgata per orbem — tells us that the **a**-ending of **vulgata** is short and that the **a** ending of **fama** is long (abl.), therefore **vulgata** modifies **bella**. Also long are diphthongs and vowels followed by two or more consonants in the same or different words. For instance, the **o** in **possumus** is long by position, that is, it is followed by two **s**'s. Also long by position is the second **u** in **possum<u>u</u>s legere**, that is, it is followed by the two consonants **s** and **l**. (Yes, sounds cross over between words in Latin scansion.) So, a vowel followed by two consonants, or **x** or **z** (which count as double consonants because of their sounds), is <u>long by position</u>.

This rule, however, is not hard and fast. Vowels appearing before the consonants **b, c, d, p,** or **t**, when followed by **l** or **r**, such as **cr** or **cl**, **pr** or **pl**, or **tr** or **tl**, may be long or short, at the poet's discretion. (Use the acronym CPT, "Consonants produce trouble," to remember the most common consonants in this series.) When these consonant combinations begin a word, they are always short, i.e., they do not count as a double-consonant in determining the quantity of the previous syllable. For instance, in the clause **ea prima piacula sunto** (6.153), the **a** in **ea** is short because **pr**, one of the exceptions, begins the next word, **prima**. Ordinarily, this vowel would have been long by position. Here are some illustrations which summarize these exceptions:

Example 1: **virginibus Tyriis mos est gestare pharetram** (vowel **e** before internal **tr** is long. 1.336)

Example 2: **sed me magna deum genetrix his detinet oris** (vowel **e** before internal **tr** is short. 2.788)

Example 3: **regnatorem Asiae. Iacet ingens litore truncus** (vowel **e** before initial **tr** is short. 2.557)

One website that describes the rules of Latin prosody contains as its last rule the disclaimer, "Poets have been known to break rules."[101]

Short Syllables

In general, if there is no reason for a syllable to be long, it is considered short. Logic and deduction are useful strategies to apply when determining the length of a syllable in Latin. For example, a single short syllable cannot appear between two long syllables (- u -) in a hexameter line. Note: although you are not required to demonstrate foot-breaks in your scansion of a hexameter line, it helps to do so in order to decide whether or not you have accurately scanned each of the first four feet. Here, then, is the formula for scanning a hexameter line:

	—	—	—	—		
Syllables	- u u /	- u u /	- u u /	- u u /	- u u /	- -
Feet	1	2	3	4	5	6

Scanning a Line of Dactylic Hexameter

1. Check to see if there are any elisions in the line and mark them.

   Arma virumque cano Troiae qui primus ab oris

   There are no elisions in this line.

2. Mark the initial syllable long (it is always long) and the final two syllables long, so that the last foot is a spondee.

   \-   - -
   Arma virumque cano Troiae qui primus ab oris

3. Mark the fifth, fourth, and third syllables from the end a dactyl, which is formulaic. The last two feet of any dactylic line on the AP Latin Exam should look like this: – u u / - -. So far, we have

   \-   - u u - -
   Arma virumque cano Troiae qui primus ab oris

4. Remember that only the first four feet are required. Remember, too, that a single short cannot appear between two longs. Mark all syllables that are long by nature or are a diphthong:

   \-   -   - -   -   - u u - -
   Arma virumque cano Troiae qui / primus ab / oris

   Note 1:

   The final **o** of verbs is always long by nature.

   Note 2:

   The **o** in **Troiae** is long because one short cannot appear between two longs in a hexameter line, i.e., you cannot have - u - over **cano Troiae**. The **i** is consonantal (= **j**).

   Note 3:

   The double-vowels **ae** and **ui** are diphthongs.

5. Mark all syllables that are long by position, i.e., are followed by two or more consonants or by **x** or **z**.

   \-   -   -   - -   -   - u u - -
   Arma virumque cano Troiae qui / primus ab / oris

6. Mark the remaining syllables short and divide the line into feet to make sure that you have the first four feet accounted for as containing either a dactyl or a spondee.

   \- u u - u u - - - - - u u - -
   Arma vir/umque ca/no Troi/ae qui / primus ab / oris
   1 2 3 4 5 6

Note:

The enclitic **-que** is not a diphthong. Its quantity is determined by its position in the line, e.g.,

u
fracti bello fatisque repulsi (short)

—
aedificant sectaque intexunt abiete costas (long by position).

Now apply these steps in scanning the following lines of the *Aeneid* for practice.

Et iam finis erat, cum Iuppiter aethere summo
despiciens mare velivolum terrasque iacentes
litora et latos populos, sic vertice caeli
constitit et Libyae defixit lumina regnis.

Answers:

\- - -u u - - - uu - uu - -
Et iam finis erat, cum Iuppiter aethere summo

\- uu- u u -uu- - - u u- -
despiciens mare velivolum terrasque iacentes (the **i** in **iacentes** is consonantal)

\- - - - - u u - - - uu - -
litora et latos populos, sic vertice caeli

\- uu- uu- - - - - u u - -
constitit et Libyae defixit lumina regnis.

Rhythm and Its Effects in the *Aeneid*

When a hexameter line consists primarily of dactyls, i.e., a predominance of short syllables, the effect is one of rapidfire or staccato action, or an expression of high emotion. Observe these examples from the *Aeneid*:

- The urgency of Hector's warning to Aeneas is evident in the jumpy interplay of dactyls and spondees:

  — u u -u u- - — uu - u u - -
  heu fuge, nate dea, teque his, ait, eripe flammis (2.289)
- The uproar in Priam's palace when the Greeks break through with a rush:

  \- u u - uu- u u- uu- u u - -
  At domus interior gemitu miseroque tumultu / miscetur (2.486)
- Dido's agitation on discovering Aeneas' plans to leave Carthage:

  \- u u- uu- u u- - - uu- -
  posse nefas tacitusque mea decedere terra (4.306)

  A predominance of spondees produces a slow or somber effect and/or creates a more thoughtful or deliberate pace.

- Nightfall settles on the land, concealing the treachery of the Greeks:

  \- - - - - - - - - u u- -

  involvens umbra magna terramque polumque (2.251)

- Priam has been slain by Pyrrhus, his life ebbing away as he witnesses the death throes of his city. The rhythm suggests the inconsistent beat of a failing heart.

  \- u u- - — - — - - u u - -

  sorte tulit, Troiam incensam et prolapsa videntem / Pergama (2.554–56)

- Cocytus, a river of the Underworld, is sluggish and slow in its flow:

  \- - - - - - - - - u u - -

  Cocytus sinu labens circumvenit atro (6.132)

Here are several for fun. Can you guess what the sounds and rhythm are describing or suggesting?

1. **Monstrum, horrendum, informe, ingens, cui lumen ademptum** (3.658)

2. **Illi inter sese multa vi bracchia tollunt** (8.452)

3. **Quadripedante putrem sonitu quatit ungula campum** (8.596)

Answers:

1. The lengthy series of elisions link together all these adjectives describing the forbidding Cyclops Polyphemus.

2. The Cyclopes, with great strength, lift their arms (they are bearing the iron tools used to forge Aeneas' shield). Note the sequence of disyllables, suggesting the intensity and continuity of their effort.

3. The thundering hooves of galloping horses.

A Summary of Scansion with Regard to the AP Latin Exam

You are:

- expected to be able to identify elisions and to mark the sound of a vowel as long or short
- allowed to mark the final syllable long

You are not:

- provided with macrons
- required to mark feet or other pertinent items, such as caesura
- tested on unusual lines

Remember, only the first four feet of a hexameter line are tested.

How Scansion Is Evaluated

Your familiarity with the scansion of dactylic hexameter is evaluated explicitly on the multiple-choice section of the Exam, and implicitly on the long and short essay questions in the free-response section. Since you are guaranteed to have a syllabus-based passage on the multiple-choice section, there is likely to be at least one question on scansion in this section. In the past, scansion questions have counted for two to five percent of your grade on this section. Here is the format of the scansion question and answer on the multiple-choice section:

The metrical pattern of the first four feet of line 3 (<u>nec quisquam</u> . . . <u>videt</u>) is

(A) spondee-dactyl-dactly-spondee

(B) dactyl-spondee-dactyl-spondee

(C) spondee-spondee-dactyl-spondee

(D) dactyl-spondee-spondee-dactyl

On the free-response section, you are not asked to comment specifically on sound or rhythm, but as you learned in Chapter 6 on writing a good essay, comments on these features of style are always useful during analysis. Avoid making easy generalizations, however, such as "These lines have a jumpy feel to them," but say, rather, "The preponderance of dactyls in these lines suggests a mood that is light-hearted and playful," then go on to explain why this observation is relevant to the theme of your essay.

Practice Questions on Elision

Mark the elisions in the following lines and then comment on how the elision contributes to the meaning. The answers are provided at the end of the questions.

1. Turbine corripuit scopuloque infixit acuto. (1.45)
2. Incute vim ventis summersasque obrue puppes. (1.69)
3. Velum adversa ferit, fluctusque ad sidera tollit. (1.103)
4. Peragro / Europa atque Asia pulsus. (1.385)
5. Taurus et incertam incussit cervice securim. (2.224)
6. Vitam exhalentem; subiit deserta Creusa. (2.563)
7. Indulge hospitio causasque innecte morandi. (4.51)
8. Fama . . . pariter facta atque infecta canebat. (4.190)
9. Corde premit gemitum lacrimasque effundit inanes. (10.465)
10. Sexum antiquum ingens, campo quod forte iacebat. (12.897)

Variant Spellings

In addition to syncope (see the definition above), two other variations in spelling commonly occur in Latin poetry. For help with an ambiguous form, look at the context.

1. Do not confuse the verb ending -**ere**, which can be a substitute for the third person plural perfect tense ending -**erunt**, with that of an infinitive. Look for the perfect stem!

    Et (cycni) coetu cinxere polum cantusque dedere (= **cinxerunt, dederunt**; note the perfect stems **cinx**- and **ded**-. 1.398)

    Ambrosiaeque comae divinum vertice odorem / spiravere. (= **spiraverunt**. 1.403–404)

    Quo primum iactati undis et turbine Poeni / effodere loco signum (= **effoderunt**. 1.442–443)

    Conticuere omnes intentique ora tenebant (= **conticuerunt**. 2.1)

2. Another variation also appears to be an infinitive, but in fact it is the second person singular of the present passive or future passive:

    Haec ara tuebitur omnes, aut moriere simul (= **morieris**. 2.524)

Practice Questions on Variant Spellings

For the underlined example of contraction or variant spelling in each sentence below, indicate its normal prose equivalent.

1. Vi superum, saevae memorem Ioninis ob iram. (1.4)

2. Audierat Tyrias olim quae verteret arces. (1.20)

3. Imperio premit ac vinclis et carcere frenat. (1.54)

4. Incubuere mari totumque a sedibus imis. (1.85)

5. O Danaum fortissime gentis / Tydide! (1.96)

Now identify the example yourself and, again, expand it to the more normal form.

6. Scuta virum galeasque et fortia corpora volvit! (1.101)

7. Nec latuere doli fratrem Iunonis et irae. (1.130)

8. Monstrarat, caput acris equi; sic nam fore bello. (1.445)

9. Pabula gustassent Troiae Xanthumque bibissent. (1.473)

10. Exstinxti te meque, soror, populumque patresque. (4.682–683)

Practice Questions on Scansion

1. Which letter is not considered a vowel in Latin, if any?

   o y i a e u

2. Why is dactylic hexameter called the "heroic hexameter"?

3. What is the minimum number of syllables found in a hexameter line?

   8 10 13 15 20

4. How many feet are found in a hexameter line?

   4 5 6 7 8 9

5. The metrical unit – u u is known as:

   spondee iamb trochee dactyl

6. The metrical unit - - is known as:

   iamb spondee dactyl trochee

7. For the purposes of the AP Latin Exam, the last two feet of a dactylic line consist of, in order:

   two dactyls two spondees dactyl and spondee spondee and dactyl

8. True or False? Elided syllables are always long.

9. A vowel followed by two consonants is long or short by position?

10. True or False? The noun **proelia** contains two diphthongs.

11. How many spondees do you find in the first four feet of each of these hexameter lines?

    Quod mare conceptum spumantibus exspuit undis. 0 1 2 3 4

    Fit sonitus spumante salo; uamque arva tenebant. 0 1 2 3 4

    Gnate, ego quem in dubios cogor dimittere casus. 0 1 2 3 4

12. Scan the following to determine whether **sola** is nominative with **leaena** or ablative modifying **rupe**.

    Quaenam te genuit sola sub / rupe leaena.

Some AP-Style Multiple-Choice Questions on Scansion

1. The metrical pattern of the first four feet of <u>huc se provecti deserto in litore condunt</u> is
   (A) spondee – dactyl – spondee – spondee
   (B) spondee – spondee – spondee – spondee
   (C) spondee -spondee – spondee – dactyl
   (D) spondee – dactyl – spondee – dactyl

2. The metrical pattern of the first four feet of <u>panduntur porte iuvat ire et Dorica castra</u> is
   (A) spondee- spondee – dactyl – spondee
   (B) spondee – spondee – spondee – dactyl
   (C) spondee – dactyl – spondee – spondee
   (D) dactyl – spondee – dactyl – spondee

3. The metrical pattern of the first four feet of <u>idque audire sat est, iamdudum sumite poenas</u> is
   (A) spondee- dactyl – dactyl – spondee
   (B) dactyl – dactyl – spondee -spondee
   (C) spondee – spondee - dactyl - dactyl
   (D) spondee – dactyl – spondee – spondee

4. The metrical pattern of the first four feet of <u>dividimus muros et moenia pandimus urbis</u> is
   (A) dactyl – spondee – spondee – dactyl
   (B) dactyl – dactyl – spondee – spondee
   (C) spondee – dactyl – spondee – dactyl
   (D) spondee – dactyl – dactyl – spondee

5. The metrical pattern of the first four feet of <u>corripiunt spirisque ligant ingentibus; et iam</u> is
   (A) dactyl – spondee – spondee – dactyl
   (B) dactyl – spondee – dactyl – spondee
   (C) spondee – dactyl – spondee – dactyl
   (D) dactyl – dactyl – spondee - spondee

How Rhythm Affects Meaning

Scan each of the following lines and then comment on how the meter or rhythm contributes to the meaning of each. Be alert for elisions.

1. Luctantes ventos tempestatesque sonoras / . . .
   Illi indignantes magno cum murmure montis. (1.53, 55)

2. Intonuere poli et crebris micat ignibus aether. (1.91)

3. Arma virum tabulaeque et Troia gaza per undas. (1.119)

4. Miscere et tantas audetis tollere moles? (1.134)

5. Fervet opus redolentque thymo fragrantia melle. (1.436)

6. Sunt lacrimae rerum et mentem mortalia tangunt. /
   Solve metus. Feret haec aliquam tibi fama salutem. (1.463–464)

7. Multa gemens largoque umectat flumine vultum. (1.465)

8. Obstipuit simul ipse simul periculosus Achates /
   laetitiaque metuque avidi coniungere dextra. (1.513)

9. Ac primum silici scintillam excudit Achates. (1.174)

10. A tergo et longum per valles pascitur agmen. (1.186)

11. Involvens umbra magna terramque polumque. (2.251)

12. Parce metu, Cytherea, manent immota tuorum. /
    fata tibi: cernes urbem et promissa Lavini. (1.257)

13. Nequiquam ingeminans iterumque iterumque vocavi. (2.770)

14. Si bene quid de te merui, fuit aut tibi quicquam /
    dulce meum, miserere domus labentis et istam. (4.317–318)

15. Et Thybrim multo spumantem sanguine certo. (6.87)

Answers to Practice Questions on Elision

1. scopulo<u>que in</u>fixit; the elision actually "fixes" or attaches Ajax to the cliff.

2. summersas<u>que ob</u>rue; the slurring of the sounds suggests the sound of the ship as it rolls over.

3. Velum adversa; fluctus <u>que ad</u> sidera; the waves are "connected to" the stars.

4. Peragro / Europa atque Asia pulsus. The journey is "lengthened" by the multiple elisions.

5. incertam incussit; this elision suggests the errant blow of the axe on the neck of the bull.

6. Vitam exhalentem; perhaps Anchises' dying gasp?

7. Indulge hospitio causasque innecte morandi; Anna suggests that Dido "connect" herself more closely to Aeneas and "weave together" reasons for him to stay in Carthage.

8. facta atque infecta; the joining of "(events) done and not done" emphasizes both.

9. lacrimasque effundit; "tears" and "pour out," when elided, have an effect that is obvious.

10. Saxum antiquum ingens; the age and size of the boulder are magnified by these words joining with the boulder itself.

Answers to Practice Questions on Variant Spellings

1. superorum
2. Audiverat
3. vinculis
4. Incubuerunt
5. Danaorum
6. virorum
7. latuerunt
8. Monstraverat
9. gustavissent
10. Exstinxisti

Answers to Practice Questions on Scansion

1. All are vowels.

2. Because dactylic hexameter is used in epic poetry, which portrays the adventures of a national hero.

3. Thirteen.

4. Six.

5. Dactyl.

6. Spondee.

7. Dactyl and spondee.

8. False.

9. A vowel followed by two consonants is (usually) long by position.

10. False; the noun **proelia** contains one diphthong, **-oe-**.

11. 3, 3, 3

- - - u u- - - - - u u- -
12. Quaenam te genuit sola sub / rupe leaena. The **a** in **sola** is long, so the answer is ablative, with **rupe**.

Answers to AP-Style Multiple-Choice Questions on Scansion

1. (B) 2. (A) 3. (D) 4. (A) 5. (B)

Answers to How Rhythm Affects Meaning

- - - - - - - - - u u - -
1. Luctantes ventos tempestatesque sonoras / . . . .

- - - - - - - - - u u - -
Illi indignantes magno cum murmure montis. (Something heavy and serious is happening here: a storm.)

- u u- u u - - - u u - u u - -
2. Intonuere poli et crebris micat ignibus aether. (Intermittent flashes of lighting and peals of thunder.)

- u u - u u - - -uu - u u - -
3. Arma virum tabulaeque et Troia gaza per undas. (Flotsam bobbing on the waves after the storm.)

- - - - - - - - - u u - -
4. Miscere et tantas audetis tollere moles? (Measured, solemn, authoritative, deliberate.)

- u u - u u- u u - - - uu - -
5. Fervet opus redolentque thymo frangrantia mella. (The beehive is alive with energy.)

- u u - - - - - - -uu - -
6. Sunt lacrimae rerum et mentem mortalia tangunt. / (Solemn spondees bemoan the fate of mortals.)

- u u - u u - uu - u u -uu- -
Solve metus. Feret haec aliquam tibi fama salutem. (A more effervescent-sounding line, encouraging and hopeful.)

\- u u - - - - - - - u u - -

7. Multa gemens largoque umectat flumine vultum. (Aeneas pours out copious tears of grief. The dactyls provide the sobs?)

\- u u - u u - u u - - - u u - -

8. Obstipuit simul ipse simul percussus Achates /
-uu - u u - u u u - - - u u - -
laetitiaque metuque avidi coniungere dextra. (The sounds and rhythm are stuttery, excited, joyful.)

\- - - uu - - - - - u u - -

9. Ac primum silici scintillam excudit Achates. (Simulates the motion and sound of metal striking flint to create sparks for starting a fire.)

\- - - - - - - - - u u - -

10. A tergo et longum per valles pascitur agmen. (The deer are strung out along a valley, grazing.)

\- - - - - - - - - u u - -

11. Involvens umbra magna terramque polumque. (All spondees suggests the slow approach of night.)

\- u u - u u -u u - - -u u- -

12. Parce metu, Cytherea, manent immota tuorum.
\- u u - - - - - - - u u - -
fata tibi: cernes urbem et promissa Lavini. (Jove is positively buoyant in the first line and more measured and serious in the second.)

\- - - - u u - uu - u u - u u - -

13. Nequiquam ingeminans iterumque iterumque vocavi. (Redundancy of dactyls suggests the echoes of Aeneas calling for Creusa.)

\- u u - - - u u- uu - uu - -

14. Si bene quid de te merui, fuit aut tibi quicquam /
-u u - uu - u u - - - u u - -
dulce meum, miserere domus labentis et istam. (The words are rapid-fire and mono- and disyllabic, as Dido heatedly confronts Aeneas.)

\- - - - - - - - - u u - -

15. Et Thybrim multo spumantem sanguine certo. (The Sibyl speaks of Rome's destiny using a solemn and somber rhythm.)

Endnotes

[99] In the Appendix for this chapter, you will find resources for Latin pronunciation and for listening to Latin poetry.

[100] The word macron may be pronounced either mā′ krŏn or mă′ krŏn. The author prefers the former.

[101] The website is *http://www.informalmusic.com/latinsoc/syllable.html*.

Chapter 10

The *Aeneid* in Review

Now that we have completed the hard part, it is time to review. We have discussed both the multiple-choice and free-response sections of the AP Latin: Vergil Exam, as well as the mechanics of poetic analysis. It is now time to revisit what you have learned about the story of the *Aeneid* in its entirety. This chapter provides you with a quick-study outline of the content of the Latin and English readings required for the AP Latin Exam, helpful print and online resources for review in the Appendix, and practice questions and answers covering the content of the entire epic.

Some Themes in the *Aeneid*

The main themes of the *Aeneid* are skillfully introduced by Vergil in the first seven lines of the poem. (Memorize these lines in meter!) These are, of course, war and a man (**Arma virumque** and **multa quoque et bello passus**); the control of men's lives by fate (**fato profugus**) and the gods (**multum ille et terris iactatus / et alto vi superum**); and the importance of having a home, a community, and gods (**dum conderet urbem / inferretque deos Latio,** etc.). What ties these themes together throughout the poem is **pietas,** or devotion to the gods, homeland, family, and friends. Here are some further thoughts on themes in the *Aeneid.*

- The triumph of Order over Disorder: the rational control of passion and the acceptance of fate.The storm scene in Book 1 represents the time of the civil wars, which were ended by Augustus, who closed the Gates of War and established the **Pax Romana**, a time of peace, order, and stability. The struggle of order (reason) versus disorder (passion) is personified by Dido.[102] Fate (the word **fatum** in its various forms appears forty times in the first three Books of the *Aeneid*), is a divine, religious principle that governs the course of history and thus the Roman Empire. Here are some additional points regarding Fate:

  The direction and destination of Aeneas' mission are preordained: Aeneas, motivated by **pietas**, follows the dictates of Fate.

  Juno, Dido, and Turnus resist Fate.

  The Romans believed that the Fates were the guiding principle in man's life. Consider the role of omens, oracles, prodigies, and prophecies in the epic.

- The significance of the Gods

  Fate is often associated with the will of Jupiter. It is unclear whether the gods themselves are subject to Fate.

  The gods, e.g., the Penates that Aeneas carries (**inferretque deos Latio**), are the transubstantiation of the identity of the Roman people.

  A return to the old-time religion is necessary to establish and maintain the stability of the new Augustan order.

- The importance of Home

  The founding of a city (Troy, Carthage, Rome) is the ultimate expression of civilization, for it serves as a refuge from the unpredictable and irrational.The wanderings of the Trojans at sea, as were those of Odysseus, are a metaphor for the uncertainty of life and therefore the significance of Home.

- The glory of Rome

  The Romans were chosen by the gods, specifically Jupiter, to rule (Book 6.847–53), and since the lineage of Emperor Augustus is divine (Venus – Aeneas – Iulus/Ascanius – **gens Iulia**), he has the divine right to rule. The *Aeneid* is Augustan propaganda.

- Nobility

  The interests of the commonwealth (finding a new Troy) are transcendant over those of the individual (Aeneas).

  The heroic warrior (Achilles) has been replaced by the heroic citizen (Aeneas); war is a means to an end, rather than an end in itself (**arma virumque**).

  Achievement requires suffering; the Stoic ideal of forebearance was the traditional expression of what was Roman.

- Acknowledgment of patriarchal primacy

  Women ultimately have subordinate roles in the *Aeneid*, e.g., Amata, Dido, and Juno.

  Women are seen as victims or as a threat to the male.

  The identity of a family derives from and is dependent upon the father or father-figure, e.g., Aeneas, Anchises, Evander, Latinus, Priam, and Turnus.

A Quick-Study of Vergil's Epic Style

- The *Aeneid* is a literary epic, whose story is modeled upon the *Iliad* and *Odyssey* of Homer. The Emperor Augustus' motivation for wanting to connect himself with the story of the settlement of Aeneas in Italy and the founding of Rome was his interest in justifying his establishment of empire by what Pharr calls "divine sanction and the weight of antiquity."[103]

In the context of the civil wars of the first century B.C., a return to the stability and traditions of the good old days, on which Augustus' rule was predicated, required formal and public acknowledgment and celebration of the role of both the gods and the family in the development of Rome.

- Vergil's sense of national pride in the glory of Rome, as well as his personal commitment to the task of composing the *Aeneid* itself, may be summed up in the sentiment **tantae molis erat Romanam condere gentem** (1.33).[104]
- The *Aeneid* is filled with Greek forms and cadences and with references and allusions to things Greek, which are products of Vergil's formal education in Rome.[105] However, Vergil reshapes the Homeric epics to Roman purposes by creating a story of personal sacrifice made in pursuit of the common good. In a sense, Vergil, who was physically weak, shy, and a "sentimental idealist," experienced life vicariously through his character Aeneas.[106]
- The story of the *Aeneid* reveals that Vergil believed that men's lives were controlled by the gods. Whether Vergil believed that the gods and fate were the same or that the gods themselves were under the control of fate is unclear in the *Aeneid* (see above).

Vergil's literary style is epic with respect to his use of the dactylic hexameter, the appearance of the gods, elaborate and allusive language, focus on a heroic character whose actions are noble, lengthy speeches, and a long but unified story of events of national significance.

"Homer is a world; Vergil, a style."[107] Vergil's style is characterized by his narrative skill. As an epic poet, Vergil:

- produces strongly-drawn main characters
- skillfully weaves long speeches into the action
- makes the action more vivid by using imagery, such as simile
- is effective in suggesting sound
- is pictorial in his descriptions
- uses verbal and situational reminiscence and foreshadowing

An Outline of the *Aeneid*

Be aware that the designation of episodes below is entirely subjective. Familiar quotations from the Latin text are provided in italics to illustrate a topic or theme. When the Latin and English passages interlock, based on the AP syllabus, that is, Latin then English then Latin, etc., summaries of the intervening English passages are provided for your convenience. This outline is not meant as a substitute for a good translation, but it is intended to help you remember the storyline.[108]

The Twelve Books of the *Aeneid*, by Episodes

Book 1 (Latin and English)

Lines to be read in Latin (1.1–519)

Episodes

1–11 The theme of the poem and invocation to the Muse

Arma virumque cano, Troiae qui primus ab oris . . . . (line 1)

12–13 Juno's jealousy and anger

Tantae molis erat Romanam condere gentem! (line 33)

34–49 The Trojans leave for Sicily.

50–75 Juno appeals to Aeolus, god of the winds.

76–101 Aeolus complies with Juno's request.

O terque quaterque beati! (line 94)

102–123 The storm shatters Aeneas' fleet.

124–156 An angry Neptune ends the storm.

Simile of the orator (lines 148–153)

157–179 The landing of the shipwrecked Trojans in Africa

180–197 Aeneas and Achates go hunting.

198–222 Aeneas encourages his comrades.

O socii. . . (lines 198–207); *forsan et haec olim meminisse iuvabit* (line 203)

223–253 Venus appears to Jupiter on behalf of her son Aeneas.

254–296 Jupiter reveals the destiny of Aeneas and of Rome.

His ego nec metas rerum nec tempora pono; imperium sine fine dedi (lines 278–79)

Romanos, rerum dominos, gentem togatam . . . . (line 282)

297–304 Jupiter sends Mercury to Carthage to insure welcome for the Trojans.

305–334 Aeneas and Achates meet Venus, disguised as a huntress.

335–371 Venus describes Dido's flight from Tyre.

dux femina facti (line 364)

372–386 Aeneas tells the sad story of the Trojans.

387–417 Venus reveals herself and covers Aeneas and Achates with a cloud.

418–440 Aeneas and Achates make their way to Carthage.

Simile of the bees (lines 430–36)

O fortunati, quorum iam moenia surgunt! (line 437)

441–465 Aeneas and Achates view the temple of Juno at Carthage.

Sunt lacrimae rerum et mentem mortalia tangunt (line 462)

466–493 The temple mural tells the story of the Trojan War.

494–519 Dido arrives at the temple.

Simile of the goddess Diana's band (lines 498–504)

Lines to be read in English (1.520–756)

Queen Dido is formally addressed by Ilioneus, one of the Trojan survivors. Aeneas and Achates remain hidden in the mist. Ilioneus describes their search for Hesperia and the circumstances that had brought them to the north coast of Africa. Dido takes pity on the shipwrecked Trojans and sends scouts to search for Aeneas and Achates. The mist parts and Aeneas stands before Dido in all his glory. He addresses the queen with thanks and embraces his comrades. Dido replies that she is familiar with the story of Troy and invites the Trojans to a banquet so that she can hear more. Aeneas sends Achates back to the ships to inform Ascanius and to bid him return with gifts for the Carthaginians. Venus sends her son Cupid to substitute for Ascanius. Dido begins to have feelings for Aeneas and invites him to tell his story as they feast.

Book 2 (Latin and English)

Lines to be read in Latin (2.1–56)

1–13 Aeneas begins his tale of the Trojan War.

Quorum magna pars fui (line 6)

14–39 The Wooden Horse

40–56 Laocoon's warning

Equo ne credite. Quicquid id est, timeo Danaos et dona ferentes (lines 48–49)

Lines to be read in English (2.57–198)

The Greek Sinon is brought before Priam. His mission is to persuade the Trojans that he has been left behind and to somehow convince them to take the Horse into the city. Sinon tells his story, in which he claims to have been wronged in a plot conceived by Odysseus. Sinon goes to admit that the Greeks had long ago desired to leave Troy, but had been prevented by storms. As a result, the Greeks sent Eurypylus to seek the advice of the Delphic oracle. The oracle advised that a blood sacrifice, like that of Iphigenia at the outset of the war, must be made. That sacrifice was to have been Sinon, who nonetheless managed to "escape." The Trojans pity Sinon and decide to take him in. To their question about the Wooden Horse, Sinon answers that it was left as a gift to Pallas Athena to atone for Odysseus' theft of the Palladium, a wooden statue of the goddess that protected Troy, from its shrine. Any attempt by the Trojans to take possession of the Horse would result in dire consequences for the Greeks.

Lines to be read in Latin (2.199–297)

199–233 The death of Laocoon and his sons

Ecce autem gemini a Tenedo tranquilla per alta (horresco referens) immensis orbibus angues (lines 203–4)

234–249 The Horse is taken into Troy.

Scandit fatalis machina muros feta armis (lines 237–38)

250–267 The return of the Greeks

268–286 Aeneas' vision of Hector in a dream

O lux Dardaniae, spes O fidissima Teucrum (lines 281–86)

289–295 Hector's warning to Aeneas

Lines to be read in English (2.298–468)

Troy is now in flames. Aeneas awakens suddenly and climbs to the roof of his house to see what is happening. He hears the sounds of war and takes up his weapons. A priest rushing by announces that Greeks have come out of the Horse and are attacking the city. Aeneas joins some fellow Trojans, who rally, despite scenes of carnage everywhere. The simile of Androgeos, who mistakes the Trojans for fellow Greeks, as one who has stepped on a snake. The Trojans attempt to save Cassandra and then flee to defend Priam's palace, where a mighty battle ensues.

Lines to be read in Latin (2.469–566)

469–485 Achilles' son Pyrrhus enters the palace.

Simile of the snake (lines 471–75)

486–505 Greeks swarm the palace.

506–525 The fate of Priam, king of Troy

526–543 The murder of Priam's son Polites

544–566 The death of King Priam

Lines to be read in English (2.567–734)

Aeneas encounters Helen, hiding inside Vesta's shrine. Aeneas casts angry words at her and then moves on. Aeneas' mother Venus appears in all her radiance and advises him to look after his father, wife, and son. The simile of the felling of the ash tree (lines 626–631). Anchises, wishing to die in his home at Troy, refuses to leave. The omen of a glowing light appearing above Ascanius' head, accompanied by thunder and a shooting star, overcome Anchises' objections. Aeneas lifts his father on his shoulders, takes his son's hand, and leads the way. They hear Greek soldiers.

Lines to be read in Latin (2.735–804)

735–767 The disappearance of Creusa and Aeneas' search

768–774 Aeneas sees a vision of Creusa.

Obstipui, steteruntque comae et vox faucibus haesit (line 774)

775–794 Creusa advises Aeneas to leave Troy without her.

Longa tibi exsilia et vastum maris aequor arandum, et terram Hesperiam venies (lines 780–81)

795–804 The Trojans take refuge in the mountains.

Book 3 (English)

The fugitive Trojans make their way to Thrace, where they meet the ghost of Trojan Polydorus. Offerings of expiation for his murder are made, followed by the departure of the fleet to the south. They reach Delos where, after an omen, a priest of Apollo advises the Trojans to "seek out their ancient mother" (Italy). On to Crete, where a plague strikes. The Penates address Aeneas and bid him go to a land called Hesperia, source of the Trojan race. A storm drives them to the islands of the Strophades where dwell Phineus and Celaeno and the Harpies. After moving on, the Trojans meet Helenus, Priam's son and now priest of Apollo and husband of Andromache, and another band of refugee Trojans. Helenus encourages the Trojans to continue their search for "the land of Ausonia."Aeneas learns of Scylla and Charybdis and then passes on to Sicily and Mt. Aetna, where the travelers meet Achaemenides, left behind by Odysseus, and Cyclops. Anchises later dies.

Book 4 (Latin and English)

Lines to be read in Latin (4.1–448)

1–30 Dido confesses to her sister Anna that she has fallen in love.

Degeneres animos timor arguit (line 13)

31–53 Anna encourages Dido.

54–64 Dido sacrifices to the gods.

65–89 Dido's emotion

90–104 Juno approaches Venus.

105–128 Venus agrees to Juno's scheme to bring Dido and Aeneas together.

129–159 The hunting party

160–172 Aeneas and Dido take shelter in a cave.

173–197 Rumor spreads the story abroad.

Fama, malum qua non aliud velocius ullum (lines 173–88)

198–221 The anger of Iarbas; Aeneas is compared to Paris for stealing another's bride.

222–278 Mercury is sent to warn Aeneas.

279–295 Aeneas makes plans to leave.

296–304 Dido's suspicions

Quis fallere possit amantem? (line 296)

305–330 Dido reproaches Aeneas the first time.

331–361	Aeneas' reply
362–392	Dido's anger increases.
393–407	The Trojans prepare to depart.
	Simile of the ants (lines 402–7)
408–436	Dido's final appeal.
	Improbe Amor, quid non mortalia pectora cogis! (line 412)
437–449	Aeneas remains steadfast in his decision.
	Simile of the oak tree in a high wind (lines 441–49)

Lines to be read in English (4.449–641)

Dido prays for death. Several portents occur, followed by Dido hearing the voice of her dead husband Sychaeus coming from the chapel. Aeneas continues to hound her in her sleep; the simile of Bacchic revelry extends her madness. Dido engages her unsuspecting sister Anna in plans for her funeral and sacrifices to the gods below. The queen delivers a grief-stricken soliloquy during which she expresses her regret at betraying Sychaeus. Mercury again appears to warn Aeneas to continue with his mission. He delivers the famous line, *Varium et mutabile semper femina* (lines 569–570). The Trojan fleet makes ready to set sail, which Dido observes from her watch-tower. She delivers a frenzied speech, invoking all manner of curses upon Aeneas. Now resigned to her fate, Dido asks nurse Barce to fetch Anna to "assist" in the ritual purification.

Lines to be read in Latin (4.642–705)

642–671	Dido's death
	Dulces exuviae (lines 651–62)
672–692	Anna's grief
693–705	Dido's spirit is set free by the goddess Iris.

Book 5 (English)

The Trojan fleet heads for Sicily, where games are held to celebrate the anniversary of Anchises' death. Fellow Trojan Acestes hosts the games, which consist of a ship race (Cloanthus), foot race (Nisus and Euryalus), boxing match (Entellus and Dares), and an archery contest in which Acestes' arrow catches fire. Ascanius leads the young men in the "Trojan Games." Juno sends Iris to the Trojan women, who then, weary of war and traveling, set the ships afire. Nautes then advises that the weak be left in Sicily with Acestes and that the Trojans move on, with the aid of Neptune, whose aid has been sought by Venus. Anchises appears to Aeneas in a dream. The helmsman Palinurus falls overboard and dies.

Book 6

Lines to be read in Latin (6.1–211)

1–13	The Trojans reach Italy and arrive at Cumae.
14–33	The Temple of Apollo, whose doors depict the story of Daedalus and the Minotaur
34–55	The Cumaean Sibyl
56–76	Aeneas prays to Apollo.
77–101	The Sibyl's prophecy *Tu ne cede malis* (line 95)
102–123	Aeneas asks to visit his father in the Underworld.
124–155	The Golden Bough *Facilis descensus Averno* (line 126)
156–184	The body of Misenus
185–211	The search for the Golden Bough

Lines to be read in English (6.212–449)

The Trojans still on the shore raise a pyre for the unfortunate Misenus and commence with the funeral after Aeneas returns. He makes an offering to the deities of the Underworld. The Sibyl descends into the Underworld, leading Aeneas. They observe Grief, Diseases, Age, Fear, Death, and cares of life, followed by monstrous creatures of various types. They arrive at the river Acheron and meet Charon, the ferryman. The riverbank is thick with the souls of the unburied, "as thick as the leaves of the forest," doomed to wander for a hundred years. Aeneas then happens upon the ghost of his former helmsman Palinurus, who had fallen overboard (end of Book 5). Charon objects to transporting a living soul, but does so. They then come upon the hell-hound Cerberus, which the Sibyl drugs with a sop. Then come the ghosts of those who died prematurely and the Fields of Mourning, wherein wander the souls of those who died for love. Aeneas meets Dido's ghost.

Lines to be read in Latin (4.450–476)

450–476	Dido refuses to acknowledge Aeneas, who is penitent.

Lines to be read in English (6.477–846)

Next come the ghosts of dead warriors; the fate of Deiphobus, son of Priam, is described. The Sibyl advises them to hurry, and they come from neutral ground to a fork, leading either to Elysium or Tartarus. Aeneas sees Phlegethon, river of fire in Tartarus, and hears the sounds of punishment, administered by Tisiphone, one of the Furies. Some famous villains are described by the Sibyl until they reach the palace of Pluto, where Aeneas places the Golden Bough. Thereupon, they reach the Elysian Fields and Anchises (666–702). Father and son walk together and come upon the river Lethe, which is explained by Anchises as the river of forgetfulness from which drink those to whom a second body is owed. Anchises philosophizes about life and then speaks about Rome's future history, the Alban kings and Romulus. Then Anchises points out to Aeneas his various Julian descendants, including Julius and Augustus Caesar. The "Parade of Heroes" begins (808–825), which contains the kings of Rome and heroes of the early Republic, followed by Caesar, Pompey, and others (826–846).

Lines to be read in Latin (6.847–901)

847–853 The mission of Rome

Excudent alii spirantia mollius aera (lines 847–53)

854–892 The young Marcellus

893–901 Return to the Upper World

Book 7 (English)

At last the Trojans arrive in Latium, where they meet Latinus, king of the Latins, and his daughter Lavinia. The story of Faunus. The Trojans "eat their tables," as prophesied. Aeneas sends a delegation, led by Ilioneus, to King Latinus and then begins to mark out the boundaries of a city. Stories are swapped, and Latinus learns that this was the original homeland of Trojan Dardanus. Latinus invites the Trojans to settle in Latium. A fearful Juno summons Allecto, changeling and dread goddess of the Underworld. Allecto stirs up trouble with Queen Amata and with the Rutulian hero Turnus, to whom Lavinia is betrothed. Ascanius, while hunting, wounds Silvia's stag, which leads to a confrontation, arranged by Allecto, between the Latins and the Trojans. Juno opens the gates of war. A great army is mustered from the Italic towns.

Book 8 (English)

The river god Tiberinus appears to Aeneas and advises him to form an alliance with the Arcadians, enemies of the Latins. Aeneas sacrifices a white sow. At Pallanteum, the Arcadian king Evander, is receptive to Aeneas' proposal. The story of Hercules and Cacus is told at the ensuing feast, as well as the history of Arcadian Rome. Venus, fearful for her son, urges Vulcan to forge mighty arms for Aeneas. The formal alliance between Trojan and Arcadian is struck. The Shield of Aeneas, which depicts Rome's future history, includes Romulus and Remus, the Rape of the Sabine Women, Porsenna's siege of Rome, the sack of the city by Gauls, Catiline and Cato, and the Battle of Actium.

Book 9 (English)

Juno sends Iris to Turnus to inform him of the latest developments. He determines to attack the Trojans while Aeneas is away, and the Trojans retreat behind their newly-constructed battlements. Turnus then moves to burn the remaining Trojan ships, which, in answer to an old blessing, are changed into sea nymphs. There follows the tragic tale of the Trojan friends Nisus and Euryalus, who attempt to take word to Aeneas. The Latins attack the Trojan fortress, but Ascanius leads a counter-attack. Turnus turns the momentum but is trapped inside the Trojan stockade. He escapes by jumping into the Tiber River.

Book 10 (Latin and English)

Lines to be read in English (10.1–419)

A council of the gods is held on Olympus, which Jupiter addresses. The king complains about the hostility between the Latins and the Trojans and reminds his fellow deities about the destiny that he has ordained for Aeneas and for Rome. Venus holds Turnus and the Rutulians responsible and pleads, once again, for her son (cf. 1.223–253). Juno gives a fierce rebuttal, in which she claims that it isn't her fault if Aeneas endeavors to marry someone else's bride (Lavinia). The gods take sides and the situation escalates. Jupiter decrees that fate will determine the outcome. As the battle rages in Italy, Aeneas arrives with a small Arcadian force led by Evander and with a huge army of Evander's Etruscan allies. Vergil now provides the "Catalogue of Ships" and identifies their Trojan captains.The throng of recently-born sea nymphs meets the returning fleet, led by the Etruscan Tarchon, and speeds it along. As the fleet approaches Italy, Turnus decides to abandon his attack and defend the coast. A Homeric battle scene ensues on the beach. Evander's young son Pallas gives a stirring speech and charges into the enemy. More blood 'n' guts.

Lines to be read in Latin (10.420–509)

420–438 Pallas invokes the river god Tiber, slays the Rutulian Halaesus, and then is confronted by Lausus, the son of Mezentius.

Da hunc, Thybri pater, ferro, quod missile libro (lines 421–23)

439–456 Turnus' sister Juturna warns him to go to the aid of Lausus. He does so.

Simile of the lion and the bull (lines 454–56)

457–478 Pallas invokes Hercules, who is then advised by Jupiter that both heroes will soon meet their fate. Pallas casts his spear, with little effect.

Stat sua cuique dies, breve et irreparabile tempus omnibus est vitae; sed famam extendere factis, hoc virtutis opus (lines 467–72)

479–500 Turnus spears Pallas and despoils the body, while boasting of victory.

501–520 Vergil apostrophizes the death of Pallas and the fate of Turnus.

Nescia mens hominum fati sortisque futurae et servare modum, rebus sublata secundis! (lines 501–2)

Lines to be read in English (10.510–908)

Bloody battle scenes ensue, with Aeneas crazed with grief over the death of Pallas. Jupiter and Juno discuss her request to save Turnus. Juno spirits Turnus away from the field by creating a ghost, with the appearance of Aeneas, that lures him away from the fighting. The deposed king of the Etruscans, cruel Mezentius, now becomes the star enemy warrior for the Latins and Rutulians. The simile of the boar (lines 707–15). Aeneas seeks out Mezentius, who defies him with a boastful speech to his son Lausus. Aeneas gravely wounds Mezentius with a spear. While delivering a hard-hearted speech, he then slays Lausus. Simile of the hailstorm (lines 803–10). Mezentius, while attempting to recover from his wounds, eulogizes his dead son and calls out for revenge upon Aeneas. Aeneas strikes Mezentius' horse, which rears up and unseats the Etruscan. Aeneas finishes him off.

Book 11 (English)

Aeneas, grieving for the death of young Pallas, arranges for the body to be sent back to Evander at Pallanteum. A 12-day truce is called to allow time for burial of the dead. The prevailing feeling seems to be that Turnus and Aeneas should settle their differences in a duel. After an angry exchange in a council of the Latins and the Rutulians, Turnus agrees to fight Aeneas. Meanwhile, the Trojans attack, divided into two forces. Turnus moves out to meet one, led by Aeneas, and Camilla, female leader of the Volscians, remains behind to secure the defenses of Laurentum. Camilla is wounded by the Tuscan Arruns, but she is spirited away by the goddess Diana. Turnus is forced to return to the leaderless city.

Book 12 (Latin and English)

Lines to be read in English (12.1–790)

Turnus realizes that the salvation of Laurentum lies with him alone. He determines to meet Aeneas in a duel and asks King Latinus to arrange this. Simile of the wounded African lion (lines 4–9). Latinus' attempts to appease the warrior fall on deaf ears. So do the entreaties of Amata. Turnus, angry over the delay, arms himself for the fight and apostrophizes his spear. Simile of the bull charging a tree (lines 101–6). Aeneas also prepares, happy that the issue will finally be decided. The Rutulian and Trojan armies come together with great pomp to confirm the agreement. Aeneas prays to the gods regarding the outcome, either way. Juno, afraid for Turnus, seeks help from his sister Juturna, a fountain nymph. Disguised as Camers, a noble Rutulian, Juturna spreads dissent among Turnus' followers. This happens while Latin and the chieftains are sacrificing to seal the agreement. At this moment, a flock of wild swans is seen in the sky attacking an eagle that is trying to carry off one of them. The Rutulians, who outnumber the Trojans, immediately sieze upon this as a sign that they should attack the Trojans. A wild free-for-all ensues. Aeneas, standing tall while trying to restore order, is wounded in the knee. Turnus, with a sudden surge of new confidence, plunges into the fighting. Aeneas is carried away and his wounds tended. Simile of Mars, the war-bringer (lines 331–339). Venus heals the wound with a magic plant from Crete, and Aeneas plunges back into the fray. Simile of the hailstorm (lines 451–458). Both warriors rage on; Juturna, in the guise of his charioteer, guides Turnus' chariot away from Aeneas. Aeneas suddenly turns his attention back to Laurentum and the Trojan army storms the walls. Queen Amata hangs herself in despair over what she believes to be Turnus' death.

Turnus turns his attention to the beleaguered city, but is encouraged to remain in battle by Juturna. Saces, a wounded Rutulian, rides up and confirms to Turnus that the city is on the verge of collapse and that the queen is dead. In anger, Turnus determines to meet Aeneas, once and for all. Simile of the mountain rockfall (lines 684–690). Aeneas and Turnus finally meet. Turnus' sword snaps when it strikes Aeneas' god-made shield (Turnus had grabbed his charioteer's sword by mistake). Aeneas pursues Turnus. Simile of the hound and the stag (lines 749–757). Aeneas' spear becomes stuck in an olive tree; Turnus prays to Faunus that the tree hold it fast. Meanwhile, Juturna has arrived with Turnus' own sword. Angry Venus comes down to free the spear for Aeneas.

Lines to be read in Latin (12.790–842)

791–842 Jupiter intervenes and forbids Juno from interfering any further. He convinces her that the Trojans have suffered enough. Juno asks that the two sides become united under the Latin name.

Quae iam finis erit, coniunx? (lines 793–806)

Occidit, occideritque sinas cum nomine Troia (line 828)

Es germana Iovis Saturnique altera proles: irarum tantos volvis sub pectore fluctus (lines 830–840)

Lines to be read in English (12.843–886)

Jove sends one of the Furies to drive Juturna back to her fountain. Simile of the speeding arrow (lines 856–860).

Lines to be read in Latin (12.887–952)

887–918 The two warriors press on and taunt each other with angry words. But Turnus says that it is not Aeneas, but the gods, who terrify him, for Jupiter is his enemy. He heaves a huge boulder at Aeneas, but misses wildly.

Non me tua fervida terrent dicta, ferox: di me terrent et Iuppiter hostis (lines 894–895)

Simile of the dream-state (lines 908–914)

919–930 Aeneas hurls his spear with all his might and wounds Turnus in the thigh.

Simile of the shot from a catapult (lines 921–923)

931–937 Turnus' last words are not a prayer for mercy, but rather an admission of guilt. "I have deserved this; you have conquered; Lavinia is your wife."

938–952 Aeneas, ready to spare Turnus, catches sight of Pallas' war-belt, which Turnus has worn ever since he slew the youth. Revenge and grief rise up in Aeneas' heart, and he plunges his sword into Turnus.

Tune hinc spoliis indute meorum eripiare mihi? Pallas te hoc vulnere, Pallas immolat et poenam scelerato ex sanguine sumit (lines 947–49)

Reviewing the *Aeneid*

The time you have remaining to review for the AP Latin: Vergil Exam in mid-May will depend upon the time it takes you to prepare the 1856 lines of the Latin syllabus of the *Aeneid.*[109] If you do not finish the Latin syllabus by the time of the Exam, you will be obliged to decide how best to proceed, that is, whether to rush through the remaining lines or stop and review what you have already done. At this time, it is probably more logical to focus on what you do know, rather than what you do not know. Worrying about what you have not done is counter-productive and will compromise what you have accomplished. Perhaps it is best to stop at some point and review, assuring yourself that you have covered enough of the syllabus and/or that your Latin skills are strong enough for you to perform satisfactorily on the Exam. During your review, you should consider the *Aeneid* in its entirety. If you have read the poem in translation the summer before your AP Latin course, you will have had a jump-start on mastering the entire poem. Your teacher may schedule some extra review sessions during or after school, but you will probably be pressed for time and energy because of the confluence of regular final exams and other AP Exams, as well as the usual flurry of activities toward the end of the school year. Some students form study-groups for cramming, while others practice by taking one or more simulated AP Latin Exams (some teachers even factor your score into your regular academic grade!) However you choose to proceed, it is best to have a plan, in order to make efficient and productive use of the time you have left.

A Sample Review Schedule for the AP Latin Exam

Here is a sample five-week Exam review schedule using this book. You can, of course, revise this, based upon how much of the required syllabus you have completed.[110] These recommendations can supplement your teacher's formal review, or they can give you some ideas about how to design your own. When you are ready to begin thinking specifically about preparing for the Exam, follow the steps recommended below. One comment before we do this: your preparation for the multiple-choice section of the Exam will be a product of your total experience reading and studying Latin; there is little to be gained from focusing on sight-reading or, for that matter, on grammar review on the eve of the Exam. In general, you should 1) read the *Aeneid* in English (again), to create or confirm your sense of the poem as a whole, 2) concentrate on (translating) those portions of the *Aeneid* in Latin that you covered earlier in the year, i.e., Books 1, 2, 4, and 6, to refresh your memory, 3) (re-)read Chapters 5 and 6 of this book on translation and essays and prepare or fine-tune yourself by using the activities and Practice Exams provided in these chapters and at the end of this book, and 4) go online to the AP Latin: Vergil website (see the Appendix for Chapter 1) and practice answering actual AP Vergil Exam questions, especially those on translation.[111] If you are truly prepared, you will only gain confidence by simulating the taking of an actual AP Vergil Exam. One final word here: misery loves company, and it is always most effective (and more fun) to review with a study-buddy or, better yet, with a small group.

Here are some more specific guidelines for the weeks before the Exam in mid-May. Remember that these are only recommendations.

Week	Activities
1	At the beginning of this first week, plan your review schedule and organize or join a study group. (Re-)read Chapters 1, 2, and 3 of this book, which will give you a general overview of the content and format of the Exam. Begin re-reading your published translation of the *Aeneid* to get a sense of the entire work, and (re-)visit the appendices of this book to discover and explore those resources that might help you review most effectively. See especially the Appendix for this chapter, the AP Vergil Metasites created by Latin teacher Tim Abney and Jerard White, and the activities and games on Vergil and the *Aeneid* at the *Quia.com* website for Latin.
2 and 3	During these next two weeks, continue (re-)reading the *Aeneid* in translation. Supplement this activity by using the overview provided above and by referring to any websites that appeal to you. Then, complete the review activities in this chapter (see below), which cover the entire *Aeneid*. (Re-)read Chapter 5 on translation and then begin to review the required Latin of Books 1, 2, 4, and 6. Open your textbook at random and practice translating five- to ten-line passages, or consult in Chapter 5 the list of passages recommended for practice. During these two weeks, it would also be useful to revisit the AP Latin: Vergil website to obtain passages for translation practice. Be sure to check your versions against the sample translation provided in the Scoring Guidelines to ensure that your translations are sufficiently literal.
4	Week Four should be devoted both to continuing your reading of the *Aeneid* in translation and to final preparations for the analytical essay questions. By now, you should have mastered the techniques of poetic analysis, but it wouldn't hurt to revisit Chapters 8 and 9, especially the activities, and the websites recommended just above. The development of skills for writing effective analytical essays takes time, however, you might find it both helpful and reassuring to return to Chapter 6 (long and short essays), Chapter 8 (using figures of speech), and the AP Latin: Vergil website to practice with AP-style and actual AP questions, respectively. By practice, we don't mean endless hours of writing (which you wouldn't do, anyway), but we do mean reminding yourself about expectations, such as how to cite Latin support correctly. Read the author's sample essays in the chapters mentoned above to remind yourself about the significance of the acronym SODA—support, organize, develop, and analyze—in writing an effective essay.
5	This final week before the actual AP Latin Exam should be devoted to completing your reading of the *Aeneid* in English. This will refresh your memory of the latter Books, which we have put aside. Your other goal should be to simulate as closely as possible, the actual experience of taking the AP Latin Exam. Use the AP-style Practice Exams provided at the end of this book. Spend the time to assess your own performance by consulting the answers. Again, the author's sample answers to essay questions are necessarily subjective, but you will receive additional reminders about some of the issues we addressed in Week Four. Discussions with a classmate or classmates will provide "feedback" and help build confidence. The final step is to take an actual AP Latin Exam under simulated conditions. Go online to the AP Latin: Vergil website, pick an Exam year at random, print out the free-response section for that year, and spend time taking the Exam and then using the Scoring Guidelines provided to help you to assess your performance.

Here is an important final point to remember throughout the final weeks of your preparation. Remain conscientious and positive, doing your best to avoid "senioritis," whether or not you are a senior. It is regrettable that some students sacrifice the work of one or more years of AP study by losing their focus at the end. Now let's find out what you know. Here are several different types of questions covering the content of the *Aeneid* as a whole. We will begin with some general open-ended questions.

Activities Reviewing the Entire *Aeneid*

Phone a Friend

Answer the following questions about Vergil and the *Aeneid*, Books 1–6.[112]

Vergil and His Times

1. Give the date and place of Vergil's birth.
2. How did his early life and education influence his writing in the *Aeneid*?
3. What political changes took place during the poet's lifetime? How did these influence his writing?
4. What did Vergil owe to Augustus? Augustus to Vergil?
5. How, when, and where did Vergil die?
6. What was the condition of the *Aeneid* at the time of his death? How do we know? What were his final wishes for the poem?
7. Translate and intrepret this inscription from Vergil's tomb:

    Mantua me genuit, Calabri rapuere, tenet nunc / Parthenope. Cecini pascua, rura, duces.

8. Why are there two accepted spellings of Vergil's name?
9. Name Vergil's three greatest works.
10. Identify the theme or subject of one of these, besides the *Aeneid.*
11. Define literary epic.
12. Name two other epics of the world's literature. In what meter were these composed?

13. Name another Roman who wrote poetry as a contemporary of Vergil.

14. What poet of the Italian Renaissance acknowledges his debt to Vergil?

Aeneas and the Aeneid*, Books 1–6*

15. What does Vergil state is the subject of the *Aeneid*? Where?

16. What is its underlying theme?

17. At what point does he begin the story? Is Book 1 first, chronologically? Arrange Books 1–6 in chronological order.

18. Give the subject of <u>each</u> of Books 1–6.

19. Give the subject of <u>each</u> of Books 7–12.

20. Of what Homeric work is each of these two "sections" of the *Aeneid* reminiscent?

21. What happens between the story of Aeneas and the founding of Rome in 753 B.C?

22. How much of the story of the Trojan War does Vergil tell? Why only that part?

23. What influences lead Aeneas to seek a home in Italy?

24. How does the poet account for the hostility of Juno? How, when, and where does she show it?

25. Identify Troy and the Trojans by another name used by Vergil. Do the same for the Greeks.

26. Discuss the use of dreams and omens in the poem. What is their general purpose?

27. Which god is most prominent in the *Aeneid*? Which goddess(es)?

28. Discuss Aeneas as an epic hero.

29. What is the meaning of **pietas**?

30. What to Vergil's mind was the destiny of Rome and what prophecies of that destiny are made in the *Aeneid*?

31. Who were the **Atridae** and what was their role in the Trojan War?

32. Who was **Aeacides**?

33. What was the name of Aeneas father? His mother? His wife? What two names was his son given?

34. Tell the story of Cassandra.

35. Identify the role of Athena/Minerva in the Trojan War.

36. Why was Italy called Hesperia?

37. Identify the referent(s) and the circumstances in which each of the following appears:
    - **Dux femina facti.**
    - **Varium et mutabile semper femina.**
    - **Sunt lacrimae rerum et mentem mortalia tangunt.**
    - **Forsitan et haec olim meminisse iuvabit.**
    - **Tros Anchisiade, facilis descensus Averno.**

38. Narrate briefly the story of Dido as told in Book 1.

39. What is the substance of Jupiter's prophecy to Venus?

40. What were the subjects of the murals that Aeneas and Achates saw on the walls of the temple of Juno at Carthage? Identify at least one specific scene.

41. Briefly discuss the role of Venus in the *Aeneid.*

42. Discuss the following, with regard to the purposes of the *Aeneid:*

    His ego nec metas rerum nec tempora pono; / imperium sine fine dedi. (1.277–278)

    Nascetur pulchra Troianus origine Caesar, / imperium Oceano, famam qui terminet astris, / Iulius, a magno demissum nomen Iulo. (1.286–288)

43. What finally induced Anchises to leave Troy?

44. What was the fate of Creusa? Why was it necessary for her to be removed from the story?

45. Tell the story of Sinon.

46. Describe Priam's death.

47. What was the two-fold origin of the Roman race? How did this fact come to light in Book 3? To what confusion did it lead?

48. Who was Helenus? What was his relationship to Andromache? To whom had she been married, previously? How did Helenus aid Aeneas, specifically?

49. Outline the story of Aeneas' stay at Carthage.

50. Why did Dido call her people **Tyrians**?

51. What historic character may Vergil have had in mind in his description of Dido?

52. What was Juno's plan in Book 4?

53. Can Aeneas' treatment of Dido be justified? If so, how?

54. How does Vergil utilize Books 1 and 4 to portray the historical relations between Rome and Carthage?

55. To what historical character as an avenger did Dido appeal?

56. Why does Vergil attribute pity for Dido's fate to Juno rather than to any other divinity? How does the goddess ultimately show compassion for Dido?

57. Identify some of the contests at the funeral games. Whose life and death were being celebrated?

58. In what way did Juno attempt to thwart the Trojans while they were in Sicily?

59. Tell the story of Palinurus. Where else do we meet him in the *Aeneid*?

60. Where did the Trojans first land in Italy?

61. Who was Aeneas' guide during his trip to the Underworld?

62. What was the story carved on the bronze doors of the temple of Apollo?

63. What is the purpose of Book 6 in the story of the *Aeneid*? What method does Vergil employ here to reveal the glory of Rome?

64. Of what would a contemporary Roman of the Augustan Age think while reading Book 6.69–70?

    Tum Phoebo et Triviae solido de marmore templum / instituam festosque dies de nomine Phoebi.

65. What specific glimpse into the future was granted to Aeneas in the Underworld? Why was Augustus reduced to tears when Vergil read these lines?

66. What specific act was Aeneas required to perform before being allowed to enter the Underworld?

67. What were the punishments of Ixion, Tantalus, Sisyphus, the Danaids (daughters of Danaus), and Tityos in Tartarus?

68. Whom, of special importance to Aeneas personally (besides his father) did he happen upon in the Underworld? Describe the mood and manner of both individuals.

69. Translate the following description of Rome's mission, as summarized by Anchises (8.852–854):

> **Tu regere imperio populos, Romane, memento**
> **(hae tibi erunt artes) pacique imponere morem,**
> **parcere subiectis et debellare superbos.**

A Match Made in Troy

Match the description or quote in the right column with the appropriate individual in the left.

Royal Family of Troy

____ Hecuba	A. she married Hector, then Helenus
____ Hector	B. he appeared to Aeneas in a dream
____ Paris	C. he was brutally murdered by Pyrrhus
____ Cassandra	D. he redeemed his son's body for burial
____ Andromache	E. she sent away her son Polydorus to save him
____ Priam	F. he slew the great Achilles
____ Polites	G. he gave a prophecy to Aeneas
____ Helenus	H. she was cursed by Apollo

Aeneas' Family

____	Anchises	A.	"Ergo age, care pater, cervici imponere nostrae."
____	Aeneas	B.	"Di patrii, servate domum, servate nepotem."
____	Venus	C.	Ilus erat, dum res stetit Ilia regno
____	Creusa	D.	"Quid tantum insano iuvat indulgere dolori, O dulcis coniunx?"
____	Ascanius	E.	"Quid meus Aeneas in te committere tantum?"

Bookin' it

Indicate in what Book of the *Aeneid* each event occurs by writing the number of the Book in the space provided. Each Book appears twice.

a. Queen Amata hangs herself in despair. ____

b. Aeneas and Achates meet Venus disguised as a huntress. ____

c. Vulcan forges a mighty shield for Aeneas. _____

d. Simile of the beehive. _____

e. Anchises dies. _____

f. Turnus spears Pallas and despoils his body. _____

g. Juno sends the Fury Allecto to stir up trouble among the Latins and Trojans. _____

h. Creusa advises Aeneas to leave Troy without her. _____

i. The Trojans finally reach Italy. _____

j. The Trojan women set their ships afire at the instigation of Juno. _____

k. Fama spreads abroad a rumor about Dido and Aeneas. _____

l. The tragic story of the Trojan friends Nisus and Euryalus. _____

m. Helenus tells Aeneas to seek out a white sow with thirty piglets. _____

n. A council of the gods is held. _____

o. Camilla is spirited away from the battlefield by the goddess Diana. _____

p. Hector appears to Aeneas in a dream. _____

q. The young Marcellus, who is destined to die prematurely, appears. _____

r. King Latinus invites the Trojans to settle in Latium. _____

s. Simile of the oak tree in a high wind. _____

t. King Evander tells the story of Hercules and Cacus. _____

u. Turnus says, "I have deserved this; you have conquered; Lavinia is your wife." _____

v. The funeral games for Anchises in Sicily. _____

w. Turnus and Aeneas decide to settle their differences with a duel. _____

x. Turnus attempts to burn the Trojan ships, but they change into sea nymphs. _____

Captain's Log

Put the following events in the order in which they appeared in the *Aeneid*, i.e., in which Book they occurred. 1 = Book 1, 2 = Book 2, etc. All 12 Books are included, one event per Book.

_____ Turnus kills Evander's son Pallas.

_____ Laocoon warns the Trojans about the wooden horse.

_____ Aeneas and the Sibyl meet Cerberus.

_____ Allecto creates hostility between the Latins and the Trojans.

_____ A storm nearly destroys the Trojan fleet.

_____ The helmsman Palinurus falls overboard and dies.

_____ Turnus attacks the Trojans while Aeneas is away at Pallanteum.

_____ The Trojans encounter many unfriendly omens during their journey.

_____ Aeneas is wounded.

_____ Aeneas' great shield illustrates the story of the future of Rome.

_____ Camilla joins the fighting.

_____ Aeneas is compared to Paris for stealing another man's bride.

Quiz dixit?[113]

Who spoke the following and to whom? Try to recall the circumstances in which each speech was given. The lines of the entire speech are provided in parentheses. The answers are provided at the end of this chapter.

Book 1

1. "Aeole, namque tibi divum pater atque hominum rex" (lines 65–75)
2. "O terque quaterque beati" (lines 94–101)
3. "Tantane vos generis tenuit fiducia vestri?" (lines 132–41)
4. "O socii (neque enim ignari sumus ante malorum)" (lines 198–207)
5. "O qui res hominumque deorumque" (lines 229–53)
6. "Parce metu, Cytherea; manent immota tuorum fata tibi" (lines 257–96)
7. "Quisquis es, haud, credo, invisus caelestibus auras vitalis carpis" (lines 387–401)
8. "Quid natum toties, crudelis tu quoque, falsis ludis imaginibus?" (lines 407–9)
9. "O fortunati, quorum iam moenia surgunt!" (line 437)
10. "Sunt lacrimae rerum et mentem mortalia tangunt" (line 462)

Book 2

1. "Infandum, regina, iubes renovare dolorem" (lines 3–13)
2. "O miseri, quae tanta insania, cives?" (lines 42–49)
3. "Equo ne credite, Teucri. Quidquid id est, timeo Danaos et dona ferentes." (lines 52–54)
4. "O lux Dardniae, spes O fidissima Teucrum" (lines 281–86)
5. "Heu! fuge, nate dea, teque his," ait, "eripe flammis" (lines 289–95)

6. "Quae mens tam dira, miserrime coniunx, impulit his cingi telis?" (lines 519–24)

7. "Referes ergo haec et nuntius ibis Pelidae genitori" (lines 247–50)

8. "Quid tantum insano iuvat indulgere dolori, O dulcis coniunx?" (lines 776–89)

Book 4

1. "Soror, quae me suspensam insomnia terrent!" (lines 9–29)

2. "Egregiam vero laudem et spolia ampla refertis tuque puerque tuus" (lines 93–104)

3. "Vade age, nate, voca Zephyros et labere pinnis Dardaniumque ducem" (lines 223–37)

4. "Dissimulare etiam sperasti, perfide, tantum posse nefas tacitusque mea decedere terra?" (lines 305–30)

5. "Ego te, quae plurima fando enumerare vales, numquam, regina, negabo promeritam" (lines 333–61)

6. "Nec tibi diva parens, generis nec Dardanus auctor, perfide, sed duris genuit te cautibus horrens Caucausus" (lines 365–87)

7. "Inveni, germana, viam (gratare sorori), qui mihi reddat eum aut eo me solvat amantem" (lines 478–98)

8. "Dulces exuviae, dum fata deusque sinebat, accipite hanc animam" (lines 651–2)

9. "Hoc illud, germana, fuit? Me fraude petebas?" (lines 675–85)

Book 6

1. "Poscere fata tempus," ait. "Deus, ecce, deus!" (lines 45–46)

2. "Sate sanguine divum, Tros Anchisiade, facilis descensus Averno" (lines 125–55)

3. "Infelix Dido, verus mihi nuntius ergo venerat exstinctam" (lines 456–66)

4. "Tu regere imperio populos, Romane, memento" (lines 847–53)

5. "Quis, pater, ille, virum qui sic comitatur euntem?" (lines 863–66)

Book 10

1. "Da hunc, Thybri pater, ferro, quod missile libro" (lines 421–23)

2. "Tempus desistere pugnae; solus ego in Pallanta feror, soli mihi Pallas debetur; cuperem ipse parens spectator adesset" (lines 441–43)

3. "Stat sua cuique dies, breve et inreparabile tempus omnibus est vitae; sed famam extendere factis, hoc virtutis opus" (lines 467–72)

4. "Arcades, haec," inquit, "memores mea dicta referte Evandro; qualem meruit, Pallanta remitto" (line 491–95)

Book 12

1. "Quae iam finis erit, coniunx? Quid denique restat?" (lines 793–806)

2. "Adiciam faciamque omnes uno ore Latinos." (lines 830–840)

3. "Quae nunc, deinde mora est? Aut quid iam, Turne, retractas?" (lines 889–93)

4. "Non me tua fervida terrent dicta, ferox: di me terrent et Iuppiter hostis" (lines 894–95)

5. "Tune hinc spoliis indute meorum eripiare mihi? Pallas te hoc vulnere, Pallas immolat et poenam scelerato ex sanguine sumit" (lines 947–49)

Danai vs. Teucri

Put the name under the correct heading of each column.

Hector	Helen	Paris	Helenus	Cassandra
Agamemnon	Hecuba	Diomedes	Priam	Menelaus
Odysseus	Polydorus	Sinon	Ascanius	Andromache

Danai	**Teucri**
____________________	____________________
____________________	____________________
____________________	____________________
____________________	____________________
____________________	____________________
____________________	____________________
____________________	____________________
____________________	____________________

Some Mixed-Up Women

Unscramble these names of female characters in the story of the *Aeneid.* Then write the letter associated with each number in the corresponding space below to solve the puzzle, which is a quote from the *Aeneid.*

CBHUAE _ _ _ _ _ _

OIDO _ _(14) _ _

DARSCNSAA _ _ _ _ _ _ _(1) _ _

SNEVU _ _ _ _ _

LEHNE _ _ _ _ _(8)

NAETAH _(11) _ _ _ _ _

MCNEODRAHA _ _ _ _ _ _ _ _ _ _(5)

RISI _ _ _(7) _

ACESRU _(12) _ _ _ _ _

LCATOLE _ _ _ _ _ _(13) _

VALNIIA _ _(9) _ _ _ _ _

NJOU _ _(2) _ _

MATAA _ _ _ _ _

LAMLIAC _ _ _(6) _ _ _ _

		X	F						F				
1	2	3	4	5	6	7	8	9	10	11	12	13	14

Aeneas' Aenigma

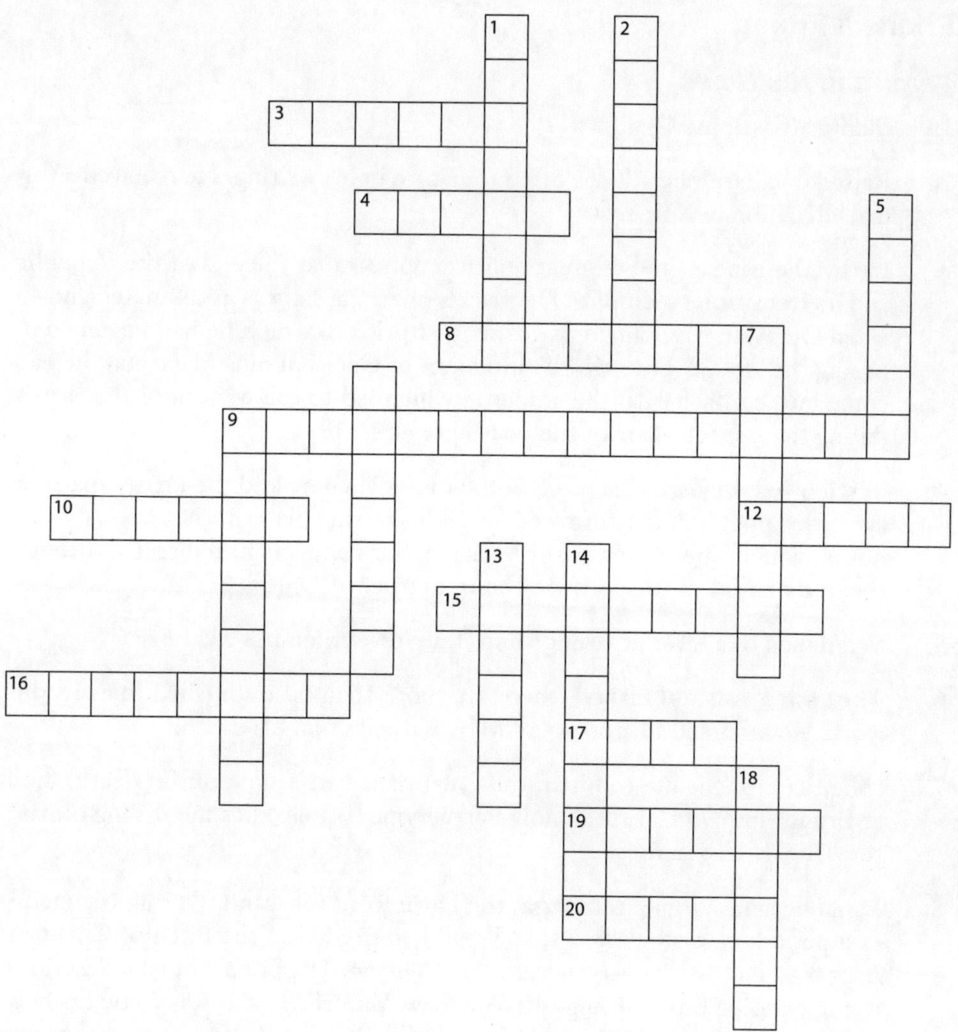

Across

3. Also spelled Virgil
4. She died by her own hand (not Dido)
6. Italia
9. First three words of the *Aeneid* (Lat.)
10. Aeneas' characteristic quality (Lat.)
12. The model for the last half of the *Aeneid*
15. The meter of the *Aeneid*
16. Confidant and political adviser to Octavian
17. *Iliad, Odyssey, Aeneid*
19. Region of Italy where Rome founded
20. He convinced the Trojans to accept the Horse

Down

1. Hill of first Roman settlement
2. Phoenician colony
5. God to whom Aeneas promised a temple
7. Aeneas met him in the Underworld
8. Replacement for Creusa
9. Helen's brother-in-law
13. God of the winds
14. Augustus' heir, mentioned in Book 6
18. Aeneas' arch-foe

Answers to Review Questions

Phone a Friend

Vergil and His Times

1. Mantua (Cisalpine Gaul), 70–19 B.C.

2. Raised on a farm, he alludes often to nature in his writing. He received a formal education in Rome.

3. He lived during a time of great political upheaval at the end of the Republic and its transition to Empire. He was 26 when Caesar was assassinated and 43 when Octavian was named Augustus, just prior to which he had begun composing the *Aeneid.* Through the influence of Gaius Cilnius Maecenas, he had come into contact with the emperor, which led to the writing of the *Aeneid* during the last ten years of the poet's life.

4. Vergil owed Augustus his place in the imperial court and the artistic patronage of his poetry. Augustus owed Vergil his lasting place in the *Aeneid,* which not only mentions the emperor by name, but connects him directly, through the **gens Iulia,** to the gods via Venus, mother of Aeneas.

5. Vergil died of a fever at Brundisium, Italy, on September 21, 19 B.C.

6. The *Aeneid* was unfinished; there are more than 50 unfinished lines in the work. He intended for the poem to be burned upon his death.

7. "Mantua brought me to birth, the Calabrians carried me off (in death) (i.e., at Brundisium, in Calabria), now Parthenope (Naples) has me. I sang of pastures, fields, and heroes."

8. Vergil became Virgil after **virga**, the Latin word for wand. During the medieval period, it was believed that Vergil had predicted the birth of Christ in *Eclogue* 4, and that he was therefore a magician. The poem actually describes the impending birth of Augustus' nephew Marcellus, who was to be his heir and who was to begin a "golden age." (Cf. Book 6.863ff.) Virgil is perhaps more common, but Vergil is more correct, as his original Latin name was **Vergilius**. Also during the Middle Ages, manuscripts of the *Aeneid* were used for bibliomancy, the *Sortes Vergilianae* (*Vergil's lottery*), in which a line would be randomly selected and interpreted in the context of a current event or personal situation.

9. *Eclogues (Bucolics), Georgics, Aeneid.*

10. The *Eclogues (Bucolics)* consist of ten selections, patterned after the Greek Sicilian poet Theocritus (his *Bucolica* means "care of cattle"), in which herdsmen converse and make songs in pastoral settings. In the Middle Ages, the Fourth Eclogue was believed to predict the birth of Christ. The *Georgics*

("Earth Poems"), ostensibly about life on the farm, have political overtones, as do the *Eclogues.*

11. An oral or folk epic evolves from the people whose civilization it describes, often transcending their factual history by incorporating legends, e.g., *Beowulf.* A literary epic is a deliberate and conscious creation of a poet about a people or civilization. The *Aeneid* is often called a "national epic" because the characteristics of the hero Aeneas are collective, rather than individual, and because the expression of those characteristics in heroic deeds serves to gratify a sense of national pride. Some consider Tolkien's *Lord of the Rings* or the Harry Potter series modern literary epics.

12. *Beowolf* (Anglo-Saxon), *Niebelungenlied* (German), and perhaps the stories of King Arthur (Celts) or El Cid (Spanish). Epic poems are typically composed in dactylic hexameter.

13. Catullus, Horace, Ovid, Propertius, Tibullus.

14. Dante Alighieri.

Aeneas and the Aeneid*, Books 1–6*

15. The subject of the *Aeneid* is the story of war and an individual man (**arma virumque cano**), the first three words of the poem.

16. Its underlying theme is the glorification of the people of Rome, esp. Augustus, as a race chosen by the gods to rule (Book 8.847–854).

17. Book 1 begins with Aeneas and the Trojans struck by a storm sent by Juno. This is not first, chronologically, as the story begins *in medias res*. The Books are to be taken in the order of 2, 3, 1, 4, 5, 6.

18. Book 1: introduction of theme; the storm and the Trojan arrival in Carthage

    Book 2: re-telling of the fall of Troy

    Book 3: adventures enroute to finding the site of a new Troy

    Book 4: Dido and Aeneas at Carthage

    Book 5: funeral games celebrating Anchises' death

    Book 6: Aeneas visits his father in the underworld

19. Book 7: the Trojans arrive in Latium; trouble brews between the Trojans and the Latins

    Book 8: Aeneas allies with Evander and the Arcadians

    Book 9: Turnus attacks the Trojan stockade and escapes capture

Book 10: council of the gods; Turnus kills Pallas and Aeneas kills Mezentius in battle

Book 11: Aeneas and Turnus agree to a duel; fighting breaks out again; Camilla

Book 12: the duel; Turnus is slain

20. The paradigm for Books 1–6 is Homer's *Odyssey*; for Books 7–12, Homer's *Iliad*.

21. If Troy fell sometime in the 12th century B.C., then there are 400 years to account for until the founding of Rome in 753 B.C. Literary tradition has it that Alba Longa was founded by Ascanius to relieve overcrowding in Lavinium and that this city became a collection point for Latin populations. The kings of Alba Longa are thought to give a direct line of descent from Ascanius to Romulus. There were 10 kings between Aeneas and Amulius, king by usurpation and younger brother of Numitor, who was the maternal grandfather of Romulus and Remus.

22. Vergil only tells the story of the fall of Troy, in Book 2, between the wooden horse and the fall of the city. This is the only part that is relevant to establishing Aeneas as a survivor and founder of a future new Troy.

23. Aeneas was advised by Hector in a dream; by his wife Creusa; by various omens after his escape, by his father in a vision, by a priest of Apollo at Delos, by Helenus, who advises him to continue to seek the "land of Ausonia," by Mercury from Jupiter, by the river god Tiberinus, etc. Also, it was reported by Vergil that Dardanus, an Arcadian Greek who was associated with the founding of Troy, was originally from Hesperia, or Italy (Book 3.163ff.).

24. Early in Book 1, Juno discusses the reasons for her anger (lines 12–30): Juno was patroness of Carthage, which was destined to be destroyed by Rome; Juno hated the Trojans because Paris had not chosen her the winner in the divine beauty contest; she also hated the Trojans because the race had sprung from Dardanus, who was the son of her husband Jupiter and Electra, her hated rival; and because Jupiter had named Ganymede, Priam's brother, as cupbearer of the gods, instead of Juno's daughter, Hebe.

25. Trojans: **Teucri** (Teucrians), **Dardanidae** (Dardanians); Greeks: **Danai** (Danaans), **Achivi** (Achaeans)

26. Dreams, oracles, omens, etc., are used to advance the story, to add elements of interest, and to demonstrate the power of fate and the divine over mortals.

27. Jupiter, Juno, and Venus appear most often in the story.

28. Aeneas is the main character in an epic whose legendary or heroic actions are central to his culture, nation, and race. Despite his human flaws, he is the

personification of the quality of **pietas,** and thus he embodies the cultural and religious beliefs that are characteristically Roman.

29. **Pietas** is devotion to gods, homeland, family, and friends. The word contains the concepts of duty and self-sacrifice.

30. Vergil's concept of Rome's destiny is perhaps summarized in Anchises' speech in Book 6, lines 847–854. Rome's future glory is revealed in three main locations in the *Aeneid:* Jupiter's long speech in Book 1, Anchises' Parade of Heroes in Book 6, and the engraved Shield of Aeneas in Book 8.

31. The **Atridae** were the sons of Atreus, who were Menelaus, king of Sparta, and Agamemnon, king of Argos or Mycenae.

32. **Aeacides** was Achilles, who was the grandson of Aeacus. The name is also used of Peleus, the son of Aeacus and Achilles' father.

33. Aeneas' family consisted of Anchises; Venus; Creusa; and Iulus/Ascanius.

34. Cassandra was the daughter of Priam and Hecuba, whose beauty caused Apollo to grant her the gift of prophecy. Since she did not love him in return, the god cursed her with the fact that no one would believe her predictions. (Book 2.246–147, 403–408)

35. Athena/Minerva, although known and portrayed as a goddess associated with war, was more a mediator and protector of the peace. To prevent the Trojan War, she passed between the two assembled armies and made both sides swear oaths of peace. Alas, a Trojan archer named Pandarus violated his oath and fired an arrow, thus beginning the actual fighting. Athena is credited with giving to Odysseus the idea of the wooden horse. Athena, of course, was also one of the goddesses involved in the Judgment of Paris.

36. Hesperia means "land to the West" (the word from which comes "vespers," prayers when the sun goes down, via the Greek and Latin words for evening), and it was towards the west that Aeneas was advised to travel in his search to find Italy.

37. Said of Dido as founder and queen of Carthage (Book 1)

    Mercury says this to Aeneas about Dido when he attempts to get Aeneas to leave Carthage (Book 2)

    Describes the melancholy of Aeneas and Achates while observing the mural of the fall of Troy on the walls of the temple of Juno at Carthage (Book 1)

    Aeneas says this to his men in the **O socii** speech after the storm (Book 1)

    The Sibyl says this to Aeneas as they prepare to enter the Underworld (Book 6)

38. Dido became infatuated with Aeneas while he was narrating the story of the fall of Troy in Book 2. She then forsook her oath to her murdered husband. Dido, through the contrivance of Juno and Venus, believed she had "married" Aeneas while together in a cave during a storm. The subsequent vacillating of Aeneas, reminded of his destiny several times by Jove through Mercury, caused the queen great anguish. When he finally determined to depart, Dido brought down curses upon him and proceeded to commit suicide.

39. Jupiter's prophecy, which foretold the ascendancy of Rome from Romulus to Augustus, was designed to reassure Venus after the Trojans were nearly destroyed by Juno's storm (Book 1.257–296).

40. The subjects of the murals were various episodes in the story of the fall of Troy (which Aeneas was about to narrate in Book 2). The most compelling scene, perhaps, was that of the ransom of Hector by his father Priam, after Achilles had desecrated Hector's body.

41. As Aeneas' mother, Venus played the role of protector and savior. She intereceded for her son with Jupiter in Books 1 and 10, protected him during Juno's plotting in Book 4 and by commissioning his great shield in Book 8, and rescued him when he had been wounded in the leg by a spear.

42. Both quotes are from Jupiter's speech in Book 1. In the first, he claims empire without limit for the Roman race, which is consistent with Vergil's purpose in using the *Aeneid* to glorify Rome. In the second, he foretells the birth and fame of Julius Caesar (and/or perhaps Augustus himself), which is consistent with the poet's purpose in commemorating the emperor's divine origins.

43. Anchises left Troy because of omens that occurred, e.g., a glowing light appearing above Ascanius' head, thunder, and a shooting star. (Book 2.679–704)

44. Vergil has Creusa disappear during the flight from Troy in order to free Aeneas to marry Lavinia when he reaches Italy. (Book 2.783–784)

45. In Book 2, Sinon is described as a Greek who, ostensibly, had escaped sacrifice at the hands of fellow Greeks and fallen into the hands of the Trojans. In reality, his mission is to gain the trust of Priam and the Trojans and convince them to take the horse into the city. This he does.

46. Priam died honorably at the hands of Achilles' son, Pyrrhus (aka Neoptolemus). The old king tried valiantly to defend his kingdom and family by strapping on his weapons and engaging Pyrrhus. Pyrrhus mocked and then slew him, leaving his headless corpse on the shore.

47. Dardanus, an Arcadian Greek who had a hand in the founding of Troy (hence **Dardanidae**; see Answer #23), was reported by Vergil in Book 3, lines 167–168, to have originated in Italy. This would imply that the Trojans were actually returning home to Italy.

48. Helenus was the son of Priam and Hecuba and twin of Cassandra. He had established the city of Buthrotum in Epirus (western Greece) and had married Andromache (former wife of Hector), after being granted freedom by Pyrrhus/Neoptolemus, whose slaves they had been since the war. Using the powers of prophecy learned from his prophetess-sister, Helenus advises Aeneas to continue to search for the "land of Ausonia," which he would know when he saw the portent of a white sow and thirty piglets. (Book 3.295–462)

49. Aeneas and some Trojan comrades were marooned on the coast of north Africa after the storm. While hunting, he met his mother Venus, disguised as a huntress, which ultimately led to Aeneas and Achates being enveloped in a fog and making their way to Carthage. After viewing murals depicting the Trojan War on the walls of the temple of Juno, Aeneas met Queen Dido and was reunited with his lost comrades. He then began an affair with the queen that ultimately led to warnings from Jupiter to get on with his mission, and to her suicide.

50. Dido came from Tyre (or alternatively, Sidon), the two main cities of Phoenicia, on the eastern coast of the Mediterranean.

51. Cleopatra.

52. Juno hoped to prevent Aeneas from meeting his destiny by keeping him in Carthage. To do this, she caused Dido to fall in love with him and subsequently created the storm during which their affections were realized. Juno suggests to Venus that they bring about a happy marriage between the two and that they settle down in Carthage, over which Juno and Venus would be patrons together.

53. Aeneas's destiny was assigned by Fate and the gods. He chose to leave Dido and Carthage because he was reminded (twice) by Jupiter that his mission to find a new homeland in Italy had not been completed.

54. In Book 1, Juno is established as the patron deity of Carthage. She gives her reasons for hating the Trojans, who are the ancestors of the Romans who will destroy her city. Book 1 also establishes Dido's back-story as queen of Carthage. In Book 4, Dido curses Aeneas and the Trojans several times, which is supposed to account for the historical enmity between Carthage and Rome. (Book 4, lines 381–387 and lines 607–629.)

55. Hannibal.

56. Juno is patron goddess of Carthage, of whom Dido is queen (see Book 1). Also, Juno has brought about the queen's death through her interference in the relationship between Dido and Aeneas. At the end of Book 4, Juno sends Iris to clip a lock of the queen's hair, thus releasing her soul.

57. The funeral games honoring Anchises consisted of a ship race, foot race, boxing match, and an archery contest.

58. During the funeral games, Juno sends Iris to the Trojan women who, weary of war and traveling, set the ships afire. Nautes then advises that the weak be left in Sicily with Acestes and that the Trojans move on, with the aid of Neptune, whose aid has been sought by Venus.

59. Palinurus, helmsman of Aeneas' flagship, is put to sleep on the job by the god Somnus, whereupon he falls into the sea and drowns.

60. The Trojans first landed at Cumae, a Greek colony along the southeastern coast near Neapolis (Naples) and site of an oracle of Apollo.

61. The Cumaean Sibyl, priestess and oracle of Apollo. Her name was Deiphobe, "God-fearer."

62. The story of Daedalus and Icarus was told in relief on the bronze doors of the temple. It was here that Daedalus finally came to earth, after losing his son, and dedicated his wings.

63. The purpose of Book 6 is to put Aeneas in contact with his father, who is now a shade in the Underworld. Aeneas needs to reaffirm that he is "on the right track." Anchises assures his son that he is and uses the so-called Parade of Heroes to personify Rome's future glory. For Julius and Augustus Caesar, see lines 789ff.

64. Augustus constructed a majestic temple of solid marble to Apollo on the Palatine Hill. Stored therein were the Sibylline oracles, which had much importance for the history of Rome. In this quote, Aeneas is promising the Sibyl such a temple in return for her assistance.

65. Aeneas was allowed to see what Augustus had hoped would be his heir to the throne, his nephew Marcellus, son of his sister Octavia (Book 6.855–885). Unfortunately, Marcellus died prematurely, which was a devastating blow to both Augustus and the Roman people.

66. Aeneas was required to obtain the Golden Bough as prescribed by the Sibyl, and take it to the palace of Pluto in the Underworld. (Book 6.140–148). He must also bury Misenus, whose unburied body on the shore was a source of pollution.

67. Ixion: he was bound to a burning wheel that spun forever.

 Tantalus: while standing in a pool, he was unable to reach the fruit hanging above him or the water beneath him, as both eluded his grasp.

 Sisyphus: eternally rolled a stone up a hill, whereupon it rolled back down just before reaching the top.

 Danaids: for murdering their husbands (all but one), they were condemned forever to carry water in leaky jars.

 Tityos: stretched out and tortured by two vultures, who ate out his liver unceasingly.

68. Aeneas met Dido, who failed to acknowledge his presence "as if she were set in flint." (Book 6.470–476). Aeneas breaks into tears of pity and regret.

69. You, Roman, remember to rule people with authority (these will be your arts) and to establish the custom of peace, to be sparing to those you rule, and to make war on the proud.

A Match Made in Troy

Royal Family of Troy: E, B, F, H, A, D, C, G

Aeneas' Family: B, A, E, D, C

Bookin' It

a. 12
b. 1
c. 8
d. 1
e. 3
f. 10
g. 7
h. 2
i. 6
j. 5
k. 4
l. 9
m. 3
n. 10
o. 11
p. 2
q. 6
r. 7
s. 4
t. 8
u. 12
v. 5
w. 11
x. 9

Captain's Log

10, 2, 6, 7, 1, 5, 9, 3, 12, 8, 11, 4

Quiz dixit?

Book 1

1. Juno to Aeolus
2. Aeneas
3. Neptune to the winds
4. Aeneas to his comrades
5. Venus to Jupiter
6. Jupiter to Venus
7. Venus to Aeneas
8. Aeneas to Venus
9. Aeneas
10. Aeneas to Achates

Book 2

1. Aeneas to Dido
2. Laocoon to the Trojans
3. Aeneas to Hector
4. Hector to Aeneas
5. Hecuba to Priam
6. Pyrrhus to Priam
7. Creusa to Aeneas

Book 4

1. Dido to Anna
2. Juno to Venus
3. Jupiter to Mercury
4. Dido to Aeneas
5. Aeneas to Dido
6. Dido to Aeneas
7. Dido to Anna
8. Aeneas to crew
9. Dido
10. Dido to the pyre
11. Anna to dead Dido

Book 6

1. Sibyl
2. Sibyl to Aeneas
3. Aeneas to Dido
4. Anchises to Aeneas
5. Aeneas to Anchises

Book 10

1. Pallas to Tiberinus
2. Turnus to the Rutuli
3. Jupiter to Hercules
4. Turnus to the Arcadians

Book 12

1. Jupiter to Juno
2. Jupiter to Juno
3. Aeneas to Turnus
4. Turnus to Aeneas
5. Aeneas to Turnus

Danai vs. Teucri

Danai: Agamemnon, Odysseus, Helen, Diomedes, Sinon, Helenus, Menelaus

Teucri: Hector, Hecuba, Polydorus, Paris, Priam, Ascanius, Cassandra, Andromache

Mixed-Up Women

CBHUAE	Hecuba	VALNIIA	Lavinia	OIDO	Dido
DARSCNSAA	Cassandra	MATAA	Amata	SNEVU	Venus
LEHNE	Helen	LAMLIAC	Camilla	NAETAH	Athena
MCNEODRAHA	Andromache			RISI	Iris
ACESRU	Creusa			LCATOLE	Allecto
				NJOU	Juno

D	U	X	F	E	M	I	N	A	F	A	C	T	I
1	2	3	4	5	6	7	8	9	10	11	12	13	14

Aeneas' Aenigma

Across

3. Vergil
4. Amata
6. Hesperia
9. arma virumque cano
10. pietas
12. Iliad
15. hexameter
16. Maecenas
17. epic
19. Latium
20. Sinon

Down

1. Palatine
2. Carthage
5. Apollo
7. Anchises
8. Lavinia
9. Agamemnon
13. Aeolus
14. Marcellus

Endnotes

[102] For many, the killing of Turnus by Aeneas at the very end of Book 12 violates the idea that **pietas** is transcendant over **furor**.

[103] Pharr/Boyd, *Aeneid*, 2001, page xvi.

[104] Augustus was, of course, Vergil's literary patron. By virtue of the emperor's **auctoritas,** he established a sort of patron-client relationship with the poet through Maecenas. The nature of their relationship was complex but intimate. According to Suetonius, the emperor exchanged letters with the poet, solicited poems from him, attended private recitations of the *Georgics* and the *Aeneid*, and was even named in Vergil's will. During his composition of the *Aeneid,* the poet no doubt was highly motivated to honor his patron's wishes by connecting him and his family with the foundation legend of Rome.

[105] Vergil probably planned on completing and polishing the *Aeneid* while in Greece in 19 B.C., but he died in that same year.

[106] For Vergil as a "sentimental idealist," see Pharr/Boyd, *Aeneid*, 2001, page 3.

[107] Mark Van Doren, American poet and critic and winner of the Pulitzer Prize.

[108] For recommended references to consult for the entire *Aeneid,* see Appendix 2. There are a number of different formats for review, e.g., outlines, summaries, and so forth.

[109] If it will make you feel any better, the "minimum essentials for meeting the requirements of the College Board" (whatever those were) in 1930 were 4500 lines of Vergil! A.A. Hamblen, "Sight Translation in the Fourth Year," *Suggestions for Teachers of Vergil in Secondary Schools,* Service Bureau of the American Classical League, Bulletin VII (April, 1930), page 37.

[110] The sample schedule provided assumes that you have completed or will complete the required reading. For the entire syllabus, see Chapter 1.

[111] Consider adapting the medieval custom of **Sortes Vergilianae** by opening your text of the *Aeneid* to the required lines at random and picking out a passage of 5–10 lines to translate.

[112] These questions are adapted versions of those designed by Elizabeth Simpson, Emma Willard School, Troy, NY, and published in *Suggestions for Teachers of Vergil in Secondary Schools*, 1930, pp. 97–104. See Endnote #109, above. If you cannot answer the questions about Vergil's life and works, see the resources listed in the Appendix for Chapter 1, under "Additional Useful Sites" and for Chapter 7, under "The Augustan Age."

[113] For several websites containing *Quia* games, on quotes from Vergil, see the Appendix for this chapter.

Chapter 11

Taking and Scoring the AP Latin Exam

"Walking the Walk"

If you are reading this chapter, you have done all the hard work of preparing for success on the AP Latin Exam, which is usually administered during the third week in May. Be aware that in recent years the AP Latin Exam has been scheduled in the very last testing slot, so if you are taking multiple AP exams, you should plan accordingly. You have spent considerable time preparing for this exam, in order to show yourself, your friends, your parents, your teachers, and your selected college or university, that you have mastered a difficult language and a difficult exam syllabus. In recent years, there has been much discussion among those who teach AP Latin about the rigorous expectations of the College Board AP Latin syllabus, as compared to semester courses on Vergil now taught in colleges and universities. This may account for the fact that comparability studies conducted by the Advanced Placement Program every five to seven years indicate that secondary students who have studied an AP subject score higher on the AP Exam than those who have had an equivalent course in college and who take the Exam.

As we have mentioned several times already, the best way to find success on the AP Latin Exam is to prepare the required readings as thoroughly as possible and to read as much Latin as you can. (For additional tips on preparing for the Exam, see the previous chapter.) We hope that you have made the most of this study guide in helping you to prepare for the Exam, whether you have done so systematically throughout an AP course, or whether you are using it during your personal or class review just before the Exam. You have "talked the talk," now it's time to "walk the walk."

Exam Day

Since you are now taking an AP Exam, you have probably reached the point in your education where you are SAT-savvy. This means that you know all the rules about how to "bubble" your answer sheet correctly, and so forth. This also means that you know that you should get a good night's rest before the exam, eat a good breakfast (or lunch), and, above all, relax! For the exam, bring several #2 pencils with erasers (for the machine-graded bubble sheet used in the multiple-choice section) and a black or blue pen (required for the free-response section). You will also need your school code, your social security number, and a photo I.D., if you are not taking the Exam at your own school. It is also helpful to have a watch, in case you are seated so that you cannot see the clock. (Do not bring your cell phone or iPod!) Also, bring an energy-boosting snack for the 10-minute break between the multiple-choice and free-response sections. The tips presented below consolidate what we have said in various places throughout this book. They also presume that you have taken practice AP Latin Exams, especially the AP-style Exams provided in this book or actual AP Latin Exams on the AP Latin website, and that you are familiar with the format, directions, and level of difficulty of the questions. This is important because you will want to spend all your mental energy during the Exam focusing on the Latin.

Multiple-Choice Section

- Before you answer the questions, read through each Latin passage. Use the reading title and the vocabulary assistance to help you understand the general theme or message. As you look over each passage, focus on noun-adjective combinations, pronoun references, verb forms (particularly participles, infinitives, and subjunctives), and the special words that define and bind together phrases, clauses, and sentences. Identify sense-units.
- Do not attempt to translate the entire multiple-choice reading passage. Translate only when the question requires you to do so.
- Read each question carefully.
- Know that the questions are asked in the sequence in which the answers are found in the Latin passage and that all questions contain both underlining of the relevant Latin and the line references needed to answer the question, e.g., <u>Troiae qui primus ab oris</u> (line 1). There are usually one or two questions per Latin sentence.
- Do not blind guess. Remember that you are penalized for wrong answers. If you can narrow your choices to two, then answer the question by making an educated guess. You are not expected to know the answer to every question or to answer every question in order to achieve a "good" score on this part of the Exam.
- Do not rush, but work at a steady pace. You should average about one minute per question, as you have 60 minutes to answer 50 questions.

Free-Response Section

- Use the 15-minute reading period productively. Look over every question in your green booklet and try to recognize the Latin passages being tested and the essential element/s of each essay question. Begin to outline or organize your answer in marginal notes and to underscore or otherwise highlight relevant Latin in the text and the prompt within the question. You may write directly on your green test booklet. (Refer back to Chapter 3 for more tips on how to use the reading period effectively.)

- Answer the five questions on the free-response section in whatever sequence makes you feel the most confident. You may wish to begin by addressing those questions which you find the easiest. If you are confronted with an unfamiliar passage, you are perhaps best served to leave this until last and then apply the principles of successful sight reading that you have learned during your time in Latin. In such situations, you will presumably have the advantage of being familiar with the literary context of the passage, even though you do not recognize it immediately in Latin.
- When you are underway, re-read each question thoroughly and answer the question asked. Avoid blathering or telling everything you know about the author or the passage. Quality, not quantity, will earn you top marks. Repeat key words from the question in your opening statement.
- Write your essays with attention to providing a beginning, a middle, and an end.
- Be familiar with the implications of the terms "literal" and "well-developed," and with the differences in expectations between a long essay and a short one.
- In essay questions, refer to the Latin throughout the passage or passages.
- Document your discussions on essays by correctly citing and translating or closely paraphrasing relevant Latin. It is customary to underline the Latin cited. Underlining the relevant Latin highlights your ability to make use of the Latin text accurately and thoughtfully in your discussion. Remember that ellipsis points may be used in citing longer clauses or sentences, however, it is a good idea to limit the length of your citations to a few relevant words. (Refer back to Chapter 6 for reminders about how to cite Latin correctly and effectively on essays.)
- Remember that you must begin the answer to each question on a fresh page of your pink free-response booklet. This does not apply to different sections of the same question. Be sure to label each question, or section of a question, accurately. Skip lines as you write to allow for editing later in the testing session.

How to Score the AP Latin Exam

The statistics provided below are those given for the 2005 AP Latin Vergil Exam, the most recently released Exam.[114] These numbers are valid only for that particular Exam and are used only for the purposes of illustration.

The Multiple-Choice Section

This section counts as 40 percent, weighted to 48 total points out of 120 possible on the Exam. Each of the four multiple-choice passages counts as 10 percent of the total Exam score.

The Free-Response Section

The free-response section counts as 60 percent of the total Exam score, weighted to 72 total points out of 120 possible on the Exam.

- **Translation 1**

  Counts for 9 points (× 1.2 = 10.8 weighted points) = 15 percent of the free-response section and 9 percent of the total Exam score.

- **Translation 2**

  Counts for 9 points (× 1.2 = 10.8 weighted points) = 15 percent of the free-response section and 9 percent of the total Exam score.

- **Long Essay**

  Counts for 6 points (× 4.2 = 25.2 weighted points) = 35 percent of the free-response section and 21 percent of the total Exam score.

- **Short Essay**

  Counts for 6 points (× 2.4 = 14.4 weighted points) = 20 percent of the free-response section and 12 percent of the total Exam score.

- **Background Question**

  Counts for 6 points (× 1.8 = 10.8 weighted points) = 15 percent of the free-response section and 9 percent of the total Exam score.

Scores on Multiple-Choice Questions

One College Board publication points out, "Generally, to obtain a total grade of 3 or higher on an AP Exam, students need to answer about 50 percent of the multiple-choice questions correctly and to do acceptable work on the free-response section."[115] Here are some performance statistics for the multiple-choice section of the 2005 released exam, indicating what range of multiple-choice scores correlated with what total scores.[116] (Percentages have been rounded up.)

	AP Latin Grade		
Multiple-Choice Score	**3**	**4**	**5**
41–48	0%	0%	100%
32–40	0%	10%	90%
23–31	18%	20%	38%
16–22	61%	20%	2%
8–15	19%	0.1%	0%

This chart tells you, for instance, that 90 percent of the students who scored a 5 on the AP Latin: Vergil Exam in 2005 scored between 32 and 40 (out of 49) answers correct on the multiple-choice section, and so forth.

Average Scores on Free-Response Questions

Here are the mean scores for the free-response questions on the 2005 and 2008 AP Latin Exams.[117] The mean score is the average score earned by all students who answered that question. Again, these scores are to be taken as points of reference and not as summaries of student performances on any other AP Latin Exam. The scores indicate average number of points earned out of the points that were available for each of the free-response questions.

	Translation 1	Translation 2	Long Essay	Short Essay	Background
2005	4.43 out of 9	3.03 out of 9	3.34 out of 6	3.28 out of 6	3.33 out of 6
	49%	34%	56%	55%	56%
2008	4.94 out of 18	7.15 out of 18	3.19 out of 6	2.85 out of 6	3.31 out of 6
	27%	40%	53%	48%	55%

Sample Scoring Worksheet[118]

Look over the scoring worksheet for 2005 provided below, followed by the scoring of a hypothetical student.

Step 1: Multiple-Choice

[__________ minus 1/3 × __________] × .9796 = __________

Number correct — Number wrong — Weighted Section I Score (Do not round scores.)

Step 2: Free-Response Section

Question 1 (Translation 1) __________ × 1.2 = __________

Question 2 (Translation 2) __________ × 1.2 = __________

Question 3 (Long Essay) __________ × 4.2 = __________

Question 4 (Short Essay) __________ × 2.4 = __________

Question 5 (Background) __________ × 1.8 = __________

Sum = __________

Weighted Section II Score

Step 3: Composite Score[119]

__________ + __________ = __________

Weighted Section I Score — Weighted Section II Score — Composite Score (Round to nearest whole number)

Step 4: Grade Conversion Chart for 2005 (see below)

Sample Student

Step 1: Multiple-Choice

[30 (Number correct) minus 1/3 × 18 (Number wrong)] × .9796 = 23.52 (Weighted Section I Score) (Do not round scores.)

Step 2: Free-Response Section

Question 1 (Translation 1)	6 (of 9 pts.)	× 1.2 =	7.2
Question 2 (Translation 2)	5 (of 9 pts.)	× 1.2 =	6.0
Question 3 (Long Essay)	4 (of 6 pts.)	× 1.2 =	16.8
Question 4 (Short Essay)	5 (of 6 pts.)	× 2.4 =	12.0
Question 5 (Background)	4 (of 6 pts.)	× 1.8 =	7.2
		Sum =	49.2 (Weighted Section II Score)

Step 3: Composite Score[120]

23.5 (Weighted Section I Score) + 49.2 (Weighted Section II Score) = 73 (Composite Score (Round to nearest whole number))

Step 4: Grade Conversion Chart for 2005

Composite Score Range	AP Grade
79–120	5
68–78	4
50–67	3
36–49	2
0–35	1

Our hypothetical student's composite score is 73, which falls within the range of 68–78 that produces a grade of 4 on the 2005 Exam. S/he did better than the average on all free-response questions (see above for the averages for each question), which compensated for a somewhat lower score on the multiple-choice section.

What Does My AP Latin Exam Score Mean?

As you have seen, your AP Latin Exam score of 5, 4, 3, 2, or 1 is calculated using a formulaic numerical assessment of your performance on the multiple-choice and free-response sections, the sum of which is converted from a composite score to the following 5-point AP scale:[121]

AP Grade	Qualification
5	Extremely well qualified
4	Well qualified
3	Qualified (considered by many to be "passing")
2	Possibly qualified
1	No recommendation

For your information, here is the breakdown of rounded scores on the AP Latin: Vergil Exams for the past five years. Seventeen percent of those taking the Exam in 2008 scored a 5, and so forth.

	2004	2005	2006	2007	2008
5	18%	19%	18%	19%	17%
4	17%	17%	18%	19%	18%
3	27%	29%	28%	25%	27%
2	20%	16%	17%	19%	16%
1	18%	19%	20%	19%	22%
Mean grade	2.97	3.00	2.96	3.00	2.92
Number students	4061	4362	4844	4929	4847

Making the Most of Your Experience with AP Latin

Before you take the AP Latin Exam, you should contact the Admissions or Classics Department of your chosen colleges or universities for information about their graduation requirements in foreign language and about what placement or credit you may earn from your performance on the AP Latin Exam. Gather information from your teacher, college or guidance counsellor, school or college alumni, catalogues and bulletins, or college/university or Classics Department websites.[122] Remember that the department in which classics courses are taught varies from institution to institution. In major universities and many liberal arts colleges, you will find a Department of Classics. Alternatively, Latin may have its own department or be taught within a classical civilization or other humanities department, such as English, comparative literature, history, or languages. Also, be aware that there is some difference among higher institutions with regard to how they view a given score on the AP Latin Exam. Although more students are taking the AP

Latin Exam, paradoxically, fewer colleges and universities seem to be accepting even high scores for credit or placement (the reasons for this vary from institution to institution).[123] Even having had the experience of taking an AP Latin course and/or Exam, you may be asked to take an "in-house" test designed by the college/university or the department that determines placement or credit. If you are asked to do this, your chances for a successful experience will certainly be increased by your background in the Advanced Placement Program. Remember, that there is much to be said for your participation in a seminar-sized class of able and motivated Latin students, led by an enthusiastic and capable instructor, all of whom are willing to accept and grow from academic challenge. This is, perhaps, more to the point of preparing for success in college. You have taken part in what many students have considered one of their best academic experiences in high school.

Endnotes

[114] One multiple-choice question on the 2005 Exam was subsequently dropped as invalid, making a total of 49 questions on the multiple-choice section of the 2005 Exam. All statistical information provided in this chapter comes from *2005 AP Latin Literature and AP Latin Vergil Released Exams* or from the AP Latin: Vergil website, unless indicated otherwise.

[115] The College Board, *A Guide to the Advanced Placement Program* (Acorn book), May 1999, page 46.

[116] *2005 Released Exams*, page 181.

[117] Interestingly, the mean scores on the translation section of the AP Latin Exam have been dropping, slowly but consistently, over the past six years, despite the emphasis placed on translation skills on the Exam. The reason for this may have something to do with the growing number of secondary programs that have adopted the so-called reading method, which emphasizes comprehension rather than translation. (See Chapter 5.) In order to "compare apples with apples," the author has converted the mean scores for 2008 into their equivalents, as the point totals for translation questions increased from 9 to 18 in that year. The mean scores were actually 4.94 pts. out of 18, or 27 percent, and 7.15 pts. out of 18, or 40 percent, for questions V1 and V2, respectively.

	2003	**2004**	**2005**	**2006**	**2007**	**2008**
Translation Question 1	4.55	4.36	4.43	3.25	3.18	(2.43)
Translation Question 2	3.78	3.44	3.03	2.96	2.85	(3.60)

[118] *2005 Released Exams*, page 180.

[119] For information about how individual translation questions and essays are scored on the AP Latin Exam, see Chapters 5 and 6, respectively.

[120] Composite score ranges are determined by formula each year by the Chief Reader. The composite score ranges provided here are accurate for the 2005 AP Vergil Exam.

[121] For many (but not all!) institutions, the AP Exam scoring scale approximates the grading scale of a college course, e.g., 5 = A, 4 = B, 3 = C, etc.

[122] For information about college and university credit policies for AP Exam scores, see Appendix 6.

[123] To the knowledge of the author there are no hard data for this claim, but the comments made by Latin teachers at professional conferences and at AP workshops, in journals and newsletters, and on the College Board's AP Latin Electronic Discussion Group (EDG), suggest that, indeed, colleges and universities are becoming more circumspect about granting credit or placement, at least for scores below 5. Students should always check the AP credit policies of the schools they are considering well in advance of their application to those schools.

PART II

Review of Grammar and Syntax

Chapter 12

Nouns

Quick Study of Noun Forms*

	1st	2nd	2nd N.	3rd	3rd N.	4th	5th
Singular							
Nom.	**tibia**	**nasus**	**bracchium**	**pes**	**caput**	**manus**	**facies**
Gen.	**tibiae**	**nasi**	**bracchi**	**pedis**	**capitis**	**manus**	**faciei**
Dat.	**tibiae**	**naso**	**bracchio**	**pedi**	**capiti**	**manui**	**faciei**
Acc.	**tibiam**	**nasum**	**bracchium**	**pedem**	**caput**	**manum**	**faciem**
Abl.	**tibia**	**naso**	**bracchio**	**pede**	**capite**	**manu**	**facie**
Plural							
Nom.	**tibiae**	**nasi**	**bracchia**	**pedes**	**capita**	**manus**	**facies**
Gen.	**tibiarum**	**nasorum**	**bracchiorum**	**pedum**	**capitum**	**manuum**	**facierum**
Dat.	**tibiis**	**nasis**	**bracchiis**	**pedibus**	**capitibus**	**manibus**	**faciebus**
Acc.	**tibias**	**nasos**	**bracchia**	**pedes**	**capita**	**manus**	**facies**
Abl.	**tibiis**	**nasis**	**bracchiis**	**pedibus**	**capitibus**	**manibus**	**faciebus**

* For a more thorough review of the basics of Latin grammar and syntax, see the author's book, *The Best Test Preparation for the SAT Subject Test: Latin*, Research & Education Association, 2006.

Quick Study of Noun Syntax

Case	Function	Description of Function	Example
Nominative			
	subject	expresses who or what is performing the action	**Servus laborat.** *The slave is working.*
	predicate nominative (complement)	restates the subject	**Senex servus est.** *The old man is a slave.*
Genitive ("of," -'s or -s')			
	possessive	expresses whose, of whom, or of what; links two nouns	**amica pueri** *the girlfriend of the boy* or *the boy's girlfriend.*
	descriptive	with accompanying adjective, describes another noun	**femina magnae pulchritudinis** *a woman of great beauty.*
	partitive	indicates a part of the whole	**satis temporis; plus vini** *enough (of) time; more wine*
	objective	expresses object of emotion	**cupiditas pecuniae** *the desire for money,* lit., *of money*
	with special words	requires translation "of"	**plenus irae; amoris gratia** *full of anger; for the sake of love*
Dative ("to" or "for")			
	indirect object	indicates "to" or "for" whom something is done, shown, told, or given	**Puer puellae osculum dedit.** *The boy gave a kiss to the girl, The boy gave the girl a kiss.*
	possession	shows ownership	**Est canis puero.** *The boy has a dog,* lit., *there is a dog to/for the boy*

Case	Function	Description of Function	Example
Dative ("to" or "for") *(cont.)*			
	reference	indicates "with reference" to whom an action is done	**Militi periculum belli verum est.** *With reference to or For the soldier, the danger of war is real.*
	double dative	dative of reference + dative of purpose	**suis saluti fuit** *he was the salvation of his men,* lit., *for the salvation for his men.*
	with verbs	intransitive verbs	**Crede mihi.** *trust me,* lit., *be trusting to me.*
		impersonal verbs	**licet mihi**, *I am permitted*, lit., *it is permitted to me*
		compound verbs	**occurrere amico** *to meet a friend*
	with adjectives	adjectives that require the meaning "to" or "for"	**similis patri** *similar to the father*
	agent	the person who must perform a necessary action	**tibi agendum est** *you must do it,* lit., *it must be done by you*
Accusative			
	direct object	receives action of verb	**Brutus Caesarem necavit.** *Brutus killed Caesar.*
	object of preposition	accompanies **per, prope**, etc.	**per viam; prope arborem** *along the road; near the tree*
	place to which	expresses motion towards with **ad**	**ad urbem** *toward the city*

Case	Function	Description of Function	Example
Accusative *(cont.)*			
	duration of time	expresses passage of time	**tres dies; abhinc duos menses** *for three days; two months ago*
	subject of infinitive	subject of infinitive in indirect statement	**Audio <u>theatrum</u> clausum esse**. *I hear that the <u>theater</u> was closed.*
	gerundive of purpose	**ad** + gerundive expresses purpose or intent	**<u>ad forum videndum</u>** *<u>to see the forum</u>*
	exclamatory	expresses an exclamation	**Me miserum!** *How unhappy I am!*
Ablative ("by," "from," "with," etc.)			
With a preposition			
	place where	used with prepositions, e.g., **in** (*in, on*), **sub**, etc., to indicate location	**in mensa; sub plaustro** *on the table; beneath the wagon*
	accompaniment	expresses partnership (*with*)	**Puer <u>cum cane</u> ambulat**. *The boy walks <u>with his dog</u>.*
	personal agent	indicates the person who completes the action of a passive verb (*by*)	**Luna <u>ab amantibus</u> conspicitur**. *The moon is seen <u>by the lovers</u>.*
	place from	used with prepositions, e.g., **a/ab, de,** or **e/ex**, to express motion away	**ab urbe, de caelo, e villis** *away from the city, down from the sky, from the villas*

Case	Function	Description of Function	Example
Ablative ("by," "from," "with," etc.) *(cont.)*			
With or without a preposition			
	manner	indicates how (*with*)	**magno (cum) murmure** *with a great rumbling*
	separation	indicates the distancing of one person/thing from another, following certain verbs (with or without **a/ab** or **e/ex**)	**(e) timore se liberavit** *he freed himself from fear*
	cause	"because of," with or without **a/ab, de, e/ex**	**(ex) vulnere dolebat** *he was in pain from (because of) his wound*
Without a preposition			
	time when	expresses a point in time (*in, on, at*)	**sexto anno; aestate** *in the sixth year; in the summer*
	time within	expresses time during which (*in, within*)	**quinque mensibus** *(with)in five months*
	means	indicates the instrument or tool with which an action is performed (*with, by*)	**Miles gladio hostem vulneravit.** *The soldier wounded his enemy with a sword.*
	comparison	expresses comparison between two persons or things	**Hic mons altior illo est.** *This mountain is higher than that.*
	degree of difference	indicates the extent to which one person/thing differs from another (*much, less*)	**Hic mons multo altior est.** *This mountain is much higher,* lit., *higher by much.*

Case	Function	Description of Function	Example
Ablative ("by," "from," "with," etc.) *(cont.)*			
With or without a preposition *(cont.)*			
	description	with accompanying adjective, describes some characteristic (a person *of*...)	**Erat vir magna fortitudine.** *He was a man of great courage.*
	respect or specification	expresses in what regard or respect something is true	**meā sententiā** *in my opinion*
	with certain verbs	accompanies specific deponent verbs	**Fruamini vitā.** *You should enjoy life.*
	ablative absolute	phrase consisting of pro/noun+ participle in ablative	**hoc facto** *after this is/was/had been done (after, when, since,* etc.)
			multis clamantibus *while many are/were shouting*
			Caesare consule *while Caesar is/was consul*
Vocative			
	direct address	naming or speaking directly to a person	**"Tite, claude ianuam."** *"Titus, close the door."*
			"Fer auxilium matri, fili." *"Help your mother, son."*
Locative (*in* or *at*)			
	place where	indicates location without a preposition (names of cities, small islands, **domus**, **rus**)	**Romae maneo.** *I am staying in Rome.*

Practice Questions: Nominative Case*

1. Ignavo servo mandata dedit. The subject of this sentence is
   (A) Ignavo (C) mandata
   (B) servo (D) he (in the verb dedit)

2. Quis erat ____?
   (A) vilicum (C) vilico
   (B) vilici (D) vilicus

3. Bacillus Bombacem** ____ punire vult.
   (A) servum (C) servo
   (B) servus (D) servorum

4. Bacillus ____ non erat.
   (A) dominum (C) dominus
   (B) domino (D) domine

Practice Questions: Genitive Case

1. Bombax plus ____ semper vult.
   (A) cibus (C) cibo
   (B) cibum (D) cibi

2. Bombax servus ____ erat.
   (A) magnae ignaviae (C) magnas ignavias
   (B) magnam ignaviam (D) magna ignavia

3. The life of a slave was often full of misery.
   (A) plena miseriā (C) plena miseria
   (B) plena miseriae (D) plena et misera

4. Canes vestigia fugitivae ancillae secuti sunt.
   (A) of the runaway maid (C) for the runaway maid
   (B) with the runaway maid (D) toward the runaway maid

* The answers to all review questions are found at the end of each chapter.

** The sentences in these practice questions include the fictional characters Bombax, a ne'er-do-well slave, Bacillus, his overseer, and Palaestra, Bombax's heartthrob.

5. For a slave, the price <u>of freedom</u> was hard work.
   (A) libertatum
   (B) libertati
   (C) libertatis
   (D) libertate

6. Bombax <u>aliquid mali</u> semper agebat.
   (A) of something bad
   (B) for something bad
   (C) something bad
   (D) with someone bad

7. ____ nomen non habuit.
   (A) Unus e servis
   (B) Unum servum
   (C) Uno servo
   (D) Unius servi

8. Servus <u>gratiam benefici</u> agit.
   (A) gratitude and kindness
   (B) gratitude or kindness
   (C) gratitude for kindness
   (D) kind gratitude

9. Bombax quinque milia ____ ambulare non poterat.
   (A) passus
   (B) passum
   (C) passus
   (D) passuum

Practice Questions: Dative Case

1. Will the master give <u>the slave</u> her freedom?
   (A) servam
   (B) serva
   (C) servae
   (D) serva

2. Bombacis tunica <u>idonea cenae</u> non erat.
   (A) suitable with dinner
   (B) suitable for dinner
   (C) a suitable dinner
   (D) for a suitable dinner

3. Necesse est ____ parcere.
   (A) miseros servos
   (B) miseri servi
   (C) miserorum servorum
   (D) miseris servis

4. <u>Dominus filio servi pecuniam libertati dedit</u>.
   (A) The master gave the slave's son freedom for his money.
   (B) The slave's son gave the master money for his freedom.
   (C) The master gave the slave's son money for his freedom.
   (D) The slaves gave the master's son money for their freedom.

5. Licebatne Bacillo servis praeesse?
   (A) Is he permitted to place Bacillus in charge of the slaves?
   (B) Did he place the slaves in charge of Bacillus?
   (C) Was Bacillus permitted to be in charge of the slaves?
   (D) Was Bacillus permitting the slaves to be in charge?

6. Nihil pecuniae Bombaci erat.
   (A) Bombax never has money.
   (B) Bombax had no money.
   (C) Bombax has no money.
   (D) There is no money for Bombax.

7. Bombax ____ epistulam amoris misit.
   (A) Palaestram
   (B) Palaestrae
   (C) Palaestra
   (D) ad Palaestram

8. The overseer Bacillus was a great help to his master.
   (A) magnum auxilium domini
   (B) magno auxilio ad dominum
   (C) magnum auxilium domino
   (D) magno auxilio domino

9. Cena ____ ponenda erat.
   (A) ab Palaestra
   (B) Palaestrae
   (C) Palaestrā
   (D) Palaestra

Practice Questions: Accusative Case

1. Bombax napped for eight hours.
   (A) octo horis
   (B) octava hora
   (C) octo horas
   (D) octavam horam

2. Bacillus iratus erat propter ____ servi.
   (A) fugā
   (B) fugae
   (C) fuga
   (D) fugam

3. Bombax cum Palaestra tres horas in horto sedebat.
   (A) three hours ago
   (B) for three hours
   (C) within three hours
   (D) at the third hour

4. In horto, statua ____ piscinam posita erat.
   (A) prope (C) de
   (B) pro (D) sine

5. Bombax ad villam <u>abhinc quattuor menses</u> pervenit.
   (A) four months later (C) within four months
   (B) after four months (D) four months ago

6. "Noli <u>in me</u> baculum vertere!" implorabat Bombax.
   (A) in me (C) into me
   (B) against me (D) on me

7. <u>Triginta milia passuum abhinc septem dies iter fecit</u>.
   (A) In seven days, he traveled three miles.
   (B) Seven days ago, he traveled three thousand miles.
   (C) Seven days ago, he traveled for thirty miles.
   (D) Within seven days, he traveled thirty miles.

8. Bombax <u>Delphos</u> iter facere volebat.
   (A) from Delphi (C) to Delphi
   (B) near Delphi (D) in Delphi

9. Bombax in agros cucurrit <u>ad fugiendum.</u>
   (A) as he was fleeing (C) at the point of flight
   (B) in order to flee (D) towards the fugitive

10. Nemo cogitat ____ diligentem servum esse.
   (A) Bombax (C) Bombace
   (B) Bombacem (D) Bombacis

Practice Questions: Ablative Case

1. Radix <u>magnitudine</u> pulli felix erat.*
   (A) by means of the size (C) because of the size
   (B) according to the size (D) except for the size

2. <u>Within three hours</u>, the dessert will have been served.
   (A) Tertiā horā (C) Tres horas
   (B) Tribus horis (D) Tertias horas

*Radix is a cook.

3. Gustatio huius cenae dignissima ____ erat.

(A) laudis (C) laudi

(B) laude (D) laus

4. Cena mensa <u>magnā curā</u> parata erat.

(A) with great care

(B) because of great care

(C) by means of great care

(D) with respect to great care

5. Radix optimus coquus ____ dubio erat.

(A) pro (C) sub

(B) de (D) sine

6. For the dinner, Radix created dishes <u>of great beauty</u>.

(A) magna pulchritudo

(B) magnae pulchritudini

(C) magna pulchritudine

(D) magnam pulchritudinem

7. Radix convivas <u>culina</u> prohibebat.

(A) from the kitchen (C) in the kitchen

(B) by means of the kitchen (D) with respect to the kitchen

8. Coquus ____ salis semper utebatur.

(A) nimium (C) nimio

(B) nimius (D) nimiam

9. The dinner lasted <u>for four hours</u>.

(A) quartā horā (C) quattuor horis

(B) quattuor horas (D) quartam horam

10. Radix pullum ____ scindebat.

(A) cum cultro (C) cultro

(B) culter (D) a cultro

11. Radix paulo melior coquus Testa erat.
   (A) a little worse cook than Testa
   (B) a little better cook than Testa
   (C) a much better cook than Testa
   (D) a somewhat worse cook than Testa

12. Pullo cocto, Radix aliquid vini bibebat.
   (A) While the chicken was cooking
   (B) After the chicken was cooked
   (C) Since the chicken is cooking
   (D) While he was cooking the chicken

Practice Questions: Vocative Case

1. ____ Catulle, desinas ineptire. (Catullus)
   (A) Misere (C) Miser
   (B) Miseri (D) Misero

2. "Extende manum, ____!" admonuit iratus Tuxtax.
   (A) Iuventius (C) Iuventi
   (B) Iuventium (D) Iuventio

3. Ignosce mihi, ____ .
   (A) grammaticus (C) grammaticum
   (B) grammatici (D) grammatice

4. The vocative singular of my friend is
   (A) mi amice (C) mi amico
   (B) meus amicus (D) mei amici

Practice Questions: Locative

1. Aeneas classem ____ ducebat.
   (A) Italiam (C) ad Italiam
   (B) Italiae (D) Italia

2. Aeneas cum Sibylla Cumis profectus est.
   (A) from Cumae (C) up to Cumae
   (B) to Cumae (D) near Cumae

3. After leaving Troy, Odysseus sailed <u>for home</u>.
   (A) domus (C) ad domum
   (B) domum (D) in domum

4. Navigavitne Aeneas <u>Syracusas</u>?
   (A) away from Syracuse (C) to Syracuse
   (B) in Syracuse (D) within Syracuse

5. Dum Aeneas ____ manebat, Dido eum amavit.
   (A) Carthagine (C) Carthaginem
   (B) Carthagini (D) Carthaginibus

6. Vergilius <u>Brundisio</u> <u>Neapolim</u> iter fecit.
   (A) from Brundisium to Naples
   (B) to Brundisium from Naples
   (C) up to Brundisium from Naples
   (D) from Brundisium and Naples

7. Vergilius <u>ruri</u> morari semper volebat.
   (A) from the country (C) in the country
   (B) to the country (D) into the country

Practice Questions on All Nouns

1. Filius senatoris ____ est.
   (A) miles (C) militis
   (B) militem (D) milite

2. Cleopatra <u>veneno</u> mortem sibi intulit.
   (A) without poison (C) for poison
   (B) poison (D) with poison

3. Aeger ____ mortuus est.
   (A) quinto die (C) quinti diei
   (B) quinque dies (D) quintum diem

4. Eratne Caesar parvus <u>in size</u>?
   (A) magnitudo (C) magnitudinem
   (B) magnitudine (D) magnitudini

5. Silvae sunt plenae <u>arborum</u>.

(A) with trees
(B) of trees
(C) trees
(D) from trees

6. Liberi aliquid ____ semper volunt.

(A) novum
(B) novi
(C) novus
(D) novo

7. <u>Erat auxilio amico</u>.

(A) He helped a friend.
(B) A friend helped him.
(C) The help was friendly.
(D) His friend was helpful.

8. <u>Viginti annos</u> vir pauper erat.

(A) After twenty years
(B) Within twenty years
(C) For twenty years
(D) On the twentieth year

9. Iuvenis suum patrem oravit, "Crede ____!"

(A) me
(B) meum
(C) mihi
(D) mei

10. Manus utiles <u>multis rebus</u> sunt.

(A) for many tasks
(B) with many tasks
(C) many tasks
(D) because of many tasks

11. Adulescens ____ cum parentibus habitabat.

(A) domo
(B) domum
(C) domus
(D) domi

12. Cicero ____ erat.

(A) consulem
(B) consule
(C) consuli
(D) consul

13. Hospites ____ manebant.

(A) in ianuam
(B) propter ianuam
(C) per ianuam
(D) ad ianuam

14. Duobus mensibus Athenas navigabit.
    (A) Within two months/from Athens
    (B) After two months/from Athens
    (C) For two months/to Athens
    (D) In two months/to Athens

15. Multi Romam ____ visitare volunt.
    (A) urbs aeterna
    (B) urbis aeternae
    (C) urbem aeternam
    (D) urbe aeterna

16. Hannibal in Italia sedecim annos manebat.
    (A) within sixteen years
    (B) for sixteen years
    (C) after sixteen years
    (D) sixteen years

17. Catilina erat vir parvae dignitatis. The expression equivalent in meaning to the underlined phrase is
    (A) parvae dignitati
    (B) parva dignitate
    (C) parvam dignitatem
    (D) parva dignitas

18. Roma maior urbs ____ erat.
    (A) Brundisium
    (B) Brundisio
    (C) Brundisi
    (D) Brundisiis

19. Illā nocte multi senatores Romā fugerunt.
    (A) For that night/to Rome
    (B) After that night/from Rome
    (C) On that night/from Rome
    (D) Because of that night/to Rome

20. Milites in hostes impetum faciebant.
    (A) toward the enemy
    (B) against the enemy
    (C) from the enemy
    (D) through the enemy

21. Miles ____ causa mortuus est.
    (A) honore
    (B) honori
    (C) honorem
    (D) honoris

22. Multa servis facienda sunt.
    (A) Many things must be done to the slaves.
    (B) Slaves have to do many things.
    (C) Many slaves must do things.
    (D) The slaves are doing many things.

23. Quot amicos habes, ____ ?
    (A) Publius
    (B) Publium
    (C) Publi
    (D) Publio

24. Mihi nomen est Perdix.
    (A) My name is Perdix.
    (B) Perdix has my name.
    (C) Perdix gave me a name.
    (D) Perdix was my name.

25. Senex prudentiā carebat.
    (A) Age and wisdom were lacking.
    (B) The old man lacked wisdom.
    (C) The wise man was old.
    (D) He lacked the wisdom of age.

26. Cena ____ placebat.
    (A) imperatori
    (B) imperatorem
    (C) imperatore
    (D) imperatoris

Answers: Nominative Case

1. **(D)**

The sentence reads "He gave orders to the lazy slave." The subject is in the verb, as none of the other forms can serve as the subject. Answers (A) **Ignavo** and (B) **servo** are in the dative case and **mandata** is (neuter) plural, whereas the verb **dedit** is singular.

2. **(D)**

Vilicus is a predicate nominative because it follows the verb and restates the subject. (A), the most likely choice but the verb **erat** cannot take a direct object. Answer (B) is genitive singular or nominative or vocative plural and (C) dative or ablative singular.

3. **(A)**

This question is designed to test the fact that a noun in apposition must agree with the noun that it defines or limits and is generally found next to the noun it defines. Therefore, the answer is **servum**, modifying **Bombacem**. Answer (B) is nominative singular and could modify **Bacillus**, but the position of the missing word makes it more likely to be taken with **Bombacem** than with **Bacillus**, and the case is wrong. Answer (C) is dative or ablative singular and (D) genitive plural, neither of which are correct choices for apposition with **Bacillum**.

4. **(C)**

Dominus is the correct answer because a predicate nominative, restating the subject, is required by the context. The obvious answer is perhaps (A) **dominum**, but an accusative direct object cannot be found with **erat**. Answer (B) is dative/ablative and (D) vocative, neither of which fits the context.

Answers: Genitive Case

1. **(D)**

The irregular noun **plus** is found with the partitive genitive, therefore, **plus cibi** "more of food (= more food)" is the best choice to complete the sentence. Answer (A) **cibus** is a distractor because it has the same ending as **plus** (which is neuter). Answers (B) accusative and (C) dative/ablative are not justifiable in the context of this sentence.

2. **(A)**

The missing expression is a genitive of description, giving the meaning "Bombax was a slave of great idleness." Answer (B) is accusative, which can't follow a form of **esse**. Answer (C) is plural and the context is singular and (D) is nominative and not appropriate here.

3. **(B)**

This question tests knowledge of the genitive case used with certain adjectives, here, **plenus, -a, -um**. So, "full of misery" is correctly translated as **plena miseriae**. Answers (A) and (C) do not make sense, as the nouns accompanying **plena** are not in the genitive, but in the ablative and nominative cases, respectively. Neither does Answer (D) "full with misery" make sense.

4. **(A)**

This question asks for recognition of **fugitivae ancillae** as genitive, rather than dative. The context of the sentence requires the sense "of the runaway maid" rather than "to/for the runaway maid," so the resulting phrase must be (A) genitive, not (C) dative. Answers (B) and (D) are ablative and accusative phrases, respectively, and therefore are not appropriate choices here.

5. **(C)**

This question simply asks for knowledge of the genitive singular ending of the 3rd declension noun **libertas**, which is **libertatis**. The other answers are (A) **libertatum**, genitive plural, (B) **libertati**, dative singular, and (D) **libertate**, ablative singular, none of which correctly translates "of freedom."

6. **(C)**

Aliquid mali is a partitive genitive, meaning "something (of) bad." The sentence reads, "Bombax was always doing something bad." Answer (A) is a distractor that incorrectly translates the genitive phrase and Answers (B) and (D) are dative "for" and ablative "with," respectively, neither of which translates the genitive form **mali** correctly.

7. **(A)**

Given the choices, this sentence requires an alternative to the partitive genitive, which is Answer (A) **Unus e servis** "one of the slaves." Answers (B), (C), and (D) do not make sense in the context of this sentence, which reads, "One of the slaves did not have a name."

8. **(C)**

This is an example of the objective genitive, requiring the sense of "for" for **gratiam benefici**, e.g., "The slave is giving gratitude for (a) kindness." The translations offered in Answers (A) and (B) require conjunctions such as **et** and **aut/vel** in the Latin, which are not found in the sentence, and (D), "kind" is an indefensible translation of the noun **benefici**.

9. **(D)**

Numbers are used in expressions of the partitive genitive, as here, **milia passuum**, "thousands of paces," or "miles." Answer (A) is genitive, but singular, and **quinque** and **milia** both require a plural to complete their meaning. Answer (B) **passum** could serve as the accusative direct object of **ambulare**, but does not link grammatically with **milia**. Answer (C) is the nominative singular of the 4th declension noun **passus** and does not have a function in this sentence, as **Bombax** is the subject.

Answers: Dative Case

1. **(C)**

This is an example of the dative as indirect object. The gender is not an issue, as all forms are in the 1st declension and feminine. Answer (A) is accusative, (B) ablative, and (D) nominative, none of which suit the context. The phrasing of the English suggests that "the slave" should be accusative, but the direct object is clearly "freedom."

2. **(B)**

This question examines familiarity with the dative case accompanying adjectives whose essential meaning includes the word "to/for," as here, **idonea cenae**, "suitable for dinner." The sentence reads, "Bombax did not have a tunic suitable for dinner." Answer (A) is an ablative phrase and (C) "a suitable dinner" incorrectly translates **idonea** as modifying **cenae**. Answer (D) is a distractor that requires the Latin to read **idoneae cenae**, "for a suitable dinner" rather than **idonea cenae**, "suitable for dinner."

3. **(D)**

Parcere is a verb that takes a dative object, hence, **miseris servis parcere**, "to be sparing to the unfortunate slaves." Answer (A) is the obvious (but incorrect!) answer as the accusative direct object of the verb, (B) is nominative plural, intended to simulate 3rd declension dative singular forms, and (C) genitive plural, does not fit the meaning of the sentence.

4. **(C)**

This intricate sentence contains two uses of the dative: indirect object (**filio**) and purpose (**libertati**). The noun **servi** in the genitive singular serves as a distractor. Translation (A) incorrectly swaps the phrase **pecuniam libertati**, "money for freedom" with "freedom for money." Translation (B) misinterprets the functions of the nouns **dominus filio**, as **dominus** is nominative and **filio** dative rather than dative and nominative, respectively. In Answer (D), if slaves (**servi**) were the subject, a plural verb would be necessary, but the verb **dedit** is singular.

5. **(C)**

This sentence contains two uses of the dative, one with an impersonal verb, Licebatne Bacillo, "Was Bacillus permitted," lit., "Was it permitted to Bacillus," and the other with a compound verb, servis praeesse, "to be in charge of the slaves". Answer (A) makes the common error of confusing the verb praeesse, "be in charge of," with praeficere, "place in charge of." Answer (B) is defensible, grammatically, but makes less sense than Answer (C) and gives the impersonal verb Licebat a personal subject ("he"). Answer (D) makes Bacillus the personal subject of Licebat and mistranslates praeesse as praeficere.

6. **(B)**

Nihil ____ Bombaci erat is an example of the possessive dative, equivalent to **Bombax pecuniam non habet**. This sentence also contains an example of the partitive genitive, **nihil pecuniae**, "nothing of money = no money." Answers (C) and (D) do justice to the Latin, but the verb tense in each should be past, not present. In Answer (A), "never" does not render **nihil** correctly.

7. **(D)**

Because motion is implied in the verb **misit**, Bombax is sending the love letter "toward" Palaestra and the preposition **ad** + accusative is used. Therefore, the dative case in Answer (B) is inappropriate here. Answer (A) "to send someone something" misrepresents an indirect object ("someone") as a direct object.

8. **(D)**

Magno auxilio domino is a double dative, expressing both reference ("to his master") and purpose ("a great help"). Answer (C) seems the most likely answer because it replicates the English, but Latin requires a dative of purpose (**magno auxilio**) rather than a predicate nominative or accusative (**magnum auxilium**) in this context. The Latin of Answer (A) incorrectly reads "a great help of the master." In the phrase **ad dominum** in (B), **ad** means "toward" and implies motion, which is not evident in the English here.

9. **(B)**

The passive periphrastic requires a dative of agent when a person is performing the obligatory action of the verb, hence, **Palaestrae**, "by Palaestra." This sentence reads, "The dinner had to be served by Palaestra." Answer (A), and perhaps (C), as ablatives of agent, are tempting answers, but the dative, and not the ablative, is found with a passive periphrastic such as **ponenda erat**. Answer (D) **cena** is preferable to **Palaestra** as the nominative subject, given the sense.

Answers: Accusative Case

1. **(C)**

"For eight hours" expresses extent of time, therefore the accusative case is needed. The ablative case, expressing other elements of time, appears in two of the other options: Answer (A) "(with)in eight hours" and Answer (B) "in/on the eighth hour." Note in this mistaken translation the use of the ordinal "eighth" (**octavam**) rather than the cardinal number "eight" (**octo**). Answer (D) **octavam horam**, "for the eighth hour," expresses an extent of time.

2. **(D)**

The preposition **propter** takes the accusative case, hence **fugam**. If **propter** is properly identified as a preposition, the two choices are Answers (A) ablative and (D) accusative. Answer (B) is a red herring, as the meaning of **propter**, "because of," might suggest an object in the genitive case, however, this is incorrect. Answer (C) **fuga**, a subject form, does not fit the grammatical requirements.

3. **(B)**

This is another accusative extent of time, this time in Latin. Answer (A) is provided as a distractor because the word "ago" in the answer would be expressed in the accusative case (i.e., **abhinc tres horas** "three hours ago"), however the adverb **abhinc** is missing. "Within three hours" and "at the third hour," indicating a point in time, require the ablative.

4. **(A)**

This question requires a specific knowledge of which prepositions are found with the accusative case and which with the ablative. **Prope** is the only choice found with the accusative, hence, **prope piscinam**, "near the fishpool."

5. **(D)**

This sentence reads, "Bombax arrived at the villa four months ago." Answers (A) and (B) require that the Latin be **post quattuor menses** or **quattuor post mensibus**, and Answer (C) the ablative phrase **quattuor mensibus**.

6. **(B)**

This question asks you to discriminate among various meanings of the preposition "in." The sentence reads, "'Don't turn the switch against me,' implored Bombax." Answers (A) and (D) are incorrect because in meaning "in" or "on" is found with the ablative case. Answer (C) "into me" makes less sense than "against me."

7. **(C)**

This sentence contains two constructions with the accusative: extent of distance, **triginta milia passuum**, "for thirty thousand paces = 30 miles," and a time expression, **abhinc septem dies**, "seven days ago." In Answer (A) the time frame and mileage are incorrect; in (B) the time frame is correct, but the mileage is not; and in (D) the distance is correct, but the time frame is incorrect.

8. **(C)**

The preposition **ad** is understood with the name of a city in the accusative of place to which. The context of the sentence implies that Bombax wished to travel to or from Delphi because the idiom **iter facere** expresses motion. This eliminates Answers (B) and (D) as choices, due to sense. As **Delphos** has an accusative ending (plural because the name **Delphi** is plural) with the understood preposition **ad,** Answer (C) is correct. For (A) to have been correct, the form **Delphis** (= **e Delphis**) would have been necessary.

9. **(B)**

In this sentence, **ad fugiendum** is a gerund of purpose, meaning "for the purpose of fleeing" or "(in order) to flee." Answer (D) is omitted because **fugiendum** does not mean "fugitive." The translations in neither (A) "as" nor (C) "at the point of" correctly translate the preposition **ad**.

10. **(B)**

The noun **Bombacem** is accusative singular and serves as the subject of the infinitive **esse** in this indirect statement. Answer (A) **Bombax**, which might be taken as the obvious answer, is incorrect because the form is nominative. Answers (C) and (D) are eliminated because **Bombace** and **Bombacis** are in the wrong cases, i.e., ablative and genitive, respectively.

Answers: Ablative Case

1. Ablative of description (C) The sentence reads, "Radix was happy because of the size of the chicken." Answers (B) and (D) do not make sense in this context and are not justifiable grammatically from the Latin provided. Answer (A) is justifiable, as **magnitudine** could conceivably be an ablative of means, but **magnitudo** is not an implement.

2. Ablative of time (within which) (B) This sentence reads "Within three hours, the dessert will have been served." Answer (A) **tertia hora** is singular and therefore incorrect, as is Answer (D) **tertias horas**, because the ordinal number **tertius** appears, instead of the cardinal **tres**. Answer (C) is an example of extent of time with the accusative "for three hours" and is therefore an incorrect translation of **tribus horis**.

3. Ablative with special adjective (B) Because the adjective **dignus, -a, -um** "worthy of" nearly always takes the ablative case, Answer (B) **(dignissima) laude** "most worthy of praise," is the correct response. Answer (A) accusative is not plausible, nor is Answer (C), which is dative. Answer (D) is tempting because **dignissima** is feminine nominative singular, as is **laus**. However, the sentence does not make sense with **dignissima laus** as the subject (which is **gustatio**).

4. Ablative of manner (A) "With great care" makes the best sense of the choices given. The sentence reads, "The dinner course had been prepared with great care." This answers the question, "How or in what manner had the dinner been prepared?" The word **magna** in the ablative preceding a noun in the ablative strongly suggests that **magnā curā** is ablative of manner. Answers (B) and (C) do not make sense in this context and the wording of (C) requires that **magnā curā** be taken as an ablative of means, but **curā** is not an implement.

5. Ablative with preposition (D) All options contain prepositions that take the ablative case, but only **sine** supplies a word whose meaning is consistent with the context: "Radix was the best cook, without a doubt."

6. Ablative of description (C) The appearance of the word "of" in the phrase "of great beauty" tempts an identification as genitive of description, but there is no

genitive option among the answers. Since the ablative case may also be used to describe someone or something, Answer (C) is correct. Answer (B) looks temptingly like a genitive, but is in fact a dative, which is unsuited to the context here. The nominative and accusative in Answers (A) and (D), respectively, have no grammatical justification for expressing the phrase "of great beauty."

7. Ablative of separation (A) The meaning of the verb **prohibebat** suggests the answer "from the kitchen" by default. This is a verb of separation, because it means to keep someone or something away. The translations in Answers (B) "by means of," (C) "in," and (D) "with respect to," are not consistent with the meaning of this verb. Therefore, **culina prohibebat** is an example of the ablative of separation, "(Radix) kept the guests (away) from the kitchen."

8. Ablative with a special verb (C) As an alert Latin student, you no doubt immediately spotted the deponent verb **utebatur**, one of the special deponents that takes an object in the ablative case, which is **nimio** in this sentence. The other forms are (A) nominative/accusative neuter, (B) nominative, and (D) accusative, respectively. Complicating matters is the appearance of the partitive genitive in this sentence, **nimio salis**, "too much (of) salt." If you answered this one correctly, way to go!

9. Accusative, duration of time (B) This is a sneaky one, as it tests your knowledge of the accusative of duration of time, reviewed in the previous chapter. Answer (A) **quartā horā**, "in the fourth hour," is ablative of time when. Answer (C), **quattuor horis**, means "(with)in four hours," ablative of time within which. Answer (D), **quartam horam** is singular and contains an ordinal, rather than a cardinal, number.

10. Ablative of means (C) The context "Radix was cutting the chicken . . ." sets up an ablative of means of instrument. Answers (A) and (D) incorrectly contain a preposition, and **culter** in (B) is nominative. Although the word **culter**, "knife," my be unfamiliar, enough lexical information is provided in the answers to lead to the correct response.

11. Ablatives of degree of difference and comparison (B) This sentence contains an ablative of degree of difference (**paulo melior**, "a little better"), together with an ablative of comparison (**Testā**, "than Testa"). The word **melior** does not mean "worse," so Answers (A) and (D) are out. Answer (C) is not appropriate because **paulo** is incorrectly translated as "much."

12. Ablative absolute (B) **Pullo cocto** contains a past participle, therefore Answers (A), (C), and (D) are all incorrect, as "While . . . cooking" or "Since cooking" would require a present participle.

Answers: Vocative Case

1. **(C)**

This line from Poem 8 reads, **Miser Catulle, desinas ineptire**, "Poor Catullus, stop playing the fool."As an adjective modifying **Catulle**, which is vocative, **Miser** must therefore also be vocative. Answer (A) **Misere** is an adverb that might mislead you into thinking that the adjective **miser** must have the same ending as its noun, **Catulle**. Neither (B) **Miseri,** genitive singular or nominative or vocative plural, nor (D) **Misero**, dative or ablative singular, agrees with **Catulle**.

2. **(C)**

The context requires the vocative form of the name **Iuventius**, based upon the answers provided. Since this name ends in **–ius**, the **–us** is dropped, leaving **Iuventi** as the vocative. Answer (A) is nominative singular, (B) accusative singular, and (D) dative or ablative singular and irrelevant to the context.

3. **(D)**

Given the forms of the answers, the word **grammaticus** "teacher" clearly belongs to the 2nd declension, leading to the choice of (D) **grammatice**, as the correct answer. The imperative **Ignosce** in the sentence requires that the missing form be vocative singular. Answer (A) is nominative, (B) genitive singular or nominative plural, and (C) accusative singular.

4. **(A)**

The correct translation of "my friend" as a vocative requires familiarity with the fact that the vocative form of the possessive adjective **meus** is irregular. Thus, **mi amice** is correct. Answer (B) is nominative, not vocative. Answer (C) **mi amico** is the contracted form of **mihi** + the dative form of **amicus**. Answer (D) **mei amici** is nominative or vocative plural.

Answers: Locative Case

1. **(C)**

Italy is a "country," not a city or small island, and therefore requires the preposition **ad**. The other cases are irrelevant, although Answer (A) **Italiam**, is a sneaky attempt to get you to nibble a red herring!

2. **(A)**

Cumis is either the ablative or dative form of **Cumae** (a name which is plural), meaning either "from Cumae" or the locative "in Cumae." Because the verb **profectus est**, "he set out," predisposes the former meaning, **Cumis** must mean "from Cumae," giving the sentence the meaning "Aeneas set out from Cumae with the Sibyl."

3. **(B)**

"Sailed for home" is motion towards a place, therefore **ad** + accusative is expected. However, the word **domus** gets special treatment among place expressions and drops the preposition, thereby omitting Answers (C) and (D). The nominative **domus** in Answer (A) has no meaning here.

4. **(C)**

Among the choices, Answers (B) and (D) can be omitted because one can't sail in a city. Since **Syracusas** is accusative (the name **Syracusae** is plural), the place preposition **ad** is understood, giving "to Syracuse." Answer (A) requires **Syracusis**, "from Syracuse."

5. **(B)**

The sentence in this question begins, "While Aeneas remained . . . ," implying "at" or "in" Carthage. These prepositions require the locative case, which for the singular 3rd declension noun **Carthago** is equivalent to the dative, **Carthagini**. None of the other answers makes sense with **manebat**: Answer (A) means "from Carthage," (C) "to Carthage," and (D) does not translate.

6. **(A)**

The ablative **Brundisio** (= **e Brundisio**) and accusative **Neapolim** (= **ad Neapolim**) mean "from Brundisium" and "to Naples." Answers (B) and (C) require **Brundisium Neapoli**, (D) **Brundisio et Neapoli**.

7. **(C)**

The verb **morari,** "to stay," creates a context that requires the locative case, meaning "in or at place." The locative form **ruri** thus means "in the countryside." Remember that **rus** is a word that does not take a preposition in place expressions. Answer (A) "from the country" requires the ablative form **rure** and (B) "to the country" and (D) "into the country" require the accusative form **rus,** which is neuter.

Answers: Practice Questions on All Nouns

1. (A) pred. nom.
2. (D) abl. means
3. (A) abl. time
4. (B) abl. respect
5. (B) gen. w/ adj.
6. (B) partitive gen.
7. (A) double dative
8. (C) acc. extent time
9. (C) dat. with verb
10. (A) dat. with adj.
11. (D) locative
12. (D) pred. nom.
13. (D) acc. prep. phrase
14. (D) abl. time within, acc. place to which
15. (C) apposition
16. (B) acc. extent time
17. (B) abl. descr.
18. (B) abl. compar.
19. (C) abl. time; abl. place from
20. (B) acc. prep. phrase
21. (A) abl. with adj.
22. (B) dative of agent
23. (C) vocative
24. (A) dat. possession
25. (B) abl. separation
26. (A) impersonal, w/**cena** as subject, dative object

Chapter 13

Pronouns

Quick Study of Demonstrative Pronouns

Hic, Haec, Hoc						
	Singular			Plural		
	M	F	N	M	F	N
Nom.	**hic**	**haec**	**hoc**	**hi**	**hae**	**haec**
Gen.	**huius**	**huius**	**huius**	**horum**	**harum**	**horum**
Dat.	**huic**	**huic**	**huic**	**his**	**his**	**his**
Acc.	**hunc**	**hanc**	**hoc**	**hos**	**has**	**haec**
Abl.	**hōc**	**hāc**	**hōc**	**his**	**his**	**his**

Ille, Illa, Illud						
	Singular			Plural		
	M	F	N	M	F	N
Nom.	**ille**	**illa**	**illud**	**illi**	**illae**	**illa**
Gen.	**illius**	**illius**	**illius**	**illorum**	**illarum**	**illorum**
Dat.	**illi**	**illi**	**illi**	**illis**	**illis**	**illis**
Acc.	**illum**	**illam**	**illud**	**illos**	**illas**	**illa**
Abl.	**illo**	**illā**	**illo**	**illis**	**illis**	**illis**

Is, Ea, Id						
	Singular			Plural		
	M	F	N	M	F	N
Nom.	**is**	**ea**	**id**	**ei**	**eae**	**ea**
Gen.	**eius**	**eius**	**eius**	**eorum**	**earum**	**eorum**
Dat.	**ei**	**ei**	**ei**	**eis**	**eis**	**eis**
Acc.	**eum**	**eam**	**id**	**eos**	**eas**	**ea**
Abl.	**eo**	**eā**	**eo**	**eis**	**eis**	**eis**

The Forms of Demonstrative Pronouns

The demonstrative pronoun (**demonstrare**, *point out*), which can serve as both a pronoun and an adjective, designates a particular person or thing. The demonstrative pronouns are:

Singular	Plural
hic, **haec**, **hoc**, *this one here*	*these ones here*
ille, **illa**, **illud**, *that one over there* or *this one, that one*	*those ones over there* *they, these ones, those ones*
is, **ea**, **id**	*he, she, it,*
īdem, **eadem**, **idem**, *the same one*	*the same ones*
iste, **ista**, **istud**, *that one over there (often shows contempt)*	

Notes:

- The pronoun **īdem**, **eadem**, **idem** consists of **is**, **ea**, **id** + the suffix -**dem**. The following forms vary from the regular forms of **is**, **ea**, **id** (the letter –**m** changes to –**n** in these forms for reasons of pronunciation):

  acc. sing., masc. and fem.: **eundem** and **eandem**

  gen. pl.: **eorundem**, **earundem**, **eorundem**

- The neuter plural form **eadem**, *the same (things)* is often used as a substantive.
- The demonstrative **iste, ista, istud** has the same forms as **ille, illa, illud.**

The Uses of Demonstrative Pronouns

Hic and **ille** have the same distinctions in meaning as in English, i.e., **hic** refers to this one right here, and **ille** to that one over there. When used as adjectives, these words have the same forms and meanings as the pronouns, but simply modify a noun in the sentence, e.g,

Demonstrative pronoun: **Hic in foro ambulabat**.

This man (or He) was strolling in the forum.

Demonstrative adjective: **Hic vir in foro ambulabat.**

This man was strolling in the forum.

In the first sentence, with no other information as to the identity of the person or thing to which the pronoun refers, **Hic** is translated as "This man" or "He" because the pronoun is masculine.

Notes:

- Use the context to distinguish the feminine form **haec** from the neuter form **haec**, which appears often as a pronoun, *these things*. Do this also when distinguishing the meaning of the feminine form **illa** from the neuter form **illa**.
- Don't confuse the demonstrative **hic**, *this*, with the adverb **hīc**, *here*.

It is important to note that the demonstrative pronoun **is**, **ea**, **id**, *this one, that one,* substitutes for the pronoun of the third person, *he, she, it*, which Latin does not have. (This demonstrative will be discussed more thoroughly in the section on personal pronouns.)

Practice Questions on Demonstrative Pronouns

1. The accusative singular of <u>īdem</u> is

   (A) idem (C) eundem

   (B) eandem (D) eorundem

2. Noli <u>ei</u> credere!

   (A) them (C) that

   (B) him (D) yourself

3. Tribunus <u>haec</u> dixit quod iratus erat.

   (A) this thing (C) these things

   (B) those things (D) that thing

4. Senatores in Curia congregant. Vidistine ____ ?

   (A) eum (C) ea

   (B) ei (D) eos

5. In Curia <u>hic</u> senator prope <u>illos</u> sedebat.

   (A) that . . . this man (C) this . . . them

   (B) these . . . those men (D) that . . . these men

6. <u>That acquaintance of yours</u> always disrupts public assemblies.

   (A) Īdem (C) Hic

   (B) Is (D) Iste

7. Censor nomina <u>illorum</u> in tabula scribit.

   (A) his (C) them

   (B) their (D) that

8. Does a praetor do <u>the same things</u> as a consul?

   (A) illa (C) eos

   (B) istos (D) eadem

9. <u>Frater huius senator est</u>.
   (A) This senator has a brother.
   (B) The brother of that man is a senator.
   (C) This man's brother is a senator.
   (D) He is the brother of this senator

10. Dabatne aedilis <u>his</u> <u>illa</u>?
   (A) these things to her
   (B) those things to them
   (C) that thing to them
   (D) her to these

11. <u>Is eis de hoc dicet</u>.
   (A) He will tell this about them.
   (B) He is telling him about this.
   (C) He is telling them about that.
   (D) He will tell them about this.

Quick Study of the Relative Pronoun

	Singular			Plural		
	M	**F**	**N**	**M**	**F**	**N**
Nom.	**qui**	**quae**	**quod**	**qui**	**quae**	**quae**
Gen.	**cuius**	**cuius**	**cuius**	**quorum**	**quarum**	**quorum**
Dat.	**cui**	**cui**	**cui**	**quibus**	**quibus**	**quibus**
Acc.	**quem**	**quam**	**quod**	**quos**	**quas**	**quae**
Abl.	**quo**	**qua**	**quo**	**quibus**	**quibus**	**quibus**

Notes:

- In prepositional phrases with forms of **qui** accompanying the word **cum**, the preposition is enclitic, i.e., it is attached to the end of the relative pronoun, e.g., **quo<u>cum</u>** or **quibus<u>cum</u>**.

The Relative Clause

The relative pronoun **qui, quae, quod**, *who, which, that*, is so called because it introduces an explanatory or descriptive clause that "relates" to another word or other words in its sentence or in a previous sentence. The verb of this clause is in the indicative and therefore its meaning is expressed as a fact. The noun or pronoun that the relative clause modifies is known as the antecedent, which is usually found immediately prior to the relative pronoun. The pronoun that introduces the relative clause agrees with its antecedent in gender and number, but not necessarily in case. In its clause, the relative pronoun performs a function independent of that of its antecedent, e.g.,

nom. acc.

Spurius quem numquam antea audivi longam orationem habebat.

relative clause

Spurius whom I had never heard before was delivering a long speech.

The relative pronoun **quem** agrees with its antecedent **Spurius** in gender (masculine) and number (singular), but not in case. Whereas the antecedent **Spurius** serves as the nominative subject in the main clause, the relative pronoun **quem** serves as the direct object of the verb **audivi** in the subordinate clause.

Tips on Translating the Relative Pronoun

- When the antecedent is a person, use *who, whom*, or *whose* when translating. When the antecedent is a thing, use *which* or *that*.
- The relative clause is a self-contained unit of thought, often framed by commas. When translating a relative clause, it is helpful to underline the clause as a separate sense unit within the sentence, e.g., **Oratio quam audivi erat longa**, *The speech that I heard was long*. When translating, avoid pulling words out of the relative clause and inserting them into the main clause, and vice versa.
- The antecedent of a relative pronoun is sometimes given in the context of the preceding sentence, leading to a situation where the relative pronoun is found at the beginning of the succeeding sentence. When translating this "linking **qui**," substitute a demonstrative, such as *this* or *these*, or a personal pronoun, such as *him*, e.g.,

  Spurius de rebus urbanis dicebat. Quibus dictis, omnes eum laudabant.

  Spurius was speaking about urban affairs. These, (words), lit., *Which, (words) having been spoken, everyone praised him.*

  Quem octo servi e foro lectica ferebant.

  Eight slaves carried him, lit., *Whom, eight slaves carried, from the forum in a limo.*

  In the first set of sentences, the form **quibus** refers to Spurius' speech about urban affairs, **de rebus urbanis**, mentioned in the previous sentence. In the second example, the relative pronoun **quem** refers back to **eum** (Spurius) in the previous sentence. In such situations, English requires that you avoid translating a word such as **quem** as a relative pronoun (*whom, which*, etc.).

- The relative pronoun can also introduce other types of clauses that have their verbs in the subjunctive mood. These clauses, such as the relative clause of purpose and the relative clause of characteristic, will be presented in a later chapter.

Quick Study of The Interrogative Pronoun

	Singular			Plural		
	M	F	N	M	F	N
Nom.	**quis**	**quis**	**quid**	**qui**	**quae**	**quae**
Gen.	**cuius**	**cuius**	**cuius**	**quorum**	**quarum**	**quorum**
Dat.	**cui**	**cui**	**cui**	**quibus**	**quibus**	**quibus**
Acc.	**quem**	**quem**	**quid**	**quos**	**quas**	**quae**
Abl.	**quo**	**quo**	**quo**	**quibus**	**quibus**	**quibus**

Notes:

- The singular forms of the interrogative pronoun are identical in the masculine and feminine. The forms of the plural are exactly the same as those of the relative pronoun.
- The interrogative adjective has the same forms as the relative pronoun.

Examples of the Use of the Interrogative Pronoun and Adjective

Interrogative Pronoun

- **De quibus Spurius orationem habebat?**

  About what (or whom) was Spurius making his speech?
- **Quos Spurius discedens e foro vidit?**

  Whom did Spurius see while leaving the Forum?

Interrogative Adjective

- **Quae oratio quam Spurius habuerat optima erat?**

  Which speech that Spurius had given was the best?
- **Cui senatori Spurius orationem scriptam dabit?**

  To which senator will Spurius give the speech after it has been written down?
- **Qua lectica Spurius domum ferebatur?**

  In which lectica was Spurius being carried home?

Practice Questions on Relative and Interrogative Pronouns

1. Senes ____ in foro vidi senatores erant.

   (A) quis (C) quem

   (B) qui (D) quos

2. The accusative singular feminine of quis is

   (A) quam (C) quae

   (B) quem (D) qua

3. Basilica quam Sempronius aedificaverat erat magna

   (A) when (C) because

   (B) that (D) since

4. At what hour will the citizens leave the assembly?

   (A) Quam horam (C) Qua hora

   (B) Quae hora (D) Quid horae

5. Consul cui fasces dati sunt imperium tenebat.

   (A) whose (C) who

   (B) whom (D) to whom

6. The senators with whom the consul was walking were his enemies.

   (A) quocum (C) quibus

   (B) post quos (D) quibuscum

7. Consul cui nomen Cicero est Arpini natus est.

   (A) whom (C) whose

   (B) who (D) with whom

8. ____ legi cives semper parent?

   (A) Quo (C) Cui

   (B) Quem (D) Quis

9. Which laws did Roman citizens disregard?

   (A) Quas leges (C) Quarum legum

   (B) Quae leges (D) Quibus legibus

10. A quibus omnes leges parebuntur?
    (A) For whom (C) From which
    (B) From whom (D) By whom

11. Qui quae vult dicit, quae non vult audiet. If stated, the antecedent of each quae would be the form
    (A) eas (C) ea
    (B) eam (D) id

12. Plebes qui ambulabant per Viam Sacram ad comitiam ibant. The most accurate substitute is
    (A) ambulaturi (C) ambulantes
    (B) postquam ambulaverant (D) quod ambulabant

13. Saxa quibus basilica aedificata erat gravissima fuerunt.
    (A) for whom (C) to which
    (B) with which (D) by whom

14. Pericula timidus quae non sunt videt. The antecedent of quae is
    (A) dangers (C) those things (understood)
    (B) the fearful person (D) she (understood)

15. Sunt quibus diversae opiniones essent.
    (A) There are those who had different opinions.
    (B) They are the ones whose opinions are different.
    (C) Those who had opinions were different.
    (D) They are the different ones who had opinions.

Quick Study of Indefinite Pronouns and Adjectives

Indefinite Pronoun M F N	Indefinite Adjective M F N
quidam, **quae**dam, **quid**dam, *a certain one*	**qui**dam, **quae**dam, **quod**dam, *a certain*
ali**quis**, *some/anyone*, ali**quid**, *some/anything*	ali**qui**, ali**qua**, ali**quod**, *some, any*
quisque, **quid**que, *each one, everyone*	**quis**que, **quae**que, **quod**que, *each, every*
quisquam, *anyone*, **quid**quam/quicquam, *anything*	(**ullus**, **-a**, **-um**, *any*)

Notes:

- **Quidam** changes **m** to **n** before **d** in the accusative singular, e.g., **quendam** and **quandam**, and in the genitive plural, e.g., **quorundam**, **quarundam**.
- **Quicquam** and **quicquid** are alternative forms of **quidquam** and **quidquid**, respectively. These changes were made for ease of pronunciation.
- Additional indefinites include **quic**umque, **quae**cumque, **quod**cumque, *whoever*, *whatever*, and **quisquis**, **quisquis**, **quidquid/quicquid**, *whoever*. These two forms, plus **quoquo**, are the only three forms of this pronoun found in classical Latin. **Quis**quam, **quis**quam, **quid**quam, *anyone*, *anything*, is usually found in a negative context, i.e., in a sentence containing words such as **nec** or **non**, **numquam**, or **negare**.
- The common indefinite phrase **si quis** means if *any(one)*.

Practice Questions on Indefinite Pronouns and Adjectives

1. Suntne aliquae leges malae?

   (A) all laws
   (B) many laws
   (C) some laws
   (D) certain laws

2. The Senate wishes to remove certain praetors from their provinces.

   (A) quidam praetores
   (B) quosdam praetores
   (C) aliquos praetores
   (D) quosque praetores

3. Si quis in forum ierit, splendida aedificia videbit.

   (A) who
   (B) anyone
   (C) someone
   (D) whoever

4. Quisquis amat, valeat; pereat qui nescit amare! (Pompeiian wall inscription)

   (A) Anyone
   (B) Someone
   (C) a certain one
   (D) Whoever

5. Aliquis aliquid de quoquam dicere potest.

   (A) He can say anything whatever about this.
   (B) Some people can speak about anything to anyone.
   (C) Every person has something to say about this certain person.
   (D) Anyone can say anything about anyone.

6. Alicui quidem roganti quam iubenti libentius paremus. This sentence means
   (A) You can catch more flies with honey than with vinegar.
   (B) Oil and water don't mix.
   (C) Birds of a feather flock together.
   (D) The end justifies the means.

7. Idem is to eundem as quidam is to
   (A) quorundam (C) quendam
   (B) quemquam (D) quemque

8. Can there be a reason for anyone to speak out against his own country?
   (A) quicquid (C) quibusque
   (B) quodam (D) cuiquam

9. ____. remedia graviora periculis sunt.
   (A) Quadam (C) Quidam
   (B) Quaedam (D) Quoddam

Quick Study of Personal Pronouns

	First person, "I," "we/us"		**Second person, "you"**	
	Singular	**Plural**	**Singular**	**Plural**
Nom.	**ego**	**nos**	**tu**	**vos**
Gen.	**mei**	**nostrum, nostri**	**tui**	**vestrum, vestri**
Dat.	**mihi**	**nobis**	**tibi**	**vobis**
Acc.	**me**	**nos**	**te**	**vos**
Abl.	**me**	**nobis**	**te**	**vobis**

The Pronoun of the Third Person (*He*, *She*, *It*, and *They*)

The demonstrative **is, ea, id** designates the person or thing about which the speaker or writer is talking or writing and therefore serves as the pronoun of the third person, *he, she, it*. The subject plurals are **ei, eae, ea**, *they*. Here are examples of the use of this demonstrative as the pronoun of the third person:

Noli dicere ea ei.
Don't say those things to him/her.

Mitte epistulam ad eum.
Send the letter to him.

Nos eos non amamus.
We do not like them.

Eis id facient.
They will do it for them.

Ite cum eis!
Go with them!

Is eam amat.
He likes her.

Note:

- Remember that third person pronouns may cross gender boundaries when expressing meaning, e.g., **Accepistine epistulam?** *Did you receive the letter?* **Eam accepi.** *I did receive it (not her).*

Personal Pronouns and Possessive Adjectives

	Singular		**Plural**	
	Personal Pron.	**Possessive Adj.**	**Personal Pron.**	**Possessive Adj.**
1st person	**ego** *I*	**meus, -a, -um** *my, mine*	**nos** *we*	**noster, nostra, nostrum** *our/s*
2nd person	**tu** *you* (alone)	**tuus, -a, -um** *your/s* (sing.)	**vos** *you* (all)	**vester, vestra, vestrum** *your/s* (pl.)
3rd person	**is, ea, id** *he, she, it*		**ei, eae, ea** *they*	

Notes:

- To express possession in the third person, Latin uses either a pronoun or an adjective. As there is no possessive adjective corresponding to the third person pronoun **is, ea, id,** the genitive form of the pronoun **eius**, *of him*, *of her*, *of it* (= *his*, *hers*, *its*) is used. (Note how much the Latin word **eius** sounds like the English word *his*!) The plurals are **eorum**, **earum**, **eorum,** *of them* (= *their*, *theirs*):

  Fortuna eius bona est.
  His/Her luck is good.

- Possession in the third person can also be expressed by using the reflexive adjective **suus**, **-a**, **-um**. This adjective corresponds to the reflexive pronoun **se** (for which, see below). The reflexive adjective **suus**, **-a**, **-um** can be singular or plural and has the meaning *his own*, *her own,* or *their own*. Here are some examples to illustrate the distinction in meaning between the use of **eius** as a possessive pronoun and that of **suus**, **-a**, **-um** as a reflexive adjective:

Possessive pronoun: **Pater se culpavit quod filium eius non agnovit.**

Father blamed himself because he did not recognize his (someone else's) son.

Nonne matres filios earum agnoscere possunt?

Surely mothers can recognize their sons (the sons of others)?

Reflexive adjective: **Pater se culpavit quod filium suum non agnovit.**

Father blamed himself because he did not recognize his own son.

Nonne matres filios suos agnoscere possunt?

Surely mothers can recognize their own sons?

Practice Questions on Possessive Pronouns and Adjectives

1. ____ omnes liberi esse volumus.

   (A) Nobis (C) Ei

   (B) Vos (D) Nos

2. The plural of tibi is

   (A) vobis (C) vestrum

   (B) vos (D) tui

3. Amici, Romani, cives, ____ venite!

   (A) nobiscum (C) cum vobis

   (B) ad vestros (D) cum nobis

4. Illum librum emi sed eum non legi.

   (A) him (C) it

   (B) his (D) them

5. Te tua, me mea delectant.
   - (A) My things please you, your things please me.
   - (B) Your things please me, my things please you.
   - (C) Your and my things please both you and me.
   - (D) Your things please you, my things please me.

6. Dic mihi haec.
   - (A) She is speaking to me.
   - (B) Tell me these things.
   - (C) Tell her this for me.
   - (D) This woman is talking to me.

7. Nec tecum possum vivere nec sine te. (Martial)
   - (A) I can live neither with you nor without you.
   - (B) I can live with you and I cannot live without you.
   - (C) You can neither live with me nor without me.
   - (D) I not am able to live with you or near you.

8. He lost his (someone else's) money.
   - (A) eorum pecuniam
   - (B) eius pecuniam
   - (C) suam pecuniam
   - (D) eam pecuniam

9. Not for ourselves alone.
   - (A) nos
   - (B) nostris
   - (C) nobis
   - (D) ad nos

10. Videsne ____ in speculo?
    - (A) te
    - (B) vos
    - (C) vestrum
    - (D) tibi

11. I am helping you.
    - (A) Tuli auxilium ad te.
    - (B) Vobis auxilio sum.
    - (C) Tu auxilium mihi das.
    - (D) Auxilium tibi venit.

Reflexive and Intensive Pronouns

The Reflexive Pronoun **Singular and Plural**	**M, F,** and **N**
Nom.	_____
Gen.	**sui**
Dat.	**sibi**
Acc.	**se**
Abl.	**se**

Note:

- There is no nominative form of the reflexive pronoun, since it must refer back to the subject.
- With the exception of the neuter nominative and accusative singular, the intensive pronoun ipse, ipsa, ipsum, has the same forms as ille, illa, illud, for which, see above.

Tips on Translating Reflexive and Intensive Pronouns

- Distinguish between the reflexive and the intensive pronoun by looking at both the placement of the word and its function. With the reflexive pronoun, the action of the verb is directed at the subject. Unlike the intensive pronoun, the case function of a reflexive pronoun is independent of that of the noun to which it refers, e.g.,

  nom. acc.
  Pater se culpavit.
  Father blamed himself.

  nom. acc.
  Pater dicit se ab alio culpatum esse.
  Father says that he (himself) was blamed by another.

  Intensive pronouns generally follow the nouns with which they combine and (unless they are substantives) behave like adjectives, i.e., agree with the noun in case, gender, and number:

  nom. nom.
  Pater ipse me non culpavit.
  Father himself did not blame me.

  The intensive pronoun can also be used to emphasize in the way that English uses the word "very," as in **vir ipse**, "that very man."

Practice Questions on Reflexive and Intensive Pronouns

Enjoy the following "sentence story"!

1. Ille consul sibi potestatem habere volebat.
   (A) himself
   (B) for himself
   (C) for him (someone else)
   (D) for them

2. The senators blamed him for his rival's death.
   (A) eum
   (B) ipse
   (C) ipsum
   (D) se

3. Consul dicit suum competitorem se occidisse.
   (A) The consul says that his rival killed him (someone else).
   (B) The consul says that he (someone else) killed his rival.
   (C) The consul says that his (someone else's) rival killed himself.
   (D) The consul says that his rival killed himself.

4. Some senators called for his removal.
   (A) sui
   (B) suum
   (C) eius
   (D) ipsius

5. Iste sciebat quosdam senatores sibi inimicos esse.
   (A) some
   (B) all
   (C) any
   (D) several

6. Certe irati senatores consuli ipso se opposuerunt.
   (A) Surely the consul himself confronted the angry senators.
   (B) Surely the angry senators themselves confronted the consul.
   (C) Surely the consul confronted the angry senators themselves.
   (D) Surely the angry senators confronted the consul himself.

7. Senatores suos secum ducebant.
   (A) The senators brought his men with them.
   (B) They were bringing with them the senators' men.
   (C) The senators brought their men with them.
   (D) The senators brought their men with him.

8. "You must give <u>yourself</u> up to justice!" shouted someone from the crowd.
   (A) se
   (B) vobis
   (C) tu
   (D) te

9. "<u>I myself</u> am not a crook!" exclaimed the consul.
   (A) Meus ipse
   (B) Ego ipse
   (C) Ille ipse
   (D) Me ipse

10. Iste <u>se ipsum</u> puniendum esse non credidit.
   (A) they themselves
   (B) he himself
   (C) he (someone else)
   (D) that one

Quick Study of Common Pronouns

Latin Form	Translation	Type	Function
hic, ille, is	*this one, that one*	demonstrative	points out specifically
qui, quae, quod	*who, which, that*	relative	describes, explains
quis, quis, quid	*who? what?*	interrogative	introduces a question
quidam, aliquis	*a certain one, someone, anyone*	indefinite	identifies vaguely
ego, tu, is, ea, id	*I, you, he, she, it*	personal	designates with reference to writer
me, te, se	*myself, yourself, him/herself/itself*	reflexive	restates the subject
ipse, ipsa, ipsum	*he himself, she herself, it (itself)*	intensive	emphasizes

Some Questions for Practice with Pronouns and Adjectives

Practice Question 1: *Hic* and *Ille*

Complete each sentence with the correct form of **hic** or **ille**, as appropriate to the context.

1. _____ (*This*) raeda _____ (*that*) urbem appropinquabat, _____ (*that*) raeda _____ (*this*) city.

2. _____ (*That*) dominus nomen _____ (*of this*) ancillae nesciebat.

3. _____ (*This*) pretium est maius quam _____ (*that*).

4. Princeps in _____ (*those*) monumentis nomen suum inscripsit.

5. Heri _____ (*these*) sacerdotes (f.) _____ (*these*) templa intraverunt.

6. _____ (*Those*) oppida sunt maiora _____ (*that*) urbe.

7. _____ (*These*) senatores cum _____ (*those*) amicis cenabant.

8. Multi _____ (*this*) pulchram villam videre volebant.

9. _____ (*This man*) est fortior quam _____ (*that*).

10. Duo servi aquam ex _____ (*this*) puteo extrahebant.

Practice Question 2: *is, ea id*

Do the same with **is, ea, id.**

1. He gave her flowers.

2. His brothers are twins.

3. She brought those things with her to the Forum.

4. They gave water to their horses.

5. Give them more!

6. The overseer gives him the water. He drinks it.

7. I fear wolves. Do you fear them?

8. They saw her.

9. I will see both him and her. Will you see them?

10. Her father is a senator.

Practice Question 3: *qui, quae, quod*

Select the form of **qui, quae, quod** that correctly completes each sentence, basing your choice on the context.

1. Ego illos servos, ____ (*whom*) ad forum duxeram, vendidi.
   (A) quos
   (B) qui
   (C) quem
   (D) quorum

2. Patronus ____ (*to whom*) cliens auxilium dederat gratus erat.
   (A) qui
   (B) quo
   (C) quibus
   (D) cui

3. Dominus servis ____ cum (*with whom*) laborabas loqui volebat.
   (A) quorum
   (B) quibus
   (C) quo
   (D) quos

4. Miles ____ (*whose*) filius meam filiam nupserat erat gloriosus.
   (A) qui
   (B) quem
   (C) cuius
   (D) quo

5. Tabellarius ____ (*whom*) per Viam Appiam iter facientem vidisti erat servus imperatoris.
   (A) qui
   (B) cuius
   (C) quam
   (D) quem

6. Dum Romae eras, ____ (*which*) aedificia vidisti?
   (A) cuius
   (B) quae
   (C) qua
   (D) quas

7. ____ (*Whose*) servos in agris laborantes conspexisti?
   (A) Qui
   (B) Quos
   (C) Quibus
   (D) Quorum

8. Canes ____ (*that*) felem petentes vidisti celerrime currebant.
   (A) qui
   (B) quos
   (C) quem
   (D) quod

9. Puella ____ (*with whom*) in foro ambulabas mea soror est.
   (A) cui
   (B) quibuscum
   (C) quacum
   (D) quocum

10. Pauperes ____ (*to whom*) patronus panem dedit maximas gratias ei egerunt.
    (A) quibus
    (B) quorum
    (C) quos
    (D) quae

Question 4: *ego, tu, nos, vos*

Form the correct Latin personal pronoun or possessive adjective to complete each sentence.

1. Give me liberty or give me death!
2. Peace be with you (sing.)
3. Grant us peace.
4. You all are my friends.
5. Come with us!
6. Our father, who are in heaven.
7. Yours, mine, and ours.
8. You too, Brutus?
9. Take me with you, friends!
10. We are happy to be going to your (sing.) house.

Question 5: *quidam, aliquis*, etc.

Select the correct indefinite pronoun or adjective.

1. ____ (*Whatever*) id est, timeo Danaos et dona ferentes.
    (A) Aliquid
    (B) Quoddam
    (C) Quidquid
    (D) Quisquis

2. Surely ____ (*someone*) will bring us help.
    (A) quisquis
    (B) quidque
    (C) quosdam
    (D) aliquis

3. Catilina cum ____ (*certain*) senatoribus ad consulatum obtinendum coniurabat.
    (A) quibusdam
    (B) quibus
    (C) quodam
    (D) quibusque

4. We caught sight of _____ (*someone*) we knew in the crowd.
   (A) quendam
   (B) aliquem
   (C) quosdam
   (D) quicquam

5. Si _____ (anyone) Romam ierit, magnifica aedificia videbit.
   (A) quisquis
   (B) quoddam
   (C) quis
   (D) quicquam

6. Quidam e senatoribus sperabant Pompeium consulem futurum esse.
   (A) Everyone
   (B) Some
   (C) A few
   (D) Several

7. Which of the following is an indefinite pronoun?
   (A) quamquam
   (B) quomodo
   (C) quidem
   (D) quicquid

8. Poteratne Cicero dicere _____ (*something*) de Catilina puniendo?
   (A) aliquid
   (B) quodam
   (C) quisque
   (D) quoquo

9. Dominus cuique servo laudem dedit.
   (A) a certain
   (B) some
   (C) each
   (D) every

10. Mali alicui semper nocent.
   (A) everyone
   (B) a few
   (C) no one
   (D) someone

Question 6: *se* and *ipse*

Fill in each blank with the correct pronoun.

1. Femina Romana ____ in speculo videbat. (ipsa, se)

2. Avaritia ____ causa belli erat. (ipsa, se)

3. Poeta moriturus dixit _____ librum non finivisse. (ipsum, se)

4. Nonne omnes Romani deis _____ sacrificaverunt? (ipsis, se)

5. Augustus _____ testimonium suum scripsit. (ipse, se)

6. Servi Romani _____ libertatem emere poterant. (ipsis, sibi)

7. Senator canem suum in lectica ____ semper ferebat. (cum ipso, secum)

8. Nomina consulum _____ in tabulis inscripta sunt. (ipsorum, se)

9. Si iudex aliquem iniuste condemnabit, _____ condemnabitur. (ipse, se)

10. Laudantne scriptores _____ semper? (ipsi, se)

Practice in Identifying the Referent of a Pronoun

Passage 1

Why Juno hates the Trojans.

Urbs antiqua fuit, Tyrii tenuere coloni,
Karthago, Italiam contra Tiberinaque longe
ostia, dives opum studiisque asperrima belli;
quam Iuno fertur terris magis omnibus unam
posthabita coluisse Samo; hic illius arma,
hic currus fuit; hoc regnum dea gentibus esse,
si qua fata sinant, iam tum tenditque fovetque.
Progeniem sed enim Troiano a sanguine duci
audierat, Tyrias olim quae verteret arces;
hinc populum late regem belloque superbum
venturum excidio Libyae: sic volvere Parcas.
Id metuens, veterisque memor Saturnia belli,
prima quod ad Troiam pro caris gesserat Argis—

Vergil, *Aeneid* 1.12-24

1. The word Quam (line 4) refers to
   (A) Urbs (line 1) (C) ostia (line 3)
   (B) Italiam (line 2) (D) asperrima (line 3)

2. The word hic in line 5 means
   (A) this (C) here
   (B) that (D) he

3. In line 5, the word illius modifies which of the following?
   (A) Tyrian settlers (C) Carthage
   (B) Juno D) Samos

4. In line 6, the word hoc actually refers to
   (A) the city of Carthage
   (B) the goddess Juno
   (C) the Tyrian settlers
   (D) the cult site of Samos

5. In line 7, qua is in the ___ case.
   (A) nominative
   (B) vocative
   (C) ablative
   (D) accusative

6. The word quae (line 9) refers to
   (A) Iuno (line 4)
   (B) Progeniem (line 8)
   (C) Troiano . . . sanguine (line 8)
   (D) arces (line 9)

7. Id (line 12) refers to
   (A) the Roman defeat of Carthage
   (B) the Trojan War
   (C) the rise of Rome
   (D) the prophetic ability of the Parcae

8. The word quod (line 13) refers to
   (A) Id
   (B) memor
   (C) Saturnia
   (D) belli

Passage 2

Cicero expresses concern about his political future.

1 L. Iulio Caesare, C. Marcio Figulo consulibus filiolo me auctum scito salva Terentia.
2 Abs te tam diu nihil litterarum! Ego de meis ad te rationibus scripsi antea diligenter.
3 Hoc tempore Catilinam, competitorem nostrum, defendere cogitamus. Iudices habemus,
4 quos volumus, summa accusatoris voluntate. Spero, si absolutus erit, coniunctiorem illum
5 nobis fore in ratione petitionis; sin aliter acciderit, humaniter feremus. Tuo adventu nobis
6 opus est maturo; nam prorsus summa hominum est opinio tuos familiares nobiles homines
7 adversarios honori nostro fore. Ad eorum voluntatem mihi conciliandam maximo te mihi
8 usui fore video. Quare Ianuario mense, ut constituisti, cura ut Romae sis.

Cicero, *Epistulae ad Atticum* I.II

In the case of the personal pronouns underlined above, identify <u>in Latin</u> the person or thing to which the pronoun refers. If the underlined word is a possessive adjective, indicate the word it modifies. Be aware that Cicero often uses a plural form of the personal pronoun or possessive adjective when referring to himself, e.g., he uses **nos** when he means **ego**.

	Pronoun	Adjective	Antecedent	Word Modified
me	___	___	________	________
meis	___	___	________	________
nostrum	___	___	________	________
quos	___	___	________	________
illum	___	___	________	________
nobis	___	___	________	________
tuos	___	___	________	________
eorum	___	___	________	________
te	___	___	________	________

Passage 3

This fragment from a comedy by the early Latin poet Quintus Ennius contains a number of indefinite pronouns. Work through the meaning and then translate it into English.

> **Cum debere carnufex cuiquam quicquam quemquem, quemque quisque conveniat, neget.**
>
> *<u>carnufex, carnuficis,</u> m., executioner, hangman; rascal, scoundrel*
>
> *<u>conveniat:</u> let (someone) sue*

Auxilia:

quisquam, quisquam, quidquam/quicquam, *anyone, anything*

quisquis, quisquis, quidquid/quicquid, *anyone, whoever*

quisque, quisque, quidque, *each one*

Answers: Demonstrative Pronouns

1. **(C)**
The form **eundem** is the equivalent of the pronoun **eum** + the suffix **–dem**, which is accusative singular. Answer (A) is neuter, (B) has the correct case but the incorrect gender (feminine), and (D) the correct gender but the incorrect case and number (genitive plural).

2. **(B)**
The verb **credere** takes an object in the dative, accounting for the appearance of **ei**, which is dative singular. Answer (A) misdirects you into considering **ei** as the nominative plural masculine form, which would produce the translation "them," actually a translation of an accusative form (vs. the nominative **ei**, "they"). This does not fit the context here. Answer (C) "that" cannot be a translation of the demonstrative **ei** without a meaning such as "that person" as a pronoun. Answer (D) requires that the **ei** be the personal/reflexive pronoun **tibi**, "yourself" (singular because the imperative is singular).

3. **(C)**
This question examines your ability to discriminate between singular and plural forms of the demonstrative pronoun **hic, haec, hoc**, and between the meanings of "this" and "that." Since this demonstrative pronoun means "this/these," Answers (B) and (D) are not options because they contain translations of **ille**, i.e., "that" and "those." The context requires that **haec** be the accusative direct object of **dixit**. Familiarity with the forms of this pronoun leads to the conclusion that **haec** is accusative plural neuter, "these things." The sentence reads, "The tribune said these things because he was angry."

4. **(D)**
This sentence completion calls for the simple direct object form **eos**, "Did you see them?" referring to the senators (masculine and plural). Answer (A) is singular, the incorrect number, (B) is dative singular or nominative plural, the incorrect cases, given the context of this sentence, and (C) is **ea,** feminine singular or nominative or accusative plural neuter. Answer (C) as a neuter plural form **ea**, "those things," is justifiable grammatically, but **ea** has no possible antecedent (**senatores** is not neuter and **Curia** is not plural). Furthermore, **ea,** as the 3rd person form "she," could not be the subject of **vidistine**.

5. **(C)**
This questions asks for discrimination between the meanings of **hic** and **ille** and between their functions as adjective and pronoun. **Hic**, as a demonstrative adjective, modifies **senator** "this (senator)" and **illos** "them" serves as the pronoun object of the preposition **prope**. For Answer (A), the Latin would be **ille. . .hunc**. In (B), the answer "these" is plural and in the sentence **hic** is singular. For (D), the

correct Latin would be **hic** and **hos**. The sentence reads, "In the Senate House, this senator was sitting near those (senators)."

6. **(D)**
The English translation of the underlined phrase contains an overtone or suggestion of contempt or distaste, requiring that the answer be (D) **iste**. The pronouns supplied in the other answers do not carry such meaning.

7. **(B)**
Illorum is a genitive (plural) form of the demonstrative pronoun, which can be deduced from the context. Answer (B) "their" is the only plural answer that expresses the idea of possession. Answer (A) "his" (Latin **eius**) is singular, (C) "them," is not genitive ("of them" would be correct), and (D) "that," is both singular and an adjective, despite having the proper basic meaning of **ille, illa, illud**.

8. **(D)**
The phrase "the same things" in the question requires a neuter plural pronoun in Latin. Answer (A) fills the bill, but does not include the meaning of "the same." Answers (B) and (C), although plural, are both masculine and therefore do not accurately translate "things." Furthermore, as with **illa** in (A), these pronouns do not carry the meaning of "the same" found in **eadem**.

9. **(C)**
This sentence is tricky, because your mind's eye wants to read it as Answer (D) "He is the brother of this senator," or something equivalent. The sentence reads, "The brother of this (man) is a senator." The genitive form **huius** does not agree with **senator** or **frater**, which are nominative. Answer (A) is incorrect because **est** does not mean "has" and (B) **huius** has a meaning of "this," rather than "that." Note that the apostrophe is used instead of the more familiar word "of" to indicate possession in the translation given in the correct answer, (C).

10. **(B)**
"Was the aedile giving those things to them?" The verb of giving implies the appearance of both a direct object (here, **illa**, "those things") and an indirect object (here, **his**, "to them"). Answer (A) "these things to her" requires that the Latin be **haec ei**, (C) "that thing to them," **illud eis,** and (D) "her to those," **his eam**.

11. **(D)**
The fact that **dicet** is in the future tense eliminates Answers (B) and (C), which have verbs in the present tense. In Answer (A), the meanings of **hoc** and **eis** are transposed, leaving Answer (D), "He (**Is**) will tell (**dicet**) (to) them (**eis**) about this (**de hoc**).

Answers: Relative and Interrogative Pronouns

1. **(D)**

The context of the missing relative pronoun suggests the word "whom" to complete the meaning of the verb, i.e., "I saw whom." As "whom" is an object form in English, an object form in Latin is required, leaving the choices of Answers (C) and (D), which are both accusative. Since the antecedent **senes** is plural, (C) **quem**, which is singular, must be eliminated. Answer (A) **quis** is an interrogative pronoun and does not relate back to an antecedent and (B) **qui** is a relative pronoun in the nominative case, which seems to be the correct answer, at first glance. Remember that the function of a relative pronoun in its clause is separate from that of its antecedent. The sentence reads, "The old men whom I saw in the forum were senators."

2. **(B)**

Option (A) **quam** seems the obvious correct answer, but this form is the accusative singular feminine form of the relative pronoun **quae** and not that of the interrogative pronoun **quis**. Answer (C) **quae,** is feminine nominative (singular or plural) and (D) **qua** is the feminine ablative singular form of the relative **quae**.

3. **(B)**

The relative pronoun **quod** in this sentence modifies **aedificium** and is the direct object of the verb **faciebant**, i.e., "The building that they were making." Answer (A) "when" is not an option for translating **quod**. **Quod** can have a causal meaning, i.e., "because" or "since," as in Answers (C) and (D), but these meanings do not make sense in the context of this sentence.

4. **(C)**

The underlined phrase "At what hour" requires an ablative of time. Since the sentence is a direct question, an interrogative adjective is needed. The underlined phrase "At what hour" requires an ablative of time. Since the sentence is a direct question, an interrogative adjective is needed. The ablative singular form of **qui, quae, quod**, which serves as the interrogative adjective, is therefore, **qua**. **Qua hora**, "At what hour?" accurately completes the meaning of the sentence. The accusative, nominative, and partitive genitive phrases in Answers (A), (B), and (D), respectively, have no grammatical meaning in this context.

5. **(D)**

In this sentence, **dati sunt** takes a dative indirect object **cui** "to whom," the antecedent of which is **consul**. The sentence reads, "The consul to whom the fasces were given held the imperium." Answer (A) "whose" is possessive genitive, the form of which would be **cuius**. Answer (B) "whom" is object accusative, the form of which is **quem**, and (C) "who" is subject nominative, the form of which is **qui**.

6. **(D)**

"With whom" is a phrase requiring the preposition **cum**. Since the antecedent **senatores** is plural, the relative pronoun must also be plural. Hence, Answer (A), which is singular, must be eliminated. Answer (B) **post quos** "after whom," changes the meaning of the original prepositional phrase and (C) breaks the general rule that the ablative of accompaniment must be found with the preposition **cum**.

7. **(C)**

Cui is the dative singular form of the relative pronoun in a dative of possession with **erat**, "The consul to whom the name was Cicero . . . ," i.e., who had the name Cicero." In the Latin sentence, Answer (A) requires the accusative form **quem**, (B) the nominative form **qui**, and (D) the ablative form **quocum**.

8. **(C)**

This is a bit tricky. Success on this question requires that you know that the verb **parere** takes a dative object. Only **cui** is dative and is therefore the correct answer. This form is an interrogative adjective modifying **legi**. Answer (A) **quo,** is ablative, (B) **quem**, perhaps the most obvious answer, accusative, and (D) **quis**, nominative. The sentence reads, "Which law do (the) citizens always obey?"

9. **(A)**

Basically, this question asks you to decide whether the English phrase "Which laws?" serves as the subject or direct object of the verb. By turning the sentence around, "Roman citizens disregarded which laws?" you can determine that the answer must be the object accusative, e.g., **quas leges**. Answer (B) **quae leges** is nominative, (C) **quarum legum** is genitive, and (D) **quibus legibus** dative or ablative.

10. **(D)**

This sentence contains the simple prepositional phrase **A quibus**, "By whom?" as the interrogative phrase to be translated. Answer (A) "For whom" is dative. Answers (B) "From whom" and (C) "From which" are ablative, but require the prepositional phrase **E quo** or **E quibus**. The sentence reads, "By whom will all laws be obeyed?"

11. **(C)**

This sentence says, "He who says (the things) that he wants will hear (the things) that he does not want (to hear)." Since the sense requires that the form **quae** be the neuter plural of the relative pronoun, the antecedent is understood as the neuter plural "things." Since "that" is the direct object in both instances, the only pronoun among the answers that is accusative plural neuter is **ea** (**quae**). If Answer (A) **eas** were the antecedent, the relative would be **quas**; if (B) **eam**, the relative would be **quam**; if (D) **id**, then **quod.**

12. **(C)**

This question asks you to substitute a similar construction for the relative clause **qui ambulabant**. The present active participles **ambulantes** can be translated as the relative clause "who were walking." Answer (A) **ambulaturi** "about to walk" is a future active participle, (B) **postquam ambulaverant** "after they had walked" is a time clause, and (D) **quod ambulabant** "because they were walking," a causal clause.

13. **(B)**

Quibus is tricky here because it is an ablative without a preposition, leading to some contextual guesstimation. The form could also be dative, of course, but the sense does not permit this use, unless it would be incorrectly taken as a possessive dative with the verb **erat**. Therefore Answers (A) and (C), which are dative, are eliminated. So, "The stones . . . the basilica had been built were extremely heavy." Answer (D) "by whom" does not relate to **saxa**, the antecedent of **quibus**, nor is a preposition found before **quibus**, which would be required for an ablative of agent, also meaning "by whom," with the passive verb. Such a sentence would not make sense, i.e, "The stones by whom . . . ." **Saxa quibus** must mean, "The stones with which or by means of which . . . ."

14. **(A)**

This sentence by Publilius Syrus says, "The fearful (person) sees dangers <u>that</u> are not even (there)." Among the answers, the antecedent of **quae** that gives the most meaningful translation is "dangers," **Pericula**, which is the direct object of **videt**. **Quae** agrees with **Pericula** as a neuter plural, leading to the meaning "Dangers that. . . ." **Quae** does not agree with Answer (B) **timidus** in gender or number. Answer (C) is grammatically conceivable, but the ensuing translation does not make sense, and (D) requires that the relative clause have a singular verb.

15. **(A)**

This sentence reads, literally, "There are those to whom there were different opinions,"i.e., who had different opinions. Thus, **quibus diversae opiniones essent** is an example of dative of possession. Also, the antecedent of the relative pronoun **quibus** is missing. In the sentence, the adjective **diversae** clearly modifies **opiniones**, which removes Answers (C) and (D). The translations of the relative pronoun and verb tense are wrong in Answer (B). The relative clause of characteristic with the subjunctive, **quibus . . . essent**, that appears in this sentence will be covered below.

Answers: Indefinite Pronouns and Adjectives

1. **(C)**

Selecting the correct answer here requires knowledge of the meaning of the indefinite adjective **aliqui**, **aliqua**, **aliquod**, "some" or "any." The Latin of Answer (A) would be **omnes leges**, (B) **multae leges**, and (D) **quaedam leges**. The sentence reads, "Are <u>some</u> laws bad?"

2. **(B)**

Proper translation of the underlined phrase requires knowledge of the meaning of the adjective **quidam**, **quaedam**, **quoddam** "a certain," which the context requires in its accusative plural form, **quosdam.** Answer (A) has the correct adjective, but in the wrong form, i.e., nominative instead of accusative. Answers (C) and (D) have the correct case endings, but neither is the correct Latin word: **aliquos** means "some" or "any" and **quosque** means "each" or "every."

3. **(B)**

When introduced by conjunctions such as **si**, the pronoun **quis** means "anyone." Translation (A) "who" for **quis,** requires that the pronoun be an interrogative and that the sentence be a direct question, which it is not. Answers (C) "someone" and (D) "whoever" are not acceptable meanings of the pronoun **quis**. The Latin for the former would be **aliquis** and for the latter **quicumque** or **quisquis**. The sentence reads, "If anyone comes into the forum, he will see magnificent buildings."

4. **(D)**

This quote is part of a Pompeiian wall inscription about love. The indefinite pronoun **quisquis** is the nominative subject of the sentence and means "whoever." The Latin for Answers (A) and (B) is **aliquis**. For Answer (C), **quidam**. The sentence reads, "Whoever loves, let him prosper; he who does not know (how) to love, let him be undone." Note the appearance of the jussive subjunctives **valeat** and **pereat**, "Let him . . . ."

5. **(D)**

This sentence contains a mouthful of three indefinite pronouns: **aliquis** "anybody," **aliquid** "anything," and a form of **quisquam** (or **quicquam**) "anyone" (or "anything"). The first is the nominative subject, the second the accusative direct object, and the third the object of an ablative preposition. Answers (A), (B), (C), all containing various elements of correctness, are designed to test your knowledge of the meanings of various indefinite pronouns. In (A), the object **aliquid** cannot mean "whatever." In (B), **quisque** does not mean "some people" nor does **de quoquam** mean "to anyone." The "about this certain person" of Answer (C) requires the ablative of the indefinite pronoun **quidam**, which is **quodam**, not **quoquam**.

6. **(A)**

This sentence says, literally, "We more readily obey someone (who is) asking (rather) than ordering." The verb **parere** takes a dative object, hence the participial phrase **alicui . . . roganti quam iubenti.** Don't be fooled into thinking that **quidem** in this sentence is another indefinite pronoun!

7. **(C)**

This analogy compares the singular subject and object forms of the demonstrative pronoun **idem** with the indefinite pronoun **quidam**. These forms illustrate the effect of assimilation in producing the spelling changes of **eundem** and **quendam**.

8. **(D)**

"For anyone" requires the dative of **quisquam**, which is **cuiquam**. Answer (A) **quicquid** is nominative or accusative singular neuter, meaning, "whatever." Answer (B) **quodam** is ablative singular of **quidam** "a certain person" and (C) **quibusque** is a plural of **quisque**, which does not fit the singular sense here.

9. **(B)**

The various possible answers tell you that what is missing is a form of **quidam**, **quaedam**, **quoddam**, the indefinite adjective. The missing adjective modifies **remedia**, which is the neuter plural subject of the verb **sunt**. Of the choices, the neuter plural form of the adjective that agrees with **remedia** is **quaedam**. Answer (A) **quadam** is ablative singular feminine, (C) **quidam** is nominative singular masculine, and (D) **quoddam** is nominative/accusative singular neuter. This sentence reads, "Some solutions are worse than the problems."

Answers: Possessive Pronouns and Adjectives

1. **(D)**

The missing pronoun must be **Nos**, in order to agree with the verb **volumus** "we wish." The appearance of the pronoun in addition to the personal ending of the verb, emphasizes that it is we who wish to be free. Answer (A) is the wrong form of the pronoun and neither (B) **Vos** "you" nor (C) **Ei** "they" agrees with the verb. The sentence reads, "We all (or All of us) wish to be free.

2. **(A)**

Tibi is dative singular. Therefore, its plural is **vobis**. Answer (B) **vos** is nominative or accusative plural, (C) **vestrum** is genitive plural, and (D) **tui** genitive singular.

3. **(A)**

Nobiscum to accompany **venite**,"You (pl.) come with us," makes the best sense. Answers (B) **ad vestros** "toward yours" and (C) **cum vobis** "with you" make no sense in the context of this sentence. Remember that the preposition **cum** is attached to the pronoun, eliminating Answer (D).

4. **(C)**

This question asks you to remember that a masculine pronoun can be translated "it" when referring to a thing (e.g., **librum**). Answer (A) "him" is a possible translation of the pronoun **eum**, but this meaning does not make sense in the specific context given. Answer (B) "his" is not a possible translation of **eum** and (D) "them" is plural, whereas **eum** is singular. This sentence reads, "I bought that book, but I didn't read it."

5. **(D)**

This sentence reads, "Your (things) please you (and) my (things) please me." The pronouns **te** and **me** are in the accusative singular and serve as direct objects in this sentence. **Tua** and **mea**, "yours" and "mine," serve as corresponding possessive adjectives used as neuter substantives, "your things" and "my things," since no nouns are provided. Answers (A) and (B) are the same, but the wording is reversed. (This is a confusing sentence!) The translation in (C) does not give the meaning of the Latin, wherein each person is pleased by his own things, not both persons by both things.

6. **(B)**

Dic "Tell" is an imperative, immediately eliminating Answers (A) and (D), which do not contain imperatives. In Answer (C), the translation "her" is incorrect for the demonstrative **haec**, which can be feminine, but is not in the dative case, as required by the translation "Tell (to) her . . . ." This form would be **huic**. In the correct answer, **haec** serves as a pronoun in the accusative plural neuter form, meaning "these things."

7. **(A)**

The meaning of this sentence depends upon correct translation of **nec . . . nec**, "neither . . . nor," and upon seeing that **cum** and **sine** are opposites, and that therefore their prepositional phrases **tecum** "with you" and **sine te** "without you" contrast. Answer (B) says the same thing in both clauses, (C) turns the thought around, and (D) **sine**, is mistranslated as "near."

8. **(B)**

In Answer (A), the pronoun **eorum** "their" is plural, whereas "his" is required in the sentence. Answer (C) contains the reflexive adjective "his own," but the sentence reads "his ("someone else's"). In Answer (D), **eam** serves as a demonstrative adjective "this or that (money)," which does not indicate possession. Answer (B) may be rendered "his money," i.e., the money of someone other than the subject.

9. **(C)**

The word "for" in the English sentence suggests the use of the dative case. Therefore, Answer (A) **nos**, which is nominative or accusative and not dative, (B) **nostros**, which is accusative and adjective, and (D) **ad nos**, which is a prepositional phrase requiring a verb of motion, are all inappropriate.

10. **(A)**

The appearance of the word **speculo** "mirror" suggests that someone is looking at himself or herself, requiring the reflexive/personal pronoun "you." This is because the subject of **vides** is in the second person, i.e., "you are looking at yourself." Answers (A) and (B) are both possible, but the verb is singular, therefore (B) is incorrect because the object pronoun **vos** is plural. Answer (C) **vestrum** "of you" or "your" does not fit the sense, and (D) is in the dative case, which is not justifiable here. The sentence reads, "Do you see <u>yourself</u> in the mirror?"

11. **(B)**
"I am helping you" may be rendered in Latin as a double dative, "I am for a help to/for you," i.e., **Vobis auxilio sum**. Answer (A) has the verb in the wrong tense, (C) transposes "you" and "me," and (D) "Help is coming to/for you" does not indicate from whom the help is coming.

Answers: Reflexive and Intensive Pronouns

1. **(B)**
"For himself" requires the dative form of the reflexive pronoun **se**, which is **sibi**. The Latin of Answer (A) is the intensive pronoun **(ille consul) ipse**, "that consul himself." Answer (C) requires the pronoun of the third person **ei** "for him" (a second party) and (D) "for them" is not reflexive, as the subject is **ille consul** "that consul."

2. **(A)**
The pronoun **eum** fits the need for an accusative form of the third person pronoun, referring to the consul. Answers (B) and (C) are intensive (nominative singular masculine and nominative/ accusative singular neuter), neither of which is appropriate to the sense here. The pronoun **se** is a reflexive pronoun of the third person in the accusative, but must refer back to **senatores** as its antecedent, which doesn't fit the sense.

3. **(D)**
This sentence contains both a reflexive adjective (**suum**) and a reflexive pronoun (**se**), both referring to the consul's rival (**competitorem**), which is found within an indirect statement. Therefore, the sentence reads, "The consul says that his (own) rival killed himself." Answers (A) and (B) require **eum**, rather than **se** (note the ambiguity of the Latin here), and Answer (C) requires the substitution of **eius** for **suum.**

4. **(C)**
"His" is not a reflexive adjective because the subject to which it refers is **senatores**, which is plural. Therefore, Answers (A) and (B) are to be discounted. Answer (D) **ipsius** is, indeed, genitive and suggests the idea of possession found in the word "his," but the meaning of the sentence does not provide an opportunity for the use of an intensive pronoun.

5. **(A)**
This question reviews the material in a previous chapter. The indefinite pronoun **quidam** can mean "some" in the plural. The sentence reads, "That one (i.e., the consul) knew that some senators were unfriendly to him." Answer (B) requires **omnes**, (C) **aliquos,** and (D) the adjective **complures.**

6. **(D)**

This sentence contains both an intensive pronoun, **(consuli) ipso** "(the consul) himself," which is dative after the compound verb **opposuerunt**, and a reflexive pronoun, **se (opposuerunt)** "(opposed) themselves (to)." In Answer (A) the translation wrongly has the consul confronting the senators. In (B), the Latin requires that the intensive pronoun be **ipsi** to modify **senatores** instead of the consul. Answer (C) is a combination of the variations found in (A) and (B), and is therefore incorrect.

7. **(C)**

The reflexive adjective **suus, -a, -um** sometimes serves as a substantive, as here, where **suos** without a modified noun means "their (own) men." Note the masculine gender. **Secum** "with themselves" behaves as other reflexive pronouns when found with **cum**, which is enclitic. In Answer (A), the translation "his men" is not reflexive with regard to the subject **senatores**, which is plural. Answer (B) omits **suos** in its translation and (D) "with him," does not correctly translate **secum**, which is reflexive.

8. **(D)**

The sentence illustrates the use of the personal pronoun as reflexive. "Yourself" or **te** is the direct object of the verb "give up" and refers back to the subject of that verb, "you." Answer (A) is in the wrong person (third) and (B) and (C) are in the wrong case, dative and nominative, respectively.

9. **(B)**

This sentence illustrates the use of the intensive pronoun emphasizing a personal pronoun, which is a common type of expression. Therefore, **Ego ipse** is the correct rendering of "I myself." Answer (A) offers an impossible combination of a possessive adjective (**meus**, "my") and an intensive pronoun (**ipse**, "himself"). Answer (D) is not an intensive, but a reflexive, pronoun in the third person and is found in the incorrect case (accusative). Answer (C) **Ille ipse** gives the incorrect meaning, "He himself."

10. **(B)**

This sentence, which combines an intensive with a reflexive, reads, "That one (i.e., the consul) believed that he himself must not be punished." **Se ipsum** serves as the subject accusative of the infinitive **puniendum esse** in an indirect statement and refers back to the subject of the main clause, **iste**. Answer (A) "they themselves" is impossible as a translation because **se ipsum** is singular. Answer (C) "he (someone else)" is not reflexive, as required by **se ipsum** in the sentence. Answer (D) is rendered by the pronoun **illum** or **istum** in Latin.

Answers to Questions for Practice with Pronouns

Practice Question 1: *hic* and *ille*

1. Haec, illam, illa, hanc
2. Ille, huius
3. Hoc, illud
4. illis
5. Haec, haec
6. Illa, illa
7. Hi, illis
8. hanc
9. Hic, ille
10. hoc

Practice Question 2: *is, ea, id*

1. Is, ei
2. Eius or Sui
3. Ea, ea, cum ea
4. Ei or Eae, eorum or earum, or suis
5. eis
6. ei, eam (**aqua** is feminine)
7. eos
8. Ei or Eae, eam
9. eum, eam, eos (defer to the masculine when the gender is uncertain)
10. Eius or Suus

Practice Question 3: *qui, quae, quod*

1. (A)
2. (D)
3. (B)
4. (C)
5. (D)
6. (B)
7. (D)
8. (B)
9. (C)
10. (A)

Practice Question 4: *ego, tu, nos, vos*

1. mihi
2. tecum
3. nobis
4. Vos, mei or meae
5. nobiscum
6. noster
7. Tuus or Vester, meus, noster
8. tu
9. me, vobiscum
10. Nos, tuam

Practice Question 5: *quidam, aliquis*, etc.

1. (C)
2. (D)
3. (A)
4. (B)
5. (C)
6. (B)
7. (D)
8. (A)
9. (C)
10. (D)

Practice Question 6: *se* and *ipse*

1.	se	6.	sibi
2.	ipsa	7.	se
3.	se	8.	ipsorum
4.	ipsis	9.	ipse
5.	ipse	10.	se

Practice in Identifying the Referent of a Pronoun

Answers to Passage 1

1. (A)	3. (B)	5. (C)	7. (A)
2. (C)	4. (A)	6. (B)	8. (D)

Translation of Passage 1 (for additional practice)

There was an ancient city, (that) the colonists from Tyre settled, Carthage, far across from Italy and the banks of the Tiber, rich in resources and fierce in its zest for war; (a city) that Juno is said to have cherished more than any in all the lands, preferred (even) to Samos; here were her arms, her was her chariot; this (city) the goddess cherished to be the realm of all nations, if in any way the fates should allow it. But in fact she had heard that there was a race, sprung from Trojan blood, that would one day overthrow the Punic towers; (she had heard) that from this source a people widely ruling and proud in war would come for the destruction of Libya: (she had heard) that the Parcae foretold (this). Fearing that, Saturnian Juno, mindful of the war of old, which she, first and foremost, had waged at Troy for her dear Argives . . . .

Answers to Passage 2

	Pronoun	Adjective	Antecedent	Word Modified
me	x		Cicero	
meis		x		rationibus
nostrum		x		competitorem
quos	x		Iudices	
illum		x		coniunctiorem
nobis	x		Cicero	
tuos		x		homines
eorum	x		adversarios	
te	x		Atticus	

Translation of Passage 2

Be informed that, when L. Julius Caesar and C. Marcius Figulus were consuls (65 B.C.), I (my family) was increased by a baby boy. Terentia doing well. Why so long without a letter from you! I wrote earlier to you completely about my situation. At this time I am considering defending Catiline, my political rival. I have the jury that I want, with the complete consent of the prosecutor. I hope that, if he is acquitted, he will be more supportive of me in the cause of (my) candidacy; but if he is not (acquitted), I shall carry on with resignation. Your early arrival (back in Rome) is important to me; there is great speculation going around that close friends of yours, men of high rank, will be opposed to my election. I realize that you will be of great value to me in winning their favor. And so, be sure that you are in Rome in January, as you have agreed.

Translation of Passage 3

Cum debere carnufex cuiquam quicquam quemquem, quemque quisque conveniat, neget.

Since the scoundrel denies that anyone (**quemquem**) owes anything (**quicquam**) to anyone (**cuiquam**), let each one (**quisque**) sue the other (**quemque**).

Chapter 14

Adjectives and Adverbs

The forms of adjectives are the same as or similar to those of nouns. Adjectives modify nouns and can even stand as nouns themselves. They are organized into two classes, based on their forms. One class has endings of the first and second declensions of nouns and is identified by the masculine, feminine, and neuter forms of the nominative singular, e.g., **laetus, laeta, laetum** (in dictionary format, **laetus, -a, -um**). The other class has endings of the third declension, e.g., **tristis, tristis, triste** (**tristis, -is, -e**).

First/second declension adjective:	**Romani qui ruri habitabant <u>laeti</u> saepe erant.** *Romans who lived in the country were often <u>happy</u>.*
Third declension adjective:	**Romani qui in urbe habitabant <u>tristes</u> saepe erant.** *Romans who lived in the city were often <u>unhappy</u>.*

An adjective must agree with its noun in case, number, and gender. In the first example above, **laeti** modifies **Romani**. Both are nominative, plural, and masculine. In the second example, **tristes** also modifies **Romani**, and both are also nominative, plural, and masculine. <u>However, an adjective is not required to have the very same ending as the noun in order for it to agree with the noun</u>. If the adjective belongs to a different declension from the noun, the endings will be spelled differently, e.g.,

Same Declensions:

First/second declension adjective and first/second declension noun	**laeti Romani**, *happy Romans*
Third declension adjective and third declension noun	**agrestis amnis**, *country stream*

Different Declensions:

Third declension adjective and first/second declension noun	**tristes Romani**, *unhappy Romans*
First/second declension adjective and third declension noun	**periculosum flumen**, *dangerous river*

Adjectives in the Positive, Comparative, and Superlative Degrees

		Singular			Plural	
		Masc.	Fem.	Neut.	Masc.	Fem.	Neut.
Nom.	1st/2nd	**laetus**	**laeta**	**laetum**	**laeti**	**laetae**	**laeta**
		laetior	laetior	laetius	laetiores	laetiores	laetiora
		laetissimus	laetissima	laetissimum	laetissimi	laetissimae	laetissima
	3rd	**tristis**	**tristis**	**triste**	**tristes**	**tristes**	**tristia**
		tristior	tristior	tristius	tristiores	tristiores	tristiora
		tristissimus	tristissima	tristissimum	tristissimi	tristissimae	tristissima
Gen.	1st/2nd	**laeti**	**laetae**	**laeti**	**laetorum**	**laetarum**	**laetorum**
		laetioris	laetioris	laetioris	laetiorum	laetiorum	laetiorum
		laetissimi	laetissimae	laetissimi	laetissimorum	laetissimarum	laetissimorum
	3rd	**tristis**	**tristis**	**tristis**	**tristium**	**tristium**	**tristium**
		tristioris	tristioris	tristioris	tristiorum	tristiorum	tristiorum
		tristissimi	tristissimae	tristissimi	tristissimorum	tristissimarum	tristissimorum
Dat.	1st/2nd	**laeto**	**laetae**	**laeto**	**laetis**	**laetis**	**laetis**
		laetiori	laetiori	laetiori	laetioribus	laetioribus	laetioribus
		laetissimo	laetissimae	laetissimo	laetissimis	laetissimis	laetissimis
	3rd	**tristi**	**tristi**	**tristi**	**tristibus**	**tristibus**	**tristibus**
		tristiori	tristiori	tristiori	tristioribus	tristioribus	tristioribus
		tristissimo	tristissimae	tristissimo	tristissimis	tristissimis	tristissimis
Acc.	1st/2nd	**laetum**	**laetam**	**laetum**	**laetos**	**laetas**	**laeta**
		laetiorem	laetiorem	laetius	laetiores	laetiores	laetiora
		laetissimum	laetissimam	laetissimum	laetissimos	laetissimas	laetissima
	3rd	**tristem**	**tristem**	**triste**	**tristes**	**tristes**	**tristia**
		tristiorem	tristiorem	tristius	tristiores	tristiores	tristiora
		tristissimum	tristissimam	tristissimum	tristissimos	tristissimas	tristissima
Abl.	1st/2nd	**laeto**	**laeta**	**laeto**	**laetis**	**laetis**	**laetis**
		laetiore	laetiore	laetiore	laetioribus	laetioribus	laetioribus
		laetissimo	laetissima	laetissimo	laetissimis	laetissimis	laetissimis
	3rd	**tristi**	**tristi**	**tristi**	**tristibus**	**tristibus**	**tristibus**
		tristiore	tristiore	tristiore	tristioribus	tristioribus	tristioribus
		tristissimo	tristissima	tristissimo	tristissimis	tristissimis	tristissimis

Notes:

- Remember that neuter comparatives have nominative and accusative singular forms that end in **-ius**, not **–ior** and **-iorem**, respectively. Remember, too, that positive and superlative forms have the same endings, i.e., those of the first/second declensions, whereas the comparative degree has third declension adjective endings.
- Six adjectives in **–lis** form the superlative by replacing the positive ending with **–illimus, -a, -um**. These adjectives are: **facilis, -is, -e**, *easy* (**facillimus, -a, -um**), **difficilis, -is, -e**, *difficult* (**difficillimus, -a, -um**), **similis, -is, -e**, *similar* (**simillimus, -a, -um**), **dissimilis, -is, -e**, *dissimilar* (**disimillimus, -a, -um**), **gracilis, -is, -e**, *graceful* (**gracillimus, -a, -um**), and **humilis, -is, -e**, *low, humble* (**humillimus, -a, -um**). Other **–lis** adjectives retain the duplicated **-ss-** in the superlative, e.g., **fidelissimus, -a, -um** and **nobilissimus, -a, -um**.

Adjectives as Nouns

Plural forms of both first/second and third declension adjectives are sometimes used as nouns. When an adjective substitutes for, or "takes the substance of," a noun in this way, it is called a substantive, which means that it can "stand by itself." Substantive adjectives appear in English, as in the title of the classic film *The Good, the Bad, and the Ugly*. **Labor omnia vincit**, *Labor conquers all (things)*, serves as the motto of the State of Oklahoma.

Multi in Campaniam se moverunt.
Many (people) have moved into Campania.

Tuleruntne bona secum?
Did they bring their possessions with them?

The following adjectives are commonly found as substantives:

First/Second Declension	Third Declension
bona, *the goods (property)*	**maiores,** *ancestors*
boni/mali, *good/bad people*	**minores,** *descendants*
multa, *many things*	**omnes,** *all men, everyone*
multi/pauci, *many/few people*	**omnia,** *all things, everything*
Romani, *Romans*	

Adjectives as Adverbs

Where English uses an adverb, Latin often uses an adjective. When you translate, let the best sense dictate the phrasing, e.g.,

Aestate laeti ad oram maritimam proficiscuntur.
In the summertime, they gladly go to the seacoast, (rather than *the glad (people) go to the seacoast.*)

Variable Adjectives (*Alius*, *Nullus*, etc.)*

Nine common adjectives of the first and second declensions are irregular in that they have **–ius** in the genitive singular and **–i** in the dative singular in all genders, e.g.,

Estne pomerium terminus totius urbis Romae?
Is the pomerium the boundary of the entire city of Rome?

Except for the variation in the nominative and accusative singular neuter, these two cases have the same endings as the demonstrative pronoun **ille**, **illa**, **illud** (for which, see the previous chapter). These variable adjectives are:

alius, alius, aliud, *another*
nullus, -a, -um, *none*
solus, -a, -um, *alone*
totus, -a, -um, *whole, entire*
ullus, -a, -um, *any*
unus, -a, -um, *one*
alter, altera, alterum, *the other*
neuter, neutra, neutrum, *neither*
uter, utra, utrum, *which (of two)*

Use the acronym **unus nauta** to remember these adjectives, i.e., unus, nullus, ullus, solus, then neuter, alter, uter, totus, alius.

Adjectives as Numbers

Cardinal Numbers	Ordinal Numbers (Nouns)	Roman Numerals (Adjectives)
unus, -a, -um, *one***	**primus, -a, -um,** *first*	**I**
duo, duae, duo, *two,* **etc.**	**secundus, -a, -um,** *second,* **etc.**	**II**
tres, tres, tria	**tertius, -a, -um**	**III**
quattuor	**quartus, -a, -um**	**IV or IIII**
quinque	**quintus, -a, -um**	**V**
sex	**sextus, -a, -um**	**VI**
septem	**septimus, -a, -um**	**VII**
octo	**octavus, -a, -um**	**VIII**
novem	**nonus, -a, -um**	**IX**
decem	**decimus, -a, -um**	**X**
undecim	**undecimus, -a, -um**	**XI**
duodecim	**duodecimus, -a, -um**	**XII**
tredecim	**tertius decimus, -a, -um**	**XIII**
quattuordecim	**quartus decimus, -a, -um**	**XIV**
quindecim	**quintus decimus, -a, -um**	**XV**
sedecim	**sextus decimus, -a, -um**	**XVI**
septendecim	**septimus decimus, -a, -um**	**XVII**
octodecim	**octavus decimus, -a, -um**	**XVIII**
duodeviginti	**duodevicensimus, -a, -um**	**XIX**

* These adjectives are often designated by the term "irregular." The term "variable" is used here to distinguish these adjectives from other irregular adjectives, for which, see below.

** For the forms of **unus**, see variable adjectives, above. **Duo** and **tres** have forms only in the plural.

viginti	**vicesimus, -a, -um**	**XX**
triginta	**tricesimus, -a, -um**	**XXX**
quadraginta	**quadragesimus, -a, -um**	**XL**
quingenta	**quingentesimus, -a, -um**	**L**
sexaginta	**sexagesimus, -a, -um**	**LX**
septuaginta	**septuagesimus, -a., -um**	**LXX**
octaginta	**octogesimus, -a, -um**	**LXXX**
nonaginta	**nonagesimus, -a, -um**	**XC**
centum	**centesimus, -a, -um**	**C**
quingenti, -ae, -a	**quingentesimus, -a, -um**	**D**
mille	**millesimus, -a, -um**	**M**

Adjectives with Expressions of Comparison

- Comparison with **quam**

  Aliquae herbae altiores quam arbores sunt.

  Some plants are taller than trees.

Note that the two items compared, **herbae** and **arbores**, are in the same case.

- Ablative of Comparison

  Aliquae herbae altiores arboribus sunt.

  Some plants are taller than trees.

Note that the two items compared, **herbae** and **arboribus**, are not in the same case, but that the second item, **arboribus**, is in the ablative and that **quam** has been omitted.

- Ablative of Degree of Difference

  Aliquae herbae multo altiores quam arbores sunt.

  Some plants are much taller (taller by much) than trees.

  Aliquae herbae paulo altiores quam arbores sunt.

  Some plants are a little taller (taller by a little) than trees.

- Superlative with **omnium**

  Illa arbor altissima omnium est.

  That tree is the tallest of all.

- **Quam** + superlative

  Rami illius arboris quam latissimi sunt.

  The branches of that tree are as widely-spread as possible, or *as widely-spread as (they) can be.*

Translation of Comparative and Superlative Adjectives

- Comparative adjectives are usually rendered in English with the suffix *–er*, e.g., **celerior**, *faster,* or with the helping words *more, rather,* or *too,* e.g., **gravior**, *more serious*, **facilior**, *rather easy*, or **saevior**, *too cruel*. Choose the meaning that best fits the context.
- Superlative adjectives are traditionally rendered in English with the suffix *–est*, e.g., **celerrimus**, *fastest,* or with the helping words *most* or *very*, e.g., **gravissimus**, *most serious*, or **facillimus**, *very easy.*

Quick Study of the Comparison of Irregular Adjectives

Positive	Comparative	Superlative
bonus, -a, -um, *good*	**melior, melius**, *better*	**optimus, -a, -um**, *best*
malus, -a, -um, *bad*	**peior, peius**, *worse*	**pessimus, -a, -um**, *worst*
magnus, -a, -um, *big*	**maior, maius**, *bigger*	**maximus, -a, -um**, *biggest*
parvus, -a, -um, *small*	**minor, minus**, *smaller*	**minimus, -a, -um**, *smallest*
multus, -a, -um, *many, much*	**plus, pluris** (gen.), *more*	**plurimus, -a, -um**, *most*

Practice Questions: Adjectives

1. Roma ____ quam Pompeii erat.

   (A) paulo minor (C) multo minor

   (B) paulo maior (D) multo maior

2. Hard work overcomes <u>all things</u>.

   (A) omnes (C) omnia

   (B) omni (D) omnibus

3. Was Caesar a better orator <u>than Cicero</u>?

   (A) Cicerone (C) quam Cicerone

   (B) Cicero (D) Ciceronem

4. Eratne Caesar ____ omnium Romanorum?
   (A) nobilissimus (C) nobilissimum
   (B) nobilius (D) nobilior

5. Bonum is to melius as multum is to
   (A) plurimus (C) plurimum
   (B) plurium (D) plus

6. The genitive singular of alter is
   (A) alteri (C) alteris
   (B) alterius (D) altero

7. Pauci sed boni.
   (A) The few are the good.
   (B) Few men, but good ones.
   (C) The good are few.
   (D) Few possessions, but good ones.

8. Facile consilium damus alii.
   (A) We give easy advice to others.
   (B) We are giving someone else advice about that which is easy.
   (C) We give advice to another easily.
   (D) The easiest advice is that which we give to others.

9. Estne Mons Olympus altior quam ____ ?
   (A) Monte Vesuvio (C) Mons Vesuvius
   (B) Montem Vesuvium (D) Montis Vesuvii

10. Which of the following is not a possible meaning of lentius?
    (A) too slowly (C) slower
    (B) rather slow (D) very slowly

Practice with Agreement of Adjectives in the *Aeneid*

Identify the Latin noun, stated or implied, described by each modifier underlined in the following passage. Then translate the noun-adjective combination.

Passage 1

Atlas, Man and Mountain

(Mercurius) iamque volans apicem et latera ardua cernit
Atlantis duri, caelum qui vertice fulcit,
Atlantis, cinctum assidue cui nubibus atris
piniferum caput et vento pulsatur et imbri;
nix umeros infusa tegit; tum flumina mento
praecipitant senis, et glacie riget horrida barba.

Vergil, *Aeneid* 4.246–251

volans ______________ Translation: ______________________________

ardua ______________ Translation: ______________________________

dur ______________ Translation: ______________________________

cinctum ______________ Translation: ______________________________

atris ______________ Translation: ______________________________

piniferum ______________ Translation: ______________________________

infusa ______________ Translation: ______________________________

horrida ______________ Translation: ______________________________

Passage 2

Cyellene's Offspring

Hic primum paribus nitens Cyllenius alis
constitit; hinc toto praeceps se corpore ad undas
misit avi similis, quae circum litora, circum
piscosos scopulos humilis volat aequora iuxta.
Haud aliter terras inter caelumque volabat
litus harenosum ad Libyae, ventosque secabat
materno veniens ab avo Cyllenia proles.

Vergil, *Aeneid* 4.252–258

paribus ______________ Translation: ______________________________

nitens ______________ Translation: ______________________________

toto ______________ Translation: ______________________________

praeceps ______________ Translation: ______________________________

similis ______________ Translation: ______________________________

piscosos ______________ Translation: ______________________________

humilis ______________ Translation: ______________________
harenosum____________ Translation: ______________________
materno ______________ Translation: ______________________
Cyllenia ______________ Translation: ______________________

Adverbs

Quick Study – Comparison of Regular Adjectives and Adverbs

	Adjectives of the 1st and 2nd Declensions	Adverbs
Positive	**laetus, -a, -um,** *happy*	**laete,** *happily*
Comparative	**laetior, laetior, laetius,** *happier*	**laetius,** *more happily*
Superlative	**laetissimus, -a, -um,** *happiest*	**laetissime,** *most happily*
	Adjectives of the 3rd Declension	**Adverbs**
Positive	**brevis, brevis, breve,** *short*	**breviter,** *shortly*
Comparative	**brevior, brevior, brevius,** *shorter*	**brevius,** *more shortly*
Superlative	**brevissimus, -a, -um,** *shortest*	**brevissime,** *most shortly*

Note:

- If the stem of a 3rd declension adjective ends in **–nt**, e.g., **diligent**- (from **diligens, diligentis**), the positive adverb adds -**er**, e.g., **diligenter**.

Uses of Adverbs

Adverbs answer the questions When?, Where?, or How? They usually modify verbs, but they can also modify adjectives or other adverbs:

With a verb: **Arbores in umbra lente crescunt.**

Trees grow slowly in the shade.

With an adjective: **Quam nobile serere arborem est!**

How noble it is to plant a tree!

With another adverb: **Ita vero, nihil tam pulchra quam arbor est.**

Truly yes, there is nothing so lovely as a tree.

Some adverbs have only a positive form, such as **heri, hodie,** or **cras**, whereas those which derive from adjectives have comparative and superlative forms that approximate their fellow adjectives. (See the chart above.) In English, adverbs derived from adjectives are usually translated by adding *–ly* to the meaning, e.g., **lente**, *slowly.*

Some Common Adverbs

Time

aliquando *at some time*
interdiu *during the day*
mane *in the morning, early*
meridie *at midday*
nocte *at night*
vesperi *in the evening*
diu *for a long time*
paulisper *for a short time*
sero *late*
iam *now, already*
iterum *again*
mox *soon, presently*
nonnumquam *sometimes*
numquam *never*
nunc *now*
saepe *often*
semper *always*
tum *then*
tunc *then*
umquam *ever*
cotidie *daily*
cras *tomorrow*
heri *yesterday*
hodie *today*
postridie *the next day*
adhuc *still*
quamdiu *how long*
quando *when*
ubi *when*

Place

hic *here, in this place*
ibi *there*
ubi *where*
eo *to that place*
huc *to this place*
quo *to what place*
hinc *from this place*
inde *from that place*
unde *from what place*
nusquam *nowhere*
undique *everywhere*
usquam *anywhere*
usque *all the way to*

Manner

cur *why*
magis *more*
quam *how*
ita *so*
itaque *therefore*
paene *almost*
quomodo *how*
sic *so, thus*
valde *very, greatly*
vix *scarcely, hardly*

Quick Study – Comparison of Irregular Adjectives and Adverbs

	Positive	Comparative	Superlative
	M F N	**M & F N**	**M F N**
Adjective	**bonus, -a, -um**, *good*	**melior, melius,** *better*	**optimus, -a, -um,** *best*
Adverb	**bene,** *well*	**melius,** *better*	**optime,** *best*
Adjective	**malus, -a, -um,** *bad*	**peior, peius,** *worse*	**pessimus, -a, -um,** *worst*
Adverb	**male,** *badly*	**peius,** *worse*	**pessime,** *worst*
Adjective	**magnus, -a, -um,** *great*	**maior, maius,** *greater*	**maximus, -a, -um,** *greatest*
Adverb	**magnopere,** *greatly*	**magis,** *more*	**maxime,** *most*
Adjective	**parvus, -a, -um,** *small*	**minor, minus,** *smaller*	**minimus, -a, -um,** *smallest*
Adverb	**paulum,** *little*	**minus,** *less*	**minime,** *least*
Adjective	**multus, -a, -um,** *many, much*	**plus** (**pluris**, gen.), *more*	**plurimus, -a, -um,** *most*
Adverb	**multum,** *much*	**plus,** *more*	**plurimum,** *most*

N.B. Be aware that a few adjectives are compared by using the adverbs **magis**, *more*, and **maxime**, *most*, e.g., **magis idoneus**, *more suitable*, and **maxime idoneus**, *most suitable*.

Practice Questions: Adjectives and Adverbs

1. Flores in horto prope arbores <u>dulces</u> redolent odores. Based on the sense, the noun modified by <u>dulces</u> is

   (A) Flores
   (B) horto
   (C) arbores
   (D) odores

2. Crescuntne flores <u>celerius</u> arboribus?

   (A) quickly
   (B) more quickly
   (C) as quickly as
   (D) most quickly

3. The form of the adverb that means <u>too easily</u> is

(A) facilius
(C) facillime
(B) facilis
(D) magis facilis

4. Which of the following adverbs has a meaning pertaining to place?

(A) postridie
(C) undique
(B) paulisper
(D) vix

5. <u>Italia est pulcherrima</u> means

(A) Italy is rather beautiful.
(C) Italy is too beautiful.
(B) Italy is very beautiful.
(D) Italy is beautiful.

6. Nonne sol maior <u>quam luna</u> est? The best substitute for the underlined phrase is

(A) lunā
(C) lunam
(B) luna
(D) lunae

7. Illud opus in horto non ____ est.

(A) facilis
(C) facile
(B) facilium
(D) facilibus

8. The positive adverb of the adjective <u>gravis</u> is

(A) grave
(C) graviter
(B) gravius
(D) gravidus

9. <u>Libere, liberius, liberrime</u>.

(A) freely, very freely, too freely
(B) freely, too freely, relatively freely
(C) free, rather free, very free
(D) freely, rather freely, most freely

10. Hoc flumen ____ quam illud fluit.

(A) lentior
(C) lente
(B) lentissime
(D) lentius

11. Heri vesperi per ripam <u>quam diutissime</u> ambulabamus.

(A) for a long time
(C) for a very long time
(B) for as long as possible
(D) for a rather long time

12. Canis nomine Fido ____ est.
    - (A) fidelissimus omnium
    - (B) fidelissimus omnibus
    - (C) fidelissime omnium
    - (D) maxime fidelis omnium

13. Parvus is to paulum as magnus is to
    - (A) magis
    - (B) maxime
    - (C) magnopere
    - (D) magnum

14. Multa ignoscendo fit potens potentior. (Publilius Syrus)
    - (A) Many things become more powerful through forgiveness.
    - (B) By being forgetful of power, many become more powerful.
    - (C) By forgiving many things, a powerful man becomes more powerful.
    - (D) Being so powerful over many things, he becomes forgiving.

15. Hi horti ____ quam illi sunt. Qui horti ____ omnium sunt?
    - (A) minores / minimi
    - (B) minori / minimorum
    - (C) minores / minime
    - (D) minoribus / minimi

16. Scribe saepissime.
    - (A) often
    - (B) very often
    - (C) as often as possible
    - (D) more often

17. Suntne canes ferociores quam feles?
    - (A) more fierce
    - (B) fierce
    - (C) more fiercely
    - (D) fiercest

18. Diligens: diligenter :: malus : _____.
    - (A) peius
    - (B) pessime
    - (C) male
    - (D) peior

19. Hic miles more seriously quam ille vulneratus est.
    - (A) gravis
    - (B) graviter
    - (C) gravior
    - (D) gravius

20. Haec femina _____ omnium est.
    - (A) felicissima
    - (B) felix
    - (C) felicior
    - (D) feliciora

21. Eratne Socrates sapientior _____?
    (A) Cicero
    (B) Ciceronem
    (C) Cicerone
    (D) Ciceronis

22. Vinum illius cauponis _____ quam huius est.
    (A) suavius
    (B) suaviorem
    (C) suavior
    (D) suavissimum

23. Equi velociter currebant.
    (A) very swiftly
    (B) more swiftly
    (C) rather swiftly
    (D) swiftly

24. Num tu cotidie in agris laboras, serve?
    (A) during the day
    (B) every day
    (C) many days
    (D) every other day

25. Boves _____ plaustrum lente trahebant.
    (A) gravis
    (B) gravium
    (C) grave
    (D) gravem

26. Ille senator erat divitissimus. Which meaning of divitissimus is not acceptable?
    (A) very wealthy
    (B) most wealthy
    (C) rather wealthy
    (D) the wealthiest

27. Which word is not an adverb of time?
    (A) aliquando
    (B) adhuc
    (C) numquam
    (D) quo

28. The adverbial equivalent of aegerrimus is
    (A) aegrius
    (B) aegre
    (C) aegerrime
    (D) aegrior

29. The phrase totius urbis is translated
    (A) of the entire city
    (B) from the whole city
    (C) in the entire city
    (D) from all the cities

30. Noster magister est _____.
    (A) intellegenter
    (B) intellegentem
    (C) intellegens
    (D) intellegente

31. Omnia omnibus.
    (A) Everyone wants everything.
    (B) All things to all people.
    (C) We cannot all do everything.
    (D) All for one and one for all.

32. Illud aedificium _____ est.
    (A) parvum (C) minorum
    (B) paulum (D) minor

33. Haec domus <u>multo maior</u> quam illa est.
    (A) much better (C) a little better
    (B) a little bigger (D) much bigger

34. Anna grieved <u>mournfully</u> over the death of her sister.
    (A) maestus (C) maestissima
    (B) maeste (D) maestum

35. Cum non esuriunt, aves <u>better</u> cantant.
    (A) optime (C) meliores
    (B) bene (D) melius

Answers: Adjectives

1. **(D)**

This sentence expresses a comparison between Rome and Pompeii. Since you should know that Rome was much larger than Pompeii, Answer (D) is preferable to (B). Answers (A) **paulo minor** "a little smaller" and (C) **multo minor** "much smaller" are not correct because they are not true. This comparative construction is an example of the ablative of degree of difference. This sentence reads, "Rome was <u>much bigger</u> than Pompeii."

2. **(C)**

Omnia "all things" appears as a substantive in this sentence. Answer (A) **omnes** can be accusative plural, as required, but would have the meaning "all people" as the masculine/feminine form. Answer (B) is dative or ablative singular and (D) dative or ablative plural, neither of which fits the meaning of "all things" as the direct object in this sentence.

3. **(A)**

Cicerone is an ablative of comparison. Answer (B) is only possible if it is accompanied by **quam**, which it is not. In (C), both options that express comparison appear together, i.e., **quam** and the ablative, which is incorrect. Answer (D) is genitive and irrelevant to the required English meaning.

4. **(A)**

"Was Caesar the most noble Roman of all?" The appearance of **omnium** in this sentence keys the need for the superlative adjective "most . . . of all." Based on the answers provided, a form of the adjective **nobilis** is missing. This adjective must modify **Romanus**, which is a nominative in apposition to the subject **Caesar**. This requirement eliminates (C), which is a superlative adjective, but in the accusative case. Answers (B) and (D) are comparative forms, respectively, neither of which correctly completes the idiomatic use with **omnium**. Because of its similarity to **Romanus**, the neuter comparative form **nobilius** surely distracted you!

5. **(D)**

This analogy compares positive and comparative forms of irregular adjectives in the neuter gender. As **melius** is the comparative form of **bonum**, you are asked to provide the comparative form of **multum** "much," which is **plus** "more." Answers (A) and (C) are both superlative, not comparative, and in (B) the genitive plural form **plurium** is reminiscent of the nominative or accusative singular neuter ending **–um**, but the declension is wrong.

6. **(B)**

Alter is an irregular adjective, which takes the unexpected genitive and dative singular endings of **–ius** and **–i**, respectively. The remaining forms of **alter, altera, alterum** have endings of the regular first/second declension adjective. Answer (A) is nominative or dative, (C) dative or ablative plural, and (D) ablative singular, which are all inconsistent with the requested genitive singular form.

7. **(B)**

This sentence contains examples of adjectives used as substantives. **Pauci** = "the few" or "few people," just as **boni** means "the good" or "good people." The sentence reads, "Few men, but good ones." (A form of the verb **esse** is often understood in mottoes.) Answers (A) and (C) omit the conjunction **sed** from their translations and (D) would require that the substantives be neuter, as implied by the word "possessions," i.e., goods.

8. **(C)**

This sentence provides an example of the neuter form of the adjective **facilis** used as an adverb, **facile,** "easily." In Answer (A) **alii** cannot be translated as "to others," which would require the dative plural form **aliis**. The translation in Answer (B) does not render **facile** correctly. Answer (D) "easiest" translates the superlative and not the positive degree as required by the form **facile** in the sentence. Also, as mentioned, "to others" is not the correct translation of **alii**.

9. **(C)**

The appearance of **quam** requires that the answer be **Mons Vesuvius**, which is nominative singular, as is its partner in the comparison, **Mons Olympus**. Answer (A) is a distractor, designed to insure that you discriminate the **quam** comparison from the ablative of comparison.The accusative and genitive answers in (B) and (D) are irrelevant.

10. **(D)**

Answer (D), "very slowly," is a superlative adverb, whereas **lentius** is either a comparative adverb, as translated in Answers (A) and (B), or a neuter comparative adjective, as in Answer (C).

Answers to Practice with Agreement of Adjectives

Passage 1

volans	(Mercurius)	Translation:	(Mercury) flying or in flight
ardua	latera	Translation:	steep sides
duri	Atlantis	Translation:	of sturdy Atlas
cinctum	caput	Translation:	(his) head/summit girded/encircled
atris	nubibus	Translation:	with dark clouds
piniferum	caput	Translation:	pine-wreathed head/summit
infusa	nix	Translation:	fallen snow
horrida	barba	Translation:	rough/shaggy beard

Passage 2

paribus	alis	Translation:	on even/equal/balanced wings
nitens	Cyllenius	Translation:	the Cyllenian, striving
toto	corpore	Translation:	with his whole body
praeceps	(Mercurius)	Translation:	(Mercury), headlong/headfirst
similis	(Mercurius)	Translation:	(Mercury) like a (bird)
piscosos	scopulos	Translation:	fish-dwelling cliffs
humilis	(Mercurius)	Translation:	(Mercury flies) low
harenosum	litus	Translation:	sandy shore
materno	avo	Translation:	from his maternal grandfather (mother's father)
Cyllenia	proles	Translation:	Cyllene's offspring

Answers: Adjectives and Adverbs, Questions 1–15

1. Adjective **(D)**

This sentence reads, "The flowers in the garden near the trees give off a sweet scent." Based purely on the ending, the adjective **dulces** could modify **Flores, arbores**, or **odores**, but based upon the sense, **odores** is the most likely noun modified. The position of the noun **odores**, perhaps a poetic counterpart to **Flores** at the front of the sentence, is meant to distract you, as **odores** would logically be found beside **dulces**.

2. Adverb **(B)**

The form **celerius** can be a comparative adjective in the nominative or accusative singular neuter form, or a comparative adverb. If **celerius** were an adjective, it would modify either the noun **flores** or the noun **arboribus**, which are neither singular nor neuter. Therefore, **celerius** must be an adverb modifying the verb **crescunt**. As an adverb, the form **celerius** is comparative, hence Answer (B), "more quickly." The Latin of Answer (A) is **celeriter**, the positive adverb, (C) the correlative expression **tam celeriter quam . . .** , and (D) the superlative adverb **celerrime**. The sentence reads, "Do flowers grow more quickly than trees?"

3. Adverb **(A)**

"Too easily" is a comparative ("too") adverb ("easily"). "Too . . ." is one of the options for translating the comparative degree of adjectives and adverbs. Of the forms provided, Answer (A) **facilius** is correct. Answer (B) **facilis** is a positive adjective "easy," (C) **facillime** a superlative adverb "very easily," and (D) **magis facilis** "more easily," which is an improper use of the comparative adverb **magis**.

4. Adverb **(C)**

Answers (A) **postridie** "on the next day" and (B) **paulisper** "for a short while" pertain to time and (D) **vix** "scarcely" expresses manner, leaving **undique** "on all sides" as an adverb answering the question "Where?" and expressing place.

5. Adjective **(B)**

This question tests knowledge of the potential variations used to express the meaning of the superlative adjective. Here, the form is **pulcherrima**. Answers (A), (C), and (D) are all unacceptable. Answers (A) "rather beautiful" and (C) "too beautiful" are variations of ways to express the comparative degree, and Answer (D) "beautiful" expresses the positive degree.

6. Adjective **(A)**

This sentence, which reads "Isn't the sun larger than the moon?" contains an expression of comparison between the sun and the moon. Of the choices offered, only the ablative of comparison, Answer (A) **luna** can substitute for the **quam** comparative construction that appears in the sentence. Answer (B) **luna** is nominative, (C) **lunam** is accusative, and (D) **lunae** genitive or dative.

7. Adjective **(C)**
The demonstrative adjective **illud** reveals the gender of **opus** to be neuter. Therefore, by the rules of agreement, the missing adjective must have a neuter ending. Furthermore, the adjective must have a nominative case ending, because it is modifying the subject, **opus**. The question of degree doesn't arise, because all answers appear in the positive degree. These limitations rule out Answer (A) **facilis**, which does not have a neuter ending, and (D) **facilibus**, which is not singular, but plural. Answer (B) provides distraction because it has an ending that is identifiable as a potential nominative or accusative neuter form of the 2nd declension. However, it is not. **Facilium** is genitive and plural. The sentence reads, "The work in the garden is not easy."

8. Adverb **(C)**
Only two of the four answers can be adverbs: Answers (B) **gravius** the comparative and (C) **graviter** the positive. Since the positive is requested, the correct answer is **graviter**. Answers (A) **grave** and (D) **gravidus** are positive adjectives.

9. Adverb **(D)**
This series represents the sequence of the various degrees of the adverb **libere**. The meaning of the word is irrelevant, as all answers have to do with being free. You should be concerned with 1) the correct part of speech, adjective or adverb, and 2) the appropriate sequence of the translations relative to the forms. Since the forms are adverbs and are given in the standard order of positive, comparative, and superlative, the correct answer is (D). Answer (C) translates adjectives, rather than adverbs. Answer (A) reverses the comparative and superlative and (B) gives redundant translations of the comparative form.

10. Adverb **(D)**
The need for a comparative adverb to accompany **quam illud** in order to complete the meaning of the sentence, "This river flows more slowly than that one," leads to Answer (D) **lentius**. Answer (A) **lentior** is comparative, but is an adjective. Answers (B) **lentissime** and (C) **lente** are incorrect forms of the degree of the adverb required by the context here.

11. Adverb **(B)**
The idiomatic expression **quam** + superlative is translated "as . . . as possible," which makes Answer (B) **quam diutissime** correct. Answer (A) requires the positive adverb **diu**, (B) the superlative adverb **diutissime** by itself, and (D) the comparative adverb **diutius**. The sentence reads, "Yesterday evening we walked along the riverbank for as long as possible."

12. Adjective **(A)**
Given the answers, the missing part of the sentence is the common phrase containing the superlative adjective plus the genitive plural form **omnium**, ". . . -est of all." The best immediate choices are (A) and (C), both of which contain a superlative. Answer (A) is correct because Answer (C) **fidelissime** is an adverb,

and an adjective is needed to modify **Fido**, as the sense suggests. Answer (B) **fidelissimus omnibus** contains the wrong form of **omnis** and (D) provides a tempting, but incorrect, phrase using the superlative adverb **maxime**.

13. Adjective **(C)**
As **paulum** "little" is the positive adverb corresponding to the positive irregular adjective **parvus** "small" you are looking for the adverbial equivalent of the positive irregular adjective **magnus** "big." This is Answer (C) **magnopere**, "greatly." Answer (A) **magis** is the comparative adverb formed from **magnus**, (B) is the superlative adverb formed from **magnus**, and (D) **magnum** is the positive adjective of **magnus** in the neuter form, which matches, incorrectly, with the positive adverb **paulum**.

14. Adjective **(C)**
Don't let the gerund in this sentence fool you into translating the adjectives incorrectly. **Multa** is used as a substantive, "many things," here, as is **potens**, "a/the powerful man." In Answer (A), the translation makes **multa** the subject, which it is not possible because the verb **fit** is singular. This version also omits the word **potens**. In Answer (B), the object of **ignoscendo** is "many things," not "power," nor does **potentior** agree with **multa**. Answer (D) omits the word **potentior** and ignores the substantive adjective **potens** as the subject of the verb **fit**. The sentence reads, "By overlooking many things (or much), a powerful (man) becomes more powerful."

15. Adjective **(A)**
Read these sentences as, "These gardens are smaller than those. Which gardens are the smallest of all?" These translations require comparative and superlative forms of the irregular adjective **parvus** to complete their meanings. In both sentences, the adjectives modify the nominative subject **horti**. Answer (B) **minori** is not a nominative form, but dative, and **minimorum** is genitive. The missing adjective in the second sentence must modify **horti** and not the genitive plural form **omnium**. Answer (C) contains an adverb **minime** and Answer (D) **minoribus** is in the ablative case, which is a diversion to fool you into considering the possible need for the ablative of comparison here.

Answers to Practice Questions: Adjectives and Adverbs, Questions 16–35

16. (C)	21. (C)	26. (C)	31. (B)
17. (A)	22. (A)	27. (D)	32. (C)
18. (C)	23. (D)	28. (C)	33. (D)
19. (D)	24. (B)	29. (A)	34. (B)
20. (A)	25. (C)	30. (C)	35. (D)

Chapter 15

Indicative Mood of Verbs: Active and Passive

The Indicative Mood

This chapter is devoted to helping you recall the forms and meanings of regular finite verbs in the indicative mood, which is the most common category of verbs in Latin. The indicative mood can express either a fact or an assertion or a direct question. There are two voices and six tenses of the indicative, active and passive. Because indicative verbs are the most frequently found in Latin, you probably learned these first and extended from them your knowledge of additional verb forms. The assumption is made here that you are generally acquainted with the grammatical terms voice, mood, tense, person, and number as they apply to verbs. Note: the forms and meanings of participles, infinitives, and irregular verbs, as well as the imperative and subjunctive moods, will be covered in subsequent chapters.

Active and Passive Voice

Voice is the aspect of the verb that expresses who is doing the action. The active voice expresses the doer of the action and the passive voice expresses the action of the verb as done to the subject:

Active: **Multas aves in prato vidimus.**
We saw many birds in the meadow.

Passive: **Multae aves a nobis in prato visae sunt.**
Many birds were seen by us in the meadow.

In the form charts provided below, the third conjugation verb **mitto, mittere, misi, missus** is used as an example because verbs from this conjugation appear most often in Latin literature. For the forms of verbs in the other conjugations, consult your textbook or grammar reference.

Principal Parts, Stems, and Tenses

The principal parts of a verb are the keys to understanding its formation.

1st princ. pt.	2nd princ. pt	3rd princ. pt	4th princ. pt.
mitto	**mittere**	**misi**	**missus**
1st person singular present tense active *I send*	present active infinitive present stem **mitte-** *to send*	1st person singular perfect tense active perfect stem **mis-** *I sent*	perfect passive participle *having been sent*

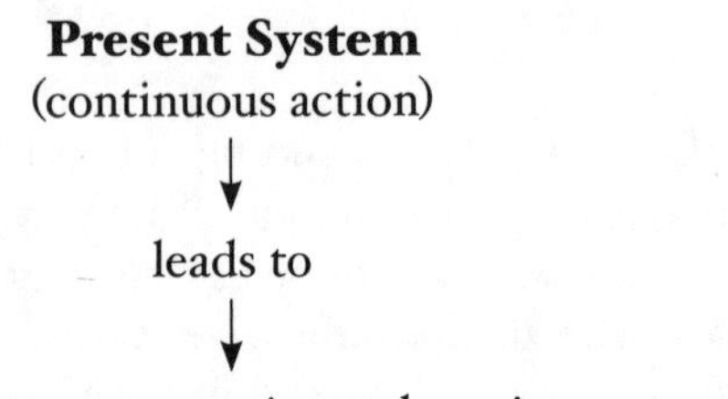

Present System
(continuous action)
↓
leads to
↓
Present tense, active and passive
Imperfect tense, active and passive
Future tense, active and passive

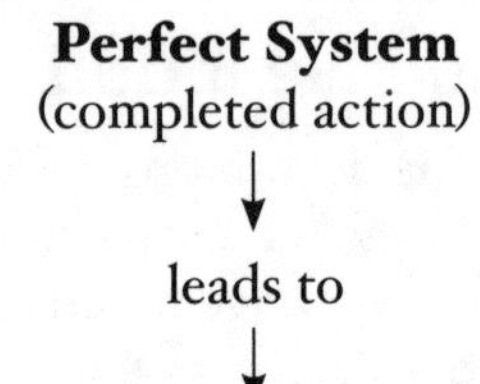

Perfect System
(completed action)
↓
leads to
↓
Perfect tense, active and passive
Pluperfect tense, active and passive
Future perfect tense, active and passive

Note: The pluperfect tense expresses an action completed before another past action, while the future perfect tense expresses an action completed before another future action.

Personal Endings

There are several different sets of personal endings for a Latin verb. The meanings of these endings, respectively, are *I, you (alone), he/she/it*, and *we, you (all), they*.

Present System, Active		Perfect Tense, Active		Present System, Passive	
Sing.	Pl.	Sing.	Pl.	Sing.	Pl.
-o or **–m**	**-mus**	**-i**	**-imus**	**-r**	**-mur**
-s	**-tis**	**-isti**	**-istis**	**-ris**	**-mini**
-t	**-nt**	**-it**	**-erunt**	**-tur**	**-ntur**
For all tenses of the active voice except for perfect and for the perfect system of the passive		For perfect active		For present, imperfect, future passive	

Translating Latin Verbs in the Indicative Mood

A synopsis is a summary of representative forms of a verb, given in the same person and number. Here is a synopsis of the main forms of the verb **mitto** in the 3rd person singular.

Active Voice

Continuous Action

Present	**mittit**	*he sends, is sending, does send*
Imperfect	**mittebat**	*he was sending, used to send, kept on sending*
Future	**mittet**	*he will send*

Completed Action

Perfect	**misit**	*he sent, has sent*
Pluperfect	**miserat**	*he had sent*
Future Perfect	**miserit**	*he will have sent*

Passive Voice

Continuous Action

Present	**mittitur**	*he is sent, is being sent*
Imperfect	**mittebatur**	*he was sent, was being sent*
Future	**mittetur**	*he will be sent*

Completed Action

Perfect	**missus est**	*he has been sent, was sent*
Pluperfect	**missa erat**	*she had been sent*
Future Perfect	**missum erit**	*it will have been sent*

Translating Ambiguous Verb Forms in the Indicative Mood

Pay special attention to forms of the indicative that are, or appear to be, ambiguous.

Forms of the imperfect and future tenses, e.g.,

susurrabat	vs.	**susurrabit**
he was whispering		*he will whisper*

Forms of the present and perfect tenses in the 3rd singular, e.g.,

Labor omnia vincit.	vs.	**Labor omnia vicit.**
he *conquers*		*he conquered*

Legit volumen. vs. **Lēgit volumen.**

He reads the scroll. *He has read the scroll.*

Forms of the present and future tenses, e.g.,

persuadet vs. **credet**

he convinces *he will believe*

regeris vs. **regēris**

you are being ruled *you will be ruled*

Forms of the 3rd plural, e.g.,

erunt, *they will be*

viderunt, *they have seen*

visi erunt, *they will have been seen*

as well as

viderant, *they had seen*

viderint, *they will have seen*

Forms of the passive voice, e.g.,

monentur vs. **monitae sunt**

they are warned *they have been warned* (not *they are warned*)

Forms of the active and passive voices, e.g.,

miseris vs. **mitteris**

you will have sent *you are being sent*

mittēris

you will be sent

"Telling the Future"

The future tense of third conjugation verbs is often confused with the present tense of verbs of the second conjugation. Here are some tips to help you to distinguish between the two.

- Know the principal parts of the verbs in question. In a second conjugation verb, e.g., **docet,** the vowel **-e-** is the stem vowel of the present tense, as indicated in the first principal part **doceo**. In a third conjugation verb, e.g., **discet**, the vowel **-e-** represents the future tense.
- Look for other indications of the future tense in the context of the sentence, e.g., the adverb **cras**, *tomorrow,* or a verb having a more obvious form of the future tense, e.g., **docebit**.
- Guess future! There are many more verbs in the third conjugation than in the second, making it much more likely that a verb with an **-e-** vowel is in the future tense than in the present.

Note: Future time may also be expressed by the use of the so-called active periphrastic, consisting of the future participle + forms of **esse**, e.g., **missurus est**, *he is about to send, going to send*. The active periphrastic is a more emphatic or definitive expression of the future tense. The future participle will be covered in a forthcoming chapter.

Quick Study Synopsis of an Indicative Verb in the Active and Passive Voices

	Active	Passive
	mitto, mittere, misi, missus	
Present System		
Present	**mittit**, *he is sending, sends*	**mittitur**, *he is being sent, is sent*
Imperfect	**mittebat**, *he was sending*	**mittebatur,** *he was being sent, was sent*
Future	**mittet,** *he will send*	**mittetur,** *he will be sent*
Perfect System		
Perfect	**misit,** *he sent, has sent, did send*	**missus est,** *he has been sent, was sent*
Pluperfect	**miserat,** *he had sent*	**missus erat,** *he had been sent*
Fut. Perf.	**miserit**, *he will have sent*	**missus erit,** *he will have been sent*

Practice Questions: Indicative Verbs

These questions approximate the types of questions on indicative verbs that are found in the multiple-choice section of the AP Latin Exam.

1. The future passive equivalent of <u>scribit</u> is

   (A) scribitur (C) scriptus est

   (B) scribebatur (D) scribetur

2. The perfect tense equivalent of <u>audis</u> is

   (A) auditus est (C) audiebas

   (B) audivisti (D) auditis

3. Hodie <u>legisti</u> librum quem heri emeras.

   (A) you are reading (C) you will read

   (B) you did read (D) you want to read

4. The active equivalent of tenebamini is
   (A) tenebas (C) tenetis
   (B) tenebatis (D) tenebaris

5. The active of positum erat is
   (A) ponebat (C) posuerat
   (B) ponebatur (D) ponit

6. Pater suum filium cognoverat.
   (A) recognized (C) has recognized
   (B) had recognized (D) was recognizing

7. Vocabamur a parentibus nostris.
   (A) We will be called (C) We were called
   (B) We are called (D) We were calling

8. The plural of tenuit is
   (A) tenuerant (C) tenuerint
   (B) tenuerunt (D) tenent

9. Prima luce sol surget.
   (A) arose (C) has risen
   (B) will rise (D) rises

10. The future tense of duco is
    (A) ducam (C) ducemus
    (B) ducebam (D) ducor

11. Dormiebatne ignavus discipulus?
    (A) Will . . . sleep? (C) Was . . . sleeping?
    (B) Can . . . sleep? (D) Were . . . sleeping?

12. The personal subject of trahimini is
    (A) tu (C) nos
    (B) ego (D) vos

13. Proximo mense ad Hispaniam mittēris.
    (A) you will be sent (C) you will have sent
    (B) you are being sent (D) you will send

14. The singular of parabamus is
    (A) paramus (C) paro
    (B) parabo (D) parabam

15. Which of the following belongs to the second conjugation?
    (A) custodio (C) iungo
    (B) navigo (D) iubeo

16. The passive of portaverunt is
    (A) portati erant (C) portati erunt
    (B) portati sunt (D) portantur

17. Quinque dies Capuae mansi.
    (A) I am staying (C) I stayed
    (B) Stay (D) To have stayed

18. Di homines semper amaverint.
    (A) they had loved (C) they will have loved
    (B) they did love (D) they will love

19. Baculum a cane receptum est.
    (A) has been fetched (C) is being fetched
    (B) had been fetched (D) has fetched

20. Si ad Cretam navigaveris, a piratis capieris.
    (A) you are being captured (C) you are capturing
    (B) you will have captured (D) you will be captured

Answers to Practice Questions: Indicative Verbs

1.	(D)	5.	(C)	9.	(B)	13.	(A)	17.	(C)
2.	(B)	6.	(B)	10.	(A)	14.	(D)	18.	(C)
3.	(B)	7.	(C)	11.	(C)	15.	(D)	19.	(A)
4.	(B)	8.	(B)	12.	(D)	16.	(B)	20.	(D)

Chapter 16

Deponent Verbs

Overview

Deponent verbs have "put aside" (**deponere**) their active forms and passive meanings. Therefore, they are verbs that have only passive forms and active meanings, e.g., **loquitur**, *he is speaking* (not *he is being spoken*). Such verbs have also been called "fake passives." Deponent verbs occur in all four conjugations and have the same forms as regular passive verbs. Even forms such as the perfect passive participle have active meanings, e.g., **locutus**, *having spoken* (not *having been spoken*). Be aware that some non-deponent verbs have an active meaning in both active and passive forms, e.g., **video**, *I see*, and **videor**, *I seem*. Imperatives, participles, and infinitives of deponent verbs will be covered in later chapters.

Deponent Verbs

Note that deponent verbs have only three principal parts:

loquor (*I speak*, first person singular, present tense passive)

loqui (*to speak*, present passive infinitive)

locutus sum (*I have spoken*, first person singular, perfect tense passive)

As with non-deponent verbs, the conjugation of a deponent verb is determined from its second principal part, e.g., **conari**, **vereri**, **loqui**, and **experiri**. The deponent verb given above belongs to the third conjugation because its present infinitive form is **loqui**. (The forms of passive and deponent infinitives will be discussed further in Chapter 23.) The present active stem is then **loque-** (from the hypothetical present active infinitive form **loquere**). The deponent verb has a present active stem that is used in some forms, such as the gerundive, e.g., **loquendum**, or the imperfect subjunctive, e.g., **loqueretur**. There are no deponent verbs in English, but there are a large number in Latin, many of which are found in compound forms. Here is an example of how deponent verbs are translated in context:

Glukos medicus se ipsum curare conatus est. Mortuus est.

Dr. Glukos tried to cure himself. He died.

Synopsis of a Deponent Verb

loquor, loqui, locutus sum	
Present	**loquuntur**, *they are speaking*
Imperfect	**loquebantur**, *they were speaking*
Future	**loquentur**, *they will speak*
Perfect	**locuti sunt**, *they have spoken*
Pluperfect	**locuti erant**, *they had spoken*
Future Perfect	**locuti erunt**, *they will have spoken*

Common Deponent Verbs

First Conjugation

arbitror, arbitrari, arbitratus sum, *think, judge*
conor, conari, conatus sum, *try, attempt*
hortor, hortari, hortatus sum, *encourage, urge on*
miror, mirari, miratus sum, *wonder*
moror, morari, moratus sum, *stay, remain*

Second Conjugation

polliceor, polliceri, pollicitus sum, *promise*
reor, reri, ratus sum, *think*
tueor, tueri, tutus sum, *protect, aid*
vereor, vereri, veritus sum, *fear, be afraid*

Third Conjugation

labor, labi, lapsus sum, *fall, slip*
loquor, loqui, locutus sum, *speak, talk*
nanciscor, nancisci, nactus sum, *obtain*
nascor, nasci, natus sum, *be born*
obliviscor, oblivisci, oblitus sum, *forget*
proficiscor, proficisci, profectus sum, *set out, depart*
queror, queri, questus sum, *complain, lament*
sequor, sequi, secutus sum, *follow*
ulciscor, ulcisci, ultus sum, *avenge*

Third-*io* Conjugation

egredior, egredi, egressus sum, *go out, leave*

ingredior, ingredi, ingressus sum, *go in, enter*

morior, mori, mortuus sum, *die*

patior, pati, passus sum, *endure, suffer, allow*

progredior, progredi, progressus sum, *go forward, proceed*

regredior, regredi, regressus sum, *go back, return*

Fourth Conjugation

experior, experiri, expertus sum, *test, try*

orior, oriri, ortus sum, *rise, get up*

Some Special Deponent Verbs

Semi-Deponent Verbs

The subcategory of deponent verbs called semi-deponents consists of verbs that are active in the present system and passive in the perfect system, e.g., **audeo, audere, ausus sum**, *I dare, to dare, I (have) dared.* In addition to **audeo**, the most common semi-deponents are **gaudeo, gaudere, gavisus sum**, *rejoice, be glad*, and **soleo, solere, solitus sum**, *be accustomed*, all of which belong to the second conjugation. Be careful to distinguish between **audeo** and **audio**!

> **Nuper vespillo Diaulus nunc medicus fieri ausus est.**
> *Diaulus, recently an undertaker, now has dared to become a doctor.*

Deponent Verbs with the Ablative Case

A small number of deponent verbs take their direct objects in the ablative case, rather than the accusative.

> **Symmachus discipulis qui manus gelatas habebant utebatur.**
> *Symmachus kept using apprentices who had cold hands.*

These verbs are:

fruor, frui, fructus sum (+ abl.), *enjoy, have benefit of*

fungor, fungi, functus sum (+ abl.), *perform, discharge*

potior, potiri, potitus sum (+ abl. gen.), *obtain, get possession of*

utor, uti, usus sum (+ abl.) *use, make use of*

vescor, vesci (+ abl.), *eat, feed on*

Note:

- Use the memory device PUFFV ("puffy") to remember these deponent verbs with the ablative case.*

* David Pellegrino, http://latinteach.com/

Several Additional Points

1) Note that the common deponent **morior** in the perfect system means *is dead* as well as *died*, i.e., **mortuus est** means *he is dead*, as well as *he died.*
2) The verb **videre** has a special sense when it appears in the passive, i.e., *to be seen* means *to seem*. In its passive forms, this verb can behave like a deponent verb, i.e., it can have an active meaning: **videor, videri, visus sum**, *I seem, to seem, I have seemed.*

Tips on Translating Deponent Verbs

Deponent verbs may be recognized through familiarity or from context. First, know the principal parts of the most common deponents, i.e., know which verbs are deponent. Secondly, use common sense to help you to determine whether a verb is passive or deponent, e.g.,

Aegri multum dolorem patiebantur.

The sick were enduring much pain.

You can deduce the fact that **patiebantur** is deponent because its meaning as a passive verb, *were being endured*, does not make sense in this context.

- Be alert to the peculiarities of some deponent verbs, e.g., semi-deponents and deponents with ablative objects.
- When working with deponent verbs, take care to distinguish among those that look alike, e.g., **miror,** *wonder at*, **morior,** *die*, and **moror,** *delay*, or **nanciscor,** *obtain*, and **nascor,** *be born*.

Practice Questions: Deponent Verbs

1. Iuvenalis loquebatur, "Mens sana in corpore sano."

   (A) was said (C) was saying

   (B) will say (D) kept on being said

2. Glukos in cubiculum ingressus est ut cum aegra Anemia loqueretur.

   (A) entered (C) has been entered

   (B) is entering (D) having entered

3. "Anemia, it is important for you to get out of the house every day," advised Glukos.

   (A) egredere (C) egressus esse

   (B) egrediendi (D) egredi

4. Anemia mortua ad inferos a Mercurio ducetur.
   (A) will lead (C) is leading
   (B) is led (D) will be led

5. Quamobrem Mercurius ____ potitus est?
   (A) caduceum (C) caduceos
   (B) caduceo (D) caduceorum

6. Vererisne mori? The closest meaning to that of the underlined word is
   (A) Timetisne (C) Timebisne
   (B) Timesne (D) Timeresne

7. Aesculapius omnes Romanos tuetur.
   (A) will protect (C) is being protected
   (B) should protect (D) protects

8. Medici Romani se ipsos curare ausi sunt.
   (A) were dared (C) have been dared
   (B) dared (D) are daring

Sententiae Antiquae

1. Cura pecuniam crescentem ____ (Horace)
   (A) sequitur (C) secuturus esse
   (B) sequi (D) secutus es

2. Non nobis solum nati sumus. (Cicero)
   (A) we have been born (C) we were being born
   (B) we are being born (D) we had been born

3. In bibliothecis ____ defunctorum immortales animae. (Pliny the Elder)
   (A) loquebatur (C) loquor
   (B) locuti erant (D) loquuntur

4. Non progredi est regredi. (Motto)
   (A) We're advancing backwards rapidly.
   (B) The good old days were best.
   (C) Man never accomplished anything without hard work.
   (D) Forward not backward.

5. "Stick to the subject, the words will follow." (Cato)
   (A) sequuntur
   (B) secuta erunt
   (C) sequantur
   (D) sequentur

Stumper: "O passi graviora, dabit deus his quoque finem!" (Vergil)
   (A) to suffer
   (B) having been suffered
   (C) having suffered
   (D) they suffered

Answers

1. **(C)**

Loquebatur is in the imperfect tense and therefore is translated "he was saying." The sentence reads, "Juvenal was saying, 'A sound mind in a sound body.'" Answers (A) and (D) also express the meaning of the imperfect tense, but in the passive voice, whereas **loquor** is a deponent verb. Answer (B) requires the future tense form **loquetur**.

2. **(A)**

As with verbs in the regular passive voice, verb forms such as **ingressus est** provide the various past tenses of deponent verbs. **Ingressus est** is a form of the perfect tense, therefore Answer (A) "entered" is correct. The sentence reads, "Glukos entered the room to speak with the ill Anemia." Answer (C) is also given in the perfect tense, but it is passive. Answer (B) "is entering" is a common incorrect translation of a passive form of the perfect system because of the appearance of the verb **est**. Answer (D) would require the past participle **ingressus**, which is only a component of the perfect passive verb form.

3. **(D)**

The phrase "to get out of" is expressed by the infinitive **egredi**. Although Answer (A) **egredere** appears to be an infinitive, it is not, because **egredior** is a deponent verb and has forms only in the passive. (The form **egredere** is a singular imperative.) This form is an alternative to the second person singular present tense form **egrederis**. Answer (B) **egrediendi** is a gerund or gerundive and (C) **egressus esse** is an infinitive, but appears in the wrong tense (perfect).

4. **(D)**

The appearance of a regular passive verb form is designed to "keep you honest." **Ducetur** "she will be led" is the future tense passive of the regular verb **ducere**. The sentence reads, "The deceased Anemia will be led by Mercury to the underworld." The other answers give translations in the active voice, in anticipation of the incorrect identification of **ducetur** as a deponent verb.

5. **(B)**

This question tests your alertness to the fact that certain deponent verbs take a direct object in the ablative case. **Potior** is one of these verbs, therefore

caduceo is the correct answer, leading to the meaning "For what reason did Mercury come into possession of the caduceus?" Answer (A) is the anticipated incorrect answer, as **caduceum** is accusative. Answers (C) and (D) are in the plural and therefore incorrect here, since "caduceus" is singular.

6. **(B)**
Vererisne is in the present tense, second person singular, "Are you afraid?" The equivalent in the active voice is **times**. Answer (A) is plural and (B) is future tense. **Vereri** is a second conjugation verb and therefore **vereris** is present tense, not future, which is **Vereberis**. Answer (D) is a form of the imperfect subjunctive. Note the deponent infinitive **mori**, "to die."

7. **(D)**
In this question, you are to decide between the present and future tenses, either of which could conceivably be expressed by the form **tuetur**. Since this verb belongs to the second conjugation, the form is in the present tense, making (D), and not (A), the correct answer. The Latin of (B) "should protect" is the subjunctive form **tueatur**. Answer (C) is not possible, since the translation "is being protected" is passive, and **tueor** is a deponent verb. The sentence reads, "Aesculapius protects all Romans." (For the ambiguity between forms of the present and future tenses, see above.)

8. **(B)**
Audeo is a semi-deponent verb, which has active meanings in the perfect system. **Ausi sunt** is in the perfect tense and has **medici Romani** as its subject. The sentence therefore reads, "Roman doctors ventured to take care of themselves." Answers (A) and (C) offer translations that are passive, which are not appropriate for a deponent form. Answer (D) is a red herring, because it contains the translation "are," a meaning of **sunt**, but not of **ausi sunt**.

Sententiae Antiquae Answers

1. **(A)**
Horace's sentence reads, "Worry follows increasing money." Therefore, a main verb is necessary to complete the meaning of the sentence. Answers (B) and (C), which are infinitives, do not serve this function. Answer (D) **secutus es** "you have followed" does not have a personal ending that agrees with the nominative subject **cura**.

2. **(A)**
Cicero's sentence reads, "We have not been born for ourselves alone." Because of the meaning "be born" in English, the verb **nascor** appears to be passive, but it is deponent. Therefore, the underlined form **nati sumus** is a form of the perfect tense, which is translated "we have been born," or better, "we are born" = "we are alive." The translations in Answers (B), (C), and (D) are in the wrong tenses, i.e., present, imperfect, and pluperfect.

3. **(D)**

Pliny says, "The undying souls of the dead speak in libraries." The nominative subject **immortales animae** requires a plural verb, a fact that drops Answers (A) and (C) from consideration. Answer (B) appears to be a likely option, but the verb **locuti erant** does not agree in gender with the subject **animae**.

4. **(D)**

The Latin reads literally, "Not to go forward is to go backward." The deponent infinitives **progredi** and **regredi** are examples of the subjective infinitive, i.e., the infinitive used as a noun subject ("going forward" and "going backward"). (For the subjective infinitive, see Chapter 23.)

5. **(D)**

"Will follow" requires a future tense in the Latin, so **sequentur** is the correct answer, as **sequor** belongs to the third conjugation. Answer (A) **sequuntur** means "they are following," (B) **secuta erunt** "they will have followed," and (C) **sequantur** "let them follow," a form of the jussive subjunctive.

Stumper:

(C)

Passi is the past participle of **patior** which, by the way, gives the English derivative "passive." Perfect passive participial forms may only be translated (literally) in the active voice if the verb is deponent, i.e., "having suffered" rather than "having been suffered," (i.e., Answer (B)). Answer (A) "to suffer" translates the infinitive form **pati**, which is similar in appearance to the participial form **passi**. Answer (D) "they suffered," **passi sunt**, includes the past participle in its form, but is a main verb.

Chapter 17

Review of Irregular Verbs

Overview

Look at the list of principal parts provided below. You will remember that irregular verbs do not necessarily conform to the patterns found in regular verbs. Irregular verbs are among the most commonly used verbs in Latin, as they are in many languages. They can stand alone, like **est**, become parts of other verb forms, such as **missus est** or **missus esse**, or be combined with prepositional prefixes to form a host of verbs that are related to them in meaning, e.g., **abesse**. Some tenses of irregular verbs conform to the patterns of regular verbs and contain familiar personal endings, but many of the forms of irregular verbs are unpredictable and must be memorized.

Principal Parts of Irregular Verbs

sum, esse, fui, *be*

possum, posse, potui, *be able, can*

eo, ire, ii (or **ivi**), *go*

fero, ferre, tuli, latus, *carry, bring*

volo, velle, volui, *wish, want*

nolo, nolle, nolui, *be unwilling*

malo, malle, malui, *prefer*

fio, fieri, factus sum, *become, happen*

Examples of irregular verbs in context:

Habentne magistri in memoria se discipulos fuisse?
Do teachers ever remember that they themselves were students?

Romani Athenas ierunt ut linguam Graecam discerent.
Romans went to Athens in order to learn the Greek language.

The Present Indicative Active of Irregular Verbs

The forms of the present tense of irregular verbs are the most unpredictable of the six tenses. Here are the forms of the present indicative of the common irregular verbs listed above, except for **nolo** and **malo**, which approximate those of **volo**. Look for patterns within the irregularities and try to remember what you have previously learned about these verbs. Notice from the principal parts given above that only two irregular verbs, **fero** and **fio**, have passive forms.

Conjugations of the Present Tense of Irregular Verbs

	esse, *be*		**posse, *be able***		**ire, *go***	
	Sing.	**Pl.**	**Sing.**	**Pl.**	**Sing.**	**Pl.**
1st	**sum**	**sumus**	**possum**	**possumus**	**eo**	**imus**
2nd	**es**	**estis**	**potes**	**potestis**	**is**	**itis**
3rd	**est**	**sunt**	**potest**	**possunt**	**it**	**eunt**
	fero, *bring*		**velle, *wish***		**fieri, *become***	
	Sing.	**Pl.**	**Sing.**	**Pl.**	**Sing.**	**Pl.**
1st	**fero**	**ferimus**	**volo**	**volumus**	**fio**	**fimus**
2nd	**fers**	**fertis**	**vis**	**vultis**	**fis**	**fitis**
3rd	**fert**	**ferunt**	**vult**	**volunt**	**fit**	**fiunt**

Indicative Active of Irregular Verbs

All tenses of irregular verbs, except for the forms of the present, behave as their regular verb counter-parts (stem + ending). For complete conjugations of these forms, consult your textbook.

Quick Study Synopses of Irregular Verbs

	esse	**posse**	**ire**
Pres.	**est**, *he is*	**potest**, *he is able*	**it**, *he is going*
Impf.	**erat**, *he was being*	**poterat**, *he was able*	**ibat**, *he was going, went*
Fut.	**erit**, *he will be*	**poterit**, *he will be able*	**ibit,** *he will go*
Perf.	**fuit,** *he has been, was*	**potuit**, *he has been able, could*	**iit** (or **ivit**), *he has gone, went*
Plupf.	**fuerat**, *he had been*	**potuerat**, *he had been able*	**ierat** (or **iverat**), *he had gone*
Fut. Pf.	**fuerit**, *he will have been*	**potuerit**, *he will have been able*	**ierit** (or **iverit**), *he will have gone*

	ferre	velle	fieri
Pres.	**fert**, *he is bringing*	**vult**, *he is wishing*	**fit**, *he is becoming*
Impf.	**ferebat**, *he was bringing*	**volebat**, *he was wishing*	**fiebat**, *he was beoming*
Fut.	**feret**, *he will bring*	**volet**, *he will wish*	**fiet**, *he will become*
Perf.	**tulit**, *he has brought*	**voluit**, *he has wished*	**factus est**, *he has become*
Plupf.	**tulerat**, *he had brought*	**voluerat**, *he had wished*	**factus erat**, *he had become*
Fut. Pf.	**tulerit**, *he will have brought*	**voluerit**, *he will have wished*	**factus erit**, *he will have become*

Sum, esse, fui, *be, exist*

1. The forms of **esse** vary the most of any irregular verb. Remember that the third person plural of the future tense is **erunt**. Be careful to distinguish this form from that of the third person plural of the perfect tense, **fuerunt**.
2. Although both **eram** and **fui** may be translated *I was*, the former is in the imperfect tense and thus the action is understood as ongoing, i.e., *I was, over a period of time*. **Fui** is in the perfect tense and shows completed action, i.e., *I was, and am no longer*.
3. Forms of the irregular verb **esse** may accompany participles in order to create other verb forms, e.g., **missus erat, missus esset, missus esse, missurus esse**, **mittendus est.** Note that when this type of combination occurs, there is a change in the meaning of the form of **esse**, e.g., **missus est** means *he has been sent*, not *he is sent*.
4. In a line of verse, forms of **esse** may be omitted from a two-part verb, such as **missurus (esse)**, due to considerations of meter or dramatic effect.

Possum, posse, potui, *be able, can*

1. The forms of **posse** derive from the adjective **potis**, meaning *able, capable*, which is attached as a prefix to various forms of **esse**. Before forms of **esse** beginning with **s-**, the **-t-** of **potis** is altered or assimilated to **-s-**, hence **potis + sum = possum** (as opposed to **potsum**). The **-t-** is retained before a vowel, e.g., **poteram** or **potuisti**.
2. In English, the past tense of *can* is *could*.

3. When translating, be careful to distinguish the imperfect indicative **poteram** from the pluperfect indicative **potueram**, and the forms of the verb **posse** from those of the regular verb **pono, ponere, posui, positus**, *put, place.*

Eo, ire, ii (ivi), *go*

1. This verb behaves as the regular fourth conjugation verb **audio** except for the future tense, where it changes to first and second conjugation forms, e.g., **ibo**, **ibis, ibit**, etc.
2. The alternative perfect tense form **ivi** is found much less often than **ii**, i.e., the form **iveram** appears less commonly than **ieram**. The forms of the perfect tense of **ire** made from the **i**-stem are **ii, isti, iit** and **iimus, istis, ierunt.** Those made from the stem **iv-** are **ivi, ivisti, ivit** and **ivimus, ivistis, iverunt.**

Fero, ferre, tuli, latus, *bring, carry*

1. This irregular verb has the endings of a regular third conjugation verb, such as **mittere**, in the present system, although the stem vowel **-e-** is missing occasionally, e.g., **ferre**, *to bring*.
2. This verb has a passive voice, the forms of which are constructed and translated in a regular manner, e.g., the synopsis **feritur, ferebatur, feretur, latus est, latus erat, latus erit**.

Volo, velle, volui, *wish, want*; nolo, nolle, nolui, *be unwilling, not wish*; malo, malle, malui, *prefer, want more*

1. These verbs often have the endings of regular third conjugation verbs, except for forms in the present tense (see the chart above, and also note the irregular forms of the present infinitives **velle, nolle**, and **malle**). The tenses of the perfect system are regularly formed.
2. Remember that the verb **nolo (non + volo)** can become a compound form in the present tense, i.e., singular, **nolo, non vis, non vult,** and plural, **nolumus, non vultis, nolunt.**

Fio, fieri, factus sum, *become, happen*; *be made*

Fio has forms much like the regular fourth conjugation verb **audio**. This irregular verb serves as the passive of the present system of the verb **facere**, e.g., **faciuntur,** *they are being made* = **fiunt,** *they become*. In the perfect system, passive forms appear as deponent verbs, e.g., **facti sunt**, *they have become.* **Fieri** can have either the meanings *become, occur*, or *happen*, or the passive meanings *be done* or *be made.* Consider both options when translating.

Common Compound Forms of Irregular Verbs

sum	eo	fero
adsum, *be present*	**abeo**, *go away, leave*	**affero**, *carry toward, bring in*
absum, *be absent*	**adeo**, *go to, approach*	**aufero**, *carry away, remove*
desum, *be down, fail*	**circumeo**, *go around*	**confero**, *bring together, collect*
intersum, *be between*	**exeo**, *go out, leave*	**defero**, *carry* or *bring down*
praesum, *be* or *preside over*	**ineo**, *go in, enter*	**effero**, *carry out, lift up, express*
prosum, *be useful, benefit*	**intereo**, *be lost, perish*	**infero**, *bring in* or *on, attack*
supersum, *be over, remain*	**obeo**, *meet, oppose, die*	**offero**, *bring to, present, offer*
	pereo, *go through, perish*	**refero**, *carry* or *bring back, return*
	praetereo, *go past, pass by*	
	redeo, *go back, return*	
	subeo, *go under, submit to*	
	transeo, *go across, cross*	

Lookalikes

Do not confuse:

- The irregular verb **sumus**, *we are*, with the adjective **summus, -a, -um**, *the top of.*
- The irregular verb **eo,** *I go*, with the adverb **eo**, *to this place*.
- Forms of the irregular verb **fero, ferre** with those of **ferio, ferire**, *strike, hit*.
- The irregular verb **volo, velle** with **volo, volare**, *fly*, and with forms of the noun **vis**, *force, strength*.
- Forms of the irregular verb **malo** (**magis** + **volo**, *wish more*) with those of the adjective **malus, -a, -um**, *bad*.

Be sure to consult the context when determining the meaning of ambiguous forms.

Tips for Translating Irregular Verbs

Practice with the forms of irregular verbs and know the principal parts so that you are familiar with the patterns within the irregularity of each verb. Be able to make distinctions in tense and meaning among forms that are similar, e.g., **erunt**, **fuerunt**, and **ierunt**, or **erant**, **fuerant**, and **ierant**.

- It is important to remember that forms of the imperfect tense **eram**, **eras**, **erat**, etc., refer to ongoing action in the past and the forms of the perfect tense, **fui**, **fuisti**, **fuit**, etc., refer to completed action in the past. Remember that, although the word "been" is used in translating forms of verbs in the perfect system of **esse**, i.e., **fuit**, *he has been*, the verb has a meaning in the active voice.
- Remember that the forms of the irregular verb **fio**, **fieri**, **factus sum** may be translated with meanings that are either active (*become, happen*) or passive (*be done* or *be made*), depending upon the context.
- The irregular verbs **ferre**, **ire**, and **sum** have many compound forms. These often exhibit assimilation, e.g., **afferre** (**ad** + **ferre**), *carry toward*, and **auferre** (**ab** + **ferre**), *carry away*.

Practice Questions

1. The perfect active indicative of sunt is

   (A) fuerunt (C) fuerant
   (B) fuerint (D) fuissent

2. The perfect active indicative of potes is

   (A) potuistis (C) potueris
   (B) potueras (D) potuisti

3. Ego magister factus eram.

   (A) I was being made (C) I had become
   (B) I was becoming (D) I have been made

4. When will we be able to live in peace and harmony?

   (A) potuerimus (C) poterimus
   (B) poteramus (D) possumus

5. We went to school.

   (A) imus (C) iimus
   (B) eamus (D) ieramus

6. Which verb is not in the present tense?

   (A) fuit (C) vult
   (B) fert (D) it

7. Coals <u>had been brought</u> to Newcastle.
   (A) ferebant (C) ferebantur
   (B) lati erant (D) lati sunt

8. Ubi leges non valent, <u>poterit</u>ne populus liber esse?
   (A) will be able (C) is able
   (B) was able (D) will have been able

9. <u>Does</u> any young person <u>prefer</u> to stay at home?
   (A) Maluitne? (C) Mavultne?
   (B) Malebatne? (D) Maletne?

10. <u>Non feremus</u>.
    (A) We are not enduring.
    (B) We shall not be endured.
    (C) We shall not endure.
    (D) We have not endured.

Stumper: The prince <u>had become</u> a pauper.
   (A) factus est (C) fecit
   (B) factus erat (D) fecerat

Sentantiae Antiquae

1. <u>Anni eunt modo fluentis aquae</u>. (Ovid) The basic meaning of this thought is
   (A) Time flies.
   (B) O the times, O the values!
   (C) Seize the day.
   (D) Make haste slowly.

2. If <u>you prefer</u> peace and quiet, take a wife of equal station. (Quintilian)
   (A) malebas (C) mavis
   (B) malueras (D) maluisti

3. In this Republic, <u>there were</u> once men of great character and reliability. (Cicero)
   (A) fuerant (C) essent
   (B) erant (D) sunt

4. Possunt quia posse videntur. (Vergil)
   (A) They could since they seemed to be able.
   (B) They can since they seemed to be able.
   (C) They could since they seem to be able.
   (D) They are able since they seem to be able.

5. Magnae res non fiunt sine periculo. (Terence)
   The basic meaning of this thought is
   (A) Always carry an umbrella.
   (B) No pain, no gain.
   (C) Only the simple things matter.
   (D) We have nothing to fear but fear itself.

Answers

1. **(A)**

The perfect tense forms of **esse** have regular endings. Answer (B) is in the future perfect tense, (C) the pluperfect indicative, and (D) the pluperfect subjunctive.

2. **(D)**

The verb **posse** has the endings of regular verbs in the perfect tense, plus the stem **potu-**, hence **potuisti** "you were or have been able" is equivalent in the perfect tense to the present tense form **potes** "you are able." Answer (A) is in the perfect tense and is in the 2nd person, but is plural. Answer (B) **potueras** is pluperfect, "you had been able" and (C) **potueris** is future perfect, "you will have been able."

3. **(C)**

The perfect system of the passive voice of **facere** is translated as a deponent verb, i.e., with the active meaning of "happen" or "become." The form **factus eram** is in the pluperfect tense, therefore the verb means "I had become." Answers (A) and (B) require **fiebam** and (C), **factus sum**.

4. **(C)**

Answer (A) is to be distinguished from the correct answer (C) because the perfect stem is found in (A) **potuerimus**, making this form future perfect. The underlined translation "will we be able" in the sentence calls for **poterimus,** a form in the future tense. Answer (B) **poteramus** is pluperfect, "we had been able," and (D) **possumus** present, "we are able."

5. **(C)**

"We went" requires a form of the imperfect or perfect tense of the verb **ire**. Since no form of the imperfect tense is available among the choices, Answer (C)

iimus, is correct. Answer (A) **imus** is in the present indicative and (B) **eamus** is in the present tense of the subjunctive mood. Answer (D) is pluperfect, "we had gone."

6. **(A)**

Answer (A) **fuit,** contains the perfect stem **fu-** and therefore is a form of the perfect tense of **esse**, "he has been" or "he was." Answers (B), (C), and (D) are all in the present tense.

7. **(B)**

The translation "had been brought" requires a passive form of the pluperfect tense of **ferre**, thus, **lati erant**. Answer (A) is in the active voice and Answers (C) and (D) are in the wrong tenses, i.e., imperfect and perfect. Remember that among irregular verbs, only **fero** and **fio** have passive forms.

8. **(A)**

Poterit is in the future tense and is thus translated "will be able." The sentence reads, "When the laws are not strong, <u>will</u> the people <u>be able</u> to be free?" Answer (B) translates a verb in the imperfect or perfect tense, (C) in the present tense, and (D) in the future perfect.

9. **(C)**

"Does prefer" requires the present tense in Latin, leading to the answer **mavult**, which is a compound form of the verb **volo**. Answer (A) **maluit** is perfect tense (note the tense indicator **-u-**), (B) **malebat** is imperfect tense, and (D) **malet** is future tense.

10. **(C)**

The **-e-** vowel present in **feremus** makes this a form of the future tense. It cannot be translated in the present tense because **ferre** is an irregular verb, rather than a verb of the 3rd conjugation. Answer (A) requires the present tense **(ferimus)**, (B) the future passive (**feremur**), and (D) the perfect tense (**tulimus**).

Stumper: (B)

The tense of the underlined verb is pluperfect, eliminating Answers (A) and (C), which are in the perfect tense. Since "had become" = "had been made," the passive form **factus erat** is required, rather than the active form **fecerat**.

Sententiae Antiquae Answers

1. **(A)**

Ovid's sentence reads, "The years go (by) in the manner of flowing water." The verb **eunt** is the present tense of **ire**. The subject of this sentence is **anni** "years" which leads to the immediate conclusion that the sentence has something to do with time.

2. **(C)**

"You prefer" requires the present tense of the irregular verb **malle** in the 2nd person, which is **mavis**. Answer (A) **malebas** means "you were preferring," (B) **malueras** "you had preferred," and (D) **maluisti,** "you (have) preferred."

3. **(B)**

The underlined verb "there were" is translated by a form of the imperfect tense of the verb **esse**, which is **erant**. (**Fuerunt** is not an option given here.) Answer (A) **fuerant** "they had been" is pluperfect tense, (C) **essent** is imperfect tense, but subjunctive, and (D) **sunt** "they are" is present tense.

4. **(D)**

This question tests command of forms of the verb **posse** and also the use of the passive of **videre** as a deponent verb. The correct answer is "They are able since they seem to be able." Since **possunt** is in the present tense, Answers (A) and (C), containing the translation "could," which expresses the past tense in English, are incorrect. Answer (B) translates the present tense form **videntur** as "seemed," which is in the past tense, and therefore also incorrect.

5. **(B)**

Terence's sentence reads, "Great events don't come about without risk." Of the answers available, the closest in meaning to this is Answer (B) "No pain, no gain."

Chapter 18

Review of Impersonal Verbs

Impersonal verbs are found in the third person singular and have the ending **-t** and the non-personal subject "it," e.g., **Claudio placet**, *it is pleasing (to) Claudius* or *Claudius is pleased*. Some impersonal verbs, such as **placet**, can be used personally, that is, the subject is expressed: **Boleti placent Claudio**, *Mushrooms please Claudius*. Impersonal verbs may also appear as gerunds or infinitives. There are about fifteen or so of these verbs that appear commonly in Latin, many of which belong to the second conjugation. Most are followed by an infinitive phrase, but some may also be followed by a subjunctive clause. When there is need for variation in tense, the tense change appears in the impersonal, e.g., **placet, placebat, placebit**. Forms of the impersonal verb are found in both the indicative and subjunctive moods. Since impersonal verbs are common in Latin but rarely appear in English, the literal translation of an impersonal construction in Latin should be rephrased in English, as in this example:

Pudebatne Claudium claudum esse?

Was Claudius ashamed to be lame? lit., *Was it shaming Claudius to be lame?*

The subject of the sentences in this chapter is the life and times of the emperor Claudius, as he is portrayed in the film series *I, Claudius*.

Impersonal Verb Accompanied by the Accusative Case and an Infinitive

Observe the function of the impersonal verbs **necesse erat** in the sentence below. Note that the impersonal is accompanied by a noun in the accusative case, plus an infinitive:

Caligula occiso, necesse erat milites (acc.) novum imperatorem eligere (infin.).

When Caligula was killed, it was necessary for the soldiers to select a new emperor.

Impersonal verbs with the accusative:

accidit, accidere, accidit, *it happens*

decet, decere, decuit, *it is proper, fitting; one should*

iuvat, iuvare, *it pleases*

necesse est, *it is necessary*

oportet, oportere, oportuit, *it is fitting; one ought* or *must*

Impersonal Verb Accompanied by the Dative Case and an Infinitive

Observe the function of the impersonal verb **libebat** in the sentence below. Note that the impersonal is accompanied by a noun in the dative case, plus an infinitive:

dat. infin.

Libebatne Claudio imperator fieri?

Was it agreeable to Claudius to become (that he become) emperor?

Impersonal verbs with the dative:

libet, libere, libuit, *it is pleasing, agreeable*

licet, licere, licuit, *it is allowed, permitted; one may*

opus est, *there is need, it is necessary*

placet, placere, placuit, *it pleases; one likes*

videtur, **videri**, *it seems*

Impersonal Verb Accompanied by the Subjunctive Mood

The sentence below illustrates the use of an impersonal verb followed by a subjunctive clause, with or without **ut**. This serves as an alternative to the impersonal verb accompanied by an infinitive, described above. The same rules apply regarding the used of the accusative or dative case;

subjunctive

Licebatne Claudio (ut) filiam fratris uxorem duceret?

Was Claudius permitted to marry (that he marry) his niece?

Impersonal Verbs Accompanied by the Accusative and Genitive or an Infinitive

This type of impersonal verb expresses feelings or emotion and is followed by the accusative (of the person or persons feeling the emotion) and the genitive (of the cause or reason for the emotion), e.g.,

acc. gen.

Non taedebat Tiberium vitae Capreis.

It was not boring Tiberius of life on Capri. (literal)

When such impersonal verbs are used, some rephrasing of the English is necessary in order to clarify the meaning of the Latin. For example, the sentence above, when rendered in better English, reads, *Tiberius was not bored with life on Capri.* Such verbs may be accompanied alternatively by an infinitive phrase, in place of the genitive case, e.g,

acc. infin.

Non paenituit Tiberium Roma egredi.

Tiberius did not regret leaving Rome, lit., *It did not make Tiberius feel regret to leave Rome.*

Impersonal verbs that express a feeling or emotion and are found with the accusative + genitive (or infinitive). Note that all belong to the second conjugation:

miseret, miserere, miseruit, *it makes one* (acc.) *feel pity* or *feel sorry for something* (gen.)

paenitet, paenitere, paenituit, *it makes one* (acc.) *regret* or *repent of something* (gen.)

piget, pigere, piguit, *it annoys, disgusts, causes one* (acc.) *to be ashamed of something* (gen.)

pudet, pudere, puduit, *it shames, makes one* (acc.) *ashamed of something* (gen.)

taedet, taedere, taesum est, *it bores, makes one* (acc.) *tired of something* (gen.)

Passive Verbs Used Impersonally

Intransitive verbs, i.e., verbs that do not take a direct object, may be used in the third person singular of the passive, with the implied subject "it," e.g.,

Ab imperatore ad munera perventum est.

The emperor arrived at the public show, lit., *It was arrived by the emperor. . . .*

Such verbs are used impersonally when the writer or speaker wishes to emphasize the action, rather than the person/s performing the action. Good English requires rephrasing of passive verbs used impersonally, e.g., **fortiter pugnabatur**, *the fighting was fierce*, lit., *it was fought fiercely*. Verbs such as **parco**, *spare*, **persuadere**, *convince*, **pugnare**, *fight*, and compound forms of **venire**, e.g., **pervenire**, *arrive*, among others, appear impersonally in the passive.

Tips on Translating Impersonal Verbs

An impersonal verb differs from a personal verb by requiring the non-personal subject "it," in most cases. After working out the meaning of the impersonal verb and its accompanying forms, recast the wording in comprehensible English.

- The impersonal verb is often found at the front of a Latin sentence, but it may be located anywhere.
- Be alert to the fact that the case of the noun or pronoun that accompanies the impersonal verb can be accusative, dative, and/or genitive.
- Note the tense of the impersonal verb and also whether it is accompanied by an infinitive phrase or a subjunctive clause.
- The semi-deponent verb **soleo, solere, solitus sum**, *be accustomed, be usual*, and the verb **debeo, debere, debui, debitus**, *owe, ought, be obligated, should*, can appear to be impersonal verbs because their forms are often found in the third person and are accompanied by an infinitive. However, they always have personal subjects, e.g.,

  Caligula solebat crudelis esse.

  Caligula was in the habit of being cruel.

  Caligula debet propter crudelitatem puniri.

  Caligula ought to be punished for his cruelty.

Practice Questions

1. In pictura moventi "Sum Claudius," multos veneno necare ____ placebat.
   (A) Liviae (C) Livia
   (B) Liviam (D) Liviā

2. Non decebat Caligulam dicere "Oderint, dum metuant."
   (A) Caligula was not allowed
   (B) It was not necessary for Caligula
   (C) Caligula was not ashamed
   (D) It was not appropriate for Caligula

3. Julia was weary of exile.
   (A) Iulia exsili taedebat. (C) Iuliam exsili taedebat.
   (B) Iuliae exsilium taedebat. (D) Iuliam exsilium taedebat.

4. Videbatur ____ Claudium stultum esse.
   (A) Livia (C) Liviae
   (B) Liviam (D) Liviā

5. Piget Liviam linguae haesitationis Claudi. The basic meaning of this sentence is that
   (A) Claudius feels pity for Livia's stuttering.
   (B) Claudius' stuttering is agreeable to Livia.
   (C) Livia permits Claudius to stutter.
   (D) Claudius' stuttering annoys Livia.

6. "Oportuit Germanos signa legionum reddere!" exclamabat Augustus.
   (A) Ought (C) Can
   (B) Did (D) Might

7. Debebatne Claudius Britanniam vincere?
   (A) was forbidden (C) was obligated
   (B) was permitted (D) was encouraged

8. Women were not allowed to be emperors.
   (A) Feminis non licet (C) Feminae non licebant
   (B) Feminae non licebat (D) Feminis non licebat

9. Tacitus scripsit Neronem Romam incendere <u>non paenitere</u>.
   - (A) did not regret
   - (B) is not permitted
   - (C) is not punished
   - (D) ought not

10. Caligula imperatore, <u>accidit</u> ut equus senator fieret.
   - (A) it happened
   - (B) it was appropriate
   - (C) it pleased
   - (D) it was necessary

11. Spectatoribus a Claudio in amphitheatro non parcebatur.
   - (A) The amphitheater was not spared by the spectators and Claudius.
   - (B) In the amphitheater, the spectators were not sparing Claudius.
   - (C) The spectators in the amphitheater were not spared by Claudius.
   - (D) In the amphitheater, Claudius was not spared by the spectators.

12. Necesse est <u>ut iussis imperatoris pareamus.</u>
   - (A) that we all speak the truth.
   - (B) that we spoke the truth.
   - (C) that we be told the truth.
   - (D) that we all may speak the truth.

13. Miseret me immaturae mortis Marcelli.
   - (A) The untimely death of Marcellus shames me.
   - (B) I am frightened by Marcellus' untimely death.
   - (C) I am enraged by the untimely death of Marcellus.
   - (D) I feel pity for the untimely death of Marcellus.

14. <u>It was agreeable</u> multis Romanis tumulum Augusti saepe visitare.
   - (A) oportebat
   - (B) licebat
   - (C) libebat
   - (D) paenitebat

15. Imperatori a senatoribus persuasum est.
   - (A) The emperor convinced the senators.
   - (B) The senators convinced the emperor.
   - (C) The citizens and emperor were convinced.
   - (D) He convinced the emperor who was a senator.

16. Romans were ashamed of the corrupt character of Tiberius.
    (A) Romanos . . . turpis ingeni
    (B) Romanis . . . turpe ingenium
    (C) Romanis . . . turpis ingeni
    (D) Romanorum . . . turpe ingenium

17. It happened ut multi imperatores se occiderent.
    (A) opus erat
    (B) taesum est
    (C) decuit
    (D) accidit

Sentientiae Antiquae

1. Infamiae suae neque pudet et taedet. (Cicero, on Verres) These words refer to
    (A) shame and weariness
    (B) regret and pity
    (C) misery and repentence
    (D) pleasure and pain

2. A liar ought to have a good memory. (Quintilian)
    (A) licet
    (B) placet
    (C) oportet
    (D) decet

3. Decet verecundum esse adulescentem. (Plautus)
    (A) It is shameful for a young person to be modest.
    (B) A young person can regret being modest.
    (C) It is proper for a young person to be modest.
    (D) There is need for young people to be modest.

4. Quodque libet facere ____ licet. (Seneca)
    (A) victor
    (B) victorem
    (C) victori
    (D) victoris

5. Placeat ____ quidquid deo placuit. (Seneca)
    (A) hominem
    (B) homo
    (C) homini
    (D) homine

Stumper: Aedificare in tuo proprio solo non licet quod alteri noceat. (Legal)
    (A) You are allowed to build whatever you like on your own property.
    (B) If someone hurts himself while building on your property, you are at fault.
    (C) You are allowed to build on your own property only what does not harm another.
    (D) No one should harm another while in a building on your property.

Answers

1. **(A)**

When used impersonally, **placere** takes a dative object, therefore the missing form of the word **Livia** should appear in the dative case, which is Answer (A). The sentence reads, "In the movie 'I, Claudius,' it was pleasing to Livia to kill many (people) with poison." Answer (B) **Liviam**, an accusative, is an obvious, but incorrect, answer. Answers (C) **Liviā** and (D) **Livia** have no function in this sentence.

2. **(D)**

As all the verbs are given in the imperfect tense, you are asked to select the correct meaning of **(non) decebat (Caligulam)**, which is "it was (not) appropriate (for Caligula)." The sentence reads, "It was not appropriate for Caligula to say, 'Let them hate (me), so long as they fear (me).'" Answer (A) "was allowed" requires **licebat**, (B) "was necessary" requires **necesse erat**, and (C) "was ashamed" **pudebat**.

3. **(C)**

Taedebat, as a verb expressing emotion, takes an accusative of the person and a genitive of the cause or reason for the emotion. In Answer (C), **Iuliam** is accusative and **exsili** genitive, giving the literal meaning "It was not wearying Julia of exile." Answers (A), (B), and D) do not have the correct combination of accusative and genitive forms: (A) has nominative and genitive, (B) dative/genitive and accusative, and (D) accusative and accusative.

4. **(C)**

This sentence reads, "It seemed to Livia that Claudius was foolish." The missing noun must be the dative form **Liviae** after the impersonal verb **videbatur**. Answers (A), (B), and (D) are all in the incorrect case, i.e., nominative, accusative, and ablative, respectively.

5. **(D)**

Piget, another verb expressing emotion, is found with the accusative, **Liviam**, and genitive, **linguae haesitationis**. (**Claudi** is simply a possessive genitive, unrelated to the use of the impersonal verb here.) Answer (A) would require an exchange of Livia and Claudius in the sentence and the appearance of the look-alike verb **pudet**. Answers (B) and (C) mistranslate **piget** as "is agreeable" and "permits," respectively.

6. **(A)**

Of the choices of meanings for **oportuit** in this sentence, "ought" is the most appropriate. Answer (B) "did" simply translates the tense of **oportuit**. Answers (C) "can" requires the verb **posse** and (D) "might" the subjunctive mood. The sentence reads, "'The Germans ought to return the legionary standards,' exclaimed Augustus." The accusative form **Germanos** is consistent with the appearance of the irregular verb **oportuit**.

7. **(C)**

This question tests your knowledge of the meaning of the verb **debere**, which has the sense of obligation, that is, something one ought to do or should do. Hence, the sentence reads, "Was Claudius obliged to conquer Britain?" The answers "forbid," "permit," and "encourage," require other verbs.

8. **(D)**

The impersonal verb **licebat** is found with the dative case, therefore Answer (D) **feminis licebat** is correct. Answer (A) **feminis licet** has the incorrect tense. Answer (B) **feminae** is singular when a plural is required ("women") and Answer (C) **feminae** incorrectly serves as the subject of the impersonal verb.

9. **(A)**

The impersonal verb **paenitet** means "regret" (as in penance and penitant), therefore Answer (A) is correct. The sentence reads, "Tacitus writes that Nero did not regret burning Rome." The infinitive **paenitere** is used in an indirect statement. Answer (B) requires the verb **licere**, (C) the verb **punire** (etymologically akin to **paenitere**), and (D) **oportere**.

10. **(A)**

This sentence reads, "While Caligula was Emperor, it happened that a horse became a senator." The meaning of the verb **accidit** is "it happens" or "it happened." The imperfect tense of the subjunctive **fieret** in the substantive result clause requires that **accidit** be translated as a past tense in this sentence. Answer (B) requires **decebat** in the Latin, (C) **placebat**, and (D) **necesse erat**.

11. (C)	13. (D)	15. (B)	17. (D)
12. (A)	14. (C)	16. (A)	

Sententiae Antiquae Answers

1. **(A)**

Since the meanings of the impersonals **pudet** and **taedet** are "it is shameful" and "it is wearisome," respectively, Answer (A) is correct. Answer (B) requires the verbs **paenitet** and **miseret**, and (C) and (D) require words that do not relate to impersonal verbs. The sentence reads, "(Verres) is neither ashamed of nor bored with his own ill fame."

2. **(C)**

The word "ought" requires the impersonal verb **oportet**. Answer (A) **licet** means "permitted" or "allowed," (B) **placet** "pleased," and (D) **decet** "fitting" or "appropriate."

3. **(C)**

Since **decet** means "it is fitting or appropriate," Answer (C) is the best response. Answers (A) "shameful" and (B) "regret" do not give acceptable meanings of the impersonal verb **decet**. Answer (D) gives the wrong sense of **decet** and translates **adulescentem** as plural.

4. **(C)**

Seneca's statement, "A victor is allowed to do whatever he likes," requires that the word **victor** be in the dative case after the impersonal verb **licet**, i.e., "it is permitted to the victor." The nominative, accusative, and genitive cases found in Answers (A), (B), and (D) are not relevant in this sentence.

5. **(C)**

This sentence reads, "Let whatever has been acceptable to god be acceptable to mankind." The dative form **deo** with the impersonal verb **placuit** prompts recognition of the fact that the case of the missing noun will also be dative, i.e., **homini**. Answer (A) is accusative, (B) nominative, and (D) ablative. Note the appearance of the independent jussive subjunctive form **placeat**, "let it be acceptable."

Stumper:

(C)

Neither Answer (B) nor Answer (D) contains in its translation the proper meaning of the impersonal verb **licet**. Answer (A) seems likely, until you notice that "whatever you like" does not correctly render **quod alteri noceat,** which means "(the type of thing) which may be harmful to another" in the original sentence. This is a relative clause of characteristic with the subjunctive.

Chapter 19

Imperative Mood: Commands

The Imperative Mood

You will remember that the term mood indicates the way in which a verb functions in a sentence. Now that you have reviewed the indicative, you will review the second mood of the three, the imperative, which expresses a command or entreaty and, in the negative, a prohibition. The imperative mood appears less often than the indicative and subjunctive moods. This chapter will present the positive and negative imperatives of regular, deponent, and irregular verbs. Although the imperative has forms in both the present and future tenses, only the present tense will be reviewed in this book.

Imperatives of Regular Verbs				
	Singular		Plural	
First conjugation (**stare**)	**Sta!**	*(You alone) stand!*	**State!**	*(You all) stand*
Second conjugation (**sedēre**)	**Sedē!**	*(You alone) sit!*	**Sedete!**	*(You all) sit*
Third conjugation (**recumbere**)	**Recumbe!**	*(You alone) recline!*	**Recumbite!**	*(You all) recline*
Fourth conjugation (**venire**)	**Veni!**	*(You alone) come!*	**Venite!**	*(You all) come!*

Notes:

- The verbs **dicere, ducere, facere**, and **ferre** have irregular forms of the present imperative: **dic, duc, fac,** and **fer**. The plurals are regular: **dicite, ducite, facite**, and **ferte** (but note the dropped **-i-** in **ferte**). This rhyme may help your memory: "**Duc, dic, fac**, and **fer**, should have an **-e**, but it isn't there." Keith Berman; see David Pellegrino, http://latinteach.com/

- When you are uncertain about whether a verb form is imperative, look at the punctuation, i.e., a command will generally be accompanied by an exclamation point, quotation marks, and a comma.* Also look for a noun of direct address, i.e., the vocative case:

  "Dicite, pueri, veritatem!"

  "Tell the truth, boys!"

Note that the addressee of an imperative is implicitly in the second person, i.e., *"(You) tell the truth, boys!"*

Prohibitions of Regular Verbs				
	Singular		**Plural**	
First conjugation (**stare**)	**Noli stare!**	*Don't stand!*	**Nolite stare!**	*Don't stand!*
Second conjugation (**sedēre**)	**Noli sedēre!**	*Don't sit!*	**Nolite sedēre!**	*Don't sit!*
Third conjugation (**recumbere**)	**Noli recumbere!**	*Don't recline!*	**Nolite recumbere!**	*Don't recline!*
Fourth conjugation (**venire**)	**Noli venire!**	*Don't come!*	**Nolite venire!**	*Don't come!*

Notes:

- Avoid translating the word **noli** in a prohibition or negative command as *I don't want*, e.g., **Noli cadere!** means *Do not fall!*, not *I don't want to fall!*
- In poetry, **ne** + imperative appears often, e.g., **Equo ne credite, Teucri** (*Aeneid* 2.48)
- The perfect tense of the subjunctive is sometimes used to express a negative command or prohibition, e.g., **Ne ceperis consilium in arena**, *Don't make your plan in the arena*. This is an alternative to the more common **noli/ nolite** + infinitive.**

* For the use of punctuation when translating, see Chapter 5. For the vocative case of nouns, see Chapter 12.

** For the use of the independent subjunctive in the perfect tense to express a negative command or prohibition, see Chapter 25.

	Imperatives of Deponent Verbs			
	Singular		Plural	
First conjugation (**morari**)	**Morare!**	*Stay!*	**Moramini!**	*Stay!*
Second conjugation (**polliceri**	**Pollicere!**	*Promise!*	**Pollicemini!**	*Promise!*
Third conjugation (**egredi**)	**Egredere!**	*Leave!*	**Egredimini!**	*Leave!*
Fourth conjugation (**oriri**)	**Orire!**	*Get up!*	**Orimini!**	*Get up!*

Notes:

- The singular imperative of a deponent verb is the same form as the alternative form of the second person singular of the present tense, i.e., **morare** (for **moraris**, *you are staying*). The plural is the same form as that of the second person plural.
- The prohibition of a deponent verb is formed in the regular fashion, i.e., **Noli egredi!** *(You alone) don't leave!* and **Nolite egredi!** *(You all) don't leave!*

	Imperatives of Common Irregular Verbs			
	Present Singular		Present Plural	
sum	**Es!**	*Be!*	**Este!**	*Be!*
fero	**Fer!**	*Bring!*	**Ferte!**	*Bring!*
eo	**I!**	*Go!*	**Ite!**	*Go!*

Practice Questions: Commands

1. ____ bene, discipule!

   (A) Notate
   (B) Nota
   (C) Notare
   (D) Nolite notare

2. Semper ____ veritatem, Doofe.

   (A) dicite
   (B) nolite dicere
   (C) dic
   (D) dici

3. ____ cum paedagogo, pueri!

   (A) Ite!
   (B) I!
   (C) Eunt
   (D) Ire

4. ____ diem, discipuli!
   (A) Carpe
   (B) Carpite
   (C) Noli carpere
   (D) Carpi

5. Noli obdormire!
   (A) Don't fall asleep!
   (B) I don't want to fall asleep!
   (C) Don't be unwilling to fall asleep!
   (D) I wish you wouldn't fall asleep!

6. Sequere praecepta.
   (A) To follow directions.
   (B) You will follow directions.
   (C) Follow directions.
   (D) Having followed directions.

7. ____ domum dum laborem confeceris.
   (A) Regredere
   (B) Regredi
   (C) Noli regredi
   (D) Regredimini

8. ____ capsam tecum, discipule!
   (A) Ferre
   (B) Ferte
   (C) Ferri
   (D) Fer

9. Es tu ipse.
   (A) Let it be.
   (B) Be yourself.
   (C) Know yourself.
   (D) You are who you are.

10. ____ verba magistri vestri, discipuli.
    (A) Audi
    (B) Audiri
    (C) Audivi
    (D) Audite

Sentententiae Antiquae

1. <u>Disce aut discede</u>. (School motto)
   (A) Teach or leave.
   (B) Learn or leave.
   (C) Behave or depart.
   (D) Dance or die.

2. Saepe stilum verte bonum libellum scripturus. (Horace) (stilum vertere = *to turn over the stilus, to erase)*

   (A) Good reading leads to good writing.

   (B) Write much to write well.

   (C) Use a good pencil when writing.

   (D) Much editing makes for good writing.

3. ____, O Veneres Cupidinesque! (Catullus)

   (A) Luge (C) Lugete

   (B) Lugeri (D) Lugere

4. ____ in arma properare, Romani! (Anon.)

   (A) Non (C) Nolle

   (B) Noli (D) Nolite

5. Ludi magister, ____ simplici turbae. (Martial)

   (A) parce (C) parcere

   (B) parcite (D) parsus

Answers to Practice Questions: Commands

1. **(B)**

   The punctuation reveals this sentence to be a direct command. Since **discipule**, a single student, is being addressed, the answer must be a singular form of the imperative, which is Answer (B) **Nota**. Answer (A) is plural, (C) is an infinitive, and (D) is a negative command.

2. **(C)**

   The implied meaning of this sentence requires the singular command, since **Doofe** is in the vocative case. The verb **dico** has an irregular form of the singular imperative, which is **dic**. The remaining answers are incorrect because (A) and (B) are plural and (D) is a present passive infinitive.

3. **(A)**

   The punctuation suggests that an imperative is required. All answers are forms of the verb **ire**, so the root meaning of the verb is not in question. The vocative **pueri** is plural, therefore requiring that the accompanying command be plural, i.e., Answer (A) **Ite!** Answer (B) is singular, (C) **eunt**, "they are going," is a form of the present tense indicative, and (D) **ire**, "to go," is the present active infinitive.

4. **(B)**

   This sentence tempts you to choose Answer (A) **Carpe**, to complete Horace's famous saying, but the vocative form **discipuli** is plural, requiring (B) **Carpite**.

Answer (C) doesn't make sense, given the implied meaning of the command, and (D) is a present passive infinitive, which could easily be mistaken as a form of the imperative, if the verb **carpere** belonged to the 4th conjugation.

5. **(A)**
   This sentence provides an example of a singular negative command or prohibition, "Don't fall asleep!" Answers (B) and (C) are typical mistaken translations of the negative imperative and (D) requires a subjunctive verb expressing a wish.

6. **(C)**
   Sequor is a deponent verb, the present infinitive of which is **sequi**, nullifying Answer (A). Answer (B) translates **sequere** as a future tense, which would be **sequeris**. Answer (D) translatesthe past participle **secutus, -a, -um**. Answer (C) is therefore correct, by default, and also because it has the form of alternative second person singular of the present tense, **sequeris**.

7. **(C)**
   The context requires a command, since the present infinitive **regredi**, Answer (B), does not make sense. Answers (A) and (C) are positive imperatives, "return," which do not fit the context of "___ home until you have completed (your) work." The prohibition **Noli regredi**, "Do not return," makes the best sense.

8. **(D)**
   Again, the punctuation and vocative cue an imperative. Answers (A) and (C) are present active and passive infinitives, respectively, and Answer (B) is plural, whereas the vocative **discipule** is singular. The sentence reads, "Bring (your) book bag with you, student!"

9. **(B)**
   Es can be either the singular form of the present imperative "be" or the second person singular of the present tense, "you are." Answers (A) and (C) are therefore out of consideration. Answer (D) is possible, but "who you are" does not translate **tu ipse**.

10. **(D)**
   The context requires a plural command, because of the vocative plural **discipuli**. Answer (A) **Audi** won't work because, although it is an imperative, it is singular, (B) **Audiri** is a present passive infinitive, "to be heard," and (C) **Audivi** is the first person singular of the perfect tense, "I (have) heard."

Sententiae Antiquae Answers

1. **(B)**
   This motto plays on the imperative singular forms of the verbs **discere** "learn" and **discedere** "leave." Answer (A) requires familiarity with the meaning of the verb **discere**, which is not "teach" (this is **docere**). Answer (C) suggests,

wrongly, that **disce** might mean "behave," given the derivative "discipline." Answer (D) is for fun.

2. **(D)**

Horace's saying reads, "Turn (your) stilus often (if you're) going to write a book (that's) good." He means by "turn your stilus often," that erasing or frequent editing is necessary for good writing. **Verte** is a singular command addressed to the reader and **scripturus** is a future active participle modifying you, the reader (the subject of **Verte**).

3. **(C)**

You might be familiar with this famous opening line from Poem 3. The punctuation requires an imperative, which must be plural, since the vocatives **Veneres** and **Cupidines** are plural. Answer (C) **Lugete** fits the requirements. Answer (A) **Luge** is a singular imperative, (B) **Lugeri** a present passive infinitive, and (D) **Lugere** a present active infinitive, none of which fits the context of the sentence.

4. **(D)**

This sentence is a negative command in the plural, as required by the punctuation and by the vocative plural form **Romani**. **Nolite** is the form needed to supplement the infinitive **properare**, therefore completing the negative imperative. The sentence reads, "Don't rush to arms, Romans!" Answer (A) **Non** has no sense here, (B) **Noli** is the singular imperative, and (C) **Nolle** the present active infinitive.

5. **(A)**

This quote from Martial asks the teacher to "spare the simple crowd," i.e., the students. The context requires a singular imperative, **parce**, because the person addressed (**magister**) is singular. Answer (B) **parcite,** is a plural imperative, (C) **parcere,** a present active infinitive, and (D) **parsus,** a perfect passive participle, none of which fits the context here.

Chapter 20

Questions and Answers

The ancient Romans expressed questions either by tone of voice or by using question words. Question words are not a specialized category of Latin grammar—they can be pronouns, adjectives, or adverbs—but they are nonetheless important because they are used often.* They may be placed in two groups, one consisting of the **n**-words, **nonne**, **num** and **–ne**, and the other consisting of question words that mostly begin with the letter **q-**, such as forms of the interrogative pronoun **quis** and **quid**.

Nonne, Num, and *-ne*

The adverbs **nonne** and **num** introduce questions to which the answer is suggested by the person asking the question. **Nonne** expects an affirmative answer, i.e., agreement with the questioner is expected. Such questions are answered by words such as **certe**, **etiam, ita** or **ita vero, sic, sane**, and **vero**, none of which are really equivalent to the simple unqualified answer "yes" in English. These words mean *surely* or *certainly* (**certe**), *even so* (**etiam**), *thus* (**ita**), *so, in this way* (**sic** = *si* in Italian or Spanish), or *indeed* or *truly* (**sane**). Repeating the verb in the original question is another way to answer in the affirmative, e.g.,

Question: **Nonne Aeneas pius erat?**

Wasn't Aeneas dutiful?

or

Aeneas was dutiful, wasn't he?

Answer: **Erat pius**, or simply, **Erat.**

The adverb **num** expects a negative answer, i.e., disagreement with the questioner is expected.** Such questions are answered by words such as **minime**, *by no means*, **haud**, *not at all*, **immo**, *on the contrary*, or simply, **non est**. **Non** does not mean "No" in Latin.

Question: **Num omnes naves Troianae deletae sunt?**

Surely all the Trojan ships were not destroyed?

or

All the Trojan ships were not destroyed, were they?

Answer: **Minime**, or **Non deletae sunt**.

---

* For more about questions, see Chapters 5 and 8.

** In an indirect question, **num** means *whether*. See Chapter 28.

The enclitic **–ne** is usually attached to the first word, or to an emphatic word, in a question of simple fact, that is, one whose answer may be either affirmative or negative.

Question:	**Adiuveruntne di Troianos?**
	Did the gods help the Trojans?
Possible Answers:	Affirmative: **Ita vero**, etc., or **Adiuverunt**.
	Negative: **Minime**, etc., or **Non adiuverunt.**

Common Q-Words That Introduce Questions

Quis? *Who?*

Quid? *What?*

Quem? *Whom?* (pl. **Quos**? *Whom?*)

Qualis? *What kind of? What sort of?*

Quando? *When?*

Quare? or **Qua re**? *Why? For what reason?*

Quocum? *With whom?* (pl. **Quibuscum**? *With whom? With what?*)

Quo? *To where?*

Quomodo? *How? In what way?*

Quot? *How many?*

Also:

Cur? *Why?*

Ubi? *Where?*

Unde? *From where?*

The answers to such questions reflect the wording of the original question, e.g.,

Who?	**Quis erat pater Aeneae?**	**Anchises (erat pater Aeneae).**
Whom?	**Quem Aeneas amavit?**	**(Aeneas amavit) Creusam.**
Where to?	**Quo Aeneas navigabat?**	**(Aeneas navigabat) ad Hesperiam.**
How?	**Quomodo Aeneas Turnum superavit?**	**Magna saevitia (Aeneas Turnum superavit).**
With whom?	**Quocum Aeneas Troia effugit?**	**Cum Ascanio (Aeneas Troia effugit).**

Practice Questions: Questions and Answers

1. Nonne odium Iunoni in omnes Troianos erat? Which is NOT a correct answer to this question?
   - (A) Ita vero.
   - (B) Erat.
   - (C) Immo.
   - (D) Vero.

2. Sicilia relicta, quo magna tempestas Troianos egit?
   - (A) ad Italiam
   - (B) Karthaginem
   - (C) Alexandriam
   - (D) ad Graeciam

3. Habebatne Aeneas viginti naves?
   - (A) Surely Aeneas had . . . ?
   - (B) Aeneas didn't have, . . . did he?
   - (C) Did Aeneas have . . . ?
   - (D) Aeneas had . . . , didn't he?

4. Aeneas did not really marry Dido, did he?
   - (A) Nonne
   - (B) –ne
   - (C) Neque
   - (D) Num

5. Quocum Aeneas Troia effugere conabatur?
   - (A) cum Creusa
   - (B) cum Priamo
   - (C) cum matre
   - (D) cum Heleno

6. Unde populi qui Italiam primum incoluerant venerunt?
   - (A) Where to
   - (B) Where from
   - (C) When
   - (D) Why

7. Wasn't Alba Longa founded by Ascanius?
   - (A) Num
   - (B) –ne
   - (C) Nonne
   - (D) Non

8. What sort of woman was Dido's sister, Anna?
   - (A) Quomodo
   - (B) Quot
   - (C) Quando
   - (D) Qualis

9. Quare Aeneas rogavit Sibyllum ut eum ad Orcum duceret?
   (A) Why (C) How
   (B) When (D) Where

10. With which of the following would you introduce a question that would expect the answer non est?
   (A) Nonne (C) Num
   (B) Cur (D) −ne

Answers to Practice Questions: Questions and Answers

1. **(C)**

Nonne introduces a question expecting the answer "Yes," which is expressed in Answers (A), (B), and (D). Answer (C), **immo**, expresses the answer "No, on the contrary." The question asks, "Did Juno feel hatred toward all the Trojans?" Note the dative of possession, **odium Iunoni . . . erat**.

2. **(B)**

The question word **quo** ("where to?") requires an answer in the accusative, which we have in all four options here. The correct answer has to do with where the Trojans were driven by the storm, which was, of course, Carthage, and not (A), Italy, (C) Alexandria, or (D) Greece.

3. **(C)**

Habebatne asks the open question, "Did Aeneas have twenty ships?" which may be answered in either the affirmative or negative. Only (C) leaves the answer open. The answers given in (A) and (D) translate the cue word **nonne** instead of the enclitic **−ne**, and Answer (B) translates the cue word **num**. None of these fit the sense required by the Latin.

4. **(D)**

The phrasing of the sentence "Aeneas did not really marry Dido, did he?" requires the interrogative adverb **num**. Answers (A) and (B) do not lead to that meaning, and **neque** does not introduce a question.

5. **(A)**

The question word **quocum** requires that the answer be an ablative of accompaniment. Since all four answers have this form, the correct response has to do with the identity of the person with whom Aeneas fled from Troy. That was Creusa, and not (B) Priam, (C) Venus, or (D) Helenus. Creusa is indeed feminine, but **quo** is the ablative singular feminine form of the interrogative pronoun (see Chapter 13).

6. **(B)**

The question word **Unde** means "From where"? Answer (A) translates **quo**, (C) **ubi** or **quando**, and (D) **cur**. The sentence reads, "From where did the people come who had first settled Italy?"

7. **(C)**

The English word "wasn't" calls for an affirmative answer, which leads to the assumption that the equivalent question word in Latin is (C) **Nonne**. Answer (A) **Num** translates as "Alba Longa wasn't . . . , was it?" and (B) **–ne** as "Was Alba Longa . . . ?" Answer (D) **Non** is not a viable option.

8. **(D)**

The **q**-word that translates "What sort of?" is **Qualis**. Answer (A) **Quomodo** means "How?" (B) **Quot** means "How many?" and (C) **Quando** means "When?"

9. **(A)**

Quare, also spelled **Qua re**, is translated as "Why?" or "For what reason?" Answer (B) "When" is **Quando**?, (C) "How" is **Quomodo**? and (D) "Where" is **Ubi**? The sentence reads, "Why did Aeneas ask the Sibyl to take him to Orcus?"

10. **(C)**

Non est is a negative reply, so the cue word must be **Num**, and not (A) **Nonne**, (B) **Cur**, or (D) **–ne**.

Chapter 21

Participles and the Ablative Absolute

A participle is a verb with an adjective ending, hence it "participates" in the functions of two different parts of speech. It serves all of the functions of an adjective, hence it modifies a noun or pronoun and agrees with the word modified in gender, number, and case. It also expresses some of the functions of a verb, hence it has past, present, and future tense, and can take an object. Participles can also serve as substantives.

Quick Study of Participles mitto, mittere, misi, missus		
	Active	**Passive**
Present	**mittens** (stem **mittent-**), *sending*	
Perfect		**missus, -a, -um**, *having been sent*
Future	**missurus, -a, -um,** *about to send*	**mittendus, -a, -um,** *about to be sent* (also known as the gerundive)*

The Present Active Participle

- Use the letters **–ns** (**mittens**) to recognize the form of the nominative singular of the present participle. The nominative singular lacks the **-nt-** of the remaining forms. Use the **-nt-** of the Latin form, e.g., **mittent-**, to identify the participle as present.
- For greater clarity in English, translate the participle as a clause:

  Exercens in palaestra, Linus sudat.

  As a verbal adjective: *Exercising in the palaestra, Linus is sweating.*

  As a clause: *While (he is) exercising in the palaestra, Linus is sweating.*

* Gerundives will be covered in Chapter 22.

- The action of the present participle takes place continuously and at the same time as the action of the main verb in a sentence. Therefore, if the main verb is found in the past tense, the present participle, in order to express contemporary action, must be translated *was___-ing*, and not *is___-ing*. Use the words *while* or *as* to translate the present participle:

  Present — Present

  Exercens in palaestra, Linus sudat.

  While (he is) exercising in the palaestra, Linus is sweating.

  Present — Present

  Present — Past

  Exercens in palaestra, Linus sudabat.

  While (he was) exercising in the palaestra, Linus was sweating.

  Past — Past

The time of the action of the participle thus correlates with that of the main verb. For present participles, the time is contemporary with that of the main verb, for past participles, the time is previous to that of the main verb, and for future participles, the time succeeds that of the main verb. Latin has no present participle in the passive.

The Perfect Passive Participle

- The perfect passive participle is the fourth principal part of the regular verb. It is also known as the past participle or as the PPP. You met this form when reviewing the perfect passive system of indicative verbs, e.g., **missus est**, *he has been sent*. As the perfect passive participle of the verb, **missus, -a, -um** is translated *having* (perfect) *been* (passive) *sent*. Latin does not have a perfect active participle, although past participles of deponent verbs have active meanings.

  Regular verb:

  Linus unctus e palaestra egressus est.

  Linus, having been oiled, left the exercise area.

  Deponent verb:

  Linus egressus e palaestra ad tepidarium iit.

  Linus, having left the exercise ground, went to the warm room.

- Unlike the action of the present participle, the action of the past participle is completed and takes place prior in time to the action of the main verb in the sentence. In the sentences just above, Linus was oiled down before he left the exercise area, and he left the exercise area before he went to the warm room. Context and knowledge of the principal parts of deponent verbs will assist you in translating correctly the participles of deponent verbs.

- Here are some common ways to translate a perfect passive participle of a regular verb using the sentence **Linus unctus egressus est:**

  Literal: *Linus, having been oiled, left.*

  As a clause: *Linus left when he was/had been oiled.*
  Linus left after he was/had been oiled.
  Linus left because he was/had been oiled.
  Linus, who was/had been oiled, left.

The Future Active Participle

- With participles, the future depends upon the past, i.e., the form of the future active participle is an extension of that of the perfect passive participle.
- Remember that a form such as **missurus** is a participle in the future tense by noting that the **-ur-** in the form reflects the -ur- in the English word "future."

  Linus dimissurus servum plus unguenti poposcit.

  Linus, about to send away the slave, asked for more oil.

- Here are some ways of expressing the future active participle in English:

About to...	*Intending to...*	*Planning to...*
Going to...	*On the point of...*	*Ready to...*

- These sentences illustrate the translation of the future active participle as a clause:

  Linus senatori in thermas ingressuro occurrit.

  Linus happened upon the senator who was going to enter the baths.

  Linus senatorem subsequens, "Nos lavaturi te salutamus!" clamavit.

  Linus, tagging along after the senator, proclaimed, "We who are about to bathe salute you!"

- The future participle sometimes appears with a form of the verb **esse** as a variant of the future tense. This is known as the active periphrastic.

  Linus sperat senatorem iocum eius risurum esse.

  Linus hopes that the senator will laugh at his joke.

The Ablative Absolute

- The ablative absolute is a participial phrase that is grammatically independent of the rest of the sentence ("absolute," fr. **absolvere**, *set free, separate*). It generally consists of a noun or pronoun that is accompanied by a present or past participle, with both forms found in the ablative case, e.g,

  Thermis aedificatis, Linus salubritate fruebatur.

  After the public baths were built, Linus enjoyed good health.

  The meaning of the ablative absolute **Thermis aedificatis** is independent of that of the main clause **Linus salubritate fruebatur.** Linus did not build the baths (but no doubt he enjoyed them!)

  Contrast the following sentence:

  Thermas aedificantes, complures servi mortui sunt.

  While they were building the baths, several slaves died.

  How do these two sentences differ in structure? In the second example, the participial phrase is not an ablative absolute because there is a direct connection between the participal phrase **Thermas aedificantes** and **complures servi mortui sunt**, the main part of the sentence. That is, the participle **aedificantes** modifies the subject of the main clause, **servi**. This participial phrase is not "absolute" or separate from the main sentence.

- In Latin, the subject of the perfect passive participle in an ablative absolute is not the same as that of the main verb; however, in English it may be expressed as such if the identity of the two subjects is clearly the same, e.g.,

  Vestimentis exutis, Linus aliquid unguenti poscebat.

  After he had taken off his clothes, Linus asked for some oil, lit.,
  After the clothes had been taken off, Linus....

  In this sentence, the person who is disrobing and Linus are clearly the same, therefore the ablative absolute may be changed from the passive to the active voice in translation. When translating in such situations, be sure to express the action of the past participle as preceding that of the main verb.

- Because there is no present active participle of the verb **esse**, this participle is understood and expressed in the English translation of a Latin sentence in which the ablative absolute seems to lack a participial form, e.g.,

  With a noun: **Lino custode, vestimenta non surripientur.**

  While Linus is on guard, the clothes will not be stolen.

  With an adjective: **Fure callido, vestimenta surripientur.**

  If the thief is clever, the clothes will be stolen.

Quick Study of the Ablative Absolute

Type 1 (with the perfect passive participle, action precedes that of the main verb)

Linteo a balneatore accepto, Linus se ipsum strenue defricabat.

After the towel had been received from the attendant, lit., *the towel having been received from the attendant, Linus vigorously rubbed himself dry.*

Type 2 (with the present active participle, action contemporary with that of the main verb)

Lino in popina bibente, amicus suus in caldario madefacit.

While Linus is drinking in the snack-bar, his friend is soaking in the hot room.

Lino in popina bibente, amicus suus in caldario madefaciebat.

While Linus was drinking in the snack-bar, his friend was soaking in the hot room.

Type 3 (with no participle)

Lino balneatore, accipietne aliquis linteum?

If Linus is the bath attendant, will anyone receive a towel?

Aqua frigidiore, Linus in frigidarium intrare non voluit.

The water being too cold, Linus did not wish to enter the cold room.
Better English, *Since the water was too cold. . . .*

Recognizing an Ablative Absolute

- Every ablative absolute must contain at least two elements, the noun or pronoun and the participle or its substitute (a second noun, an adjective, or a pronoun).
- Often the noun or pronoun and participle are found in close proximity, but there may be additional, intervening words. The noun or pronoun regularly appears before the participle.
- The ablative absolute usually appears early in the sentence.
- As an independent thought unit in a sentence, the ablative absolute is usually (but not always) set off by commas from the rest of the sentence.

Translating an Ablative Absolute

The "Type 1" ablative absolute, that is, the ablative absolute containing a past participle, is by far the most common. When translating, begin by rendering the participle literally, i.e., **Thermis aedificatis**, *The baths having been built*. Use *having been* _____ as your memorized or default translation of the past participle. Then move on to other possibilities that might better express the meaning in English. As with other participial constructions, the ablative absolute can be translated as a clause that expresses time (*after, when*) or cause (*since*). The decision is up to you, the reader, to determine the best contextual sense of an ablative absolute, e.g.,

Thermis aedificatis, cotidie multi se lavare poterant.

Temporal: *After/When the baths had been built . . .*

Causal: *Since/Because the baths had been built . . .*

The ablative absolute may also coordinate with the main clause and serve as a second main verb, e.g., *The baths had been built and . . .*

Here are some additional examples of ablatives absolute translated as clauses:

Lino morante, amici in apodyterium intraverunt.

While Linus was loitering, his friends entered the dressing room.

Vestimentis exutis, Linus amicos deridentes eum audiebat.

After he had taken off his clothes, Linus heard his friends laughing at him.

Hoc audito, Linus linteo se celavit.

When he (had) heard this, Linus hid himself with a towel.

Amicus molestus, Lino verecundo, linteum surripuit.

Since Linus was (being) bashful, his pesky friend stole away the towel.

Tips on Translating Participles

Please refer to the following sentence with respect to the tips below:

Linus unguentum et strigilem ferens, in pavimento lapsus est.

While Linus was carrying the oil and strigil, he slipped on the tiled floor.

- Participles are verbal adjectives and must modify a noun or pronoun in the sentence. The participle follows the rules of noun-adjective agreement in Latin. When translating a participle, locate the participle (**ferens**) and then link it with the pronoun or noun modified (**Linus**).
- The participle **ferens** represents one of two actions in the sentence in which it appears. The expression in English of the time of the action of the participle depends upon the tense of the main verb of the sentence. **Ferens** is expressed as *was carrying* because the main verb **lapsus est** is in the past tense.

- The participle as a verbal adjective is found in a participial phrase, which is a group of words without a subject or verb and containing a participle, e.g., **unguentum et strigilem ferens**. In Latin, the participle is found at the end of the phrase, as **unguentum et strigilem ferens**, whereas in English, the participle is found at the beginning, *carrying oil and a strigil*.
- Participial phrases are usually translated as subordinate clauses that express particular circumstances of time (*while, when*) or cause (*since, because*). The phrase underlined above is expressed as a temporal clause, *while Linus was carrying*.
- Participial phrases can be found at the beginning, middle, or end of a Latin sentence.
- The word modified by the participle usually precedes it: **Linus . . . ferens**.
- The phrase in which a participle is found is often framed by commas.

Practice Questions on Participles and the Ablative Absolute

1. Lavantes, furibus vestes surripientibus, custodes conducebant.
   (A) because their clothes had been stolen by the thieves
   (B) since the thieves had stolen the clothes
   (C) because the thieves were stealing the clothes
   (D) while the thieves are stealing the clothes

2. Cicero scripsit, "Signa rerum futurarum a dis ostenduntur."
   (A) having been
   (B) being
   (C) about to be
   (D) had been

3. The voices of the men singing annoyed me while I was soaking in the hot bath.
   (A) cantantium/madefaciens
   (B) cantantis/madefacientes
   (C) cantantium/madefacientem
   (D) cantantes/madefaciente

4. The girls were going to hurry into the changing room.
   (A) festinaturae erant
   (B) festinaturae fuerant
   (C) festinaturae sunt
   (D) festinaturi erant

5. Select the translation of the sentence that is not correct.

   Servi strigilibus homines unctos defricabant.

   (A) While the men were being oiled down, the slaves were scraping them with strigils.

   (B) The slaves were scraping with strigils the men who had been oiled down.

   (C) The slaves were oiling down the men and then scraping them with strigils.

   (D) After the men had been oiled down, the slaves scraped them with strigils.

6. His rebus factis, athletae in palaestram ierunt.

   (A) While these things were being done

   (B) After these things were done

   (C) About to do these things

   (D) While doing these things

7. Exercens athleta plus unguenti rogat.

   (A) While exercising
   (C) Having exercised

   (B) About to exercise
   (D) Who was exercising

8. "We who are about to bathe salute you!" the men proclaimed to the attendants.

   (A) lavantes
   (C) lavandi

   (B) lauturi
   (D) lauturos

9. Select the translation of the underlined participial phrase that is not correct.

   Illa, vix patiens vaporem, e caldario egrediebatur.

   (A) since she was barely enduring the steam

   (B) barely enduring the steam

   (C) because she is barely enduring the steam

   (D) who was scarcely enduring the steam

10. Linus paucos lavantes in frigidario vidit.

    (A) having been bathed
    (C) having bathed

    (B) about to bathe
    (D) bathers

11. Which of the following accurately substitutes for Profecti ad thermas . . . ?

    (A) Postquam ad thermas profecti erant . . .

    (B) Ad thermas proficiscentes . . .

    (C) Cum ad thermas proficiscebantur . . .

    (D) Dum ad thermas proficiscuntur . . .

12. We gave money to the beggars <u>who were lingering</u> in the entryway.
   (A) moratis
   (B) cum morati erant
   (C) quamquam morabantur
   (D) morantibus

13. Linus <u>regressus</u> ad tepidarium in aquam insiluit.
   (A) returning
   (B) who was returning
   (C) having returned
   (D) about to return

Sententiae Antiquae

1. Who can deceive <u>one who is in love</u>? (Vergil)
   (A) amatam
   (B) amandam
   (C) amaturam
   (D) amantem

2. Why are you laughing? <u>When the name has been changed</u>, the story is told about you. (Horace)
   (A) Mutans nomen
   (B) Mutato nomine
   (C) Mutatis nominibus
   (D) Mutatum nomen

3. A word <u>to the wise</u> is sufficient. (Terence)
   (A) sapienti
   (B) sapiens
   (C) sapientes
   (D) sapientem

4. O vos ____ graviora, dabit deus his quoque finem. (Vergil)
   (A) passa
   (B) passus
   (C) passi
   (D) passos

5. The skill of an orator <u>about to recite</u> pleases those <u>who are going to listen</u>. (Quintilian)
   (A) dicturi/auditura
   (B) dicentis/audientes
   (C) dicti/auditos
   (D) dicturi/audituros

Participles in the *Aeneid*

Passage 1

Circle the seven participles appearing in this passage from Book 6. Three are deponent, one of which is a substantive.

Venus has sent doves to guide Aeneas.

1 Sic effatus vestigia pressit
2 observans quae signa ferant, quo tendere pergant.

Pascentes illae tantum prodire volando
quantum acie possent oculi servare sequentum.
Inde ubi venere ad fauces grave olentis Averni,
tollunt se celeres liquidumque per aera lapsae
sedibus optatis gemina super arbore sidunt,
discolor unde auri per ramos aura refulsit.

***Aeneid* 6.197–204**

Passage 2

Circle all six participles in this passage from Book 2 and draw an arrow to the word each modifies. Be careful of infinitives in ellipsis that appear to be participles.

Laocoon addresses his fellow Trojans.

Primus ibi ante omnes magna comitante caterva
Laocoon ardens summa decurrit arce,
et procul, "O miseri, quae tanta insania, cives?
Creditis avectos hostes? Aut ulla putatis
dona carere dolis Danaum? Sic notus Ulixes?
Aut hoc inclusi ligno occultantur Achivi,
ait haec in nostris fabricata est machina muros,
inspectura domos venturaque desuper urbi,
aut aliquis latet error; equo ne credite, Tecuri.
Quidquid id est, timeo Danaos et dona ferentes."

***Aeneid* 2.40–49**

Answers to Practice Questions on Participles and the Ablative Absolute

1. Ablative absolute **(C)**

This question tests your ability to translate an ablative absolute containing a present participle when the main verb is in a past tense. The present participle must be translated in the past because its action must be contemporary with that of the main verb, which is past. The translations in Answers (A) and (B) provide past actions that are completed, "had been stolen" and "had stolen," which would require perfect passive participles. The translation in Answer (D) "are stealing" is not contemporary with the time of the main verb **conducebant**, which is in the imperfect tense.

2. Future participle **(C)**

Answer (C) translates the underlined form **futurarum** correctly as the future participle of the verb **esse**. The sentence reads, "Indications of future events, lit., things about to be are revealed to the world by the gods." Answer (A) translates a perfect active participle, which doesn't exist as a form except in the case of deponent verbs. Answers (B) and (D) are in the wrong tenses.

3. Present participle **(C)**

"Of the men singing" requires a form that is genitive plural and "annoyed me (while I was) soaking" a form that is accusative singular to modify **me**, leading to **cantantium/madefacientem**. Although the verbs may be unfamiliar, their forms should not. **Madefaciens** in Answer (A) is nom. sing. and does not agree with **me**, the direct object of the verb "annoyed" in the sentence. Answer (B) contains forms that are gen. sing. and nom./acc. pl., which are incorrect. Answer (D) contains forms that are also in the incorrect case and number (nom./acc. pl. and abl. sing.)

4. Active periphrastic **(A)**

This question tests your familiarity with the active periphrastic. "(They) were going to hurry" requires a future active participle "going to hurry" and the auxiliary verb "(they) were," which is **erant**. Answer (B) translates as "had been about to hurry," and (C) "are about to hurry." Answer (D) "were about to hurry" provides the correct translation, but the participle **festinaturi** has a masculine ending where a feminine ending, modifying "the girls," is required.

5. Perfect passive participle **(A)**

This sentence reads literally, "The slaves were scraping with strigils the men <u>having been oiled down</u>." The participle is **unctos**, the perfect passive participle of **unguere** modifying **homines**, which is the direct object of the verb **defricabant**. Answer (A) requires a present participle to render the meaning "while," which is an action contemporary with that of the main verb, rather than prior to it, as required by the perfect passive participle **unctos**.

6. Ablative absolute **(B)**

"After these things were done" is a condensation of "these things having been done," a more literal translation of the ablative absolute **His rebus factis**. Answer (D) requires the present participle "while doing" (**facientes**) and (C) the future participle "about to do" (**facturi**), both directly modifying **athletae** and thus not ablative absolutes. Answer (A) renders a present passive participial form ("were being done"), which is inexpressible in Latin.

7. Present participle **(A)**

Exercens is the nominative singular form of the present participle modifying **athleta**, the subject of the sentence. Answer (B) "about to exercise" translates the future participle **exerciturus**, (C) "having exercised" gives an impossible meaning of **exercens**, and (D) "was exercising" requires that the main verb be **rogabant**, a past tense. The sentence reads, "<u>While exercising</u>, the athlete is requesting more oil." Note the appearance of the partitive genitive.

8. Future participle **(B)**

This sentence requires a future participle, "about to bathe," modifying the subject "we,"which is the form **lauturi** (remember that the masculine ending is preferred when the gender is not specified). Answer (A) **lavantes** is a present participle, "bathing," and (C) **lavandi** a gerund or gerundive form that is not appropriate in this context. Answer (D) **lauturos** is a future participle, but has an accusative ending, rather than the necessary nominative.

9. Present participle **(C)**

Vix patiens vaporem is a present participial phrase that must be rendered as continuous action in the past tense in order to be contemporary with the time of the main verb **egrediebatur**, which is in the imperfect tense. Answer (C) is incorrect because the translation "is enduring" cannot properly render **patiens**, since the main verb is in the past tense.

10. Present participle as substantive **(D)**

The sentence reads, "Linus saw few (people) bathing, i.e., few bathers, in the cold room." Answer (A) calls for a perfect passive participle, **lautos**, and Answer (B) a future participle, **lauturos**. Answer (C), "having bathed," requires a perfect active participle, which is an impossible translation of **lavantes**, since **lavo** is not a deponent verb.

11. Past participle of a deponent verb **(A)**

The original phrase reads, "(They) having set out for the baths . . . . Answer (A) correctly reads "After they had set out for the baths . . . , which is a past completed action. The remaining answers contain continuous actions: (B) "Setting out for the baths," (C) "When they were setting out for the baths," and (D) While they are setting out for the baths."

12. Present participle **(D)**

"Who were lingering" requires a present participle, as the main verb "gave" is in the past tense and the action of "lingering" is continuous, hence **morantibus**. The case is dative, modifying "to the beggars." Answer (A) is a present participle, but in the gen. sing., and (B), "who had lingered," has the incorrect tense. Answer (C), "although they were lingering" does not translate the original wording correctly.

13. Past participle **(C)**

Regressus is a deponent verb, so the translation is active, "having returned." Answers (A) and (B) "returning" and "who was returing" require the present participle, **rediens**. Answer (C), "about to return," is future, **regressurus**.

Sententiae Antiquae Answers

1. Present participle as substantive **(D)**

The present participle **amantem** correctly expresses the present time given in the phrase "one who is in love," i.e., a lover. Answer (A), amatam, is a past participle, and (C) is future. Answer (B) is a gerundive, or future passive participle, which will be covered in the next chapter.

2. Ablative absolute **(B)**

The ablative absolute **mutato nomine** correctly translates the time clause "When the name has been changed." Answer (A) **mutans nomen** contains a present participle, which does not correctly render the meaning. Answer (C) **mutatis nominibus** is an ablative absolute, but has forms in the plural, whereas the singular is required. Answer (D) **mutatum nomen** is a phrase with the past participle, but does not make sense in the context.

3. Present participle, substantive **(A)**

This question presents the participle **sapiens** as a substantive, i.e., "the one being wise," "the wise." Since the English requires a dative form, "to the wise," **sapienti** is the correct answer. Answer (B) is nominative, (C) nom/acc. plural, and (D) accusative singular, none of which fits the context.

4. Past participle, deponent **(C)**

All answers are in the perfect passive participial form of the deponent verb **patior, pati, passus sum**. This participle, when translated in the active voice, means "having suffered." All that's left to do is to determine the function, or case, of the missing participle. The form modifies the vocative form **vos**, given the sense, so it must be vocative plural, ergo, **passi**. Answer (A) tempts you to use the participle to modify **graviora**, but this word serves as the (neuter plural substantive) direct object. Answer (B) **passus** is singular, not plural, and (D) **passos** is accusative, not vocative, as required by the context. The sentence reads, "O you having suffered (who have suffered) rather serious trials, god will make an end to these, too."

5. Future participle **(D)**

"About to recite" and "going to listen" both require future active participles. The first participle modifies "of an orator," which requires a form in the genitive case. The clause "who are going to listen" modifies "those," which serves as the accusative direct object. (There are no dative forms offered as answers, so a verb other than **placere** for "please" must be assumed.) The forms in Answer (D) **dicturi/audituros** fulfil all the requirements and provide the correct answer. Answer (A) **dicturi/auditura** contains future participles, but **auditura** does not modify "those (people)," which is personal and not neuter. Answers (B) and (C) contain participles other than those in the future tense, i.e., **dicentis** (present) and **dicti/auditos** (past).

Answers to Participles in the *Aeneid*

Passage 1

1. **effatus** (line 1)
2. **observans** (line 2)
3. **Pascentes** (line 3)
4. **sequentum** (line 4)
5. **olentis** (line 5)
6. **lapsae** (line 6)
7. **optatis** (line 7).

Passage 2

1. **comitante caterva** (line 1)
2. **Laocoon ardens** (line 2)
3. **inclusi Achivi** (line 6)
4. **machina inspectura** (lines 7-8)
5. **machina ventura** (lines 7-8)
6. **Danaos ferentes** (line 10).

Chapter 22

The Gerund, Gerundive, and Supine

The Gerund

The gerund is a verbal noun that has characteristics of both a verb and a noun, e.g.,

Possumus discere multa de deis Romanis legendo.

We can learn much about the Roman gods by reading.

The gerund is formed by adding **-nd-** to the present stem of the verb, together with the endings of the second declension singular noun in all cases but the nominative. The gerund serves the functions of a noun in these cases and is translated with *–ing*, e.g., *reading.*

	Forms	Common Uses
Nom.	______	
Gen.	**legendi**, *of reading*	purpose with **causa** or **gratia**
Dat.	**legendo**, *to, for reading*	indirect object or with special adjectives
Acc.	**legendum**, *reading*	purpose with **ad**
Abl.	**legendo**, *by, with reading*	means/instrument or with **de**, **e/ex,** or **in**

Note:

- There is no nominative form of the gerund. The subjective infinitive **legere**, *reading*, is substituted. (For this type of infinitive, see Chapter 23.)

The Gerundive (Future Passive Participle)

The gerundive is a verbal adjective formed by adding **-ndus, -a, -um** to the present stem of the verb, e.g., **legendus, -a, -um.** As a verbal adjective, the gerundive agrees with a noun:

Possumus discere de deis Romanis fabulis legendis.

We can learn about the Roman gods by reading stories, lit., *by stories about to be read.*

In the sentence given above, note that the gerundive **legendis** is attracted into the ablative case in agreement with the noun **fabulis**, *by (means of) stories*. You would normally expect the accusative form **fabulas** to serve as the direct object of **legendis**, but the Romans preferred to use a gerundive, i.e., **fabulis legendis,** instead of a gerund, i.e., **fabulas legendo**, when a direct object was involved.

Notes:

- The form of both the gerund and gerundive may be recognized by the **-nd-**, deriving from **gerendus**, **-a**, **-um**, *about to be done*, which is the gerundive form of the Latin verb **gerere**.
- You may remember that the gerundive serves as a verbal adjective by learning the phrase "The gerundive is an adjective."

Simple Gerundive

The gerundive is found in all noun cases, e.g.,

Dative: **Orpheus apud inferos lyram modulatus est acquirendae uxori.**

Orpheus played his lyre in the underworld to gain possession of his wife.

Ablative: **Lyrā modulandā Orpheus bestias flexit.**

Orpheus charmed the beasts by playing his lyre.

Gerundive of Purpose (with *Ad*, *Causa*, or *Gratia*)

The gerundive accompanying **ad** (+ acc.), *to, in order to*, **causa** (+ gen.) or **gratia** (+ gen.), *for the purpose of, for the sake of*, indicates purpose or intent, e.g.,

Icarus alte volabat caeli tangendi causa.

Icarus flew high for the sake of touching the sky.

Daedalus mare investigabat ad filium mortuum inveniendum.

Daedalus searched the sea in order to find his dead son.

Gerundive of Obligation (Passive Periphrastic)

The gerundive is commonly used with a form of the verb **esse** to express necessity or obligation. When the gerundive has this function, it has meanings such as *must be*, *ought to be, should be.* This use is known either as the gerundive of obligation or the passive periphrastic, the latter of which is a time-honored Greek term which roughly means "roundabout." Any tense of the verb **esse** may be used, e.g.,

Medusa necanda est. *Medusa has to be (must be) killed.*

Medusa necanda erat. *Medusa had to be killed.*

Medusa necanda erit. *Medusa will have to be killed*, etc.

Note:

- The gerundive of obligation is frequently used in indirect statements and indirect questions. For more on these constructions, see Chapters 23 and 28, respectively.

Indirect statement: **Perseus scit Medusam necandam esse.**
Perseus knows that Medusa must be killed.

Indirect question: **Perseus non rogavit cur Medusa necanda esset.**
Perseus did not ask why Medusa had to be killed

When an intransitive verb, that is, a verb which does not take a direct object, appears in the passive periphrastic, the gerundive is translated impersonally, i.e., has "it" as its subject. For better English, transform the passive voice to the active, e.g.,

Ad Graias Perseo eundum est.

Perseus must go to the Graiae, lit., *It must be gone by Perseus to the Graiae.*

Dative of Agent

You will note in the previous example that **Perseo** is expressed in the dative case. In the passive periphrastic, the person who must perform the obligation expressed in the verb is found in the dative case, a use known as the dative of agent. (The ablative of personal agent with **a/ab** is not used with this construction. For this usage, see Chapter 12.)

Quick Study of the Gerund and the Gerundive

The Gerund	The Gerundive
is a verbal noun	is a verbal adjective
corresponds to the English verbal noun in *-ing*, e.g., **mittendum**, *sending*	agrees with a noun or pronoun, e.g., **ad epistulam mittendam**, *for the purpose of sending the letter*
is present and active in meaning	is future and passive in meaning
is found only in the gen., dat., acc., and abl., sing. forms of the second declension	is found in all case forms of the first/second declension adjective

The Supine

Just as the gerund is a verbal noun, so is the supine. It is formed from the fourth principal part of the verb, but has a different meaning from that of the perfect passive participle. Only two cases invite review: the accusative, e.g., **narratum**, and the ablative, **narratu.** Note that the endings of the supine are those of the fourth declension noun. The supine is used with the accusative to express purpose, e.g.,

narratum, *to tell*, and with the ablative to express respect or specification, e.g., **narratu**, *with respect to telling*. Use the context to distinguish between **narratum** as a supine, *to tell*, and **narratum** as a perfect passive participle, *having been told*.

Supine showing purpose: **Hercules ad inferos Cerberum captum iit.**
Hercules went to the underworld to capture Cerberus.
(Note that the meaning of **captum** as "having been captured" does not make sense here.)

Supine showing respect: **Cerberus tria capita habebat (horribile visu!)**
Cerberus had three heads (horrible to see!)

Notes:

- Verbs that govern the accusative supine usually express motion, as in the example just above.
- The supine as ablative of respect is found with certain neuter adjectives, e.g., **facile/difficile,** *easy/difficult*, **horribile,** *dreadful*, **mirabile,** *remarkable*, **miserabile**, *wretched,* and **optimum**, *best*. (For the ablative of respect, see Chapter 12.)

Practice Questions: The Gerund, Gerundive, and Supine

1. Quod erat demonstrandum.

   (A) What was being shown (C) What had to be shown

   (B) What has to be shown (D) What is being shown

2. Prometheus ignem surripuit hominis ____ causa.

   (A) adiuvandus (C) adiuvandis

   (B) adiuvandi (D) adiuvandum

3. Minotauro necato, ____ domum redeundum est.

   (A) Theseus (C) Theseo

   (B) Theseum (D) Thesea

4. Theseus navigavit ad Cretam ut Minotaurum necaret. The best substitute for this clause is

   (A) necare Minotaurum

   (B) ad Minotaurum necandum

   (C) quod Minotaurus necabitur

   (D) Minotauro necato

5. Sisyphus scivit saxum sibi semper volvendum esse.
   (A) Sisyphus knows that he will always roll the stone.
   (B) Sisyphus knew that he must roll the stone forever.
   (C) Sisyphus knew that the stone had always been rolled by him.
   (D) Sisyphus knew that he was going to roll the stone forever.

6. Arachne melius Minerva ____ texere poterat.
   (A) mirabilis dictu (C) mirabile dictu
   (B) mirabile dictum (D) mirabilis dictum

7. Multi venerunt ad videndum Pegasum. The construction that has the same basic meaning is
   (A) Pegasum visum (C) Pegaso viso
   (B) quod Pegasum videbant (D) videntes Pegasum

8. Daphne fugiente, Apollini celerrime currendum erat. The basic meaning of this sentence is that
   (A) Daphne had to run after Apollo
   (B) Apollo had to run after Daphne
   (C) Apollo has to run after Daphne
   (D) Apollo was running from Daphne

9. Hercules duodecim labores complevit laborando diligenter.
   (A) for working (C) about to work
   (B) by working (D) having worked

10. Pyramus Thisben visam amavit. Which of the following is not correct?
   (A) Pyramus loved to look at Thisbe.
   (B) Pyramus saw Thisbe and fell in love with her.
   (C) Pyramus loved Thisbe after seeing her.
   (D) When he had seen her, Pyramus loved Thisbe.

Sententiae Antiquae

1. Wise thinking is the source of writing well. (Horace)
   (A) scribendum (C) scribendi
   (B) scribendae (D) scribendorum

2. Gossip gains strength by going (as it goes). (Vergil)
   (A) iens (C) eundo
   (B) eundum (D) euntem

3. Caesari omnia uno tempore erant agenda. (Caesar)
   (A) Everything was being done by Caesar at the same time.
   (B) Caesar had to do everything at the same time.
   (C) Caesar was about to do everything at the same time.
   (D) Everything was done to Caesar at the same time.

4. Mea Musa a componendo carmine teneri non potest. In this sentence, Ovid says that
   (A) creating his verse cannot be kept from the Muse.
   (B) his Muse keeps him from creating verse.
   (C) his Muse cannot keep him from creating verse.
   (D) his Muse cannot be kept from creating verse.

5. Regulus laudandus est in conservando iure iurando. (Cicero)
   (A) Regulus ought to be praised for keeping his oath.
   (B) Regulus is praising those who keep their oath.
   (C) Regulus had to be praised for keeping his oath.
   (D) Regulus is being praised for keeping his oath.

The Gerund and Gerundive in the *Aeneid*

Locate and identify the gerund, gerundive, or gerundive of obligation in each sentence from the *Aeneid*. Then translate the sentence. Some context is provided.

1. *Jupiter reassures Venus.*

   At puer Ascanius triginta magnos volvendis mensibus orbes (annorum) imperio explebit. (1.268–269)

2. *Venus cloaks Aeneas and Achates in a foggy mist.*

   At Venus obscuro gradientes aere saepsit ne quis posset veniendi poscere causas. (1.411-414)

3. *The Trojans decide to take the Horse to the citadel.*

   Ducendum (esse) ad sedes simulacrum orandaque (esse) divae numina conclamant. (2.232–233)

4. *Creusa advises Aeneas about his future.*

"Longa tibi exsilia (ferenda sunt) et vastum maris aequor arandum (est tuis navibus) et terram Hesperiam venies." (2.780–781)

5. *Anna encourages her sister to try to win Aeneas.*

"Indulge hospitio causasque innecte morandi." (4.50–51)

6. *Rumor grows as it goes.*

Fama mobilitate viget viresque adquirit eundo. (4.175)

7. *Aeneas prepares to set sail.*

Aeneas Mnesthea Sergestumque vocat (ut) classem aptent taciti sociosque ad litora cogant, arma parent et quae rebus sit causa novandis dissimulent. (4.288–291)

8. *Aeneas accepts responsibility.*

"Ego te, qua plurima fando enumerare vales, numquam, regina, negabo promeritam (esse de me)." (4.333–335)

9. *Aeneas attempts to reassure Dido.*

At pius Aeneas lenire dolentem (reginam) solando cupit et dictis avertere curas. (4.393–394)

10. *Aeneas completes his promise to the Sibyl.*

Aeneas finem dedit ore loquendi. (6.76)

11. *Anchises reveals to Aeneas his future.*

Quae postquam Anchises natum per singula duxit incenditque animum famae venientis amore, exim bella viro memorat quae deinde gerenda (sint). (6.888–890)

12. *Turnus sends the slain Pallas back to Evander with these words.*

"Quisquis honos tumuli, quidquid solamen humandi est, largior." (10.493–494)

13. *Aeneas challenges Turnus.*

"Non cursu, saevis certandum est communis armis." (12.890)

Answers to The Gerund, Gerundive, and Supine

1. Gerundive of obligation **(C)**

Demonstrandum is a gerundive modifying the relative pronoun **quod**, whose antecedent is the unstated pronoun **id**. The appearance of the verb **erat** defines the construction **erat demonstrandum** as a gerundive in a passive periphrastic, meaning "(that) which had to be demonstrated (was, in fact, demonstrated)." This Latin phrase, abbreviated Q.E.D., is often found at the end of mathematical proofs.

2. Gerundive of purpose **(B)**

This question evaluates your knowledge of the gerundive of purpose with **causa**. The sentence reads, "Prometheus stole fire <u>for the sake of helping</u> mankind." Since **causa** takes the genitive case, its object is **hominis,** to be modified by the gerundive **adiuvandi**. Answer (A) is nominative singular, (B) dative/ablative plural, and (D) masculine accusative singular or neuter nominative/accusative singular, all designed to prompt consideration because of the similarity of their endings to those already found in the sentence.

3. Dative of agent **(C)**

The periphrastic **redeundum est** in this sentence requires that Theseus be dative of agent, i.e., **Theseo**. The sentence reads, "After the Minotaur was killed, <u>Theseus</u> was obliged to return home." **Theseo . . . redeundum est**, which is an example of the passive periphrastic used with an intransitive verb, reads, literally, "It must be returned home by Theseus. . . ." Answer (B) might seem to be a good choice, since **Theseum** appears to agree with **redeundum est**, but the accusative case is not justifiable. Answers (A) and (D) have no sense here.

4. Gerundive of purpose **(B)**

The gerundive of purpose, **ad Minotaurum necandum,** "for the purpose of killing the Minotaur," may be substituted for **ut Minotaurum necaret**, which is an **ut** clause of purpose with the subjunctive. The infinitive in Answer (A) is not generally used to express purpose. Answer (C) is a causal clause, "because the Minotaur will be killed," which changes the meaning, and the ablative absolute in Answer (D) expresses that the Minotaur had already been killed.

5. Gerundive of obligation **(B)**

The periphrastic **volvendum esse** is found in the context of an indirect statement following the verb **scivit**. This construction requires the use of an infinitive. The sentence reads, literally, "Sisyphus knew that he must roll the stone forever, lit., that the stone must always be rolled by him." Note that **sibi**, the dative of agent, replaces the accusative form **se**, which would ordinarily be the subject accusative of the infinitive.

6. Supine **(C)**

The supine phrase **mirabile dictu**, a favorite of Vergil, here completes the sentence "Arachne was able to weave better than Minerva (<u>remarkable to say</u>!)" The supine as ablative of respect ("remarkable with respect to saying so") is found with the neuter form of **mirabilis**, hence, Answers (A) and (D) must be omitted, as **mirabilis** is masculine/feminine. Because the meaning of this sentence does not require a supine of purpose, Answer (B) **mirabile dictum** may be eliminated.

7. Gerundive of purpose; supine **(A)**

The acceptable substitute for the gerundive of purpose, **ad videndum Pegasum**, is the supine phrase **Pegasum visum**. The sentence reads, "Many came to see Pegasus." Answer (B) is a causal clause that does not express purpose, nor do the participial phrases given in Answers (C) and (D).

8. Gerundive of obligation **(B)**

The sentence reads, "Since Daphne was fleeing, Apollo had to run very quickly." The passive periphrastic construction with an intransitive verb, **currendum erat**, expresses necessity in past time. **Apollini** is dative of agent. Answers (A) and (D) reverse the meaning, and Answer (C), which is not in past time, requires the form **currendum est**.

9. Gerund **(B)**

Since **laborando** serves the function of a noun in this sentence, Answer (B) "by working," which serves as an ablative of means, is correct. If **laborando** were a gerundive, it would modify another word. The sentence reads, "Hercules completed the twelve Labors by working tirelessly." Answer (C) "about to work" translates a future active participle and (D) "having worked" translates a perfect active participle, which has no form in Latin. Answer (A) is a potential translation of **laborando**, but has no contextual meaning in this sentence.

10. Perfect passive participle **(A)**

"To look at" incorrectly translates the perfect passive participle **visam** as a supine. The accusative form of the supine ends in **–um**, i.e., **visum**. Answers (B), (C), and (D), are acceptable ways of translating **visam** as a past participle.

Sententiae Antiquae

1. Gerund **(C)**

"Of writing" is a noun, therefore requiring that the gerund **scribendi** have its ending in the genitive case. Answer (A) **scribendum** could be a gerund, but is not in the genitive case. Answers (B) **scribendae** and (D) **scribendorum** must be gerundives, because of their adjectival endings.

2. Gerund **(C)**

"By going" is a gerund, here serving the function of the ablative of means. This quote from Vergil's *Aeneid* is the source of the motto of the State of New Mexico, **Crescit eundo**. All answers are forms of the irregular verb **ire**: Answer (A) **iens** is a present participle in its nominative (masculine, feminine, neuter) or accusative singular (neuter) form and (D) **euntem** is an accusative singular form of the present active participle, neither of which may be translated as "by going." Answer (B) **eundum** may be seen as a gerund, but the accusative case is not justified by the context.

3. Gerundive of obligation **(B)**

This sentence contains the passive periphrastic **erant agenda**, with **Caesari** serving as dative of agent. Answers (A), (C), and (D) do not express the idea of necessity or obligation, but of past continuous action ("was being done"), future action ("was about to do"), or past completed action ("was done"), respectively. Note the word order of **erant agenda**.

4. Gerundive **(D)**

The core of the meaning of this sentence is the prepositional phrase that includes a gerundive, **a componendo carmine**, "from composing verse." The use of the ablative here contains the idea of separation. Answer (A) is incorrect because the prepositional phrase given above does not serve as the subject of the sentence. In Answers (B) and (C), the Muse is not "keeping him from creating verse," as there is no Latin pronoun "him" in the original sentence. This sentence translates, "However, my Muse cannot be kept from creating verse."

5. Gerundive of obligation **(A)**

The correct answer to this question centers on the expression of the meaning of the periphrastic, **laudandus est**. Answers (B) "is praising" and (D) "is being praised" can be eliminated because they do not express obligation. Answer (C) "had to be praised" can be eliminated because it expresses past time.

Answers to The Gerund and Gerundive in the *Aeneid*

1. At puer Ascanius triginta magnos volvendis mensibus orbes (annorum) imperio explebit. (1.268-269) (gerundive)

But the boy Ascanius will complete with (his) rule thirty great years with their passing months.

2. At Venus obscuro gradientes aere saepsit ne quis posset veniendi poscere causas. (1.411-414) (gerund with **causas**)

But Venus cloaked them while proceeding in a fog so that no one could ask about the reasons for (of) their coming.

3. Ducendum (esse) ad sedes simulacrum orandaque (esse) divae numina conclamant. (2.232-233) (gerundives of obligation in indirect statement with **conclamant**.)

They (The Trojans) cry that the image must be taken to (her = Athena's) temple and that the divinity of the goddess must be supplicated.

4. "Longa tibi exsilia (ferenda sunt) et vastum maris aequor arandum (est tuis navibus) et terram Hesperiam venies." (2.780-781) (gerundives of obligation, in ellipsis)

"Long exile (must be endured) by you and the vast open space of the sea must be plowed (by your ships) and you will arrive at the land of Hesperia."

5. "Indulge hospitio causasque innecte morandi." (4.50-51) (gerund)

"Treat (him) with hospitality and weave together reasons for him to stay (for his staying)."

6. Fama mobilitate viget viresque adquirit eundo. (4.175) (gerund)

Rumor grows strong with (its) movement and gains strength as it goes (by going).

7. Aeneas Mnesthea Sergestumque vocat (ut) classem aptent taciti sociosque ad litora cogant, arma parent et quae rebus sit causa novandis dissimulent. (4.288-291) (gerundive with **rebus**)

Aeneas calls Mnestheus and Sergestus to outfit the fleet in silence, gather (their) comrades at the shore, prepare (their) armament, and hide (what is) the reason for (their) new undertaking.

8. "Ego te, qua plurima fando enumerare vales, numquam, regina, negabo (te) promeritam (esse de me). (4.333-335) (gerund)

"I will never deny, Queen, that you have deserved of me the very most that you are able to count in speech (by speaking)."

9. At pius Aeneas lenire dolentem (reginam) solando cupit et dictis avertere curas. (4.393-394) (gerund)

But dutiful Aeneas wishes to comfort the grieving queen with sympathy and deflect her troubles with words.

10. Aeneas finem dedit ore loquendi. (6.76) (gerund; note the pleonasm with **ore**)

Aeneas made an end of speaking (with his mouth).

11. Quae postquam Anchises natum per singula duxit incenditque animum famae venientis amore, exim bella viro memorat quae deinde gerenda (sint). (6.888-890) (gerundive of obligation in indirect question)

After Anchises led his son through (the scenes) one by one and set his soul on fire with desire for (his) forthcoming fame, thereupon he recounts for the man the wars which must then be waged.

12. "Quisquis honos tumuli (est), quidquid solamen humandi est, largior." (10.493-494) (gerund)

"Whatever honor there is in a tomb, whatever consolation there is in burial (of burying), I grant it."

13. "Non cursu, saevis (nobis) certandum est communis armis." (12.890) (impersonal gerundive of obligation)

"Not in a race, but hand to hand with savage weapons must we do battle."

Chapter 23

Infinitives and Indirect Statement

Quick Study of Infinitives

mitto, mittere, misi, missus		
	Active	**Passive**
Present	**mittere**, *to send*	**mitti,** *to be sent*
Perfect	**misisse**, *to have sent*	**missus esse**, *to have been sent*
Future	**missurus esse**, *to be about to send*	**missus iri**, *to be about to be sent* (rare)

Quick Study of the Infinitives of Irregular Verbs

Present	Perfect	Future
esse, *to be*	**fuisse**, *to have been*	**futurus esse**, *to be about to be*
posse, *to be able*	**potuisse**, *to have been able*	
ire, *to go*	**iisse**, *to have gone*	**iturus esse**, *to be about to go*
ferre, *to bring*	**tulisse**, *to have brought*	**laturus esse**, *to be about to bring*
velle, *to wish*	**voluisse**, *to have wished*	
nolle, *to be unwilling*	**noluisse**, *to have been unwilling*	
malle, *to prefer*	**maluisse**, *to have preferred*	
fieri, *to become*	**factus esse**, *to have become*	

Notes:

- **Fero** is the only irregular verb with passive infinitive forms: **ferri**, *to be brought*, and **latus esse**, *to have been brought*.
- The word **fore** is often used as a substitute for **futurum esse**.

Uses of the Infinitive

Subjective infinitive and objective infinitive

The infinitive, usually the present active infinitive, may be used as a subject or object of the main verb. Subjective infinitives are considered neuter singular nouns:

subjective

Dulce et decorum est pro factione mori.

It is sweet and glorious to die for one's racing team, i.e., *Dying is sweet. . . .**

The infinitive may also serve as the direct object of a verb:

objective

Vincere quam vinci auriga mavult.

A charioteer prefers victory to defeat, lit., *to win, rather than to be defeated.*

Complementary infinitive

The complementary (not complimentary!) infinitive completes the meaning of another verb. The other verb is often irregular, e.g.,

Potestne Limax hoc certamen vincere?**

Is Limax able to win this race?

Nonne Limax metam vitare vult? Eheu!

Surely Limax wants to avoid the turning post? Oops!

Quadrigas fregisse videtur.

He seems to have broken his chariot.

Tips on Translating Infinitives

- When translating, consider the context of the sentence in which the infinitive is found. Look for a controlling verb in the case of a complementary infinitive.
- The literal translation of an infinitive, *to* ___, will not always be appropriate to the context in which the infinitive is found, e.g., as a subject or object or in indirect statement. Be alert for the use of an adjective + **esse** that may appear to be a perfect passive infinitive, e.g.,

Adjective + **esse**:	**Auriga putat se peritum esse.** *The charioteer thinks that he (himself) is experienced.*
Perfect Passive Infinitive:	**Auriga putat se victorem pronuntiatum esse.** *The charioteer thinks that he (himself) was declared the winner.*

* After the famous saying by Horace, **Dulce et decorum est pro patria mori**, *It is sweet and glorious to die for one's country.*

** "Limax" means "slug" or "snail."

- The literal translation of an infinitive rarely shows or expresses purpose, i.e., *in order to___*. For the latter, a gerund or gerundive of purpose (**ad** or **causa/gratia** + the gerund or gerundive) or a clause of purpose (**ut** + subjunctive) is used. (For the gerund/gerundive of purpose, see the previous chapter. For the purpose clause with **ut**, see Chapter 27.
- Also, especially in poetry, an alternative form of the perfect tense, such as **sumpsere**, may fool you into thinking that it is the present infinitive **sumere**. Closer inspection reveals that it is the perfect stem, e.g., **sumps** –, that precedes what appears to be an infinitive ending. The form **sumpsere** is, in fact, an alternative to the third person plural of the perfect tense, **sumpserunt**, *they have obtained*, and not the present active infinitive **sumere**, *to obtain*. See Chapter 9.
- Subjunctive verbs formed from the present and perfect active infinitives are not to be confused with the infinitives themselves, e.g., **esse** is a present infinitive, whereas **essem** is an imperfect subjunctive, and **egisse** is a perfect infinitive, while **egisset** is a pluperfect subjunctive. (The forms of the subjunctive will be reviewed in Chapter 24.)

Indirect Statement

The infinitive may be used to report what someone hears, says, thinks, etc. This grammatical construction is known as indirect statement or accusative and infinitive. The following sentences illustrate the grammatical differences between direct and indirect statement:

Direct statement: **Auriga quadrigas magna arte agit.**
The charioteer drives the chariot with great skill.

Indirect statement: **Dicit aurigam quadrigas magna arte agere.**
He says that the charioteer drives the chariot with great skill.

Verbs of mental or verbal action, e.g., **dicit**, are followed by a subject accusative, e.g., **aurigam**, and an infinitive, e.g., **agere**, unless they introduce a direct quotation. Such verbs should be remembered, because of the frequency with which the indirect statement occurs in Latin. (This might lead you to think that the ancient Romans were gossipy!) A memory device such as "M and M (mind and mouth) verbs" may help you to remember the following verbs that commonly introduce indirect statements in Latin:

arbitrari, *think*
audire, *hear*
cognoscere, *recognize*
credere, *believe*
dicere, *say*
intellego, *know, understand*
negare, *deny*
putare, *think*
scire, *know*
sentire, *feel, perceive*
sperare, *hope*
videre, *see*

An infinitive has a definite relationship in time with that of the main verb of the sentence. Look at the following examples:

Conspiciebamus Limacem equos pascere.
We saw that Limax was feeding his horses.

Limax putabat Velocem optimum equum fuisse.
Limax thought that Velox had been the best horse.

Because the infinitive **pascere** in the first example is given in the present tense, its action is contemporary with or happening at the same time as that of the main verb **conspiciebamus**, which is past tense. Therefore, the "feeding" and the "seeing" must be expressed as happening at the same time. In the second example, the infinitive **fuisse** is in the past tense, indicating that its action has already happened relative to that of the main verb **putabat**. But the action of the main verb **putabat** is also past tense, leading to the conclusion that Velox had been the best horse before Limax thought about it. This relationship may be thought of as "past (main verb) – past (infinitive) – *had*." In the table below, note that infinitives in the present tense are translated at the same time as the main verb, those in the perfect tense are translated at a time before the main verb, and those in the future tense at a time after the main verb.

Quick Study of Indirect Statement

The Active Infinitive in Indirect Statement		
Present Main	**Limax dicit se quadrigas agere.** *Limax says that he drives (is driving) the chariot.*	Present Infinitive
Present Main	**Limax dicit se quadrigas egisse.** *Limax says that he drove (has driven) the chariot.*	Past Infinitive
Present Main	**Limax dicit se quadrigas acturum esse.** *Limax says that he will drive the chariot.*	Future Infinitive
Past Main	**Limax dicebat se quadrigas agere.** *Limax said that he was driving the chariot,* i.e., he said this at the same time as he was driving.	Present Infinitive
Past Main	**Limax dicebat se quadrigas egisse.** *Limax said that he had driven the chariot,* i.e., he drove before he spoke about it.	Past Infinitive
Past Main	**Limax dicebat se quadrigas acturum esse.** *Limax said that he would drive the chariot.*	Future Infinitive

The Passive Infinitive in Indirect Statement		
Present Main	**Limax dicit a se quadrigas agi.** *Limax says that the chariot is (being) driven by him.*	Present Infinitive
Present Main	**Limax dicit a se quadrigas actas esse.** *Limax says that the chariot has been driven by him.*	Past Infinitive
Past Main	**Limax dicebat a se quadrigas agi.** *Limax said that the chariot was (being) driven by him,* i.e., he said this at the same time that he was driving.	Present Infinitive
Past Main	**Limax dicebat a se quadrigas actas esse.** *Limax said that the chariot had been driven by him,* i.e., he drove before he spoke about it.	Past Infinitive

Tips on Translating Indirect Statement

- Look for a verb of mental or verbal action that introduces an infinitive with a subject accusative.
- Distinguish between reflexive and non-reflexive subjects of the infinitive, e.g., **se**, *himself*, and **eum**, *him*, i.e., someone other than the subject of the main verb. (For reflexive pronouns, see Chapter 13.)
- In indirect statement, when the infinitive has a compound or two-part form, i.e., perfect passive or future active, the participial portion of the infinitive agrees in gender and number with its subject, which will be accusative, e.g.,

  Perfect passive: **Auriga vidit mappam demissam esse**.
  The charioteer saw that the white starting cloth had been dropped.

  Future active: **Sperabat se metam primo circumiturum esse.**
  He was hoping that he (himself) would go around the turn post first.
- The indirect statement will never have quotes around it.
- For the best sense, insert the word "that" after the main verb in the English translation, even though this word does not appear in the Latin. Do not use the word "to" when translating an infinitive in an indirect statement, e.g.,

  Limax dicit se victorem esse.

  Incorrect: *Limax says he (himself) to be the winner.*

  Correct: *Limax says that he (himself) is the winner.*

- Remember that it is the time relationship between the main verb and the infinitive that you are translating, i.e., it is the tense of the infinitive relative to that of the main verb that determines the meaning of the indirect statement. Take special care with sentences containing a main verb in the past tense, e.g., **dicebat**, *he was saying*, when found with an infinitive either in the present tense, e.g., **esse**, *was*, or the past tense, e.g., **fuisse**, *had been*. When faced with an example of the latter, where the tenses of both the main verb and the infinitive are past, remember the acronym PPH, "past-past-*had*." If you are uncertain about how to express the time relationship, turn the indirect statement into a direct statement:

  Indirect: **Limax dicebat se quadrigas egisse**. (Note that the infinitive is in the past tense.)
  Limax said that he ____ the chariot.

  Direct: Limax said, "*I drove the chariot.*"
  i.e., he had already driven the chariot at the time he spoke.

  Therefore: *Limax said that he had driven the chariot.*

- The form **esse** is often omitted from the perfect or future active infinitive, e.g., **missum** (**esse**) or **missurum (esse),** and their meanings assumed or understood from context.

Practice Questions: Infinitives and Indirect Statement

1. "Don't fall out of your chariot, Limax!" laughed the spectators.

   (A) Non cadere (C) Noli cadere
   (B) Nolite cadere (D) Non licet cadere

2. Finire : finiri :: vincere : ________

   (A) vinci (C) vince
   (B) vici (D) victi

3. Spectator animadvertit that charioteer e curru cecidisse.

   (A) ille auriga (C) illi aurigae
   (B) illum aurigam (D) illos aurigas

4. Limax putavit se a multis non fautum esse.

   (A) has not been favored (C) was not favored
   (B) is not favored (D) had not been favored

5. Infelix auriga semper sperat crastinum diem melius ________.

   (A) fuisse (C) fuerat
   (B) fore (D) erit

6. Limax dixit se scire <u>velle</u> quot factiones contenderent.
   (A) has wanted
   (B) was wanting
   (C) wants
   (D) will want

7. <u>Making an effort is noble</u>.
   (A) Conans est nobilis.
   (B) Conari est nobile.
   (C) Conatus est nobiliter.
   (D) Nobiliter conatur.

8. "Miror tot milia virorum cupere equos et in curribus homines videre," inquit Plinius.
   (A) Pliny doesn't understand why so many people like chariot racing.
   (B) Pliny wonders what it would be like to be a charioteer.
   (C) Pliny thinks that everyone should experience chariot racing.
   (D) Pliny says that both horses and charioteers often act like children.

9. Limax scivit <u>sibi carceres purgandos esse</u>.
   (A) that he is going to clean out the stalls
   (B) that he must have the stalls cleaned out
   (C) that he must clean out the stalls
   (D) that he will be invited to clean out the stalls

10. <u>Sperat auriga diu se victurum</u>.
   (A) The charioteer, going to live for a long time, is hopeful.
   (B) The charioteer hoped that he would live for a long time.
   (C) He hopes that the charioteer will live for a long time.
   (D) The charioteer hopes that he will live for a long time.

Sentententiae Antiquae

1. Identify the item that is <u>not</u> one of the three components necessary for an indirect statement.

   <u>Ait omnia pecunia effici posse</u>. (Cicero)
   (A) Ait
   (B) posse
   (C) omnia
   (D) effici

2. We often see that the victor <u>has been overcome</u> by the vanquished. (Dionysius Cato)
   (A) superavisse
   (B) superatum esse
   (C) superare
   (D) superaturum esse

3. If you wish to be loved, love! (Seneca)

   (A) Si vis amari, ama!　　(C) Si vis amari, amate!

   (B) Si vis amare, ama!　　(D) Si vis amatus esse, ama!

4. He preferred to be good rather than to seem good. (Sallust)

   (A) esse . . . videre　　(C) fuisse . . . visus esse

   (B) esse . . . videri　　(D) esse . . . vidisse

5. ____ quid antequam natus sis acciderit id est semper esse puerum. (Cicero)

   (A) Noli nescire　　(C) Nesciendus

   (B) Nescire　　(D) Nesciri

6. Pudor doceri non potest, nasci potest. (Publilius Syrus)

   (A) Modesty cannot be learned, it can be obtained.

   (B) One cannot be taught modesty, one is born with it.

   (C) Teaching is not shameful, it can be a product of birth.

   (D) He cannot teach modesty, but he can obtain it.

7. He is ungrateful who denies that he has received a kindness that he has received. (Cicero)

   (A) accipi　　(C) accipere

   (B) acceptum esse　　(D) accepisse

8. Ego verum amo; verum volo mihi dici. (Plautus)

   (A) to be spoken　　(C) to speak

   (B) to have spoken　　(D) to have been spoken

9. Making a mistake is human. (Seneca)

   (A) Errans est humanus.　　(C) Errare humanum est.

   (B) Esse humanus est error.　　(D) Errans est humanus.

Infinitives and Indirect Statement in the *Aeneid*

Underline the main verb, the subject accusative, and the infinitive when you encounter an indirect statement in the sentences below. Translate all sentences, giving attention to the tenses of the verbs.

1. *Juno has heard that the Fates have preordained the fall of Carthage.*

   Iuno audierat sic volvere Parcas. (1.22)

2. *Juno complains that Athena has been able to do what she herself has not.*

   "Pallasne exurere classem Argivum atque ipsos potuit summergere ponto?" (1.39–40)

3. *Juno flatters Aeolus.*

   "Tibi divum pater atque hominum rex et mulcere dedit fluctus et tollere vento." (1.65–66)

4. *Aeneas' first speech.*

   "O terque quaterque beati, quibus ante ora patrum Troiae sub moenibus altis contigit oppetere (mortem)!" (1.95–96)

5. *Neptune becomes aware of the storm.*

   Interea magno misceri murmure pontum emissamque (esse) hiemem sensit Neptunus. (1.124–125)

6. *Neptune reminds the winds that he is master of the sea.*

   "Dicite (regi vestro = Aeolus) non illi imperium pelagi saevumque tridentem, sed mihi sorte datum (esse)." (1.137–139)

7. *Aeneas' "O socii" speech.*

   "Forsan et haec olim meminisse iuvabit." (1.203)

8. *Venus seeks reassurance from Jove.*

   "Certe hinc Romanos olim volventibus annis, hinc fore ductores . . . pollicitus (es)." (1.234-237)

9. *Aeneas tells of the Greek deception.*

   Nos (Danaos) abiisse rati (sumus) et vento petiisse Mycenas. (2.25)

10. *Laocoon attempts to convince the Trojans not to trust the Greeks.*

    Laocoon, ardens summa decurrit ab arce, et procul, "Creditis avectos (esse) hostes? Aut ulla putatis dona carere dolis Danaum?" (2.41–44)

Answers to Infinitives and Indirect Statement

1. Prohibition **(C)**

   The negative command "Don't fall," **Noli cadere,** represents one of the varied uses of the infinitive. Answer (A) is not a negative command, (B) is plural (Limax is being addressed in the original sentence), and (D) is not a command, but an infinitive phrase with an impersonal verb.

2. Present passive infinitive **(A)**

   The present active infinitive of **finio** is to the present passive as the present active infinitive of **vinco** is to the present passive, which is **vinci**. Answer (B) **vici** is the third principal part or perfect tense, first person singular. Answer (C) **vince** is the present imperative and (D) **victi** a form of the perfect passive participle.

3. Subject accusative **(B)**

The subject of an infinitive in an indirect statement is in the accusative case. Of the choices provided, **illum aurigam** is in the accusative case and in the singular, as required by "that charioteer." Answer (A) **ille auriga** presents what would have been the subject of the direct statement. Answer (C) **illi aurigae** is dative and (D) **illos aurigas** is plural.

4. Indirect statement **(C)**

In this sentence, the main verb **putavit** is past and the infinitive **favere** is present, so the meaning of the infinitive must be expressed in a manner that is contemporary with that of the main verb. The Latin for Answer (A) would be **favisse**, for (B) **fauturos esse**, and for (D), the main verb must be present tense, **putat**.

5. Indirect statement with **fore** **(B)**

In this sentence, the verb **sperat** is a verb of mental action, which prompts an indirect statement, of which **crastinum diem** is the subject and **fore** (= **futurum esse**) the infinitive. The sentence reads, "The unsuccessful charioteer always hopes that tomorrow <u>will be</u> better." Answer (A) **fuisse** translates as "has been" and (C) and (D) are not infinitives, but pluperfect and future tense forms of the verb **esse**.

6. Indirect statement **(B)**

The main verb **dixit** in this sentence keys an indirect statement, the subject of which is **se** and the infinitive **velle**. The combination of the main verb in the past tense and the infinitive in the present tense leads to the translation "was wanting." Answer (A) "has wanted" is **voluisse**. Answer (C) "wants" is a literal translation of the infinitive **velle**, but, given the context, the infinitive cannot have this meaning. Answer (D) "will want" cannot translate the present active infinitive **velle**. The sentence reads, "Limax said that he <u>was wanting</u> to know how many racing teams were in contention."

7. Subjective infinitive **(B)**

This sentence contains the subjective infinitive of the deponent verb **conari** "to try" = "trying." Therefore **Conari est nobile** is the correct answer. Since a subjective infinitive is considered equivalent to a neuter noun, the adjective **nobile**, which is neuter, is correct. The obvious but incorrect answer is (A), while (C) **Conatus est nobiliter** expresses the action in past time. Answer (D) **Nobiliter conatur**, meaning "He is trying nobly," is also incorrect.

8. Indirect statement **(A)**

Pliny said, "I wonder that so many thousands of men want to watch horses and people standing in chariots." Answers (B), (C), and (D) contain various inaccuracies in their translations. Note that there are two indirect statements following the main verb **miror** and connected by **et.**

9. Indirect statement with passive periphrastic **(C)**

This sentence contains an indirect statement in which the infinitive consists of **purgandos esse**, a gerundive in the passive periphrastic construction, which expresses necessity. The subject of the infinitive has reverted from accusative to dative as the agent of the necessary action. Therefore, **se** becomes **sibi.** Answer (A) "is going to clean out" is **(se) . . . purgaturum esse**. Answer (B) "must have the stalls cleaned out" is in colloquial English and cannot express the Latin in the original sentence because it makes it sound as though someone else will do it. In Answer (D) the Latin for "he will be invited" is not found in the original. Poor Limax, who even has to clean out the stalls!

10. Indirect statement **(D)**

The sentence reads, "The/A charioteer hopes that he will live for a time." The subject of the sentence, **auriga,** is put in a secondary position to tempt you into thinking that it is the subject of the infinitive, which is **se**. Note the ellipsis of the future infinitive **victurum (esse)**. Answer (A) requires a future participle in the nominative case, **(auriga) victurus**. Answer (B) requires a main verb that is in the past tense and not the present. Answer (C) requires that **auriga** be **aurigam** in order to serve as the accusative subject of the infinitive **victurum (esse)**. Remember that **auriga** is masculine.

Sententiae Antiquae Answers

1. **(D)**

Effici is a complementary infinitive dependent upon **posse** in this sentence. **Posse**, the subject of which is **omnia**, is the infinitive in the indirect statement following **ait**. The sentence reads, "He says that all things can be accomplished with money."

2. Indirect statement **(B)**

The underlined phrase "has been overcome" requires an infinitive that is perfect and passive, e.g., **superatum esse**. Answer (A) **superavisse** is active, and (C) **superare** and (D) **superaturum esse** are in the wrong tenses and voices (present and future active).

3. Complementary infinitive **(A)**

Answer (B) is incorrect because the infinitive **amare** is active and does not correctly express "to be loved." In Answer (C) the imperative is plural, whereas the singular is required, as indicated by the 2nd person singular form **vis**. Answer (D) offers the incorrect translation in the past tense, "If you wish to have been loved, love!"

4. Complementary infinitive **(B)**

Answer (C) is immediately rejected because **fuisse**, "to have been" does not correctly translate the infinitive "to be," as required in the original sentence. Answers (A) and (D) have the incorrect form of the infinitive, as **videre** means "to see" and **vidisse** "to have seen." "To seem" requires the present passive infinitive, which is **videri**, "to be seen" = "to seem."

5. Subjective infinitive **(B)**
Cicero's famous thought contains a subjective infinitive, **nescire**, "not knowing." The sentence reads, "Being unaware of what happened before you were born is always to be a child." The infinitive acts as the antecedent of the pronoun **id**. Note the two subjunctive clauses within this sentence: **quid . . . acciderit** and **antequam natus sis**.

6. Complementary infinitive **(B)**
In Answer (A) **doceri** is incorrectly translated as "learned" (this is **disci**). Answer (C) "Teaching is not shameful" reverses the thought of the original sentence, "Shame cannot be taught." Answer (D) incorrectly translates the passive infinitive **doceri** as active and misreads **nasci** as the infinitive of **nanciscor**, "obtain," rather than **nascor**, "be born."

7. Indirect statement **(D)**
The verb "denies," which introduces the indirect statement "that he has received," is in the present tense and active voice. The corresponding form of the infinitive "he has received" is the perfect active form **accepisse**. Answer (A) **accipi** is present passive, which has a contextual meaning "he is received." Answer (B) **acceptum esse** is perfect passive, "he has been received," and (C) **accipere** is present active, "he is receiving."

8. Complementary infinitive **(A)**
Dici is the present passive infinitive of the verb **dicere**. The sentence reads, "I love (what is) true, i.e., the truth; I wish the truth to be spoken to me." Answer (B) "to have spoken" is the perfect active infinitive **dixisse**, (B) "to speak," the present active form **dicere**, and (D) "to have been spoken" the perfect passive form **dictum esse**. Note the substantive adjective **verum.**

9. Subjective infinitive **(C)**
This famous saying contains the subjective infinitive **errare** modified by the neuter adjective **humanum**, a gender required by the use of the infinitive as a noun.

Answers to Infinitives and Indirect Statement in the *Aeneid*

1. Iuno audierat sic volvere Parcas. (1.22) (indirect statement)
Juno had heard that the Fates were unrolling (the thread) in this way.

2. "Pallasne exurere classem Argivum atque ipsos potuit summergere ponto?" (1.39–40) (complementary infinitive)
"Could Pallas Athena set fire to the Greek fleet and sink (the Greeks) themselves in the sea?"

3. "Tibi divum pater atque hominum rex et mulcere dedit fluctus et tollere vento." (1.65–66) (objective infinitive)
"The father of the gods and the king of men gave to you (the power) to calm the waves and raise them up with the wind."

4. "O terque quaterque beati, quibus ante ora patrum Troiae sub moenibus altis contigit oppetere (mortem)!" (1.95–96) (subjective infinitive)
"O three and four time blessed are those for whom the encounter with death has occurred before the countenances of their fathers beneath the high walls of Troy!"

5. Interea magno misceri murmure pontum emissamque (esse) hiemem sensit Neptunus. (1.124–125) (indirect statement with ellipsis of **emissam esse**)
In the meantime, Neptunus perceived that the sea was thrown into turmoil with a great roaring sound and that a winter storm had been sent forth.

6. "Dicite (regi vestro = Aeolus) non illi imperium pelagi saevumque tridentem, sed mihi sorte datum (esse)." (1.137–139) (indirect statement with ellipsis of **datum esse**)
"Tell your king that rule over the sea and the savage trident was granted by lot not to him, but to me."

7. "Forsan et haec olim meminisse iuvabit." (1.203) (subjective infinitive)
"Perhaps one day it will delight you to remember these things (remembering these things will delight you)."

8. "Certe hinc Romanos olim volventibus annis, hinc fore ductores . . . pollicitus (es). (1.234–237) (indirect statement with **fore** = **futuros esse**)
"Surely you promised that one day, as the years rolled by, the Romans would be leaders . . . ."

9. Nos (Danaos) abiisse rati (sumus) et vento petiisse Mycenas. (2.25) (indirect statement)
We thought that (the Greeks) had departed and had made for Greece on the wind.

10. Laocoon, ardens summa decurrit ab arce, et procul, "Creditis avectos (esse) hostes? Aut ulla putatis dona carere dolis Danaum?" (2.41–44) (indirect statements, the first with ellipsis of **avectos esse**)
Laocoon, fired up, runs down from the high citadel and, far away (shouts), "Do you believe that the enemy has sailed off (been carried away)? Or do you think that any gifts of the Greeks lack treachery?"

Chapter 24

Forms of the Subjunctive

The Subjunctive Mood

The subjunctive is the third of the three moods of finite verbs.* Remember from your review of the indicative and imperative moods that mood indicates the function of a verb in a sentence. You have met the indicative mood, which indicates a statement of fact or an assertion, as well as a direct question, and the imperative mood, which expresses a command. The third mood, the subjunctive, is used to express a non-factual or hypothetical action, such as a possibility or wish, often requiring in English an auxiliary or helping verb such as *might, should,* or *would*:

Indicative: **Libertus gladiator esse volebat.**
The freedman wanted to be a gladiator.

Imperative: **"Noli esse gladiator!" dicebat amicus.**
"Don't be a gladiator!" his friend said.

Subjunctive: **Amicus mirabatur cur libertus gladiator esse vellet.**
The friend wondered why the freedman wished to be a gladiator.

The use of the subjunctive, such as "I wish I were in Rome now" (not "was"!) or "Be it ever so humble...," has virtually disappeared from English. In Latin, verbs found in the subjunctive mood have a variety of uses, including serving as the verb with independent meaning found in a main clause or as the verb in a variety of subordinate or dependent clauses. The subjunctive appears most commonly as the verb of a dependent clause, as in the example provided above. This is evident from the meaning of its Latin root **subiungere**, *to subjoin, subordinate.* It has been observed that the subordinating nature of the Latin language, that is, the fact that a single main idea can establish control or priority over secondary or dependent thoughts in a sentence, reflects the martial character of the Romans and the direct authority that they established over other peoples.

There are four tenses of the subjunctive, with no forms in the future or future perfect tenses. The expression of the tense of a subjunctive verb is the same as its indicative equivalent, e.g., the imperfect subjunctive **mitteret**, *he was sending*, translates just as the imperfect indicative **mittebat**, *he was sending*. The meaning of a subjunctive verb is dependent upon and derived from its context.

---

*For convenient online summaries of the subjunctive, go to *http://en.wikibooks.org/wiki/Latin/Lesson_1-Subjunctive* and *http://dl.ket.org/latin3/grammar/home.htm.*

Present Subjunctive: Active and Passive

	1st Conj.	2nd Conj.	3rd Conj.	4th Conj.
Present Active	**pugnet**	**deleat**	**mittat**	**custodiat**
Present Passive	**pugnetur**	**deleatur**	**mittatur**	**custodiatur**

Notes:

- Formation: The vowel that marks the present subjunctive for the second, third, and fourth conjugations is -**a**-, e.g., **deleat, mittat**, and **custodiat**. Since the stem vowel of the first conjugation in the indicative is already **-a-,** the present subjunctive of that conjugation is formed using the vowel **-e-**, e.g., **pugnet.** "Let's eat caviar" or "We hear a liar" are memory devices that might help you remember the stem vowels of the four conjugations that are found in the present subjunctive.*
- The first person singular, or "I" form, of each tense in the active voice ends in **–m**, e.g., **mittam, mitterem, miserim, misissem**. The remaining personal endings for all tenses of the subjunctive are the same as those of indicative verbs. The present subjunctive is most often found by itself in a main clause and also in "should . . . would" conditional clauses. For these uses, see the following chapters.

Imperfect Subjunctive: Active and Passive

	1st Conj.	2nd Conj.	3rd Conj.	4th Conj.
Imperfect Active	**pugnaret**	**deleret**	**mitteret**	**custodiret**
Imperfect Passive	**pugnaretur**	**deleretur**	**mitteretur**	**custodiretur**

Note:

- The imperfect subjunctive is regularly used in purpose, result, and **cum** clauses, present contrary to fact conditions, and optative subjunctive expressions with **utinam**. It is perhaps the most commonly used of subjunctive forms. For these uses, see the following chapters.

* Mastery of sequence of tenses is not required for the AP Latin Exam. If you are interested in reviewing this, see *http://dl.ket.org/latin3/grammar/indirect1.htm*.

Perfect Subjunctive: Active and Passive

	1st Conj.	2nd Conj.	3rd Conj.	4th Conj.
Perfect Active	**pugnaverit**	**deleverit**	**miserit**	**custodiverit**
Perfect Passive	**pugnatus sit**	**deletus sit**	**missus sit**	**custoditus sit**

Notes:

- The perfect tense active gives the appearance of the future perfect tense active (for which, see Chapter 15). Note, however, that the first person singular of the perfect active subjunctive is **miserim**, whereas that of the future perfect indicative is **misero**. All other forms are the same.
- The perfect tense appears the least often of the four tenses of the subjunctive. It occurs independently as a potential subjunctive, and in conditional, result, and indirect question clauses. For these uses, see the following chapters

Pluperfect Subjunctive: Active and Passive

	1st Conj.	2nd Conj.	3rd Conj.	4th Conj.
Pluperfect Active	**pugnavisset**	**delevisset**	**misisset**	**custodivisset**
Pluperfect Passive	**pugnatus esset**	**deletus esset**	**missus esset**	**custoditus esset**

Note:

- The pluperfect tense of the subjunctive appears frequently in past contrary to fact conditions, in **cum** clauses, and as an optative subjunctive expressing an unfulfilled wish in past time. For these uses, see the following chapters.

Quick Study Synopsis of Subjunctive Verbs

	Active	Passive
Present	**mittat**	**mittatur**
Imperfect	**mitteret**	**mitteretur**
Perfect	**miserit**	**missus sit**
Pluperfect	**misisset**	**missus esset**

Synopses of Deponent Verbs in the Subjunctive

1st conj: **hortor, hortari, hortatus sum**
2nd conj: **vereor, vereri, veritus sum**
3rd conj: **loquor, loqui, locutus sum**
4th conj: **orior, oriri, ortus sum**

	1st Conj.	2nd Conj.	3rd Conj.	4th Conj.
Pres.	**hortetur**	**vereatur**	**loquatur**	**oriatur**
Imperf.	**hortaretur**	**vereretur**	**loqueretur**	**oriretur**
Perf.	**hortatus sit**	**veritus sit**	**locutus sit**	**ortus sit**
Pluperf.	**hortatus esset**	**veritus esset**	**locutus esset**	**ortus esset**

Synopses of Irregular Verbs in the Subjunctive

sum, esse, fui **possum, posse, potui** **eo, ire, ii/ivi** **fero, ferre, tuli, latus** **volo, velle, volui** **fio, fieri, factus sum**

	sum	possum	eo	fero	volo	fio
Pres.	**sit**	**possit**	**eat**	**ferat**	**velit**	**fiat**
Imperf.	**esset**	**posset**	**iret**	**ferret**	**vellet**	**fieret**
Perf.	**fuerit**	**potuerit**	**ierit** **iverit**	**tulerit**	**voluerit**	**factus sit**
Pluperf.	**fuisset**	**potuisset**	**isset** **ivisset**	**tulisset**	**voluisset**	**factus esset**

Notes:

- Be reminded that the perfect stem of the verb **ire** is found variously as **i-** and **iv-**. Thus, **isset** and **ivisset** are both correct.
- In addition to the passive forms of **fieri**, given above, the verb **ferre** contains passive forms of the subjunctive, e.g., present tense, **feratur**, imperfect tense, **ferretur**, perfect tense, **latus sit,** and pluperfect tense, **latus esset**.

Tips on Mastering Forms of the Subjunctive

The present and perfect subjunctive forms are sometimes mistaken for their present, future, and future perfect indicative counterparts, e.g., the present subjunctive **mittat** can be mistaken for the present or future indicative, **mittit** or **mittet.** You should assume that a verb form containing the ending vowel **-a-** is in the present subjunctive, since this vowel characterizes the present subjunctive of three conjugations (second, third, and fourth), whereas it characterizes the indicative of only one, the first. Therefore, such a verb form has a much greater chance of being subjunctive than indicative.

Use the context to distinguish the perfect subjunctive **miserit** from the future perfect indicative form **miserit**. (Remember, however, that the first person singular of the perfect subjunctive is **-erim**, e.g, **miserim**, whereas the future perfect indicative form is **–ero**, e.g., **misero**.) To differentiate between ambiguous forms, know principal parts and use contextual clues.

As was mentioned in the previous chapter on infinitives, the imperfect and pluperfect tenses of the subjunctive, both active and passive, are formed from the present and perfect infinitives. Avoid confusing forms of the subjunctive with those of the infinitive.

	Present Active	Perfect Active
Infinitives	**mittere**	**misisse**
	Imperfect, Active and Passive	Pluperfect, Active and Passive
Subjunctives	**mitteret, mitteretur**	**misisset, missus esset**

Remember that a verb in the subjunctive mood can be found both independently as a main verb and in a clause that is dependent upon the main verb.

Subjunctive in a main clause:	**Fiat lux.**
	Let there be light.
Subjunctive in a subordinate clause:	**Deus imperavit ut lux esset.**
	God commanded that there be light.

Subjunctive verbs, whether independent or dependent, express non-factual or hypothetical situations. Use words such as *can, could, may, might, should,* or *would* when translating.

Chapter 25

Independent Subjunctives

A subjunctive verb may be found independently in a sentence, i.e., by itself in a main clause, as opposed to serving as the verb in a dependent clause:

Independent (main clause): **Pugnent omnes gladiatores fortiter.**
Let all gladiators fight bravely!

Dependent (subordinate clause): **Gladiatores pugnant ut vivant.**
Gladiators fight so that they may live.

The presentation in this chapter is limited to independent uses of the subjunctive, which include polite command and encouragement (jussive and hortatory), questions in which the speaker or writer expresses doubt or disbelief by "thinking aloud" (deliberative), wishes that cannot or may not be fulfilled (optative), and the possibility that something may happen or might have happened (potential). The actions of such verbs in the subjunctive, as opposed to those in the indicative, may not actually take place or have taken place and are therefore to be considered hypothetical. English words such as *can, could, may, might, should,* and *would* best express the meaning of the various uses of the independent subjunctive. You should concentrate on determining the suitable English meaning from context. For example, **Ne pugnent** has meanings such as, *Let them not fight*, *If only they wouldn't fight*, or *They should not fight*, depending upon the circumstances. For the forms of the independent subjunctive, which are found most often in the present tense, see the previous chapter.

Uses of the Independent Subjunctive

Jussive and hortatory subjunctives

Perhaps the most common uses of the independent subjunctive are the jussive and the hortatory.

Jussive: **"Cedant togae armis!" exclamabant gladiatores.**
"Let the togas yield to arms!" yelled the gladiators.

Hortatory: **Ne pugnemus, mi Maxime, atque vivamus.**
Let us not fight, my Maximus, and let us live.

Descriptive Label	Function	Tenses used	Negative
Jussive (iubere, *order*)	polite command	present (*Let him/them...*)	**ne**
Hortatory (hortari, *urge*)	encouragement	present (*Let us...*)	**ne**

Notes:

- Because the uses and meanings of the jussive and hortatory are substantially identical (distinguished by whether the first or third person is being addressed), the forms are often combined into a single category and translated "*Let*...." You may enjoy remembering this usage as the "Caesar salad" subjunctive, i.e., *Lettuce do this, lettuce do that*.*
- For an example of the jussive subjunctive, keep in mind the well-known saying **Caveat emptor**, *Let the buyer beware*, i.e., be an informed consumer.
- When the second person (*you*) is required in the expression of a command, Latin prefers the imperative mood of the verb, e.g., **Cape consilium in arena!** *(You) make your plan in the arena!***
- The perfect tense of the subjunctive is sometimes used to express a negative command or prohibition, e.g., **Ne ceperis consilium in arena**, *Don't make your plan in the arena*. This is an alternative to the more common **noli/nolite** + infinitive (for which, see Chapter 19).

Deliberative subjunctive

Unlike the direct question, which is found with the indicative mood (see Chapter 15), the deliberative question with the subjunctive is expressed as a question to oneself, with no answer expected. This type of question can imply doubt, indignation, surprise, or confusion, e.g.,

Androcles leoni se oppositurus erat. "Quid faciam?" gemuit.
Androcles was about to face the lion. "What should I do?" he groaned.

Descriptive Label	Function	Tenses used	Negative
Deliberative (**deliberare**, *consider*)	self-question	present (*Am I to? Should I?*) imperfect (*Was I to?*)	**non**

Note:

- The difference between a direct question with the indicative and a deliberative question is that the former expresses a fact and the latter a non-fact:

* From a roundtable sharing discussion, Oklahoma Classics Association workshop, 1996.

** The example sentences in this section derive from Roman *sententiae*: **Cedant arma togae**, *Let arms yield to the toga* (Cicero), i.e., the military should be subordinate to the government; **Vivamus, mea Lesbia, atque amemus**, *Let us live, my Lesbia, and let us love* (Catullus); **Gladiator in arena consilium capit**, *The gladiator makes his plan in the arena* (Seneca), i.e., the gladiator must be able to think on his feet and adjust to circumstances.

Direct question: **Quod consilium in arena capis?**
What plan are you making in the arena?

Deliberative question: **Quod consilium in arena capias?**
What plan should you make in the arena?

Optative subjunctive

The optative subjunctive expresses a wish felt or spoken by the speaker or writer. It is found either independently or as a clause, and most often with the particle **utinam** (negative **utinam ne**), which has the meanings *if only, would that, I wish (that), may*. A clause introduced by **utinam** usually expresses a wish incapable of fulfilment, or a regret. It is most often found with the imperfect or pluperfect tense:

Imperfect tense: **Lanista cogitabat, "Utinam meliores gladiatores haberem."**
The trainer was thinking, "I wish that I had better gladiators (but I do not)" or *"I regret that I do not have..."*.

Pluperfect tense: **Utinam naumachiam in amphitheatro vidissemus.**
If only we had seen a sea battle in the amphitheater (but we did not) or *"I regret that we did not see..."*.

Descriptive Label	Function	Tenses used	Negative
Optative (**optare**, *choose*)	wish	present (*if only*, *may*, *hope*, possible future) imperfect (*if only...were*, unaccomplished present) pluperfect (*if only...had*, unaccomplished past)	**ne**

Notes:

- The present tense is used when the wish is conceived of as possibly coming true in the future:

  Utinam sis victor, Anxi.*
  If only you would be the victor, Anxius or
  May you be the victor, Anxius (and you very well may be).

- For testing purposes, the optative subjunctive is usually found with **utinam**. However, the optative may also appear independently of this particle when its meaning has the effect of a jussive/hortatory or a conditional, as in a prayer, e.g.,

  Di me adiuvent.
  May the gods help me or *If only the gods would help me.*

*Anxius is the name of a fictional gladiator.

- The imperfect tense is used when expressing a wish that is unaccomplished or incapable of fulfillment in present time:

  Lanista cogitabat, "Utinam meliores gladiatores haberem."
  The trainer was thinking, "I wish that I had better gladiators (but I do not)" or *"I regret that I do not have . . ."*

- The pluperfect tense is used when expressing a wish that is unaccomplished or incapable of fulfillment in the past:

  Utinam naumachiam in amphitheatro vidissemus.
  If only we had seen a sea battle in the amphitheater (but we did not) or *I regret that we did not see . . . .*

Potential subjunctive

The potential subjunctive is an independent subjunctive that expresses an action as possible or conceivable in past, present, or future time. It is translated as *can, could, may, might, should,* or *would* in the present (occasionally the perfect) tense when referring to present or future time and *could have, might have*, or *would have* in the imperfect tense when referring to past time.

Present or Future time: **Spartacus Romanos superet.**
Spartacus may defeat the Romans (and there is the possibility that he might).

Past time: **Nemo hoc crederet.**
No one would have believed this (but there is the possibility that they might have).

Descriptive Label	Function	Tenses used	Negative
Potential (**posse**, *be able*)	possibility	present (*may, could, would, should,* present or future) imperfect (*might have, could have, would have*, past)	**non**

Quick Study of Independent Subjunctives

Present Time			
Romae vivam.	*Let me live in Rome.*	hortatory	exhortation
Romae vivat.	*Let him live in Rome.*	jussive	polite command
Vivamne Romae?	*Should I live in Rome?*	deliberative	self question
(Utinam) Romae vivam.	*May I live in Rome.*	optative	wish
	I wish I could live in Rome.	optative	wish
	If only I might live in Rome.	optative	wish
Utinam Romae viverem.	*If only I were to live in Rome.*	optative	wish
Romam vivam.	*I could live in Rome.*	potential	possibility
	I may or *might live in Rome.*	potential	possibility
Past Time			
Viveremne Romae?	*Was I to live in Rome?*	deliberative	self question
Utinam Romae vixissem.	*If only I had lived in Rome.*	optative	wish
Romae viverem.	*I might have/could have/would have lived in Rome.*	potential	possibility

Tips on Translating Independent Subjunctives

- The present tense is the tense most often found in the various uses of the independent subjunctive.
- When in the process of identifying and translating a subjunctive verb as independent, look carefully at the environment of the verb. When translating, observe the context to help you to make an "educated guess" about whether or not the verb is subjunctive. For instance, observe this sentence from Horace:

  Non omnis moriar, multaque pars mei vitabit Libitinam.

  I will not perish altogether, and indeed a great part of me will elude Libitina (goddess of the dead.)
- The verb **moriar** could mean either *I will die* (future indicative) or *Let me die* (present subjunctive). The context of this verb, which includes the more obvious future form **vitabit**, will help you to determine that the best meaning is *I will die*. (Of course, you've probably already decided this since you know that **non** negates **moriar** here, whereas **moriar** as a hortatory subjunctive would be negated by **ne**!)
- Translation of the present subjunctive can be confusing, because of the variety of its functions (exhortation, wish, possibility, etc.). Similar blurring of intent or tone has taken place in English, e.g., "I would be careful" could be conceived of as advice (hortatory), a wish (optative), the main clause of a condition ("if I were you"), etc. It is important to let the context of the sentence dictate how you express the meaning of the present subjunctive. Use words such as *can, could, may, might, should*, and *would*, as well as *let*.

Practice Questions: Independent Subjunctives

1. May she rest in peace.

   (A) Requiescit
   (B) Requiescens
   (C) Requiesce
   (D) Requiescat

2. Sit tibi terra levis. (= S.T.T.L., often inscribed on Roman tombstones.)

   (A) The earth is gentle upon you.
   (B) Be gentle upon the earth.
   (C) You are resting gently in the earth.
   (D) May the earth be gentle upon you.

3. Palmam qui meruit, ferat. (Lord Nelson)
   (A) Whoever deserves the palm will display it.
   (B) He who has earned the palm, let him display it.
   (C) He is displaying the palm which he earned.
   (D) Whoever wants the palm should display it.

4. Would that we had been less desirous of life. (Cicero)
   (A) fuissemus (C) fueramus
   (B) essemus (D) fuerimus

5. Sit. (The Beatles)
   (A) It is. (C) Let it be.
   (B) He can. (D) Would that it were.

6. Quid agam? (Cicero)
   (A) What should I do? (C) What have I done?
   (B) What was I to do? (D) What had I done?

7. Dum inter homines sumus, colamus humanitatem. (Seneca)
   (A) While we are among men, let us cherish humanity.
   (B) We must cherish humanity while we are among men.
   (C) We do cherish humanity as long as we are among men.
   (D) While we were among men, we should have cherished humanity.

8. Let us hope for what we want, but let us endure whatever happens. (Cicero)
   (A) Speramus . . . ferimus (C) Speramus . . . feramus
   (B) Speremus . . . feremus (D) Speremus . . . feramus

9. Utinam populus Romanus unam cervicem ____! (Suetonius, quoting Caligula)
   (A) habet (C) haberet
   (B) habuerat (D) habebat

10. Quod sentimus loquamur; quod loquimur sentiamus. (Seneca)
    If we were to negate the subjunctive verbs in this sentence, we would use the word . . . .
    (A) non (C) nihil
    (B) ne (D) nonne

11. Utinam ratio duxisset, non fortuna. (*pace* Livy)
    (A) might guide (C) had guided
    (B) would guide (D) was guiding

12. Utinam liberorum nostrorum mores non ipsi perderemus. (Quintilian)
    (A) Would that we might not ruin our children's character.
    (B) I wish that we will not ruin our children's character.
    (C) If only we had not ruined our children's character.
    (D) We were not ruining our children's character.

13. Let us rejoice, therefore, while we are young! (Medieval song)
    (A) Gaudemus (C) Gaudete
    (B) Gaudebimus (D) Gaudeamus

14. Which word is not appropriate for translating the independent subjunctive?
    (A) should (C) may
    (B) might (D) will

15. Fortunam citius invenias quam retineas. (Publilius Syrus)
    (A) you will find (C) you may find
    (B) you find (D) you might have found

Independent Subjunctives in the *Aeneid*

Translate these sentences, each of which contains one or more independent subjunctives. Those appearing in the first five sentences are underlined for you. Some context is provided.

1. Aeneas to Venus:

   "Sis felix nostrumque leves, quaecumque, laborem." (1.330)

2. Aeneas to Dido and the Carthaginians:

   "Quis talia fando Myrmidonum Dolopumve aut duri miles Ulixi temperet a lacrimis?" (2.6–8)

3. Aeneas deliberates about how to approach Dido:

   Heu quid agat? Quo nunc reginam ambire furentem audeat adfatu? Quae prima exordia sumat? (4.283–284)

4. Dido's dying words:

   (Dido) dixit, et os impressa toro, "Moriemur inulta, sed moriamur!" ait. (4.659-660)

5. Anna to Dido:

   "Idem ambas ferro dolor atque eadem hora <u>tulisset</u>." (4.679)

6. Pallas to Hercules:

   "Cernat semineci sibi me rapere arma cruenta victoremque ferant morientia lumina Turni." (10.462–463)

7. Pallas to the Rutulians:

   "Cuperem ipse parens spectator adesset." (10.443)

8. Jupiter to Juno:

   "(Decuit) aut ensem (quid enim sine te Iuturna valeret?) ereptum reddi Turno et vim crescere victis?" (12.798–799)

9. Juno to Jupiter:

   "Ne vetus indigenas nomen mutare Latinos neu Troas fieri iubeas Teucrosque vocari." (12.823–825)

10. Juno to Jupiter:

   "Sit Latium, sint Albani per saecula reges, sit Romana potens Itala virtute propago." (12.826–828)

Answers to Practice Questions: Independent Subjunctives

1. Jussive **(D)**

The famous epitaph R.I.P., **Requiescat in pace**, is an example of the jussive subjunctive in the present tense. Answer (A) **Requiescit** is in the present indicative form, (B) **Requiescens** is the present participle, and (C) **Requiesce** the singular form of the present imperative.

2. Jussive **(D)**

The verb **sit** in this epitaph is also a jussive subjunctive. Answer (A) requires a verb that is present indicative and (B) a present imperative. Answer (C) also requires a present indicative and mistranslates the other words in the epitaph.

3. Jussive **(B)**

Since **ferat** is a form of the present subjunctive, Answer (B) "...let him display it" is the best translation. Answer (A) requires the future tense **feret** and (C) the present tense **fert**. Answer (D) translates **meruit** incorrectly.

4. Optative **(A)**

"Would that" introduces the subjunctive of a wish, therefore, "we had been" must be a subjunctive form in the pluperfect tense. This is **fuissemus**. Answer (B)

essemus is in the wrong tense (imperfect), (C) **fueramus** is in the correct tense (pluperfect) but wrong mood (indicative), and (D) **fuerimus** is in the wrong tense and mood (future perfect indicative, "we will have been") or simply the incorrect tense (perfect subjunctive, "we have been").

5. Jussive **(C)**
"Let it be" is an obvious answer if you're a Beatles fan! Answers (A) and (B) call for the indicative mood and (D) is optative in past time.

6. Deliberative **(A)**
Quid agam? is a classic example of the use of the subjunctive mood in a deliberative question. The real question here is, "What is the tense of the verb **agam**?" Well, the answer is the present tense, leading to Answer (A) "What am I to do?" Answers (B) "What was I to do," (C) "What have I done," and (D) "What had I done," all have incorrect verb tenses.

7. Hortatory **(A)**
In this sentence, you should focus your thinking on the mood and tense of the main verb **colamus**. Since the verb **colo, colere** belongs to the third conjugation, this form is a hortatory subjunctive in the present tense, i.e., "Let us cherish." Answer (B) "We must cherish (humanity)" requires a construction that expresses necessity or obligation, e.g., **(humanitas) nobis colenda est**, (C) "We do cherish," is **colimus** and (D) "We should have cherished" is **coluerimus**.

8. Hortatory **(D)**
Determining the correct answer to this question requires familiarity with the principal parts or forms of the regular verb **spero, sperare** and the irregular verb **fero, ferre**. (These may be deduced from the answers provided.) **Sperare** belongs to the first conjugation, so Answers (A) and (C) are incorrect, since **speramus** is in the present indicative and the hortatory or present subjunctive is required by the English meaning. Answer (B) **feremus** is in the future tense, leaving **feramus** as the correct answer.

9. Optative **(C)**
The appearance of the particle **utinam** defines this sentence as a wish, which requires a subjunctive verb. Since **haberet** is the only subjunctive appearing among the choices, it is the correct answer. Answer (A) is present indicative, (B) pluperfect indicative, and (D) imperfect indicative. In this wish, Caligula wanted the people to have one head so he could decapitate them all at once.

10. Hortatory **(B)**
The hortatory subjunctive forms **loquamur** and **sentiamus** require the negative **ne**. Answers (C) and (D) do not require the subjunctive and Answer (B), when found with the subjunctive, is most commonly used in the context of the result clause, i.e., **ut non**.

11. Optative **(C)**
The subjunctive verb **duxisset** in this wish is in the pluperfect tense, hence, "had guided" is the correct response. (Note that all forms in the answers appear in the active voice.) Answers (A) "might guide" and (B) "would guide" are in the present tense (**ducat**) while (D) "was guiding" is in the imperfect tense (**duceret**).

12. Optative **(A)**
The tense of the verb **perderemus** in this wish introduced by **utinam** is imperfect, which nullifies the translations in Answers (B) and (C). These contain verbs in the future and pluperfect tenses, respectively. Answer (D) is not possible because the translation is phrased as a (factual) assertion, not a wish, therefore requiring the indicative mood.

13. Hortatory **(D)**
This famous song, often sung or played at graduations, is an encouragement to celebrate. Therefore, the hortatory subjunctive **Gaudeamus** "Let us rejoice" is correct. Answer (A) **Gaudemus** "We are rejoicing" is in the present indicative, (B) **Gaudebimus** "We shall rejoice" is in the future indicative, and (C) **Gaudete** "Rejoice!" is a plural imperative.

14. **(D)**
The word "will" is only used in the indicative mood, because it implies a statement that is going to come true. The words "should," "might," and "may" are all used to express meanings that are only potentially true, and are thus subjunctive.

15. Potential **(C)**
This sentence, which reads, "You <u>may come upon</u> fortune sooner than (you may) hold onto it, "contains two potential subjunctives, **invenias** and **retineas**, expressing possibilities capable of realization. Answers (A) and (B) are in the future and present tenses of the indicative, respectively, and as such make assertions of fact, rather than possibility. Answer (D) "you might have found" translates a potential subjunctive in the imperfect tense (**invenires**), rather than the present (**invenias**), and expresses past time.

Answers to Independent Subjunctives in the *Aeneid*

1. "<u>Sis</u> felix nostrumque <u>leves</u>, quaecumque, laborem." (1.330) (optatives, expressing wishes that might be fulfilled in future time)
"May you be favorable and lighten our burden, whoever (you are)."

2. "Quis talia fando Myrmidonum Dolopumve aut duri miles Ulixi <u>temperet</u> a lacrimis?" (2.6–8)
(deliberative question)

"Who of the Myrmidons and Dolopes or what soldier of cruel Odysseus could refrain from tears in recounting such things?"

3. Heu quid agat? Quo nunc reginam ambire furentem audeat adfatu? Quae prima exordia sumat? (4.283–284) (deliberative questions)
Alas, what should he (Aeneas) do? With what speech should he now dare to address the raging queen? What opening words should he undertake first?

4. (Dido) dixit, et os impressa toro, "Moriemur inulta, sed moriamur!" ait. (4.659–660) (hortatory)
Dido spoke and said, having buried her face in the couch, said, "I will die unavenged, but let me die!"

5. "Idem ambas ferro dolor atque eadem hora tulisset." (optative, expressing unaccomplished wish in the past)
"If only the same pain of the sword, the same hour, had taken (us) both!"

6. "Cernat semineci sibi me rapere arma cruenta victoremque ferant morientia lumina Turni. (10.462–463) (jussive)
"May Turnus see that I am stripping the bloody arms from him, half-dead, and may his dying eyes suffer (me) as victor."

7. "Cuperem ipse parens spectator (Evander) adesset." (10.443) (**cuperem** is a potential subjunctive expressing a possibility in past time; **adesset** is optative, implying a wish that cannot be accomplished in the present)
"I could wish that my father himself were present as an observer (but he is not).

8. "(Decuit) aut ensem (quid enim sine te Iuturna valeret?) ereptum reddi Turno et vim crescere victis?" (12.798–799) (potential, expressing a possibility in past time)
"Was it fitting that the lost sword be returned to Turnus (for what good would Juturna have been without you?) and that the might of the conquered grow stronger?"

9. "Ne vetus indigenas nomen mutare Latinos neu Troas fieri iubeas Teucrosque vocari." (12.823–825) (hortatory)
"May you not command that the native Latins change their ancient name nor become Trojans and be called Teucrians."

10. "Sit Latium, sint Albani per saecula reges, sit Romana potens Itala virtute propago." (12.826–828) (jussive)
"Let there be Latium, let Alban kings endure throughout the ages, let Roman descendants be strong in Italian valor."

Chapter 26

Conditional Sentences

Conditional, or "if-then," sentences in Latin are complex in that they really express two ideas, one in a main or independent clause, the other in a subordinate or dependent clause, e.g., "If you understand this, then you understand conditional sentences." A conditional sentence contains a conditional clause, or condition, which consists of the *if*-clause introduced by **si** (or its negative equivalent **nisi**, *if . . . . not, unless*) and ending with a verb. In the conditional sentence given above, the conditional clause is "If you understand this." The *then*-clause serves as the main or independent clause, also known as the conclusion. In the sentence above, the main clause is "then you understand conditional sentences." The *if*-clause is traditionally known as the protasis (Greek for "premise"), and the *then*-clause as the apodosis (Greek for "outcome"). Note that the word "then" is not necessarily expressed in the English translation.

condition/subordinate or dependent clause/protasis

[Si Lesbia Catullum amabit], ipse laetus erit.

conclusion/main or independent clause/apodosis

[If Lesbia will love / loves Catullus], (then) he will be happy.

The clauses in conditional sentences may be found with verbs in either the indicative or the subjunctive mood, and in any tense. There are three main types of conditional sentences, which are classified as simple, future less vivid or "should . . . would," and contrary to fact. Simple conditionals have the indicative in both clauses, the future less vivid conditional has the present subjunctive in both clauses, and contrary to fact conditionals have a past tense of the subjunctive in both clauses. In this chapter you will read about the Roman poet Catullus, who had a love affair with a woman to whom he gave the name "Lesbia."

Conditionals with the Indicative Mood

Simple Conditional Sentences

This type of conditional sentence, also known as a "factual" or "open" condition, makes a simple statement. Simple conditionals have verbs in the indicative mood in both clauses. Use of the indicative implies that the condition is happening or is likely to happen. Any tense may be used. If the tense used is future or future perfect in the *if*-clause and future in the *then*-clause, then the sentence is classified as a future more vivid conditional. Here are some examples:

Simple Conditions:

Si Lesbia Catullum amat, ipse laetus est.

If Lesbia loves Catullus (and very possibly she does), (then) he is happy.

Si Lesbia amabat Catullum, ipse laetus erat.

If Lesbia loved Catullus (and very possibly she did), he was happy.

Future More Vivid Conditions:

Si Lesbia Catullum amabit, ipse laetus erit.

If Lesbia will love Catullus, (and very possibly she will), he will be happy.

Si Lesbia Catullum amaverit, ipse laetus erit.

If Lesbia will have loved Catullus (and very possibly she will have), he will be happy.

Note:

- In simple and future more vivid conditional clauses, it is better to translate verbs in the future and future perfect tenses as present tenses in English, e.g.,

Si Lesbia Catullum amaverit, ipse laetus erit.

If Lesbia loves, lit., *will have loved, Catullus, he will be happy.*

Conditionals with the Subjunctive Mood

Future Less Vivid (*"should . . . would"*) Conditional Sentences

This type of conditional, sometimes called "ideal," expresses a remote future possibility, i.e., a condition that may possibly (but improbably) be true or realized in the future. These appear with the present subjunctive in both clauses and may be translated traditionally, if somewhat archaically, by "should" in the *if*-clause and "would" in the *then*-clause, e.g.,

Si Lesbia Catullum amet, ipse laetus sit.

If Lesbia should love Catullus (and it is possible, but unlikely, that she does), he would be happy.

Note:

- This type of conditional sentence is less frequent than the other two types.

Contrary to Fact (or Contrafactual) Conditional Sentences

Such conditionals express conditions and conclusions that could not possibly happen or be true. The verbs of these conditionals, which are also known as "imaginary" or "unreal," are both subjunctive. In present time, or present contrary to fact, the imperfect subjunctive appears in both clauses; in past time, or past contrary to fact, Latin uses the pluperfect subjunctive in both clauses:

Si Lesbia Catullum amaret, ipse laetus esset.

If Lesbia were to love Catullus (but she does not), he would be happy (but he is not).

Si Lesbia Catullum amavisset, ipse laetus fuisset.

If Lesbia had loved Catullus (but she did not), he would have been happy (but he was not).

Mixed Conditions

The tenses or moods of both clauses in a conditional sentence need not be the same. Mixed conditionals may be found containing clauses 1) with different tenses of the subjunctive, 2) with an indicative paired with an independent subjunctive, 3) with a subjunctive *if*-clause paired with an imperative, or with various other combinations. The meaning of such sentences is usually apparent from the sense implied by the context, e.g.,

Mixed tenses: **Essetne Catullus laetus, si Lesbia eum amavisset?**
Would Catullus be happy (now), if Lesbia had loved him (previously)?

Mixed moods: **Si Lesbia Catullum amat, gaudeamus.**
If Lesbia does love Catullus, let us be delighted.

Mixed moods: **Si putatis Lesbiam Catullum amare, gaudete!**
If you think that Lesbia does love Catullus, be glad!

Quick Study of Conditional Sentences

Type	Verbs in Clauses	Meanings of Verbs: Dependent clause / Main clause
Simple (likely to happen)	indicative	*If he does..., then he is....* *If he did,..., then he was....*
Future more vivid (likely to happen)	future, future perfect indicative	*If he will (have)..., then he will....* (Best translated in the present)
Future less vivid (possible, but unlikely)	present subjunctive	*If he should..., then he would...*
Present contrary to fact (impossible or unreal)	imperfect subjunctive	*If he were to..., then he would....*
Past contrary to fact (impossible or unreal)	pluperfect subjunctive	*If he had..., then he would have....*

Tips on Translating Conditional Sentences

- Conditional sentences present few problems in translation because they are very similar to English.
- The conclusion or *then*-clause may precede the condition or *if*-clause in the word order of a Latin sentence for emphasis or other considerations, e.g.,

Fuissetne Catullus laetus, si Lesbiam in matrimonium duxisset?

Would Catullus have been happy if he had married Lesbia?

Always read through in Latin the entirety of a Latin sentence before determining its meaning.

- In the *if*-clause or condition, translate future and future perfect tenses in the present tense.
- Note that all three types of conditional sentences in Latin reveal something about the truth of what is being said or written, i.e., simple conditions reveal that it is likely that the condition is true, future less vivid conditions reveal the possibility that the condition may be true, and contrary to fact conditions express that it is impossible that the condition is true.

Practice Questions on Conditional Sentences

*Catullus is to be imagined as speaking in many of these sentences.**

1. Si vales, Lesbia, gaudeo.
   (A) If you are well, Lesbia, I am happy.
   (B) If you should be well, Lesbia, then I would be happy.
   (C) If you were well, Lesbia, then I would be happy.
   (D) If you will be well, Lesbia, then I am happy.

2. Si pulchram Lesbiam vidisses, certe eam amavisses.
   (A) you would love
   (B) you had loved
   (C) you would have loved
   (D) you were loving

3. O di, si vitam puriter agam, eripiatis hanc pestem perniciemque mihi.
   (A) If I will lead an upright life, you will take away . . . .
   (B) If I should lead an upright life, you would take away . . . .
   (C) If I were to lead an upright life, you would take away . . . .
   (D) If I am leading an upright life, you should take away . . . .

4. Si cum passere ludere possem, tristes curas animi levarem.
   (A) If I can play with the sparrow
   (B) If I am able to play with the sparrow
   (C) If I were able to play with the sparrow
   (D) If I should be able to play with the sparrow

5. Si Lesbiam in matrimonium ducere velim, dicatne "Ita vero"?
   (A) should wish
   (B) will wish
   (C) am wishing
   (D) was wishing

* Several answers in this practice exercise are derived directly from the poems of Catullus: question 3, Poem 76.19-20; question 4, Poem 2.9-10; question 6, Poems 5 and 7; question 7, Poem 77.3-4; and question 10, Poem 13.4-7.

6. Mortuus essem, nisi mea puella mihi mille basia daret.
   (A) I would die if I gave my girl a thousand kisses.
   (B) Unless I were to give my girl a thousand kisses, I would die.
   (C) If I would not have given my girl a thousand kisses, I would die.
   (D) I would die unless my girl were to give me a thousand kisses.

7. Si meam Lesbiam ames, Rufe, misero mihi intestina eripias. This sentence tells us that
   (A) There is no information as to whether or not Rufus loves Lesbia.
   (B) It is possible, but unlikely, that Rufus loves Lesbia.
   (C) Rufus could not, in any way, love Lesbia.
   (D) It is a fact that Rufus loves Lesbia.

8. Sepulcrum mei fratris visam, si ego ipse ad Bithyniam iero.
   (A) if I go to Bithynia
   (B) if I had gone to Bithynia
   (C) if I would have gone to Bithynia
   (D) if I were going to Bithynia

9. Si navis mihi non fuisset, ad Sirmionem navigare non____ . .
   (A) potero (C) potuissem
   (B) possem (D) poteram

10. Si candidam puellam et vinum attuleris, mi Fabulle, bene cenabis.
    Which of the following is not an acceptable translation of attuleris?
    (A) you will have brought (C) you will bring
    (B) you bring (D) you brought

Sententiae Antiquae

1. Discere si quaeris, doce. Sic ipse doceris. (Medieval)
   (A) if you will seek (C) if you will be sought
   (B) if you are sought (D) if you seek

2. If anyone should violate this, I wish that he would live for a long time in pain. (From a tombstone)
   (A) violaverit (C) violavisset
   (B) violaverat (D) violabat

3. Si ea defendes quae ipse recta esse senties. (Cicero)
   (A) If only you will stand by what you feel to be correct.
   (B) If only you should stand by what you would feel to be correct.
   (C) If only you had stood by what you would have felt to be correct.
   (D) If only you were standing by what you saw to be correct.

4. The whole world would perish if compassion were not to end bad feelings. (Seneca the Elder)
   (A) pereat . . . finiat
   (B) periet . . . finiet
   (C) periret . . . finiret
   (D) perebat . . . finiebat

5. Salus omnium una nocte amissa esset, nisi Catilina captus esset. (Cicero) The tense and voice of the subjunctive verbs in this sentence are
   (A) imperfect passive
   (B) imperfect active
   (C) pluperfect passive
   (D) present passive

6. Minus saepe erres, si scias quid nescias. (Publilius Syrus)
   (A) If you knew what you did not know
   (B) If you know what you did not know
   (C) If you should know what you do not know
   (D) If you knew what you do not know

Stumper: Which of the following conditional sentences contains a future more vivid condition?
   (A) Dices "heu" si te in speculo videris. (Horace)
   (B) Si tu eo die fuisses, te certo vidissem. (Cicero)
   (C) Laus nova nisi oritur, etiam vetus amittitur. (Publilius Syrus)
   (D) Si quietem mavis, duc uxorem parem. (Quintilian)

Conditional Sentences in the *Aeneid*

Underline each protasis or *if*- clause (the first three are done for you). Then, identify the type of clause, and translate the entire sentence accordingly. A brief context is provided.

1. Juno's plans for Carthage:

   Hoc regnum dea gentibus esse, si qua fata sinant, iam tum tenditque fovetque. (1.17–18)

2. The orator simile:

   Tum, pietate gravem ac meritis si forte virum quem conspexere, silent arrectisque auribus astant. (1.151–152)

3. Venus to Aeneas and Achates:

   "Monstrate (eam mihi), mearum vidistis si quam hic errantem forte sororum." (1.321–322)

4. Aeneas to Venus:

   "O dea, si prima repetens ab origine pergam et (si) vacet (tibi) annales nostrorum audire laborum, ante diem clauso componet Vesper Olympo." (1.372–374)

5. Aeneas complains about the gods:

   "Et, si fata deum, si mens non laeva fuisset . . . Troia nunc staret, Priamique arx alta maneres." (2.54–56)

6. Hector to Aeneas, in a dream:

   "Si Pergama dextra defendi possent, etiam hac defensa fuissent." (2.292–292)

7. Hecuba to Priam:

   "Non tali auxilio nec defensoribus istis tempus eget; non, si ipse meus nunc adforet Hector." (2.521–522)

8. Dido appeals to Aeneas:

   "Si te nulla movet tantarum gloria rerum . . . Ascanium surgentem et spes heredis Iuli respice, cui regnum Italiae Romanaque tellus debetur." (4.272–276)

9. Dido rebukes Aeneas:

   "Si non arva aliena domosque ignotas peteres, et Troia antiqua maneret, Troia per undosum peteretur classibus aequor?" (4.311–313)

10. Dido wants something to remember Aeneas by:

    "Saltem si qua mihi de te suscepta fuisset ante fugam suboles, si quis mihi parvulus aula luderet Aeneas, qui te tamen ore referret, non equidem omnino capta ac deserta viderer." (4.327–330)

11. Dido to her funeral pyre:

    "Felix (fuissem), heu nimium felix, si litora tantum numquam Dardaniae tetigissent nostra carinae." (4.657–658)

12. The effect of the news of Dido's suicide:

    Resonat magnis plangoribus aether, non aliter quam si immissis ruat hostibus omnis Karthago aut antiqua Tyros, flammaeque furentes culmina perque hominum volvantur perque deorum. (4.669–670)

13. At the temple of Apollo at Cumae:

    Quin protinus omnia perlegerent oculis, ni iam praemissus Achates adforet atque una Phoebi Triviaeque sacerdos. (6.33–35)

14. Anchises to Aeneas:

    "Nimium vobis Romana propago visa (esset) potens, superi, propria haec si dona fuissent." (6.870–871)

Answers to Practice Questions: Conditional Sentences

1. Simple **(A)**

This is a simple conditional sentence with the indicative, stating as a fact that if Lesbia is well, then Catullus is happy. Answer (B) "If you should be well" contains a translation that requires a "should . . . would" condition, (C) "If you were well" a present contrary to fact condition, and (D) "If you will be well" a future more vivid condition with the future tense. This sentence greets Lesbia as if in a letter or note.

2. Past contrary to fact **(C)**

This condition is revealed by the appearance of the pluperfect subjunctive form **amavisses**. The sentence reads, "If you had seen the gorgeous Lesbia, you would have loved her." Answer (A) requires the imperfect subjunctive form **amares** in a present contrary to fact condition. Answer (B) "you had loved," although in the proper tense, is a statement requiring the indicative mood, i.e., **amaveras**, as is (D) "you were loving," i.e., **amabas**.

3. Future less vivid **(B)**

That this sentence is a "should . . . would" conditional is indicated by the present subjunctive form **eripiatis**. The verb **agam** could, of course, be a form of the future indicative, but this possibility is negated by the appearance of **eripiatis**. This sentence, taken from Catullus Poem 76, reads, "O gods, if I should lead an upright life, you would snatch away from me this plague and pestilence" (i.e., Lesbia). Answers (A) and (D) require the indicative mood. Answer (C) is phrased as a present contrary to fact clause, "If I were to lead . . . ," which would require a verb in the imperfect subjunctive, i.e., **agerem**.

4. Present contrary to fact **(C)**

The underlined clause is part of a present contrary to fact conditional sentence. The appearance of the verb **possem** in the imperfect tense of the subjunctive leads to the translation "If I were able." Answers (A) and (B) express the same thing in different ways, both requiring the indicative, since they are assertions. Answer (D) "If I should be able . . ." translates a future less vivid clause, which is **Si . . . possim**. This sentence, from Catullus Poem 2, reads, "If I were able to (could) play with the songbird, I would relieve the sad cares of my heart."

5. Future less vivid **(A)**
This condition sentence contains a "should . . . would" condition, requiring the present subjunctive **(velim)** in the protasis, or *if*-clause, and in the apodosis, or *then*-clause (**dicat**). Answer (B) "will" requires the future indicative (**volam**), (C) the present indicative (**volo**), and (D) the imperfect indicative or subjunctive (**volebat** or **vellet**).

6. Present contrary to fact **(D)**
This sentence is a present contrary to fact condition, containing the verbs **essem** and **darem**, both in the imperfect tense. Unless Lesbia were to give Catullus a thousand kisses (which she will not), he would die (but he will not). Answer (A) does not translate **nisi** correctly, (B) turns the thought around and has Catullus giving Lesbia the kisses, and (C) translates the tense of the verb **darem** incorrectly as "would have given."

7. Future less vivid **(B)**
This is a "should...would" conditional sentence, expressing the fact that it is possible, but unlikely, that if Rufus should love Lesbia, he would tear out Catullus' guts. Answer (C) requires a contrary to fact condition, which is impossible, given the present tenses of the verbs, and (D) requires that the Latin express a simple factual condition, but the verbs are subjunctive.

8. Future more vivid **(A)**
This sentence reads, "<u>If Catullus goes to Bithynia</u>, he will visit his brother's grave." The use of the future and future perfect tenses **visam** and **iero** reveal this sentence to be a future more vivid conditional. Remember that in English the present tense may be used to express future time in such a context. Answers (B) and (D) are past contrary to fact conditions requiring the pluperfect subjunctive and (C) is a present contrary to fact condition, which requires the imperfect subjunctive. The verb **ierit** in the *if*-clause is a future perfect indicative form (or a perfect subjunctive, which doesn't fit the context).

9. Past contrary to fact **(C)**
This sentence reads, "If I had not had a ship, <u>I would</u> not <u>have been able</u> to sail to Sirmio." This is a past contrary to fact condition, which requires the pluperfect subjunctive in both the protasis and apodosis of the sentence. Answer (A) **potero** is future indicative, (B) **possem** is imperfect subjunctive, and (D) **poteram** imperfect indicative.

10. Future more vivid **(D)**
The future indicative verb form **cenabis** reveals that **attuleris** is in the future perfect tense in a sentence that expresses a future more vivid condition. As a past tense, Answer (D) "you brought" is the only translation that does not have an acceptable meaning of the future perfect tense.

Sententiae Antiquae Answers

1. Simple **(D)**

This simple conditional sentence reads, "If you seek to learn, teach. And so you yourself are taught." The verb **quaeris** is present active indicative. Answer (A) requires the future tense (**quaeres**), (B) the present passive (**quaereris**), and (C) the future passive (**quaēreris**).

2. Future less vivid **(A)**

The perfect subjunctive may appear in "should...would" conditions such as this. The non-factual nature of the statement removes Answers (B) and (D), which are indicative, from consideration. Answer (C) **violavisset**, which is in the pluperfect tense, cannot produce the translation "should violate," which expresses a meaning that derives from the present system of verbs.

3. Future more vivid **(A)**

This sentence expresses the future more vivid condition **Si . . . defendes**, "If you (will) defend...," **senties**, "(then) you will feel." The translation in Answer (B) "If you should stand" requires a "should...would" condition with the present subjunctive, (C) "If you had stood" requires a past contrary to fact condition with the pluperfect subjunctive, and (D) "If you were standing," a present contrary to fact condition with the imperfect subjunctive.

4. Present contrary to fact **(C)**

Seneca's thought expresses a contrary to fact condition in present time, as the imperfect subjunctive is suggested by the translation "were to end." Thus, the forms **periret** and **finiret** are correct. Answer (A) contains verbs in the present subjunctive, (B) in the future indicative, and (D) in the imperfect indicative, none of which fit the sense required.

5. Past contrary to fact **(C)**

Amissa esset and **captus esset** are forms of the pluperfect passive subjunctive in a past contrary to fact conditional sentence. The sentence reads, "The safety of everyone would have been lost in a single night, if Catiline had not been captured."

6. Future less vivid **(C)**

This sentence reads, "You would be wrong less often, if you (should) know (that) which you do not know." The main clause of this future less vivid condition contains the indirect question **quid nescias**. The translations in Answers (A) and (D) contain verbs in the past tense, which the original sentence does not contain. The meaning of the sentence in Answer (B) is rendered by the indicative in a simple condition.

Stumper: (A)

The correct answer reads, "You will say 'Ugh!' if you see yourself in the mirror." This sentence contains verbs in the future (**Dices**) and future perfect (**videris**) tenses. Answer (B) reads, "If you had been (there) on that day, I surely would have seen you," a past contrary to fact condition. Answer (B) reads, "Unless brand new praise is forthcoming, even the previous (praise) is lost," a simple condition. Answer (D) "If you prefer peace, marry a wife of equal (station)" is another simple condition with the indicative.

Answers to Conditional Sentences in the *Aeneid*

1. Juno's plans for Carthage:

Hoc regnum dea gentibus esse, si qua fata sinant, iam tum tenditque fovetque. (1.17–18) (mixed condition, future less vivid in the *if-* clause with indicative in main clauses)

The goddess even then planned and cherished the hope that this should be the kingdom (over all) nations, if the fates should in any way allow (it).

2. The orator simile:

Tum, pietate gravem ac meritis si forte virum quem conspexere, silent arrectisque auribus astant. (1.151–152) (simple condition)

Then, if by chance they caught sight of some man, noble in integrity and service, they are silent and stand by with ears at the ready.

3. Venus to Aeneas and Achates:

"Monstrate (eam mihi), mearum vidistis si quam hic errantem forte sororum." (1.321–322) (mixed simple condition, with imperative in the main clause)

"If by chance you have seen any (one) of my sisters wandering about here, point her out to me."

4. Aeneas to Venus:

"O dea, si prima repetens ab origine pergam et (si) vacet (tibi) annales nostrorum audire laborum, ante diem clauso componet Vesper Olympo." (1.372–374) (protases of two future less vivid conditions mixed with the future tense **componet** in the main clause)

"O goddess, if I should proceed, retracing from the first beginning, and you should have the free time to hear the accounts of our struggles, sooner will the evening (star) lay the day to rest after heaven (the doors of Olympus) has been shut."

5. Aeneas complains about the gods:

"Et, si fata deum, si mens non laeva fuisset . . . Troia nunc staret, Priamique arx alta maneres." (2.54–56) (mixed contrary to fact condition with pluperfect **fuisset** in the *if*-clause and then **staret** and **maneres** in the main clauses)

"And, if the fates of the gods (and) if their disposition had not been unfavorable, Troy would now be standing and, high citadel of Priam, you would remain.

6. Hector to Aeneas:

"Si Pergama dextra defendi possent, etiam hac defensa fuissent." (2.292–292) (mixed contrary to fact condition with imperfect **possent** in the *if-* clause, and pluperfect **fuissent** in the main clause)

"If Troy's citadel (Pergama) could be defended by (anyone's) right hand, it would have been defended by this one."

7. Hecuba to Priam:

"Non tali auxilio nec defensoribus istis tempus eget; non, si ipse meus nunc adforet Hector." (2.521–522) (**adforet = adesset**; present contrary to fact condition)

"Not such support (as yours) nor these defenders does (this) crisis lack; no, even if my Hector himself were now here."

8. Dido appeals to Aeneas:

"Si te nulla movet tantarum gloria rerum . . . Ascanium surgentem et spes heredis Iuli respice, cui regnum Italiae Romanaque tellus debetur." (4.272–276) (simple condition)

"If no glory of such plans moves you . . . consider the growing Ascanius and the promise of your heir Iulus, to whom the kingdom of Italy and Roman land are due."

9. Dido rebukes Aeneas:

"Si non arva aliena domosque ignotas peteres, et Troia antiqua maneret, Troia per undosum peteretur classibus aequor?" (4.311–313) (present contrary to fact)

"If you were not seeking foreign lands and unknown homes, and if ancient Troy were (still) remaining, would Troy still be sought across the billowy sea in ships?"

10. Dido wants something to remember Aeneas by:

"Saltem si qua mihi de te suscepta fuisset ante fugam suboles, si quis mihi parvulus aula luderet Aeneas, qui te tamen ore referret, non equidem omnino capta ac deserta viderer." (4.327–330) (mixed contrary to fact condition, **fuisset** and then **luderet, referret, and viderer**)

"At any rate, if any child had been born to me from you, if some tiny Aeneas were to play in my hall, whose face, at least, would remind (me) of you, I would not seem utterly vanquished and deserted.

11. Dido to her funeral pyre:

"Felix (fuissem), heu nimium felix, si litora tantum numquam Dardaniae tetigissent nostra carinae." (4.657–658) (past contrary to fact)

"I would have been happy, alas too happy, if only the Trojan ships had never touched our shores."

12. The effects of Dido's suicide:

Resonat magnis plangoribus aether, non aliter quam si immissis ruat hostibus omnis Karthago aut antiqua Tyros, (non aliter quam si) flammaeque furentes culmina perque hominum volvantur perque deorum. (4.669–670) (future less vivid)

Heaven resounds with great wailing, no differently than if all Carthage or venerable Tyre should fall after the enemy has been let in, (no differently than if) raging flames should roll through the homes of both men and gods.

13. At the temple of Apollo at Cumae:

Quin protinus omnia perlegerent oculis, ni iam praemissus Achates adforet. (6.33–35) (present contrary to fact; **ni = nisi; adforet = adesset**)

In fact they would have examined everything (of the story of Daedalus) if Achates, having been sent ahead, were not present now.

14. Anchises to Aeneas:

"Nimium vobis Romana propago visa (esset) potens, superi, propria haec si dona fuissent." (6.870–871) (past contrary to fact)

"Too mighty would the Roman race have seemed to you, O gods, if these gifts (i.e., Marcellus) would have been lasting."

Chapter 27

Subordinate Clauses with *Ut*

As you have been reminded in the past two chapters, subjunctive verbs are found both independently in main clauses and as verbs in dependent clauses, which are also known as secondary or subordinate clauses. In Chapter 13, you reviewed dependent clauses with the indicative, introduced by the relative pronoun **qui, quae, quod**. Dependent clauses with the subjunctive are usually introduced by words such as **si, quis, cum**, or, as presented in this section, the adverb **ut**, e.g.,

main/independent clause subordinate/dependent clause

Omnes milites ferociter pugnant [ut hostes superent].

All soldiers fight hard [in order to defeat the enemy].

In the sentence above, the main thought is that all soldiers fight hard. Secondary to this thought and dependent upon it is the purpose clause "in order to defeat the enemy," which gives additional information about the main thought. Such clauses can be "triggered" or set off by a word in the main clause that provides a context for the dependent clause, such as **tam** with this result clause:

Milites tam ferociter pugnabant [ut hostes superarentur].

The soldiers fought so hard [that the enemy was defeated].

Subjunctive verbs, whether independent or in dependent clauses, express wishes, possibilities, doubts, opinions, and so forth, whereas indicative verbs express statements of fact. In this and the next two sections, you will review the ways to identify various subjunctive clauses, as well as the ways in which they differ in meaning. Only the most common subordinate clauses with the subjunctive are presented in these chapters, because these types appear most frequently in Latin literature. The presentations for review are organized according to the word that introduces the dependent clause, such as **ut**, **quid**, or **cum**. In this chapter, you will review four clauses introduced by the adverb **ut**: purpose, result, indirect command, and fear. Brackets [ ] are used to designate the subordinate clause.

Types of *Ut* Clauses with the Subjunctive

The adverb **ut** introduces several different types of subjunctive clauses and is also found in a clause with the indicative. The negative of these clauses varies with the type of clause. The terms used to identify **ut** clauses, such as purpose or result, give insight into their meanings.

Purpose Clause with *Ut*

Although there are several different ways to express in Latin the idea of the purpose or intent of an action, the **ut** clause is perhaps the most common. This clause is also known as a "final" clause. The negative is **ne.** When translating, use wording such as *to, in order to, so that,* or *for the purpose of*, and render the verb by using the helping verbs *may* or *might*. Most often, the present or imperfect tense is found in a purpose clause, e.g.,

Gloriosus miles esse vult [ut ipse praeclarissimus fiat].

Gloriosus wants to be a soldier [in order to become famous].

Gloriosus praeclarissimus esse volebat [ut puellae eum amarent].

Gloriosus wanted to be famous [so that girls might like him].

Notes:

- Whereas the infinitive is used in English to express purpose, this use appears rarely in Latin, and then only in poetry.
- For the relative purpose clause and a summary of purpose constructions in Latin, see the next chapter.

Result Clause with *Ut*

The result clause, also called a "consecutive" clause, begins with **ut** (negative **ut non**) and ends with a subjunctive verb, usually in the present or imperfect tense. This clause, however, is set up by a "trigger word," such as **adeo, ita, sic,** or **tam,** which mean *so, to such an extent*, **talis, -is, -e**, *of such a kind,* **tantus, -a, -um**, *of such a size*, or **tot**, *so many.* Such words appear outside of and preceding the **ut** clause. When translating **ut** in a result clause, use the word *that* (= *with the result that*):

Gloriosus <u>tam</u> defessus est [ut Rubiconem transire non possit].

Gloriosus is <u>so</u> weary [that he cannot cross the Rubicon River]

Rubico flumen <u>ita</u> vivum fluebat [ut Gloriosus lapsus in aquam caderet].

The Rubicon River was running <u>so</u> fast [that Gloriosus slipped and fell in].

Notes:

- Sometimes the perfect subjunctive, instead of the imperfect, is found in the result clause if the past event whose action is being described <u>actually occurred</u>:

Gloriosus <u>talis</u> conspiciebatur [ut alii milites riserint].

Gloriosus was such a sight [that the other soldiers (in fact) laughed].

- A variation of the result clause, often referred to as a substantive (noun) clause of result, appears with verbs of causing or happening, such as **facere ut**, *to bring it about that*, or with several impersonal verbs, such as **accidit ut, evenit ut**, or **fit/fiebat ut**, *it happens/happened that*, or **fieri potest ut**, *it may be that, it is possible that*. For example,

  Caesar faciebat [ut Romani urbem Romam oppugnarent].

  Caesar was bringing it about [that Romans were attacking Rome].

Indirect Command

You might expect a highly structured and militaristic society such as that of the Romans to have several different ways to express the idea of command. You have reviewed the direct command (imperative mood, Chapter 19) and the independent subjunctive with the force of a gentle command (jussive and hortatory, Chapter 25). The indirect command expresses or reports a command as second hand communication, i.e., states what the original command was. Also known as the jussive clause, jussive noun clause, or substantive noun clause of purpose, the indirect command is a substantive or noun clause that consists of **ut** (or **ne**) + the subjunctive and answers the implied question "What is commanded?" A substantive is anything that takes the place of a noun, including a verbal clause:

Centurio Glorioso imperat.

The centurion gives an order to Gloriosus.

What direct command does the centurion give? **"Desili de nave."** The order "Jump down from the ship" becomes the direct object of the verb **imperat**, i.e., that which was ordered. The direct command **"Desili de nave"** now becomes the substantive clause, or indirect command, **ut de nave desiliret.** The translation of **ut** in this type of subjunctive clause is *to* . . . or *that* . . . , e.g.,

Direct command:	**"Desili de nave, Gloriose!" centurio imperat.** *The centurion commands, "Jump down from the ship, Gloriosus!"*
Indirect command:	**Centurio Glorioso imperat [ut de nave desiliat].** *The centurion commands Gloriosus [to jump down from the ship].*

Notes:

- The above sentence could be written alternatively as:

  Centurio imperat [ut Gloriosus de nave desiliat].

  The centurion orders [that Gloriosus jump down from the ship].

  In this sentence, Glorious is not the direct recipient of the centurion's command (the word **Gloriosus** is found inside the dependent clause), but receives the command through another.

- For the Romans, the use of verbs that mean *bid, order, request*, as well as *invite, persuade, beg*, or *pray,* carried weight and required a response. The following verbs introduce an indirect command:

hortari, *encourage, urge*
imperare (+ dat.), *order*
invitare, *invite*
mandare, *command*
monere, *advise, warn*
obsecrare, *beg, beseech*
orare, *plead, pray*
persuadere (+ dat.), *persuade, convince*
petere, *ask*
praecipere (+ dat.), *instruct*
rogare, *ask*

- Remember the verbs listed above by using the convenient, if goofy, acronym "HIPPIPROMMO."
- Most of the verbs above take a direct object in the accusative case. The verbs **imperare, persuadere**, and **praecipere**, however, take the dative case.

Centurio Glorioso imperabat ut de nave desiliret.

The centurion was ordering Gloriosus to jump down from the ship.

- The verb **iubere**, which also has the meaning *order*, is not followed by the indirect command but takes the infinitive with subject accusative, e.g.,

Centurio Gloriosum desilire iubebat.

The centurion was ordering Gloriosus to jump down.

Fear Clause

Fear clauses are structured like other **ut** clauses with the subjunctive, except that the meanings of **ut** and **ne** are unique. Their meanings are reversed, that is, **ut** and **ne** have meanings that are the opposite of those found in other **ut** clauses. They express in a different way what was originally an independent jussive clause in the context of the emotion of fear or apprehension, e.g., **Vereor. Ne cadas**! *I'm scared. May you not fall!* became **Vereor ne cadas**, *I'm scared that you may fall.* Thus, **ne** expresses the positive, *that...*, and **ut** the negative, *that...not*, following words that suggest or mean fear or apprehension. That which is feared is expressed in the fear clause. The fear clause, like the indirect command, is a noun or substantive clause, in that it serves as the direct object of the main verb and answers the implied question "What is feared?" Verbs that introduce a fear clause include **metuere, pavere, timere,** and the deponent **vereri**, e.g.,

Gloriosus veretur [ut scuto defendatur].

Gloriosus fears [that he may not be protected by his shield].

Timebatne Gloriosus [ne in testudine nigresceret]?

Was Gloriosus afraid [that it would be dark inside the "tortoise"]?

Notes:

- Alternatively, the verbs of fearing listed above may be accompanied by an infinitive, e.g.,

Gloriosus metuebat a castris discedere.

Gloriosus was afraid to leave camp.

Quick Study of *Ut* Clauses with the Subjunctive

Type Clause	Main Clause Cue	Introductory Word	Meaning of Clause	Subjunctive
Purpose	[none]	**ut**	*to, in order that, so that*	present, imperfect
		ne	*so that . . . not, not to . . .*	
Example:	**Gloriosus se celabat ut diu dormiret.** *Gloriosus was hiding in order to sleep for awhile.*			
Result	**adeo, ita, sic, tam**, etc.	**ut**	*that, with the result that*	present, imperfect, perfect
		ut non	*that . . . not*	
Example:	**Iste tam bene se celaverat ut centurio eum invenire non posset.** *He had hidden so successfully that the centurion couldn't find him.*			
Indirect Command	verb of command or persuasion	**ut**	*that*	present, imperfect
		ne	*that . . . not*	
Example:	**Scelesto invento, centurio ei imperavit ut matellas vacuefaceret.** *When the rascal had been found, the centurion ordered him to empty the chamber pots.*			
Fear	word of fearing	**ne**	*that*	present, imperfect
		ut	*that . . . not*	
Example:	**Gloriosus timuerat ne centurio ei noceret.** *Gloriosus had feared that the centurion might harm him.*			

Tips on Translating *Ut* Clauses

- When translating **ut** clauses, look for a cue word in the main clause that may "trigger" or set up the specific meaning of the subordinate clause, e.g., **ita** or **tam** (result), **hortari** or **imperare** (indirect command), or **timere** or **vereri** (fear). Remember that "trigger words" are found outside of and preceding the subjunctive clause. It is helpful to bracket the subjunctive clause in order to indicate that it contains information which is separate from that of the main clause of the sentence.
- **Ut** clauses are generally found with the present or imperfect subjunctive and follow the rules of sequence of tenses.
- Most **ut** clauses are best translated using the words *that . . .* or *to . . . .*

- Occasionally, and most often in poetry, **ut** can have the meaning *how* and introduce an indirect question:

  Gloriosus dicit se nescire ut res sit.

  Gloriosus says that he does not know how the situation stands.

- The adverb **ut** may also be found with a verb in the indicative, in which case it has the meaning of *as* or *when*, e.g.,

  Gloriosus, ut centurio imperaverat, pilum iecit.

  Gloriosus, as the centurion had ordered, threw the spear.

- The use of **ut** extends to the introduction of similes, where it may correlate with a word such as **sic** or **ita** (*so*):*

  Ut aries portam percutit, sic Gloriosus in hostem se propellit.

  Just as a battering-ram smashes a city gate, so does Gloriosus drive himself forward into the enemy.

Practice Questions: Subordinate Clauses with *Ut*

1. Admonebitne Caesar suos ut Britanni suas facies tingant?
   (A) that the Britons dye their faces
   (B) to dye his own face like the Britons
   (C) that his men will dye the faces of the Britons
   (D) that the Britons dye the faces of centurions

2. Suntne tot barbari in Gallia ____ Caesar eos vincere ____?
   (A) non . . . potest (C) ne . . . potest
   (B) ut . . . non possit (D) ne . . . possit

3. Are soldiers afraid to die?
   (A) ut . . . moriantur (C) ut . . . morerentur
   (B) ne . . . moriuntur (D) ne . . . moriantur

4. Traiano imperatore, accidit ut Dacii ____ .
   (A) victi sunt (C) vincerentur
   (B) victuri sint (D) vincebantur

5. Miles bibebat ad bellum obliviscendum. Which answer provides the closest substitute?
   (A) ut bellum oblivisceretur (C) quia bellum obliviscebatur
   (B) bello oblito (D) obliviscens bellum

---

* For more on correlatives, see Chapter 30.

6. ____ superbus Gloriosus erat ut multos amicos non haberet.

   (A) Tamen (C) Tandem

   (B) Tam (D) Tunc

7. Gloriosus, ut hostes conspexit, arborem ascendit.

   (A) in order to see the enemy

   (B) to see the enemy

   (C) with the result that he saw the enemy

   (D) when he saw the enemy

Sententiae Antiquae

1. Non ut edam vivo sed ut vivam edo. (Quintilian)

   (A) I do not eat to live, but I live to eat.

   (B) I should not live to eat, but I should eat to live.

   (C) I do not live to eat, but I eat to live.

   (D) I will not live so that I may eat, but I will eat so that I may live.

2. The fruit vendors ask that you make. M. Holconius Priscus aedile. (from a Pompeiian election poster)

   (A) ut vos facitis (C) ne vos faciatis

   (B) ut vos faceretis (D) ut vos faciatis

3. Feminae spectatum veniunt et veniunt ut ipsae ____ . (Ovid)

   (A) spectentur (C) spectent

   (B) spectarentur (D) spectantur

4. Orandum est ut sit mens sana in corpore sano. (Juvenal)

   (A) that there will be (C) that there be

   (B) that there was (D) that there must be

5. Nemo adeo ferus est ut mitescere non possit. (Horace)

   (A) was not able (C) has not been able

   (B) will not be able (D) is not able

6. Cito scribendo non fit ut bene scribatur; bene scribendo fit ut cito. (Quintilian)

   (A) that it is written well

   (B) as it should be well written

   (C) in order to write well

   (D) that it was written well

Subordinate Clauses with *Ut* in the *Aeneid*

Translate the following sentences containing **ut** clauses, which are underlined. Observe whether each is indicative or subjunctive. Some context is provided.

1. Mercury visits Carthage:

   Haec ait et Maia genitum demittit ab alto, ut terrae utque novae pateant Karthaginis arces hospitio Teucris, ne fati nescia Dido finibus arceret. (1.297–300)

2. Shipwrecked Aeneas explores the coast:

   At pius Aeneas per noctem plurima volvens, ut primum lux alma data est, exire locosque explorare novos . . . constituit. (1.305–307)

3. Venus cloaks Aeneas and Achates:

   At Venus obscuro gradientes aere saepsit, cernere ne quis eos neu quis contingere posset. (1.411–412)

4. Aeneas bemoans the fall of Troy:

   "Iubes renovare dolorem, Troianas ut opes et lamentabile regnum eruerint Danai." (2.3–5)

5. Jupiter chastizes Juno for her interference :

   "Desine iam tandem precibusque inflectere nostris, ne te tantus edat tacitam dolor et (ne) mihi curae saepe tuo dulci tristes ex ore recursent." (12.800–802)

6. Juno defends her actions to Jupiter:

   "Iuturnam misero (fateor) succurrere fratri suasi . . . non ut tela tamen, non ut contenderet arcum." (12.813–815)

Answers to Practice Questions: Subordinate Clauses with *Ut*

1. Indirect command **(A)**

   The appearance of the verb **Admonebit** defines the clause **ut...tingant** as an indirect command with its subjunctive verb in primary sequence. The sentence reads, "Will Caesar advise his men that the Britons dye their faces?" For various reasons, the remaining answers do not translate the Latin correctly. Answers (C) and (D) translate as part of the subordinate clause elements that are really part of the main clause.

2. Result clause **(B)**

   The word **tot** preceding the clause cues this as a result clause. The sentence reads, "Are there so many barbarians in Gaul that Caesar cannot defeat them?"

This **ut** result clause requires a subjunctive verb in primary sequence, as the main verb is in the present tense, which removes Answers (A) and (C) from consideration. The negative of a result clause is not **ne**, as in Answer (D), but **ut non**.

3. Fear clause **(D)**
   This fear clause is in primary sequence, which requires that the subjunctive be in the present tense, as in the clause **ne...moriatur**. Remember that the meanings of **ut** and **ne** are reversed in fear clauses! Answer (A) disregards this fact, (B) does not contain a subjunctive verb, and in (C), the tense of the verb **moreretur** is not justifiable, given the present tense of the main verb.

4. Substantive result clause **(C)**
   This sentence reads, "While Trajan was emperor, it came to pass (happened) that the Dacians were conquered." The appearance of **accidit** sets up a result clause requiring a subjunctive verb, which eliminates Answers (A) **victi sunt** and (D) **vincebantur**. Answer (B) **victuri sint** is subjunctive, but has a meaning in the active voice, i.e., "about to conquer," which does not fit the context. Therefore, Answer (C) **vincerentur** is correct.

5. Purpose clause **(A)**
   The purpose clause **ut...oblivisceretur** "(in order) to forget the war" is the best substitution for the underlined gerundive of purpose **ad bellum obliviscendum**. The original sentence reads, "The soldier drank for the purpose of forgetting the war." Answer (B) is an ablative absolute, (C) a causal clause, and (D) a present participial phrase, none of which fit the context. (For the gerundive of purpose, see Chapter 22.)

6. Result clause **(B)**
   The sense of the thought here, "Gloriosus was so arrogant that he did not have many friends," leads to the conclusion that this sentence contains a result clause. Of the choices, the word **tam**, "so...," introduces the result clause **ne... haberet** in secondary sequence. None of the adverbs in Answers (A), (B), and (C) are relevant to defining an **ut** clause with the subjunctive.

7. **Ut** + indicative **(D)**
   This sentence reads, "When he saw the enemy, Gloriosus climbed a tree." Because the verb **conspexit** is indicative, **ut** must be translated "as" or "when." Answers (A) and (B) call for purposes clauses, and (C) for a result clause, all requiring subjunctive verbs.

Sententiae Antiquae Answers

1. Purpose clause **(C)**
   Quintilian's sentence contains two purpose clauses, **ut...edam** and **ut vivam**. Answer (A) reverses the two clauses, Answer (B) requires independent subjunctives in the present tense, and (D) mistranslates the tenses of the verbs **vivere** and **edere**.

2. Indirect command **(D)**

Ut vos faciatis idiomatically translates "that you vote." This clause is an indirect command introduced by the verb "ask" in the main clause of the English sentence and requiring a subjunctive verb in primary sequence. Answer (A) is not a subjunctive clause, (B) has the verb in the wrong tense, and (C) **ne vos faciatis**, incorrectly negates the original positive statement.

3. Purpose clause **(A)**

This sentence, which reads, "They come to see (and) to be seen themselves," referring to women at the races, contains a purpose clause with its verb in primary sequence (**spectentur**, after **veniunt**). Answer (B) **spectarentur** is in the imperfect tense in secondary sequence, (C) **spectent** is active and doesn't fit the context, and (D) **spectantur** is in the indicative mood. Note the supine of purpose, **spectatum**, for which, see Chapter 21.

4. Indirect command **(C)**

Ut sit is an indirect command after the verb **orare** in the periphrastic **orandum est**. Juvenal's famous statement says, "(We) must maintain that there be a sound mind in a sound body." Answer (A) requires the "future subjunctive" form (**futura sit**), (B) the imperfect tense (**esset**), and (D) an expression of necessity in the clause.

5. Result clause **(D)**

The appearance of **adeo** keys the result clause **ut non mitescere possit**. The present tense of the subjunctive verb **possit** is correctly translated "is not able" or "cannot." The sentence reads, "No one is so fierce that he cannot be tamed."

6. Substantive result clause **(A)**

The underlined clause is a substantive result clause following the verb **fit**. Quintilian's thought reads, "Not by writing quickly does it come about that it is written well; by writing well, it comes about that (it is written) quickly." Note the condensation of the Latin, with the omission of **scribatur** in the second half of the sentence. In Answer (B), the translation "as" for **ut** requires an indicative verb, whereas **scribatur** is subjunctive. Answer (C) "in order to" is phrased as a purpose clause and has the verb in the active voice, and (D) incorrectly translates the tense of **scribatur** as imperfect.

Answers to Subordinate Clauses with *Ut* in the Aeneid

1. Mercury visits Carthage:

Haec ait et Maia genitum demittit ab alto, ut terrae utque novae pateant Karthaginis arces hospitio Teucris, ne fati nescia Dido finibus arceret. (1.297–300) (purpose)

He says these things and sends down from on high the son of Maia, so that the lands and the new towers of Carthage may lie open in hospitality for the Trojans, and so that Dido, ignorant of fate, might not keep them away from her territory.

2. Shipwrecked Aeneas explores the coast:

At pius Aeneas per noctem plurima volvens, ut primum lux alma data est, exire locosque explorare novos . . . constituit. (1.305–307) (indicative)

But dutiful Aeneas, turning over (in his mind) much throughout the night, when first the kindly light of day arrived, decided to set out and explore the new places.

3. Venus cloaks Aeneas and Achates:

At Venus obscuro gradientes aere saepsit, cernere ne quis eos neu quis contingere posset. (1.411–412) (negative purpose)

But Venus cloaked them, as they went, with a concealing mist, so that no one might see or touch them.

4. Aeneas bemoans the fall of Troy:

"Iubes renovare dolorem, Troianas ut opes et lamentabile regnum eruerint Danai." (2.3–5) (indirect question)

"You bid (me) to renew the pain (of) how the Greeks brought down the might of Troy and its kingdom full of woe."

5. Jupiter chastizes Juno for her interference:

"Desine iam tandem precibusque inflectere nostris, ne te tantus edat tacitam dolor et (ne) mihi curae saepe tuo dulci tristes ex ore recursent." (12.800–802) (indirect commands after **precibus**)

"Stop now and yield to my entreaties, so that such great grief (of yours) may not consume you in silence and so that (your) sad cares may not often return to me from your sweet mouth."

6. Juno defends her actions to Jupiter:

"Iuturnam misero (fateor) succurrere fratri suasi . . . non ut tela tamen, non ut contenderet arcum." (12.813–815) (indirect commands after **suasi**; **non ut** is poetic for **ne**; these could also be viewed as negative result clauses)

"I convinced Juturna (I confess it) to help her unfortunate brother . . . but not to aim the arrow, not to bend the bow."

Chapter 28

Subordinate Clauses with Q-Words

During your review, you have met the relative, or **qui**, clause with the indicative, e.g., **Cicero qui consul erat**, *Cicero who was a consul* (Chapter 13) and the deliberative question with the independent subjunctive, e.g., **Quid agam**? *What should I do?* (Chapter 25). There are several different types of subjunctive clauses that are introduced in Latin by question words or by a word that begins with the letter **q**. Because of the similarity in the appearance of these clauses, it is appropriate to consider them together.

Types of Subjunctive Clauses Introduced by Q-Words

The most common subjunctive clauses introduced by a **q**-word are the indirect question, relative clause of characteristic, and causal clause. In the context of these clauses, we will also review doubt clauses and the relative, or **qui**, purpose clause.

Indirect Question

Indirect questions are to direct questions as indirect commands are to direct commands. They express the fact that someone is reporting a direct question, e.g.,

Direct question: **"Quid agis?" Cicero rogabat.**
"How are you doing?" Cicero asked.

Indirect question: **Cicero rogabat [quid agerem]**.
Cicero asked [how I was doing].

An indirect question consists of a dependent subjunctive clause that is introduced by a "question word" such as **cur, quid, quis, quomodo, ubi,** or **unde**. Such clauses are set up or "triggered" by an indicative verb of asking, wondering, or knowing, such as **quaerere**, **mirari,** or **scire**, respectively. The indicative verb of the main clause is the same type of verb as that which introduces an indirect statement (for which, see Chapter 23). When working out the meaning of a Latin sentence containing an indirect question, look for the following components: a verb of verbal or mental action, a question word, and a subjunctive verb, e.g.,

Direct question: *"Scribax, why haven't you written those letters yet?"*

verb of verbal action — question word

Indirect question: **Atticus rogat Scribacem cur illas epistulas nondum scripserit].**

subjunctive verb — indirect question clause

Atticus is asking (his scribe) Scribax why he has not yet written the letters.

Compare these other indirect expressions:

Direct statement: *"I lost my pen," Scribax said.*

verbal action — subj. acc. — infinitive

Indirect statement: **Scribax dicit se stilum suum amisisse.**

Scribax says that he lost his pen.

Direct command: *"Get another pen, Scribax!"*

command verb — **ut** or **ne**

Indirect command: **Atticus Scribaci imperavit ut alterum stilum obtineret.**

subjunctive verb

Atticus ordered Scribax to get another pen.

The subjunctive verb in an indirect question is translated in the same tense as it would be if it were an indicative verb. Remember that indirect questions in Latin will never contain question or quotation marks. Use your "I.Q.!"

Notes:

- Take care to distinguish the indirect question clause from other types of **q**-clauses, such as the relative clause found with the indicative (for which, see Chapter 13).
- In an indirect question, the Romans often preferred to emphasize the question by placing it first in the sentence, e.g.,

  [Quid sit futurum cras] fuge quaerere. (Horace)

  Stop asking [what may happen tomorrow].

- Since a direct question may be expressed by using a verb in the future tense, it should be remembered that, in an indirect question, the active periphrastic (future participle + form of **esse** in the subjunctive) may be used to express future time, e.g.,

  Scribax scire voluit quot epistulas ipse scripturus esset.

  Scribax wanted to know how many letters he was about to transcribe.

  The future participle plus a form of esse is called an active periphrastic.

Double Indirect Questions

Indirect questions can be alternative or double, i.e., more than a single question may be asked in a sentence, such as the following questions introduced by **utrum...an**, *whether...or*:

Atticus mirabatur [utrum Scribax ignavus an stultus esset].

Atticus was wondering [whether Scribax was lazy or foolish].

Indirect Clauses Expressing Doubt

An indirect question may express doubt in the following ways:

1) the subjunctive clause of doubt is introduced by the words **num** or **an**, *whether*, preceded by a verb of questioning or doubting, such as a form of the verb **dubitare**, *doubt*, or the phrase **dubium est**, *there is doubt that*, e.g,

Aliqui dubitant [num Cicero carmina scripserit].

Some people doubt [whether Cicero wrote poetry].

Note:

- Remember that the interrogative particle **num** can also introduce a direct question with the indicative, to which a negative answer is expected. (See Chapter 20.)

2) the negative subjunctive clause of doubt is introduced by the word **quin**, *that*, preceded by the stated or implied negative of the doubting word or expression, e.g., **non dubitare** or **non dubium est** (= **sine dubio**):

Est non dubium [quin Caesar ad Ciceronem epistulas scripserit].

There is no doubt, or It is doubtless [that Caesar wrote letters to Cicero].

Relative Clause of Characteristic

This type of subjunctive clause, which is introduced by a relative pronoun, describes a type of person or thing, rather than one that is actual or specific. This type of relative clause describes a general quality or characteristic of the antecedent. Such clauses follow indefinite words phrases such as **nemo est qui** (*there is no one who...*), **is est qui** (*he is the type* or *kind of person who...*), and **sunt qui** (*there are those of the sort who...*). The relative clause of characteristic is generally found with the present subjunctive. Be especially careful to distinguish the relative characteristic clause with the subjunctive from the explanatory relative clause with the indicative. The explanatory clause provides (more) factual information about the antecedent:

Relative clause with the indicative: **Tiro est scriba [qui diligens est].**
Tiro is the (particular) scribe [who is careful].

Relative clause with the subjunctive: **Tiro est scriba [qui diligens sit].**
Tiro is the (type of) scribe [who is careful].

Additional examples of relative clauses of characteristic:

Nemo est [qui omnes epistulas Ciceronis legerit].

There is no one (in the opinion of the writer) [who has read all of Cicero's letters].

Erant [qui dicerent] Tironem scribam optimum omnium esse.

There were those [who said] that Tiro was the best secretary of all.

Relative Purpose Clause

The relative, or **qui**, clause with the subjunctive can also be used to express purpose:

Cicero Terentiae dedit epistulam [quam legeret].

Cicero gave Terentia a letter [to read, i.e. that she was to read].

In such situations, the relative pronoun (**quam**), refers back to a particular antecedent (**epistulam**), while at the same time indicating purpose or intent (**legeret**).

Note:

- When translating a relative clause, identify the antecedent of the relative pronoun, determine if the verb of the clause is indicative or subjunctive, and then consider the contextual sense of the **qui** clause carefully before deciding upon its meaning. If the verb of the relative clause is in the indicative, the clause gives a factual description of something or someone. If the verb is in the subjunctive, it describes a general type of person or indicates the purpose of some other action.

Quick Study of Expressions of Purpose

Gerundive of purpose	
Cicero iter facit ad amicum visendum. *Cicero is traveling to visit a friend.*	See Chapter 22.
Supine	
Cicero iter facit visum amicum. *Cicero is traveling to visit a friend.*	See Chapter 22.
Ut purpose clause	
Cicero iter facit ut amicum visat. *Cicero is traveling to visit a friend.*	See Chapter 27.
Relative purpose clause	
Cicero epistulam mittet quae dicat se venire. *Cicero will send a letter to say that he is coming.*	See above.

Causal Clauses

Causal clauses are dependent clauses introduced by explanatory words such as **quod, quia,** or **quoniam**,* all meaning *because*, or *since*. Such clauses are found with either the indicative or the subjunctive. When the indicative is used, the writer/speaker is taking responsibility for the reason, i.e., the reader must assume that the explanation is viewed by the writer as a known fact. When the subjunctive is found in the dependent clause, the reason is viewed as that of someone other than the writer/speaker, i.e., it is alleged, e.g.,

Indicative (fact):

Cicero orationes Philippicas habebat [quod Antonius tyrannus erat].

Cicero delivered the Philippics [because Antony was a tyrant, as far as the speaker of the sentence is concerned*]*.

Subjunctive (allegation):

[Quia Cicero rem publicam servavisset], "Pater Patriae" salutabatur.

[Since Cicero had saved the state, in the opinion of someone other than the writer*], he was saluted as "Father of his Country."*

Note:

- When **quod** is found in a clause with its verb in the indicative mood, be careful to use context in order to determine whether **quod** has the meaning *because* (causal) or *which, that* (relative):

  Quod causal (indicative-factual):

  Cicero scripsit De Natura Deorum [quod credit] deos esse.

  Cicero wrote "On the Nature of the Gods" [because he believes] that the gods existed.

  Quod relative (indicative-factual):

  Placebatne Ciceroni nomen [quod ei datum erat]?

  Was Cicero pleased with the name [that had been given to him]?

* For causal clauses introduced by **cum**, see the next chapter.

Quick Study of Q-Clauses

Type of clause	Introductory word	Meaning	Function
Indicative (factual)			
Relative	**qui, quae, quod**	*who, which, that*	explains, describes
Causal	**quod, quia, quoniam**	*since, because*	gives a reason as a fact
Subjunctive (non-factual)			
Indirect question	**cur, quid, quis, quomodo, ubi**, etc.	*why, what, who, how, when*, etc.	restates a question
Double indirect question	**utrum . . . an**	*whether...or*	restates more than one question
Doubt clauses	**num** **quin**	*whether* *that*	expresses uncertainty (**dubitare, dubium est**) expresses certainty (**non dubitare**)
Relative characteristic	**qui, quae, quod**	*the type who...*	describes a type
Relative purpose	**qui, quae, quod**	*to, in order to*	indicates purpose (relates to antecedent)
Causal	**quod, quia, quoniam**	*since, because*	gives a reason as an allegation

Practice With Q-Clauses

Look carefully at the prior and succeeding context of a **q**-word in the clause in order to determine its meaning. Is there a word in the main clause that "sets up" the meaning expressed in the subordinate clause? Does an indicative or subjunctive verb appear in the dependent clause? Now review what you know about **q**-word clauses by bracketing the clause in each sentence below and then inspecting its context. Finally, translate the entire sentence:

1. **Antonius qui inimicus Ciceronis erat illum necare voluit.**
2. **Quot senes libellum De Senectute legerint, Cicero scire vult.**
3. **Estne Cicero qui virtutem optimam esse credat?**
4. **Cicero de philosophia scripsit quod cara Tullia mortua esset.**

5. **Cicero orationem habebat quae Milonem defenderet.**
6. **Legimus orationes Ciceronis quod de Romanis nos certiores faciunt.**

Practice with Indirect Expressions

You have now met three different types of expressions that are "indirect": an infinitive clause and two subjunctive clauses. Each reports in second-hand fashion an original statement, command, or question. To test your command of indirect expressions, translate the following sentences and then create in English the original direct expression:

Indirect statement: **Multi sciunt Ciceronem Arpini natum esse.**

Indirect command: **Aliquis Ciceroni persuasit ut Tusculi habitaret.**

Indirect question: **Scitne quisquam in quo loco Cicero mortuus sit?**

Practice Questions: Q Clauses

1. Cicero scire vult <u>quis</u> sibi nomen "Tully" <u>dederit</u>.
   (A) who will have given
   (B) who was giving
   (C) who had given
   (D) who has given

2. Cicero Milonem ____ quia Clodium per Viam Appiam occidisset.
   (A) defendebat
   (B) defendet
   (C) defenderet
   (D) defenditur

3. Non dubium erat ____ Cicero clementiam Caesaris ____ .
   (A) qui . . . colat
   (B) ne . . . coleret
   (C) quin . . . coleret
   (D) quin . . . colebat

4. Quid agas, cura ut sciam.
   (A) Take care that I know where you are going.
   (B) Take care to know who you are.
   (C) Take care that I know how you are doing.
   (D) Take care to know what you are doing.

5. Cicero mirabatur quomodo cum senatoribus <u>gratiam habiturus esset</u>.
   (A) has gained favor
   (B) was going to gain favor
   (C) is going to gain favor
   (D) will be able to gain favor

6. Erant qui non credidit Ciceronem militem fuisse.
   (A) There are those who do not believe that Cicero was a soldier.
   (B) There were those who believe that Cicero was not a soldier.
   (C) There were those who did not believe that Cicero had been a soldier.
   (D) There were those who did not believe that Cicero was a soldier.

7. Nemo scivit utrum Hortensius an Cicero optimus orator ____.
   (A) factus est (C) factus esset
   (B) fiebat (D) facturus esse

8. Nemo est qui dubitet quin Cicero bonus consul fuerit.
   (A) There is no one who will doubt that Cicero would have been a good consul.
   (B) There is no one who does not doubt that Cicero was a good consul.
   (C) There is no one who doubts that Cicero was a good consul.
   (D) There is no one who doubts that Cicero was not a good consul.

Sententiae Antiquae

1. Videtis quantum scelus contra rem publicam vobis <u>nuntiatum sit</u>. (Cicero, on Catiline)
   (A) has been reported (C) was being reported
   (B) had been reported (D) is reported

2. Scire ubi aliquid invenire ____ , ea maxima pars eruditionis est. (Anon.)
   (A) posses (C) potueras
   (B) potes (D) possis

3. <u>Quod</u> cum animadvertisset Caesar naves militibus compleri iussit. (Caesar)
   (A) Because (C) The fact that
   (B) What (D) This

4. Malum est consilium quod mutari non ____ . (Publilius Syrus)
   (A) potuerit (C) potuisset
   (B) posset (D) potest

5. Odi et amo. <u>Quare id faciam</u>, fortasse requiris. (Catullus)
   (A) Why I have done this (C) Why I do this
   (B) Why I will do this (D) Why I will have done this

6. Multi cives ea pericula quae imminent neglegunt. (Cicero)
   (A) which might be imminent
   (B) which are imminent
   (C) which were imminent
   (D) which will be imminent

7. Quis dubitet num in virtute felicitas sit? (Cicero)
   (A) Who would doubt whether there is happiness in virtue?
   (B) Who would doubt whether or not there is happiness in virtue?
   (C) Who doubts whether virtue is happiness?
   (D) Who will doubt whether he is happy in his virtue?

8. Caesar milites reprehendit quod sibi ipsi iudicavissent quid agendum esset. (Caesar)
   (A) because they had (in fact) decided for themselves what had to be done.
   (B) because they were deciding for themselves what he must do.
   (C) because they did the thing which they had decided.
   (D) because they had (according to others) decided for themselves what had to be done.

Stumper: Do both of the following have the same meaning?

(A) Yes (B) No

Exegi monumentum aere perennius. (Horace)
Nihil est manu factum quod tempus non consumat. (Cicero)

Subordinate Clauses with Q-Words in the *Aeneid*

Translate the following sentences from the *Aeneid* containing subjunctive clauses introduced by **q**-words. First, underline the clause(s) and then translate the entire sentence. The first one is underlined for you. Some context is provided.

Indirect Question

1. Shipwrecked Aeneas on the African coast:

   At pius Aeneas . . . quas vento accesserit oras, qui (eas) teneant, quaerere constituit. (1.305-308)

2. Aeneas views the murals in the temple of Juno:

   Namque videbat, uti bellantes Pergama circum hac fugerent Grai, (uti hac) premeret Troiana iuventus; (uti) hac Phryges (fugerent), (uti hac) instaret curru cristatus Achilles. (2.466-468)

3. Aeneas surveys the scene as Troy falls:

   Respicio et, quae sit me circum copia, lustro.

4. Aeneas considers when to approach Dido with the news that he is leaving:

   (Sentit) sese . . . temptaturum (esse) aditus et, quae mollissima fandi tempora (sint), quis rebus dexter modus (sit). (4.293-294)

5. Sibyl to Aeneas:

   "Si tanta cupido (menti tuo) est bis Stygios innare lacus . . . accipe quae (tibi) peragenda (sint) prius." (12.133-136)

6. The Trojans discuss what to do about Misenus' body:

   Multa inter sese vario sermone serebant, quem socium exanimem vates, quod corpus humandum diceret. (6.160-162)

7. Aeneas observes Venus's doves:

   Sic effatus vestigia pressit, observans quae signa ferant, quo tendere pergant. (6.197-198)

8. Anchises instructs Aeneas:

   (Anchises) Laurentesque docet populos urbemque Latini, et quo quemque modo fugiatque feratque laborem. (6.891-892; note the tmesis of **quo . . . modo**; take **quemque** with **laborem**)

9. Turnus falters:

   Rutulos aspectat et urbem cunctaturque metu letumque instare tremescit, nec quo se eripiat, nec qua vi tendat in hostem, nec currus usque videt aurigamve sororem. (12.915-918)

Relative Clauses with the Subjunctive

Note that the grammatical identity of the relative characteristic clause is the same as that of the relative purpose clause. The meaning must be based upon the reader's perception of the context, i.e., does the clause give a generalized description or does it indicate the reason why something may be done?

10. Juno learns of the fate of Carthage:

    Progeniem sed enim Troiano a sanguine duci audierat Tyrias olim quae verteret arces. (1.19-20)

11. Aeolus' authority:

    Sed pater omnipotens . . . regemque dedit qui foedere certo et premere et laxas sciret dare iussus habenas. (1.60-63)

12. Venus to Jupiter:

    "Certe hinc Romanos (futuros esse), . . . hinc fore ductores . . . qui mare, qui terras omnes dicione tenerent, pollicitus (es)." (1.234-237)

13. Venus to Aeneas:

    "Quisquis es, haud, credo, invisus caelestibus auras vitales carpis, Tyriam qui adveneris urbem." (1.387-388)

14. Laocoon's sacrilege:

    Scelus expendisse merentem Laocoonta ferunt, sacrum qui cuspide robur laeserit et tergo sceleratam intorserit hastam. (2.229-231)

15. Juno releases Dido's soul:

    Tum Iuno omnipotens . . . Irim demisit Olympo, quae luctantem animam nexosque resolveret artus. (4.693-695; note that this relative clause has causal force)

Answers to Practice Questions on Q-Clauses

1. **{Qui . . . erat}**

   Antony, who was a personal enemy of Cicero, wished to kill him.

2. **{Quot . . . legerint}**

   Cicero wants to know how many elderly men have read his treatise "On Old Age."

3. **{qui . . . credat}**

   Is Cicero the type of man who believes that virtue is the greatest (good)?

4. **{quod . . . mortua esset}**

   Cicero wrote about philosophy because his dear Tullia had died.

5. **{quae . . . defenderet}**

   Cicero gave a speech to defend Milo.

6. **{quod . . . faciunt}**

   We read the speeches of Cicero because they inform us about the Romans.

Discussion of Answers

Sentence 1 contains a relative clause of fact with the indicative (see Chapter 13). Sentence 6 contains a **quod** causal clause with the indicative, also indicating a factual statement. The remaining sentences contain clauses with subjunctive verbs. Remember that subjunctive verbs are used in clauses that express hypothetical or non-completed actions. In Sentence 2, Cicero does not yet know for a fact how many men have read his essay (indirect question). Sentence 3 describes the type of man Cicero might be (relative clause of characteristic). In Sentence 4, the subjunctive is used because it is the opinion of someone other than the writer that Cicero wrote philosophy because his daughter had died (causal clause with the subjunctive). The use of the subjunctive in the clause in Sentence 5 tells us that Cicero gave the speech in order to defend Milo (relative purpose clause).

Answers to Practice with Indirect Expressions

Indirect statement:	*Many know that Cicero was born at Arpinum.*
Direct statement:	"Cicero was born at Arpinum."
Indirect command:	*Someone persuaded Cicero to live in Tusculum.*
Direct command:	"Live in Tusculum, Cicero!"
Indirect question:	*Does anyone know where Cicero died?*
Direct question:	"Where did Cicero die?"

Answers to Practice Questions: Q-Clauses

1. Indirect question **(D)**

This sentence contains an indirect question in primary sequence, with the main verb in the present tense and the subjunctive verb **dederit** in the perfect tense. The sentence reads, "Cicero wants to know <u>who has given</u> him the name "Tully." **Dederit** could be identified as a future perfect tense, as is suggested in Answer (A) "who will have given," but the question word **quis** requires that the verb be subjunctive in an indirect question. Answers (B) and (C) require verbs in secondary sequence, which do not correlate with the tense of the main verb.

2. Causal clause **(A)**

A main verb in the past tense is required because the subjunctive verb of the causal clause, **quia...occidisset**, is in the pluperfect tense. Answers (B) and (D) are in the future and present tenses, respectively, and Answer (C) is in the imperfect tense, but is subjunctive, which does not fit the context of the main or independent clause. The sentence reads, "Cicero <u>was defending</u> Milo since he had killed Clodius along the Appian Way."

3. Doubt clause **(C)**

The words **non dubium** introduce a doubt clause with its verb in secondary sequence after **erat**. This sentence reads, "There was no doubt <u>that Cicero respected</u> Caesar's clemency." The verb in Answer (A) is in the wrong tense of the subjunctive, Answer (B) contains **ne**, an incorrect particle for a doubt clause, and (D) **quin...gaudebat** is a clause with a verb in the indicative, rather than the required subjunctive.

4. Indirect question and indirect command **(C)**

This sentence, which contains two subjunctive clauses, reads, "Take care that I know how you're doing." **Quid agas** is an indirect question following the verb **sciam**. **Ut sciam**, after **cura**, has the force of an indirect command. Answer (A) mistranslates the indirect question that contains the idiomatic expression **Quid agis?** "How are you?" Answers (B) and (D) imply that the subject of the verb **sciam** is in the second person, rather than the first. (For indirect command, see the previous chapter.)

5. Indirect question **(B)**

This sentence contains an example of the "future subjunctive," that is, the use of the future active participle with a subjunctive form of the verb **esse** as an active periphrastic. The **q**-word **quomodo** introduces the indirect question clause. The sentence reads, "Cicero was wondering how <u>he was going to gain favor</u> with the senators." Answers (B) and (C) incorrectly translate **esset** in the perfect and present tenses, respectively, and the translation in (D) assumes the future tense of the verb **posse**, which does not appear in the sentence.

6. Relative clause with the indicative **(C)**

The accuracy of the translation of this sentence depends upon the correct rendering of the tenses of the three verbs: **erant, credidit**, and **fuisse**. **Qui non credidit** is a relative clause with the indicative, indicating that it was considered a fact that some did not believe that Cicero had been a soldier. The verb **erant** is in the imperfect tense, eliminating Answer (A). In Answer (B), **non** incorrectly negates **esse** and in (D), the infinitive is translated incorrectly, that is, "was a soldier" requires the infinitive **esse** instead of **fuisse**. (See Chapter 23.)

7. Indirect question **(C)**

This sentence reads, "No one knew whether Hortensius or Cicero <u>had become</u> the best orator." **Utrum** and **an** introduce double indirect questions that require the subjunctive mood, which is **factus esset**. Answers (A) **factus est** and (B) **fiebat** are indicative, and Answer (D), **facturus esse**, a future infinitive, is a distractor which presumes that you will be misled by the verb **scivit**.

8. Relative clause of characteristic and doubt clause **(C)**

The correct translation is "There is no one who doubts that Cicero was a good consul." This sentence contains two subordinate clauses with the subjunctive. **Qui dubitet** is a relative clause of characteristic with a verb in the present subjunctive in primary sequence, describing a type of person who doubts. The appearance of **dubitet** in this clause introduces a clause of doubt, **quin . . . fuerit**. Answer (A) incorrectly translates **dubitet** as a future tense, therefore making the original characteristic clause an explanatory relative clause. The translation in Answer (B) "does not doubt" incorrectly negates the verb **dubitet**, creating a meaning that is the opposite of that of the original sentence. In the same way, Answer (D) incorrectly negates the subordinate verb **fuerit**.

Sententiae Antiquae Answers

1. Indirect question **(A)**

Nuntiatum sit is a form of the perfect passive subjunctive (for which, see Appendix 12), here found in an indirect question introduced by **quantum**. The sentence reads, "You see how much evil against the State (i.e., by the Catilinarian conspirators) has been reported to you all." The remaining answers translate the verb **nuntiatum sit** in the incorrect tense, i.e., (B) pluperfect (**nuntiatum esset**), (C) imperfect (**nuntiaretur**), and (D) present (**nuntiatur**).

2. Indirect question **(D)**

As all the verbs in this sentence are found in the present tense, the primary sequence is used, eliminating Answer (A), which is in the imperfect tense. The subjunctive mood is required because the missing form completes an indirect question introduced by **ubi**, thereby eliminating Answers (B) **potes** and (C) **potueras**, which are both indicative. The sentence reads, "Knowing (To know) where you can find something, that is the most important part of being educated."

3. (Ambush question!) **(D)**

The form **quod** is a relative pronoun refering to some previous antecedent that is neuter singular. Answers (A), (B), and (C) do not fit the context of the meaning, which is, "When Caesar had noticed this, he ordered the ships to be filled up with soldiers." It is tempting to connect **quod** with the following subjunctive verb **animadvertisset**, but this verb follows **cum** in a circumstantial clause. (This will be reviewed in the next chapter.)

4. Relative clause with the indicative **(D)**

Quod . . . potest is a simple relative clause, describing **malum consilium**. An indicative verb is therefore required in the subordinate clause, hence **potest**. The sentence reads, "It is a bad plan that cannot be changed." Answer (A) as a form of the future perfect indicative does not make sense, and as a form of the perfect subjunctive, is out of place in an explanatory relative clause. Answers (B) and (C) are subjunctive, and not justifiable in the context of this sentence.

5. Indirect question **(C)**

The indirect question **quare id faciam**, dependent upon **requiris**, is found in Catullus, Poem 85. This sentence reads, "I hate and I love. Why I do this, perhaps you ask." As the verbs are all in the present tense, the sequence is primary. Answer (A) mistranslates the tense of **faciam** as perfect, (B) as a future indicative, and (D) as a future perfect indicative.

6. Relative clause with the indicative **(B)**

The relative clause **quae imminent** describes its antecedent **ea pericula**, and thus requires the indicative mood. The sentence reads, "Many citizens disregard those dangers which are imminent." Answer (A) "might be imminent," as a non-fact, requires the subjunctive. Answers (C) and (D) translate the tense of **imminent** incorrectly as imperfect and future.

7. Doubt clause **(A)**

The doubt clause **num . . . sit** is introduced by the deliberative question **Quis dubitet**? "Who would doubt?" Answers (B) and (C) incorrectly negate the verb **sit** and (D) contains two errors: the verb **dubitet** is not in the future tense and **felicitas** is not an adjective, but a noun.

8. Causal clause and indirect question **(D)**

This sentence contains two subjunctive clauses, a causal clause with the subjunctive, **quod . . . iudicavissent (iudicavissent)**, indicating that the speaker/writer is doubtful of the reason given by Caesar, and an indirect question, **quid agendum esset**, whose verb is a passive periphrastic. Answer (A) is incorrect because it suggests that the statement is factual, which would require the verb **iudicaverit**, in the indicative mood. The verb tense of **iudicavissent** in Answer (B) is translated incorrectly, and Answer (D) gives a wholesale mistranslation of the Latin.

Stumper: (B)

Horace's line reads, "I have built a monument more lasting than bronze," i.e., something timeless. Cicero says, "There is nothing made by (man's) hand that time does not consume," i.e., all things are transitory. These statements obviously oppose one another in meaning.

Answers to Subordinate Clauses with Q-Words in the *Aeneid*

Indirect Question

1. Shipwrecked Aeneas on the African coast:

At pius Aeneas . . . quas vento accesserit oras, qui (eas) teneant, quaerere constituit. (1.305–308)

But dutiful Aeneas decided to explore what lands (shores) he reached with the wind (and) who might dwell there.

2. Aeneas views the murals in the temple of Juno:

Namque videbat, uti bellantes Pergama circum hac fugerent Grai, (uti hac) premeret Troiana iuventus; (uti) hac Phryges (fugerent), (uti hac) instaret curru cristatus Achilles. (2.466–468; note the gapping)

For in this (picture) he observed how the Greeks, fighting around the Pergama, fled, (in this one how) the Trojan youth pressed (them) hard, in this one (how) the Phrygians (fled), (and in this one how) Achilles with the crested helmet in hot pursuit in his chariot.

3. Aeneas surveys the scene as Troy falls:

Respicio et, quae sit me circum copia, lustro.

I look back and assess what force is around me. (2.564)

4. Aeneas considers when to approach Dido with the news that he is leaving:

(Sentit) sese . . . temptaturum (esse) aditus et, quae mollissima fandi tempora (sint), quis rebus dexter modus (sit). (4.293–294)

Aeneas decides that he will try (to find) an opening, what time may be the kindest for the telling, what method might be appropriate for the stuation.

5. Sibyl to Aeneas:

"Si tanta cupido (menti tuo) est bis Stygios innare lacus . . . accipe quae (tibi) peragenda (sint) prius." (12.133–136)

"But if you have such a desire to swim the Stygian lake twice, hear what (you) must do first."

6. The Trojans discuss what to do about Misenus' body:

Multa inter sese vario sermone serebant, quem socium exanimem vates, quod corpus humandum diceret. (6.160–162)

Many things were they discussing among themselves with different points of view, (that is), of which dead companion, of what body to be buried the seer was speaking.

7. Aeneas observes Venus's doves:

Sic effatus vestigia pressit, observans quae signa ferant, quo tendere pergant. (6.197-198)

Having spoken in this way he checked his steps, observing the signs that they (the birds) bring (and) where they proceed to go.

8. Anchises instructs Aeneas:

(Anchises) Laurentesque docet populos urbemque Latini, et quo quemque modo fugiatque feratque laborem. (6.891–892; note the tmesis of **quo . . . modo**; take **quemque** with **laborem**)

He instructs him (Aeneas) about the Laurentine people and the city of Latinus, and how he should flee or face each challenge.

9. Turnus falters:

Rutulos aspectat et urbem cunctaturque metu letumque instare tremescit, nec quo se eripiat, nec qua vi tendat in hostem, nec currus usque videt aurigamve sororem. (12.915–918)

Turnus looks on his Rutulians and the city and hesitates in fear and trembles at the death that threatens, and he does not see where he might escape, by what means he might attack his foe, nor does he see his chariot anywhere, or his sister, the charioteer.

Relative Clauses with the Subjunctive

10. Juno learns of the fate of Carthage:
Progeniem sed enim Troiano a sanguine duci audierat Tyrias olim quae verteret arces. (1.19–20)

But she had heard that a race was arising from Trojan blood to overthrow the Tyrian towers one day. (This could also be considered a relative characteristic clause referring back to ***progeniem****, "a race of the sort that might overthrow the Tyrian towers one day.")*

11. Aeolus' authority:
Sed pater omnipotens . . . regemque dedit qui foedere certo et premere et laxas sciret dare iussus habenas. (1.60–63)

But the all-powerful father gave (them) a king who, under fixed agreement, knew both (when or how) to tighten and loosen the reins on command. (This clause can also be considered a relative purpose clause, i.e., "gave them a king, to know both . . ."

12. Venus to Jupiter:
"Certe hinc Romanos (futuros esse), . . . hinc fore ductores . . . qui mare, qui terras omnes dicione tenerent, pollicitus (es)." (1.234–237)

"Surely you promised that from them the Romans would arise, from them they would be rulers, who would hold the sea (and) all lands under their sway." (Again, the clauses here might well be considered relative purpose clauses, referring back to ***Romanos****.)*

13. Venus to Aeneas:
"Quisquis es, haud, credo, invisus caelestibus auras vitales carpis, Tyriam qui adveneris urbem." (1.387–388)

"Whoever you are, you do not, I believe, breathe mortal air hated by the gods, you who have arrived at the Tyrian city."

14. Laocoon's sacrilege:
Scelus expendisse merentem Laocoonta ferunt, sacrum qui cuspide robur laeserit et tergo sceleratam intorserit hastam. (2.229–231)

They say that Laocoon deservedly paid the price for his transgression, who defiled the sacred wood with his spear and hurled the ill-fated shaft into its body. (This relative clause has causal force, i.e., "he paid the price for his transgression because he defiled . . .)

15. Juno releases Dido's soul:
Tum Iuno omnipotens . . . Irim demisit Olympo, quae luctantem animam nexosque resolveret artus. (4.693–695)

The all-powerful Juno sent Iris down from Olympus to set free her struggling soul and (from) her confining limbs.

Chapter 29

Subordinate Clauses with *Cum*

The word **cum** has two basic functions in Latin: as a preposition governing an object in the ablative case, e.g., **cum laude**, *with praise*, and as a conjunction that joins a dependent clause to a main clause, e.g., **[Cum strenuissime laboravisset], summam laudem recepit,** *[Since he had worked the hardest], he received the greatest praise*. There are three major types of **cum** clauses found with the subjunctive: causal, circumstantial, and concessive (the "three C's"). In such clauses, the word **cum** means *since, when*, or *although*, depending upon the context. A variation of the circumstantial clause that expresses action at a specific time appears with its verb in the indicative mood. **Cum** clauses with verbs in the subjunctive are found in the imperfect and pluperfect tenses and follow the rules for sequence of tenses.

Types of *Cum* Clauses

Cum Causal Clause (*Since, Because*)

When the **cum** clause expresses the reason why the action of the main clause occurred, **cum** means *since* or *because* and is followed by a subjunctive verb, e.g.,

> **[Cum Troianos superare non possent], Graeci equum ligneum aedificaverunt.**
>
> *[Since they were unable to defeat the Trojans], the Greeks constructed a wooden horse.*
>
> **Laocoon [cum hasta equum percussisset] a serpentibus necatus est.**
>
> *Laocoon [because he had struck the horse with a spear], was killed by serpents.*

Notes:

- **Cum** clauses are generally located close to the front of the sentence.
- The clause **quae cum ita sint**, *since these things are so*, appears often in prose.
- For causal clauses introduced by **q**-words, see the previous chapter.

Time Clauses (*When*)

Cum Circumstantial and Temporal Clauses

When a dependent **cum** clause expresses the general circumstances, situation, or conditions in which the action of the clause occurs, a subjunctive verb is used, and **cum** means *when*. The circumstantial clause is found with the imperfect or pluperfect subjunctive and refers to past time. **Cum** meaning *when* may also be found with a past tense of the indicative, but in this case, the **cum** clause indicates or dates a specific or precise point in time, and is sometimes accompanied by a clarifying phrase or word, such as **eo tempore**, *at that time,* or **tum**, *then*. When the clause has this meaning, it is generally referred to as a temporal clause.

Circumstantial (+ subjunctive):

> **[Cum manes ad Acherontem flumen pervenissent], Charon eos scapha transportavit.**
>
> *[When souls had reached the river Acheron], Charon carried them across in a boat.*

Temporal (+ indicative):

> **[Cum ad Acherontem pervenerat], tenuitne Aeneas obolum?**
>
> *[(At the time) when he had reached the Acheron], did Aeneas have the fare?*

Notes:

- A famous example of the **cum** temporal clause is Cicero's saying, **Cum tacent, clamant**, *When they are silent, they cry aloud*, meaning that they (i.e., the senators) have made their feelings clear without having to express them. In **cum** clauses, the appearance of **cum** with the indicative is much less frequent than with the subjunctive.

Time Clauses with the Indicative (When, As soon as)

Temporal or time clauses introduced by words such as **ubi,** *when,* and **simul atque** or **simul ac,** *as soon as*, are found with the indicative and express pure time.

Cum Concessive Clause *(Although)*

The word concessive implies that the statement within the **cum** clause is granted or assumed as true by the speaker or writer. In this context, **cum** means *although* and introduces a clause with its verb in the subjunctive mood. The concessive **cum** clause is often (but not always) accompanied by the word **tamen**, *nevertheless*, in the main clause:

> **[Cum Vergilius de armis viroque caneret], (tamen) de femina optime scripsit.**
>
> *[Although (or Granted that) Vergil sang about arms and a man], (nevertheless) he did his best writing about a woman.*

Note:

- The word **quamquam**, meaning *although*, also introduces concessive clauses, either with the indicative or the subjunctive, depending upon whether or not the clause contains a statement of fact. In the first example below, the use of the indicative verb **nolebat** suggests that the writer believes that Aeneas was unwilling to kill Turnus.

Quamquam Aeneas Turnum occidere nolebat, tamen eum ferro confodit.

Although Aeneas did not wish to kill Turnus, he nonetheless stabbed him with a sword.

Conversely, in the next sentence, the use of the subjunctive verb **nollet** indicates that the writer does not believe that Aeneas was unwilling to kill Turnus.

Quamquam Aeneas Turnum occidere nollet, tamen eum ferro confodit.

Although Aeneas did not wish to kill Turnus, he nonetheless stabbed him with a sword.

Tips on Translating *Cum* Clauses

When translating **cum** clauses, which are almost all grammatically identical, try one meaning of **cum**, then another, etc., to see which meaning makes the best sense in the context of the sentence. **Cum** clauses are regularly found with subjunctive verbs in either the imperfect or pluperfect tense. Be especially alert for the appearance of **cum** as a preposition. Questions on standardized tests are not designed to be misleading and will rarely present you with a grammatical decision that is not clearly defined. and so, because of its ambiguity, the **cum** clause is often tested in the reading passages of the multiple-choice section, where more context is available. A question might read: "In line such and so, **cum** is translated (A) when (B) with (C) although (D) since" or "The first sentence (**Cum . . . esset**) tells us that . . . ."

Quick Study of *Cum* Clauses

Type of clause	Cue in main clause	Meaning of clause	Function
Indicative			
Temporal	**eo tempore, tum**	*when, whenever*	specific time
Subjunctive			
Causal		*since, because*	gives a reason
Circumstantial		*when*	general circumstance
Concessive	**tamen**	*although*	truth granted by writer

Practice Questions: Cum Clauses

1. Cum Augustus novam Romam aedificare vellet, tamen dicebat "O fortunati, quorum iam moenia surgunt!"
   (A) When
   (B) Because
   (C) Provided that
   (D) Although

2. Cum Aeneas Carthagine excessisset, Dido se necare constituit.
   (A) Since Aeneas left Carthage
   (B) When Aeneas leaves Carthage
   (C) When Aeneas had left Carthage
   (D) Since Aeneas was leaving Carthage

3. When Troy had been captured, it was burned.
   (A) Troia cum capta esset, incensa est.
   (B) Troia dum capiebatur, incensa est.
   (C) Troia capta, incensa erat.
   (D) Troia cum caperetur, incendebatur.

4. Vergilius cum apibus avibusque ruri libenter habitabat.
   (A) when
   (B) with
   (C) since
   (D) although

5. Cum Vergilius mortuus sit, Aeneis non completa est.
   (A) While Vergil was dying
   (B) After Vergil died
   (C) When Vergil dies
   (D) Because Vergil died

6. When Aeneas heard Cerberus barking, the Sibyl said, "Cave canem, Cave canem, Cave canem!"
   (A) audiret
   (B) auditus erat
   (C) audivisset
   (D) audit

7. Eodem tempore cum Vergilius de Marcello . . . , Augustus lacrimavit.
   (A) legit
   (B) legeret
   (C) legat
   (D) legisset

8. Romani, cum crederent Aeneam gentem togatam condidisse, Aeneidem legebant.
   (A) since they believed
   (B) whenever they believe
   (C) after they believed
   (D) although they believe

9. Troianis fugientibus, cum Creusa e conspectu . . . tum Aeneas ad urbem rediit.

   (A) abiisset (C) abit
   (B) abeat (D) abierat

10. Cum Augustus de Livia certior factus esset, cogitavit, "Dux femina facti."

   (A) Because Augustus is informed about Livia
   (B) When Augustus was informed about Livia
   (C) When Augustus had been informed about Livia
   (D) Since Augustus was being informed about Livia

Sententiae Antiquae

1. A man is outside of his body at that very moment when he is angry. (Publilius Syrus)

   (A) cum iratus est (C) cum iratus sit
   (B) cum iratus esset (D) cum iratus esse potest

2. Satis est beatus qui potest cum vult mori. (Publilius Syrus)

   (A) He is happy enough who wants to die when he can.
   (B) Happy enough is the one who can die when he wants.
   (C) He who dies can be happy enough whenever he wants.
   (D) Because he wants to die, he who is happy enough can.

3. Quae cum ita sint, Catilina, ... (Cicero)

   (A) Since these things are this way
   (B) Whenever this is true
   (C) Although this was the case
   (D) Whatever things are so

4. Quod bellum oderunt, cum fide de pace . . . . (Livy)

   (A) agerent (C) egissent
   (B) agebant (D) aguntur

5. You hope (to see) a fox's tail at the very moment when you see his ears. (Medieval)

   (A) cum vidisti (C) cum videas
   (B) cum vides (D) cum visurus es

Stumper: Cum essent civium domini, libertorum erant servi. (Pliny the Younger)

(A) Seeing that they were (C) Since they had been

(B) Although they were (D) Provided they are

Answers to Practice Questions: *Cum* Clauses

1. Concessive **(D)**

The appearance of the word **tamen** in the main clause cues the **cum** clause in this sentence as concessive. The sentence reads, "Although Augustus wished to build a new Rome, nevertheless he said, 'O fortunate are they whose walls are already rising!'" which is a quote from Book 2 of the *Aeneid*. The translations in Answer (A) "When" and (B) "Because" are possible grammatically, but less likely than "Although," because of **tamen**. Answer (B) "Provided that," which is a provisional clause, does not fit the context.

2. Circumstantial **(C)**

This sentence requires decisions about the type of clause and the tense of the verb. Since the verb **excessisset** is in the pluperfect tense, Answers (A), (B), and (D) are incorrect because they offer translations in the simple past, present, and imperfect tenses, respectively. The clause is translated as circumstantial because the only answer with the subordinate verb in the correct tense is introduced by the word "when." The sentence reads, "When Aeneas had left Carthage, Dido decided to kill herself."

3. Circumstantial **(A)**

The subordinate clause in this sentence can be found either with an indicative or a subjunctive verb. Answer (B) provides Latin that does not give the translation "When Troy had been captured." Answer (C) is incorrect because the verb of the main clause, the pluperfect form **incensa erat**, does not translate "it was burned" correctly. Answers (A) and (D) contain subjunctive verbs, so the decision becomes one of tense. The original sentence reads "had been captured," which requires a pluperfect passive verb form in the subordinate clause. This is **capta esset**. Answer (D) gives the verb **caperetur** in the imperfect tense.

4. Prepositional phrase **(B)**

This question is included to "keep you honest" about the possibility that **cum** can be a preposition followed by a noun in the ablative case, as here: **cum apibus avibusque**. The sentence reads, "Vergil gladly lived in the country with the birds and bees."

5. Causal **(D)**

The **cum** clause in this sentence makes the best sense as a causal clause, "Because Vergil died, the *Aeneid* was not completed." Answers (A) "While Vergil was dying" and (C) "When Vergil dies" do not translate the perfect subjunctive form **mortuus sit** correctly. Answer (B) "After Vergil died" does not give an appropriate rendering of the conjunction **cum**.

6. Circumstantial **(A)**

Since the choices of answers provide two verbs in the indicative and two in the subjunctive, the decision must be made on the basis of tense. Answers (B) and (C) are incorrect because they are pluperfect and the imperfect or perfect is required to translate "When Aeneas heard...." Answer (C) **audit** is in the present tense, leaving **audiret**, an imperfect subjunctive form in secondary sequence, as the correct answer. Hopefully, you enjoyed the humor of this sentence!

7. Temporal **(A)**

The time phrase "at the moment" specifies the time of the action of the verb in the **cum** clause, thus requiring an indicative verb in a temporal clause. As Answers (B) **legeret**, (C) **legat**, and (D) **legisset** are all forms of the subjunctive, Answer (A) **legit** is correct.

8. Causal **(A)**

This sentence reads, "<u>Since</u> the Romans believed that Aeneas had founded the toga-ed race, they read the *Aeneid*." Answers (B) and (C) do not correctly translate the **cum** of the subordinate clause in this sentence. Answer (D) "although" is possible grammatically, but even if the clause **cum crederent** were concessive (note that the following "trigger word" **tamen** is missing), this clause does not make sense when translated as concessive.

9. Temporal **(D)**

The correlative "time words," **tum...cum**, "at the time when...," specify the time of the action of the clause, thereby establishing it as a temporal clause with the indicative. The correct answer is therefore **abierat.** Answers (B) and (C) are in the present tense, which is incorrect in a sentence that contains **rediit**, a verb that requires the secondary sequence in the subordinate clause. Answer (A) **abiisset,** would make the clause circumstantial and the time element more generalized. The sentence reads, "While the Trojans were fleeing, Aeneas returned to the city at the time when Creusa <u>had vanished</u>."

10. Circumstantial **(C)**

The tense of the verb in the subordinate clause determines which answer is correct. As **factus esset** is a form of the pluperfect passive, Answer (C) is correct. Answer (A) requires the present tense and Answers (B) and (D) "was informed" and "was being informed" require the imperfect tense.

Sententiae Antiquae Answers

1. Temporal **(A)**

The appearance of "at that very moment" in the sentence creates a specific time frame for the action of the subordinate clause, which is a temporal clause with the indicative. Answers (B) and (C) contain subjunctive clauses with subjunctive verbs in the imperfect and present tenses, respectively, and Answer (D) is not a correct translation because the verb **potest** does not appear in the original sentence.

2. Temporal **(B)**
The use of the indicative in the subordinate clause **cum vult** means that Publilius Syrus is saying that he who dies at the very moment that he wishes is happy. Answers (A), (C), and (D) all change the meaning of the original statement by altering the elements contained in the **cum** clause.

3. Causal **(A)**
Answer (C) contains a mistranslation of the present subjunctive verb **sint** and (D) a mistranslation of the relative pronoun **quae**, which refers to some antecedent that is unidentified here. When **cum** means "whenever," the indicative mood is used, eliminating Answer (B).

4. Prepositional phrase **(B)**
Cum fide is a prepositional phrase, which removes from consideration the use of **cum** in a subordinate clause and any need for the subjunctive, eliminating Answers (A) and (C) The present passive form in Answer (D) does not make sense in the context here. The sentence reads, "Because they hated war, they were acting <u>with reliability</u> concerning peace."

5. Temporal **(B)**
Answer (A) **cum vides** is the only choice that contains a verb in the correct tense. Answers (A) and (D) all contain verbs in incorrect tenses, i.e., perfect indicative and the future tense in an active periphrastic construction. Answer (C) is incorrect because **cum** circumstantial clauses are found with verbs in the imperfect or pluperfect tenses, and **videas** is in the present tense. This sentence indicates that at the specific time when you see the ears of a fox, i.e., his head, then he probably sees you, and you may be in danger. At the time when you see the tail, i.e., his back, he has passed by and you are safe.

Stumper: **(B)**
Answers (C) and (D) are incorrect because they contain incorrect translations of the underlined verb **essent**, which is in the imperfect tense. Answer (A) contains a verb that is correctly translated ("they were") but has a less acceptable meaning than that of Answer (B) in its context. The sentence reads, "<u>Although they were</u> the masters of the citizens, they were the slaves of freedmen." Note the omission of **tamen**.

Chapter 30

Latin Sentence Structure

Conjunctions

Although conjunctions are rarely considered an important feature of reading Latin, they are the "connective tissue" of a Latin sentence and therefore are important for comprehension and translation. Conjunctions are indeclinable words that join together words, phrases, clauses, and sentences. They are used to connect two ideas of equal importance (coordinating) or to attach a dependent or secondary idea to a main thought (subordinating). Since dependent clauses appear frequently in Latin, subordinating conjunctions are most important for understanding the relationship between the dependent clause and the main clause:

Coordinating conjunction: **Cicero in rostra ascendit <u>et</u> orationem habuit.**
Cicero mounted the Rostra <u>and</u> gave a speech.

Subordinating conjunction: **Orationem habuit <u>ut</u> Pompeium laudaret**.
He gave the speech <u>to</u> praise Pompey.

Important Coordinating Conjunctions

et **-que** **atque** **ac**	*and*	**neque** **nec**	*nor, and not*
aut **vel** **-ve**	*or, either*	**sive** **seu**	*whether, or*
sed **at**	*but*	**autem**	*however*
nam **enim**	*for*	**quare (qua re)** **quamobrem** **(quam ob rem)**	*wherefore, for which reason*
ergo **itaque** **igitur**	*therefore*		

Important Subordinating Conjunctions

Causal:	**cum** **quod** **quia** **quando** **quoniam**	*because, since*
Conditional:	**si** **nisi**	*if* *if not, unless*
Concessive:	**cum** **etsi** **quamquam**	*although*
Interrogative:	**num** **utrum** **utrum . . . an**	*whether* *whether . . . or*
Purpose/ Result	**ut** **ne** **ut . . . non**	*to, in order to, that, so that* *that . . . not, lest* *so that . . . not* (result)
Temporal:	**cum**	*when*

The Conjunction *-que*

The conjunction **–que**, which means *and*, is usually joined to the second of a combination of two words that are closely connected in meaning, e.g., **(in) terra marique**, *on land and sea,* or **Senatus Populusque Romanus (SPQR)**, *the Senate and People of Rome*. Here is an example in context:

Servi Ciceronis fortiter fideliterque ei serviebant.

Cicero's slaves served him bravely and faithfully.

When connecting clauses, **-que** is usually attached to the first word of the connected clause. The conjunction does not always connect the word to which it is attached with the word or those words immediately preceding it, but may be separated by intervening words:

Atticus Ciceroni [discedenti] e Curia [procedentique] ad bibliopolam occurrit.

Atticus happened upon Cicero [who was leaving the Senate House] and [proceeding to the bookseller].

[Epistula a Tirone scripta est], [iussuque Ciceronis ad Atticum missa est].

[The letter was transcribed by Tiro] and [was sent to Atticus at Cicero's bidding].

Some Sentences Containing *-que* from the *Aeneid*

1. **Arma virumque cano, Troiae qui primus ab oris Italiam fato profugus Laviniaque venit litora.** (1.1–3)

   The enclitic **–que** joins **Arma** with **virum** and **Italiam** with **Lavinia . . . litora**.

2. **Dum conderet urbem inferretque deos Latio.** (1.5–6)

   The enclitic **–que** connects the clauses **Dum conderet urbem** and **(dum) inferret deos Latio**.

3. **Genus unde Latinum Albanique patres (sunt) atque altae moenia Romae.** (1.6–7)

   The enclitic **–que** combines **Genus unde Latinum (est)** with **(unde) Albani patres (sunt)**; the coordinating conjunction **atque** combines both of these with **altae moenia Romae (sunt)**.

4. **Urbs antiqua fuit (Tyrii tenuere coloni) Karthago, Italiam contra Tiberinaque longe ostia, dives studiisque asperrima belli.** (1.13–14)

   The enclitic **–que** joins **Italiam** with **Tiberina ostia** and **dives** with **studiis asperrima belli**.

5. **Id metuens veterisque memor Saturnia belli.** (1.23)

   The enclitic **–que** connects **Id metuens (Saturnia)** with **veteris memor Saturnia belli**.

6. **Manet alta mente repostum iudicium Paridis spretaeque iniuria formae.** (1.26–27)

   -Que combines **iudicium Paridis** and **spretae iniuria formae**.

7. **Ipsa Iovis rapidum iaculata e nubibus ignem disiecitque rates evertitque aequora ventis.** (1.42–43)

   The double **–que** connects **disiecit rates** and **evertit aequora ventis**.

8. **Hic vasto rex Aeolus antro luctantes ventos tempestatesque sonoras imperio premit ac vinclis et carcere frenat.** (1.52–54)

   Note the variety of coordinating conjunctions appearing here: **-que, ac,** and **et**. The first joins **luctantes ventos** with **tempestates sonoras** and the second two, when taken together, have the meaning equivalent to **et . . . et**, i.e., *both . . . and* (*with both chains and confinement*).

Practice with the Coordinating Conjunction *–que*

Mark the **–que** and then indicate what elements of the Latin that this conjunction joins together. The answers follow.

1. **"Tu das epulis accumbere divum nimborumque facis tempestatumque potentem."** (1.79–80)

2. **Insequitur clamorque virum stridorque rudentum.** (1.87)
3. **"Ubi tot Simois correpta sub undis scuta virum galeasque et fortia corpora volvit!"** (1.100–101)
4. **Talia iactanti stridens Aquilone procella velum adversa ferit, fluctusque ad sidera tollit.** (1.102–103)
5. **Unum (navem), quae Lycios fidumque vehebat Oronten . . .** (1.113)
6. **"Iam caelum terramque meo sine numine, venti, miscere . . . audetis?"** (1.133–134)
7. **"Maturate fugam regique haec dicite vestro."** (1.137)
8. **Sic ait, et dicto citius tumida aequora placat collectasque fugat nubes solemque reducit.** (1.142–143)
9. **Vos et Scyllaeam rabiem penitus<u>que</u> sonantes accestis scopulos.**
10. **What is the meaning of "O qui res hominumque deorumque . . . regis"?** (1.229–230)

Answers

1. **"Tu das epulis accumbere divum nimborum<u>que</u> facis tempestatum<u>que</u> potentem."** (1.79–80)

   Joins **(me) nimborum facis (potentem)** with **facis (me) tempestatum potentem**.

2. **Insequitur clamor<u>que</u> virum stridor<u>que</u> rudentum.** (1.87)

   Joins **clamor virum** with **stridor rudentum**.

3. **"Ubi tot Simois correpta sub undis scuta virum galeas<u>que</u> et fortia corpora volvit!"** (1.100–101)

   Joins **scuta virum** with **galeas**.

4. **Talia iactanti stridens Aquilone procella velum adversa ferit, fluctus<u>que</u> ad sidera tollit.** (1.102–103)

   Joins **velum adversa ferit** with **fluctus ad sidera tollit**.

5. **Unum (navem), quae Lycios fidum<u>que</u> vehebat Oronten . . .** (1.113)

   Joins **Lycios** with **fidum Oronten**.

6. **"Iam caelum terram<u>que</u> meo sine numine, venti, miscere . . . audetis?"** (1.133–134)

   Joins **caelum** with **terram**.

7. **"Maturate fugam regi<u>que</u> haec dicite vestro."** (1.137)

   Joins **Maturate fugam** with **regi haec dicite vestro**.

8. **Sic ait, et dicto citius tumida aequora placat collectas<u>que</u> fugat nubes solem<u>que</u> reducit.** (1.142–143)

   Joins **tumida aequora placat** with **collectas fugat nubes** with **solem reducit**.

9. **Vos et Scyllaeam rabiem penitus<u>que</u> sonantes accestis scopulos.**

   Et and **-que**, *both . . . and*, join **Scyllaeam rabiem** with **penitus sonantes scopulos**.

10. **What is the meaning of "O qui res hominum<u>que</u> deorum<u>que</u> . . . regis"?** (1.229–230)

    "O (you) who rule over the affairs of <u>both</u> mortals <u>and</u> gods . . . ."

Words that Correlate and Coordinate

Latin sentences often contain words that correlate, that is, they have partners or are paired. Such words are known as correlatives. These words are usually separated within the sentence, so, as you begin to comprehend the meaning, it is best to be alert to the possibility that their partners may appear further along. Here are some common examples of correlatives:

Correlative Conjunctions

ibi . . . ubi	*there . . . where*
non solum . . . sed etiam	*not only . . . but also*
talis . . . qualis	*such . . . as*
tantus . . . quantus	*so great . . . as (great)*
tot . . . quot	*so many . . . as (many)*
tum . . . cum	*then . . . when*

In addition, some adverbs, as well as conjunctions, coordinate with one another, that is, they are found in pairs, e.g.,

Correlative Adverbs

aut . . . aut (or **vel . . . vel**)	*either . . . or*
cum . . . tum	*while . . . so also* or *at the same time*
et . . . et (or **-que . . . -que**)	*both . . . and*
modo . . . modo	*now . . . now*
neque . . . neque (nec . . . nec)	*neither . . . nor*
nunc . . . nunc (or **iam . . . iam**)	*now . . . now*
sive (**seu** or enclitic **-ve**) **. . . sive** (**seu** or enclitic **-ve**)	*whether . . . or, if . . . if*
tam . . . quam	*so (as) . . . as*

The following pairs of indefinite pronouns are also used in this way:

alius . . . alius	*the one . . . another*
alii . . . alii	*some . . . others)*
alter . . . alter	*the one . . . the other*

Examples of How Correlatives Work

In the following example of the use of correlatives, **quam** correlates with **tam**:

Ea tam antiqua est quam Amphitheatrum Flavium!

She is so (or as) old as the Colosseum!

Such sentences are often condensed. The expanded original reads:

Ea tam antiqua est quam Amphitheatrum Flavium (antiquum est).

She is so (or as) old as the Colosseum (is old).

In the following sentence, note the relationship between **tantam** and **quanta**:

Dives tantam pecuniam habebat quanta erat numquam satis.

The rich man had so (or as) much money as was never enough, lit., *so much money as much (as) was never enough.*

The relative adjective **quanta** must agree in gender and number (feminine singular) with that of its correlative antecedent **tantam**, but observe also that its case (nominative) is determined by how it functions within its clause, i.e., **quanta (pecunia)** serves as the subject of its clause, whereas **tantam pecuniam** serves as the direct object of the main clause.

Idioms

An idiom (fr. Greek, "one's own," "personal") is an expression in one language that cannot be expressed precisely in another or has a meaning that requires familiarity with the cultural context of the language, e.g., English "to bum a ride." Idioms are found regularly in Latin and should be considered in any thorough review of the language. Here are some common Latin idioms:

bellum gerere, *to wage war*
certior facere, *to inform*
consilium capere, *to make a plan*
gratias agere, *to thank*
in animo habere, *to intend*
in memoria habere, *to remember*
orationem habere, *to deliver a speech*
proelium committere, *to begin battle*
iter facere, *to make a journey, travel*
vitam agere, *to live one's life*

Thoughts About the Structure of a Latin Sentence

Remember that Latin, when expressing a thought, makes use of participles and dependent clauses more often than English does. When in Rome, do as the Romans do. Think like a Roman!

Latin: *After this was done, he did that.*

English: *He did this and then he did that.*

- Latin regularly (but not always!) places the most emphatic words at the beginning and end of a clause or sentence. The intervening words contribute to the overall sense.

- The words within word groups or "sense units" in a Latin sentence are not mixed together except in poetry, when a particular effect is desired by the poet. Consider the following prose sentence:

  Urbe Roma condita, multi mirabantur num Romulus deus facturus esset.

  After Rome had been founded, many wondered whether Romulus would become a god.

  Words from the main clause **multi mirabantur** may not intrude upon or interject themselves into the ablative absolute **urbe Roma condita**. No elements from either of these constructions may intrude upon the dependent clause **num . . . facturus esset**, and so forth. However, one word group may contain another.

- Patterns of word order do appear in Latin sentence structure (see more below). "Normal" word order in a Latin sentence consists of subject – indirect object – direct object – adverb and prepositions – verb, with the result that the subject and verb "bookend" the thought. Remember that such a pattern is common, but not obligatory.

- Remember, too, that the functional meaning of a Latin word derives from its ending, which forces your mind's eye to work from right to left, or backwards, through a word, e.g., in translating **mittebat**, you read **-t**, *he*, **-ba-**, *was*, **mitte-**, *sending*. This puts your mind, which is trained to read English from left to right, at odds with itself and creates a sort of mental tension that must be reduced through practice in translation.

- No doubt you have observed that Latin can express the same thought in fewer words than English. As the Romans, at least early in their history, were spare and economical by nature, their language is often condensed or elliptical, leaving out verbal elements whose meaning is "understood," i.e., must be deduced from context. This is known as gapping.

  Qui non est hodie, cras minus aptus erit.

  (He) who is not (ready) today will be less ready tomorrow.

  If the Latin were expanded, it would read:

  (Is) qui non (aptus) est hodie, cras (ille) minus aptus erit.

Some Observations About Word Order

A Word or Two about Adjectives and Word Order

Roman writers, especially poets, often separated an adjective from its noun for visual or phonetic effect, e.g.,

"O <u>miseri</u>, quae tanta insania, <u>cives</u>?" (Laocoon, in the *Aeneid*)

O <u>pitiable</u> <u>citizens</u>, what madness is this?"

In the following line, Horace describes a maid embraced by a youth while both are surrounded by roses:

Quis multa **gracilis** [te] **puer** in rosa?

What ***slender boy*** *(embraces) [you] amid many a rose?*

Although an adjective or adverb generally precedes the word that it modifies (with a few exceptions, such as **res publica** or **populus Romanus**), an adjective can also be found after the noun it modifies. When two adjectives modify the same noun, they can be connected with **et**, e.g., **Tiberis erat flumen celere et turbidum**, *the Tiber was a swift, wild river*. Note that the conjunction is omitted in English. It is most important to be familiar with the forms of adjectives and nouns and to think clearly about your options regarding the words that may or may not go together in a noun-adjective combination.

Some Additional Observations Regarding Word Order

- The first position in a sentence is emphatic.
- The more unusual the position of a word, the more emphatic its meaning.
- A name or a personal pronoun often stands in an emphatic place.
- Demonstrative, interrogative, and possessive adjectives regularly precede their nouns, e.g., **haec mater**, **Quae mater**? and **mea culpa**.
- The adjective precedes the noun modified, just as the adverb precedes the verb. Adjectives used as attributes are usually placed after the noun modified, e.g., **senator prudens, servus ignavissimus**.
- Certain common conjunctions, such as **itaque**, regularly come first in a sentence, whereas words such as **autem, enim, igitur, quidem, quoque**, and **vero** are never found first. **Quidem** and **quoque** immediately follow the words they emphasize.
- A preposition regularly precedes its noun, e.g., **in hoc signo vinces**; a prepositional phrase often immediately precedes the verb to which it is connected.
- When a form of **esse** is used as the main verb, it regularly stands first, or before its subject, e.g., **Est prudens**, *He is wise*.
- The negative, such as **haud, non, neque**, precedes the word it affects.

Practice Exams

AP Latin: Vergil

Practice Exam 1

AP Latin: Vergil

Multiple-Choice Section

TIME: 60 Minutes
50 Questions

DIRECTIONS: Each reading passage is followed by a series of questions and incomplete statements that are related to the passage. Select the best answer or completion and fill in the appropriate oval on your answer sheet.

A sad time in the Underworld

"O nate, ingentem luctum ne quaere tuorum;
ostendent terris hunc tantum fata neque ultra
esse sinent. Nimium vobis Romana propago
visa potens, superi, propria haec si dona fuissent.
Quantos ille virum magnam Mavortis ad urbem
campus aget gemitus! Vel quae, Tiberine, videbis
funera, cum tumulum praeterlabere recentem! . . .
Heu! miserande puer, si qua fata aspera rumpas,
tu Marcellus eris! Manibus date lilia plenis,
purpureos spargam flores animamque nepotis
his saltem accumulem donis et fungar inani
munere."

1. This speech is given by whom to whom?
   (A) the Cumaean Sibyl to Aeneas
   (B) Venus to Juno
   (C) Jupiter to Hercules
   (D) Anchises to Aeneas

2. The common prose equivalent of the grammatical construction ne quaere (line 1) is

   (A) non quaere
   (B) noli quaerere
   (C) nolite quaerere
   (D) ne quaeras

3. In lines 1–3 (O . . . sinent), the speaker is advising the listener not to grieve because

   (A) the deceased is not worthy of grief
   (B) the departed person is not related to the listener
   (C) the entire Roman Empire will be mourning
   (D) the deceased is not fated to live long

4. Line 4, the missing word that completes visa is

   (A) est
   (B) esse
   (C) sum
   (D) esset

5. Si dona fuissent (line 4) is translated as

   (A) If the gifts had been . . .
   (B) If the gifts are . . .
   (C) If the gifts were to be . . .
   (D) If the gifts should be . . .

6. The case of virum (line 5) is

   (A) accusative
   (B) genitive
   (C) vocative
   (D) nominative

7. Which of the following figures of speech is found in lines 5–6 (Quantos . . . gemitus)?

   (A) personification
   (B) ellipsis
   (C) hyperbaton
   (D) asyndeton

8. Line 5–6 (Quantos . . . gemitus) imply that

   (A) the god Mars will bring grief to the city
   (B) there will be a funeral in the Campus Martius
   (C) Mars will be acknowledged as patron god of Rome
   (D) in the Campus Martius many men will die

9. The verb praeterlabere (line 7) is translated
   (A) to glide past
   (B) glide past
   (C) you will glide past
   (D) about to glide past

10. Which of the following figures of speech is found in lines 8–9 (Heu . . . eris)?
   (A) polysyndeton
   (B) apostrophe
   (C) chiasmus
   (D) aposiopesis

11. As an historical figure, Marcellus (line 9) was destined to be
   (A) Julius Caesar's son
   (B) conqueror of Hannibal
   (C) the son of Romulus
   (D) Augustus' heir

12. In lines 9–12 (Manibus . . . munere), we learn that Anchises wants to
   (A) honor his ancestors
   (B) remember past times
   (C) say prayers
   (D) perform a ritual burial

13. The metrical pattern of the first four feet of line 11 is
   (A) spondee-dactyl-spondee-spondee
   (B) spondee-dactyl-dactyl-spondee
   (C) dactyl-spondee-spondee-spondee
   (D) dactyl-spondee-spondee-dactyl

The Sabine women prevent war

Iam stabant acies ferro mortique paratae
iam lituus[1] pugnae signa daturus erat,
cum raptae veniunt inter patresque virosque
inque sinu natos, pignora[2] cara, tenent.
Ut medium campi scissis tetigere capillis,
in terram posito procubuere genu,
et quasi sentirent, blando clamore nepotes
tendebant ad avos[3] bracchia parva suos . . .
Tela viris animique cadunt, gladiisque remotis
dant soceri[4] generis accipiuntque manus,
laudatasque tenent natas, scutoque[5] nepotem
fert avus: hic scuti dulcior usus erat.

1 lituus, -i, m.: bugle, war trumpet
2 pignus, pignoris, n.: pledge, token
3 avus, -i, m.: grandfather
4 socer, soceri, m.: father-in-law
5 scutum, -i, n.: shield

14. In lines 1–2 (Iam . . . erat), we learn that
   (A) the battle lines were ready
   (B) the signal for battle had been given
   (C) the fighting was just under way
   (D) the fighting was fierce and to the death

15. Which of the following figures of speech occurs in line 1 (Iam . . . paratae)?
   (A) transferred epithet
   (B) metonymy
   (C) prolepsis
   (D) polysyndeton

16. In line 3, raptae is translated
   (A) having captured
   (B) while capturing
   (C) about to capture
   (D) having been captured

17. In line 4, the subject of tenent is
   (A) raptae (line 3)
   (B) patresque virosque (line 3)
   (C) natos (line 4)
   (D) pignora (line 4)

18. In line 5, tetigere is translated

(A) touch
(B) they touched
(C) to have touched
(D) to touch

19. In lines 5–8 (Ut . . . suos), we learn that

(A) the women covered their heads
(B) the women embraced their husbands around the knees
(C) the young children held out their arms to their grandfathers
(D) the older folk wept and grieved for their misfortune

20. In line 7, quasi sentirent is translated

(A) as if they understood
(B) which they understood
(C) so that they might understand
(D) since they understand

21. In line 8, ad avos . . . suos means

(A) to his own grandfather
(B) to someone else's grandfathers
(C) to the grandfathers themselves
(D) to their own grandfathers

22. Which of the following figures of speech occurs in lines 9–10 (Tela . . . manus)?

(A) metaphor
(B) chiasmus
(C) zeugma
(D) polyptoton

23. In line 9, gladiis remotis is translated

(A) while putting away their swords
(B) after they had put away their swords
(C) when their swords were being put away
(D) as they were about to put away their swords

24. In lines 11–12 (laudatasque . . . usus erat), we learn that

(A) gifts were exchanged by the adversaries
(B) grandfathers carried their grandsons on their shields
(C) sons praised and embraced their fathers
(D) children were returned to their parents

25. In line 12, dulcior means

(A) sweeter
(B) very sweet
(C) rather sweetly
(D) much sweeter

Why Fabricius recommended an enemy for the consulship

Fabricius Luscinus magnā gloria vir magnisque rebus gestis fuit. P. Cornelius Rufinus manu quidem strenuus et bellator bonus militarisque disciplinae peritus admodum fuit, sed furax homo et avaritiā acri erat. Hunc Fabricius non probabat neque amico utebatur osusque[1] eum morum causā fuit. Sed cum in temporibus rei publicae difficillimis consules creandi forent et is Rufinus peteret consulatum competitoresque eius essent inbelles quidam et futtiles,[2] summa ope adnixus est Fabricius uti Rufino consulatus deferretur. Eam rem plerisque admirantibus, quod hominem avarum cui esset inimicissimus, creari consulem vellet, "Malo," inquit, "civis me compilet,[3] quam hostis vendat."

1 osus, -a, -um, adj: having hated
2 futtilis, -is, -e, adj.: good for nothing, worthless
3 compilo, -are, -avi, -atus: to rob

26. In lines 2–3 (P. Cornelius . . . fuit), we learn that Rufinus was

(A) antagonistic and vengeful
(B) skilled in matters of war
(C) inexperienced as a leader
(D) tough but undisciplined

27. The case of disciplinae (line 3) depends on

(A) bellator (line 2)
(B) militarisque (line 3)
(C) peritus (line 3)
(D) fuit (line 3)

28. Lines 3–4 (sed . . . erat) tell us that Rufinus was also

(A) cruel
(B) clever
(C) ambitious
(D) greedy

29. In lines 4–5 (Hunc . . . fuit), we are told that Fabricius
    (A) respected Rufinus, but did not like him
    (B) thoroughly disliked Rufinus because of his character
    (C) considered Rufinus a friend, despite his shortcomings
    (D) disapproved of Rufinus, but did not hate him

30. In lines 5–6 (Sed . . . forent), we learn that, during the Republic, consuls
    (A) had to be elected in troubled times
    (B) made the times more difficult
    (C) could be appointed rather than elected
    (D) sometimes failed to deal with a crisis

31. In line 6, forent is an alternative to the more traditional form
    (A) fuerunt
    (B) futurum esse
    (C) essent
    (D) fuisse

32. In lines 6–7 (et . . . futtiles), we learn that
    (A) the enemies of Rufinus were seeking the consulship
    (B) Rufinus intended to make war on the consuls, who were his enemies
    (C) His rivals for the consulship planned to kill Rufinus
    (D) Rufinus' political adversaries were weak

33. In line 6, peteret is subjunctive because it completes
    (A) a causal clause (since)
    (B) an indirect statement
    (C) a concessive clause (although)
    (D) a purpose clause

34. In line 8 (summa . . . deferretur), we learn that Fabricius
    (A) worked hard to defeat Rufinus
    (B) requested that Rufinus postpone his bid for office
    (C) used all his resources to support Rufinus' candidacy
    (D) purchased the consulship for himself

35. The words Eam rem (line 9) refer to
    (A) the perilous state of the Republic
    (B) Rufinus' character
    (C) the weakness of the opposing candidates
    (D) Fabricius' support of Rufinus' candidacy

36. The case of plerisque admirantibus (line 9) depends upon
    (A) Eam rem (line 9)
    (B) esset inimicissimus (lines 9–10)
    (C) creari consulem vellet (line 10)
    (D) inquit (line 10)

37. Lines 9–10 (Eam . . . vellet) tell us that many people were wondering
    (A) why Fabricius wanted a personal enemy to become consul
    (B) if Fabricius himself wanted to become consul
    (C) whether a greedy man could become consul
    (D) why Rufinus wanted to become consul

38. Lines 10–11 (Malo . . . vendat) are translated
    (A) The citizen who robs me and then sells me to the enemy is wicked.
    (B) I prefer that a citizen rob me than an enemy sell me.
    (C) The citizen who sells me to an enemy, robs me.
    (D) I would rather have a citizen rob me than an enemy.

Martial describes an acquaintance

Vicinus meus est manuque tangi
de nostris Novius potest fenestris.
Quis non invideat mihi putetque
horis omnibus esse me beatum,
iuncto cui liceat frui sodale?[1]
Tam longe est mihi quam Terentianus,
qui nunc Niliacam regit Syenen.[2]
Non convivere, nec videre saltem,[3]
non audire licet, nec urbe tota
quisquam est tam prope tam proculque nobis.
Migrandum est mihi longius vel illi.
Vicinus Novio vel inquilinus[4]
sit, si quis Novium videre non vult.

1 sodalis, -is, m.: close friend
2 Niliacam . . . Syenen: Syene, located on the Nile River
3 nec . . . saltem: "not even"
4 inquilinus, -i, m.: fellow tenant

39. In lines 1–2 (<u>Vicinus</u> . . . <u>fenestris</u>), we learn that Martial and Novius
    (A) use the same window
    (B) like to leave windows open
    (C) are close neighbors
    (D) share a room

40. In line 3, <u>Quis non invideat mihi</u> is translated
    (A) Who does not envy me
    (B) Who would not envy me
    (C) Whom would I not envy
    (D) He who does not envy me

41. In line 5 (<u>iuncto</u> . . . <u>sodale</u>), why does Martial think that most people would consider him fortunate?
    (A) His friends envy him.
    (B) He has a friend close by.
    (C) His friends enjoy getting together with him.
    (D) He makes his friends happy.

42. The noun-adjective combination <u>iuncto</u> . . . <u>sodale</u> (line 5) takes its case from
    (A) the pronoun <u>cui</u>
    (B) the verb <u>liceat</u>
    (C) the verb <u>frui</u>
    (D) the general sense of the context

43. In line 6, the words <u>Tam</u> . . . <u>quam</u> mean
    (A) Now . . . then
    (B) So . . . than
    (C) As . . . as
    (D) So . . . that

44. Martial's point in lines 6–7 (<u>Tam</u> . . . <u>Syenen</u>) is that
    (A) Terentianus is as far from him as the Nile is from Syene.
    (B) Rome is a less friendly place than Africa.
    (C) Novius has a friend in Africa named Terentianus.
    (D) Novius might as well be in Africa.

45. The case of <u>Syenen</u> (line 7) is
    (A) nominative
    (B) genitive
    (C) accusative
    (D) vocative

46. In lines 8–10 (Non . . . nobis), Martial declares that
   (A) no one is farther away from him than his neighbor
   (B) he enjoys the company of his neighbors
   (C) there is no one in the entire city, near or far, who is not his friend
   (D) people in a large city should avoid each other

47. Which of the following figures of speech occurs in lines 8–10 (Non . . . nobis)?
   (A) litotes
   (B) anaphora
   (C) zeugma
   (D) chiasmus

48. Line 11 (Migrandum . . . illi) is translated
   (A) He and I ought to move away together.
   (B) I should move closer to him.
   (C) He intends to move farther away from me.
   (D) I must move farther away or he must.

49. In line 13, sit is translated
   (A) he is
   (B) let him be
   (C) I wish that he were
   (D) Be!

50. The figure of speech that appears in lines 12–13 (Vicinus . . . vult) is
   (A) alliteration
   (B) polyptoton
   (C) chiasmus
   (D) ellipsis

STOP

This is the end of the Multiple-Choice Section of the AP Latin: Vergil Exam. If time remains, you may check your work only in this section. Do not begin the Free-Response Section until instructed to do so.

Practice Exam 1

AP Latin: Vergil

Free-Response Section

TIME: 2 hours (including a 15-minute reading period)

DIRECTIONS: Answer ALL FIVE of the questions in this Section, following directions carefully.

Question 1 – Vergil (15 percent)

(Suggested time – 10 minutes)

"Romulus excipiet gentem et Mavortia condet
moenia Romanosque suo de nomine dicet.
His ego nec metas rerum nec tempora pono;
imperium sine fine dedi. Quin aspera Iuno,
quae mare nunc terrasque metu caelumque fatigat,
consilia in melius referet, mecumque fovebit
Romanos, rerum dominos, gentemque togatam."

***Aeneid* 1.276–82**

Give a literal translation of the passage above.

Question 2 – Vergil (15 percent)

(Suggested time – 10 minutes)

Begin your answer to this question on a fresh page.

Tum genitor natum dictis adfatur amicis:
"Stat sua cuique dies, breve et inreparabile tempus
omnibus est vitae; sed famam extendere factis,
hoc virtutis opus. Troiae sub moenibus altis
tot gnati cecidere deum, quin occidit una
Sarpedon, mea progenies; etiam sua Turnum
fata vocant metasque dati pervenit ad aevi."

***Aeneid* 10.466–72**

Give a literal translation of the passage above.

Question 3 – Vergil (35 percent)

(Suggested time – 45 minutes)

Begin your answer to this question on a fresh page.

(A)

"Quid tantum insano iuvat indulgere dolori,
O dulcis coniunx? Non haec sine numine divum
eveniunt; nec te hinc comitem asportare Creusam
fas, aut ille sinit superi regnator Olympi.
Longa tibi exsilia et vastum maris aequor arandum,
et terram Hesperiam venies, ubi Lydius arva
inter opima virum leni fluit agmine Thybris:
illic res laetae regnumque et regia coniunx
parta tibi; lacrimas dilectae pelle Creusae."

***Aeneid* 2.776–84**

(B)

"O tandem magnis pelagi defuncte periclis
(sed terrae graviora manent), in regna Lavini
Dardanidae venient (mitte hanc de pectore curam),
sed non et venisse volent. Bella, horrida bella,
et Thybrim multo spumantem sanguine cerno.
Non Simois tibi nec Xanthus nec Dorica castra
defuerint; alius Latio iam partus Achilles,
natus et ipse dea; nec Teucris addita Iuno
usquam aberit, cum tu supplex in rebus egenis
quas gentes Italum aut quas non oraveris urbes!

Causa mali tanti coniunx iterum hospita Teucris
externique iterum thalami."

***Aeneid* 6.83–94**

In these speeches, Aeneas listens to two descriptions of what his fate in Italy will be. In a well-developed essay, compare and contrast these two speeches, commenting on how the tone reflects the circumstances in which each is given.

(Remember to support what you say by making direct reference to the Latin **throughout** each passage. Cite and translate or closely paraphrase the relevant Latin. Do not simply summarize or paraphrase what the poem says.)

Question 4 – Vergil (20 percent)

(Suggested time – 20 minutes)

Begin your answer to this question on a fresh page.

(A)

"Mene incepto desistere victam
nec posse Italia Teucrorum avertere regem?
Quippe vetor fatis. Pallasne exurere classem
Argivum atque ipsos potuit summergere ponto
unius ob noxam et furias Aiacis Oilei?
. . .
Ast ego, quae divum incedo regina Iovisque
et soror et coniunx, una cum gente tot annos
bella gero. Et quisquam numen Iunonis adorat
praeterea aut supplex aris imponet honorem?"

***Aeneid* 1.37–41, 46–49**

(B)

"Antenor potuit mediis elapsus Achivis
Illyricos penetrare sinus atque intima tutus
regna Liburnorum et fontem superare Timaevi . . .
nunc placida compostus pace quiescit.
. . .
Nos, tua progenies, caeli quibus adnuis arcem,
navibus (infandum!) amissis unius ob iram
prodimur atque Italis longe disiungimur oris.
Hic pietatis honos? Sic nos in sceptra reponis?"

***Aeneid* 1.242–245, 250–253**

Both passages above express or allude to the anger of Juno. In a **short** essay, discuss how the poet uses the examples of the fate of others to communicate the extent of the goddess's wrath towards Aeneas.

(Remember to support your observations from the **entire text** of each passage and translate or closely paraphrase from the Latin text.)

Question 5 – Vergil (15 percent)

(Suggested time – 20 minutes)

Begin your answer to this question on a fresh page.

Hybris is a Greek term that means exaggerated pride, which is often accompanied by stubbornness. In ancient literature, this flaw often led to dishonor, punishment, or even death. **Choose one character from Group A and one character from Group B.** In a **short** essay, discuss how the behavior of these two characters illustrates the idea of *hybris*. Provide specific details in your discussion.

Group A	Group B
Allecto, one of the Furies	Dares or Entellus, boxers at the funeral games
Amata, queen of the Latins	Mezentius, Etruscan ally of the Rutuli
Juturna, sister of Turnus	Turnus, king of the Rutuli

END OF AP LATIN: VERGIL PRACTICE EXAM 1

Practice Exam 1

AP Latin: Vergil

Answer Key

List of Authors and Passages Appearing on This Exam

Multiple-Choice[1]

Required Author Passage

"A sad time in the Underworld" (*Aeneid* 6.868–874, 882–886)

Sight Passages

"The Sabine women prevent war" (Ovid, *Fasti* 3.215–222, 225–228)

"Why Fabricius recommended an enemy for the consulship" (Aulus Gellius, *Noctes Atticae* 4.8)

"Martial describes an acquaintance" (Martial, *Epigrams* 1.86)

Free-Response

Translation 1: *Aeneid* 1.276–282

Translation 2: *Aeneid* 10.466–472

Long Essay: *Aeneid* 2.776–784, 6.83–94

Short Essay: *Aeneid* 4.23–29, 6.469–474

Identification: Allecto, Amata, and Juturna; Dares/Entellus, Mezentius, and Turnus

[1] Translations of all multiple-choice passages can be found at the end of the Detailed Explanations of Answers to the Multiple-Choice Questions.

Answers to the Multiple-Choice Questions: Vergil, Practice Exam 1

A Sad Time	Sabine Women	Fabricius	Martial
1. (D)	14. (A)	26. (B)	39. (C)
2. (B)	15. (B)	27. (C)	40. (B)
3. (D)	16. (D)	28. (D)	41. (B)
4. (D)	17. (A)	29. (B)	42. (C)
5. (A)	18. (B)	30. (A)	43. (C)
6. (B)	19. (C)	31. (C)	44. (D)
7. (C)	20. (A)	32. (D)	45. (C)
8. (B)	21. (D)	33. (A)	46. (A)
9. (C)	22. (C)	34. (B)	47. (B)
10. (B)	23. (B)	35. (C)	48. (D)
11. (D)	24. (B)	36. (D)	49. (B)
12. (D)	25. (A)	37. (A)	50. (A)
13. (A)		38. (B)	

Practice Exam 1

AP Latin: Vergil

Detailed Explanations of Answers to Multiple-Choice Questions

"A sad time in the Underworld"

1. **(D)**

The mention of the Underworld in the title cues the fact that this passage is from Book 6 of the *Aeneid.* **O nate**, "my son" (line 1), refers to Aeneas, as throughout the *Aeneid.* This passage comes from the "Parade of Heroes," where Anchises describes to Aeneas the future history of Rome. In this particular passage, Anchises mournfully describes the fact that Marcellus, waiting for passage to the Upperworld, is destined to die young (see lines 8–9). In line 1, he advises Aeneas not to mourn for "one of your own" (**tuorum**), referring to Marcellus as his future ancestor. Marcellus, son of Augustus' sister Octavia and Augustus' heir-designate, died in 23 B.C. He was buried in Augustus' own mausoleum (see lines 6–7) and his name was memorialized in the Theater of Marcellus. Vergil himself died a few years later.

2. **(B)**

The particle **ne** + the present imperative is a common poetic substitute for the imperative of **nolo** + present infinitive found in prose. For review of the imperative, see Chapter 19.

3. **(D)**

Lines 2–3 translate "The fates will only reveal him to the earth nor will they allow him to stay longer." Cf. line 8, "if only you could break the harsh (bonds of) fate." Thus, Answer (D) "the deceased is not fated to live long" is correct.

4. **(D)**

Answer **(D) esset** is correct because **visa esset** is the pluperfect subjunctive form necessary to complete the then–clause of the condition **si . . . fuissent**, to mean "if the gifts had been . . . (then) the Roman race would have seemed . . . ." The omission of **esset** is due to ellipsis. The subject of **visa esset** is **Romana**

propago (line 3). For subjunctive forms, see Chapter 24, and for conditional sentences, see Chapter 26.

5. **(A)**

Si dona fuissent (line 4), "If the gifts had been," is the conditional or *if*-clause in a past contrary to fact conditional sentence. The tense of **fuissent** is pluperfect. The tense of the translated subjunctive verb in Answer (C) "If the gifts were to be" requires the imperfect tense (**essent**) in a present contrary to fact condition. For conditional clauses, see Chapter 26.

6. **(B)**

Virum is syncope for **virorum**, genitive plural, as often in Vergil. **Virum** completes (**Quantos**) . . . **gemitus** (line 6), the direct object of **aget**. For syncope, see Chapter 9.

7. **(C)**

The adjective-noun combination **Quantos . . . gemitus** (lines 5–6) frames the entire sentence and emphasizes the extent of the grief being described, hence this figure is hyperbaton. **Quantos . . . gemitus** is the accusative direct object of **ille . . . campus . . . aget** (lines 5–6), referring to the grief that Marcellus' death will elicit. For figures of speech, see Chapter 8.

8. **(B)**

Answer (B) "there will be a funeral in the Campus Martius" is correct because lines 5–6 say, "How much grieving (**Quantos . . . gemitus**) of men (**virum**) will that Field (**ille . . . campus**) bring (**aget**) to the great city of Mars!"

9. **(C)**

Praeterlabere = praeterlabēris, which is the second person, future indicative passive form of the deponent verb **praeterlabor, praeterlabi, praeterlapsus sum**, *to pass by*. **Praeterlabere** means something like "you will glide past." The subject is **Tiberine**, the river god Tiber, which is in the vocative singular. For variations in the spelling of Latin verbs, such as **praeterlabere**, see Chapter 9.

10. **(B)**

Anchises digresses to address Marcellus directly, **miserande puer . . . tu Marcellus eris**, in lines 8–9. This is an example of apostrophe, for which, see Chapter 8.

11. **(D)**

Marcellus was the first choice of Augustus to succeed him as Emperor. This is a background fact question.

12. **(D)**

The Latin translates, "Give me lilies with full hands (i.e., handsful of lilies, still a flower commonly associated with funerals), let me scatter the purple flowers and at least heap up the dead soul of my ancestor with these gifts and perform this meaningless ritual (i.e., the gesture will be meaningless because it won't prevent Marcellus from dying young).

13. **(A)**

Don't forget to incorporate the elision of **saltem** with **accumulem** into your scansion. The line reads

- - - u u - - - - - u u - -
his saltem accumulem donis et fungar inani. For scansion, see Chapter 9.

"The Sabine women prevent war"

14. **(A)**

Answer (A) is correct, because the Latin of lines 1–2 does not give any indication that the battle (between the Romans and the Sabine men) was already under way. These lines are translated, "Now the battle lines (**acies**) were standing fast (**stabant**), prepared for the sword and for death (**ferro mortique paratae**), now the bugle (**lituus**) was ready to give the signal (**signa daturus erat**) for attack (**pugnae**)."

15. **(B)**

The word **ferro**, iron or steel, the material of which the weapon is made, substitutes in line 1 for the weapon itself. This is an example of metonymy. For figures of speech, see Chapter 8.

16. **(D)**

Raptae is a perfect passive participle of **rapio, rapere, rapui, raptus**, serving here as a substantive, i.e., "those women (note the feminine ending) having been abducted," "the abducted women" (hence, the "rape" of the Sabine women). For more on participles, see Chapter 21.

17. **(A)**

The subject of **tenent**, as it is of **veniunt**, previously, is **raptae** (line 3). See the previous answer for the use of a participle as a noun. This part of the sentence translates, "when the abducted women (**raptae**) came between (**veniunt inter**) the fathers and husbands (not simply "men" for **virosque**) and held to their bosoms (**in sinu . . . tenent**) their sons, dear pledges (of love) (**pignora cara**)".

18. **(B)**

Tetigere is a poetic alternative for **tetigerunt**, the third person plural of the perfect active indicative = "they touched." Thus, Answer (B) is correct. For alternative verb forms, see Chapter 9.

19. **(C)**

This sentence says, "When they reached (**tetigere**) the middle of the field, their hair shorn (in grief) (**scissis . . . capillis**) they sank (**procubuere**) to the ground on bended knee (**posito . . . genu**) and, as if they understood, with a persuasive call (**blando clamore**), the grandsons reached out their tiny arms to their grandfathers." Thus, Answer (C) "the younger children held out their arms to their grandfathers" is correct.

20. **(A)**
Quasi sentirent is a present contrary to fact conditional clause. The verb is imperfect subjunctive, because the idea that the children understood what was happening was imaginary or could not possibly happen, which emphasizes the importance of what was actually happening, i.e., that they were being encouraged to make contact with their grandfathers (**tendebant ad avos bracchia parva suos**). Thus, Answer (A) "as if they understood (but they did not)" is the correct answer. For conditionals, see Chapter 26.

21. **(D)**
Answers (A) and (C) are incorrect because each child was calling his grandfather (**avum** is accusative). Answer (B) is incorrect because the child was seen by the grandfather, rather than vice versa (**visum [est]** is passive). Thus, Answer (D) "to their own grandfathers" is correct.

22. **(C)**
In line 11 we find a "one for two," an example of zeugma. The subjects of the single verb **cadunt** are both **tela**, "weapons," and **animi**, "their hostility," i.e., how they felt. Thus, the men are dropping both an object and a feeling. For more on figures of speech, see Chapter 8.

23. **(B)**
Gladiisque remotis is an ablative absolute, "after they had put away their swords." The key to the correct answer is the word "after," since **remotis** is a past participle. Answer (A) "while . . . " indicates an action contemporary with that of the main verb, i.e., a present participle. Answer (C) "were being" is an ongoing or continuous action, whereas in a past participle such as **remotis**, the action has been completed. In Answer (D) "were about to" the meaning is in the future tense. The translation in Answer (A) is acceptable in the active voice because the identity of those putting away their swords is made clear by the context. Technically, **gladiis remotis** means "(their) swords having been put away," with no understanding of who it was that had put them away. For the ablative absolute, see Chapter 21.

24. **(B)**
Answer (C) is tempting, but **natas** means daughters, not sons (gotcha!). Nothing was exchanged or returned, so Answers (A) and (D) are incorrect. The Latin that leads to the correct answer (B) translates, "(each) grandfather carried his grandson on his shield: this was a sweeter use of the shield."

25. **(A)**

Dulcior is a comparative adjective modifying **usus**. The correct answer is therefore (A) "sweeter." Answer (B) "very sweet" is in the superlative degree (**dulcissimus**), Answer (C) "rather sweetly" is a comparative adverb (**dulcius**), and Answer (D) "much sweeter" (**multo dulcior**) is an example of the ablative of degree of difference, for which, see Chapter 12. For forms of adjectives and adverbs, see Chapter 14.

"Why Fabricius recommended an enemy for the consulship"

26. **(B)**

Lines 1–2 tell us that Rufinus was skilled in hand-to-hand combat (**manu . . . strenuus**) and a fine warrior (**bellator bonus**), who was thoroughly experienced in military training (**militarisque disciplinae peritus**). Thus, Rufinus may be said to have been "skilled in matters of war" (Answer A).

27. **(C)**

Disciplinae is genitive because this case is required by the meaning of the adjective **peritus, -a, -um**, "experienced in" (literally "experienced of"). The genitive case establishes a connection between two nouns or between a noun and certain adjectives. See Chapter 12.

28. **(D)**

The answer is (D) greedy, because we are told in lines 2–3 that Rufinus was thievish (**furax**) and fiercely greedy (**avaritia acri**).

29. **(B)**

Hunc Fabricius non probabat tells us that "Fabricius did not approve of him (**Hunc** =Rufinus)," **neque amico utebatur**, that "he did not accept him as a friend," and **osusque eum morum causa fuit**, that "he (Fabricius) hated him because of his character (**morum causa**)." Thus, Answer (B) is correct. Answers (A), (C), and (D) all require some degree of acceptability of Rufinus by Fabricius, which is not indicated in the Latin.

30. **(A)**

The grammar of the clause **cum . . . creandi forent** (line 4) makes this sentence tricky. **Forent** is a substitute for the more common form of the imperfect subjunctive, which is **essent.** In its more familiar form, **creandi essent** is a gerundive of obligation whose subject is **consules**, giving the meaning "the consuls must be, or had to be, elected." The subjunctive mood is required in the form **essent** because **creandi essent** completes a **cum** causal clause, according to the best sense of the context. Thus, this part of the sentence reads, "But since in the very troubled times (**in temporibus . . . difficillimis**) of the Republic (or state,

rei publicae), consuls had to be elected . . . . " For the gerundive of obligation, see Chapter 22; for **cum** clauses with the subjunctive, see Chapter 29.

31. **(C)**
See the answer to the previous question.

32. **(D)**
In line 5, the subjunctive clause (**cum**) **is Rufinus peteret consulatum** is another second clause introduced by **cum,** which is an understood or gapped repetition of the **cum** found at the beginning of the sentence. This clause tells us that Rufinus was seeking the consulship. A third subjunctive clause, also dependent upon **cum**, is **competitoresque . . . futtiles**, which tells us that Rufinus' (**eius**) adversaries for the consulship were **inbelles** (also spelled **imbelles**). . . **et futtiles** (also spelled **futiles**), meaning "unwarlike and ineffective." Thus, Answer (D) "Rufinus' political adversaries were weak" is correct.

33. **(A)**
As indicated previously, the sense of the sentence in lines 4–6 (**Sed . . . deferretur**) requires that **cum . . . forent . . . peteret . . . essent** be translated as causal clauses, "Since . . . . " Answer (B) is impossible because there is no infinitive in this sentence; the **cum** concessive clause in Answer (C) is usually found with **tamen**; and, although an **ut** purpose clause does appear in this sentence (**uti . . . . deferretur**), it is separate and grammatically distinct from the **cum** clauses found in the earlier part of the sentence. Thus, Answer (A) causal clause is correct. For **ut** clauses, see Chapter 27; for **cum** clauses, see Chapter 29.

34. **(C)**
In lines 5–6, **summa ope ādnixus est Fabricius** tells us that Fabricius labored with great resources so that the consulship would be given to Rufinus (**uti Rufino consulatus deferretur**). Thus, Answer (C) "used all his resources to support Rufinus' candidacy" is correct. There is no indication in this passage that Fabricius himself had political ambitions (Answer D), or that he had interfered in any other way with Rufinus' candidacy (Answers A and B).

35. **(D)**
The phrase **Eam rem** (line 9) refers to the situation described in the immediately previous clauses, **summa ope adnixus est Fabricius uti Rufino consulatus deferretur**, i.e., Fabricius' support of Rufinus' candidacy for the consulship. The other three answers, (A), (B), and (C), refer to information provided earlier in the same sentence, or in previous sentences.

36. **(D)**
Plerisque admirantibus is in the dative case after **inquit** in the next line. This has the meaning, "To many wondering . . . , he said . . . . " The adjective **inimicus**, "unfriendly to" (Answer B) is found with the dative case, but it is not to be

considered in the context of the participial phrase **plerisque admirantibus**. For the dative case, see Chapter 12.

37. **(A)**

Lines 6–7 (**Eam . . . vellet**) tell us that "To many (people) wondering at the state of affairs wherein he (Fabricius) wanted a greedy man, to whom he was most unfriendly, to be elected consul." Thus, Answer (A) "why Fabricius wanted a personal enemy to become consul" is correct. The Latin does not support the other interpretations.

38. **(B)**

Fabricius' punchline says, "I prefer that a citizen rob me than (that) an enemy sell (me)." The other answers do not do justice to the Latin as it stands.

"Martial describes an acquaintance"

39. **(C)**

In lines 1–2, Martial indicates that he and Novius are close neighbors by saying, "Novius is my neighbor and can be reached (by hand) from my window." **Nostris**, incidentally, is an example of the use of poetic plural (= **meis**). Answers (A) and (B) use the word **fenestris** as a distractor. Answer (D) goes too far past the meaning of **vicinus**.

40. **(B)**

This is a deliberative question with the subjunctive, "Who would not envy me?" Answer (B), as a statement of fact, requires the indicative mood, but **invideat** is subjunctive. Answer (C) swaps **Quis** with **mihi**, which is the dative object of **invideat**, making the sentence in Latin, **Cui ego non invideam?** Answer (D) is not a question. For this use of the independent subjunctive, see Chapter 25.

41. **(B)**

Lines 3–4 set up the answer to this question. "Who would not envy me and (who would not) think that I am happy all the time, I who (**cui**) am allowed (**licet**) to enjoy (**frui**) close companionship (**iuncto sodale**)?" Martial is saying that a neighbor who lives as close as Novius does to him, and the companionship that this implies, is ordinarily cause for feelings of satisfaction.

42. **(C)**

The deponent verb **fruor, frui, fructus sum**, "to enjoy," takes the ablative case, therefore Answer (C) the verb **frui** is correct. **Cui** itself is the dative object of **liceat** (Answers A and B). For special deponent verbs, see Chapter 16.

43. **(C)**

Tam and **quam** are correlatives, which requires that they take their meaning as a pair. The sentence in which these words are found (line 6) reads, "(He) is as far away from me as Terentianus." Answer (C) is therefore correct. For correlatives, see Chapter 30.

44. **(D)**

The sentence in lines 6–7 reads, "(He) is as far away from me as Terentianus, who now governs Syene, on the Nile." This implies that Novius might as well be in Africa with Terentianus, which is Answer (D).

45. **(C)**

Syenen (line 7) is accusative (the name of the city is Greek). The Greek ending **–n** becomes the Latin ending **–m**; both are accusative singular. See Chapter 8.

46. **(A)**

In lines 8–9, the series of instances in which Martial may not rely upon his neighbor Novius (neither enjoying his company nor seeing nor hearing him) leads to the conclusion in lines 9–10 that "there is no one in the entire city so near and yet so far from me." Answer (A) "no one is farther away from him than his neighbor," is therefore correct; the other answers give inaccurate meanings. Note the reappearance of the poetic plural, **nobis**.

47. **(B)**

The repetitions of **non**, **nec,** and **tam** in lines 8–10 are all examples of anaphora, which creates a cumulative effect. For figures of speech, see Chapter 8.

48. **(D)**

The gerundive of obligation **Migrandum est** is impersonal, requiring the subject "it" literally, "It must be moved." **Mihi**, a dative of agent, is the one who "must be moved." To create better sense, the passive is turned around to become active, i.e., "It must be moved by me" becomes "I must move." **Illi**, which refers to Novius, also serves as a dative of agent with **Migrandum est**. Thus, the correct answer is (D) "I must move farther away or he must (move farther away)." For the gerundive of obligation, see Chapter 22.

49. **(B)**

In lines 12–13, Martial explains what he meant in the previous line. **Sit** is the jussive use of the present subjunctive, requiring the translation "let," e.g., "Let the one who does not want to see Novius be his neighbor or his roommate." Answer (A) requires the Latin word **est**, (C) **(velim) esset**, and (D) **esto.**

50. **(A)**

Note the emphatic use of the letter **v** in the final two lines: **Vicinus Novio vel . . . Novium videre . . . vult**. For alliteration and other figures of speech, see Chapter 8.

Translations of the Multiple-Choice Passages

"A sad time in the Underworld"

"O son, do not ask about the immense sorrow of your (people); the fates will only reveal him (Marcellus) to the earth and not allow him to remain any longer. The Roman race (would have) seemed too mighty to you, gods, if these gifts (i.e., Marcellus) had been lasting. How much grieving of men that Field (of Mars) will bring to the great city of Mars! Or what funeral service, O Tiber, will you see when you will glide past the freshly-built tomb! . . . Woe, pitiable youth, if in any way you could disrupt the fates, you will be Marcellus! Give me lilies with full hands, let me scatter the purple flowers and at least heap up the dead soul of my ancestor with these gifts and perform this hollow/empty gesture."

"The Sabine women prevent war"

Now the battle lines were standing fast, prepared for the sword and for death, now the bugle was ready to give the signal for attack, when the abducted women came between the fathers and husbands and held to their bosoms their sons, dear pledges of love. When they reached the middle of the field, their hair shorn (in grief), they sank to the ground on bended knee and, with a persuasive call, the grandsons, as if they understood, reached out their tiny arms to their grandfathers. The weapons and hostility dropped away from the men and, their swords having been put away, the fathers-in-law gave and received the hands (i.e., shook the hands) of their family (members) [or, the fathers-in-law of the family gave and received hands, i.e., shook hands], and praised their daughters and held onto them, and (each) grandfather carried his grandson on his shield: this was a sweeter use of the shield.

"Why Fabricius recommended an enemy for the consulship"

Fabricius Luscinus was a man of great reputation and great deeds. P. Cornelius Rufinus, indeed was skillful in hand-to-hand (combat) and a fine warrior and completely experienced in military matters, but a man thievish and fiercely greedy. Fabricius did not approve of him nor associated with him as a friend, and hated him because of his character. But since there was need of electing consuls during the trying times of the Republic, and Rufinus sought the consulship and his political opponents were unwarlike and feeble, Fabricius strove with great resources in order that the consulship should be given to Rufinus. To many wondering at this state of affairs, the fact that he wanted a greedy man to whom he was a sworn enemy to be elected consul, Fabricius said, "I would prefer that a citizen rob me, than an enemy sell me."

"Martial describes an acquaintance"

Novius is my neighbor and can be touched by hand from my window. Who would not envy me and think me happy all the time, I who am permitted the joy of close companionship? He is as far away from me as Terentianus, who now governs Syene on the Nile. I may not enjoy his company, nor even see or hear him, who is so near and yet so far from me. Either I must move away or he must. If anyone does not want to see Novius, let him be his neighbor or roommate.

Answers to Free-Response Section

Question 1

Translation

"Romulus will take up the line and found the walls of Mars and will call (the people) Romans after his own name. Upon these I place boundaries of neither territory nor time; I have granted empire without limit. Yes, even harsh Juno, who now in her fear harrasses the sea, the lands, and the sky, will change her counsel for the better, and with me will cherish the Romans, masters of the world, and the toga-ed race."

Grading

18 pts. total. Round up your score.

1. *Romulus excipiet gentem*
2. *et Mavortia condet moenia*
3. *Romanosque . . . dicet*
4. *suo de nomine*
5. *his ego . . . pono*
6. *nec metas . . . nec tempora*
7. *rerum*
8. *imperium . . . dedi*
9. *sine fine*

10. *quin aspera Iuno*
11. *quae . . . metu . . . fatigat*
12. *mare nunc terrasque . . . caelumque*
13. *consilia . . . referet*
14. *in melius*
15. *mecumque*
16. *fovebit Romanos*
17. *rerum dominos*
18. *gentemque togatam*

Acceptable Translations for Translation Question 1, Vergil: Practice Exam 1

For instructional purposes, more grammatical and syntactical information is provided here than is usually found in the grading reports on the translation question.

1. *Romulus*: Romulus

   excipiet: (he) will accept/take up/receive

   gentem: line/people/race/nation/offspring/descendants/clan; **must be object of** *excipiet*

2. *et*: and

   Mavortia: of Mars/deriving from or coming from the god Mars/Martian; **must modify** *moenia*

   condet: (he) will found/establish/set up/build

   moenia: walls/city walls/city fortifications

3. *Romanosque*: Romans/the Romans/Roman people/Roman race

   dicet: (he) will call/name/designate/denote

4. *suo de nomine*: after/from/by/according to his own name; **"his own" or "his" are both acceptable for *suo***

5. *his*: on these/upon these/with respect to these; **the reference is to *Romanos*, line 2**

   ego pono: I put/place/set/establish//lay out

6. *nec . . . nec*: neither . . . nor

   metas: boundary/limit; **the literal meaning of *metas* as "turning posts" or "goals" may be used; may be translated as singular**

   tempora: time/period or extent of time; **may be translated as singular** *rerum*: of empire/of the world; = *orbis terrarum*; **may be taken with both** *metas* and *tempora*

7. *imperium*: empire/command/rule/mastery/authority/sovereignty; **must be object of** *dedi*

   dedi: (I) gave/granted/bestowed/offered; **"have given" or "did give" is acceptable**

8. *sine fine*: without end/limit/boundary/border; **must be construed with** *imperium*

9. *quin*: yes, even/rather/nay, rather/but, indeed

   aspera: harsh/bitter/cruel/wild/rough/difficult

   Iuno: Juno; **must be subject of** *referet* **and** *fovebit*

10. *quae*: who

    metu: because of /in her fear/apprehension/dread/anxiety; **must be construed with** *fatigat*

    fatigat: (she) harrasses/wears out/wearies/tires/fatigues/vexes

11. *mare nunc terrasque . . . caelumque*: now the sea, (and) the lands, and the sky; **must be objects of** *fatigat*

12. *consilia*: counsel/plans/resolve/judgment/deliberation; **must be the object of** *referet*; **may be translated as** *singular*

    referet: change//bring back/return/restore

13. *in*: for the better/in or with respect to

    melius: the better

14. *mecum*: and with me/and together with me/and along with me

    -que: and

15. *fovebit*: (she) will cherish/foster/support

    Romanos: the Romans/the Roman people/the Roman race; **must be object of** *fovebit*

16. *rerum*: of empire/of the world [= *orbis terrarum*; cf. line 3]

    dominos: masters/lords/possessors/owners; **must be in apposition to** *Romanos*

17. *gentemque togatam*: the toga-ed race/the nation or race wearing or clad in togas; **also in apposition to** *Romanos*

Question 2

Translation

Then the father (Jupiter) addresses his son (Hercules) with kindly words: "To each person his own day is designated; brief and irretrievable is the time of life for all; but to extend (your) reputation by actions, this is the task of courage. Beneath

Troy's high walls so many sons of gods fell (died), indeed together (with them) Sarpedon, my own son, died; and so his own destiny summons Turnus and he has arrived at the limit of his life that has been assigned."

Grading

18 pts. total.

1. *tum genitor*
2. *natum . . . adfatur*
3. *dictis . . . amicis*
4. *stat sua . . . dies*
5. *cuique*
6. *breve et inreparabile*
7. *tempus omnibus est vitae*
8. *famam extendere factis*
9. *hoc . . . opus virtutis*
10. *sub moenibus altis Troiae*
11. *tot gnati . . . deum*
12. *cecidere*
13. *quin occidit una Sarpedon*
14. *mea progenies*
15. *etiam sua Turnum fata vocant*
16. *pervenit*
17. *metasque . . . ad*
18. *dati . . . aevi*

Acceptable Translations for Translation Question 2, Vergil: Practice Exam 1

For instructional purposes, more grammatical and syntactical information is provided here than is usually found in the grading reports on the translation question.

1. *tum*: then/next/thereupon/at that time

   genitor: father/forefather/Jupiter
2. *natum*: son/child/offspring; **the addition of "Hercules" is acceptable here**

   adfatur: (he) addresses/approached/speaks to
3. *dictis*: word/speech; **must reflect ablative**

   amicis: kindly/friendly/favorable/pleasing

4. *stat*: (it) is designated/appointed/exists/stands/remains/is fixed
   sua: one's own/his or her own; **must modify** *dies*
   dies: day/lifetime/span of life; **must be subject of** *stat*
5. *cuique*: each person/every person/everybody/each one
6. *breve*: brief/short/small/quick/short-lived/fleeting
   et: and
   inreparabile: irretrievable/unrecoverable/irreplaceable/temporary
7. *tempus*: time; **must be subject of** *est*
   omnibus: for all or everyone/with respect to all or everyone; may be rendered as "everyone's"
   est: (it) is
   vitae: life; **must be construed with** *tempus*
8. *famam*: reputation/fame/public opinion/repute
   extendere: extend/prolong/expand/stretch out/embellish/enlarge
   factis: action/deed/act/exploit; **must reflect ablative**
9. *hoc*: this; **must modify** *opus*
   opus: task/work/labor/job
   virtutis: courage/valor/strength/manliness/bravery
   (est): **understood in ellipsis**
10. *sub*: under/beneath
    moenibus: the walls/city walls/city fortifications
    altis: high/tall/lofty/towering/soaring/steep
    Troiae: of Troy/Troy's; **must be construed with** *moenibus*
11. tot: so many; **must modify** *gnati*
    gnati: son/offspring/progeny; **must be subject of** *cecidere*
    deum: god/the divine/deity; **must be genitive plural, taken with** *gnati*
12. *cecidere*: (they) fell/fell down/dropped/died/were destroyed or killed
13. *quin*: yes even/rather/nay rather/but indeed
    occidit: (he) died/fell dead/perished/was killed
    una: together/with
    Sarpedon: Sarpedon; **subject of** *occidit*
14. *mea progenies*: my son/progeny/offspring/child; **must be in apposition to** *Sarpedon*

15. *etiam*: also/besides/even

    sua . . . fata: his (Turnus') own fate/destiny/future; **may be translated as singular; subject of** *vocant*

    Turnum: Turnus

    vocant: (they) summon/call/beckon/designate
16. *pervenit*: (he) has arrived/arrived at/reached/come to/approached
17. *metasque*: the boundary/limit/turning post/goal; **may be translated as singular**

    ad: at; **must be taken with** *metas*
18. *dati*: (having been) assigned/alloted/given/provided/apportioned/meted out; **must be taken with** *aevi*

    aevi: life/age/life-time/span of life/period of years; **must be construed with** *metas*

Question 3

Long Essay

For the grading scale used for evaluating essays, see Chapter 6. Here are some high points of each speech to consider in your comparative analysis, followed by a sample essay. Such observations, which will set up your formal essay, may be made in writing during the 15-minute reading period. The sample essays may seem overly thorough, but the author is attempting to accommodate the wide range of answers that will be given by users of this book.

(A) *Aeneid* 2.776–84:

- Creusa takes her leave of Aeneas after Troy has fallen
- Creusa reassures the worried Aeneas (insano . . . dolori, frantic grief) that what she is doing is sanctioned by the gods (Non . . . eveniunt).
- Jupiter, ruler of the high gods, does not allow him (nec fas [est] . . . sinit) to take Creusa from here as his companion.
- Aeneas will experience lengthy exile (longa exsilia) and wander the vast ocean (vastum arandum) before reaching Hesperia.
- He will find there the Lydian/Etruscan Tiber flowing with gentle stream (leni fluit agmine) among the rich fields (arva opima).
- There Aeneas will find happiness (res laetae), a kingdom (regnum), and a royal wife (regia coniunx).
- Creusa continues to reassure Aeneas by advising him not to mourn (lacrimas pelle) and that she knows that he loves her (dilectae Creusae).

(B) *Aeneid* 6.83–94:

- The Cumaean Sibyl foretells Aeneas' destiny
- The Sibyl begins by reassuring Aeneas that he has already survived the great perils of the sea (magnis pelagi periclis), but tempers this with a warning of dangers ahead on land (terrae graviora manent).
- She also reassures the Trojans (mitte hanc de pectore curam) that they will reach their goal in the realm of Lavinium, but will regret coming (non et venisse volent).
- The Sibyl speaks of grim wars and the Tiber flowing with blood. There will be rivers like those at Troy, and a Greek camp (Dorica castra). There will be another Achilles (=Turnus), who will also be goddess-born.
- Juno will continue to harrass the Trojans (nec usquam aberit) and force them to seek aid (cum tu supplex in rebus egenis) from those already settled in Hesperia, i.e., Evander and the Arcadians.
- The cause of the hostilities will again be a foreign bride (coniunx hospita) and an immigrant marriage (externique thalami). Iterum alludes to Lavinia as a second Helen.

Sample Long Essay

These two speeches, the first of which (A) was given by Creusa and the second (B) by the Cumaean Sibyl, have several things in common and many differences. They are both addressed to Aeneas by women and both outline his future as leader of the Trojans; however, they differ in factual detail and in tone. The first speech may be said to be "Odyssean" in that it focuses on the upcoming journey of Aeneas after the fall of Troy (longa . . . venies) and the rewards of finding "home" (lines 6–8). The second speech may be seen as "Iliadic," in that it focuses on the conflict upon the Trojan arrival in Italy (sed terrae graviora manent and bella . . . cerno, lines 2–5).

In Speech (A), Creusa attempts to reassure her husband, as they are soon to be parted, that Aeneas' destiny is the will of the gods (i.e., Jupiter), as opposed to Speech (B), which, although somewhat reassuring that the Trojans will gain a foothold in Italy (in regna . . . curam, lines 2–3), emphasizes the fact that Juno will continue to haunt them (nec Teucris . . . aberit, lines 8–9).

In Speech (A), the tone is upbeat—when Aeneas reaches Hesperia, he will find the gentle flow of the Lydian Tiber (Lydia was the reputed home of the Etruscans, who were countrymen of the Trojans in both Asia Minor and Italy) and fertile farmland (arva inter opima, lines 6–7). He will find happiness (res laetae), a kingdom (regnum) and a royal wife (regia coniunx). On the other hand, in Speech (B), the Sibyl, in graphic and foreboding terms (sed terrae graviora manent . . . sed non et venisse volent, lines 2–4), warns Aeneas of the trials to come. Note the contrast between the description of the Tiber with its gentle flow (leni fluit agmine Thybris) in Speech (A) and the Tiber foaming with blood (Thybrim multo spumantem sanguine) in Speech (B). These trials include war and bloodshed (bella . . . cerno, lines 4–5), and a second battle for survival against new "Greeks" and a new Achilles (Turnus, lines 7–8), the cause of which will be a foreign bride, Lavinia (coniunx iterum hospita and externique thalami, lines 11–12), just as Helen was the cause of the Trojan War. In Speech (A), emphasis is given to what Aeneas will find in Hesperia, i.e., "a land of milk and honey" (ubi Lydius. . . Thybris, lines 6–7). In Speech (B), the Sibyl mentions what Aeneas will not find, i.e., welcome assistance (cum tu supplex . . . urbes, lines 9–10).

On the other hand, each speaker briefly adopts the tone of the other in describing the realities of Aeneas' situation. Creusa warns Aeneas that "long exile" and "the vasty deep" lie ahead (A, line 5). The Sibyl congratulates Aeneas on surviving thus far (O tandem . . . periclis, B1–2, and mitte . . . curam, B3). The tone of Speech (A) then is one of cautious optimism because Creusa is trying to persuade her husband to look forward, and not back. The tone of Speech (B) is more foreboding and pessimistic, if not realistic: Dardanidae venient . . . sed non et venisse volent (B, lines 3–4).

Creusa's speech is more calming and reassuring (note the various noun-adjective combinations dulcis coniunx, comitem Creusam, arva opima, leni agmine, res laetae, and dilectae Creusae). She still loves her husband (O dulcis coniunx, line 2), and knows that he loves her, (dilectae . . . Creusae, line 9). Creusa is hopeful and encouraging, which reassures both Aeneas and the reader. On the other hand, the Sibyl's speech is threatening and ominous (note the pejorative accumulation of horrida, spumantem sanguine, in rebus egenis, mali tanti, externique thalami). Through these grim words, Vergil elicits in the reader feelings of sympathy and compassion for Aeneas and the Trojans. The edgy tone of the Sibyl in Speech (B) reminds both Aeneas and the reader that, although many hardships have been endured (magnis . . . periclis), the struggle is not yet over. Ultimately it is Aeneas' triumph over such misfortunes that makes him truly pius and that allows him to enjoy the fruits of his labors of which Creusa speaks.

Question 4

Sample Short Essay

In Passage [A], Juno delivers a soliloquy in which she expresses her helplessness (Me . . . victam, 1) and subsequent outrage (ast ego, 6–9) at not being able to have the success in punishing Aeneas that Minerva had with the Greek, Ajax. In Passage [B], Venus uses the example of the Trojan Antenor to demonstrate to Jupiter that other Trojans have been successful in resettling, so why not her son, Aeneas? She concludes by complaining that the reason for this is Juno's anger (iram, 6).

In Passage [A], Juno is upset at being unable to keep Aeneas from reaching Italy (nec . . . regem, 2). She recalls that Minerva, a lesser goddess, had been successful in punishing the mortal Ajax, a Greek, by burning and sinking his fleet (exuere classem, summergere [in] ponto, 3–4). Ajax had desecrated Minerva's temple (ob noxam et furias, 5) during the sack of Troy by abducting Cassandra, who had sought sanctuary there. In the portion of the text not provided, Juno implies that if such an act was worthy of the dramatic punishment of being struck by Jove's thunderbolt and pinned to a sharp rock cliff, then Aeneas, a Trojan, deserved much worse, because a Trojan had slighted her beauty during the judgment of Paris. And she is, after all, queen of the gods and the wife of Jupiter. This magnifies Juno's current feelings of helplessness, and thus her anger toward Aeneas and the Trojans (lines 6–8). She closes with emotional rhetorical questions that claim, as a consequence of this helplessness, a loss of respect for her divinity, i.e., quisquam numen Iunonis adorat? and supplex aris imponet honorem?, 8–9). (The reader imagines the pitch of the goddess's voice rising with the emotion of these last words.)

In Passage [B], the goddess Venus also uses an example of the fate of a mortal to make her point. This time, the mortal is a Trojan, Antenor, a survivor of the fall of Troy (mediis elapsis Achivis, 1). In this example, the outcome is successful, that is, Antenor has managed to settle a new community in Italy (Antenor potuit Illyricos penetrare sinus, etc., 1–2). This causes the goddess to feel helpless at not being able to aid her son Aeneas in achieving the same success. For this frustration, she blames Juno, whom she does not name: unius ob iram prodimur, 6–7. Note here the interjection of the word infandum, "unspeakable", which punctuates the emotion that Venus is expressing. This and other words expressing betrayal and disconnection, such as prodimur and disiungimur (11), suggest turmoil, which brings an effective contrast with the tranquillity found by Antenor in Italy (previously, placida compostus pace quiescit, 4). Thus, Venus uses the example of Antenor to illustrate to the king of the gods that he has not yet fulfilled his promise to allow Aeneas and his comrades to settle in Italy. Venus, as did Juno, closes her speech with two rhetorical questions that challenge the respect and credibility received by a god (honos, 8; cf. honorem, A9), this time by Jupiter himself, as a result of Juno's interference.

In Passages [A] and [B], Vergil uses descriptive examples to convey the consequences of Juno's wrath for Aeneas, which profoundly heighten the reader's understanding and appreciation of the meaning of the poet's dedicatory lines, quidve dolens regina deum tot volvere casus insignem pietate virum, tot adire labores impulerit. (Note: My students are asked to memorize the first eleven lines of the *Aeneid*.)

Question 5

Because it is difficult to do justice to this question in the space provided here (there are nine possible combinations of characters that can be discussed), you are given some information about each character which is relevant to the topic of *hybris*. Compare the content of your own answer with those given below. On the actual AP Vergil Exam, a short analytical essay is expected.

Group A

Allecto: One of three Furies who drove their victims insane (furor). Allecto serves as Juno's henchwoman in Book 7, first stirring up trouble by alienating both Amata and Turnus to the idea of a Trojan presence in Italy, using the vision of a terrible snake, then by causing Ascanius to wound a pet stag of the Latins while hunting. Although it was the nature of the Furies to stand for the rightness of things and the natural order, they often persecuted mortals who broke "natural laws." It was in regard to the latter that Allecto was hybristic, because her duties as accomplice to Juno took her "out of bounds" with respect to what had been preordained by the Fates, i.e., Aeneas' success.

Amata: From her first appearance in Book 7, when Aeneas and the Trojans arrive in Latium, to her suicide in Book 12, Amata attempts to "get her way" by promoting the cause of Turnus as Lavinia's true future husband. Despite the oracle that Lavinia is to marry a foreigner, Amata remains steadfast in her self-destructive plans for her daughter (although she becomes more reasonable when she joins King Latinus in attempting to persuade Turnus to withdraw during a truce). In Book 7, she yields to the poisonous words of the Fury Allecto and hides Lavinia in the woods and continues thereafter to interfere with what others consider are the best interests of her daughter. At the end of the Aeneid, on the mistaken assumption that Turnus is dead, she hangs herself. That Amata's single-minded determination is the cause of her own downfall is an example of hybris.

Juturna: Juturna, Turnus' sister, is active in the story of Book 12. She is less a victim of her own choices than the other characters on this list, as she is manipulated by Juno to protect her brother and thus to interfere with the destiny of the Trojans in Italy. She assumes the guise of Turnus' charioteer and saves him more than once on the battlefield. Her resolute, almost obsessive, concern for her brother does not lead to her destruction, as she is a water nymph. Juturna jumps into a river and disappears from the story at the end of Book 12.

Group B

Dares or Entellus: Dares and Entellus were contestants in the boxing event at the funeral games for Anchises described in Book 5. Dares' attitude toward himself and his opponent was something like that of a modern professional wrestler: disdain and arrogance. Entellus, after defeating Dares, showed poor sportsmanship by bragging about his feat and flaunting his victory over Dares. The moral is clear: humility is a virtue, arrogance (hybris) a vice.

Mezentius: Etruscan king and father of Lausus, Mezentius appears primarily in Book 10, where he is an ally of Turnus against Aeneas and the Trojans. He had been exiled from his home city for cruelty. Mezentius has the character of Plautus' Miles Gloriosus, a swaggering braggart. After Lausus, who had defended his father in battle, is killed by Aeneas, Mezentius' shame at the fact that his son died in his place drove him into a frenzy of rage and despair. Fearless and defiant until his death, Mezentius was subsequently killed by Aeneas. Excessive pride was Mezentius' downfall.

Turnus: Turnus is the anti-hero (some would say hero) of Books 7–12 because he serves as the chief antagonist of Aeneas. In fighting against the newcomer Trojans, he proves himself valiant but hot-headed. Turnus shows a moment of nobility when he takes exception to Juno saving him from battle by tricking him with a ghost-phantom of Aeneas. But it is in Book 10 where Turnus sows the seeds of his own destruction by slaying Pallas, the young son of King Evander, and then by mocking the dead youth and taking his swordbelt. His provocative, if not sacrilegious, behavior earned him an apostrophe from Vergil declaring that it was Turnus' time to die. At the end of Book 12, it is Aeneas' recognition of the swordbelt on Turnus' shoulder that causes him to kill Turnus on behalf of Pallas.

Practice Exam 2

AP Latin: Vergil

Multiple-Choice Section

TIME: 60 Minutes
50 Questions

DIRECTIONS: Each reading passage is followed by a series of questions and incomplete statements that are related to the passage. Select the best answer or completion and fill in the appropriate oval on your answer sheet.

Aeneas confronts Turnus

Stetit acer in armis
Aeneas volvens oculos dextramque repressit;
et iam iamque magis cunctantem flectere sermo
coeperat, infelix umero cum apparuit alto
balteus et notis fulserunt cingula bullis
Pallantis pueri, victum quem vulnere Turnus
straverat atque umeris inimicum insigne gerebat.
Ille, oculis postquam saevi monimenta doloris
exuviasque hausit, furiis accensus et ira
terribilis: "Tune hinc spoliis indute meorum
eripiare mihi? Pallas te hoc vulnere, Pallas
immolat et poenam scelerato ex sanguine sumit."

1. In lines 1–2 (<u>Stetit</u> ____ <u>repressit</u>), we learn that Aeneas is
   (A) taking the fight to Turnus
   (B) convinced that the fight is over
   (C) vigilant but non-combative
   (D) lacking the weapons to continue the fight

2. Cunctantem (line 3) is a
   (A) noun
   (B) subjunctive
   (C) gerundive
   (D) participle

3. The noun sermo in the context of line 3 refers to the previous speech of
   (A) Turnus
   (B) Juturna
   (C) Jupiter
   (D) the Rutulians

4. In lines 3–4 (et ____ coeperat), we learn that Aeneas had begun to
   (A) speak
   (B) change his mind
   (C) grow more confident
   (D) interrupt Turnus

5. In lines 4–5 infelix ____ balteus is an example of
   (A) asyndeton
   (B) hyperbaton
   (C) simile
   (D) transferred epithet

6. Quem (line 6) refers to
   (A) the swordbelt
   (B) Pallas
   (C) the wound inflicted by Turnus
   (D) Turnus

7. In line 7, straverat is translated
   (A) he was throwing down
   (B) he threw down
   (C) he had thrown down
   (D) he had been thrown down

8. In lines 4–7 (infelix ____ gerebat), we learn that Aeneas
   (A) saw Pallas' dead body on the ground
   (B) wept upon seeing Pallas' wounds
   (C) noticed Turnus wearing Pallas' swordbelt
   (D) tore the swordbelt from Turnus' shoulder

9. The metrical pattern of the first four feet of line 7 is
   (A) dactyl-spondee-spondee-dactyl
   (B) spondee-dactyl-dactyl-spondee
   (C) spondee-spondee-dactyl-dactyl
   (D) dactyl-dactyl-dactyl-spondee

10. The figure of speech that appears in lines 8–9 (oculis ____ hausit) is

(A) hendiadys
(B) asyndeton
(C) chiasmus
(D) transferred epithet

11. The case of indute (line 10) is

(A) ablative
(B) accusative
(C) nominative
(D) vocative

12. In lines 10–11, (Tune) ____ eripiare mihi? is translated

(A) Are you snatching me away?
(B) Are you being snatched away from me?
(C) Will I snatch you away?
(D) Are you to be snatched away from me?

13. In lines 11–12 (Pallas ____ sumit), who is represented figuratively as striking Turnus' death blow?

(A) Mars
(B) the goddess of vengeance
(C) Aeneas
(D) Pallas

Romulus reacts to news of his brother's death

Haec ubi rex didicit,[1] lacrimas introrsus obortas
devorat et clausum pectore vulnus habet.
Flere palam non vult exemplaque fortia servat,
"Sic"que "meos muros transeat hostis," ait.
Dat tamen exsequias[2] nec iam suspendere fletum
sustinet, et pietas dissimulata patet,
osculaque applicuit posito suprema feretro[3]
atque ait, "Invito frater adempte, vale!"
Arsurosque artus unxit. Fecere, quod ille,
Faustulus et maestas Acca soluta comas.
Tum iuvenem nondum facti flevere Quirites.
Ultima plorato subdita flamma rogo[4] est.

1 Haec ubi rex didicit: in this version of the story, Remus had been killed by Celer, who had been put in charge of building Rome's walls.
2 exsequiae, -arum, f.pl.: funeral rites
3 feretrum, -i, n.: bier to carry the body to the grave
4 rogus, -i, n.: funeral pyre

14. In lines 1–2 (Haec ___ habet), we learn that Romulus
    (A) could not contain his grief
    (B) suppressed his grief
    (C) increased his grief
    (D) felt no grief

15. In line 1, the verbal form obortas is a
    (A) deponent
    (B) present subjunctive
    (C) gerund
    (D) main verb

16. As indicated in line 3 (Flere ___ servat), it appears that Romulus
    (A) wept openly
    (B) was pleased at the news
    (C) did what everyone expected
    (D) grieved privately

17. In line 4, transeat hostis is translated
    (A) let the enemy go across
    (B) the enemy is passing over
    (C) the enemy will go over
    (D) he may overtake the enemy

18. In line 5, the phrase nec iam means
    (A) not only now
    (B) no longer
    (C) and yet not
    (D) never again

19. In lines 5–8 (Dat ___ vale), we learn that Romulus was unable to conceal his grief
    (A) during the funeral rites
    (B) after he had buried his brother
    (C) when he kissed the funeral bier
    (D) after he had bid his brother farewell

20. Which of the following figures of speech appears in lines 7–8 (osculaque ____ vale)?
    (A) hendiadys
    (B) interlocked word order (synchysis)
    (C) hyperbole
    (D) polysyndeton

21. In line 8 (Invito ____ vale), Romulus' final words to his brother imply that
    (A) his brother had welcomed death
    (B) his brother's body had been stolen
    (C) his brother had died prematurely
    (D) he had wanted his brother to die

22. Which of the following is closest in meaning to Arsurosque artus unxit (line 9)?
    (A) He cremated the body and then annointed it.
    (B) He annointed the body about to be cremated.
    (C) With great skill, he prepared the body to be cremated.
    (D) He embraced the body before cremation.

23. In line 9, the form Fecere is
    (A) future indicative
    (B) perfect indicative
    (C) present infinitive
    (D) present imperative

24. Which of the following figures of speech is found in line 10 (Faustulus ____ comas)?
    (A) transferred epithet
    (B) metonymy
    (C) litotes
    (D) aposiopesis

25. Line 12 (Ultima ____ est) is translated
    (A) The final lament is given over the burning pyre.
    (B) Romulus, as a final act of grief, ignited the pyre.
    (C) After the pyre was arranged, the wretched fire was finally lit.
    (D) At last the fire has been placed beneath the lamentable pyre.

Pliny congratulates a friend

Recte fecisti, Valeri, quod gladiatorum munus Veronensibus nostris promisisti, a quibus olim amaris suspiceris ornaris. Inde etiam uxorem carissimam tibi et probatissimam habuisti, cuius memoriae aut opus aliquod aut spectaculum atque hoc potissimum, quod maxime funeri, debebatur. Praeterea tanto consensu rogabaris, ut negare non constans, sed durum videretur. Illud quoque egregie, quod tam facilis tam liberalis in edendo fuisti; nam per haec etiam magnus animus ostenditur. Vellem Africanae[1], quae coemeras plurimas, ad praefinitum diem occurrissent: sed licet cessaverint[2] illae tempestate detentae, tu tamen meruisti ut acceptum tibi fieret, quod quo minus exhiberes[3] non per te stetit. Vale.

1 Africanae, -arum, f.pl.: = Africanae ferae, panthers
2 licet cessaverint: "granted that they were late"
3 quo minus exhiberes: "that you could not show them"

26. In lines 1–2 (Recte ____ ornaris), we learn that Valerius
   (A) is a well-known gladiator in Verona
   (B) wants to win votes by sponsoring games
   (C) is being honored by gladiatorial games
   (D) has sponsored games in Verona

27. The figure of speech that occurs in amaris susceperis ornaris (line 2) is
   (A) alliteration
   (B) asyndeton
   (C) hyperbole
   (D) ellipsis

28. In lines 2–5 (Inde ____ debebatur), we learn that Valerius' wife
   (A) was deceased
   (B) was a wealthy and powerful woman
   (C) was not loved or respected by her husband
   (D) cared little for the games

29. The case of the noun memoriae (line 3) depends upon
   (A) uxorem (line 2)
   (B) cuius (line 3)
   (C) funeri (line 5)
   (D) debebatur (line 5)

30. Complete the following translation of lines 5–6 (Praeterea ____ videretur): "Moreover, you were asked by so many people ____ "
   (A) that to deny that you were not strong-minded would seem shameless
   (B) that to refuse would seem not resolute, but rude
   (C) that those who did not seem to agree with you were considered harsh, rather than steadfast
   (D) that no one appeared to deny your determination and toughness

31. In line 6, Illud is the direct object of
   (A) fecisti (understood from line 1)
   (B) edendo (line 7)
   (C) fuisti (line 7)
   (D) the verb est (understood)

32. In the context of line 7, edendo is translated
   (A) must sponsor
   (B) having sponsored
   (C) sponsoring
   (D) about to be sponsored

33. In lines 6–8 (Illud ____ ostenditur), Pliny characterizes Valerius as generous because
   (A) Verona had never had gladiatorial games before
   (B) he had honored his wife with the show
   (C) he was efficient and lavish in giving the games
   (D) public games were usually financed by the state

34. The adjectives facilis (line 6) and liberalis (line 7) modify
   (A) Illud
   (B) Pliny, understood
   (C) Valerius, the subject of fuisti
   (D) animus (line 7)

35. The words Vellem Africanae ____ ad praefinitum diem occurrissent (lines 8–9) are translated
   (A) I wished that the panthers had arrived on the appointed day.
   (B) I want you to know the panthers will arrive as scheduled.
   (C) I wished I knew on what day the panthers would arrive.
   (D) If only the panthers had arrived on the day I wished.

36. The verb occurrissent (line 9) is translated

(A) they were arriving

(B) they would arrive

(C) they will have arrived

(D) they had arrived

37. The clause that ends with the subjunctive verb exhiberes (line 11) is introduced by

(A) licet (line 9)

(B) ut (line 10)

(C) quod (line 10)

(D) quo minus (line 10)

38. In lines 10–11 (tu ____ stetit), Pliny assures Valerius that

(A) Pliny will take responsibility for what happened

(B) Valerius deserves credit for his intentions

(C) Valerius can display the panthers at another time

(D) No one will blame him

A festival celebrates the blessings of the farm

Luce sacra requiescat humus, requiescat arator,
et grave suspenso vomere[1] cesset opus.
Solvite vincla iugis; nunc ad praesepia[2] debent
plena coronato stare boves capite.
Omnia sint operata deo;[3] non audeat ulla
lanificam pensis[4] imposuisse manum.
Vos quoque abesse procul iubeo, discedat ab aris,
cui tulit hesterna gaudia nocte Venus.
Casta placent superis: pura cum veste venite
et manibus puris sumite fontis aquam.
Cernite, fulgentes ut eat sacer agnus ad aras
vinctaque post olea[5] candida turba comas.

1 vomer, vomeris, m.: ploughshare
2 praesepium, -i, n.: manger; corn crib
3 deo: Bacchus or Ceres
4 pensum, -i, n.: a portion of wool weighed out to a spinner as a day's task; "a day's work"
5 olea, -ae, f.: the olive (tree, branch, leaf, fruit)

39. As we learn from lines 1–2 (Luce ____ opus), the poet asks that the festival include

(A) a day of rest for all

(B) more rigorous work than usual

(C) postponement of all work but the ploughing

(D) only light chores

40. The word grave (line 2) modifies

(A) arator (line 1)
(C) vomere (line 2)
(B) suspenso (line 2)
(D) opus (line 2)

41. In lines 3–4 (Solvite ____ . capite), we learn that

(A) the farm equipment should be cleaned

(B) corn cribs should be decked with wreaths

(C) oxen are to be prepared for sacrifice

(D) the cattle should be fed well

42. In line 5, Omnia sint operata deo is translated

(A) All things have been done for the god

(B) Let the god do all things

(C) Let all things be done for the god

(D) All things are being done by the god

43. In line 6, the case of pensis depends upon

(A) Omnia . . . deo (line 5)
(C) lanificam . . . manum (line 6)
(B) audeat (line 5)
(D) imposuisse (line 6)

44. In lines 7–8 (Vos ____ Venus), we learn that those who have been recent lovers

(A) are especially welcome at the festival

(B) must stay away from the festival

(C) may be present, but not at the altars

(D) may be together only the night of the festival

45. In line 8, Venus is an example of which figure of speech?

(A) transferred epithet
(C) metonymy
(B) hendiadys
(D) onomatopoeia

46. In lines 9–10 (Casta ____ aquam), we learn that festival celebrants are to
   (A) wash their garments in the pure spring water
   (B) draw the spring's water with pure hands
   (C) make chaste offerings to the gods
   (D) purify themselves after they arrive

47. Line 11 (Cernite ____ aras) is translated
   (A) See how the shining lamb goes to the sacred altars
   (B) O shining ones, tell us when the sacred lamb will go to the altars
   (C) Determine whether the sacred lamb will go to the shining altars
   (D) Observe how the sacred lamb goes to the shining altars

48. In line 11 (Cernite ____ aras), which figure of speech occurs?
   (A) hyperbaton
   (B) hyperbole
   (C) anaphora
   (D) polysyndeton

49. The first four feet of line 11, which is dactylic, are
   (A) dactyl-dactyl-spondee-spondee
   (B) dactyl-spondee-spondee-dactyl
   (C) dactyl-spondee-dactyl-dactyl
   (D) spondee-dactyl-dactyl-spondee

50. Line 12 (vinctaque ____ comas) describes the
   (A) celebrants annointing their heads with oil
   (B) harvesting of olive branches
   (C) celebrants in festival attire
   (D) honoring of the farm's crops

STOP

This is the end of the Multiple-Choice Section of the AP Latin: Vergil Exam. If time remains, you may check your work only in this section. Do not begin the Free-Response Section until instructed to do so.

Practice Exam 2

AP Latin: Vergil

Free-Response Section

TIME: 2 hours (including a 15-minute reading period)

DIRECTIONS: Answer ALL FIVE of the questions in this Section, following directions carefully.

Question 1 – Vergil (15 percent)

(Suggested time – 10 minutes)

"Dis equidem auspicibus reor et Iunone secunda
hunc cursum Iliacas vento tenuisse carinas.
Quam tu urbem, soror, hanc cernes, quae surgere regna
coniugio tali! Teucrum comitantibus armis
Punica se quantis attollet gloria rebus!
Tu modo posce deos veniam, sacris litatis
indulge hospitio causasque innecte morandi."

Aeneid **4.45–51**

Give a literal translation of the passage above.

Question 2 – Vergil (15 percent)

(Suggested time – 10 minutes)

Begin your answer to this question on a fresh page.

Sic Turno, quacumque viam virtute petivit,
successum dira dea negat. Tum pectore sensus
vertuntur varii; Rutulos aspectat et urbem
cunctaturque metu letumque instare tremescit,
nec quo se eripiat, nec qua vi tendat in hostem,
nec currus usquam videt aurigamve sororem.

***Aeneid* 12.913–18**

Give a literal translation of the passage above.

Question 3 – Vergil (35 percent)

(Suggested time – 45 minutes)

Begin your answer to this question on a fresh page.

(A)

At domus interior gemitu miseroque tumultu
miscetur, penitusque cavae plangoribus aedes
femineis ululant; ferit aurea sidera clamor.
Tum pavidae tectis matres ingentibus errant
amplexaeque tenent postes atque oscula figunt.
Instat vi patria Pyrrhus: nec claustra nec ipsi
custodes suffere valent.

***Aeneid* 2.486–92**

(B)

It clamor ad alta
atria; concussam bacchatur Fama per urbem.
Lamentis gemituque et femineo ululatu
tecta fremunt, resonat magnis plangoribus aether,
non aliter, quam si immissis ruat hostibus omnis
Karthago aut antiqua Tyros, flammaeque furentes
culmina perque hominum volvantur perque deorum.

***Aeneid* 4.665–71**

In each of these two passages, a household is thrown into an uproar. In a well-developed essay, compare and contrast the manner in which each each is described.

(Remember to support what you say by making direct reference to the Latin **throughout** the passages. Cite and translate or closely paraphrase the relevant Latin. Do not simply summarize or paraphrase what the poem says.)

Question 4 – Vergil (20 percent)

(Suggested time – 20 minutes)

Begin your answer to this question on a fresh page.

Constitit et lacrimans, "Quis iam locus," inquit "Achate,"
quae regio in terris nostri non plena laboris?
En Priamus. Sunt hic etiam sua praemia laudi;
sunt lacrimae rerum et mentem mortalia tangunt.
Solve metus; feret haec aliquam tibi fama salutem."
Sic ait atque animum pictura pascit inani
multa gemens, largoque umectat flumine vultum. . .
Ter circum Iliacos raptaverat Hectora muros
exanimumque auro corpus vendebat Achilles.
Tum vero ingentem gemitum dat pectore ab imo,
ut spolia, ut currus, utque ipsum corpus amici
tendentemque manus Priamum conspexit inermes.

***Aeneid* 1.459–65, 483–87**

In this passage, Aeneas expresses deep emotions with regard to what he and Achates are seeing. In a **short** essay, discuss now the poet uses his craft to develop sympathy for Aeneas and the Trojans.

(Remember to support your observations from the **entire text** of each passage and be sure to cite and translate or closely paraphrase directly from the Latin text.)

Question 5 – Vergil (15 percent)

(Suggested time – 25 minutes)

Begin your answer to this question on a fresh page.

In the *Aeneid*, lesser deities often appear in the story to further the interests of another character or an event. **Select one deity from each group below** and discuss the way in which that deity furthers the cause of an individual or an incident in the story. The deities in Group A might be considered to have a positive effect, whereas the deities in Group B a negative one.

Group A	**Group B**
Cupid, son of Venus	Allecto, a Fury
Sea Nymphs	Iris, messenger goddess
Vulcan, blacksmith god	Juturna, sister of Turnus

END OF AP LATIN: VERGIL
PRACTICE EXAM 2

Practice Exam 2

AP Latin: Vergil

Answer Key

List of Authors and Passages Appearing on This Exam

Multiple-Choice[1]

Required Author Passage

"Aeneas confronts Turnus" (*Aeneid* 12.938–949)

Sight Passages

"Romulus reacts to the news of his brother's death" (Ovid, *Fasti* 4.845–855)

"Pliny congratulates a friend" (Pliny, *Epistulae* 6.34)

A festival celebrates the blessings of the farm" (Tibullus, *Elegies* 2.1.5–16)

Free-Response

Translation 1: *Aeneid* 4.45–51

Translation 2: *Aeneid* 12.913–918

Long Essay: *Aeneid* 2.486–492, 665–671

Short Essay: *Aeneid* 1.456–465, 483–487

Identification: Allecto, Cupid, Sea Nymphs, and Vulcan; Allecto, Iris, and Juturna

[1] Translations of all multiple-choice passages can be found at the end of the Detailed Explanations of Answers to the Multiple-Choice Questions.

Answers to the Multiple-Choice Questions: Vergil, Practice Exam 2

Aeneas	Romulus	Pliny	Festival
1. (C)	14. (B)	26. (D)	39. (A)
2. (D)	15. (A)	27. (B)	40. (D)
3. (A)	16. (D)	28. (A)	41. (D)
4. (B)	17. (A)	29. (D)	42. (C)
5. (B)	18. (B)	30. (B)	43. (D)
6. (B)	19. (A)	31. (A)	44. (B)
7. (C)	20. (B)	32. (C)	45. (C)
8. (C)	21. (C)	33. (C)	46. (B)
9. (D)	22. (B)	34. (C)	47. (D)
10. (A)	23. (B)	35. (A)	48. (A)
11. (D)	24. (A)	36. (D)	49. (C)
12. (D)	25. (D)	37. (D)	50. (C)
13. (D)		38. (B)	

Practice Exam 2

AP Latin: Vergil

Detailed Explanations of Answers to Multiple-Choice Questions

"Aeneas confronts Turnus"

1. **(C)**

Lines 1–2 translate "Aeneas stood fierce in arms, shifting his eyes, and he restrained his weapon-hand." Thus, the correct answer is (C) "vigilant but non-combative."

2. **(D)**

Cunctantem is a present participle (note the **–nt-** in the form) modifying **eum** (Aeneas), understood. Answer (A) noun is incorrect, as **cunctantem** would not make sense in this context as a substantive. In Answer (C), the gerundive **cunctandum**. For participles, see Chapter 21.

3. **(A)**

From your familiarity with the story of Book 12, you should know that Turnus' speech (**sermo**) of resignation and defeat in the lines previous to the multiple-choice passage had given Aeneas pause.

4. **(B)**

Lines 3–4 read, "And now, and now (Turnus') words had begun to sway him more (**magis . . . flectere**) as he hesitated (**cunctantem**)," so Answer (B) "change his mind" is correct. Note the emphatic use of repetition in **iam iamque** (line 3).

5. **(B)**

These lines contain an example of hyperbaton because the adjective **infelix** is widely separated from the noun it modifies, **balteus**, in order to emphasize the swordbelt's ill-fortune. The words **infelix . . . balteus** also "wrap around" Turnus' shoulder!

6. **(B)**

In line 6, the pronoun **quem** introduces a relative clause describing **Pallantis pueri**. **Quem** serves as the object of **Turnus straverat** (lines 6–7) and is modified by the perfect passive participle **victum**. For relative pronouns, see Chapter 13.

7. **(C)**

Straverat is the pluperfect tense of **sterno, sternere, stravi, stratum**, to throw down, lay someone low. Therefore, Answer (C) "he had thrown down" is correct. For the forms and meanings of indicative verbs, see Chapter 15.

8. **(C)**

Lines 4–7 translate, "when the luckless swordbelt (**infelix . . . balteus**) high on his (Turnus') shoulder (**umero cum . . . alto**) came into his (Aeneas') view (**apparuit**) and the belt (**cingula**) of the youth Pallas (**Pallantis pueri**) shone (**fulserunt**) with its familiar studs (**notis . . . bullis**), (the youth) whom Turnus had thrown down (**straverat**), overcome by a wound (**victum . . . vulnere**), and (Turnus) was wearing it on his shoulders (**umeris . . . gerebat**) as the token of a foe (**inimicum insigne**)." The correct answer is, therefore, (C) "(Aeneas) noticed Turnus wearing Pallas' swordbelt."

9. **(D)**

Answer (D) dactyl-dactyl-dactyl-spondee is correct. Be sure to include the two elisions, **atque umeris** and **inimicum insigne**, in your scansion. The **–que** in **atque** is short and the second elision is long by position, i.e., it is followed by two consonants, **ns-**. For scansion, see Chapter 9.

10. **(A)**

In lines 8–9, note that Aeneas really does not see both "the reminder of cruel grief" (**saevi monimenta doloris**) and the swordbelt (**exuviasque**). As required by the sense, **saevi monimenta dolori** is really in apposition to **exuvias.** Therefore, this is an example of hendiadys and Answer (A) is correct. For figures of speech, see Chapter 8.

11. **(D)**

Indute is a perfect passive participle with a vocative ending, modifying **Tu** (=Turnus). For participles, see Chapter 21.

12. **(D)**

Lines 10–11 are translated, "Are you, adorned with the plunder of one of mine (**meorum**), to be snatched away from me?" **Eripiare** is a form of the present subjunctive passive of the verb **eripio, eripere** in a deliberative question. The form **eripiare** is condensed from **eripiaris**. For deliberative questions, see Chapter 25; for alternative verb forms, see Chapter 9.

13. **(D)**
In lines 11–12, Aeneas pathetically invokes the name of Pallas, in whose name he is striking the fatal blow. "Pallas (is the one who) makes a death-sacrifice of you (**immolat**) with this wound, Pallas (is the one who) exacts retribution (**poenam . . . sumit**) from your villainous blood."

"Romulus reacts to news of his brother's death"

14. **(B)**
In lines 1–2, the relevant words **lacrimas . . . habet** translate, "he (Romulus) chokes back the tears having welled up inside and keeps the wound closed away in his heart." The correct answer is therefore (B) "suppressed his grief."

15. **(A)**
Although the **–as** ending of **obortas** could lead you to Answer (B) a present subjunctive (see Chapter 24), or (D) a main verb (first conjugation, present tense indicative), the verb **oborior, oboriri, obortus sum** is deponent, that is, it is passive in form and active in meaning. Therefore, **obortas** is a perfect passive (past) participle modifying **lacrimas**. For deponent verbs, see Chapter 16; for past participles of deponent verbs, see Chapter 21.

16. **(D)**
Line 3 answers the question by translating "He does not wish to weep openly and maintains (= wishes to maintain) strength as an example." Therefore, Answer (D) "grieved privately" is correct.

17. **(A)**
The verb of this famous saying is a jussive subjunctive, which required the meaning of "let." The verb form required by Answer (B) is present tense, **transit**, and Answer (C) future tense, **transibit**. **Hostis** is a nominative subject and cannot serve as the direct object of **transeat**, therefore Answer (D) "he may overtake the enemy" is incorrect. The entire sentence translates, "Let the enemy cross over my walls and this (**sic**) will happen," i.e., the enemy will die, just as Remus did. For the forms and uses of the independent subjunctive, see Chapter 25.

18. **(B)**
Nec iam, "no longer," is an idiomatic phrase commonly found throughout Latin literature.

19. **(A)**
Lines 5–6 say, "However, he conducts the funeral rites (and) no longer able to hold back the tears, his hidden devotion is disclosed and he presses final kisses (on the body) placed on the bier." The finality implied in Answers (B) and (D) is not present or suggested in these words. The sequence of the Latin in this sentence implies that Romulus had "broken down" during the funeral rites, which presumably took place before transport to the grave on the bier.

20. **(B)**

The words that interlock are **osculaque** with **suprema** (accusative plural, neuter) and **posito** with **feretro** (ablative singular, neuter), giving **osculaque . . . posito suprema feretro** as the synchysis. For figures of speech, see Chapter 8.

21. **(C)**

Ovid takes this famous line directly from Catullus, Poem 101, on the death of the poet's brother. It reads, "Brother, taken away from me against your will, farewell." The words **invito** and **adempte** imply an early/unexpected death, giving (C) "his brother had died prematurely" as the correct answer. **Ademptus** is the perfect passive participle of **adimo, adimere, ademi, ademptus** and has a vocative ending, modifying **frater.**

22. **(B)**

This sentence requires careful reading, as the sense requires that the future active participle **arsuros** be translated with a passive meaning: Romulus annointed (**unxit**) the body (**artus**, accusative plural) about to be cremated (**arsuros**, modifying **artus**, a fourth declension noun). The correct sequence is reversed in Answer (A); Answer (B) mistakes **artus**, "limbs," for a form of **ars, artis**, "skill"; and Answer (D) mistranslates **unxit** (for **iunxit**?). The use of **artus** for body is an example of synecdoche. For the future active participle, see Chapter 21.

23. **(B)**

Fecere is a poetic condensation of **fecerunt**, which is third person plural, perfect active indicative = "they made" or "they did." It cannot be a form of the future tense (Answer A), a present infinitive (Answer C), or a present imperative (Answer D) because the stem **fec-** is in the perfect tense. For alternative verb forms, see Chapter 9.

24. **(A)**

In line 10, the ending of the adjective **maestas** requires that it modify the noun **comas**, but it is not the hair that is sad, but Acca herself. Therefore, the meaning of **maestas** may be transferred to **Acca** from **comas** (note also the juxtaposition of **maestas** with **Acca**). For figures of speech, see Chapter 8.

25. **(D)**

Break down this sentence by noticing the interlocking of **ultima . . . flamma** with **plorato . . . rogo** and the separation of the elements of the main verb, which is **subdita . . . est**. The adjective **ultima** may be translated adverbially, as Answer (D) "at last." The verb **subdo, subdere, subdidi, subditum** means *to place under*. **Plorato . . . rogo** is an ablative absolute meaning "the funeral pyre having been lamented, or, "after the funeral pyre was lamented." Hence, the correct answer is (D) "At last the fire has been placed under the pyre after it was lamented, i.e., the lamentable pyre."

"Pliny congratulates a friend"

26. **(D)**

Answer (D) "has pledged to present games in Verona" is correct because Line 1 reads, "You have done well, Valerius, because you have sponsored gladiatorial games for our fellow Veronese."

27. **(B)**

The listing of three verbs in a row without punctuation – **amaris suspiceris ornaris** – is asyndeton. Normally, you would find **amaris et suspiceris et ornaris**. See Chapter 8 for figures of speech.

28. **(A)**

That Valerius' wife was deceased is surmised from the past tense of the verb, i.e., **uxorem . . . habuisti**, the use of the words **memoriae** (line 3) and **funeri** (line 4), and Pliny's comment here that gladiatorial combats are particularly suitable for funeral tributes (their original function). The sentence in lines 2–4 reads, "From there (Verona) you had a wife very dear and most acceptable to you, to whose memory you owe either some public work (**opus**) or show (**spectaculum**), and this is very much the kind of show that is especially appropriate (**hoc potissimum quod maxime**) for a funeral."

29. **(D)**

The case of the noun **memoriae**, dative, depends upon the verb **debebatur**, used impersonally (line 4): "to the memory of whom (**cuius**, i.e., the wife) . . . there was owed." Avoid taking both **memoriae** and **cuius** as genitive. For the dative case, see Chapter 12.

30. **(B)**

This is a tricky sentence. The key to the meaning is the observation of **negare** as a subjective infinitive, i.e., **negare** serves as the subject of the result clause **ut . . . videretur**. Subjective infinitives serve as neuter nouns, therefore **constans** and **durum** modify **negare**. For this use of infinitive, see Chapter 23.

31. **(A)**

In lines 1–5, Pliny congratulates Valerius for having done well (**recte fecisti**) in proposing the games. Thereafter, he concentrates on talking about the games themselves. Therefore, **illud quoque egregie** correctly follows after **fecisti**, understood: "You did that admirably, too, the fact that (**quod**) . . . ." Thus, the correct answer is (A) **fecisti** (understood from line 1).

32. **(C)**

The correct translation of the gerund **edendo** is Answer (C) "sponsoring." The ablative case is used after the preposition **in**. Answer (A) is a red herring, designed to get you to think about the distinction between a gerund and a passive periphrastic. The perfect active participle in Answer (B) "having sponsored," cannot be expressed directly in Latin, as **edo, edere** is not a deponent verb. The meaning given in Answer (D) "about to be sponsored" requires a future passive participle or gerundive, which is an adjective; **edendo** functions as a noun here. For more on gerunds and gerundives, see Chapter 22.

33. **(C)**
Answer (C) is correct because Pliny characterizes Valerius in line 5 as **tam facilis tam liberalis**, "so efficient (and) so lavish" (in giving the games). Note the asyndeton.

34. **(C)**
Answer (A) is incorrect because **facilis** and **liberalis** cannot modify **Illud**, which is neuter. There is no reason to assume that these adjectives modify Pliny, understood, (Answer B) as there is no reference to him in this sentence. Answer (D), **animus**, although appropriate in case, gender, and number, appears in the main clause that follows the clause in which **facilis** and **liberalis** appear. The answer is (C), Valerius, the addressee of the letter, who is described here as "efficient" (**facilis**) and "lavish" (**liberalis**) in his productions.

35. **(A)**
As given, the sentence reads "If only (**Vellem**) the panthers (**Africanae**) . . . had arrived (**occurrissent**) on the appointed day (**ad praefinitum die**)." **Vellem** is optative subjunctive, for which, see Chapter 25. For the form of **occurrissent**, see Chapter 24. Answer (A) is correct because the renderings of the verb tenses in Answers (B) "will arrive," (C) "would arrive," and (D) "had wished," are incorrect.

36. **(D)**
The form **occurrissent** is pluperfect active subjunctive following **Vellem**, which expresses the wish, "If only they had arrived." The tenses of Answers (A) and (B) are incorrect (imperfect and present), and the mood of Answer (C) is indicative.

37. **(D)**
The words **quo minus** (sometimes spelled **quominus**) introduce the subjunctive clause **quo minus . . . exhiberes**. **Quo minus** is found with the subjunctive when hindering or preventing is stated or implied, as it is here. Answer (A) **licet** governs **cessaverint**; Answer (B) **ut** introduces a clause with **fieret**; Answer (C) **quod** introduces a causal clause with **stetit**. For subjunctive clauses, see Chapters 26–29.

38. **(B)**
The Latin says, "you nonetheless deserved that the credit (**acceptum**, a financial term referring to something entered into the credit column) should go (**fieret**) to you, because (**quod**) it was not your fault (**non per se stetit**, an idiomatic use of **stetit**) that you could not show them (**quo minus exhiberes**)." Therefore, Answer (C) "Valerius deserves credit for his intentions" is correct.

"A festival celebrates the blessings of the farm"

39. **(A)**

The required lines (1–2) tell us "the earth and the ploughman should have a day of rest on festival day (**luce sacra**) and that, with the plough lifted (**suspenso vomere**), the heavy work should cease." "The plough lifted" refers to the removal of the ploughshare from the earth. Answer (A) "a day of rest for all" is the correct answer. Note the metonymy of light (**Luce**) for day.

40. **(D)**

The adjective **grave** modifies the neuter noun **opus**. Do not be distracted by the e-ending of **vomere**, which is ablative with **suspenso** in an ablative absolute. Note the use of hyperbaton in **grave . . . opus**.

41. **(D)**

Lines 3–4 are translated, "Now the oxen, with garlanded heads, should stand at feeding troughs that are full," leading to Answer (D) "the cattle should be fed well." The other answers exploit, but confuse, the wording of this sentence. **Solvite vincla iugis** refers to loosening the harnesses from the yokes.

42. **(C)**

Answer (C) "Let all things be done for the god" correctly translates **Omnia sint operata deo** (line 5). **Sint** is a jussive subjunctive, the subject of which is the substantive **omnia**, modified by the adjective **operata**. **Deo** refers, presumably, to Bacchus, Ceres, or some other divinity associated with fertility or the farm. At the beginning of the poem, which is not provided here, both of these deities are invoked in celebration of the festival. For independent subjunctives, see Chapter 25.

43. **(D)**

In line 6, the dative case of **pensis** depends upon the compound verb **imposuisse**. This portion of the sentence reads, "let no one (**nec . . . ulla**) dare to have applied (**imposuisse**) her spinner's hand (**lanificam . . . manum**) to the **pensum** (the day's work)." For the dative case, see Chapter 12.

44. **(B)**

The translation of lines 7–8 leads to the meaning, "I bid you all be far away; let him depart from the altar to whom Venus (love) brought pleasure last night (**hesterna gaudia nocte**)." Thus, Answer (B) "must stay away from the festival" is correct. Use scansion to determine whether **hesterna** is accusative modifying **gaudia** or ablative with **nocte**. (It is the latter.)

45. **(C)**

The substitution of **Venus** for love or passion is metonymy. For figures of speech, see Chapter 8.

46. **(B)**

The possible answers require careful reading! Answer (B) "draw the spring's water with pure hands" is correct. Answer (A) "wash their garments in pure spring water" incorrectly translates **pura cum veste venite** ("arrive with purified garments") and Answer (C) "make chaste offerings to the gods with pure garments" incorrectly interprets **casta placent superis** ("purity is pleasing to the gods)." Answer (D) "draw purified water by hand from the spring" is incorrect because **puris** modifies **manibus** and not **aquam**.

47. **(D)**

Answer (D), "Observe how the sacred lamb goes to the shining altars," is correct. Answer (A) reverses **fulgentes** (shining) and **sacer** (sacred); Answer (B) incorrectly renders **fulgentes** as vocative; and Answer (C) incorrectly translates **eat** as future tense. **Eat** is present subjunctive of the verb **eo, ire** in an indirect question introduced by **ut**. For irregular verbs, see Chapter 17; for present participles, see Chapter 21; for subjunctive clauses with **ut**, see Chapter 27.

48. **(A)**

The word **fulgentes** is pulled away from the prepositional phrase **ad aras** and placed in an emphatic position, framing the activity anticipated to take place at the altar: fulgentes ut eat sacer agnus ad aras. For anastrophe and hyperbaton, see Chapter 8.

49. **(C)**

- uu - - - u u- u u - u u - -

Line 11 is scanned Cernite fulgentes ut eat sacer agnus ad aras, dactyl-spondee-dactyl-dactyl.

50. **(C)**

Answer (A) sacrificial procession refers to the preceding line. Answer (B) exploits the appearance of the word **olea** (olive tree) as a distractor and Answer (D) exploits the context of the poem, which is about farming. This difficult final line is rendered "behind it (referring to the procession taking the sacrificial lamb to the altar) a throng (garbed) in white (cf. line 9), their hair bound up (literally, bound up as to their hair, or with regard to their hair) with olive branches (**vinctaque olea . . . comas**)." The past participle **vinctaque** (from **vincio,** not **vinco**) modifies **candida turba**.

Translations of the Multiple-Choice Passages

"Aeneas confronts Turnus"

Aeneas stood fierce in arms, shifting his eyes, and he restrained his weapon hand; and now, and now (Turnus') words had begun to sway him more as he hesitated, when the luckless sword-belt high on his (Turnus') shoulder came into his view and the belt of the youthful Pallas shone with familiar studs, (Pallas the youth) whom Turnus had thrown down, overcome by a wound, and he (Turnus) was wearing it on his shoulders as a token of the foe. He (Aeneas), after he caught sight of the swordbelt, testament to cruel grief, inflamed with madness and frightful with anger, proclaimed "Are you, adorned with the plunder of one of mine, to be snatched away from me? Pallas (is the one who) makes a sacrifice of you with this death-blow, Pallas (is the one who) exacts retribution from your villainous blood."

"Romulus reacts to news of his brother's death"

When the king (Romulus) learned this (that his brother had been killed), he chokes back the tears having welled up inside and keeps the wound closed away in his heart.[1] He does not wish to weep openly and he maintains strength as an example. "Let it be the same for (any) enemy who should cross my walls," he says. Nonetheless, he conducts the funeral rites (and), no longer able to hold back the tears, his hidden devotion is disclosed and he presses final kisses (on the body) placed on the bier, and says, "O brother, taken from me before your time, farewell!" (Romulus) annointed the body about to be cremated. Both Faustulus and Acca, having loosened her hair in grief, did what he had done. Then the not-yet-citizen Quirites wept for the youth. At last the fire has been placed under the pyre after it was lamented, i.e., the lamentable pyre.

"Pliny congratulates a friend"

You have done well, Valerius, because you have sponsored gladiatorial games for our fellow citizens of Verona, by whom for a long time now you are loved, respected, and honored. You had a wife, also from there (Verona) who was very dear to and most compatible with you, to/in whose memory you owe either some public work or show, and this is very much the kind of show that is especially appropriate for a funeral. Moreover, you were asked by so many people, that to refuse would seem not stubborn, but rude. You did that admirably too, the fact that you were so efficient and lavish in producing (the games); for even through things like this, the true spirit (of generosity) is shown. If only the panthers, which you had purchased

[1] The verbs in the present tense in this passage may be translated as past.

in quantity, had arrived on the appointed day: but granted that they, having been delayed by a storm, were late, you nonetheless deserved that the credit should go to you, because it was not your fault that you could not show them. Farewell.

"A festival celebrates the blessings of the farm"

On (this sacred day) let the earth rest, let the ploughman rest and, with the plough lifted (from the soil), the heavy work should cease. Loosen the harness from the yokes; now the oxen with garlanded heads should stand at feeding troughs that are full. Let all things be done for the god; let no one dare to have applied her spinner's hand to the day's work. Also, I bid that you be far away, let him depart from the altar to whom love brought pleasure last night. Purity is pleasing to the gods: come with pure garments and draw the spring's water with pure hands. Look how the sacred lamb proceeds to the shining altar and behind (it) the white-robed throng, their hair bound up with olive leaves.

Answers to Free-Response Section

Question 1

Translation

"Indeed, I think that, with the guidance of the gods and with Juno favorable, the Trojan ships have held their course here on the wind. What a city you will see here, sister, what a kingdom you will see rise up by way of such a marriage! To what heights will Punic glory rise with Trojan arms accompanying (us)! Only ask the gods for pardon and, sacrifices having been offered, be generous with (your) hospitality and weave together reasons for him to stay."

Grading

18 pts. total; round up your score.

1. *dis equidem auspicibus*
2. *reor Iliacas carinas . . . tenuisse*
3. *et Iunone secunda*
4. *hunc cursum*
5. *vento*
6. *quam tu. . . hanc urbem . . . cernes*

7. *quae . . . regna*
8. *coniugio tali*
9. *Teucrum*
10. *comitantibus armis*
11. *Punica . . . gloria*
12. *quantis rebus*
13. *attollet*
14. *tu modo posce deos veniam*
15. *sacris litatis*
16. *indulge hospitio*
17. *causasque innecte*
18. *morandi*

Acceptable Translations for Question 1, Vergil: Practice Exam 2

For instructional purposes, more grammatical and syntactical information is provided here than is usually found in the grading reports on the translation question.

1. *dis*: gods

   equidem: indeed/surely/truly

   auspicibus: favor/auspices/patronage/guide; **must be taken with dis**

2. *reor*: (I) think/suppose/reckon/be of the opinion

   Iliacas: Trojan/Ilian

   carinas: keels; synecdoche for ships/boats; **subject of** *tenuisse*

   tenuisse: hold/keep/preserve/maintain; **must be construed with** *reor*

3. *et*: and

   Iunone: Juno

   secunda: favorable/following/propitious/aiding; **must be taken with** *Iunone*

4. *hunc cursum*: this course/journey/direction/way; **must be object of** *tenuisse*

5. *vento*: wind; **must reflect ablative**

6. *quam*: What/How great; **must be taken with** *hanc urbem*

   hanc urbem: this city

   tu: you

   cernes: (you) will see/observe/witness/perceive/regard

7. *quae*: what; **must be taken with** *regna*

   regna: kingdom/realm/dominion/sovereignty; **may be translated as singular**

8. *coniugio*: marriage/wedlock/wedding/union; **must reflect ablative**

   tali: such/of such a kind; **must be taken with** *coniugio*

9. *Teucrum*: Trojan/Teucrian/Teucri; **must be construed with** *armis*

10. *comitantibus*: accompany/join/escort/attend/follow

    armis: arms/weapons

11. *Punica*: Punic/Carthaginian

    gloria: glory/renown/fame/pride/achievement

12. *quantis*: what/such great

    rebus: the meaning here is equivalent to *gloria*: heights/honor/acclaim/esteem/prestige

13. *attollet*: (it) will rise/elevate/climb/raise or lift up/soar

14. *modo*: only/just now

    tu . . . posce: ask for/seek from/request of or from/inquire of/call upon/demand

    deos: the gods; **must be object of** *posce*

    veniam: pardon/favor/grace/indulgence/good will; **must be object of** *posce*

15. *sacris*: sacred or holy things/sacrifices; **must be taken as substantive**

    litatis: to make a favorable sacrifice/appease/pacify/placate

16. *indulge*: be generous/be kind/favor/indulge

    hospitio: hospitality/welcome/reception; **must be construed with** *indulge*

17. *causas*: reason/cause/pretext/inducement/excuse; **must be object of** *innecte* **and complete** *morandi*

    innecte: weave/connect/fasten/tie or bind together

18. *morandi*: of/for staying/remaining/delaying/lingering

Question 2

Translation

And so to Turnus, with whatever courage he sought a way (to win), the dread goddess denies success. Then different imaginings spin around in his mind; he observes the Rutulians and his city and hesitates through fear and trembles that death is imminent, neither does he see to where he might escape, nor in what way he might attack the enemy, nor (does he see) his chariot anywhere, or his sister, the charioteer.

Grading

18 pts. total; round up your score.

1. *sic Turno*
2. *quacumque*
3. *viam . . . petivit*
4. *virtute*
5. *successum . . . negat*
6. *dira dea*
7. *tum pectore*
8. *sensus . . . varii*
9. *vertuntur*
10. *Rutulos aspectat et urbem*
11. *cunctaturque*
12. *metu*
13. *letumque instare*
14. *tremescit*
15. *nec quo se eripiat*
16. *nec qua vi tendat in hostem*
17. *nec currus usquam videt*
18. *aurigamve sororem (videt)*

Acceptable Translations for Question 2, Vergil: Practice Exam 2

For instructional purposes, more grammatical and syntactical information is provided here than is usually found in the grading reports on the translation question.

1. *sic*: thus/and so/therefore

   Turno: Turnus; **must be indirect object of** *negat*
2. *quacumque*: whatever

   virtute: courage/bravery/fortitude/fearlessness/valor/boldness; **must reflect ablative**
3. *viam*: way/path/means/method

   petivit: (he) sought/looked for/determined/strove after/endeavored to obtain

4. *successum*: success/accomplishment/fulfilment/attainment

   negat: (she) denies/refuses/rejects/turns down

5. *dira*: dread/terrible/horrible or horrifying/fearful/cruel/deadly

   dea: goddess

6. *tum*: then/thereupon/at that time

   pectore: mind or heart/seat of consciousness; **must be construed as ablative with** *in*

7. *sensus*: imaginings/visions/perceptions/feelings; **must be plural, subject of** *vertuntur*

   varii: different/diverse/various/manifold/variant/dissimilar; **must modify** *sensus*

8. *vertuntur*: spin/turn/turn around/whirl/wheel/fly about/roll around; **may be translated as active**

9. *Rutulos*: Rutuli/Rutulians/people of Turnus; **must be object of** *aspectat*

   aspectat: (he) observes/sees/gazes on/looks at

   et: and

   urbem: city; **must be object of** *aspectat*

10. *cunctatur*: (he) hestitates/delays/stays/remains/lingers/bides time; **Turnus is acceptable as subject**

    -que: and

11. *metu*: fear/dread/apprehension/fright/terror; **must reflect ablative**

12. *letum*: death/ruin/annihilation; **subject of** *instare*

    -que: and

    instare: be imminent/threaten/press upon/be close/pursue; **must be construed with** *tremescit*

13. *tremescit*: (he) dreads/fears/trembles at

14. *nec*: neither/and . . . not/nor; **must negate** *videt*

    quo: to anywhere

    se eripiat: (he) may or might escape/rescue himself/snatch himself from

15. *nec*: same as in #14.

    qua vi: in what or which way/with what force/by what means; **must reflect ablative**

    tendat: (he) may or might strive after/make for/contend with; **must be construed with** *in hostem*

16. *nec*: same as in #14
    currus: chariot; **may be translated as singular**
    usquam: anywhere/in any place
    videt: (he) sees/notices/heeds/takes note of/regards
17. *aurigam*: charioteer/chariot driver; **must be taken with** *sororem*
    -ve: = *vel*, or; **must connect** *aurigam sororem* **with** *currus*
    sororem: sister

Question 3

Long Essay

For the grading scale used for evaluating essays, see Chapter 6. Here are some high points of each description to consider in your comparative analysis, followed by a sample essay. Such observations, which will set up your formal essay, may be made in writing during the 15-minute reading period. The sample essays may seem overly thorough, but the author is attempting to accommodate the wide range of answers that will be given by users of this book.

(A) The Greeks are sacking Troy and Pyrrhus is breaking into the interior of the palace.

- The inner house is full of shrieks (gemitu), uproar (misero tumultu), and confusion (miscetur).
- The vaulted halls echo (ululant) with women's cries (pangoribus . . . femineis); the noise reaches to the very stars. The diction creates an atmosphere of noise and confusion; the interlocking of cavae plangoribus aedes femineis) through synchysis causes the women's wailing to "echo" against the valuted halls; ad sidera is hyperbole and ululant onomatopoeia.
- The panic-stricken women (pavidae . . . matres) roam through the immense quarters, clasp and hold tight to the door-posts (amplexaeque tenent postes) and plant kisses on them (oscula figunt). The interlocking of fear, halls, and women in pavidae tectis matres ingentibus (4) accentuates the interrelationship of all three. The chiasmus of tenent postes atque oscula figunt (5) gives the impression that the women are actually embracing and kissing the door-posts.
- Pyrrhus appears suddenly, with instat in prime position in the line. The juxtaposition and alliteration of vi patria Pyrrhus adds to the intensity of his dramatic entrance. Neither the bolts nor the guards are strong enough to withstand him. The hard c of nec claustra nec . . . custodes suggests the sounds of hacking or knocking at the interior doors.

(B) Carthage reacts to the news that Queen Dido has killed herself.

- This passage also begins with noise (a single shriek?) raised to the heights (ad alta atria; cf. Passage A, line 3). Note the hyperbaton concussam . . . urbem that frames bacchatur Fama, which runs riot inside the shaken city.

Bacchatur is a metaphor that suggests the wild uncontrolled behavior of the worshippers of Bacchus.

- The halls resonate with the sobbing (lamentis), groaning (gemitu), and wailing of women (femineo ululatu). Cf. gemitu, Passage A, line 1, and femineis ululant, line 3.
- The heavens echo (resonat . . . . aether) with loud laments (magnis plangoribus). Next comes a simile comparing the noise and confusion with that of a city, such as Carthage or Tyre, falling to the enemy (immissis . . . hostibus). Note the hyperbole of resonat . . . aether (cf. Passage A, line 3) and the whoosh of s's in line 5, which suggest the onrush of the enemy. The enjambment of Karthago aut antiqua Tyros adds drama.
- Further description of a sacked city describes the raging flames (flammaeque furentes) rolling over the rooftops (culmina) of the houses of men and gods.

Sample Long Essay

These two passages, which describe the downfalls of two households at two different times and places, are remarkable similar in setting, tone, diction, and imagery. Death and destruction are common elements. Passage (A) depicts the noise and confusion in the inner palace of Priam during the sack of Troy. Passage (B) describes the noise and confusion in the inner palace of Dido (and in the city of Carthage) after the news has been received that Dido has killed herself.

As mentioned, both narratives describe their respective scenes as noisy, confused, and filled with grief. The same words are sometimes used: Passage (A) plangoribus, ululant, clamor; Passage (B) clamor, ululatu, plangoribus. In Passage (A), words expressing disorientation and despair include gemitu, tumultu, pavidae, and amplexaeque . . . figunt (line 5); in Passage (B), concussam, bacchatur, immissis ruat hostibus (line 5), and furentes, all onomatopoetic, or nearly so. There is a preoccupation with the structure of both households or cities as if they were almost living beings and participants in the commotion: Passage (A) domus interior (line 1), cavae . . . aedes (line 2), tectis. . . ingentibus (line 4), tenent postes (line 5), and nec . . . claustra . . . valent (lines 6–7); Passage (B) ad alta atria (1–2), tecta (line 4) and culmina (line 5). All this adds to the reader's sense of mayhem and chaos and to the sense that both buildings and people are vulnerable during a crisis. Also in both instances, women are depicted as the true victims of what has happened, at least with regard to their reactions: Passage (A) plangoribus. . . . femineis ululant (lines 2–3) and pavidae matres (line 4), etc.; Passage (B) femineo ululatu (line 3), and perhaps bacchatur (line 2). Vergil uses exaggeration (hyperbole) in both scenes to pump up the action: Passage (A) ferit aurea sidera clamor (line 3), "the noise reaches the golden stars," and (B) resonat magnis plangoribus aether (line 4), "the high heavens resound with great shrieks."

Word order also contributes to the reader's appreciation of what is happening: interlocking is used effectively in Passage (A) where the wailing of the women seems to "echo" from the vaulted halls (cavae plangoribus aedes femineis, lines 2–3). The interlocking of fearful, halls, and women in pavidae tectis matres ingentibus (line 4) accentuates the interrelationship of all three. Word-pictures also contribute to the description of the uproar. In Passage (A), line 5, tenent . . . figunt depicts the women actually "embracing" (amplexaeque) the door-posts; in Passage (B), the hyperbaton of concussam . . . urbem in line 2 frames bacchatur Fama, which literally "runs riot" inside the shaken city.

The differences between these two passages are few but significant. In Passage (A), all the action seems to funnel down into the dramatic arrival of a single individual, Pyrrhus, who becomes a catalyzing element in the destruction of the royal family and of Troy by killing King Priam. The prime position of instat and the juxtaposition and alliteration of vi patria Pyrrhus in line 6, add to the dramatic intensity of the warrior's entrance. In Passage (B), the final three lines employ a simile which compares the downfall of Carthage, which is implied by the death of Dido, to the sack of a great city by an enemy. Note that the houses of the gods are destroyed in the simile in Passage B, which perhaps suggests purification by fire for the pollution brought upon Carthage by Dido's broken vow. Did Vergil have in his files a stock description for depicting the downfall of a household?

Question 4

Short Essay

For the grading scale used for evaluating essays, see Chapter 6. Here are some high points of the passage to consider in your comparative analysis.

- Aeneas and Achates, hidden from view by a mist, inspect the murals in the Temple of Juno at Carthage. The first reaction of Aeneas is weeping (lacrimans). He asks Achates, in a tone of despair, what region of the earth has not heard of their tragedy? Note the ellipsis of est; abbreviated sentence structure is a feature of expressions of high emotion.
- Aeneas spots the dead Priam and makes the ironical observation that these are the rewards of virtue. He also speaks of compassion (lacrimae) for suffering (rerum) and mortal woes (mortalia) touching the human heart (mentem). Note the compressed sentence structure of En Priamum and the emphatic repetition of sunt (3–4). The words lacrimae and mortalia contribute to the development of pathos.
- Aeneas then does an "about face" by reverting to a condensed version of his previous "O socii" speech. He advises Achates (whose presence allows Aeneas to vocalize his thoughts and thus heighten our sympathy for both) not to fear: "the struggle you witness here (i.e., our fama or reputation) will bring us salvation." Metus is another charged word; note the poetic plural, which multiplies the fear.
- Aeneas then does another "about face" and relapses into despair as he studies "the empty picture" (pictura . . . inane). He groans and his face be-

comes wet with a flood of tears. Note the evocative words gemens, umectat, and largo . . . flumine, the metaphorical use of pascit, and the solemn m-sounds throughout the passage.

- The final five lines describe significant events of the war and Aeneas' reaction upon seeing them portrayed on the mural. The postponement of the subject Achilles in the sentence of lines 8–9 is notable in developing anticipation, as if Aeneas was hoping to defer his grief over such painful memories. There are many significant words and phrases used in these lines: exanimum . . . corpus, corpus amici, tendentem manus Priamum . . . inermes. Aeneas' reaction to all this is a tremendous groan (ingentem gemitum dat pectore ab imo). Note the sound play of ingentem gemitum, which suggests the groans themselves. The anaphora of ut, the asyndeton, and the enjambment of inermes are all emphatic and therefore contribute to developing in the reader a sense of compassion for Aeneas and the Trojans.

Sample Short Essay

In this passage, Vergil provides the reader with many opportunities to develop and heighten a sense of pathos or compassion. Word selection, the sounds of words, the use of altered sentence structure through abbreviation and repetition, the use of imagery, and the interplay of dialogue and narrative description all contribute. The subject of Aeneas' attention in this passage, i.e., events of the Trojan War as portrayed on the murals of the Temple of Juno at Carthage, certainly warrants an emotional reaction on the part of Aeneas, as he himself was a participant in those tragic events.

This passage teems with words that communicate or suggest the grief and pain suffered by Aeneas and Achates while viewing the murals. Words such as lacrimans (line 1), lacrimae (line 4), largoque umectet flumine vultum (line 7), and ingentem gemitum . . . pectore ab imo (line 10) all denote the tearful pain and suffering experienced by Aeneas. Additional words are suggestive: mortalia (line 4), metus (line 5), inani (line 6), exanimum . . . corpus (line 9), corpus amici (line 11), and tendentem manus Priamum . . . inermes (line 12).

Vergil also uses words whose sounds evoke the solemnity of remembering trauma and death. Consonance of m-sounds is found throughout the passages, especially in lines 4, 7, 10, and 12. Also, the interplay of ingentem and gemitum suggests the sounds made by Aeneas when he groans and moans. Events or speeches of high emotion usually contain some alteration in sentence structure, as events speed up or slow down. Vergil's "craft" here includes the use of short sentences, such as En Priamum (line 3), examples of ellipsis (est in line 5), the use of anaphora (sunt . . . sunt, lines 3–4, and ut, line 11), and asyndeton (line 11).

Because the use of elaborate imagery in this passage would detract from the simplicity of the emotions portrayed here, figurative speech contributes little to developing pathos in the reader. Exaggeration (hyperbole) appears in flumine (line 7), exaggerating the amount of weeping, and pectore ab imo (line 10), amplifies the expressiveness of the groan. Animum . . . pascit (line 6) expresses the image that Aeneas is "grazing" as he looks at the pictures.

The use of dialogue between Aeneas and Achates, including a rhetorical question (lines 1–2), spliced into the descriptive narrative, personalizes the emotions and allows Aeneas to make observations that heighten his own feelings (lines 6–7).

When we first meet Aeneas in the Aeneid, he is lamenting the fact that he did not die at Troy. We learned at that time that it was acceptable in a warrior culture, even for heroes, to break down and cry. In the passage here, Vergil is masterful in portraying the humanity of Aeneas without sacrificing our appreciation of the hero's sense of himself as a man.

Question 5

Because it is difficult to do justice to this question in the space provided here (there are nine possible combinations of characters that can be discussed), you are given below some information about each "lesser deity." Compare the content of your own answer with those provided. On the actual AP Vergil Exam, a short analytical essay is expected.

Group A

Cupid: The son of Venus appears in the latter stages of Book 1 and precipitates the action in the next three Books. Upon being invited by Queen Dido to a banquet, Aeneas sends back to the ships for his son Ascanius. Venus, fearful of Juno's continuing interference, disguises her son Cupid as Ascanius. At the banquet, Dido embraces Ascanius/Cupid and then falls passionately in love with Aeneas. This scene leads in Book 2 to Aeneas' narration of the Trojan War and in Book 3 to his account of his travels, which then lead to the subsequent relationship between Dido and Aeneas described at length in Book 4. Though acting in a minor role, Cupid precipitates momentous events in the Aeneid.

Sea Nymphs: In Book 9, Jupiter, at the behest of his mother Cybele, changed the Trojan ships, which had been torched by Turnus and the Rutulians, into sea nymphs, who swam away unharmed. They return to the Latin coast as Aeneas arrives with Evander's fleet, which had sailed down the Tiber. Cymodocea, one of the sea nymphs, tells Aeneas of the transformation of the Trojan fleet and promises help in the rescue of Ascanius and the Trojans beleaguered by Turnus.

Vulcan: Vulcan, who is the blacksmith of the gods and husband of Venus, has a small but significant role in the drama of the Aeneid. In Book 8, Venus asks Vulcan to forge weapons and armor for her son, which with the help of the Cyclopes, he does. These weapons preserve Aeneas' life in the fighting that lies ahead, especially during his duel with Turnus in Book 12. In a magnificent ecphrasis that rivals Jupiter's speech to Venus in Book 1, Vergil uses the engraving on the shield to portray the future history of Rome. The center of the shield depicts the Battle of Actium, in which Octavian defeated Antony and Cleopatra, paving the way for Octavian to become Augustus, Vergil's literary patron. Without Vulcan's participation in the story of the Aeneid, Aeneas himself, although a demigod, would have risked death.

Group B

Allecto: One of three Furies who drove their victims insane (furor). Allecto serves as Juno's henchwoman in Book 7, first stirring up trouble by alienating both Amata and Turnus to the idea of a Trojan presence in Italy, then by causing Ascanius to wound a pet stag of the Latins while hunting. She appears both disguised as an old woman and in her real role as a terrible Fury.

Iris: Iris, a messenger goddess, plays a minor role in each of her several appearances in the Aeneid. In each, the goddess acts a handmaid to Juno and therefore implicitly is an adversary of Aeneas. Prompted by Juno, Iris cuts a lock of Dido's hair, which frees Dido's spirit to go to the Underworld, bringing closure to the story in Book 4. In Book 5, she is sent by Juno to stir up discontent among the Trojan women, which leads to the torching of the Trojan ships. Finally, in Book 9, Iris is sent by Juno to advise Turnus and the Rutulians to attack the Trojans in the absence of Aeneas, who has gone to seek help from Evander.

Juturna: Juturna, Turnus' sister, is active in the story of Book 12. She is manipulated by Juno to protect her brother, and thus interferes with the success of Aeneas and the Trojans in Italy. She assumes the guise of Turnus' charioteer and saves him more than once on the battlefield. Her resolute, almost obsessive, concern for her brother does not lead to her destruction, as she is a water nymph. Juturna jumps into a river and disappears from the story.

ANSWER SHEETS

AP Latin

Practice Exam 1

AP Latin: Vergil

Multiple-Choice Section

Answer Sheet

1. Ⓐ Ⓑ Ⓒ Ⓓ	18. Ⓐ Ⓑ Ⓒ Ⓓ	35. Ⓐ Ⓑ Ⓒ Ⓓ
2. Ⓐ Ⓑ Ⓒ Ⓓ	19. Ⓐ Ⓑ Ⓒ Ⓓ	36. Ⓐ Ⓑ Ⓒ Ⓓ
3. Ⓐ Ⓑ Ⓒ Ⓓ	20. Ⓐ Ⓑ Ⓒ Ⓓ	37. Ⓐ Ⓑ Ⓒ Ⓓ
4. Ⓐ Ⓑ Ⓒ Ⓓ	21. Ⓐ Ⓑ Ⓒ Ⓓ	38. Ⓐ Ⓑ Ⓒ Ⓓ
5. Ⓐ Ⓑ Ⓒ Ⓓ	22. Ⓐ Ⓑ Ⓒ Ⓓ	39. Ⓐ Ⓑ Ⓒ Ⓓ
6. Ⓐ Ⓑ Ⓒ Ⓓ	23. Ⓐ Ⓑ Ⓒ Ⓓ	40. Ⓐ Ⓑ Ⓒ Ⓓ
7. Ⓐ Ⓑ Ⓒ Ⓓ	24. Ⓐ Ⓑ Ⓒ Ⓓ	41. Ⓐ Ⓑ Ⓒ Ⓓ
8. Ⓐ Ⓑ Ⓒ Ⓓ	25. Ⓐ Ⓑ Ⓒ Ⓓ	42. Ⓐ Ⓑ Ⓒ Ⓓ
9. Ⓐ Ⓑ Ⓒ Ⓓ	26. Ⓐ Ⓑ Ⓒ Ⓓ	43. Ⓐ Ⓑ Ⓒ Ⓓ
10. Ⓐ Ⓑ Ⓒ Ⓓ	27. Ⓐ Ⓑ Ⓒ Ⓓ	44. Ⓐ Ⓑ Ⓒ Ⓓ
11. Ⓐ Ⓑ Ⓒ Ⓓ	28. Ⓐ Ⓑ Ⓒ Ⓓ	45. Ⓐ Ⓑ Ⓒ Ⓓ
12. Ⓐ Ⓑ Ⓒ Ⓓ	29. Ⓐ Ⓑ Ⓒ Ⓓ	46. Ⓐ Ⓑ Ⓒ Ⓓ
13. Ⓐ Ⓑ Ⓒ Ⓓ	30. Ⓐ Ⓑ Ⓒ Ⓓ	47. Ⓐ Ⓑ Ⓒ Ⓓ
14. Ⓐ Ⓑ Ⓒ Ⓓ	31. Ⓐ Ⓑ Ⓒ Ⓓ	48. Ⓐ Ⓑ Ⓒ Ⓓ
15. Ⓐ Ⓑ Ⓒ Ⓓ	32. Ⓐ Ⓑ Ⓒ Ⓓ	49. Ⓐ Ⓑ Ⓒ Ⓓ
16. Ⓐ Ⓑ Ⓒ Ⓓ	33. Ⓐ Ⓑ Ⓒ Ⓓ	50. Ⓐ Ⓑ Ⓒ Ⓓ
17. Ⓐ Ⓑ Ⓒ Ⓓ	34. Ⓐ Ⓑ Ⓒ Ⓓ	

Free-Response Section

Use the following pages to prepare your essays.

Free-Response Section *(Continued)*

Practice Exam 2

AP Latin: Vergil

Multiple-Choice Section

Answer Sheet

1. Ⓐ Ⓑ Ⓒ Ⓓ	18. Ⓐ Ⓑ Ⓒ Ⓓ	35. Ⓐ Ⓑ Ⓒ Ⓓ
2. Ⓐ Ⓑ Ⓒ Ⓓ	19. Ⓐ Ⓑ Ⓒ Ⓓ	36. Ⓐ Ⓑ Ⓒ Ⓓ
3. Ⓐ Ⓑ Ⓒ Ⓓ	20. Ⓐ Ⓑ Ⓒ Ⓓ	37. Ⓐ Ⓑ Ⓒ Ⓓ
4. Ⓐ Ⓑ Ⓒ Ⓓ	21. Ⓐ Ⓑ Ⓒ Ⓓ	38. Ⓐ Ⓑ Ⓒ Ⓓ
5. Ⓐ Ⓑ Ⓒ Ⓓ	22. Ⓐ Ⓑ Ⓒ Ⓓ	39. Ⓐ Ⓑ Ⓒ Ⓓ
6. Ⓐ Ⓑ Ⓒ Ⓓ	23. Ⓐ Ⓑ Ⓒ Ⓓ	40. Ⓐ Ⓑ Ⓒ Ⓓ
7. Ⓐ Ⓑ Ⓒ Ⓓ	24. Ⓐ Ⓑ Ⓒ Ⓓ	41. Ⓐ Ⓑ Ⓒ Ⓓ
8. Ⓐ Ⓑ Ⓒ Ⓓ	25. Ⓐ Ⓑ Ⓒ Ⓓ	42. Ⓐ Ⓑ Ⓒ Ⓓ
9. Ⓐ Ⓑ Ⓒ Ⓓ	26. Ⓐ Ⓑ Ⓒ Ⓓ	43. Ⓐ Ⓑ Ⓒ Ⓓ
10. Ⓐ Ⓑ Ⓒ Ⓓ	27. Ⓐ Ⓑ Ⓒ Ⓓ	44. Ⓐ Ⓑ Ⓒ Ⓓ
11. Ⓐ Ⓑ Ⓒ Ⓓ	28. Ⓐ Ⓑ Ⓒ Ⓓ	45. Ⓐ Ⓑ Ⓒ Ⓓ
12. Ⓐ Ⓑ Ⓒ Ⓓ	29. Ⓐ Ⓑ Ⓒ Ⓓ	46. Ⓐ Ⓑ Ⓒ Ⓓ
13. Ⓐ Ⓑ Ⓒ Ⓓ	30. Ⓐ Ⓑ Ⓒ Ⓓ	47. Ⓐ Ⓑ Ⓒ Ⓓ
14. Ⓐ Ⓑ Ⓒ Ⓓ	31. Ⓐ Ⓑ Ⓒ Ⓓ	48. Ⓐ Ⓑ Ⓒ Ⓓ
15. Ⓐ Ⓑ Ⓒ Ⓓ	32. Ⓐ Ⓑ Ⓒ Ⓓ	49. Ⓐ Ⓑ Ⓒ Ⓓ
16. Ⓐ Ⓑ Ⓒ Ⓓ	33. Ⓐ Ⓑ Ⓒ Ⓓ	50. Ⓐ Ⓑ Ⓒ Ⓓ
17. Ⓐ Ⓑ Ⓒ Ⓓ	34. Ⓐ Ⓑ Ⓒ Ⓓ	

Free-Response Section

Use the following pages to prepare your essays.

Free-Response Section *(Continued)*

AP LATIN

Appendices

Appendix I

Print and Online Resources for AP Latin

Chapter 1
The Content and Format of the AP Latin Exam

College Board Resources for AP Latin

- *Latest edition of the AP Latin Course Description*, also known as the Acorn book (published biennially; last published for the 2010 and 2011 exams) (Item # 080082753). Download from the AP Latin: Vergil Course Homepage or the AP Latin: Vergil websites, listed below. For a quick study of the course, see the Wikipedia article at http://en.wikipedia.org/wiki/AP_Latin_Virgil.
- *2005 AP Latin Literature and Latin: Vergil Released Exams*, complete multiple-choice and free-response sections of both the Vergil and Literature exams (Item #050081722)

  Note: The AP Latin Literature Exam is no longer offered.
- *1999 AP Latin Literature and Latin: Vergil Released Exams* (Item #255180)
- *AP Latin Teacher's Guide*, Jeff S. Greenberger, ed., n.d. (Item #989390)
- Relevant issues of *The Classical Outlook* (Journal of the American Classical League, published quarterly by the American Classical League, Miami University, Oxford, OH 45056).

  Note: Each year, the Chief Reader publishes in *The Classical Outlook* an analytical report on the AP Latin Exam. This report provides valuable feedback on how the expectations of the teachers who designed the exams were met by the students who took the exams. This report, which also includes scoring guidelines and sample student and Reader responses, is especially useful because it provides insight into the grading of literal translations required on the free-response sections. See most recently, Mary Pendergraft, 2009, "The Grading of the 2008 Advanced Placement Examinations in Latin: Vergil," *CO* (Fall, 2008), Vol. 86, No. 1, pp. 49–60.

  The materials listed above are available from the College Board Store at the website http://store.collegeboard.com/enter.do.

College Board and Related Websites

- AP Central

  http://apcentral.collegeboard.com/apc/Controller.jpf

  The official College Board website for Advanced Placement

- AP Latin Web Guide

  http://apcentral.collegeboard.com/apc/members/courses/teachers_corner/155475.html.

  Contains links to online resources for the study of Vergil and the *Aeneid*, including the Latin Library at Ad Fontes Academy and *Quia*.

- AP Latin: Vergil Course Homepage

  http://apcentral.collegeboard.com/latinvergil

  or

  http://apcentral.collegeboard.com/apc/public/courses/teachers_corner/2260.html

  Links to much information about the Course and Exam; primarily for the teacher (lesson plans, teaching strategies, articles on course content, plus the downloadable Acorn book and the *AP Latin Teacher's Guide*).

- The AP Latin: Vergil Exam

  http://apcentral.collegeboard.com/apc/members/exam/exam_questions/4558.html

  Contains a history of the AP Latin Exam, a link to the multiple-choice information in the Acorn book, and links to the free-response sections of the Exams themselves from 1999 to the present, plus scoring guidelines and samples of student responses with commentary from 1999 to the present.

- Latin: Vergil http://www.collegeboard.com/student/testing/ap/sub_latinverg.html?latinvergil

  Contains the Exam syllabus plus a link to and information from the Acorn book, including abilities tested and tips on how to respond to the various free-response questions. In the left margin, there are links to the free-response questions from the Exams of 2001–2009, plus scoring guidelines (2004–2009), grade distributions, etc.

  See also:

- An Unofficial Website for AP Latin (Ginny Lindzey and the Texas Classical Association)

  http://txclassics.org/old/aplatin.htm

  Mostly for teachers, but some good resources for students, too.

- Latinteach.org

  http://latinteach.com/Site/RESOURCES/Entries/2008/6/13_Teaching_Vergil.html

Check out the links to recent articles and resources, both in print and on the web.

- "Useful Internet Links for AP Latin" (Barbara F. McManus and Marianthe Colakis, VRoma = Virtual Rome, Miami University, Oxford, OH)

  http://www.vroma.org/~bmcmanus/aplinks.html, also contained in the *AP Latin Teacher's Guide,* for which, see above.

  Notes to teachers: For sample AP Latin course syllabi, consult the *AP Latin Teacher's Guide*, the AP Latin: Vergil Homepage (for both of which, see above) and the school website at http://www.mfrance.org/AP_Latin_Syllabus.pdf (also in html).

  To participate in the AP Latin Electronic Discussion Group (EGD), sponsored by the College Board and for teachers only, go to http://apcentral.collegeboard.com/apc/public/homepage/4631.html.

Print Texts and Ancillary Materials for Vergil's *Aeneid*

For Pre-AP and an Introduction to the Aeneid

Daniel H. Garrison, *The Language of Virgil: An Introduction to the Poetry of the Aeneid*, Peter Lang Publishing, 1987. Vocabulary, exercises on grammar and syntax, scansion of selections from Book 1.

LeaAnn A. Osburn, Thomas J. Sienkewicz, *Vergil, A LEGAMUS Transitional Reader*, Bolchazy-Carducci, 2004. About 200 lines from Books 1, 2, and 4, presented in a step-by-step manner to assist the student in making the transition between "made-up" and authentic Latin. Authentic passages are presented first in a simplified, rearranged, or shortened Latin version. Contains grammar review and exercises.

Henry L. Philip, *Ecce Aeneas*, Oliver and Boyd/Longman, 1986. A textbook in the British style, with selections from Books 1 and 2; facing vocabulary and notes.

Rose Williams, *Vergil for Beginners: A Dual Approach to Early Vergil Study*, Bolchazy-Carducci, 2006. Six short selections from Books 1, 2, 4, and 6, with a playlet introducing the storyline, Latin to Latin and Latin to English vocabulary aids, and text-based grammar exercises.

Standard Student Texts Covering the AP Latin Syllabus

Note: The text used for the AP Latin Exam is Sir Roger A.B. Mynors' edition of Vergil's *Opera* in the Oxford Classical Text series. All editions are paperback unless noted otherwise.

Barbara Weiden Boyd, *Vergil's Aeneid: Selections from Books 1, 2, 4, 6, 10, and 12,* Bolchazy-Carducci, 2004, paperback. Revision of Clyde Pharr's text, plus Books 10 and 12. Running vocabulary, and notes at the bottom. Pharr's revised edition of Books 1–6 (1964) is still available in hardcover.

Richard A. Lafleur, Alexander G. McKay, *A Song of War: Readings from Vergil's Aeneid*, Prentice-Hall, 2003. Includes all passages on the AP syllabus, with facing vocabulary and commentary.

Ancillaries for Students and Teachers

Henry V. Bender, David J. Califf, *Poet and Artist: Imaging the Aeneid*, Bolchazy-Carducci, 2004. This Latin student text contains a CD of the Ogilby engravings (in PowerPoint and PDF format) that illustrated Dryden's translation of the *Aeneid*. The images are correlated with the Latin texts required for the AP Latin Exam and with questions to be used as guidelines. No vocabulary or notes.

Charles Rowan Beye, *Ancient Epic Poetry*, 2nd ed., Bolchazy-Carducci, 2006. The classic work on the subject; includes chapters on Homer, Apollonius, Vergil, Gilgamesh.

Katherine Bradley, Barbara Weiden Boyd, *A Vergil Workbook*, Bolchazy-Carducci, 2006. Exercises on content, translation, meter, grammar, syntax, vocabulary, figures of speech, and literary analysis; covers the AP Latin syllabus and includes sample AP questions. Teacher's Guide with answers.

Richard A. LaFleur, ed., *Latin for the 21st Century: From Concept to Classroom,* Scott-Foresman, Addison-Wesley, 1998. Chapters on various aspects of teaching and learning Latin, including several articles on AP, written by career high school and college Latin teachers.

Archibald A. Maclardy, *Parsed Vergil*, Bolchazy-Carducci, 2005. Book 1 completely scanned and parsed.

Christine G. Perkell, *Reading Vergil's Aeneid: An Interpretive Guide*, University of Oklahoma, 1999. Essays on the various Books and presentation of critical interpretations; all Latin is translated. Scholarly.

David Ross, *Virgil's Aeneid: A Reader's Guide*, Wiley-Blackwell, 2007. Chapters include "Virgil's Hero (Aeneas)," "The Victims," (Dido, Turnus, et al.), "Fate and the Gods," "Virgil's Troy." Scholarly.

Rose Williams, *The Labors of Aeneas: What a Pain it was to Found the Roman Race*, Bolchazy-Carducci, 2003. A light-hearted and illustrated retelling of the story of Aeneas.

Jan M. Ziolkowski, Michael C.J. Putnam, eds., *The Virgilian Tradition: The First Fifteen Hundred Years,* Yale Univ., 2008. Vergil as seen by himself and by his contemporaries; influence on later Latin writers; Vergil as performed or declaimed; primary sources for Vergil's biography; Vergil's remains and grave; the burning of the *Aeneid;* images of Vergil; Vergil's texts and their uses (mss.); commentary tradition; Vergilian legends. Scholarly.

Note for teachers: See also "Communicating in Latin," at http://www.latinteach.com/Site/RESOURCES/Entries/2008/5/19_Communicating_

in_Latin.html for links to Latin audio files, MP3 recordings, podcasts, Nuntii Latini, information about S.A.L.V.I.'s *Rusticatio* programs, et al.

Webliography of Online Sites Useful for AP Latin

Online Latin Texts of the Aeneid

- *Aeneid:* Text and Resources (The Vergil Project, Joseph Farrell, Univ. Pennsylvania)

  http://ccat.sas.upenn.edu/vergil/index.php/document/index/word_id/59707

  This site, which contains a new series of web pages produced by the Vergil Project, promises to be most useful for students of Vergil. It contains a complete interactive text of the *Aeneid* (u's for v's, however), 25 lines per frame, with a unique "slider" search engine by Book and line. Macrons can be hidden or not, as the user prefers, and there is the opportunity to use a clickable word-by-word English translation (the "mouse hover textual aid"). Additional reading assistance is provided re. the grammar and syntax of each word, plus a concordance and other resources.

- *Aeneid* Book 1, lines 1–100 in Several Formats (William Harris, Middlebury College)

  http://community.middlebury.edu/%7Eharris/Classics/VergilAen1uncial.html

  The first 100 lines in typical modern format; then in all caps, but with word separation; finally, an example with all caps and no word separation.

- Bibliotheca Augustana (Ulrich Harsch, Augsburg University, Germany)

  http://www.fh-augsburg.de/~harsch/Chronologia/Lsante01/Vergilius/ver_intr.html

  Unannotated texts, plus additional resources in Latin.

- The Latin Library at Ad Fontes Academy

  http://thelatinlibrary.com

  Unannotated texts of the *Aeneid,* Book by Book.

- The Perseus Digital Library (under "Popular Texts," click on "Vergil, *Aeneid*" for Greenough's Latin text, 1900)

  http://www.perseus.tufts.edu

  Latin hypertexts and online parsers. For another site with Greenough's Latin text, see http://www.forumromanum.org/literature/vergilx.html.

- Vox-Latina-Gottingensis

  http://www.vox-latina-gottingensis.de/scripta/vergil/invergil.htm

  Book by Book text of the *Aeneid*, with every line numbered.

School Websites for AP Latin

- AP Vergil's *Aeneid* (Timothy S. Abney, Marquette High School, Chesterfield, MO)

  http://abney.homestead.com/aeneid.html

  Teacher's metasite chock full of goodies for AP Latin, Vergil, and the *Aeneid* (content, vocabulary, figures of speech, passages for sight reading practice, quotes, and helpful writing tips and grammar review materials). Books 1, 2, 4, 6, 10–12, minor contributions for Books 3, 5, and 8. Updated regularly. See also, Virgilius.org (new website by Tim Abney, 2009)

  http://virgilius.org/index.html

  "Bringing Vergil's *Aeneid* to the World Wide Web." Includes 41 useful and active but difficult to read links for Vergil and the *Aeneid* and 14 for AP Latin, plus daily quotations, ancient artwork, figures of speech, and a FAQs section. A special running banner presents *Aeneid* 1.1–7. A promising work in progress.

- AP Vergil (Dr. Melissa Bishop, Boston Latin School, Boston, MA)

  http://latinresources.homestead.com/apvergil.html

  Contains vocabulary review lists ("magic lists"), rhetorical devices (link to Ross Scaife's Univ. Kentucky website), good quick-study of scansion, and an outline of the *Aeneid*, including episodes in the "Odyssean" and "Iliadic" portions of the *Aeneid* that are associated with the Homeric texts.

- Mr. J's Vergil Page (Bruce M. Johnson, Park View High School, VA)

  http://www.hoocher.com/vergil.htm

  Includes useful teacher-produced articles on the Augustan Age, common characteristics of an epic hero (incl. Carl Jung's attributes of a hero), and an outline of the mythological background of the Trojan War.

- AP Vergil Free-Response Questions (Michael B. Myer, Heathwood Hall Episcopal School, SC)

  http://www.heathwood.org/myer/5/APVFRquestions99–09.xls

  Excel spreadsheet of AP Vergil free-response questions, including location of passage(s), year examined, and type of question (translation, long essay, etc.).

- Pittsford Mendon High Latin Home Page (David Pellegrino, Pittsford High School, Pittsford, MI)

  http://www.pittsfordschools.org/webpages/dpellegrino/index.cfm

  Contains a handy compendium of free-response questions from previous AP Latin Exams, correlated with the Book and line numbers of the passage/s tested. Click on "AP Latin Questions" in the menu and use "Latinteach" as the password.

- Locus Publicus Linguae Latinae (Jerard White, Franklin Road Academy, Nashville, TN)

  http://www.frapanthers.com/teachers/white/vergil_links.htm

  Teacher's metasite contains links to Latin texts of all passages required for the Vergil Exam, using teacher-produced texts, some useful miscellaneous links, and a chronology of Vergil's life correlating with a chart of contemporary historical events. See also http://www.frapanthers.com/teachers/white/APL_handouts.htm for additional resources on figures of speech and scansion.

Other Websites Devoted to Vergil

Collections of Links

- Vergil: Some Links to Online Resources (Jim O'Hara, UNC-Chapel Hill) http://www.unc.edu/~oharaj/VergilLinks.html.
- The Virgil Home Page (Steven Hale, DeKalb College)

  http://facstaff.gpc.edu/~shale/humanities/literature/world_literature/virgil.html

Additional Useful Sites

- *Aeneid* (Roger Dunkle, Classics Technology Center, Ablemedia)

  http://ablemedia.com/ctcweb/netshots/vergil.htm

  Hypertext discussion of literary epic; historical background for Vergil; comments on reading the *Aeneid*; questions on the comprehension and interpretation of Books 1, 2, 4, 6, 8, and 12.

- "Classical Epic" (Robin Mitchell-Boyask, Temple Univ.)

  http://www.temple.edu/classics/epicsyl03.html and epic.html

  Course syllabus and links to background resources for Homer, Apollonius, Vergil, et al.

  See also the course syllabus for "The Epic Tradition" (Rob S. Rice, Univ. Pennsylvania), http://ccat.sas.upenn.edu/rrice/clas160.html.

- The Vergil Project (Joseph Farrell, Univ. Pennsylvania)

  http://vergil.classics.upenn.edu/

  Resources for students, teachers, and readers of Vergil. For the unique presentation of Vergil's *Aeneid* on this site, see the description above under "Online Latin Texts of Vergil."

- The Vergilian Society (Steven Tuck, Miami Univ., Oxford, OH)

  http://vergil.clarku.edu/

  Information about the Villa Vergiliana Study Center at Cumae, announcements of annual summer tours, *Vergilius* journal, et al.

- Virgil.org (David Scott Wilson-Okamura)

  http://virgil.org

  Thorough collection of information about Vergil's life and works, including information about the commentator Servius, the Latin text of "The Thirteenth Book of the *Aeneid*," etc., plus a search engine for the *Aeneid*. Also includes Mantovano's online discussion group for Vergil.

Quia Websites for study of the *Aeneid*

For *Quia*, go to http://www.quia.com/shared/latin.

- AP Vergil (Virginia Kehoe, Wichita Collegiate School, Wichita, KS)

  http://www.quia.com/pages/wcslatapvergil.html

  Quia Web page for AP Vergil, including vocabulary and content games, such as matching, flashcards, Concentration, and word search, for the LaFleur text edition and also the foldout word list of the Pharr/Boyd edition.

- Dripping Vergil (Ginny Lindzey, Dripping Springs High School, TX)

  http://www.quia.com/pages/drippingvergil.html

  An excellent site with a huge number of links to *Quia* activities and games, most for the LaFleur text of the *Aeneid*, including engaging Viqua hidden picture games. Covers content, vocabulary, figures of speech, quizzes on sets of lines (but not on entire Books). Many links to additional useful websites.

Chapter 4: The Vocabulary of Vergil's *Aeneid*

Vocabulary Components of Some Current Latin Textbook Programs

Note: The following site has *Quia* vocabulary games for *Ecce Romani*, and the Cambridge and Oxford Latin Course textbook programs: Learning Latin Online (Magister Horan, Fox Lane High School, Mount Kisco, NY) at http://www.magisterhoran.com/.

Cambridge Classics Course (CLC) / Cambridge School Classics Project (CSCP)

- See the official CLC website at http://www.cambridgescp.com/page.php?p=clc^top^home.

  For text-based vocabulary games, see http://www.cambridgescp.com/page.php?p=clc^oa_games^intro.

  For vocab testers, see http://www.cambridgescp.com/page.php?p=pe^vt^intro.

- All-Level Latin Site (Myrna Copeland, L.V. Berkner High School, Richardson, TX) http://www.quia.com/pages/copeland.html

Teacher-created *Quia* games for all 40 stages of CLC.

- Cambridge Classics Course Latin Vocabulary Tester (Vergil)

  http://www.cambridgescp.com/ws2_tlc/vocab/aqa_a2.html

  Clickable multiple-choice definitions of Latin words, with varying parameters of time, etc.; Latin to English and English to Latin.

- Cambridge Latin Course Vocabulary Games

  http://www.magisterhoran.com/CambridgeLatinCourse.html

  Quia matching, flashcard, Concentration games for Units I-IV, Stages 1–39.

- *Quia* activities and quizzes for the CLC (Mrs. Lukes, St. Paul VI Catholic High School, Fairfax, VA)

  http://www.quia.com/pages/pvilatin1cambridge.html.

  For CLC Latin I, Stages 1–20.

Ecce Romani

- See the official *Ecce Romani* site at

  http://www.phschool.com + appropriate chapter webcode from the textbooks. For online vocabulary activities, et al., for each chapter of Books I and II, see http://www.phschool.com/atschool/ecce_romani/program_page.html.

- Practice Activities for *Ecce Romani* (Timothy S. Abney, Marquette High School, Chesterfield, MO)

  http://abney.homestead.com/ecce1.html and /ecce2.html

  Many chapter by chapter online exercises and activities, including vocabulary, plus links to appropriate *Quia* pages; updated regularly.

- *Ecce Romani* Latin Course (Magister Horan, Fox Lane High School, Mount Kisco, NY)

  http://www.magisterhoran.com/EcceRomaniLatinCourse.html

  Chapter by chapter links to *Quia* activities and games.

- *Ecce* Vocabulary (David R. Pellegrino, Pittsford Mendon High School, Pittsford, MI)

  http://people.umass.edu/glawall/EcceVocab.pdf

  Vocabulary lists for *Ecce* I (1–27) and IIA (28–42), 2nd ed., alphabetized and by frequency.

- *Ecce Romani* Vocabulary Games (Kentucky Educational Television)

  http://www.dl.ket.org/latin1/vocab/ecce_games/

  Online matching, phrasing, and spelling games for Book I, Chapters 1–27. For cumulative review word lists and an *Ecce Romani* Vocabulary Lookup tool, see http://www.dl.ket.org/latin1/vocab/. (Macromedia Flash Player software)

- *Ecce Romani* Vocabulary Lists (Magistra Good, Mariemont City Schools, Cincinnati, OH)

  http://www.mariemontschools.org/bowman/ecce_romani_vocabulary_lists.htm

  Book I, Chapters 1–17, in multi-chapter groupings. Also *Quia* activities at http://www.quia.com/pages/magistragood.html.

- *Quia* Activities for *Ecce Romani* (Nancy Granducci, Ogden High School, Ogden, UT)

  http://www.quia.com/pages/latin1.html

  Vocabulary for Books I and II.

- *Quia* Activities for *Ecce Romani* (Patricia Kessler, Joe E. Newsome High School, Lithia, FL)

  http://www.quia.com/pages/kessler.html

  Quia for Books I and II.

Latin for Americans (LFA)

- *Latin for Americans Webs* (Kim Ashcraft, Summit Country Day School, Cincinnati, OH)

  http://www.summitcds.org/ashcraft/latin_for_americans_websites.htm

  Comprehensive site for LFA; links to *Quia* games for this text. See also relevant *Quia* items listed at Forum Regalium (Rebecca Bush, Hamilton Southeastern High School, Fishers, IN), http://www.hse.k12.in.us/staff/RBUSH/latin_ii_practice.htm#Quia%20Activities.

Oxford Latin Course (OLC)

- See the official website

  http://www.ats-group.net/languages/language-oxford-latin.html.

- BYKI, List Central (Latin; lists with the tag "Oxford")

  http://www.byki.com/tag/Oxford

  Transparent Language flashcards for Chapters 1–26; commercial vendor.

- Internet Workbook for the *Oxford Latin Course* (Robert W. Cape, Jr., Austin College, TX)

  http://artemis.austincollege.edu/acad/cml/rcape/latin/

  Chapter by chapter activities for Books I, II, III. Includes L-E and E-L vocabulary flashcards and links to *Quia* games.

- Oxford Latin Course Vocabulary Games

  http://www.magisterhoran.com/Oxford_Latin_Course.html

Links to *Quia* matching, flashcard, Concentration games for Books I, II, and III. (Java)

- *Oxford Latin Course*, Part I (John Gruber-Miller, Cornell College)

  http://www.cornellcollege.edu/classical_studies/scriba/

  Scriba computer software 1.0 to enhance study of Part I of OLC (1st ed.); replicates and expands textbook exercises and vocabulary.

- Online Latin Drills (OLC, 2nd ed.) (Prof. Margaret B. Phillips, Univ. Missouri at St. Louis, MO, via Classics Technology Center, Ablemedia)

  http://ablemedia.com/ctcweb/showcase/phillipslatindrills.html

  Online chapter by chapter drills for all three books; mostly grammar.

Online Resources for Building a Basic Latin Vocabulary

Note:

Centaur Systems (*Latina,* Version 4.5, Rob Latousek)

http://www.centaursystems.com/catalog/latina.html.

Popular software, for home or school, titled *Latin Flash Drill* (declensions and conjugations) and *Latin Vocabulary Drill*, which is correlated with most Latin textbooks currently in use. For Windows and Mac, both networkable.

Online Latin Dictionaries and Word Search Engines

- The Latin Lexicon (William Whitaker)

  http://latinlexicon.org/word_study_tool.php; see also Whitaker's *Words* at http://ablemedia.com/ctcweb/showcase/whitakerwords.html.

  Contains Latin to English and English to Latin dictionaries with search engine, and a comprehensive list of links to online Latin dictionaries. This site also includes software for making and printing vocabulary flashcards. See also http://en.wikipedia.org/wiki/William_Whitaker's_Words for links.

- Latin Dictionary and Grammar Aid (Ken Cawley, Univ. of Notre Dame).

  See also the Latin dictionary and grammar aid search engine at http://archives.nd.edu/latgramm.htm

- Latin Vocabulary Tool (Perseus)

  http://www.perseus.tufts.edu/cgi-bin/vocab?lang=la

  Lists vocab of *Aeneid* by frequency (all, top 90 percent, etc.) and by individual Book. The accompanying Perseus Vocabulary tool lets users set up the parameters of their vocabulary searches within a given author and title.

Word Lists

- Basic Latin Vocabulary (in order of frequency in classical Latin) (Prof. R.O. Fink)

  http://www.wfu.edu/-ulery/VOCABULARY.htm.

Lists of 999 Latin words in Excel format (no lexical information or meanings).

- The Fourteen Hundred (Laura Gilmore, Danville High, Danville, PA)

  http://www.quia.com/pages/1400latin.html

  Quia games with 1400 basic words divided into 14 installments.

- FreeLatin Website (Tom McCarthy)

  http://www.perlingua.com/LatinHome/LatVocab/LatVocab.htm

  Includes Diederich's *First 300 Latin Words in Order of Frequency* (1938), in both card and list form.

- Latin Vocabulary: High Frequency Latin Word Forms, roughly in order of frequency (2nd ed.) (Claude Pavur, St. Louis Univ.)

  http://www.slu.edu/colleges/AS/languages/classical/latin/tchmat/grammar/vocabulary/hif-ed2.html.

  Words are listed in frequencies of 3000's, e.g., 1–3000, 3001–6000, etc., to 18,653 (u = v, j = i). Does not include Vergil, but does includes post-classical sources. No lexical information.

- Latin Wordstock (Sumair Mirza and Jason Tsang)

  http://www.classicsunveiled.com/romevd/html/vocabmain.html

  Easy Latin words organized into four alphabetized groups; each group contains six identifications of a Latin or English word or cognate, with clickable answers. Includes derivatives.

- 1000 Essential Latin Words, Grouped by Frequency (ancienthistory.about.com website),

  http://ancienthistory.about.com/gi/dynamic/offsite.htm?site=http%3A%2F%2Fwww.perseus.tufts.edu%2F%7Eamahoney%2Flatin_vocab.pdf.

  No lexical information.

- 125 Hard Little Words (Jerard White, Franklin Road Academy, Nashville, TN)

  http://www.frapanthers.com/teachers/white/pdfs/hard_little_words.pdf

  Alphabetized list of Latin prepositions, adverbs, and conjunctions, with meanings.

- Two Hundred Essential Latin Words (more or less) (Anne Mahoney, Boston University)

  http://www.bu.edu/mahoa/vocab200.html

  Alphabetized lists of Latin words by part of speech; derived from common prose authors.

Flashcards

- Flashcard Exchange

  http://www.flashcardexchange.com/tag/aeneid

Create your own flashcards online or share those of other students. Use the keyword "Aeneid." For another website on which you can create our own flashcards, go to The Latin Lexicon.

- Aeneid Flashcard Set (Quizlet, Brainflare, Inc.)

  http://quizlet.com/subject/aeneid/.

  Many teacher-produced vocabulary flashcard and other activities, starting with tasks titled Familiarize, Learn, and Test, followed by various games, such as Scatter and Space Race; includes voice recognition activities (Voice Race, Voice Scatter). Printable flashcards.

- Those Annoying Little Words ("Magistra," Seymour, IN)

  http://www.quia.com/jfc/355750.html

  Online flashcard drill over 50 adverbs, conjunctions, and prepositions.

  See also:

- Latin Scrabble (The Pixie Pit, via J.W. Spear and Son PLC, and Hasbro, Inc.)

  http://thepixiepit.co.uk/scrabble/latin.htm

  Online Scrabble in Latin (and 11 other languages), for 2–4 players (e-mail addresses and monetary subscription required).

Word Formation in Latin

Print

- Donald M. Ayers, Thomas D. Worthen, R.L. Cherry, *English Words from Latin and Greek Elements,* Univ. Arizona, 1986, 2nd ed., revised. A standard college text, with workbook.
- Harvey and Johannah Bluedorn, *Vocabulary Bridges from English to Latin and Greek,* Trivium Pursuit, 2001. Good for homeschoolers.
- William J. Dominik, *Words and Ideas*, Bolchazy-Carducci, 2002. Etymology text organized by the contexts in which the words are found, e.g., myth, medicine, politics and law, etc.
- Elizabeth Osborne, Paul Moliken, Larry Knox, *Vocabulary from Latin and Greek Roots,* Prestwick House, Inc., 2003, six books. Organized by word families.
- Timothy Rasinski, Nancy Padak, Rick M., Ph.D. Newton, Evangeline, *Greek and Latin Roots: Keys to Building Vocabulary*, Shell Education Pub., 2008. Designed for young students, but a useful tool for any language student and teacher.
- Waldo E. Sweet, Glenn M. Knudsvig, *A Course on Words*, Univ. Michigan Press, 1989. A high school and college workbook on the subject, written by two distinguished classicists.

Websites

- Greek and Latin Elements in English (Wikipedia)

  http://en.wikipedia.org/wiki/Greek_and_Latin_roots_in_English

  List of prefixes and roots, with English meanings and examples.
- Latin Derivatives: English Words from Latin (Eugene R. Moutoux, Eastern High School, Louisville, KY)

  http://www.geocities.com/gene_moutoux/latinderivatives.htm

  1750 derivatives used in original English sentences, with appropriate Latin lexical information. Includes printout quizzes.
- Vocabula: An Autodidactic Course in Latin Vocabulary Building (Prof. Emerita C.A.E. Luschnig, Univ. Idaho)

  http://www.class.uidaho.edu/luschnig/Latin%20Vocab/Index.htm

  Four alphabetized Latin to English wordlists plus exercises based on sayings, quotations, and mottoes; vocabulary based on Wheelock and Colby.

Resources for Building a Vergilian Vocabulary

Print

- "Four Approaches to the AP Latin Curriculum" (Jo Green, Westlake High School, Austin, TX), *Teacher's Guide to AP Latin*, pp. 111–112. Vocabulary tips and suggestions for vocabulary games for AP Latin.

Online

- AP Vergil's *Aeneid* (Timothy S. Abney, Marquette High School, Chesterfield, MO)

  For flashcard activities in the vocabulary section, organized alphabetically by Latin word in Pharr's general vocabulary, go to

  http://abney.homestead.com/aeneid.html#anchor_13111.
- AP Vergil Wordlist (Dennis De Young, Montgomery Bell Academy, Nashville, TN) http://home.montgomerybell.edu/-deyound/ and

  http://home.montgomerybell.com/%7Edeyound/2005Vergillist.doc

  Contains an alphabetized list of all Latin words, with meanings (but no lexical information), for those passages specific to the AP Latin syllabus. After the general wordlist there are three word frequency lists: words used 15 times or more, 9–14 times, and 5–8 times.
- *Aeneid* Vocabulary: words used over 50 times (Ruth Sameth, Monacan High School, Richmond, VA)

  http://www.quia.com/jg/46150.html

Typical *Quia* activities, such as matching, flashcards, Concentration, and word search.

- "Vocabulary Building" (Ginny Lindzey, An Unofficial Website for AP Latin)

  http://txclassics.org/old/teachingap.htm

  Feedback from teachers, via the AP Latin EDG, on how best to help Vergil students build their vocabulary. Includes link to De Young's list (see above).

Quia Vocab Builders for the *Aeneid*

For the *Quia* Latin site, go to http://www.quia.com/shared/latin.

http://latinresources.homestead.com/apvergil.html (Dr. Melissa Schons Bishop, Creative Classical Curriculum, Orlando, FL)

"Magic lists" of vocab with meanings for each of the required Latin portions of the *Aeneid* and http://www.quia.com/pages/apv.html

Eight sets of Java games on vocab.

http://www.quia.com/pages/danvillelatinap.html (Magistra Gilmore, Milton Area School District, Milton, PA)

Sets of Java games on the required lines of Book 1 and part of 2.

http://www.quia.com/pages/wcslatapvergil.html (Virginia Kehoe, Wichita Collegiate School, Wichita, KS)

Chapter vocabulary of the LaFleur text, as well as Pharr/Boyd's general vocab.

http://www.quia.com/pages/drippingvergil.html (Ginny Lindzey, Dripping Springs High School, Dripping Springs, TX)

Vocabulary activities for the LaFleur text.

http://www.quia.com/pages/pvilatin4drills.html (Magistra Lukes, St.Paul VI Catholic High School)

Vocabulary activities for the Pharr/Boyd general vocabulary and for the LaFleur text.

http://www.quia.com/pages/maretvergil.html (Magistra McGlennon, The Maret School, Washington, DC)

One set of Java games on words that appear in the *Aeneid* more than 23 times.

http://www.quia.com/pages/aeneid.html (Mr. Odhner, Academy of the New Church, Bryn Athyn, PA)

Vocabulary of Book 1, in installments, and small parts of Books 2 and 4.

http://www.quia.com/pages/latinapvergil.html (Ruth Sameth, Monacan High School, Richmond, VA)

Vocabulary by each of two semesters, plus some additional vocabularies, incl. several for the LaFleur text.

Quizlet Vocab Builders for the *Aeneid*

http://quizlet.com/928015/latin-ap-voc-review-flash-cards/ (Larka)

General vocabulary review (176 words, random)

http://quizlet.com/885449/aeneid-book-one-jupiter-venus-speech-vocab-flash-cards/ (raquelagr)

Book 1, Jupiter-Venus speech vocab (27 words, E-L)

http://quizlet.com/788006/aeneid-vocabulary-part-ii-flash-cards/ (crslocke)

Aeneid vocabulary Part II (79 words, E-L)

http://quizlet.com/973169/latin-vi-aeneid-1–final-vocab-flash-cards/ (raquelagr)

Book 1 (76 words)

http://quizlet.com/540295/aeneid-vocab-book-2–flash-cards/ (Larke)

Book 2 (189 words and forms)

http://quizlet.com/121299/latin-vocab-ii-199–297–469–566–735–804–flash-cards/ (JZang 21)

Sections of Book 2 (112 words)

http://quizlet.com/1045640/the-aeneid-terms-a-h-flash-cards/ (QuietChivalry)

Words A-H (101 words)

Chapter 5
The Free-Response Section: Translation

Resources for Translating Latin

Print

- "Four Approaches to the AP Latin Curriculum" (Jo Green, Westlake High School, Austin, TX), *Teacher's Guide to AP Latin*, pp. 113–114. Games for reading and translating.
- B. Dexter Hoyos 1, "Cutting Down (Out?) Translation in Latin," *Texas Classics in Action* (Summer, 1997), pp. 14–25.
- B. Dexter Hoyos 2, *Latin – How to Read It Fluently: A Practical Manual,* Classical Association of New England (CANE) Instructional Materials, Univ. Massachusetts, Amherst, MA, 1997.
- B. Dexter Hoyos 3, "Translating: Facts, Illusions, Alternatives," *Committee for the Promotion of Latin (CPL) Online 3.1* (Fall, 2006), pp. 1–12.

- William J. Mayer, "Translating Latin Literally," *Teacher's Guide to AP Latin,* Jeff S. Greenberger, ed., pp. 29–35.
- Daniel V. McCaffrey, "When Reading Latin, Read as the Romans Did," *Classical Outlook* (Winter, 2009), Vol. 86, No. 2, pp. 62–66.
- Mary Pendergraft, "The Grading of the 2008 Advanced Placement Examinations in Latin: Vergil," *Classical Outlook* (Winter 2009), Vol. 86, No. 2, pp. 49–60.
- David Perry, "Using the Reading Approach in Secondary Schools," *Latin for the 21st Century: From Concept to Classroom,* Richard A. Lafleur, ed., Scott Foresman, Addison Wesley, Glenview, IL, 1998, pp. 105–116.
- Karen Lee Singh, "Grammar Translation in High School," *Latin for the 21st Century: From Concept to Classroom,* Richard A. Lafleur, ed., Scott Foresman, Addison Wesley, Glenview, IL, 1998, pp. 90–104.
- David West, "How to Read a Bit of Latin," *Didaskalos* 3, 3 (1971), pp. 110–115.

Online

- Latinteach.org

  http://www.latinteach.com/Site/RESOURCES/Entries/2009/2/11_Latin_Language_Teaching_Methodologies.html and http://www.latinteach.com/Site/RESOURCES/Entries/2008/5/20_Teaching_Latin_Grammar.html

Computer Software for Translating Latin

Note: these software programs are commercial, but academic in intent. Avoid commercial websites that offer translators or translation services!

- *Lectrix* is a software program designed to assist in teaching the translation of Latin literature, including Vergil's *Aeneid,* Book 9. Although this program does not accommodate the passages required for the AP Latin program, it does provide valuable resources for practice with sight reading. Published by Cambridge Greek and Latin Classics (CGLC), *Lectrix* contains a Latin hypertext that correlates with a dictionary and parser, plus separate panes with commentary and a newly-commissioned English translation that can be opened at the user's discretion. For an overview, go to http://cambridge.org/online/lectrix/default.htm.
- *QuickLatin* is a "Latin-to-English translation assistant" (not a translator) that contains a dictionary and parsing capabilities, plus some sentence-handling abilities. The vocabulary is based on William Whitaker's *Words* 1.97 Latin to English dictionary program, for which see the Appendix for Chapter 4. Go to http://www.quicklatin.com. See also the Latin translation assistant for Whitaker's *Words* at http://www.inrebus.com/assistant.php. Free download of interface.

Chapter 6
The Free-Response Section—
The Long and Short Essays

Resources for Writing Essays

Note: Although some of the resources cited below are more appropriate for English than for Latin, there is some value in looking at the broader context of poetic analysis.

Recommended Print Resources for Poetic Analysis in English

- Edward Hirsch, *How to Read a Poem and Fall in Love with Poetry*, A Harvest Book, Harcourt, Inc., San Diego, CA, 1999.
- Laurence Perrine and Thomas R. Arp, *Sound and Sense: An Introduction to Poetry*, 8th ed., Harcourt Brace College Publishers, Fort Worth, TX, 1992.
- John R. Trimble, *Writing with Style: Conversations on the Art of Writing*, 2nd ed., Prentice Hall, Upper Saddle River, NJ, 2000.

See online:

- Questions to Ask of Any Poem (George Mason University Writing Center) http://www.gmu.edu/departments/writingcenter/handouts/poetry.html

Writing an Effective Essay in English

- The Writing Center Guide to Taking Essay Tests (George Mason University Writing Center)

  http://www.gmu.edu/departments/writingcenter/handouts/essaytes.html
- Writing Tips: In-Class Essay Exams (Univ. Illinois at Champaign-Urbana)

  http://www.english.uiuc.edu/cws/wworkshop/writer_resources/writing_tips/in-class_essay_exams.html

Analysis of Latin Poetry

Print

- William S. Anderson, *The Art of the Aeneid*, 2nd ed., Bolchazy-Carducci, Inc., 2005. Excellent Book-by-Book analysis of Vergil's style.
- Richard Heinze, Fred Robertson, ed., *Vergil's Epic Technique*, 2nd ed. (first written in German in 1903, but still useful), Duckworth Publishers, 2004.
- Gilbert Highet, with introduction by Michael C. J. Putnam, *Poets in a Landscape*, NYRB Classics, 2010. An engaging look at Roman poets and how their Italian environments affected both their lives and their writing.

- Roger A. Hornsby, *Patterns of Action in the Aeneid: An Interpretation of Vergil's Epic Similes*, Univ. Iowa Press, 1970.
- W.R. Johnson, *Darkness Visible: A Study of Vergil's Aeneid,* new edition, Univ. California Press, 1979. Authoritative discussion of Vergilian imagery and its Greek models.
- Brooks Otis, Virgil: *A Study in Civilized Poetry*, Univ. Oklahoma Press, 1995.
- Viktor Poschl, *The Art of Vergil: Image and Symbol in the Aeneid*, translated by Gerda Seligson, Greenwood Press reprint, new edition, 1986. Brief but imaginative discussion of Vergilian imagery.
- Kenneth Quinn, *Virgil's Aeneid: A Critical Description*, reprinted by Bristol Phoenix Press, Univ. Exeter, 1968/2006. A "critical description of the *Aeneid's* structure and aspects of its composition," including a detailed analysis of each Book.

Collections of Essays

- Steele Commager, ed., *Virgil: A Collection of Critical Essays*, Prentice Hall, 1967. Includes 12 articles from books and journals. Those by Clausen, Parry, Knox, and Brooks have become must-reads for Vergil students.
- Stephanie Quinn, ed., *Why Vergil? A Collection of Interpretations*, Bolchazy-Carducci, 2000. Contains a large number of articles and excerpts on Vergilian themes.
- S.J. Harrison, ed., *Oxford Readings in Vergil's Aeneid*, Oxford Univ. Press, 1990. A collection of essays by British scholars of Vergil, representing a broad range of recent criticism on the *Aeneid*.

Essay Writing on the AP Latin Exam

Print

- Jill Crooker, "Teaching Short Essay Writing Skills," *Teacher's Guide – AP Latin*, Jeff S. Greenberger, ed., The College Board, n.d., pp. 37–41. Some techniques helpful for writing essays.
- Sally Davis, "Answering an AP Exam Essay Question," *Teacher's Guide – AP Latin*, Jeff S. Greenberger, ed., The College Board, n.d., pp. 43–49. The application of SWIMTAG to a passage from Ovid.

Online

- Sally Davis, SWIMTAG (Kentucky Educational Television, Joan Jahnige) http://www.dl.ket.org/latinlit/carmina/terminology/swimtag.htm, also available at the Davis website, http://www.latinamagistra.com/swimtag.pdf, or at http://www.magisterwebb.com/ma/swimtag.pdf

- Ginny Lindzey, "Teaching AP: Teaching Tips: Essay Writing Skills," (An Unofficial Website for AP Latin, Texas Classical Association)

  http://txclassics.org/old/teachingap.htm

  Feedback from AP teachers on the subject, including SWIMTAG.
- Linda Montross, "How to Write a Critical Essay on Latin Poetry" (Kentucky Educational Television, Joan Jahnige) http://www.dl.ket.org/latinlit/carmina/terminology/howtowrite.htm

Chapter 7 The Free-Response Section— The Global Question

Print

- "Four Approaches to the AP Latin Curriculum" (Jo Green, Westlake High School, Austin, TX), *Teacher's Guide to AP Latin*, pp. 116–117. Contains a list of fourteen ideas for Latin projects on the content of Books 7–12 of the *Aeneid.*

Print and Online Resources on Epic Poetry

Print

- Charles Rowan Beye, *Ancient Epic Poetry*, 2nd ed., Bolchazy-Carducci, Mundelein, IL, 2006. The classic work on the subject; includes chapters on Homer, Apollonius, Vergil, Gilgamesh.
- John Miles Foley, *A Companion to Ancient Epic* (Blackwell Companions to the Ancient World), Wiley-Blackwell, 2008.
- Katherine Callen King, *Ancient Epic* (Blackwell Introductions to the Classical World), Wiley-Blackwell, 2009.

Online

- *Aeneid* (Roger Dunkle, Classics Technology Center, Ablemedia)

  http://ablemedia.com/ctcweb/netshots/vergil.htm

  Hypertext discussion of literary epic; historical background for Vergil; comments and questions on reading the *Aeneid* as an epic poem.
- Classical Epic (Eugene Cotter, Seton Hall University)

  http://pirate.shu.edu/~cottereu/outlines.htm#Aeneid%20Topics

  Resources for a college course in classical epic (outlines of topics and questions on the *Iliad, Odyssey*, and *Aeneid*).

- Classical Epic (Robin Mitchell-Boyask, Temple Univ.)

  http://www.temple.edu/classics/epicsyl03.html and epic.html

  Course syllabus and links to background resources for Homer, Apollonius, Vergil, et al. See also the course syllabus for "The Epic Tradition" (Rob S. Rice, Univ. Pennsylvania), http://ccat.sas.upenn.edu/rrice/clas160.html.

- The Epic Hero: Common Elements in Most Cultures (Bruce M. Johnson, Park View High School)

  http://www.hoocher.com/theepichero.htm

Homer's *Iliad* and *Odyssey*, and the Story of Troy

Film

- Documentary series *In Search of the Trojan War* (Michael Wood, 1985, six episodes), with now-updated companion book by the same title (Univ. California Press, 1998).
- Feature length film *Troy* (2004, 2 hrs., 43 mins.)

Print

- Barry Strauss, *The Trojan War: A New History*, Simon and Schuster, 2006. A readable history of Troy, incorporating new interpretations and recent theories.

Online

- Wikipedia hypertext article on Homer

  http://en.wikipedia.org/wiki/Homer;

  for the Trojan War, see http://en.wikipedia.org/wiki/Trojan_War

- Yahoo/Geocities site on Homer and Troy

  http://www.geocities.com/Pentagon/Quarters/2471/Troy.html#Troy

  Comprehensive hypertext archaeological and literary history of Troy, glossaries of gods and goddesses and Greeks and Trojans, images.

- The Aftermath: post-*Iliad* through the *Odyssey* (Donna Patrick, et al., Ablemedia, Classics Technology Center)

  http://ablemedia.com/ctcweb/consortium/aftermathpath.html

  Multi-resource exercise takes students from the death of Patroclus in the *Iliad* to Odysseus' arrival in Ithaca. Links to illustrations and lines in Homer (Samuel Butler's translation at Perseus).

- The Historical World Behind the Trojan War (Wilfred E. Major)

  http://home.att.net/~a.a.major/waroutline.html

  Nicely illustrated, with competent discusson.

- Homer in a Changing Tradition (William Harris, Middlebury College)

  http://community.middlebury.edu/~harris/Humanities/homer.html

  Nine-part essay covering topics in Homeric scholarship.

- The Legend of the Trojan War (Ian Johnston, Malaspina University-College, Nanaimo, British Columbia, CAN)

  http://www.mala.bc.ca/~johnstoi/clas101/troy.htm

  Prose outline of the events of the Trojan War up to the escape of Aeneas; includes "The Cultural Influence of the Legend of the Trojan War."

- Mortal Women of the Trojan War (Stanford Univ.)

  http://www.stanford.edu/~plomio/history.html

  A quick-study, with links to mini-biographies of mortal women appearing in the epics.

- Pages on the Trojan War and on Troy (Greek Mythology Link, Carlos Parada)

  http://homepage.mac.com/cparada/GML/index.html

  Go to Section VII for links to a number of interesting articles covering topics during and after the Trojan War.

- The Sequence of Major Events in the Trojan War (N.S. Gill, ancienthistory.about.com)

  http://ancienthistory.about.com/cs/troyilium/a/trojanwar.htm

  Includes a good collection of links on various Homeric questions and a review of the movie *Troy.* See also the ancienthistory.about.com site http://ancienthistory.about.com/od/troyilium/Trojan_War_From_Helen_of_Troy_to_Homer_and_Schliemann.htm.

- Troy VIIa and the Historicity of the Trojan War (Lesson 27, Prehistoric Archaeology of the Aegean, Dartmouth Univ.)

  http://projectsx.dartmouth.edu/history/bronze_age/lessons/les/27.html

  A brief discussion of the evidence and of possible alternate locations of Troy. See also http://www.historywiz.com/trojanwar.htm.

- ThinkQuest Website on Homer's *Iliad* and *Odyssey* (Tony Arkwright, et al.)

  http://library.thinkquest.org/19300/data/homer.htm

  Includes interactive "Virtual *Iliad*" and "Virtual *Odyssey*"; useful background information on Homer.

- The Trojan War: Mythological Background (Bruce M. Johnson, Park View High School)

  http://www.hoocher.com/trojanwar.htm

  Outline of major episodes in the *Iliad* and *Aeneid*, esp. those involving gods and goddesses.

The Trojan War Illustrated

- Images of the Trojan War Myth (Robin Mitchell-Boyask, Temple Univ.)

  http://www.temple.edu/classics/troyimages.html

  Links to Greek pottery paintings illustrating events before, during, and after the War.

- The Trojan War: An Illustrated Companion

  http://www.philipresheph.com/demodokos/index.htm

  Engaging collection of ancient and modern paintings, sculpture, etc., organized by topic. Click on the painting on the homepage. The section on Aeneas is under construction.

- The Trojan War (B. Precourt, Univ. Wisconsin-Milwaukee)

  http://www.uwm.edu/Course/mythology/1100/twar1.htm

  Competent narrative, interspersed with pottery and paintings, both ancient and modern.

  Support for a college course on classical mythology.

The Underworld

- The Underworld (Joan Jahnige, Kentucky Educational Television)

  http://www.dl.ket.org/latin1/mythology/1deities/underworld/intro.htm

  Includes links to characters and places, with some illustrations.

- "The Underworld Adventure of Aeneas in the *Aeneid*" and "*Aeneid* VI: Hades' Realm" (about.com) http://ancienthistory.about.com/library/weekly/aa082200a.htm

  With glossary entries, links to related subjects, and information on the corresponding passages in the *Odyssey*

The Augustan Age

- Rome: The Age of Augustus (Richard Hooker, Washington State Univ.)

  http://www.wsu.edu/~dee/ROME/AUGUSTUS.HTM

  Brief overview, with links to discussions of **pietas** and **virtus**.

- Augustus: Images of Power (Mark Morford, Univ. Virginia)

  http://etext.virginia.edu/users/morford/augimage.html

  Pictures and brief discussions of the visual symbols of Augustan propaganda: the Augustan mausoleum, the *Ara Pacis*, the Prima Porta statue of Augustus, and the *Gemma Augustea.*

- Caesar Augustus, An Annotated Guide to Online Resources (David Wilson-Okamura, virgil.org)

  http://virgil.org/augustus

Links to primary sources (incl. the *Res gestae*), to articles on many topics of the Augustan Age, recent historical fiction, et al. For the Latin text of the *Res gestae*, see also http://www.csun.edu/-hcfll004/resgest.html.

- The Emergence of the Augustan Age (Bruce M. Johnson, Park View High School)

  http://www.hoocher.com/theemergenceoftheaugustanage.htm

  Convenient chronological outline of events in Roman history from the death of Caesar to 29 B.C.

- A Literary History of the Augustan Age (Bruce M. Johnson, Park View High School)

  http://www.hoocher.com/literaryhistory.htm

- Patron Augustus-Client Rome (Sondra Steinbrenner, ancienthistory.about.com)

  http://ancienthistory.about.com/gi/dynamic/offsite.htm?site=http://roman%2Dempire.net/articles/article%2D010.html

  Excellent exploration of the symbols of Augustan *auctoritas*.

- Princeps: The Life of Augustus Caesar (Suzanne Cross)

  http://web.mac.com/heraklia/Augustus

  Recent and thoroughgoing online appreciation of Octavian/Augustus. Good collection of links. For more of these, see http://www.csun.edu/-hcfll004/histlink.html.

- Rome: Republic to Empire (Barbara F. McManus, VRoma)

  http://www.vroma.org/-bmcmanus/romanpages.html

  Illustrated synopsis of the historical background of Augustan rule, via articles "Antony, Octavian, and Cleopatra" and "Augustus and Tiberius."

Chapter 8
Techniques of Poetic Analysis—Figures of Speech

The following sites are by and for English students, but are also useful to Latin students. Be advised, however, that not all figures of speech in English have exact equivalents in Latin, and vice versa.

Figures of Speech in English

- Literary Terms (maintained by students in Ted Nellen's high school Cyber English class)

  http://www.tnellen.com/cybereng/lit_terms/

- Virtual Salt: A Handbook of Rhetorical Devices (Robert A. Harris)

  http://www.virtualsalt.com/rhetoric.htm

  Thorough list, with numerous examples in English and a self-test. Produced by a writer.

General Reference Websites for Figures of Speech in AP Latin

- Chiasmus, at Latin via Proverbs (Laura Gibbs, Univ. Oklahoma)
  http://latinviaproverbs.pbworks.com/Chiasmus

  Contains an interesting method of learning chiasmus, i.e., via proverbs, e.g., **Mors sequitur, fugit vita**.
- Chiasmus: Correspondence and Reversal http://grammatice.blogspot.com/2009/05/chiasmus-correspondence-and-reversal.html An extremely thorough explication of the figure, with many examples.
- Chiasmus at DrMardy.com (Dr. Mardy Grothe)
  http://www.drmardy.com/chiasmus/definition.shtml.

  Dr. Mardy's site for "lovers of wit and wordplay" includes a whole series of pages devoted just to chiasmus (in English): He explains here the ABBA designation often used by classicists.
- Figures of Speech (Bruce M. Johnson, teacher's website)
  http://www.hoocher.com/figuresofspeech.htm

  Definitions of required figures, with examples mostly from Catullus and the *Aeneid.*
- Flashcard Exchange
  http://flashcarddb.com/cardset/7255–latin-rhetorical-devices-and-figures-of-speech-flashcards

  Definitions of 37 terms, designed for Catullus, but helpful for Vergil.
- Glossary of Rhetorical Terms with Examples (Ross Scaife, Univ. Kentucky)
  http://www.uky.edu/AS/Classics/rhetoric.html

  Twenty-six of the 34 figures required by the College Board are found here, with English and Latin examples.
- Interpreting Poetry (Joan Johnige, Kentucky Educational Television)
  http://www.dl.ket.org/latinlit/carmina/index.htm

  Click on "Interpreting Poetry," then "Rhetorical Terms." Definitions of 25 terms, with examples from Catullus and Horace. Includes caesura, diaeresis, hiatus.
- Literary Devices (Jerard White, teacher's AP Latin Website)
  http://www.frapanthers.com/teachers/white/literary_devices.htm

  Figures are designated as AP or non-AP; includes the 34 for AP, plus anastrophe, caesura, elision, framing, the golden line, hiatus, rhetorical question, and syzygy.
- Betsy Prueter's Literary Devices (teacher's website)
  http://www.prueter.org/bill/literarydevices.html

  Thirty-seven terms, with English and Latin examples. Includes caesura, homeoteleuton, and "peripaty."

- Silvae Rhetoricae (Gideon O. Burton, Brigham Young University)

  http://humanities.byu.edu/rhetoric/Figures/Figures-Overview.htm

  Contains a useful search engine (Search the Forest); English and Latin examples, categorized.

Activities and *Quia* Games for Mastering Figures of Speech in Latin

For *Quia* activities in Latin, go to http:www.quia.com/shared/latin; there is a link to all activities at the bottom of the page.

- AP Vergil's *Aeneid* (Tim Abney, AP Vergil Website)

  Figures of Speech Definitions

  http://abney.homestead.com/files/aeneid/tropedefinitioncards.htm

  Clickable exercises that ask for definitions of 22 figures.

  See also AP Vergil website main page,

  http://abney.homestead.com/aeneid.html

  Click-and-drag matching exercises for many figures found in the required Books of the *Aeneid*, Book by Book, and praise for a good score. A valuable resource!

  See also Flashcards: Figures of Speech in the *Aeneid*, http://abney.homestead.com/files/aeneid/aeneidtropeflashcards1.htm

  Identify the Latin example in the pop-up window.

- Figures of Speech Exercises (Linda Fleming, St. Thomas Episcopal School, Houston, TX)

  http://ablemedia.com/ctcweb/consortium/figuresofspeechintro.html

  Activities for the first half of Book 2. See also Figures of Syntax Exercises and Figures of Rhetoric Exercises. Matching figures with definitions and with Latin examples and for the first half of Book 2. With answers.

- *Aeneid*, Book 1, Figures of Speech (Magistra Hynes, Catholic Memorial, Boston, MA)

  http://www.quia.com/jg/578774.html

  Concentration, flashcards, matching, word search on poetic devices.

- *Quia* (Ruth Sameth, Monacan High School, Richmond, VA)

  http://www.quia.com/jg/11339.html

  Concentration, flashcards, matching, word search on poetic devices. See also Hangman (Mrs. Maida, Creekside Intermediate School, Houston, TX)

  http://www.quia.com/hm/80390.html

- Dripping Vergil (Ginny Lindzey, Dripping Springs High School, TX)

  http://www.quia.com/pages/drippingvergil.html

An excellent site with a huge number of links to *Quia* activities and games, most for the LaFleur text of the *Aeneid*, including engaging Viqua hidden picture games. Covers content, vocabulary, figures of speech, quizzes on sets of lines (but not on entire Books). Many links to additional useful websites.

- Rhetorical Devices (in the *Aeneid*) (Magistra Higley, Pequannock High, Pompton Plains, NJ)

  http://www.quia.com/jg/424704.html

  Concentration, flashcards, matching, word search on poetic devices.

- Rhetorical Devices (in the *Aeneid*) (Magistra McGlennon, Maret School, Washington, DC)

  http://www.quia.com/jg/518288.html

  Concentration, flashcards, matching, word search on poetic devices.

  Also, Concentration, flashcards, matching, word search on poetic devices. Vergil-Figures of Syntax and Rhetoric, http://www.quia.com/hm/169239.html and http://www.quia.com/hm/301630.html (both pages have Hangman)

- Rhetorical Devices (in the *Aeneid*) (Mr. Odhner, Academy of the New Church, Bryn Athyn, PA)

  http://www.quia.com/jg/591066.html

  Concentration, flashcards, matching, word search on poetic devices.

- Vergil-Figures of Syntax and Rhetoric (Dr. Melissa Schons Bishop, Creative Classical Curriculum, Orlando, FL)

  http://www.quia.com/hm/235647.html

  Hangman.

Chapter 9
Techniques of Poetic Analysis—Meter and Scansion

Pronunciation of Latin

The standard reference book on the subject is W. Sidney Allen, *Vox Latina: A Guide to the Pronunciation of Classical Latin*, 2nd ed., Cambridge Univ. Press, 2008.

- On the Importance of Macrons in Latin Instruction (Richard LaFleur, Latinteach article)

  http://latinteach.com/Site/ARTICLES/Entries/2008/9/4_Richard_LaFleur_-_On_the_Importance_of_Macrons_in_Latin_Instruction.html

  On the importance of achieving correct pronunciation in learning Latin.

- Latin-Pronunciaton (N.S. Gill, About.com guide for Latin)

  http://ancienthistory.about.com/od/pronunciation/Latin_Pronunciation.htm

  A short series of links to websites on the subject, including stress vs. intonation. The linked article Latin Pronunciation Demystified (Michael A. Conington, Univ. Georgia) is worth a look.

- Latin Course for the Virtual School of Languages (free online Latin course at Sprachprofi, after Judith Meyer, Cursus Novus Compactus)

  http://www.sprachprofi.de.vu/

Reading the *Aeneid* Aloud

Clive Brooks, *Reading Latin Poetry Aloud: A Practical Guide to Two Thousand Years of Verse,* with two audio CDs. Cambridge Univ. Press, 2007. See also, *Latin Aloud* (Emeritus Professor Robert P. Sonkowsky, Bolchazy-Carducci, 2007), 101 Latin Masterworks read on CD using the Restored Classical Pronunciation. Includes all AP Vergil selections. For a sample audio-file of *Aeneid* 2.40–56, go to http://www.bolchazy.com/prod.php?cat=latin&id=00007. See also the Society for the Oral Reading of Greek and Latin Literature (SORGLL) at http://www.rhapsodes.fll.vt.edu/ (*Aeneid,* Books 1.1–49 and 4.296–396).

- "*Aeneid* 0 (Zero)" (Anthony Gibbins, Sydney, Australia)

  http://www.eclassics.ning.com

  Introduction to an on-going attempt by a Latin teacher to read the entire *Aeneid* in Latin; see also TuTubusLatinus on YouTube. Includes Latin text and an interesting lesson in translating *Aeneid* 1.195–197.

- The Harvard Classics Poetry Recital site (Tom Jenkins, Trinity Univ., San Antonio, TX) http://www.fas.harvard.edu/-classics/poetry_and_prose/poetry.html

  Oral recitations by Wendell Clausen, et al., in Latin, from Books 1 (1–11, 195–207, 588–610), 4 (331–361), 6 (12–41, 15–204, and 450–474), 12 (926b-952). Quicktime and RealPlayer.

- Hear the *Aeneid!* (Tim Abney's AP Vergil Website)

  http://abney.homestead.com/aeneid.html.

  Contains links to many of the other websites listed here.

- Hexametrica: An Introduction to Latin Hexameter Verse (Dan Curley, Skidmore College)

  http://www.skidmore.edu/academics/classics/courses/metrica/scansion.html

  Thorough presentation of all aspects of the hexameter line; geared toward students of Vergil. Best website on the subject. Contains audio component to illustrate points about scansion.

- Reading Latin Poetry: Reading Latin Verse Aloud: Metre and Scansion (Andrew Wilson, The Classics Pages), http://www.users.globalnet.co.uk/-loxias/latinverse.htm

  A few of the basics on hexameter, plus some lines of Vergil read aloud in meter; RealAudio.

- Vergil's *Aeneid* (read by Wilfried Stroh)

  http://wiredforbooks.org/aeneid/

  Book 4; RealAudio, MP3 file.

- Viva Voce: Roman Poetry Recited (by Vojin Nedeljkovic)

  http://web.archive.org/web/20070205171203/dekart.f.bg.ac.yu/-vnedeljk/VV/VergA4–9.mp3

  Book 4.9–29, with Latin text; MP3 file.

- Why I Read Latin Aloud (Laura Gibbs, latinviaproverbs.com)

  http://latinviaproverbs.pbworks.com/audio

  A brief diatribe on the subject.

  See also:

  Toddler Reads Latin Aloud (eclassics website)

  http://eclassics.ning.com/video/727885:Video:4408

  Improving Your Latin Listening Skills (David de Padua)

  http://eclassics.ning.com/video/727885:Video:4406

  Impressive video presentation by a Philippine student.

  Nuntii Latini (Finnish Broadcasting Company, YLE Radio 1, since 1989)

  http://www.yleradio1.fi/nuntii/

  Weekly review of world news in classical Latin, with an English translation. RealAudio.

Websites on Latin Meter and Scansion

- For a basic online introduction to the topic, see the Wikipedia article "Latin Poetry,"

  http://en.wikipedia.org/wiki/Latin_poetry

- A Brief Guide to Quantity of Latin Syllables in Latin Prosody (Later Latin Society)

  http://www.informalmusic.com/latinsoc/syllable.html

  Very thorough catalogue of quantities by individual syllable.

- Guides for Interpreting Poetry (Joan Jahnige)

  http://www.dl.ket.org/latinlit/carmina/terminology/

  Includes links to scansion rules and terminology, and rules for elision; focus on lyric.

- How to Read Latin Poetry (William Harris, Middlebury College)
  http://community.middlebury.edu/~harris/LatinBackground/PoetryandReadingVerse.html
  A rather genteel article on the subject by an emeritus professor.
- How to Scan Poetry in Latin (A teacher-produced PowerPoint presentation, Orange County Public Schools network, Orlando, FL))
  http://teacher.ocps.net/jodi.katz/media/howtoscanpoetryinlatin.ppt
  A step-by-step description; the lack of directions is a bit off-putting for someone inexperienced in using PowerPoint, but be patient.
- Scansion of Poetic Meter (Jerard White, Franklin Road Academy, Nashville, TN)
  http://www.frapanthers.com/teachers/white/scansion.htm#dactylic
  A very quick study. See also,
  http://www.frapanthers.com/teachers/white/pdfs/vergil/dactylic_aen_1_1-4.pdf
  Printable pdf worksheet for scanning the first four lines of the *Aeneid*, Book 1.
- Scansion Rules, Guides and Techniques (N.S. Gill, About.com guide) http://ancienthistory.about.com/od/scansion1/Scansion_Rules_Guides_and_Techniques.htm
  Links, esp. Scansion of Latin Poetry. See also, Latin Meter,
  http://ancienthistory.about.com/od/latinlanguage/qt/LatinMeter.htm.

Chapter 10 Resources for Reviewing the *Aeneid*

Quick Studies

- Bookrags
  http://www.bookrags.com/notes/and/SUM.htm
  Contains glossaries of characters, names/places, quotes, articles on the role of gods and goddesses, historical subtexts, omens and prophecies, women, discussion/thought topics, detailed hypertext summaries by book.
- CliffNotes
  http://www.cliffsnotes.com/WileyCDA/LitNote/id-3.html
  Summaries, commentaries, glossaries for each book; a "character map" and character analyses, the *Aeneid* as a national epic; quiz and essay questions.
- PinkMonkey
  http://www.pinkmonkey.com/booknotes/monkeynotes/pmAeneid02.asp
  Book by Book summaries.

- Sparknotes

  http://www.sparknotes.com/lit/aeneid/

  Excellent online quick study of the *Aeneid*: context, plot overview, character list, character analysis, themes and symbols, study questions, quiz.

  Also:

- Wikipedia hypertext article on the *Aeneid*

  http://en.wikipedia.org/wiki/Aeneid

  An excellent quick-study, divided into Journey to Italy (Books 1–6) and War in Italy (Books 7–12), with a map of Aeneas' journey. Good external links.

- Greek Mythology Link (Carlos Parada, s.v. "Aeneas")

  http://homepage.mac.com/cparada/GML/Aeneas.html

  Nice summary of Aeneas's life, with a map of his journeys and a genealogical chart.

  Outlines, Summaries, and Study Guides

- Outline of Vergil's *Aeneid* (Ross Scaife, University of Kentucky)

  http://www.uky.edu/AS/Classics/aeneidout.html

  Book-by-Book outline of the high points, with line numbers; support for a college course on Vergil.

- Study Guide for the *Aeneid* (University of Central Oklahoma)

  http://www.libarts.ucok.edu/english/faculty/spencer/worldlit/aeneid1.html

  Comprehensive synopses of Books 1, 2, 4, and 6. Some humor!

- Vergil Study Guide (Diane Thompson, Northern Virginia Community College)

  http://novaonline.nvcc.edu/eli/eng251/virgilstudy.html

  Includes "Aeneas-A New Kind of Hero," "The Dido Problem-Passion and Politics," "Gods, the Will Of Jupiter, Destiny/Fate." Also, a glossary of characters and deities in the *Aeneid*.

  Maps of Aeneas' Journey (Books 1–6)

- Greek Mythology Link (Carlos Parada)

  http://homepage.mac.com/cparada/GML/Aeneas.html

  Map of Aeneas' journey. See also the Wikipedia website, s.v. "Aeneid."

- Virgil.org (David Wilson Okamura's site)

  http://virgil.org/maps/

  Maps of Aeneas in Italy and the Underworld.

Study Questions and Activities for Reviewing the *Aeneid*

- AP Vergil site (Tim Abney, Marquette High School)

  http://abney.homestead.com/aeneid.html

  Valuable metasite for clickable interactive exercises on content, vocabulary, sight reading, scansion, and figures of speech, by book of the *Aeneid*, including Books 10–12. See also, Virgilius.org (new website by Tim Abney, 2009)

  http://virgilius.org/index.html

  "Bringing Vergil's *Aeneid* to the World Wide Web." Includes 41 useful and active links (but difficult to read) for Vergil and the *Aeneid* and 14 for AP Latin, plus daily quotations, ancient artwork, and figures of speech, and a FAQs section. A special running banner presents *Aeneid* 1.1–7.

- Locus Publicus Linguae Latinae (Jerard White, Franklin Road Academy, Nashville, TN)

  http://www.frapanthers.com/teachers/white/vergil_links.htm

  Teacher's metasite contains links to Latin texts of all passages required for the Vergil Exam, using teacher-produced texts, some useful miscellaneous links, and a chronology of Vergil's life correlating with a chart of contemporary historical events.

- *Aeneid:* Exercises in Reading Comprehension and Interpretation (Roger Dunkle, Ablemedia, Classics Technology Center)

  http://ablemedia.com/ctcweb/netshots/vergil.htm

  Good comments on literary epic and the historical background. Exercise in reading comprehension and interpretation, from Books 1, 2, 4, 6, 8, and 12.

- Quick Summary Outline of the *Aeneid* (Eugene Cotter, Seton Hall University)

  http://pirate.shu.edu/-cottereu/aeneid.htm

  Twelve individual topics and themes, with discussion questions. Click on "Course Outline of the *Aeneid* Topics." Images of Sibyl's cave and Lake Avernus. Nice collection of links, especially to David Wilson-Okamura's Virgil.org map collection.

- Review Questions over the Myths of Early Rome and the *Aeneid* (Jean Alvares, Montclair State University)

  http://chss2.montclair.edu/classics/aeneidetc.htm

  Clickable multiple-choice questions, with answers. The pop-up windows are fun!

- Self-Quiz on Vergil's *Aeneid* (Brooklyn College, CUNY)

  http://academic.brooklyn.cuny.edu/classics/hansen/assign3.htm (Books 1, 2, 4, and 12)

  http://academic.brooklyn.cuny.edu/classic/wilson/core/aeneid6q.htm (Book 6)

  Includes links to Ablemedia ("Study Guide"), cited above. Scroll down until you find what you want (annoying use of color on the background information). Good multiple-choice questions in self-quizzes for Books 1, 2, 4, and 12, with answers.

- Study Guide for Vergil's *Aeneid* (Robin Mitchell-Boyask, Temple University)

  http://www.temple.edu/classics/aeneidho.html

  Analytical review of Books 1–3, 4–6, 7–9, 10–12, via questions and comments.

- Study Guide, The *Aeneid* (William A. Johnson, Univ. Cincinnati)

  http://classics.uc.edu/-johnson/epic/study_guide4.html

  Includes one-sentence capsule summaries, Book by Book; list of principal deities; *precis* of each Book with principal episodes and (new) characters. For even shorter capsule summaries, see http://www.unbsj.ca/arts/classics/courses/clas1502/aenout.html.

- Vergil, *Aeneid*: Study Questions for Books 1–6 (RJS, Columbia University)

  http://humanities.psydeshow.org/reference/aeneid-study-qq-1.htm#

  Questions and suggestions for review, Book by Book, for Books 1–6.

- Virgil's *Aeneid* (David Silverman, Reed College)

  http://academic.reed.edu/humanities/110Tech/Aeneid.html

  FAQs and answers, and basic facts; some useful comments on the *Aeneid* by modern critics.

  Note: For the use of note cards for review of the *Aeneid,* see Jerard White's AP Latin website,

  http://www.frapanthers.com/teachers/white/pdfs/ap_worksheets/vergil_note_cards.pdf.

Quia Games

N.B. Go to http://www.quia.com/shared/latin and click at the bottom of this page to see all activities. All *Quia* sites listed below were active as of summer, 2009.

Quia and Other Self-Quizzes on the Story and Characters of the *Aeneid*

- AP Vergil (Timothy S. Abney, Marquette High School, Chesterfield, MO)

  http://abney.homestead.com/aeneid.html

  Clickable activities, with answers, on all aspects of the *Aeneid*; includes links to some *Quia* sites; Books 1, 2, 4, 6, 10–12, minor contributions for Books 3, 5, and 8.

- Life of Vergil (Ruth Sameth, Mondacan High School, Richmond, VA)

  http://www.quia.com/jg/155688.html

  Matching, flashcards, Concentration, word Search.

- Background Information on the *Aeneid* (Ruth Sameth, Mondacan High School, Richmond, VA)

  http://www.quia.com/cb/1492.html

  Challenge Board.

- Myth-Folklore: Vergil's *Aeneid* Reading (Virginia Kehoe, Wichita Collegiate School, Wichita, KS)

  http://www.quia.com/quiz/1859471.html?AP_rand=1006834073

  Random sequencing of many True-False questions on content.

- Practice Quizzes on the Content of *Aeneid,* Books 1, 2, 3, 4, 5, 6, and 7–12 (Ruth Sameth, Mondacan High School, Richmond, VA)

  http://www.quia.com/pages/latinapvergil.html

  Matching, flashcards, Concentration, word search; Ordered List for Book 4 events.

- *Aeneid* Practice Questions (Magistra McGlennon, Maret School, Washington, DC)

  http://www.quia.com/rr/216282.html

  Rags to Riches, *ala* TV gameshow "Do You Want to Be A Millionaire?"

- *Aeneid* Jeopardy (Magistra McGlennon, Maret School, Washington, DC)

  http://www.quia.com/cb/211354.html?AP_rand=80447003

  Challenge Board.

- 05 Aeneas (Magistra, Academy of the New Church, Bryn Athyn, PA)

  http://www.quia.com/quiz/1505327.html

  Multiple-choice; may take only once.

- Aeneas Troia effugit (Vergilius Madrinan, Teaneck High School, Teaneck, NJ)

  http://www.quia.com/pop/50116.html

  Multiple-choice questions in Latin.

- *Aeneid,* Book 2, lines 1–297 (Magistra Hynes, Catholic Memorial High School, Boston, MA)

  http://www.quia.com/hm/258282.html

  Hangman.

- *Aeneid,* Book 2, lines 2.298–565 (Magistra Hynes, Catholic Memorial High School, Boston, MA)

  http://www.quia.com/hm/285240.html

  Hangman.

- *Aeneid,* Book Quizzes (Karl Muller, Mercersberg Academy, Mercersberg, PA)

  http://www.quia.com/profiles/kmuller11

  Ten to 12–question short-answer ("Scavenger Hunt") quiz on each Book.

- *Aeneid* Practice Questions (Magister Allen, Woodward Academy, Atlanta, GA)

  http://www.quia.com/cb/174697.html?AP_rand=233410533&playHTML=1

  Jeopardy-type games to help learn story and characters

- *Aeneid,* Parts 3 & 4 (Magister Allen, Woodward Academy, Atlanta, GA)

  http://www.quia.com/rr/182676.html

  Rags to Riches.

- Dripping Vergil (Ginny Lindzey, Dripping Springs High School, TX)

  http://www.quia.com/pages/drippingvergil.html

  An excellent site with a huge number of links to *Quia* activities and games, most for the LaFleur text of the *Aeneid*, including engaging Viqua hidden picture games. Covers content, vocabulary, figures of speech, quizzes on sets of lines (but not on entire Books). Many links to additional useful websites.

- *The Iliad* or War of Troy (Eddy Gliniecki and Maria Lago, The Hawthorns School, Bletchingley, U.K.)

  http://www.quia.com/rr/81166.html

  Rags to Riches.

- Characters in Book 1 (Mr. Odhner, Academy of the New Church, Bryn Athyn, PA)

  http://www.quia.com/jg/591351.html

  Matching, Flashcards, Concentration, Word Search.

- Vergil: Characters in Books I-VI (no attribution)

  http://www.quia.com/jg/419151.html

  Matching, flashcards, Concentration, word search.

- Vergil-Characters in Books I-VI (Dr. Melissa Schons Bishop, Creative Classical Curriculum, Orlando, FL)

  http://www.quia.com/jg/807240.html

  Matching, flashcards, Concentration, word search. Also quizzes for Books 1, 2, and 3.
- Self-Quiz, Vergil's *Aeneid,* Book 1 (Donna Wilson, Brooklyn College, NY)

  http://academic.brooklyn.cuny.edu/classic/wilson/core/aeneid1q.htm

  Ten self-scoring multiple-choice questions per Book (Books 1, 2, 4, 6, 8). For those on subsequent books, see the links under each book on Tim Abney's website.
- Vergil Questions (Mr. S. Gilmore, Milton Area School District, Milton, PA)

  http://mysite.verizon.net/sgilmore1/vergilques.htm

  Open-ended questions and answers for each Book.

Latin Quotes from the *Aeneid*

- *Aeneid,* Quotations, Book 1 (Magistra McGlennon, Maret School, Washington, DC)

  http://www.quia.com/jg/513873.html

  Matching, flashcards, Concentration, word search.
- AP Vergil (Timothy S. Abney, Marquette High School, Chesterfield, MO)

  http://abney.homestead.com/aeneid.html

  Clickable activities identifying the speakers of Latin quotes from the *Aeneid,* Book-by-Book.
- Vergil's *Aeneid:* Quotations (from the entire work) (Magistra McGlennon, Maret School, Washington, DC)

  http://www.quia.com/cz/46832.html

  Cloze (completion).
- *Aeneid,* Book 1 Quotes (Magistra Hynes, Catholic Memorial High School, Boston, MA)

  http://www.quia.com/jg/578783.html

  Matching, flashcards, Concentration, word search.
- Quotes, All Book 1 (Dr. Melissa Schons Bishop, Creative Classical Curriculum, Orlando, FL)

  http://www.quia.com/jg/807245.html

  Matching, flashcards, Concentration, word search. Also games for Books 2 and 3.

- Vergil Quotes (no attribution)

  Book 1: http://www.quia.com/jg/484416.html

  Book 2: http://www.quia.com/jg/484417.html

  Matching, flashcards, Concentration, word search

- Vergil's *Aeneid* (Quotes) (Magistra Higley, Pequannock High, Pompton Plains, NJ)

  http://www.quia.com/cz/16239.html

  Cloze (complete) game.

Quizlet

- *Aeneid* Flashcard Sets

  http://quizlet.com/subject/aeneid

  50 sets of review items, written by students and teachers. Compete for scores!

Appendix 2

Translation (Chapter 5)

Another way to look at the process of getting the meaning to unfold as you proceed through the Latin is to use what Hoyos calls "line analysis." (Hoyos, *Latin—How to Read It Fluently: A Practical Manual,* pp. 36ff.[1]) Below is the author's adaptation of this technique, which represents a sort of sentence "diagramming," using the passages translated in Chapter 5.[2] Each sense-unit is placed on a new line and its function determined by its placement, i.e., subordinate elements are indented from main clauses.

Line	Sense-unit	Grammatical function
1	Fracti bello	participial phrase
	fatisque repulsi	participial phrase
2	ductores Danaum	beginning of first main clause; embraces abl. absolute
	tot iam labentibus annis	participial phrase; abl. absolute
3	instar montis	appositive, with **equum**
	equum . . . aedificant,	end of first main clause
	divina Palladis arte	adjectival phrase
4	intexunt . . . costas	second main clause
	sectaque. . . abiete;	participial phrase
5	votum	beginning of third main clause; embraces prep. phrase
	pro reditu;	prepositional phrase
	simulant	end of third main clause
	ea fama vagatur.	fourth main clause

[1] The author would like to express his gratitude to Prof. Hoyos for sharing the initial concept and for guiding subsequent discussion, and to David Perry, Caroline Kelly, and the others of the *Ecce Romani* III revision team (4th ed.) who contributed to the development and adaptation of the version of line-analysis presented here.

[2] For sentence diagramming, see Eugene R. Moutoux, "Sentence Diagrams: One Way of Learning English Grammar," http://www.geocities.com/gene_moutoux/diagrams.htm and the humorous "Diagramming Sentences: A Brief Introduction," Capital Community College Foundation, http://grammar.ccc.commnet.edu/GRAMMAR/diagrams/diagrams.htm. For diagramming sentences in Latin, see Barbara F. McManus, "Diagramming Latin Sentences, Part I," http://www2.cnr.edu/home/bmcmanus/diagraminglatin.html.

Below is a more detailed example of the same concept. Words in boldface denote the core of each main clause, i.e., subject, verb, object. Nouns and adjectives with a single underline go together grammatically in their line and words that are double-underlined go together, but are found in different lines of the text below. Subordinate or dependent elements and descriptive expressions are indented.

Line	Sense-unit	Grammatical function
1	Fracti bello	participial phrase
	fatisque repulsi	participial phrase
2	**ductores** Danaum	beginning of first main clause; embraces abl. absolute
	tot iam labentibus annis	participial phrase; abl. absolute
3	instar montis	appositive, with **equum**
	equum . . . **aedificant**,	end of first main clause
	divina Palladis arte	adjectival phrase
4	**intexunt** . . . **costas**	second main clause
	sectaque. . . abiete;	participial phrase
5	**votum**	beginning of third main clause; embraces prep. phrase
	pro reditu	prepositional phrase
	simulant;	end of third main clause
	ea fama vagatur.	fourth main clause

Appendix 3

SWIMTAG (Chapter 8)

In Chapter 8, which presented some techniques of poetic analysis, we introduced SWIMTAG, a creation of Latin teacher Sally Davis.[1] To refresh your memory, SWIMTAG, which is actually S W² I M² T² A G when expanded, means Sounds, Word order, Word choice, Images, Meter, Mood, Tone, Theme, Allusions, and Grammar. For the various figures and devices mentioned below, return to Chapter 8. Finally, remember to use SWIMTAG as a means to the end of producing a well-developed critical essay rather than as an end in itself.

1. Sounds

What sounds do you hear when you say the words? How do these affect the meaning? What sounds create what effects? What evidence is there of alliteration, assonance, consonance, onomatopoeia, rhyme, or sound play?

- The consonants B, C, D, G, P, and T give an abrupt, harsh, rigid sound:
  Taurus et incertam excussit cervice securim. (*Aeneid* 2.224).
- F, H, S, and Z are soft, soothing sounds, as in wind, the sea, whispers, or sleep; sibilation can also indicate evil, as in the hissing of a snake:
  Praecipitat suadentque cadentia sidera somnos. (*Aeneid* 2.9).
  Ardentesque oculos suffecti sanguine et igni. (*Aeneid* 2.210)
- L and R are liquid sounds, used with laughing, singing, or flowing water:
  Unde loquaces lymphae desiliunt tuae. (Horace, *Odes* 3.13.15–16)

---

[1] The author would like to thank Sally Davis for permission to use SWIMTAG in this book. This outline may also be found on Sally Davis' website, http://www.latinamagistra.com/swimtag.pdf, or at Joan Jahnige's Kentucky Educational Television website, http://www.dl.ket.org/latinlit/carmina/terminology/swimtag.htm.

See also:

Ginny Lindzey, "Teaching AP: Teaching Tips: Essay Writing Skills" (An Unofficial Web Site for AP Latin, Texas Classical Association), http://txclassics.org/old/teachingap.htm. Feedback from AP teachers on the subject, including SWIMTAG.

Linda Montross, "How to Write a Critical Essay on Latin Poetry" (Kentucky Educational Television, Joan Jahnige) http://www.dl.ket.org/latinlit/carmina/terminology/howtowrite.htm. A slight variation on SWIMTAG.

- M and N are longer, heavy sounds, suggesting humming, moaning, or rumbling, often expressing through alliteration, consonance, or assonance the solemnity of sadness or death:

  Si quicquam mutis gratum acceptumve sepulcris. (Catullus, 96.1)

  O multum miseri meus illiusque parentes. (Ovid, *Metamorphoses* 4.155)

- O and U are impressive, round, or substantial; the interjection **O!** is often used in high-sounding apostrophes:

  O patria, O divum domus Ilium et incluta bello. (*Aeneid* 2.241)

2. Word order

Why does the poet place the words where he does? How does the position of a word or words affect or contribute to the meaning? Look for:

- first and last position
- series of words, phrases, clauses (build up or let down)
- juxtaposition, oxymoron (surprise, double-take)
- asyndeton (non-stop action)
- ellipsis
- chiasmus (balance, completion, embracing)
- synchysis (interlocks word meanings literally or impressionistically)
- framing (words actually surround central objects)
- tmesis (overturning, emphasis)

3. Word choice (aka Diction)

Unusual words—unusual use of ordinary words.

- echoes (law, religion, other literature)
- exotic or foreign words
- puns
- other wordplay

4. Images

What pictures form in your mind as you read?

- similes, metaphors, hyperbole
- contrast, colors
- concrete objects
- action sequences

5. Meter[2]

Combine with Sound—often reflects pace or mood; 3+ dactyls or spondees in any line = special effects

- dactyls = faster, lighter, lilting
- spondees = slower, heavier, grander
- elisions = halting, emotional, fearful?

6. Mood

Look at adjectives and verbs. What mood is conveyed?

- formal
- tragic
- frightening
- joyous
- foreboding
- humorous

7. Tone

Can you sense or infer the author's attitude about the characters or the action? Is he

- sympathetic
- sarcastic
- amused
- judgmental

8. Theme

Does the passage relate to the overall theme of the work?

- references to philosophical or political beliefs
- illustrates purpose of the work
- does its universalize the story

9. Allusions

Note:

- proper nouns
- characters and/or places from myths

[2] Meter is covered in Chapter 9.

- customs
- beliefs
- history or geography

10. Grammar

Look at:

- pattern of verb tenses (unexpected?)
- person of verb (who speaks to whom? is there an exchange?)
- passive verbs
- imperatives and gerundives
- interjections
- complex sentence structure
- where are the adjectives
- short or abrupt sentences

Appendix 4

A Summary of Subordinate Clauses (Chapter 29)

Clause of Anticipation (*Before*)

Time clauses introduced by anticipatory words such as **antequam** and **priusquam**, *before,* are found with both indicative and subjunctive verbs. In indicative clauses, which refer strictly to the time of something that has actually occurred, the present, perfect, and future perfect tenses are used. In subjunctive clauses, when expectancy or action that did not actually occur is expressed in past time, the imperfect tense is used:

Indicative (actually happens/happened):

Priusquam Aeneas ad Italiam pervenerat, magna tempestas coorta est.

Before Aeneas had reached Italy, a great storm arose.

Subjunctive (anticipated as happening):

Antequam omnes naves delerentur, vis tempestatis cecidit.

Before all the ships were destroyed, the force of the storm weakened.

Dum Clauses with the Indicative (*While, As long as*)

The adverbs **dum** or **donec** + the indicative express an actual fact in pure time and mean *while, as long as*, depending upon the context:

Dum Troiani ad Italiam navigabant, Palinurus in mare cecidit.

While the Trojans were sailing to Italy, Palinurus fell overboard.

Dum Clauses with the Subjunctive (*Until*)

Dum or **donec** also can have the meaning *until* when expressing expectancy or anticipation. In this case the verb of the dependent clause is subjunctive:

Aeneas multa passus est dum conderet urbem. (Vergil)

Aeneas endured many things until he could found the city.

Dum Provisional Clauses (*Provided that, If only*)

Dum (often strengthened by **modo** = **dummodo**) + the present or imperfect subjunctive can also be translated *provided that* or *if only*, in which case the clause is known as a clause of proviso:

Oderint dum metuant. (Attributed to Caligula by Suetonius)

Let them hate me provided that they fear me.

Quick Study of Time Clauses

Type of clause	Introd. word	Meaning of clause	Function
Indicative			
Temporal	**cum**	*when*	specific time
	ubi,	*when*	pure time
	simul atque/ac	*as soon as*	
	dum **donec**	*while, until* *as long as*	fact in real time
	antequam, priusquam	*before*	actual time
Subjunctive			
Circumstantial	**cum**	*when*	general circumstance
Anticipatory	**antequam, priusquam**	*before*	anticipation
	dum	*until*	intention, expectancy
Provisional	**dum(modo)**	*provided that*	conditional wish

Quick Study of Subordinate Clauses

Indicative (Factual)	
1. Relative	**Plinius homo erat cui imperator credidit.** (Chapter 13)
who, which, that	*Pliny was a person whom the emperor trusted.*
2. **Quod** Causal	**Plinius praefectus creatus est <u>quod officiosus erat</u>.** (Chapter 28)
because, since	*Pliny was appointed an official <u>because (it was a fact that) he was dutiful</u>.*
3. **Cum** Temporal	**<u>Eodem tempore cum Plinius natus est</u>, suus pater Comi habitabat.** (Chapter 29)
when	*<u>At the time when Plinus was born</u>, his father was living at Comum.*

5. **Dum** Temporal	**Dum Plinius in Bithynia erat, multas epistulas ad imperatorem misit.** (Appendix 4)
while, as long as	*While Pliny was in Bithynia, he sent many letters to the emperor.*
6. Anticipatory	**Plinius consul Romae erat priusquam proconsul in Bithynia fuit.** (Appendix 4)
before	*Pliny was a consul in Rome (in fact) before he was governor.* of Bithynia.
Subjunctive (Non-factual)	
7. Conditional	**Nisi Mons Vesuvius erupuisset, urbs Pompeii mansisset.** (Chapter 26)
if	*If Mount Vesuvius had not erupted, the city of Pompeii would have remained.*
8. **Ut** Purpose	**Quintilianus Plinium docebat ut melius scriberet.** (Chapter 27)
to, in order that	*Quintilian taught Pliny to write better.*
9. **Ut** Result	**Tantum periculum erat ut multi Pompeiis fugerent.** (Chapter 27)
that	*The danger was so great that many fled from Pompeii.*
10. Substantive Result	**Plinius effecit ut complures proconsules damnarentur.** (Chapter 27)
that	*Pliny brought it about that several governors were condemned.*
11. Indirect Command	**Plinius Christianis imperabat ne in unum locum congregarent.** (Chapter 27)
that	*Pliny ordered the Christians not to gather together in one place.*
12. Fear	**Hodie multi timent ne Vesuvius iterum erupturus sit.** (Chapter 27)
(that)	*Today many are afraid that Vesuvius is going to erupt again.*
13. Indirect Question	**Secundus cognoscere voluit cur amicus Tacitus annales scripsisset.** (Chapter 28)
who, what, why	*Secundus wanted to know why his friend Tacitus had written the Annals.*

14. Relative Characteristic	**Secundus homo erat qui eruditionem magni aestimaret.** (Chapter 28)
the type who, that	*Secundus was the type of person who thought highly of education.*
15. Relative Purpose	**Plinius legatum misit qui imperatorem de Christianis certiorem faceret.** (Chapter 28)
to, in order to	*Pliny sent an envoy to inform the emperor about the Christians.*
16. **Quod** Causal	**Quod multi Christiani essent, multi delatores erant**. (Chapter 28)
since, because	*Because there were many Christians, there were many informers.*
17. **Cum** Causal	**Cum Christiani in provincia essent, Plinius consilium Traiani petebat.** (Chapter 29)
since, because	*Since there were Christians in the province, Pliny sought the advice of Trajan*
18. **Cum** Circumstantial	**Cum Plinius proconsul in Bithynia esset, cives florebant.** (Chapter 29)
when	*When Pliny was proconsul in Bithynia, the citizens were prosperous.*
19. **Cum** Concessive	**Cum Bithynia provincia Romana esset, tamen cives Graece loquebantur.** (Chapter 29)
although	*Although Bithynia was a Roman province, nevertheless the citizens spoke Greek.*
20. Doubt	**Dubitatne aliquis num Plinius epistulas scripserit?** (Chapter 28)
to have doubt	*Does anyone doubt whether Pliny wrote letters?*
21. Negative Doubt	**Est non dubium quin Plinius suum patruum dilexerit.** (Chapter 28)
not to have doubt	*There is no doubt that Pliny held his uncle in high regard.*
22. Anticipatory	**Priusquam de Vesuvio scribere posset, patruus Plini mortuus est.** (Appendix 4)
before	*Before he could write about Vesuvius, Pliny's uncle died.*

23. Anticipatory	**Plinius exspectabat dum audiret nuntium ex imperatore.** (Appendix 4)
until	*Pliny was waiting to hear,* lit., *until he should hear, news from the emperor.*
24. Proviso	**Licebat servis custodes in Bithynia esse dummodo fideles essent.** (Appendix 4)
provided that, if only	*Slaves were allowed to be guards in Bithynia, provided that they were trustworthy.*

Appendix 5

Credit and Placement in the AP Program

Here is a list of colleges and universities that receive the largest numbers of AP scores, based on those who attended the recent National Faculty Colloquium for AP Latin, November 2008.[1] This list has been correlated with that given at the College Board website, dated 2008: "The 200 Top Colleges and Universities Receiving the Most AP Grades (2008)," http://professionals.collegeboard.com/prof-download/200_Top_Colleges_11-3.pdf.

For a search engine that connects you to specific colleges and universities with AP credit policy information, go to http://collegesearch.collegeboard.com/apcreditpolicy/index.jsp, and type in the name of the college or university that you are considering. There is no statistical data currently available that provides a look at which colleges and universities offer credit or placement or both, by subject.[2] Please consult your guidance counselor, college advisor, or the print or online information available from the admissions department of the colleges or universities to which you are applying. Sometimes this information is also available on departmental websites. In the list below, all are universities unless designated otherwise.

---

[1] Obtained from an e-mail received from Mary Pendergraft, Chief Reader for the 2009 AP Latin Exam, July 6, 2009. See also the following College Board websites for additional relevant information:

http://www.collegeboard.com/student/testing/ap/about.html.
The College Board claims that over 90 percent of American colleges and universities grant placement or credit or both on the basis of AP Exam scores.

http://professionals.collegeboard.com/data-reports-research/ap/data.
Contains many links to various reports containing AP Program participation and performance statistics.

http://www.collegeboard.com/prod_downloads/research/RDGuideUseCBTest020729.pdf.
Contains "Guidelines on the Uses of College Board Test Scores and Related Data."

http://www.collegeboard.com/about/news_info/ap/independent-survey.html.
Summary of the results of an independent survey of public school teachers with regard to their satisfaction with the AP Program, conducted by the Farkas Duffett Research Group and funded by the Fordham Foundation. See the report by Ann Duffett and Steve Farkas, "Growing Pains in the Advanced Placement Program: Do Tough Trade-offs Lie Ahead?" (April 29, 2009) at http://edexcellence.net/index.cfm/news_advanced-placement-program-study. See also the Fordham Foundation's website at http://fordhamfoundation.org and type in "College Board AP Program" for additional such articles.

[2] In an e-mail dated August 18, 2009, this author was assured by James Monk, the College Board's Associate Director, World Languages and Cultures, Advanced Placement Program, that the AP Program's College and University Services unit is "in the second year of a two-year project to create a searchable database of higher ed[ucation] credit and placement figures across the more than thirty AP subjects." The plan is to have this database up and running by the end of the fiscal year, presumably mid-2010.

Top Colleges and Universities Attending the 2008 National Faculty Colloquium for AP Latin that Received the Most AP Grades in 2008

Top 50

Boston
Duke
Florida State
Michigan State
Northwestern
New York
Ohio State
Texas A&M
Arizona
Cal-Berkeley
Cal-Davis
UCLA
Cal-Santa Cruz
Colorado
Maryland
Michigan
Minnesota
Notre Dame
Texas-Austin
Washington
Wisconsin-Madison

51-100

Brown
College of William and Mary
George Washington
Harvard
Louisiana State
Miami University of Ohio
Princeton
Rice
Connecticut
Pennsylvania
Vanderbilt
Washington-St. Louis

101-150

Fordham
Johns Hopkins
Temple
Villanova

151-200

Rochester

Not listed in the top 200

Bowdoin College
Colgate
Davidson College
Dickinson College
Hunter College
Kenyon College
Oberlin College
Scripps College
Swarthmore College
Vassar College
Virginia
Virginia Tech

Top 50 Colleges and Universities Receiving the Most AP Grades in 2008

Texas-Austin
Florida
UCLA
Texas A&M
Cal-Berkeley
Cal-San Diego
Georgia
Michigan
Central Florida
Illinois-Urbana
Cal-Irvine
North Carolina-Chapel Hill
Cal-Davis
Florida State
Cal-Santa Barbara
Wisconsin-Madison
Penn State
New York University
Virginia Polytechnic Institute
Ohio State
Washington
Southern Cal
Virginia
Maryland
Michigan State
North Carolina State-Raleigh
South Florida
Georgia Tech
Arizona State
Cornell
Colorado-Boulder
Stanford
Purdue
Cal-Santa Cruz
Boston
Baylor
Rutgers
Indiana
Minnesota
Cal-Riverside
Arizona
Cal Poly State
Oklahoma
Clemson
Northwestern
Cal State-Long Beach
Notre Dame
Duke
San Diego State

AP LATIN

Index

Index

A

B

C

D

E

U

V

W

X

Z

INSTALLING REA's TestWare®

SYSTEM REQUIREMENTS

Pentium 75 MHz (300 MHz recommended), or a higher or compatible processor; Microsoft Windows 98 or later; 64 MB Available RAM; Internet Explorer 5.5 or higher.

INSTALLATION

1. Insert the AP Latin: Vergil TestWare® CD-ROM into the CD-ROM drive.
2. If the installation doesn't begin automatically, from the Start Menu, choose the RUN command. When the RUN dialog box appears, type d:\setup (where D is the letter of your CD-ROM drive) at the prompt and click OK.
3. The installation process will begin. A dialog box proposing the directory "Program Files\REA\AP_LatinVergil" will appear. If the name and location are suitable, click OK. If you wish to specify a different name or location, type it in and click OK.
4. Start the AP Latin: Vergil TestWare® application by double-clicking on the icon.

REA's AP Latin: Vergil TestWare® is **EASY** to **LEARN AND USE**. To achieve maximum benefits, we recommend that you take a few minutes to go through the on-screen tutorial on your computer. The "screen buttons" are also explained there to familiarize you with the program.

SSD ACCOMMODATIONS FOR STUDENTS WITH DISABILITIES

Many students qualify for extra time to take the AP Latin: Vergil exam, and our TestWare® can be adapted to accommodate your time extension. This allows you to practice under the same extended time accommodations that you will receive on the actual test day. To customize your TestWare® to suit the most common extensions, visit our Website at *www.rea.com/ssd*.

TECHNICAL SUPPORT

REA's TestWare® is backed by customer and technical support. For questions about **installation or operation of your software**, contact us at:

Research & Education Association
Phone: (732) 819-8880 (9 a.m. to 5 p.m. ET, Monday–Friday)
Fax: (732) 819-8808
Website: www.rea.com
E-mail: info@rea.com

Note to Windows XP Users: In order for the TestWare® to function properly, please install and run the application under the same computer-administrator level user account. Installing the TestWare® as one user and running it as another could cause file access path conflicts.